GUIDE TO
EUROPEAN COMPANY LAWS

AUSTRALIA
LBC Information Services—Sydney

CANADA and USA
Carswell—Toronto

NEW ZEALAND
Brooker's—Auckland

SINGAPORE and MALAYSIA
Thomson Information (S.E. Asia)—Singapore

GUIDE TO
EUROPEAN COMPANY LAWS

Second Edition

By

JULIAN MAITLAND-WALKER

MAITLAND WALKER
SOLICITORS
Minehead and London

LONDON
SWEET & MAXWELL
1997

Published in 1997 by Sweet & Maxwell Limited of
100 Avenue Road, Swiss Cottage,
London NW3 3PF
(http://www.smlawpub.co.uk)
Phototypeset by Selwood Systems,
Midsomer Norton
Printed and bound in Great Britain by
Butler & Tanner Ltd,
Frome and London

No natural forests were destroyed to make this product;
only farmed timber was used and replanted

A CIP catalogue record for this book is available from the British Library

ISBN 0 421 57900 5

Preface

The increasing internationalisation of trade and commerce together with the steady progress towards a fully integrated single European market means that it is increasingly difficult for lawyers trained in one country to ignore developments in other jurisdictions.

Clients will inevitably be involved in cross-frontier trade. Questions will arise with a multi-jurisdictional perspective, ranging from an assessment of a business partner or customer's credit status to the choice of the appropriate corporate vehicle for outward investment.

These questions raise issues of tax law, debt-enforcement procedures and other specialised areas but every case is grounded upon the need for an appreciation of the basic rules of business establishment. We need to know how enterprises in different jurisdictions operate and the rules and restrictions to which they are subject before we can deal with the more specific problems which might arise.

Increasingly, legal advisers are being asked to advise on matters outside their competence, outside their training. Clearly, the right approach is to do so only in consultation with those having the necessary expertise, but it is desirable nevertheless to know something of the background if only to be equipped to ask the right questions.

The object of this Guide is to provide that overview; to furnish the reader with a basic outline of corporate establishment throughout Western Europe so that he or she may have a sufficient starting point from which to seek the necessary specialist advice. I am indebted to each of the national contributors for their assistance in assembling the Guide. Their forbearance in accepting the constraints set by a uniform format for each section, which I have tried to adopt for ease of reference, is matched by the skill with which they have applied their expertise in the text.

The Second Edition has been expanded to include the majority of countries in what was formerly Eastern Europe and reflects the major changes in these countries as they adopt corporate regularity frameworks, very similar to those in other market economies. The extension of coverage reflects the increasing integration of European trade.

Julian Maitland-Walker
August 11, 1997

CONTENTS

* *Full particulars of each author are listed in the Appendix.*

Luxembourg (Tom Loesch)

Netherlands (Gerard Carrière)

Norway (Bjorn Blix)

Sweden (Mats Koffner)

Switzerland (Jean-Paul Aeschimann and François Rayroux)

United Kingdom (Julian Maitland-Walker)

European Community (Julian Maitland-Walker)

Table of Statutes

TABLE OF E.C. LEGISLATION

AUSTRIA

SECTION 1

CLASSIFICATION OF BUSINESS ORGANISATIONS: INTRODUCTION*

A.1.0 The Austrian commercial and civil law recognises different legal forms for economic activities. Under Austrian law, most of these legal forms can be divided into the three following categories:

—sole proprietorship
—partnerships
—limited liability companies

These three legal categories, mentioned above, will be explained in the following study. Such legal forms which are of minor economic importance will not be discussed.

A.1.1 Sole Proprietorships

Sole proprietorship is a legal form which is frequently used. It is also one of the simplest business forms. The main characteristic feature of the sole proprietorship is, in the economic and judicial sense, the undivided authority of the sole proprietor.

The sole proprietor is a private individual who is able to run his business without any restrictions from shareholders or another joint proprietor. The sole proprietor has all the rights and, of course, all the obligations of the business. He takes all the profits and all the risks of the business's losses.

There are no restrictions as to the liability of the sole proprietor to his creditors. As the private assets of the sole proprietor cannot be legally separated from the business assets, the sole proprietor is liable with the whole of his assets to his business creditors.

It is possible for the sole proprietor to separate his private assets from his business assets in the organisational and factual sense, but such a separation has no importance to the proprietor.

In Austria, the sole proprietorship is not regulated by any special legal regulations. Therefore, the general rules of commercial law (Handelsgesetzbuch) will apply to the sole proprietor. It must be pointed out that under the regulations of the

---

* *Dr Franz Pegger, Greiter Pegger Kofler & Partner (full particulars are listed in the Appendix).*

commercial law, generally, the sole proprietor must use his own name as his trading name, but it is possible under special circumstances for him to run a business under a name which differs from his civilian name. This name does not create a separate subject along with the merchant, as he carries the rights and obligations of his business as an individual.

Regulations affecting the name of a merchant's business fall under the general rules of commercial law. This is the name under which the merchant runs his business and gives his signature.

The business name is registered in a special court register (Firmenbuch) and other traders are prohibited from trading under a similar name.

A.1.1.1 *Branches*

If the merchant runs his business from different places, then they must be divided into a head office (registered office) and branches. Both the head office and any branches can be, in the legal sense, not only the place of performance and/or delivery, but also the place from which the merchant can sue or be sued. Usually, any branches must adhere to the Austrian registration requirements.

The corresponding regulations for a head office or the place of business also apply for applications, subscriptions, registrations and notifications for a branch of the sole proprietor. They also apply to a legal entity which has its head office in a foreign country or a commercial company which is domiciled abroad, so long as the foreign law does not make divergences necessary.

Consequently, the following information must be registered in the Commercial Register (Firmenbuch):

(1) the registered number of the business;

(2) business name;

(3) the legal structure of the business, *i.e.* sole proprietor/partnership, etc.;

(4) the registered office and the delivery address;

(5) particulars of the type of business;

(6) branches, to include the proper address for deliveries and also their business names, should these be different to the business name of the head office;

(7) date of the business's establishment;

(8) name and date of birth of the sole proprietor. In respect of other legal entities, the names of any authorised representatives together with the commencement date of the representation and the manner thereof;

(9) if there are any authorised persons of the business (Prokurist), their names and addresses should be stated and also their commencement date and manner of their representation;

(10) agreements under §§ 25.2 and 28.2 of the Commercial Code;

(11) duration of the business, should this be limited;

(12) name and address of the liquidator if the business is in liquidation and the date of appointment and manner of his authorised representation;

(13) the provided limitations of the right of disposal, which fall under the execution and insolvency law, for the registration in the Commercial Register, the annulment of these and the name of the legal representative;

(14) the rejection of any bankruptcy petitions because the business has not enough assets to fulfill bankruptcy procedures;

(15) a legal succession and its legal grounds;

(16) any other registrations, which are legally provided for.

A.1.2 Partnerships

Austrian law recognises different forms of partnerships. These businesses are covered by the Commercial and Civil Code or by special laws.

Two distinctive business which are covered by the Commercial Code are the general partnership (Offence Handelsgesellschaft: OHG) and limited partnership (Kommanditgesellschaft: KG). These businesses are very similar. The main difference is that, in the limited partnership, a proportion of the partners have a limited liability whereas the remaining partners are fully liable for any debts of the partnership.

In addition to the two above-mentioned partnerships, the Commercial Code also recognises the dormant partnership Stille Gesellschaft). This is formed by two partners. One of the partners has a business relationship with the other, but the dormant partner is not represented to the public as being a member of the partnership.

A new form of partnership has now been passed by Austrian law on April 25, 1990. This is the "Erwerbsgesellschaft". This is a partnership which is based on joint businesses which use a joint business name. This form of partnership has been passed for special cases where, according to the Commercial Code, the establishment of a general or limited partnership is not possible. Here one must, once again, distinguish between a general "Erwerbsgesellschaft" (Offene Erwerbsgellschaft: OEG) and a limited "Erwerbsgesellschaft" (Kommanditerwerbsgesellschaft: KEG). The liability of the individual partners in the latter partnership is limited, according to the Commercial Code, in a similar way to that of the limited partnership.

Additionally, there is also the "Erwerbsgesellschaft" which is covered by the Civil Code. This partnership was regulated by the Civil Code in 1811. Originally, this was meant for all types of partnerships, but especially for public limited companies. In the meantime, other forms of partnerships are regulated by special laws, so the scope for this particular form of partnership is very limited. One usually finds this type of partnership in Joint Ventures, cartels, ad hoc partnerships cooperation contracts and syndicate contracts.

A.1.2.1 *General partnerships (Offene Handelsgesellschaft: OHG)*

There are three criteria for the determination of the term "general partnership":

(a) the partners' liability is unlimited in respect of partnership debts;

(b) the partners act together in business, under the same business name;

(c) the partnership is formed for the purpose of operating a commercial business.

The partnership is not a legal body but under the name of the business, the partnership can acquire rights and can enter into commitments. It can purchase titles to land and is able to sue and be sued under the partnership name.

Not only individual persons, but also legal entities can have a share in a general partnership. Also, one general partnership can have a share in another general partnership. One partner cannot, however, have several partnership shares in the same general partnership.

A foreign limited liability company (see below) can only have a share in a general partnership, if it has a branch in Austria (in all likelihood not true for companies having their seat within the EEA).

A trustee or a personal representative can have a share as a partner in a general partnership. In this case, the unlimited liability in respect to the partnership's debts is borne by the trustee and not any beneficiary.

A general partnership is established between the partners as soon as the partnership agreement is concluded. The conclusion of the partnership agreement is not regulated by any kind of form. Therefore, the partners can conclude the partnership agreement expressly (which is orally or in writing) or implicitly. Alterations to the partnership agreement do not require any specific form. Should alterations be made, the consent of *all* the partners is necessary, unless there is a provision to the contrary in the partnership agreement. For example, that a majority of the partners pass any vote for alteration.

The partnership agreement does not have to be presented before the Registration Court. A general partnership must be registered in the Commercial Register in writing and the Registration Court must be specially informed of the following points:

(a) the business name;

(b) head office of the business;

(c) name, profession and place of residence of the partners;

(d) the legal form of such partners who are partnerships or other legal entities themselves;

(e) power of representative regulations, should these differ from the legal representative regulations;

(f) any authorised persons, should these be appointed at the establishment of the partnership.

The firm must take the name of all the partners or can be shortened to that of some of the partners' names, in which case, it must be indicated that this is a partnership (*e.g.* "... & Co." or "OHG"). It is sufficient to use surnames.

Under Austrian law, every partner has the right and is obliged to run the business (internal management) on his own behalf and on behalf of the other partners. Only acts which are not part of the normal business require the consent of all the partners. Alterations to these legal regulations can be made by contractual agreement.

Each partner has the power to act on behalf of the partnership as a whole (external representation). This applies also to acts which are not part of the normal business. Alterations to these legal regulations can be made by contractual agreement.

Unless there is any contrary agreement, the partners all make the same contribution to the partnership. The partnership agreement usually specifies what contribution each partner brings into the partnership. It is possible that, instead of a partner bringing in money or a contribution in kind, he takes over the business management and the representation. If a partner doesn't bring in money or a contribution in kind and also doesn't take over the business management and representation, then his contribution is his liability for partnership debts.

Concerning the partner's liability, the following points should be noted:

(a) the partner's liability is not restricted to a specific amount;

(b) the partnership agreement cannot restrict a partner's liability to a specific amount;

(c) a partner is liable with all his private assets and not just to the amount of his contribution;

(d) a creditor can sue a partner without having to sue the partnership first;

(e) the partner is directly liable to the creditor, which means that the creditor doesn't have to go against the partnership before enforcing his claim.

(f) each partner is liable for the whole debt of the business. The creditor can, therefore, select any partner who can pay the claim.

A creditor can claim from the partnerships assets or from the private assets of each partner. The partnership's assets are, under the civil law, "Gesamthandeigentum", which means that *all* the aspects belong to *all* the partners, and are not specifically assigned to any individual partners.

Should a partner enter a partnership, which has already been established, he is liable for all the existing debts of the partnership at the time of his entry.

Should a partner leave a partnership, he is liable for all debts incurred by the partnership up to the time of his leaving the partnership. Here, a limitation period of five years applies for any of his liabilities incurred as a partner.

Under the Commercial Code, a partnership can be dissolved when:

(a) the partnership's duration period expires;

(b) it is decided by a partnership resolution;

(c) bankruptcy proceedings are commenced over the partnership's assets;

(d) a partner dies unless otherwise provided for in the partnership agreement;

(e) bankruptcy proceedings are commenced over a partner's assets;

(f) the partnership is terminated by a judicial decision.

Other reasons for dissolving a partnership can be provided for in the partnership agreement.

A.1.2.2 Limited partnership (Kommanditgesellschaft: KG)

The limited partnership can be considered as a special form of a general partnership. Principally, according to the Commercial Code, the regulations for the general partnership also apply to the limited partnership.

Contrary to the general partnership, the limited partnership recognises two groups of partners. At least one partner's liability must be limited to a specific amount of his contribution towards the business assets. This partner is called a limited partner (Kommanditist). At least one other partner must have unlimited liability. This unlimited liability corresponds with the liability of a partner in a general partnership. The partner with the unlimited liability is called a general partner (Komplementär). A partner can only be one of the other. A partner cannot be both limited and a general partner.

A foreign limited liability company can be a limited partner, even if it doesn't have an inland branch, but it cannot be a general partner.

As the limited partners have limited liabilities, they are normally excluded from the business management. This task is assigned to the general partners, although usually, exceptional transactions will need the limited partner's consent. The business management can be regulated in other ways, as long as it is provided for in the partnership agreement.

Based on the partnership agreement, the external representation applies only to the general partners. Even though the limited partner can be responsible for the internal management, he cannot represent the partnership externally as a partner. He can only represent the partnership externally via a special authorisation.

The contribution of a limited partner must be defined, showing separately his business contribution and his liability contribution. The business contribution is that which is determined in the Partnership Agreement. The liability contribution is the amount by which he is limited towards the business debts. Such amounts can differ from one another.

As soon as the limited partner has satisfied his liability contribution, he is released from any further liability towards the creditors.

For the purpose of the limitation of liability, one or more limited liability companies can be general partners in a limited partnership (*e.g.* "GmbH & Co. KG"). In such a case, mostly the shareholders of the limited liability companies are also limited partners of the limited partnership.

Although these limited liability companies have unlimited liability in the partnership, this will, in effect, only be for the limited amount of assets which are at the company's disposal. The liability of the limited partners is limited to their shareholding in the company. The liability of the persons concerned therefore, even with the limits of a Partnership, can be limited considerably. Usually, the larger creditors (*i.e.* banks, etc.) demand special liability declarations from the limited partners or shareholders of the company.

A.1.2.3   *Dormant partnerships (Stille Gesellschaft: StG)*

The essence of the dormant partnership is that one of the two partners is a dormant (or sleeping) partner. Therefore, this partnership is only an internal partnership, which is not registered in the Commercial Register (Firmenbuch) and does not have its own business.

Externally, the proprietor of the trade business always acts on his own behalf.

There can be only two partners in a dormant partnership; the proprietor and the dormant partner. Should more than one person want an interest in the same trade business of the same proprietor, then more than one dormant partnership must be established. It is possible however, that all the persons, who want an interest in the same business, form a non-trading partnership and then, as one body, become a dormant partner in the business of the proprietor. The proprietor can be a sole trader, a partnership or other legal entity.

In this type of partnership, one defines between a "real" dormant partnership and an "unreal" dormant partnership. In the real dormant partnership, the dormant partner invests an amount of money in the partnership and accepts a return on his investment. He has no interest in the management of the partnership and at the end of his involvement, he is repaid his capital sum without any value increase.

In the latter, the dormant partner has a share in the value increase of the business assets, *i.e.* in the going concern value and in the dormant reserves, or he is granted a certain power in the business management or other special rights.

The dormant partnership does not own any assets itself, and does not have any creditors. For debts incurred, only the proprietor is liable towards the creditors. The dormant partner is not liable. Even if the dormant partner manages the business or is *de facto* principal, he is not liable towards the creditors.

According to Austrian law, the dormant partner must bring a capital contribution into the business. The nature, extent and point of time can be determined by the dormant partner himself.

The contribution must be transferred to the proprietor's capital. As well as the transfer of the contribution, a permission for use is possible.

Should the proprietor go bankrupt, then the dormant partner has the standing of an ordinary creditor in his claim.

The dormant partnership can be dissolved for the following reasons:

(a) the partnerships contractual duration period expires;

(b) mutual agreement of both partners;

(c) death of the proprietor; this is comparable to the termination of a partnership or the dissolution of a limited liability company, should these be business owners;

(d) commencement of bankruptcy proceedings over the proprietor's assets;

(e) commencement of bankruptcy proceedings over the dormant partner's assets;

(f) by a routine termination within the legal time-limit;

(g) dissolution caused by an important reason without observing a special time-limit;

(h) notice given by a dormant partner's creditor;

(i) attainment of the partnership's purpose.

Other reasons for the dissolution of the dormant partnership can be determined by contract.

A.1.2.4 *Registered "Erwerbsgesellschaft" (EEG)*

The Austrian commercial law distinguishes between merchants and small traders. The business of a small trader does not extend to the size of a small scale business. As a general partnership and a limited partnership can only be established for a merchant trade business, this type of business is not at the disposition of the small trader. The legal form which was passed by law on January 1, 1991 for the registered "Erwerbsgesellschaft" allows the operation of a small trade business. This legal form can apply also to professions other than traders (*i.e.* solicitors, tax advisors, etc.).

The registered "Erwerbsgesellschaft" (EEG) is very similar to the general and limited partnerships. The legislation refers to the legal forms of both these partnerships for the applicable legal form for the registered "Erwerbsgesellschaft" (EEG).

The EEG can be formed as soon as it is registered in the Commercial Register. The business name to be registered must give an indication as to the legal form. Professional persons can, make use of this legal form and as such can use the terms "partnership" or "and partner" as an indication as to the legal form. An EEG can establish branches, which can be registered accordingly.

Under commercial law, the EEG is not obliged to keep business accounts An obligation to keep business accounts can, however, be enforced on the grounds of tax regulations.

A.1.2.4.1 Offene (general) Erwerbsgesellschaft (OEG) The OEG is a partnership which is modelled on the general partnership (OHG). Also, the legal regulations for the OHG are to be applied correspondingly. Therefore, the partnership is an OEG, when *none* of the partners has a limited liability towards the creditors. A partnership, with this form of business, must use the term "offene Erwerbsgesellschaft" or the abbreviation "OEG".

A.1.2.4.2 Kommandit (limited) Erwerbsgesellschaft (KEG) This form of business is modelled on the limited partnership. The regulations for the limited partnership in the Commercial Code also apply to the KEG.

The KEG distinguishes itself from the OEG since one or more partners' liability is limited to the amount of a specific capital contribution towards the partnerships' debts. These partners are called limited partners.

A.1.2.5 *Civil partnerships (Bürgerlich rechtliche Erwerbsgesellschaft: GesBR)*

This form of partnership is subject to the regulations of the Civil Code. The regulations of the Commercial Code do not principally apply.

Although, under Austrian company law, special legal forms have been created by specific laws, this form of partnership is given quite a lot of importance. One often finds this form of partnership, for example when the partners only want to settle one specific business transaction. These "ad hoc" partnerships can appear as partnerships in the building trade or as syndicates for the awarding of credits or the issuing of securities. Also cartels, co-operation contracts and joint ventures can be organised under this legal form. If necessary, a commercial business, which is established by registration in the Commercial Register, can be treated as a "GesBR" before registration.

The "GesBR" does not have its own legal personality. The assigned assets belong to all the partners together. The business capital is a special capital, which is separated from the partner's private capital.

If nothing else is provided for, a partner normally only has rights and liabilities for his share of the business claims and debts. The partners are liable for business liabilities, with the whole of their business capital as well as their private capital, but only for their own share. There are, however, individual cases where the partners are jointly and severally liable. This applies especially when the "GesBR" is a small trader. A partner cannot assert business claims without the authorisation of the other partners, unless he himself gives a security or demands payment to the court.

11

The partnership is established with the completion of the partnership agreement. This does not need any particular form. In individual cases, where a partnership has a specific purpose, a special form may be necessary. In special cases, an inventory must be set up for the validity of the partnership agreement.

All alterations to the partnership agreement must have the consent of all the partners, unless there is a special provision for a different arrangement in the partnership agreement. Due to the lack of legal personality, and without an appropriate special stipulation, the "GesBR" cannot be registered in a public register. Therefore, the "GesBR" is not registered in the Commercial Register nor in the Land Register.

The business management is the duty of all the partners with respect to the general administration. The principle of the whole business management applies, whereby decisions need a majority vote. The partners in the majority cannot make a decision without first giving the minority the chance to be heard. Further protection in favour of the minority is provided for in decisions concerning extraordinary measures.

The "GesBR" can be dissolved for the following reasons:

(a) if the partners' contractual duration period expires;

(b) a dissolution by a decision of the partners;

(c) fulfilment of the purpose of the partnership;

(d) loss of all the partners' contributions, as long as they are not liable to make additional contributions;

(e) dissolution of a partnership with unlimited duration by notice;

(f) dissolution of a partnership with limited duration, when an important reason exists.

The partners can, of course, make other provisions for dissolution in the partnership agreement.

A.1.2.6 *General provisions*

Usually, a partnership contract has no special form of requirements. In a few exceptional cases, especially in relation to the purpose of the partnership, a special form (written form, notarial act, etc.) may be necessary.

The "offene Handelsgesellschaft", "Erwerbsgesellschaft", "offene Erwerbsgesellschaft" and "Kommandit-Erwerbsgesellschaft" must be all registered in the Commercial Register. These partnerships must register the Commercial Register number, name and legal form of the partnership, the registered address and the address for deliveries, a short description of the line of business, completion date of the partnership agreement, names and dates of birth of the persons authorised to represent the business, as well as the commencing date and manner of the power of representation and any duration of the partnership. When establishing these partnerships, great emphasis is laid on the completion of the partnership agreement. The registration formalities are pushed more into the background. The civil partnership (GesBR) and the dormant partnership (StG) do not have to be registered in the Commercial Register.

The number of partners (with the exception of the dormant partnership) is not limited by law. Normally, the number of partners who are personally liable are, if anything, smaller, as the partnership is marked with a special trust basis. Normally, only the "Kommanditgesellschaft" or the "Kommandit-Erwerbsgesellschaft" is suitable for a larger number of partners.

The partner's contribution can be paid in cash or by other non-cash contributions. A partner's contribution can be in the form of work performed or the taking over of liabilities. The partners can also assign objects to the partnership, for use only.

Normally, the partners have no restrictions on the valuation of the non-cash contributions. Exceptions exist for limited partners, whose liability contributions are limited towards the partnership's debts and therefore, in relation to the creditors, the value of their contributions can only correspond with the real amount which was contributed at the establishment of the partnership.

SECTION 2

CORPORATIONS

A.2.1 Introduction

The special feature of the companies which will be discussed in this section, is that they are corporate bodies. Under Austrian law, corporations are independent legal entities. They can own their own assets and are liable for their own debts.

As discussed in section 1, the business management and representation in partnerships is the duty of the partners. In corporations, this is the duty of the company itself. The respective managers of the company are individual persons and do not have to be shareholders.

In this section, the "Aktiengesellschaft" (AG) and the "Gesellschaft mit beschränkter Haftung" (GmbH) will be discussed. Apart from these companies, there are other legal forms and judicial persons to which great importance is given in economic life. For example, the co-operative society where the business is responsible for the promotion of purchases and the members' economy. Due to the special way in which these companies are formulated, and their particular methods of operation, especially in the credit system and agricultural sector, a representation is not needed.

A.2.2 Aktiengesellschaft (AG)

This corporation is more usually used for large companies and differs from the GmbH in that it is a stock or listed company. The filing and registration requirements are, therefore, more stringent than for the GmbH.

The legal form of an AG is regulated in the Austrian Company Act (Aktiengesetz) 1965. This Act defines this limited company as:

(a) a company with its own legal personality;

(b) having shareholders who make contributions;

(c) the shareholders have shares in the share capital of that company;

(d) the shareholders have no further liability for the debts of the company outside their own shareholding.

The company is therefore able to sue and be sued in its own name, and has its own legal duties, rights and obligations. It is the sole owner of the company assets, and has sole liability for the company's debts.

Shareholders are not co-owners of the company's assets, but rather members of the company. Shareholders can be individual persons, partnerships and other companies. Persons without Austrian citizenship can also be shareholders.

An essential criterion of the AG is that the shareholders have no further liability other than their shareholding for the company's debts. The creditors can only claim against the company's assets. The AG as a company has an unlimited liability in itself, but the liability is, of course, limited to the amount of assets available and does not affect the shareholders. Each AG has an obligatory minimum share capital. This must be determined with a nominal amount in schillings.

A.2.2.1 Formation (Gründung)

The formation is an essential stage of the AG. When all the requirements of the formation are fulfilled, the AG then has its own legal personality. To avoid any misuse, there are a great number of provisions which complicate the publicity of the formation, the raising of capital, the calling in of a notary, necessity of an audit and the special form of the registration.

Normally, the formation is effected in one of two ways:

(i) standard formation;

(ii) successive formation.

In the *standard formation*, all the shares are allotted to the founders of the company. The following steps are necessary for the standard formation:

(a) determination of articles of association by the founders which is recorded by a notary;

(b) subscription for shares by the founders;

(c) appointment by the subscribers of the first supervisory board (Aufsichtsrat);

(d) appointment by the subscribers of the auditor (Abschlußprüfer) for the first annual audit;

(e) appointment of the management board (Vorstand) by a resolution of the supervisory board;

(f) a formation report is to be written by the subscribers;

(g) a formation audit by the management board members;

(h) a formation audit by the supervisory board members;

(i) in some cases it is necessary to have an audit made by auditors who are appointed by the registration court;

(j) the assessment and payment of the capital transaction tax as well as obtaining the clearance certificate;

(k) payment of the cash contributions by the subscribers;

(l) obtaining the expert opinion from the Chamber of Commerce concerning the business name of the AG of (not compulsory, but advisable in doubtful cases);

(m) obtaining the necessary permissions from the Trade Office;

(n) should a non-resident subscriber have shares, a permit from the Austrian National Bank must be obtained, whereby, presently, a general permit is given by the National Bank;

(o) registration of the AG at the competent Registration Court by all the subscribers, as well as the members of the management and supervisory board;

(p) registration of the AG in the Commercial Register (Firmenbuch);

(q) publication of the registration.

The AG gains its legal personality as soon as it is registered in the Commercial Register. If the subscribers carried out business before registration of the AG, the registered AG will then take over all rights and duties of that business. Publicising the registration does not of itself give legal existence for the company.

The shares of the *successive formation* need not all be taken over by the subscribers. The special features of this formation process can be seen as follows:

(a) the rest of the shares are offered for subscription;

(b) the subscription of the shares takes place by the issue of a certificate of subscription (Zeichnungsschein);

(c) as soon as the subscription of all the shares has taken place, the founders call the first shareholders' meeting (Erste Hauptversammlung);

(d) the shareholders' meeting appoints the first supervisory board and the auditor for the first year-end closure;

(e) the supervisory board then appoints the first management board;

(f) the company applies for registration in the Commercial Register;

(g) after the application, the Registration Court calls a shareholders' meeting of all the shareholders of whom it has been notified;

(h) the shareholders' meeting is managed by the Registration Court and is defined as a constituent shareholders' meeting and this determines the formation of the company;

(i) after the determination of the company's formation, the registration takes place.

Under Austrian company law, only two founders are necessary for the formation of an AG. Two trustees can also take part in the formation. These trustees have the same full liability as the founders. Trust foundations normally occur when, after the formation of the company, all of the shares are joined together and are in the possession of one shareholder. The founders can normally be represented at the formation by someone with a certified power of authorisation.

A public notary must be present at the formation. He must make an official record of each formation procedure and notarially attest certain signatures.

A.2.2.1.1 Articles of association (Statuten) The determination of the articles of association by the subscribers is the same as a contract. All the founders must take part. A decision of the majority is not possible. The determination of the articles must be officially recorded by a public notary. If it is not officially recorded, a registration in the Commercial Register cannot take place.

The articles have an optional and an obligatory content. The obligatory content is:

(a) business name and registered office of the company;

(b) purpose of the company;

(c) amount of share capital (Grundkapital), furthermore whether bearer shares or registered shares are to be issued;

(d) nominal amount of each share; if there are more than three classes of share, then these must be defined;

(e) manner of the constitution of the management board (number of management board members);

(f) form of publication of the company.

Should the legal provisions be supplemented or should they vary, special provisions must be made in the Articles. Obligatory provisions cannot, of course, be amended by the Articles.

A.2.2.1.2 Registered office Under Austrian company law, the registered office of the AG is the place where the company has its business, where the business management is or where the administration takes place. These provisions can be diverged from if there is an important reason. An example would be competition considerations.

An AG can only have one registered office. It is possible to move the registered office in Austria. An amendment to the articles would be necessary. Should the registered office be moved abroad, this would result in the dissolution of the company. The location of the registered office is, in different respects, of great importance. This determines which is the competent court and results in different tax consequences.

A2.2.1.3 Business name Generally, the name of the AG is derived from the objects of the company. This is called a "Sachfirma". Exceptions are permitted only in limited circumstances. In exceptional cases (*e.g.* company takeover), the name of a person can be contained in the company name, or a mixture of a person's name and the object of the company. The company must always have the letters AG in its name, which stands for "Aktiengesellschaft".

A.2.2.1.4 Duration The articles can limit the duration of the AG. However, at the time of dissolution, the company is still not at an end. It stops being a company as advertised and becomes a company in liquidation. If a duration time-limit is given, then a resolution of the shareholders' meeting for the dissolution will not be necessary.

If an AG is formed without a duration time-limit, then the company will continue until a reason for dissolution is given.

Apart from the expiry of the company's duration, other reasons for dissolution are as follows:

(a) a decision of the shareholders' meeting with a three-quarters majority: provisions can be made in the articles to raise this majority or that any such decision also depends on other conditions;

(b) commencement of insolvency proceedings over the assets of the company because of an inability to pay or excessive indebtedness;

(c) decision of the Insolvency Court of rejection of the commencement of insolvency proceedings due to the lack of procedure costs;

(d) declaration of nullity because of the invalidity of important provisions of the articles;

(e) cancellation *ex officio* of the company because of the invalidity of the provisions of the articles;

(f) cancellation of the company because of lack of assets by application from the Chamber of Commerce or the authorities or other official bodies.

Other reasons for the dissolution of the company can be provided for in the articles.

A.2.2.1.5 Share capital (Grundkapital) The share capital is a nominal capital, which must be determined by the articles. The shareholders commit themselves to raising this share capital in favour of the company. An alteration to the share capital must be provided for in the articles. The increase or reduction of the share capital must be registered.

Under Austrian law, the minimum of share capital is 1,000,000 Sch. In the formation of a company by cash subscription, at least one-quarter of the share capital must be paid in. If the issuing amount for the shares is higher than the nominal amount, then the difference must be paid in full by the date of the formation of the company. One exception is the investment company, whose share capital amounts to 10,000,000 Sch and must be paid in cash as a whole.

Generally, it is possible for there to be a contribution in kind instead of cash. Therefore other assets besides cash can be contributed to the AG. In this connection, the creditors and other shareholders (apart from the founders) need special protection. Therefore special measures are taken, such as inspections by all shareholders, supervisory board members, management board members, legally appointed auditors of the formation and by the Registration Court. Also, the founders, the supervisory board and management board members are answerable if the value of the contribution is not adequate. If a contribution in kind is overvalued, then the shareholder is liable for the difference.

A.2.2.2 *Company shares*

To have an interest in an AG, one must hold a share, which means a person has the right of membership of the AG. This right of membership contains property and participation rights as well as the right to claim new issue shares when the share capital is increased.

Each share issued represents a fraction of the share capital. They can be nominal shares in the amount of 100 Sch, 500 Sch and 1,000 Sch or multiple shares of 1,000 Sch. Austrian company law only recognises shares with a nominal value (Nennwertaktien) and not no-par-value shares (Quotienaktien), as in the Anglo-American field.

The shares take the form of special deeds. These deeds differ in their transferability and are as follows:

(a) general share certificates with no shareholder's name written thereon;

(b) share certificates with the name of the shareholder on them;

(c) share certificates with shareholders' names thereon and subject to restricted transfer rights.

As well as the actual share deed, dividend and renewal coupons are issued.

Differences between the ordinary and a preference share must be defined. The ordinary share is the normal type of share. The preference shares have special preferences (especially in respect to dividends). Normally, these shares have no right of vote. Multiple voting rights are forbidden.

A.2.2.2.1   Share purchase   When a company has a standard formation, the founders purchase shares by taking them over at the formation. In contrast, when a company has a successive formation, only part of the shares are taken over by the founders at the formation and the rest of the shares are offered for subscription. Subscriptions are made via a written certificate of subscription.

In the certificate of subscription, the interested party state their offer to take over the share, which can be accepted or rejected by the founders. Of course, the founders are also entitled to apply for subscription.

Before the shares are issued, interim certificates (Interimscheine) can be issued. These are investment certificates which are made out in the name of the interested party. They can only be issued after the registration of the company in the Commercial Register.

Interim certificates are only issued so long as the contribution has not been fully paid or until the founders' shares have been printed. These are only printed after the nominal amount or the increased issuing amount has been fully paid.

With respect to the purchasing of shares which are already in circulation, this differs from share type to share type:

(a) the transmission of unnamed shares is made by contractual agreement and mere transfer;

(b) named shares without transfer restrictions are transferred by indorsement or by universal succession: a transfer entry in the Share Register is also necessary; but this entry only determines who the shareholder is;

(c) for transmission of registered shares with restricted transfer, the consent, *e.g.* of the other shareholders, is necessary: this consent, however, can only be refused if the shareholders have an important reason for doing so.

Apart from the right to purchase a share at the formation of the company or by legal succession, there are other special forms of purchase:

(a) a takeover of shares due to an increase of the share capital;

(b) a share purchase by the conversion of convertible bonds;

(c) a share purchase due to a company merger.

A.2.2.2.2 Membership rights and duties There is a distinction between general and special membership rights. All the shareholders are entitled to the general membership rights. These are the right to the pro rata profit, the right to purchase new issued shares, the right to an equity interest in the remaining assets after liquidation, right to participation in the shareholders' meeting as well as the right to demand information, to contest and the right to oppose.

Individual shareholders can be granted special rights. Under these special rights, one often finds the right to preferential dividends, the right to determine supervisory board members, the right to use specific facilities/equipment free of charge or the right to a higher liquidations quota.

There are specific rights in Austrian company law to protect the minority, which the shareholders can assert jointly if the proper conditions have been met according to the size of the minority.

The shareholder's main obligation is to pay for the full amount of his shares. The shareholder is not allowed to set off a claim against the AG with this obligation for payment. The company can set this claim off, so long as it is not doubtful or uncertain. The articles can provide that the shareholder does specified acts (e.g. works) for the company. These performances are not money payments. The shareholders are not obliged to pay additional contributions. Should the share capital be increased, the shareholder is free to subscribe for shares.

If a shareholder is behind in his payments for his contribution, he can be sued or expelled from the company by a forfeiture of shares procedure. The shareholder loses all his shares and cannot reclaim payments of contributions which he has already paid. The predecessors of the defaulting shareholder, who can be seen from the share register, can be claimed on by recourse. Should this also be unsuccessful, then the shares are either sold or put up for public auction. If the debts are still not covered, then the shareholder remains liable for his debts. If a profit is made from the sale of the shares, the defaulting shareholder is not entitled to the difference.

A.2.2.2.3 Increase and decrease of share capital An *increase of the share capital* is a measure designed to obtain more capital in the company. However, not every increase actually brings more capital into the company. This is the difference between an effective increase and a nominal increase.

The *effective* increase, where new capital/assets are brought into the company, can be found in the following forms:

(a) standard capital increase (ordentliche Kapitalerhöhung);

(b) authorised capital increase (genehmigtes Kapital);

(c) conditional capital increase (bedingte Kapitalerhöhung).

A capital increase can be in the form of cash or contributions in kind. A capital increase requires a qualified majority decision of the shareholders' meeting. Should there be more than one type of share, then separate decisions must be made.

The shareholder has a "Bezugsrecht". This is the right to subscribe to shares of a new issue in the proportion of his existing share interest. However, a qualified decision of the shareholders' meeting can bar this right, under the condition that they have an appropriate reason for doing so. Should the decision be passed by the shareholders' meeting without an appropriate reason, this can be contested. Such an appropriate reason is, for instance, the issuance of shares preferably to employees.

A capital increase must be registered at the Registration Court. The decision of the shareholders' meeting to increase the capital must be registered in addition to the execution. The capital increase comes into effect as soon as the execution is registered.

Apart from this normal form of capital increase (standard capital increase), Austrian company law also recognises an authorised capital increase. A capital increase can be provided for in the articles or by an amendment to the articles at a later date. This requires a decision of a 75 per cent majority of the shareholders. Should this be the case, the management board can be authorised to increase the capital by issuing new shares.

This authorisation is limited for a maximum period of five years. This gives the management the option to wait for favourable market conditions. Such authorisation must also be registered at the Registration Court.

The conditional capital increase serves as a preparation measure for the merging of companies or for the granting of a "Bezugsrecht" to proprietors for convertible bonds. The conditional capital is not allowed to exceed half of the share capital which was available at the time when the decision was made. Here, it is also necessary to have a 75 per cent majority of the shareholders' votes.

A nominal capital increase leads to the conversion of reserves into share capital. The shareholders' position, with respect to the assets, does not generally change. This capital increase does not bring new capital into the company. The shareholders of the company receive bonus shares.

Also, a reduction of the share capital requires a 75 per cent majority vote of the shareholders' meeting. In individual cases, this requirement can be increased.

A capital reduction is effective when the share capital is reduced and the shareholders' equity is paid back or when the shareholders are released from their obligation to make contributions. Here, one must note the special conditions for the protection of the creditors. The Court Register must be notified of this decision and consequently registered. The company must also notify the creditors of this decision, who then have six months in which to contact the AG in respect of their debts. The AG must satisfy these demands or give some kind of guarantee.

A regular capital reduction cannot be made to reduce the share capital below the minimum amount of 1,000,000 Sch, unless there is also a capital increase at the same time which brings the share capital above the minimum amount.

Another form of capital reduction is the nominal reduction. In this form of reduction, the shareholders do not receive any repayment. The losses are eliminated by entering them in the accounts with the share capital. Thus, the creditors receive a special protection, as further distribution of the profits is limited. For example, the distribution of a dividend, which exceeds more than 4 per cent of the share capital, is only permissible after a period of two years after the decision for a nominal reduction was made. There are other limitations which also must be observed.

A capital reduction can be made, by a provision in the articles, to shares by compulsory or voluntary redemption which is passed by the shareholders' meeting with a 75 per cent majority. Capital reduction is subject to special regulations for the protection of creditors.

A.2.2.2.4 Purchase of own shares by the AG The purchase of own shares by the company is very limited, so as to give the creditors extra protection. Austrian law only recognises very few cases where the AG can purchase its own shares:

(a) to avoid imminent heavy damage to the AG;

(b) if the purchase of the shares is free of consideration or is executed through a buying commission by a bank;

(c) if the acquisition is effected by universal succession;

(d) if the shares are to be offered to the employees of the AG or of an affiliate corporation, with the exception of members of the board (Vorstand, Aufsichtsrat) and other executive employees, and if these shares are to be issued within one year;

(e) if the shares are to be offered to executive employees and members of the board of the AG or of an affiliate corporation, whereby the shares have to be issued within 18 months after the shareholders' meeting has granted such an offering and issuing of shares;

(f) if the shares are used to compensate minority shareholders, as far as it is prescribed by law;

(g) for the redemption of shares according to the rules for the decrease of the stated capital.

In the cases (a), (d), (e) and (f), the purchase is only permitted if the purchased shares do not exceed 10 per cent of the share capital including already purchased shares.

Of course, the attachment of own shares as well as the purchase of shares by a subsidiary company from a parent company is not allowed or at least very limited.

A.2.2.2.5 Share register When the AG issues registered shares or interim certificates, it is obliged to keep a share register. This is obligatory and irrespective of the number of shareholders.

The management board is obliged to keep the share register. The registered shares must be entered in the share register with the proprietor's name, profession and place of residence. Only the shareholder himself is to be entered in the share register and not a creditor with a right of lien nor an usufructuary. The first entry of a registered share or an interim certificate must be made by the company itself.

Should it be the case that a share is transferred, this has to be reported to the

AG. The share is to be presented to the AG and consequently entered in the share register. The legal succession in the equity interest is irrespective of the transfer entry in the share register.

When a registration is made in the share register, it only has the effect that the person who is registered is considered as a shareholder and is subject of the rights and obligations towards the company.

An inspection of the share register is not regulated by law. In the administration of justice, the shareholder has an enforceable right to inspect the share register. The shareholder can inspect the entire share register and, therefore, the entries of the other shareholders.

The share register is especially important when recourse is taken against the predecessor of a defaulting shareholder, as the name of the predecessor can be seen from the share register.

A.2.2.3   Company's bodies

In contrast to partnerships, alterations to the functions, rights, obligations and structure of the various company bodies by the articles are very limited. Principally, the functions of the company's bodies can also be performed by persons who are not shareholders.

The AG has four compulsory bodies;

(a)   management board (Vorstand);

(b)   supervisory board (Aufsichtsrat);

(c)   shareholders' meeting (Hauptversammlung);

(d)   auditors (Abschlußprüfer).

The functions of these bodies are exactly defined by law and cannot be altered by the articles of association.

The management board has the duty to manage the business and to represent the AG. The supervisory board appoints, dismisses and also supervises the management board. The shareholders' meeting passes decisions about the appointment and dismissal of the supervisory board and the auditors, as well as about fundamental questions concerning the company. The auditors are obligated to control the accounts.

Apart from these compulsory bodies, other bodies can be provided for in the articles of association. These additional bodies cannot, of course, be given functions which have already been assigned by law to one of the aforementioned compulsory bodies. One of these additional bodies, which one comes across quite frequently, is the advisory board (Beirat).

A.2.2.3.1   Management board (Vorstand)   The management board is obliged to manage the business of the company and bears this responsibility alone. They

23

manage the business internally and represent the company externally.

A.2.2.3.1.1 Appointment and dismissal The members of the management board are appointed by the supervisory board for a maximum of five years. The management board can consist of one or more members, who must be natural persons. The number of persons in the management board is determined by the articles of association as are other conditions such as citizenship or residence qualifications. Usually, the management board has more than one member. In individual cases, there are special regulations by which the management board must have at least two members.

The reappointment of a management board member is possible. For such reappointments to be effective, there must be written confirmation from the chairman of the supervisory board.

In the absence of sufficient appointments by the supervisory board, the court can be asked to intervene.

As the supervisory board's function is to control the management board, a supervisory board member cannot also be a member of the management board. Should a management board member be unable to carry out his function, a member of the supervisory board can temporarily replace him. During this time, he is not allowed to perform his function as a supervisory board member.

The function of a management board member is determined by his appointment. However, the legal relationship between the company and the management board members still must be regulated. Legally, this is qualified as an employer/employee relationship. The difference is, however, that it has its own responsibility and nobody can burden it with instructions.

Should the supervisory board have good reasons, it can revoke the appointment of a management board member and also the nomination of the management board's chairman. Grounds for revocation are grave breach of duty; incapability for orderly business management; withdrawal of confidence by a shareholders' resolution, etc.

The revocation of the appointment is effective, unless the court considers such revocation is ineffective. However, revocation does not normally affect the contract of employment. This would depend on the nature of the reason for revoking board membership.

A member of the management board has the right to resign from office if he has an important reason for doing so. Without good reason, he needs acceptance of his resignation from the supervisory board.

Every alteration which takes place within the management board has to be entered in the court register. Every new member of the management board must submit his signature to the court.

A.2.2.3.1.2 Rights and duties Only the management board is authorised and obligated to manage the business. This cannot be withdrawn from the management board. Also, the business management cannot be taken over by another body of the company. Neither the supervisory board nor the shareholders can give the management board instructions regarding the business management.

The management board must manage the business to the benefit of the company, while, at the same time, taking the shareholders' interest into consideration, as well as that of any employees and any public interest. The management board must abide by the articles regarding the objects of the company.

The business management is determined by the management board as a group. Therefore, no member can be excluded from the management of the business. In individual cases, the supervisory board can appoint a member of the management board as the chairman. The chairman shall have the casting vote. According to Austrian company law, the management board can only pass decisions if there is a majority of votes. Any exceptions can be regulated by the articles.

It frequently happens that the company's business is dividend between different management board members who are given different fields of responsibility. This division can be made by the supervisory board. Also, the supervisory board can lay down the rules of procedure for the management board. This does not interfere with the responsibility of the individual management board members.

On the running of the business management, only the management board members have the right to represent the company. Only in a few individual cases is this right of representation given to other bodies of the company. Normally, the members of the management board must represent the company collectively. However, a diverging decision can be determined in the articles.

With respect to the management board's authority, there are certain restrictions concerning the business management. Certain business acts should only be carried out if the consent of the supervisory board is given—for example, the purchase and sale of the shares, companies and immovable properties, etc. Big investments, the raising of large credits and the establishment and closure of branches also rank among the acts to which the supervisory board must give its consent before they are carried out. Also, any change to the principles of business policy need the consent of the supervisory board. External acts are normally effective, even if the supervisory board has not given consent. In individual cases, the management board is liable for any damages or losses.

Some business transactions need the consent of the shareholders, especially the issuing of convertible bonds or the completion of merger agreements. Also, annual accounts must be audited and this has to be accepted by the supervisory board as well as the management board.

If there are more restrictions concerning the management board's authority, these do not affect the validity of legal transactions with a third party. However, the third party cannot demand performance if the acts of the management board are not in the interests of the company and the third party was aware or should have been aware of this fact.

Often, the company is represented by at least two members of the management board or by one member and a "Prokurist". Every member of the management board has the authority to receive declarations and documents. Every member of the management board has both the duty of good faith and also a fiduciary duty towards the company.

25

The management board members are subject to a strict prohibition on competition. They cannot carry on a trade business nor do business in a branch of the company, either for their own account or for the account of a third party, without the consent of the supervisory board. Also, they are not allowed to have an interest in another company as a personally liable partner. Should a member violate this restriction, he is liable in damages to the company. The company can demand that any business made on the member's own account is accounted for to the company. In any case, any remuneration/profit received by the member is to be paid into the company. This is subject to a limitation period of three months.

The giving of loans to the members of the management board is restricted. Should a loan be more than a member's monthly wage, it needs the consent of the supervisory board.

The business management is not only controlled by the supervisory board. The shareholders can decide, with a simple majority, to have a special examination of any business transactions carried out and can appoint an examiner for this purpose.

During the shareholders' meeting, the management board is obliged to give the shareholders information. This information must be conscientiously given and accurate. Information can be refused to be given, should this be of a disadvantage to the company or is privileged due to national security.

The management board must give a regular report to the supervisory board. This must be at least a quarterly report about the company's business transactions and the general situation.

A.2.2.3.1.3 *Meetings*

There is no requirement concerning the number of meetings which the management board must hold. This is, however, not the case for the supervisory board. It is the management board's responsibility to decide how often a meeting is held. The diligence of the business manager is to be taken into account.

In individual cases, it depends on the management board's rules of procedure as to how necessary the meetings are. By violation of the necessary standard of care due to the lack of care or due to an insufficient number of meetings, the management board can be held liable.

A.2.2.3.1.4 *Liability of the management board members*

Normally, liability claims against the members of the management board occur very seldom. There are, however, strict liability provisions which cannot be modified in favour of the members by the articles. In Austria, there are very few cases as to the question of the management board members' liability, as this is normally regulated by way of settlement.

The members of the management board administrate the company's assets and are subject to a special standard of care. They must apply the diligence of a conscientious business manager. Should they not do this, then this is a breach of their duty and justifies a claim for damages. Should such a claim occur, the member can justify himself by giving counter-evidence that he exercised the legal standard of care.

The general rule is that all members who are at fault are jointly and severally liable. The members who have different responsibilities, and therefore are not at fault, are still not free from their collective responsibility for the business management. Every member has the duty, to a reasonable extent, to keep a check on the business management of his colleagues in their particular fields of responsibility. Should he violate this duty, he will be held liable.

The management board is not liable to the company if it acts according to a decision passed at the shareholders' meeting. However, this does not exclude claims for damages by creditors who cannot claim any damages from the company. Even if a particular action is consented to by the Supervisory Board, the members' liability towards the company still remains.

Examples of a management board member's liability are where:

(a) contributions are refunded to the shareholders;

(b) interest or shares in the profits are paid to the shareholders;

(c) the company purchases its own shares by subscription, takes them in pledge or by redemption;

(d) shares are issued before all the capital is paid in;

(e) the company's capital is distributed; or

(f) loans are granted. It is possible for the company to waive a claim for damages. However, this is only possible after a period of five years beginning from the date of the claim and with the consent of the shareholders, as long as there is no opposition from a special minority. The same applies to damage claims which are regulated by way of settlement.

A.2.2.3.2 Supervisory board (Aufsichtsrat) The supervisory board is a compulsory body of the company. Only this body can use this special name. The supervisory board is a completely separate body to the management board.

A.2.2.3.2.1 Appointment and dismissal The number of supervisory board members is restricted by law. This states that the supervisory board shall consist of at least three members. This number can be increased by the articles.

The maximum number of members allowed depends on the share capital as follows:

Share Capital	Maximum Number of Members
Up to 5,000,000 Sch	7
More than 5,000,000 Sch and up to 50,000,000 Sch	12
More than 50,000,000 Sch	20

27

According to Austrian employment law, the works council can appoint members of the supervisory board. These members are not taken into consideration in the above-mentioned minimum and maximum figures.

The appointment of supervisory board members can be made as follows:

(a) election by the shareholders in a general meeting;

(b) appointment by an individual shareholder;

(c) appointment by the court;

(d) appointment by the works council.

Normally, the supervisory board members are elected by the shareholders on a simple majority. A representative of the minority can be elected on to the supervisory board, so long as he has at least one-third of all the shareholders' votes. Generally all board members may be re-elected (and such appointments can be revoked) by a 75 per cent majority, subject to modification in the articles. However, shareholder members only face re-election four years after their initial appointment.

The articles may provide that certain shareholders have the right to appoint not more than one-third of the supervisory board members. This excludes the members who are appointed by the works council. If the shareholder does not use this right, the seat on the supervisory board remains vacant. The duration of the appointed member's function is unlimited.

Board members can also be appointed by the court on an application by the management board, by another supervisory board member or by a shareholder. This only applies when an appointment resolution has remained inquorate for three months.

According to the Austrian constitutional employment law (Arbeits-verfassungsgesetz), employees' representatives from the competent personnel bodies are to be appointed as members of the supervisory board. Here, the principle of the one-third apportionment applies. One out of every three supervisory board members must be an employees' representative. If there is an odd number of members, the number of employees' representatives is increased by one.

The names of the members of the supervisory board are entered into the Commercial Register. Any change in the supervisory board must be published in the company's notification papers by the management board. This also applies to the employees' representatives on the supervisory board. The supervisory board must have a chairman and at least one vice-chairman. Both persons are elected by the supervisory board. Other internal rules for this body are included in the articles.

In all cases, a supervisory board member's appointment may be revoked by the person or body responsible for the appointment, or if the member ceases to hold the necessary or relevant qualifications, *e.g.* an employees' representative is no longer also a member of the works council.

A.2.2.3.2.2   Rights and duties   The rights and duties of the supervisory board are clearly regulated by Austrian law. The articles can assign further duties to the supervisory board.

Essential duties of the supervisory board are as follows:

(a) appointment of the management board;

(b) control of the business management, *i.e.* supervising and checking the management board to see if it is working legally and economically, but not interfering directly or giving instructions to the board;

(c) to manage the accounts;

(d) to call a shareholders' meeting;

(e) to present certain business management matters, for which its consent is needed, for adoption before the shareholders' meeting;

(f) to represent the company in law suits against the management board;

(g) to grant loans to members of the management board.

To be able to carry out it duties of control, the supervisory board has the right to inspect all information and to demand a report from the management board. The supervisory board is obliged to observe a similar standard of care to that of the management board. This applies to all members of the supervisory board, including those appointed by the works council. The members must carry out their assigned duties themselves and must not delegate to others.

Remuneration can be granted to the supervisory board members for their performance, so long as the financial and legal position of the company permits it. This remuneration can be provided for in the articles. A reduction of the remuneration which is provided for in the articles can be made at any time, so long as there is a simple majority of votes in favour of this. If remuneration is not provided for in the articles, then this can be determined by the shareholders' meeting.

A.2.2.3.2.3 Meetings The number of necessary supervisory board meetings held in one business year depends on the requirements of the company. Legally, three meetings per year are to be held. A higher number can be determined in the articles or in the internal rules of the supervisory board.

Every member of the supervisory board, or the management board as a whole, can demand that the chairman of the supervisory board call a meeting without delay; the rounds and the purpose for this must be given. In such a case, the meeting must be held within two weeks after it has been called. Should the chairman of the supervisory board fail to do this, the applicant can call a meeting of the supervisory board himself.

Generally, only members of the supervisory board take part in the supervisory board meetings. Members of the management board can take part in these meetings if they receive an invitation from the chairman of the supervisory board or from the supervisory board as a whole. For consultation on individual matters, experts or other consulting persons can take part in these meetings.

Decisions passed by the supervisory board are made orally in the meetings. If all the members of the supervisory board unanimously agree, then no meeting is necessary and a written resolution can be passed. Voting by telephone is not allowed.

Generally, the supervisory board member has the duty to take part in the meetings himself. However, the articles may allow a member to appoint another member to represent him under the power of a written authorisation. The chairman cannot pass his duty as chairman to another person. Unless otherwise stated in the articles, a quorum for board meetings is three members, excluding proxies. Normally, the supervisory board passes decisions with a simple majority but in certain cases the articles may provide for exceptions to this rule.

A.2.2.3.2.4 Legal liability of the supervisory board members The supervisory board members also have the duty of a certain standard of care, just as the management board members have. Should they violate this duty, then they are personally liable for damages. According to the decided case law, the members must have a higher degree of experience and knowledge than an average business person. In particular, they must have the ability to recognise and deal with difficult legal and economic situations.

A.2.2.3.3 Shareholders' meeting (Hauptversammiung)

A.2.2.3.3.1 General provisions The shareholders' meeting is also a compulsory body of the AG. The shareholders can only exercise their rights in the shareholders' meeting. This meeting is for basic decisions of the AG and has only a restricted scope of duties. The duties are determined by the Austrian company law and the range of these duties can be expanded by the articles. Questions as to the business management can only be decided or passed by the shareholders if this is demanded by the management board, or to a limited extent by the supervisory board, that they should do so.

The shareholders' meeting has the following duties:

(a) to elect and dismiss the supervisory board members;

(b) to pass decisions for a special examination of business operations and to appoint the auditors;

(c) to make decisions to modify the articles or other basic decisions (capital increase, capital reduction, convertible bonds, mergers, liquidation of the company, etc.);

(d) to make decisions regarding the agenda of the annual meeting.

Normally, it is necessary to distinguish between an ordinary and an extraordinary shareholders' meeting. The ordinary shareholders' meeting is held at regular intervals and has the following duties:

(a) to take notice of the annual accounts and business reports and to put them up for discussion;

(b) to make decisions about the distribution of the profits;

(c) to make decisions about the acceptance of the supervisory board members' report and that of the management board;

(d) to elect the auditors.

A.2.2.3.3.2 Calling a shareholders' meeting There is no procedural difference in calling either an ordinary or an extraordinary shareholders' meeting: both must be called in the proper way. The management board is obliged to call a shareholders' meeting if legal questions or matters under the terms of the articles are to be dealt with; whereas the supervisory board is authorised to call a meeting if it considers it necessary to do so. In both cases, before the meeting is called, the relevant board must come to a decision on the particular subject in question.

According to the existing rights of the minority, a shareholders' minority of 5 per cent of the share capital can call a shareholders' meeting, although the articles can reduce this minority. The minority can demand that the management board or the supervisory board call a shareholders' meeting. It must, however, inform the respective board of the reason for calling the shareholders' meeting. Should the management board or the supervisory board not perform their duty in this respect, the minority can be authorised by the court to call the meeting themselves.

The calling of a shareholders' meeting is to be published in all the company newspapers. Should the number of shareholders be small and their shares are secured, then an announcement in the papers is not made.

There must be at least 14 days' notice of the shareholders' meeting. If there are a large number of shareholders, this time limit is usually extended by the articles to enable the shareholders to deposit their share certificates up to a certain day before the shareholders' meeting. This is the only way in which the shareholders' right to vote can be examined.

The various points on the agenda of the shareholders' meeting must be stated when the shareholders' meeting is called. These points must be published at least seven days before the meeting. Should a larger majority than a simple majority be necessary for certain decisions, then the time-limit increases from seven to 14 days. The exact time and place of the shareholders' meeting must be made known.

If the calling of a shareholders' meeting is faulty, the decisions passed in this meeting are usually considered as null and void. This does not apply if all the shareholders are present or represented at the meeting. In individual cases of a faulty calling of the shareholders' meeting the decisions will stand but can be appealed against by the shareholders.

A.2.2.3.3.3 Location of the meeting If the articles are silent as to the location the shareholders' meeting must be held at the registered office of the company. If the company's shares are admitted for quotation on the Austrian stock exchange, then the shareholders' meeting can be held at the seat (*i.e.* the same town) of this stock exchange. Other locations for the shareholders' meeting can be determined in the articles.

The articles may not allow the person who is authorised to call a shareholders' meeting to choose the location; however, the articles can provide a choice of locations. An exception is holding a shareholders' meeting abroad. Such a provision in the articles is null and void.

A.2.2.3.3.4 Quorum As long as there is no provision under Austrian law nor in the articles that there be a special limit for the quorum, the shareholders' meeting is competent to pass a resolution independent of the number of shareholders who were present or represented. In such a case, the presence of only one shareholder is enough.

However, the articles can determine that the quorum of the shareholders' meeting depends on the presence of a specific number of shareholders or a specific percentage of the share capital. In that case, the articles should determine what conditions are needed so that a further meeting is competent to pass a resolution, if the first meeting was inquorate.

A.2.2.3.3.5 Decision-making One of the duties of the shareholders' meeting is to make resolutions. The shareholders have a right to all information before a resolution is made. Also, the shareholders can discuss the motion. The resolutions are passed by a simple majority of the valid votes unless the law or the articles state otherwise.

A qualified majority is required for the alteration of the company's objects, the ordinary capital increase, liquidation of the company, the continuation of the liquidated company, dismissal of the supervisory board members, the issuing of convertible bonds and for alterations to the articles. The articles themselves may vary the qualified majority, or amend the need for one.

The individual shareholder's right to vote depends on the nominal amount of the share which he holds. Under Austrian law if a shareholder has more than one share, the articles can specify that his voting right is limited to a maximum amount. A shareholder with more than one vote can divide his votes. Also, syndicate contracts with a commitment to vote a certain way are allowed.

Should a resolution which was made with the proper majority have an inherent defect, then this resolution can be null and void. Other offences against Austrian company law or the articles can be appealed against within one month; otherwise the resolution remains valid.

A.2.2.3.4 Auditors The annual company accounts and the annual business report must be examined by auditors. The auditors' report can only be presented to the supervisory board after the annual accounts and the annual business report have been examined by the auditors. The approval of the annual accounts cannot be obtained without the auditors' examination.

The provisions for the examination of the annual accounts have been altered under the Accounting Act (Rechnungs-legungsgesetz) 1990, which came into effect for business years commencing on or after January 1, 1992. However, it has always been the case that the annual accounts and the statement of affairs are then subject to the examinations of the auditors.

According to the new Act, the examination of the annual accounts must ascertain whether the legal regulations and the additional provisions of the articles have been observed. The statement of affairs must be examined to see if it conforms with the annual accounts and to make sure that other details in the statement of affairs do not give a misleading impression of the company's situation. The auditor is a necessary body of the company.

A.2.2.3.4.1 Appointment of auditors According to the present situation under Austrian company law, the auditors are elected at the shareholders' meeting. This also applies under the Austrian Accounting Act. One or more auditors can be elected by the shareholders. Normally, the shareholders elect only one auditor.

The auditors who are elected by the shareholders receive their orders from the management board. According to the Accounting Act, from 1992 the auditors will receive their orders from the supervisory board. This is to be given without delay. This order can only be revoked if another auditor is appointed.

According to Austrian company law, the supervisory board can revoke the elected auditors at any time without giving any reasons for doing so. An amendment to this has now been included in the new Accounting Act. The request for examination can only be withdrawn from the auditor, when important reasons are given which refer to the auditor as a person. This must be decided by the court, whereby, the supervisory board or a certain minority of the shareholders must make an application to the court first. This application must be made within one month after the day when the auditors were elected.

The auditors are to be elected annually, during the business year. Should an election not be made before the business year expires, then the auditors are to be appointed by the court. This appointment cannot be contested. If an auditor is appointed by the court, then according to Austrian company law, he can only be removed by the court. An important reason for this has to be given. Differences of opinion between the company and the auditors cannot be considered as important reasons. Even if the auditor is dismissed, he still has to inform the company of the result of his examination.

A.2.2.3.4.2 Powers and duties The auditor has a right of access to all information concerning the company. He can demand any explanations and proofs which he considers necessary for a precise examination. All books and papers of the company are to be submitted to the auditor. Furthermore, he can examine the stock of the company's assets and all its debts.

He can demand information about the parent company and its subsidiary, should he feel it necessary for a detailed examination. It is the auditor's duty to summarise the end result by making an examination report and to ascertain whether the book-keeping, the annual accounts, and the business or situation report are in accordance with the regulations. The auditor must also state in his report how much necessary information was given to him by the management board.

Should the auditor, during his examination, come across facts which could jeopardise the company's existence or which could heavily restrict the company's future development, this must be stated in his report. The same applies if he should discover that the management board has breached the articles or any provisions under Austrian company law. If the auditor has no objections after the end of his examination, he must certify the financial statement. If there are objections, the auditor must make this certification subject to a reservation or refuse to certify the financial statement at all.

The auditor is obliged to carry out his examination conscientiously and impartially. The auditor is also obliged not to disclose or exploit business or company secrets. Should the auditor violate his duties, he is then liable for damages. According to the new Accounting Act, the liability for damages for persons who act negligently is limited to 5,000,000 Sch.

A.2.2.4 *Works council*

The Works Council can be defined as the representative body of the workforce who are elected by the employees to represent them.

Under the Labour Relations Law of 1974, any corporation which employs five or more persons must allow employee representatives to have a voice and a significant right of participation in decisions concerning the employees. The number of employee representatives varies according to the total number of employees. The management of the corporation must therefore consult with and agree with the works council on matters such as working hours, payment of wages, holidays and welfare arrangements. The works council also has a say in individual personnel matters and must be consulted and its consent obtained in circumstances such as hiring and firing employees. If no agreement can be reached, the final decision lies with the labour court. The works council also has a right to information on personnel matters and has a right to inspect personnel files.

The Labour Relations Law ensures that for every two supervisory board members appointed in accordance with the "Aktiengesetz" and the articles, there must be one further employee representative. If there is an odd number of members, the number of employees representatives is increased by one. The employees can appoint whomsoever they wish to represent them. Usually, these will be members of the workforce. The members of the supervisory board who have been appointed by the workforce can also be dismissed by them.

A.2.3   Gesellschaft mit beschränkter Haftung (GmbH)

The legal form of the GmbH is regulated in Austrian law for private limited companies (GmbH-Gesetz), which was enforced in 1906. This law does not define the term "GmbH". This corporation is created by law usually for smaller businesses whereby the members want to limit their liabilities for business transactions. This is the most common form of corporation in Austria. In comparison to the AG, this corporate form gives far more organisational flexibility. Therefore, some larger companies still choose this legal form.

The characteristic features of this company are:

(a)   the company has its own legal personality;

(b)   the shareholders own portions of the nominal capital;

(c)   the capital is made up of initial contributions;

(d)   the shareholders are not liable for the liabilities of the company.

Therefore, the GmbH can sue and be sued in its own name. It owns the whole of its assets and is independently liable for all its debts. The shareholders are not joint owners of the assets. They are members of the company. Natural and legal persons can be shareholders, and they do not have to have Austrian citizenship.

The shareholders are not liable to the creditors for the debts of the company. They have only to satisfy their agreed contribution. The company (GmbH) has an unlimited liability towards the creditors. Of course, the company is, *de facto*, only liable to the extent of its own assets. It is a legal requirement that every GmbH has a nominal capital. This must be fixed with a nominal amount in Austrian schillings.

From the legal point of view, the AG and the GmbH are very similar. The main difference is that the legal regulations concerning a GmbH are much more flexible. Therefore, the shareholders have a greater opportunity to co-ordinate the company to suit their particular requirements, which is different to the AG.

A.2.3.1   *Formation*

The formation of the GmbH is much simpler than that of the AG. The main difference is that, generally, no examination by experts is necessary. The GmbH can only be established by way of a standard formation. Here, the successive formation is unknown.

The GmbH is formed as follows:

(a)   the execution of the shareholders' agreement, in the form of a notarial act; this agreement determines the internal rules of the company and therein the shareholders' portion of the nominal capital is specified;

(b) appointment of the supervisory board members; this is only necessary if it is obligatory to do so, due to the size of the company or if a voluntary supervisory board is provided for in the shareholders' agreement.

(c) appointment of the managing board, which is notarially attested; this step can be avoided if the managers are already determined in the shareholders' agreement;

(d) assessment and payment of the capital investment tax an obtaining the clearance certificate from the tax authorities;

(e) payment of the contributions; contributions in kind are to be fully paid up, whereas by cash contributions, at least 25 per cent must be paid up, so long as altogether 250,000 Sch are paid into the company; should the total amount of all the cash contributions not reach this amount, due to the fact that contributions in kind were brought into the company, then also the smaller cash contributions are to be fully paid up;

(f) obtaining an expert's opinion from the Chamber of Commerce about the wording of the business name (not compulsory, but advisable in doubtful cases);

(g) obtaining any necessary permissions from the trade authorities or from any other authorities;

(h) should a shareholder be resident abroad, then the permission of the Austrian National Bank must be obtained, whereby, at present, a general permission is given by the National Bank;

(i) the application for registration of the company at the court;

(j) the registration of the company in the Commercial Register;

(k) publishing the registered entry.

Since July 1, 1996, it is possible that only one person establishes a GmbH. In that case, the shareholders' agreement is replaced by a declaration on the establishment of the GmbH. The rules for the shareholders' agreement apply accordingly to that declaration.

A.2.3.1.1 Articles of association (shareholders' agreement) The shareholders' agreement must be concluded by *all* the subscribers. A resolution of the majority is not possible. As in the case of the AG, the GmbH also has an obligatory content in the shareholders' agreement. This can be supplemented by other points. The mandatory points are as follows:

(a) business name and location of the company;

(b) objects of the company;

(c) the amount of the nominal capital (Stammkapital);

(d)   the amount of each shareholder's contribution.

So long as the shareholders have made no further alterations these provisions are to be observed. The shareholders can, however, make other alterations in the shareholders' agreement which either diverge from or supplement these legal provisions. Most of these legal provisions are optional. There are only a few provisions, especially those for the protection of the minority and the creditors, which cannot be amended.

A.2.3.1.2   Registered office (Sitz)   According to Austrian company law, the location of the company must be in Austria. No other provision can be made. The shareholders can determine the location of the company independently as to where the effective location is. By an amendment to the shareholders' agreement, the location of the company can be moved. To move the location of the company abroad is not possible without the liquidation of the company. The location of the GmbH is also very important as this determines the competent court. Furthermore, the location may be important concerning various tax consequences.

A.2.3.1.3   Business name   Austrian law allows a greater range of possibilities for the name of the GmbH than the AG. The company's name can be a personal name or derived from the objects of the company or both. Should the company's name be a personal name, then this name must be the same as at least one of the shareholders. Likewise, if the company's name is that of the objects, then this must refer to the objects of the company. It follows that if the name is mixed, then the personal name and the objects can be jointly used.

A.2.3.1.4   Duration   The shareholders' agreement can determine that after a certain time, the company will be dissolved. Fundamentally, the company is not finished at the time of dissolution, as the phase of liquidation, which comes after dissolution, follows.
Reasons for the dissolution of a GmbH which has no limited duration are as follows:

(a)   resolution of the shareholders, whereby the simple majority is enough (other provisions can be made in the shareholders' agreement);

(b)   a merger;

(c)   opening of bankruptcy proceedings;

(d)   by order of the administrative authority;

(e)   decision of the Registration Court.

Further reasons for the dissolution of the company can be provided for in the shareholders' agreement.

A.2.3.1.5   Nominal capital (Stammkapital)   The nominal capital is determined in the shareholders' agreement. The shareholders commit themselves to raising at least this capital amount. An alteration of the amount of capital needs an amendment to the shareholders' agreement.

According to Austrian company law, a minimum capital of 500,000 Sch is required. It must be noted that, at the establishment of the company, cash contributions do not have to be fully paid, but one-quarter of the contractually agreed cash contributions must be paid. However, all the cash contributions together must at least amount to 250,000 Sch.

If cash contributions and contributions in kind are agreed upon, then the cash contributions are to be fully paid if all the cash contributions, which are normally paid, do not reach the amount of 250,000 Sch. Contributions in kind must be fully paid. By observing certain conditions, the whole capital can be raised by contributions in kind.

A.2.3.2 *Membership*

A shareholder's interest in the company is expressed by his quota in the company (Geschäftsanteil). Having these shares, the shareholders are granted property and participation rights, as well as further investment rights in the case of a capital increase.

The share in the company is the personal property of the shareholder. He can either sell it, pledge it or use it as he thinks fit. The share is not represented by a document of title. The share is determined by the contribution (Stammeinlage) taken over by the shareholder to a specific amount. Individual shareholders can be granted with special rights. These rights can be granted to the shareholders alone or also to their legal successors.

The shareholder has always one block quota in the company. This fact does not change if he increases his capital investment in the company, but his quota is merely enlarged. As documents of title are not allowed to be issued for shares, there are no dividends or renewal coupons. Of course, a document of proof can be issued. However, on no account do these documents have the character of a transferable security.

A.2.3.2.1 Purchase of a quota in the company When a notarial act concerning the establishment of the company is signed or a takeover declaration during a capital increase is signed, the shareholder takes over an initial contribution. He commits himself to paying this either in cash or in kind. With this takeover, the shareholder acquires a quota in the company.

A quota can generally not be divided. If a person is a shareholder already, his share can be increased by either the purchase of another shareholder's share or by the participation in a capital increase. In such cases, the shareholder increases his one share and does not have many shares.

Existing shares can generally be freely transferred. This can, however, be restricted in the interest of the other shareholders or for the protection of the company. This restriction of transfer does not have to affect all shareholders in the same way. This restriction can also have a time limit. The possibility of the transfer restriction can secure these particular advantages of partnership. Should a share be transferred without observing the restrictions, then this transfer is null and void.

The transfer of shares must be by way of a notarial act. An oral declaration or a written transfer is not enough. If this formal requirement is not observed, the transfer is ineffective.

The shareholders' agreement may grant pre-emption rights to co-shareholders, although these rights can be granted to affect only a few shareholders if necessary. Should a shareholder die, his shares are normally freely inheritable. The shareholders' agreement can also provide for restrictions in such a case. This way, the shareholders can protect themselves from undesirable shareholders becoming members.

A.2.3.2.2 Shareholders' rights and duties In the GmbH, a distinction can be drawn between the general rights and the special rights of individual shareholders. The general rights are a share in the profits, the right to take part in a capital increase, the right to a share of the remaining assets after a liquidation, the right of participation in the shareholders' meeting as well as rights of information and minority rights.

The special rights of individual shareholders are rights which are granted to shareholders in the shareholders' agreement and cannot be withdrawn without the consent of the individual shareholder. In this connection, one often finds the special right to be involved in the business management, the right to appoint members of the supervisory board, the right to name managers or "Prokurists", special rights to inspect the books, controlling rights, the right to call a shareholders' meeting and the right to an increased share of the profits and the remaining assets after liquidation. Also, a stronger right to vote can be granted to individual shareholders.

The company law for GmbHs also recognises the right of protection for the minority, although this is to a smaller extent similar to that of the AG.

The shareholders can remove a manager who is also a shareholder through the courts, so long as an important reason is given. Furthermore, individual shareholders have the right to inspect the shareholders' register, the register of the company minutes and the commercial books of the company. They can demand that the annual accounts are transferred to them and a
that they receive a copy of any decisions in the register of company minutes.

The shareholders are not obliged to pay any additional contributions to their initial contribution. However, a duty to pay additional contributions can be provided for in the shareholders' agreement. In this case, the amount of the additional contributions must be determined by reference to either a fractional amount or a multiple amount of the initial contribution. An unlimited additional contribution duty is inadmissible in Austria.

As is quite often happens that the nominal capital of the GmbH is only partly paid up, the question of the legal consequences for a delay in paying a contribution has a lot of significance. Should a shareholder not pay his contribution within the given period, the shareholder can be sued by the company. The shareholder at fault is obliged to pay interest on the default and also, if necessary, compensation for damages. A contractual penalty can be agreed upon in the shareholders' agreement.

Should the shareholder still not pay after being granted a period of grace, he can be excluded from the company. Through a forfeiture procedure, the shareholder loses his position as shareholder. If he pays the outstanding amount at a later date, he cannot regain his position as shareholder. The initial contributions which have already been paid up to the time of expulsion may not be repaid to the shareholder. Also the predecessors of the shareholder are liable for the outstanding amount.

Apart from the duty to pay an initial contribution, the shareholders have a duty of good faith towards the other shareholders. How far this duty of good faith goes, depends on whether the company has a more personal or capitalistic nature.

A.2.3.2.3 Increase and decrease of capital A decision of the shareholders is necessary to *increase* the capital and to do so, they must alter the articles. This amendment to the articles needs a 75 per cent majority of the votes of the shareholders in a meeting. Other requirements to increase the capital can be determined in the shareholders' agreement. The decision to increase the capital must be notarially attested. Every shareholder has a subscription right, unless it is otherwise determined in the shareholders' agreement. This subscription right must be exercised within four weeks.

To increase the capital, the shareholders must make a subscription declaration. This is made by way of a notarial act. After subscription and payment of the minimum amount, the capital increase must be applied for registration at the Registration Court and entered in the commercial register.

Capital increases can be either in the form of cash contributions or contributions in kind and, if necessary, must observe special regulations. The law for the GmbH does not recognise the "conditional capital increase" nor an "authorised capital" as in the AG. The GmbH can also make a nominal capital increase. The increase comes from the company's assets. The capital increases without the issuing of new shares.

There are two forms of capital *decrease* under the GmbH law:

(a) ordinary capital decrease:

(b) decrease by redeeming the quota (Geschäftsanteile).

For an ordinary capital decrease, a decision to alter the articles is necessary. It needs, once again, a 75 per cent majority. The decision is to be registered at the Registration Court and then published. The creditors must be notified of this decision. They then have three months in which to contact the GmbH in respect of their debts. Creditors who do not contact the GmbH are assumed to be in favour of this decision. The demands of the creditors are to be satisfied or must be given a guarantee or security.

A decrease by the redemption of the quota is possible without the creditors being notified. The repayment of initial contributions to the shareholders must either come from the profits or the company's reserve funds.

A.2.3.2.4   Purchase of own shares by the company   Under the GmbH law, the company is not allowed to purchase its own shares. Any such purchase is ineffective. This also applies to the forfeiture of shares. An acquisition by the company of a share in that company is possible by way of enforcing a judgment against a shareholder, if by this method the claim of the company can be satisfied. A purchase by a subsidiary of the company is also inadmissible.

A.2.3.2.5   Registration with the Commercial Register   Any transfer of shares, change of name or address of the shareholders as well as of their capital contributions, have to be immediately registered with the Commercial Register. The executive officers (Geschäftsführer) are responsible for that registration.

A.2.3.3   *Companies bodies*

Also in the GmbH, the functions of the company bodies can be exercised by non-shareholders. However, it is the general practice that the shareholders take over these functions. This is because a great number of GmbHs are personally co-ordinated.

The GmbH has two obligatory bodies:

(a)   managers (Geschäftsführer);

(b)   shareholders' meeting (Generalversammlung).

The GmbH does recognise a supervisory board. Under certain conditions, a compulsory supervisory board must be set up. Otherwise, the shareholders are free to decide if they want a supervisory board, and if so, this must be determined in the shareholders' agreement. If by law or in the shareholders' agreement a supervisory board is determined, then an auditor must also be appointed.

A.2.3.3.1   Managers (Geschäftsführer)   The GmbH must have one or more managers and they are bound to run the business. Unlike the AG, here the managers are more closely linked with the shareholders and are dependent on their decisions.

A.2.3.3.1.1   Appointment and dismissal   The managers are appointed by a decision of the shareholders. This decision is either made by the shareholders in a meeting or can be made in writing. A shareholder can already be appointed as a manager in the shareholders' agreement. This is, however, only for the duration of his participation in the GmbH. A person who is not a shareholder cannot be appointed in the shareholders' agreement.

The shareholders' agreement can grant individual shareholders the right to name a manager or the appointment of a manager can be dependent on the consent of a certain shareholder. It is inadmissible that the shareholders' agreement has a provision which allows the supervisory board, provided there is one, to appoint managers. Should it be the case that there is a lack of the necessary managers for the representation of the company, an application can be made that the court appoint the necessary manager.

The appointment of a manager can be made for a limited or an unlimited period. Repetition of an appointment is allowed. Should it be necessary, it can be decided that the duration of the appointment is automatically extended.

Generally, the appointment of managers can be revoked by the shareholders at any time. This revocation is immediately effective. This decision can be passed by a simple majority.

When the appointment of the manager is made in the shareholders' agreement, the admissibility of revocation can be restricted so that important reasons are necessary. It is also possible that a special right for the business management is granted to a shareholder. In such cases the shareholder, who is then a manager, must give his consent to the revocation. Should he not give his consent, he can also be dismissed by a decision of the court, as there would be an important reason.

A.2.3.3.1.2 *Rights and duties* Only the manager has the right and duty to run the business. Contrary to the AG, the manager of the GmbH is bound by the decisions of the shareholders as a whole and, of course, the supervisory board can give instructions. Individual shareholders, however, cannot give instructions.

Should more than one manager be appointed, then they run the business together. Decisions must be agreed upon unanimously. There is the possibility, however, to divide the different spheres of responsibility among the individual managers. This does not alter the fact that the individual managers still have the responsibility for the whole business management.

The shareholders' agreement can provide that each manager is individually authorised with the business management. If, in such a case, one manager objects to the actions of another manager, then these must not take place. Other particulars to this can be regulated in the shareholders' agreement.

The manager's authority of business management is partly restricted:

(a) certain transactions can only be entered into if they have the consent of the supervisory board (if it exists): for example, the purchase and sale of interests, businesses or immovables, the establishment and closure of branches, big investments and unusual loans;

(b) for certain transactions, a decision by the shareholders is needed: for example, the collection of payments of the initial contributions or a decision as to whether to confer "Prokura" or commercial authority on the whole business;

(c) further restrictions can be imposed on the managers in the business management by the shareholders' agreement or by a decision passed by the shareholders.

The managers do not *only* run the business. They also represent the GmbH in and out of court. This manner of representation to third parties cannot be restricted by the shareholders' agreement.

Unless there are no diverging regulations in the shareholders' agreement, all the managers are authorised to represent the company collectively. The shareholders' agreement can more specifically authorise each manager to represent the company himself or that his representation is limited to, *e.g.* representing the company with another specified person.

As far as third parties are concerned, there can be no restriction placed on a manager's power to represent the company. For example, they can sell the whole company or immovables. An internal business restriction of the right to represent the company does not prevent the validity of representation acts in an external relationship. In such a case, the manager is liable for damages. However, if a manager and a third person work together to purposely damage the company, the business transactions are null and void.

The manager administrates outside capital. He has, therefore, a special duty of good faith. He is not allowed to use his position for his own interest. He is not allowed to use his authority for purposes which are not those of the company.

Without the company's approval, the manager is not allowed to enter into transactions in his line of business for his own account or for the account of another. Nor can he have a personal interest in another business of the same line. He is not allowed to have a function as a member of the management board, supervisory board or be a manager in another competing company. This competition prohibition can be extended, restricted or completely set aside by the shareholders' agreement.

It is important that this prohibition of competition does not apply to the shareholders. Should a shareholder, however, also be a manager, then he must observe this competition prohibition. The manager also has an inseparable duty of discretion and secrecy.

A.2.3.3.1.3 Meetings There is no special legal regulation which determines how often the appointed managers have to have meetings. Therefore, it is left up to the managers' duty of care and responsibility to decide among themselves when the necessary meetings which are for the welfare of the company should take place. In individual cases, internal rules can exist for the managers which regulate this question of meetings.

A.2.3.3.1.4 Managers' liabilities The managers must have the diligence of a prudent business person. This is the standard of qualification and knowledge which must be expected in their relevant line of business.

The managers are responsible for the whole area of management of the GmbH. If this is divided into departments, then each manager is responsible for his department. The rest of the managers have a duty of supervision and are liable, should they violate this duty.

Should the managers violate their obligation, then they are jointly liable for any damages which occur. They are especially liable when:

(a) company assets are distributed illegally or contrary to the shareholders' agreement: this especially refers to the repayment of initial contributions or additional contributions;

(b) when they continue to trade and make payments when it should be clear for them that the company is insolvent.

The managers are also liable for damages from any legal transactions which were entered into in their own or in another name without obtaining the consent of the supervisory board or the other managers first. The managers are generally not liable if they acted on the instructions of the supervisory board or the shareholders. The GmbH's damages claims are subject to a limitation period of five years. This time-limit starts at the time the claim for damages occurred.

A.2.3.3.2 Supervisory board   In a GmbH, the supervisory board is normally only an optional body, and so is different to that of the AG. As long as there are no legal determinations, the shareholders can decide whether they establish a supervisory board or not.

There are cases where a supervisory board is obligatory.

Apart from these exceptions, the shareholders can determine in the shareholders' agreement that a supervisory board as obligatory or whether a supervisory board in the future will depend on a shareholders' decision.

Here, it is also the initial task of the supervisory board to supervise the business management of the GmbH. So long as it is provided for in the shareholders' agreement or in the shareholders' decisions, the supervisory board can interfere directly with the business management by giving instructions to the managers.

A.2.3.3.2.1 Appointment and dismissal   Under the GmbH law, the supervisory board consists of a minimum of three members. It can consist of more members, so long as the shareholders' agreement does not contain any restrictions. Austrian law does not restrict the number of members, unlike the AG. The aforementioned number is only for the members who are appointed by the shareholders. The representatives of the works council are not to be considered here.

The appointment of a supervisory board member can be made as follows:

(a) election by a shareholders' decision;

(b) appointment by an individual shareholder;

(c) appointment by the court;

(d) appointment by the works council.

Normally, a supervisory board member is elected by the shareholders' decision. This decision can be made in a shareholders' meeting or, in any case, in writing.

A simple majority of the votes is enough. It can be determined in the shareholders' agreement that a greater majority is necessary.

The shareholders' agreement can provide a nomination right to certain shareholders. The other shareholders' consent to the proposed supervisory board member is implied unless there are important reasons against this.

So long as at least three supervisory seats are to be allocated, the owners of one-third of the nominal capital can demand a special election. A person who receives one-third of all votes in the ballots is to be appointed as a member of the supervisory board.

It can be determined in the shareholders' agreement that individually named shareholders or shareholders who have a minimum capital interest have a special right to appoint members of the supervisory board. This right to appoint members can only be granted to shareholders whose share in the company is subject to restricted transfer rights.

An appointment can be made by the court if the quorum required for a resolution is not available for a period of more than three months. The court can only appoint the members who would have been appointed by the shareholders.

According to the Austrian Labour Relations Act, the employees have the right to delegate a representative for the supervisory board at the time when a supervisory board exists or should exist. The principle of a one-third parity applies. This means that for every two members appointed by the court or the shareholders' agreement, a third member is to be appointed by the works council. If there is an uneven number, another member is appointed by the works council.

Therefore, the legal minimum number of supervisory board members results in a total number of five. The GmbH law sets a limited period for the appointment of supervisory board members. They cannot be appointed for longer than a period ending with the shareholders' approval of the fourth annual financial statement. The first business year, where the supervisory board is elected, is not to be taken into account. Therefore, the duration of their function amounts to five to six years. A re-election is possible.

The elected member does not have any claim to the performance of his duties. The member can be dismissed at any time, without there being an important reason for this. The law determines a 75 per cent majority of the votes. This can be amended in the shareholders' agreement.

If the member is appointed by one or more shareholders, there is no limited period for his appointment. Shareholders who have the right to appoint members can also dismiss them at any time. Should a shareholder lose the right of appointment, he cannot dismiss the member whom he appointed in the first place. This dismissal is then the task of the shareholders as a whole.

A minority of 10 per cent of the nominal capital can demand the legal dismissal of a supervisory board member, should there be important reasons for this. Legally appointed supervisory board members are to be officially dismissed if the reason for the appointment is abolished. The employees' representatives cease their function on the supervisory board if they are dismissed by the body authorised to appoint them, if they resign voluntarily or if they retire from the works council.

A.2.3.3.2.2 Rights and duties The duty of the supervisory board is to supervise the business management. They have to check the legality, economic efficiency and the expediency of the business management. It is not enough to check the management board's actions after they have been accomplished, they must check the business management constantly.

Normally, the supervisory board cannot interfere with the business management, as the managers have the sole responsibility. The difference with the AG is that here the shareholders' agreement or a resolution of the shareholders can determine that the supervisory board has the right to give *instructions* for the business management.

Furthermore, the managers are obliged to give the supervisory board a full report. The number of reports in a business year is not determined by law. The supervisory board can, however, demand a report concerning the activities of the company. This right applies to the whole supervisory board. An individual member of the supervisory board also has the right to demand such a report for the whole supervisory board.

The supervisory board can inspect and review all books and documents of the company, as well as all its assets. It can also instruct individual members of the supervisory board or special experts to carry out this inspection.

If it is necessary for the company's well-being, the supervisory board must call a shareholders' meeting. If this is the case, the supervisory board must observe the general regulations for the calling of a meeting.

As already mentioned, the consent of the supervisory board is needed for specific business transactions. These business transactions are of an extraordinary nature, such as the purchase and sale of shares, immovables, large investments or the taking out of loans. Should the supervisory board refuse to give its consent, then the managers must obtain a resolution by the shareholders.

Furthermore, the supervisory board must inspect the annual statement of accounts, the business report and the proposed profit distribution.

In individual cases, the supervisory board can represent the company in business matters which involve the managers or in the conduct of a lawsuit against the managers.

The individual supervisory board members have if necessary, a right to claim remuneration. The work of the supervisory board can either be free or for payment. The activities of the employees' representative are always free of charge and on an honorary basis.

A.2.3.3.2.3 Meetings The number of supervisory board meetings to be held in one business year normally depends on the necessity for these meetings. According to Austrian company law, the supervisory board must meet at least three times per business year.

The chairman has the duty to call a meeting. Should a supervisory board member or a manager demand this, the chairman must call a supervisory board meeting without delay. The meeting must take place within two weeks. If two supervisory board members or the business manager demand a meeting and this is not opposed, then these persons can call the meeting themselves.

Normally, only the members of the supervisory board can attend these meetings. The members of the management board can also attend due to their obligation to report and give information. There can be no provision in the shareholders' agreement which enlarges the number of persons allowed to be present.

The managers have no right to attend. If their participation is refused, then this must be accepted. A supervisory board member can be represented by another supervisory board member, or by someone else who does not belong to the supervisory board. In both cases this must be provided for in the shareholders' agreement.

At least three supervisory board members must take part in the supervisory board meeting, otherwise no valid decisions can be passed. A decision without the necessary quorum is null, and void.

For decisions passed by the supervisory board, a special necessity for a majority is not provided for under Austrian law. Therefore, the principle of a simple majority applies. In the shareholders' agreement, it can be determined that, for individual matters, a qualified majority is necessary.

A.2.3.3.2.4 Liability of the supervisory board members The supervisory board member is liable for the activities of the company if he has violated his duty of care. Therefore, it must be thoroughly invested if a member is negligent and if he has violated his duty of care. Should the company be damaged by a resolution of the supervisory board, then it must be investigated to what extent the individual member took part. If the member is overruled in a decision, he is only liable if he purposely withheld his misgivings from the supervisory board.

The regulations for the managers' liability are also to be correspondingly applied for the supervisory board members' liability. The managers and the members of the supervisory board have individual liability if they are in breach of their duty towards the company.

A.2.3.3.3   Shareholders' meeting (Generalversammlung)

A.2.3.3.3.1 General provisions The shareholders' meeting is an obligatory body of the company. In this meeting, the shareholders can apply their rights. It is the main decision-making body of the company.

The shareholders can also apply their rights outside the shareholders' meeting. They can make written decisions or give their consent orally or in writing for specific measures. In such cases, all the shareholders must take part, which is contrary to the rules of the shareholders' meeting.

The shareholders' meeting makes decisions for the following matters:

(a)   investigation and approval of the annual accounts;

(b)   distribution of the net profits, should this be subject to a special decision from year to year in the shareholders' agreement;

47

(c) approval of the managers' acts;

(d) approval of the existing supervisory board acts;

(e) collection of payments for the initial contribution;

(f) collection and repayment of additional payments;

(g) the decision whether Prokura or trade authority is to be distributed in the whole business;

(h) measures for the investigation and supervision of the business management;

(i) the assertion of damage claims against the managers, supervisory board, etc.;

(j) appointment and dismissal of members of different company bodies.

The shareholders' agreement can specify which measures and matters are reserved for the shareholders to decide about. They have the special duty to pass a decision over the annual accounts, the distribution of the net profits, and the approval of the different bodies. Furthermore, the managers must call a shareholders' meeting if it is in the interest of the shareholders (*e.g.* loss of half of the initial capital). The supervisory board also has the right to call a shareholders' meeting, if it is in the interest of the company. The shareholders' agreement might state that other persons, *i.e.* individual shareholders, have the right to call a shareholders' meeting. A minority of 10 per cent of the nominal capital can demand a shareholders' meeting in writing. If this is refused, the minority has the right to call a meeting itself.

The calling of a shareholders' meeting must be made by way of a registered letter. Seven days' notice must be given between the calling and the day of the meeting. This time-limit can be altered in the shareholders' agreement. In the calling of a shareholders' meeting, the points on the agenda are to be stated. If the points on the agenda are not given three days before the meeting, any decisions made can be contested.

A.2.3.3.3.2 Location of meeting Normally, the meeting is to be held at the registered office of the company. It can be stated otherwise in the shareholders' agreement. A shareholders' meeting can, if necessary, be held abroad. However, if this meeting must be recorded by a notary, then only an Austrian notary can do this. Shareholders' decisions which are to be entered into the commercial register especially need to be recorded by a notary. In such cases, the shareholders' meeting must be held in Austria. Independent of this, simple written decisions can, of course, be made by the shareholders abroad.

A.2.3.3.3.3 Quorum The shareholders' meeting is competent to pass decisions, if the part of the nominal capital which is determined either by law or in the shareholders' agreement is present or represented. If there are no particular provisions made by law or in the shareholders' agreement, then 10 per cent of the nominal capital is enough for the quorum.

It can be determined in the shareholders' agreement that it is necessary for a higher part or even the whole of the nominal capital to be present.

If the meeting is not competent to pass decisions, an indication can be made as to the incompetency of the meeting and a second meeting, with the same points on the agenda, can be called. Unless it is otherwise determined in the shareholders' agreement, this meeting is competent to pass decisions, independent of how much of the initial capital is present or represented.

A.2.3.3.3.4 Majorities Shareholders' decisions are passed by a simple majority of the votes unless it is otherwise provided for in the shareholders' agreement. Principally, the shareholders' agreement can determine a qualified majority or further requirements. In individual cases, shareholders can be granted a right of veto. Austrian company law recognises individual cases where a qualified majority is required.

It is important that the dissolution of the GmbH is not bound by a qualified majority. Therefore, the dissolution of the company can be decided by a simple majority.

A.2.3.3.3.5 Records Orally passed shareholders' decisions in the shareholders' meeting have to be immediately laid down in written form. These records as well as decision that have been passed in written have to be kept with the GmbH. Every shareholder has the right to inspect these records. A copy of these decisions has to be sent to each shareholder.

A.2.3.3.4 Annual accounts (auditors) All companies which are obliged to have a supervisory board have the duty of examining the audit annually. This is modelled after the statutory audit of the AG. The annual accounts have to be inspected, which consist of the balance and the profit and loss account. Furthermore, the book-keeping and the inventory are to be inspected. Also, the financial accounting, after taking into consideration all documents which are necessary for the rendering of accounts, is to be inspected. Also, the managers' report, which explains the annual accounts, is to be inspected by the auditors.

This annual audit is only to inspect legality and the regularity of the annual accounts. It does not inspect the economic efficiency or the expediency.

The GmbH's right to inspect is very similar to that of the AG. Regarding the duty to disclose the financial conditions, there are some differences.

The duty of publicity does not depend on the existence of a supervisory board, but on the fulfilment of specific criteria, whereby small corporations, medium corporations and big corporations are to be distinguished.

Small corporations are such corporations, which do not exceed at least two of the three following criteria:

(a) 37,000,000 Sch—balance sheet total;

(b) 74,000,000 Sch—turnover in the last 12 months before the balance sheet date;

(c)   an average of 50 employees in that year.

Medium corporations are such corporations which exceed at least two of the three criteria for small corporations, but do not exceed at least two of the three following criteria:

(a)   150,000,000 Sch—balance sheet total;

(b)   300,000,000 Sch—turnover in the last 12 months before the balance sheet date;

(c)   an average of 250 employees during that year.

Big corporations are such corporations that exceed at least two of the three criteria above. A corporation is in any case considered to be big, if its shares or other securities are traded at a stock exchange in a Member State of the European Union or European Economic Area.

A.2.3.3.4.1   Appointment   The appointment and the choice of the auditors is made by the company. It can determine one or more auditors. In the normal practice, however, only one auditor is appointed.

The auditors are commissioned by the managers. Under the Austrian Accounting Act 1990, there is an alteration that companies, where a supervisory board exists, commission the auditors through the supervisory board.

Managers, the supervisory board or a minority of 10 per cent of the initial capital can oppose the choice of auditors if an important reason is given. This is then decided by the court. Should the court grant this opposition, then the court must appoint a new auditor. The election of the auditors can be revoked by a shareholders' decision before the inspection is completed.

A.2.3.3.4.2   Rights and duties   As the annual audit of the GmbH is more or less the same as the statutory audit of the AG, this can be referred to in the explanation for the AG.

A.2.3.4   *Works council*

The rules affecting a works council in a GmbH are the same as for the AG and as explained above (see A.2.2.4). The number of employees' representatives depends upon the number of people employed. The GmbH must adhere to the provisions of the Austrian labour relations law and ensure that the works council participates in and is consulted on matters affecting the company personnel.

The duty of publicity does not depend on the existence of a supervisory board, but on the fulfilment of specific criteria, whereby small corporations, medium corporations and big corporations are to be distinguished.

Small corporations are such corporations, which do not exceed at least two of the three following criteria:

(a) 37,000,000 Sch—balance sheet total;

(b) 74,000,000 Sch—turnover in the last 12 months before the balance sheet date;

(c) an average of 50 employees in that year.

Medium corporations are such corporations which at least exceed two of the three criteria for small corporations, but do not exceed at least two of the three following criteria:

(a) 150,000 Sch—balance sheet total;

(b) 300,000 Sch—turnover in the last 12 months before the balance sheet date;

(c) An average of 250 employees during that year.

Big corporations are such corporations that exceed at least two of three criteria above. A corporation is in any case considered to be big, if its shares or other securities are traded at a stock exchange in a member state of the European Union or European Economic Area.

In any event the works council is influential in matters of the company concerning the employees and is able to ensure that the company also acts in its employee's interests.

In a GmbH, the supervisory board is generally discretionary, but if it exists the same rules that one-third of the members must be appointed by the workforce apply.

SECTION 3

COSTS OF INCORPORATION

A.3.1 Incorporation Taxes (Gründungssteuer)

On the formation of a business enterprise in Austria, the business is subject to formation charges and taxes. There is, however, a distinction between the costs of formation of a partnership and a corporation.

For all partnership agreements, there are no charges (Gebühren) due on the completion of the agreement. Furthermore, if the capital investment in a partnership is raised, there are no charges due. The same is true for the transfer of a quota in a partnership to another partner or a third person.

Should, however, a corporation with limited liability be the personally liable partner of a limited partnership, then the rules for corporations apply.

At the formation of a corporation (GmbH, AG, GmbH & Co. KG, GmbH & Co. KEG), the Capital Transfer Tax Act (Kapitalverkehrsteuergesetz) forsees a tax in the amount one per cent of the capital contribution. The basis of assessment is usually the cash contribution or the value of the non-cash investment.

For the transfer of the share of a GmbH or a quota in a GmbH & Co. KG/KEG, 2.5 per cent capital transfer tax are to be paid.

For the transfer of a share of an AG, 0.15 per cent capital transfer tax is to be paid.

A.3.2 Registration Charges by the Commercial Register

When a business is registered in the Commercial Register, the following flat-rate charge is to be paid:

(a) Sole proprietorship 640 Sch

(b) OHG, KG and EEG 1,170 Sch

(c) GmbH and AG of the nominal capital 0.55%

Also, when registering branches in the Commercial Register, the following charges are to be paid:

(a) Sole proprietorship 370 Sch

(b) OHG, KG and EEG 640 Sch

(c) GmbH and AG 3,420 Sch

Should the nominal capital of a GmbH or an AG be increased, then a charge of 0.45 per cent of the increase is to be paid.

Any amendment to the partnership agreement is subject to Register charges:

(a) Sole proprietorship 370 Sch

(b) OHG, KG and EEG 640 Sch

(c) GmbH and AG 900 Sch

These charges are normally due at the application for registration.

A.3.3   Legal Costs

It is difficult to determine the charges for a solicitor's advice or the participation of a notary in the formation of a company.

Special tariff rules apply for the solicitor and the notary. These rules allow different charges for the solicitor and the notary depending on the value of the legal matter.

The solicitor can claim payment for *all* his individual services, *e.g.* letters, conferences, commissions, written pleadings, etc.: each service is subject to a special tariff and is charged as such. However, it is possible to come to an agreement with an Austrian solicitor so that he charges on an hourly basis.

The drawing-up and the implementation of a partnership agreement usually costs between 30,000 Sch and 40,000 Sch. The costs of formation of a GmbH are usually in the range of at least 30,000 Sch and 60,000 Sch, and for the formation of an AG a minimum of between 40,000 Sch and 80,000 Sch.

These charges cover the solicitor's/notary's advice, their representation activities and their professional fees. We must, however, point out that in individual cases (depending on the expense and difficulty of the particular case) these charges can be more expensive.

A.3.4   Incorporation Charges by the Chamber of Commerce

The amount of incorporation charges laid down by the Chamber of Commerce depends on the individual commercial trade of the business. It is normally the case that, for businesses like the OHG or the KG, the regular incorporation charges must be paid. Double incorporation charges are to be paid for a GmbH or an AG.

BELGIUM

CORPORATE OPTIONS*

B.1.0 Under Belgian law, commercial or civil activities can be conducted through the following structures:

—a sole trader;

—a representative office;

—a branch;

—a partnership without legal personality; or

—a legal entity (that is, an enterprise with a distinct legal personality).

B.1.1 Sole Trader

A sole trader is an individual who operates a business on his or her own rather than through a partnership or corporate body. According to Belgium's Commercial Code, anyone who performs "commercial acts", whether as a principal or subsidiary activity, will qualify as a trader. The Commercial Code contains an exhaustive list of such "commercial acts". This list includes, among others, the purchase of merchandise for resale or rental, purchase of a business, operation of a manufacturing enterprise, performance of public or private works, operation of a supply or transport business, performance of any banking, stock exchange or brokerage transactions, and operation of an insurance business. The practice of certain liberal professions, such as architecture, medicine and dentistry, is deemed to be legally, or at least ethically incompatible with the status of a trader.

Under Belgian law, there exist no special statutory rules governing the operation of a business by a sole trader. Therefore, the general rules of the Commercial Code constitute the body of law relevant to the sole trader. Because sole traders are commercial actors, they cannot claim the protection of Belgium consumer laws. Also, sole traders are individuals and are thus exempt from a number of rules and restrictions applicable to corporations, such as minimum capital requirements,

* *Steven De Schrijver and Markus Wellinger, Van Bael & Bellis (full particulars are listed in the Appendix). The authors wish to acknowledge gratefully the editorial assistance they have received from Mr Mark Johnston.*

restrictions on the distribution of profits, certain audit and accounting requirements, and financial disclosure obligations.

A sole trader can conduct his or her business under his or her own name or under a trade name. A trade name is the name under which the trader runs his or her business. A trader can prevent a third party from using a trade name or term that is confusingly similar to his or her trade name.

A sole trader must register with the Trade Registry (Handelsregister/Registre de Commerce) of the judicial district in which he or she operates. This entails the trader filing his or her name, trade name, address and a description of his or her commercial activity with the registry. The purpose is to enable third parties to verify the identity of persons with whom they are dealing. If the sole trader is involved on a regular basis in the delivery of goods or the offering of services to third parties, he or she must also register with the VAT authorities. In addition to the records which must be kept for VAT and other taxation purposes, a sole trader must also maintain a simplified bookkeeping system. A trader's profits will be taxed as personal income, at the tax rates applicable thereto.

A sole trader's business is not distinct from the trader, thus there is no distinction between the business capital of the sole trader and his or her personal funds. This means that the sole trader takes all the profits of his or her business activity, but also has personal and unlimited liability for his or her business debts and obligations. As such, if a trader cannot satisfy his or her business obligations, he or she can be declared bankrupt and be forced to liquidate his or her personal assets to satisfy outstanding debts.

B.1.2 Representative Office

The most straightforward way for a foreign company to operate in Belgium is either to incorporate a Belgian subsidiary or to establish a registered branch office. However, Belgium's courts have held that, in some limited circumstances, a foreign company may operate through a representative office without using either of these structures. A foreign company may do so if its activities in Belgium are *strictly* limited to (i) providing or collecting information, lobbying, or similar activities, or (ii) establishing business contacts in Belgium or negotiating transactions that will be effected outside of Belgium.

A representative office is not subject to the registration, publication, and accounting requirements that are imposed on registered branches or subsidiaries in Belgium.

However, representative offices can be of limited practical utility, and are only suitable to foreign companies in a limited range of circumstances. The following are some of the practical and legal difficulties associated with operating through a representative office, rather than a branch or subsidiary:

(1) In practice, a representative office provides an insufficient base for conducting business for any considerable period. If the office's activities fall outside of

the permissible scope described above, it could be deemed to operate as a branch and thus subject to the registration, publication and accounting requirements applicable to a branch. Failure to comply with these requirements could expose the representative office to substantial fines.

(2) Third parties are sometimes reluctant to deal with a representative office, since it has no officially recognised status under Belgian law and no record of it exists in Belgium's Trade Registries.

(3) A representative office may not be able to recover VAT it pays on its purchases of goods or services.

(4) A representative office may encounter difficulties that are not typically faced by branches or subsidiaries, such as opening bank accounts, subscribing to telephone, electricity and other utility services, and receiving registered letters or parcels.

B.1.3   Branch (Bijkantoor/Succursale)

Foreign companies may also establish registered branches to carry out their business activities in Belgium. A branch is a subordinate enterprise that operates for the account of and under the direction of a foreign parent company. The branch is not a separate legal entity; it forms a single entity with its parent company. Below, we will define the characteristics of a branch, discuss how branches are established, the publicity requirements applicable and the operational aspects of a branch.

B.1.3.1   *Definition and main characteristics of a branch*

Under Belgian case law and according to legal commentators, a branch is a permanently established enterprise that regularly carries out activities falling within the commercial purpose of its foreign parent company. A branch has a separate office but has no distinct legal personality of its own. It is managed by a person entitled to enter into legal obligations *vis-à-vis* third parties on behalf of the branch's foreign parent.

The important legal consequences that flow from this definition can be summarised as follows:

(a) a branch has no legal personality distinct from that of its parent company;

(b) a branch is a subordinate establishment subject to direction by its parent company; and

(c) the branch's parent company has unlimited responsibility for the operations of the branch.

59

It also follows from the foregoing definition that a foreign company will be deemed to have a branch in Belgium if the following three conditions exist:

(1) The foreign company has an office in Belgium where the business activity of the company is carried out in a permanent manner and through which the company can be contacted by potential customers. The office need not be located in premises owned by the foreign company, and, in fact, it may be located on the premises of another, unaffiliated company.

(2) The foreign company regularly exercises business activities or performs commercial acts in Belgium that fall within or are consistent with its corporate purpose.

(3) The foreign company is represented in Belgium by a representative who is legally entitled to commit the foreign company contractually.

B.1.3.2 *The establishment of a branch*

In order to establish a branch in Belgium, a foreign company must fulfil certain formalities that are similar to formalities required to incorporate a subsidiary. Specifically, it must publish certain information in the annexes to the *Belgian Official Journal* ("Belgisch Staatsblad"/"Moniteur Belge") and register the branch with the Trade Registry of the judicial district where the branch operates.

The following specific steps should be taken by a foreign company to establish a branch in Belgium:

(1) The foreign company's board of directors should adopt a resolution that provides for the establishment of a branch in Belgium. The resolution should contain the following information:

(a) the permissible scope of the branch's activities;

(b) the name and powers of the legal representative of the branch; and

(c) the address of the branch.

(2) An original and a copy of the following documents should be submitted for certification to a notary public in the jurisdiction of the foreign company's incorporation:

(a) the foreign company's original articles of incorporation;

(b) the most recent version of the foreign company's charter (and/or amended articles of incorporation, as applicable); and

(c) the above-mentioned resolution of the foreign company's board of directors.

(3) The foreign company should submit the certified copies of such documents to the authorities in its country of incorporation who hold the power to affix an

apostille to such documents pursuant to the Hague Treaty for the Abolition of the Requirement of Legalisation of Foreign Official Documents of October 5, 1961. The apostille is a statement indicating that the notary public's signature on the documents is authentic. Documents bearing the apostille can be used for legal purposes in Belgium, including the registration of a branch. If the parent company is incorporated in a country that has not acceded to the Hague Treaty, then a full chain of signature legalisations must be followed, unless a specific bilateral agreement exists between Belgium and the foreign company's country of incorporation.

(4) The aforementioned documents must be translated into Dutch, French or German (depending upon the region in Belgium in which the branch's office will be registered) by a certified translator.

(5) The documents and translations thereof must be filed with the Companies' Registry (Dienst Akten van Vennootschappen/Service Actes de Sociétés) of the Commercial Court having jurisdiction over the branch. The branch must also be registered with the Trade Registry of the same Commercial Court. For purposes of this registration, specific information on the foreign company, the branch and the legal representative must be filed with the Trade Registry.

(6) A notice of the branch's establishment must then be published in the annexes to the *Belgian Official Journal*. The notice must contain specific information as defined in the Royal Decree of November 30, 1935 co-ordinating the Laws on Commercial Companies, as amended (the "Law").

(7) If the Belgian branch will sell goods or offer services to third parties on a regular basis, then the foreign parent must apply to the Belgian VAT authorities for a VAT number. For this purpose, the legal representative of the branch must file a so-called "Declaration of Initiation of Economic Activity" (Aangifte van de aanvang van een werkzaamheid/Déclaration de commencement d'activités) with the Belgian VAT authorities. The authorities should assign a VAT number to the branch within approximately two weeks following submission of the request and declaration.

(8) Finally, if the foreign company is under a legal obligation in its country of incorporation to disclose its annual accounts, it will also have to file its annual accounts, together with its consolidated annual accounts, with the Belgian National Bank. These accounts must be in the form in which they have been drawn up, audited and made public under the laws governing the foreign company. In other words, a foreign company does not have to follow the legal format applicable to Belgian companies for the filing of annual accounts. The filing must include an unofficial Dutch, French or German translation (depending on the place where the branch is registered) of the annual accounts. If the foreign company is not subject to such a financial disclosure obligation, one will not be imposed upon its Belgian branch.

61

B.1.3.3 *Public disclosure obligations*

Once the branch has been set up, its foreign parent must publicly disclose the following facts within 30 days of their occurrence:

(a) any modification of the information and documents (including the articles of incorporation and the charter of the foreign parent) filed with the Companies Registry and the Trade Registry;

(b) the liquidation of the foreign parent;

(c) if the foreign parent is to be liquidated, the appointment, identity and powers of the responsible liquidators;

(d) any bankruptcy or similar proceeding involving the foreign parent; and

(e) the closure of the branch.

In addition, the foreign parent must disclose its consolidated annual accounts, and its own individual accounts if these must be kept and separately disclosed in its jurisdiction of incorporation, each year within one month following its general shareholders' meeting or, at the latest, within seven months after the closure of its fiscal year.

B.1.3.4 *Some operational aspects of a branch*

A particular body of rules applies to the Belgian branch of a foreign company. Some of these rules are briefly enumerated below:

(1) All documents of a commercial nature, including the branch's letterhead, official stationery, invoices and order forms, must include the following information:

(a) the name and address of the branch;

(b) an indication that it is a branch office of the foreign parent;

(c) the name, legal form (*e.g.* limited liability company) and address of the registered office of the foreign company;

(d) if the foreign company is registered in its country of origin, the name of the registry in which it is registered and its registration number;

(e) the name of the Trade Registry in Belgium where the branch is registered and the branch's registration number;

(f) the name of the bank where the branch has opened its account and its account number; and

(g) the branch's VAT number, if any.

(2) The Belgian branch of a foreign company is required to keep separate books for its operations in accordance with Belgian accounting standards. However, this requirement does not apply to branches (i) that earn no revenue from the sale of products or services to third parties or to their foreign parent companies and (ii) whose operating costs are borne by their foreign parent companies.

B.1.4 Partnerships Without Distinct Legal Personality

Under Belgian law, civil or commercial activities can also be carried out through a partnership without distinct legal personality. However, like sole traders, such partnerships do not have a distinct legal personality. This characteristic has the following consequences for forming and operating such partnerships:

(1) No formalities need to be followed to establish a partnership. In principle, an informal agreement between its partners is sufficient.

(2) A partnership does not have a legal personality or capital distinct from that of its partners. Thus, a partnership's creditors have direct recourse to the partners who are jointly and severally liable for the debts of the partnership.

(3) Legal actions can only be filed by all partners acting jointly on behalf of the partnership.

The following are types of partnerships that exist under Belgian law.

B.1.4.1 *Civil company (Burgerlijke Vennootschap/Société Civile)*

A civil company is a type of partnership that can be used to engage in civil (*i.e.* non-commercial) activities. This type of partnership is governed by the Civil Code rather than the Law.

A civil company's partners are jointly and severally liable for honouring its valid commitments of the civil company. Although the partners can limit their liability in the partnership agreement, such limitations are only enforceable against those third parties who explicitly accept and agree to them.

As will be explained below, a civil company can also take the form of a commercial company listed in the Law, in which case it is referred to as a civil company that has taken the form of a commercial company (Burgerlijke vennootschap die de vorm van een handelsvennootschap heeft aangenomen/Société civile ayant emprunté la forme commerciale).

B.1.4.2 Temporary commercial association (Tijdelijke Handelsvereniging/Association Commerciale Momentanée)

A temporary commercial association is another type of partnership, the characteristic feature of which is its limited duration. It provides a structure under which two or more businesses may transact business under a common name, usually in connection with a specific project or series of projects. Its life is typically limited to the duration of such project or projects.

This form of partnership is often used within the framework of joint ventures as, for example, joint ventures of construction companies formed to take part in public works projects. As with other forms of partnerships, a temporary commercial association does not have a distinct legal personality or distinct capital. Thus, its partners are jointly and severally liable for its debts and other obligations.

B.1.4.3 Commercial association in participation (Handelsvereniging bij Wijze van Deelneming/Association Commerciale en Participation)

A commercial association in participation is, roughly speaking, also a form of partnership. In this business form, the partners select one partner or several partners to represent the partnership in one transaction or a series of transactions. In principle, the agreement between the partners, which typically specifies the scope of the partnership arrangement, is unknown to third parties that transact partnership business with the appointed partner(s), and the appointed partner(s) transact(s) such business in its (their) own name(s). Consequently, third parties have no legal relationship with the other partners and are unable to proceed against them for any claims they may have against the appointed partner(s).

This form of business arrangement is often used by groups of banks seeking to make investments. The object of the agreement could be, for example, the purchase of securities or real estate. The association allows them to pool their resources and share investment risk for a discrete activity, usually of limited duration.

B.1.5 Legal Entities

B.1.5.1 Introduction

The last type of business structure discussed is the legal entity. Under Belgian corporate law, there are a wide variety of legal entities. Although all share the characteristic of a legal personality distinct from their owners, partners or members, they can be distinguished on the basis of the nature of their activities, their corporate purpose or the identity of their members. Such distinctions need to be borne in mind when choosing a legal structure for operating in Belgium.

The principal distinctions by which legal entities can be classified can be summarised as follows:

(a) between commercial companies and civil companies which have taken the form of a commercial company;

(b) between companies with a social motive and those that have a commercial or profit motive; and

(c) between companies of persons and capital companies.

These distinguishing characteristics will serve to help introduce the many types of co-operatives, associations, partnerships and companies that may be set up under Belgian law.

B.1.5.1.1 Commercial companies and civil companies which have taken the form of a commercial company   The legal entities that may exist under the Law can be divided into commercial companies and civil companies which have taken the form of a commercial company. They can be distinguished based on the nature of the activities in which companies of each type engage.

Commercial companies are companies that have as their purpose the exercise of a commercial activity, regardless of whether or not they have a profit motive. Such commercial companies are automatically treated as traders within the meaning of the Commercial Code. This means that any act of a commercial company is necessarily assumed to have a commercial character. Typical commercial activities include the manufacture of products, purchase and resale of goods, provision of services and financing or leasing operations.

As explained above in Section 1.4.1, civil activities can be carried out through a civil company, which does not have a distinct legal personality. However, an alternative is to create a civil company in the form of a commercial company. Such companies are referred to as civil companies which have taken the form of a commercial company. They have as their purpose the exercise of a civil activity and thus are not necessarily viewed and treated as traders. As such, their activities are not automatically deemed to have a commercial character, and will only be qualified as such if they are *per se* commercial in nature. Typical civil activities include farming and mining; intellectual activities, such as making a movie, teaching a language or other course of study or creating an art work; and the practice of liberal professions, such as law, medicine, and architecture.

Five essential distinctions can be drawn between civil companies that have taken the form of a commercial company and commercial companies:

(a) such civil companies cannot be summoned before Belgian commercial courts;

(b) such civil companies cannot be declared bankrupt;

(c) such civil companies must be registered in the Registry for civil companies that have taken the form of a commercial company ("Register van de burgerlijke vennootschappen die de vorm van een handelsvennootschap hebben aangenomen"/"Registre des sociétés civiles ayant emprunté la forme commerciale") rather than the corresponding Companies' Registry;

(d) in case of insolvency, the directors of such civil companies cannot be held liable for simple or fraudulent bankruptcy; and

(c) such civil companies are not obliged to keep the books and records that commercial companies must maintain under Belgian law.

The types of company that can be formed to perform either commercial or civil activities include:

—the general partnership;

—the limited partnership;

—the partnership limited by shares;

—the co-operative company;

—the private limited liability company; and

—the public limited liability company.

B.1.5.1.2 Companies with a social or profit motive In general, civil and commercial companies are assumed to operate with a profit motive. Under Belgian law, profit has traditionally been equated with appreciable monetary enrichment, either in the form of earnings and dividends or of capital gains. However, the last substantial amendments to the Law broadened the concept of "profit" to include any "direct or indirect economic advantage for the partners or shareholders". This notion embraces both the avoidance of losses and the saving of costs as forms of profit.

The Law, however, has also recognised that the pursuit of profits need not be an essential characteristic of a company. Thus, it has recognised and sanctioned the formation of enterprises that have a social or non-commercial motive. The forms of non-profit companies recognised under Belgian law are discussed below.

B.1.5.1.2.1 Company with a social motive (Vennootschap met Sociaal Oogmerk/Société à Finalité Sociale, abbreviated "V.S.O."/"S.F.S.") A relatively new type of company that may carry out either commercial or civil activities and which does not directly or indirectly allocate its profits to its partners or shareholders has been established under Belgian law. It is the so-called "company with a social motive". This new type of company has been established to achieve, among others, the following objectives:

(a) the promotion of enterprises that advance social or environmental programs or goals;

(b) the promotion of employee participation in the management of enterprises; and

(c) the provision of a legal structure for enterprises that have as their principal objective the rendering of services to the community.

In principle, any form of commercial legal entity can be organised as a company with a social motive. However, the most appropriate vehicle would seem to be the co-operative company with limited liability. The Law also provides that existing companies can be transformed into companies with a social motive.

A company with a social motive may be established like any other company, except that any reference to the corporate form must include the words "with a social motive". As a company with a social motive may not aim to enrich its partners or shareholders, its charter must contain a number of specific provisions guaranteeing that (i) the partners or shareholders will not seek (or seek only in a very limited manner) an economic advantage from the company's operations and (ii) the social motive of the company will be preserved. If the charter of a company that holds itself out as a company with a social motive does not contain the mandatory provisions referred to above, or if a company with a social motive acts against the provisions of its charter, any partner or shareholder, interested third party or a public prosecutor may sue for the company's dissolution in the competent court.

When a company with a social motive is liquidated, the proceeds from the liquidation, after payment of the company's debts and the refunding of the partners' or shareholders' investments, must be given to a recipient that is closely connected with the social goal(s) that the company purportedly attempted to advance.

B.1.5.1.2.2 Association without a profit motive (Vereniging Zonder Winstoogmerk/ Association Sans But Lucratif, abbreviated "V.Z.W."/"A.S.B.L.") The association without a profit motive is regulated by the Law of June 27, 1921 (hereinafter, the "Association Law") rather than the Law, and it can be described as an association that does not exercise any industrial or commercial activity and does not seek to provide its members with any personal advantage. The Law does not require that such associations completely refrain from profit-making activities. Rather, it permits them to engage occasionally in accessory, profit-making activities as long as such activities are linked to their principal purpose and directly further achievement of such purpose. Associations without a profit motive can also provide some limited moral or even material benefits to their members as long as these benefits are not of a monetary or financial nature. For example, they may organise entertainment activities for their members or provide members with access to library, study or sports facilities.

An association without a profit motive may acquire a distinct legal personality if it fulfils the following conditions:

(a) it must have its registered office in Belgium;

(b) it must have a minimum of three members;

(c) at least three-fifths of its members must be Belgian nationals or registered foreign residents then residing in Belgium;

(d) its charter must comply with the Association Law; and

(e) its charter and the names, professions and addresses of its directors must be published in the annexes to the *Belgian Official Journal*.

A distinction is made between an association's full members and its affiliated members. The association's charter usually sets forth the respective rights of full members and affiliated members. Full members generally enjoy greater rights and prerequisites than do the affiliated members, including the right to participate in the association's annual meetings. The conditions for association membership are specified either in an association's charter or can be adopted by a vote of members at an association's general meeting, by the board of directors or by a special committee of the board of directors. Association membership can be terminated either by the member himself or by the vote of two-thirds of the association's members.

B.1.5.1.2.3 International associations (Internationale Vereniging/Association Internationale) Belgium is one of the few countries that has established a particular legal regime for international non-profit associations. The Law of October 25, 1919, as modified by the Law of December 6, 1954 (hereinafter the "International Association Law"), enables an international non-profit association to acquire distinct legal personality by complying with the following conditions:

(a) the association must be open to Belgian nationals and to foreigners;

(b) the registered office of the association must be established in Belgium;

(c) the board of directors of the association must have among its members at least one Belgian national;

(d) the association may not have a profit-making purpose;

(e) the association must have as its purpose the advancement of a philanthropic, religious, scientific, artistic or educational objective;

(f) the charter of the association must comply with the International Association Law; and

(g) the charter of the association, as well as the names, professions and addresses of its directors, must be published in the annexes to the *Belgian Official Journal*.

In order to establish an international association in Belgium, an application must be made to the Belgian Ministry of Justice. For this purpose, the charter of the association must be submitted to the Ministry. In practice, it is advisable to first submit a draft of the charter to the Ministry and to see its opinion before submitting it to a vote by the association's general assembly. It should be noted that the charter must be signed by every founding member of the association, each of whom must be identified as a natural person or as a representative of a legal entity. In addition the name, profession, address and nationality of each of the association's directors must be set forth in the charter. Finally, the charter must contain an explanation of the purposes and activities of the association.

Assuming that the necessary criteria are met, a royal decree (executed by the Minister of Justice) granting the association independent legal status will be issued. The Royal Decree, as well as the charter of the association, must then be published in the annexes to the *Belgian Official Journal*. The association will officially obtain its independent legal status on the tenth day after such publication.

B.1.5.1.2.4 Institutions of public utility (foundations) The Association Law that governs associations without a profit motive also regulates institutions of public utility or foundations. In principle, this law permits anyone who obtains necessary government approval, to establish a foundation with a distinct legal personality and allocate all or part of his or her assets to it. Such a foundation must pursue a philanthropic, religious, scientific, artistic and educational purpose, and may not seek any profit.

To obtain an independent legal status for a foundation, its founder or founders must submit its charter to the Ministry of Justice for approval. The charter must contain a number of specific provisions, including a statement of the foundation's purpose or purposes and directions for the disposition of the Institution's assets on its dissolution.

Once the Ministry has approved its charter, a foundation must publish it and the Ministry's approval in the annexes to the *Belgian Official Journal*. The foundation will only be deemed to have acquired a legal personality on the tenth day after the publication of these documents. Once formed, extensive governmental control is exercised over foundations to ensure that they operate to further the purposes for which they were formed.

B.1.5.1.3 Companies of persons or capital companies In a "company of persons", such as a general partnership, limited partnership, or co-operative company with unlimited liability, the identity of the specific partners is innate in the business form. In a capital company, on the other hand, its members or shareholders are separate from its identity. They are connected with the company only by their individual contributions or investments in exchange for shares. Examples of capital companies include partnerships limited by shares and public limited liability companies. A third class of companies has characteristics of both companies of persons and capital companies. These are known as "mixed companies". Examples under Belgian law include private limited liability companies and limited liability co-operative companies.

B.1.5.2 *Partnerships With Legal Personality*

B.1.5.2.1 General partnership (Vennootschap Onder Firma/Société en Nom Collectif, abbreviated "V.O.F."/"S.N.C.") A general partnership is a partnership formed by two or more partners, which can be either natural persons or legal entities, in order to carry out commercial activities under a common name. The name of a general partnership may only contain the name of the partners.

A general partnership has a distinct legal personality in that it can both sue and be sued in its own name. This does not affect the liability of the partners for the debts of the partnership, which remains unlimited, joint and several, even if only one of the partners assumed the debt on behalf of the partnership. However, a third party cannot pursue a claim against a partnership's partners for acts of the partnership until the partnership itself has been found liable. Each of the partners is deemed to have authority to act on behalf of the partnership.

Partners in a general partnership can make a contribution of their labour, which makes this corporate form very suitable for practitioners of independent professions, such as attorneys.

The general partnership must be established in writing either by a notarial deed or a private contract. An excerpt of this document must be published in the annexes to the *Belgian Official Journal* There is no minimum capital requirement for forming a general partnership.

B.1.5.2.2 Limited partnership (Gewone Commanditaire Vennootschap/Société en Commandite Simple) A Limited Partnership is formed by one or more general or managing partners and one or more limited or silent partners. Managing partners are jointly and severally liable for the debts of a partnership and manage a partnership's operations. Limited partners only invest in the partnership and are only liable for the amount which they have agreed to invest. However, a limited partner must refrain from performing any managerial acts with respect to the partnership, even by virtue of a proxy, to preserve their limited liability exposure. If a limited partner fails to do so, he or she will be considered a managing partner and will be held jointly and severally liable with other managing partners for the partnership's obligations.

The name of a limited partnership must contain the name of one or more of the managing partners and may not contain the name of any limited partner.

Limited partnerships must be established in writing either by a notarial deed or by a private contract. An excerpt of this document must be published in the annexes to the *Belgian Official Journal*. There is no minimum capital requirement for the formation of a limited partnership.

This type of partnership was formerly used in commercial navigation, but is now no longer common in Belgium.

B.1.5.2.3 Partnership limited by shares (Commanditaire Vennootschap op Aandelen/Société en Commandite par Actions) A partnership limited by shares is a partnership formed by one or more partners and one or more shareholders, the corporate name of which may only contain the name of one or more of the partners. The partners of such a partnership are jointly and severally liable for the debts of the partnership and are responsible for managing the partnership. Its shareholders are only liable for the capital that they have agreed to contribute, and they must refrain from interfering with the management of the partnership. The only exception to this last rule is where a shareholder is appointed to act as a proxyholder for the partnership.

The partnership limited by shares is to a large extent governed by the rules under the Law that are applicable to the public limited liability company.

Such partnerships can only be established by notarial deed. An excerpt of the deed must be published in the annexes to the *Belgian Official Journal* and the deed itself must be registered with the Trade Registry of the judicial district in which the partnership operates.

Each partner has a right to veto decisions concerning modification of the partnership's charter and partnership acts that limit the partnership's operations *vis-à-vis* third parties.

Shares in this type of partnership can only be transferred to third parties if the partnership agreement explicitly provides therefore. The partnership can also raise funds by publicly offering its shares.

B.1.5.2.4 The co-operative company with unlimited liability (Cooperative Vennootschap met Onbeperkte Aansprakelijkheid/Société Coopérative à Responsabilité Illimitée, abbreviated "C.V.O.A."/"S.C.R.I") A co-operative company is defined by the Law as a company formed by shareholders who invest or contribute varying amounts. There are two different forms of co-operative companies, namely the co-operative company with unlimited liability, in which the shareholders are jointly and severally liable for the co-operatives' debts without limitation, and the co-operative company with limited liability, in which the shareholders' liability for the company's debts and other obligations is limited to their individual contributions.

The co-operative company has long been used to create companies with independent legal personality without having to comply with the strict incorporation rules governing limited liability companies. Although the rules governing the co-operative company have become much stricter as a result of amendments to the Law by the laws of July 18, 1991 and April 13, 1995, the co-operative company is a business form that offers flexibility with regard to restrictions on external representation, the organisation of general shareholders' meetings and changes of shareholders. This form of legal entity is used frequently in agriculture (central buying organisations) and by liberal professions (doctors, attorneys, accountants).

The two forms of co-operative company have a number of common features:

(a) the company must have a specific name which does not contain the name of any of its shareholders;

(b) the company must have at least three shareholders, but there is no maximum limit on the number of permissible shareholders;

(c) the share capital of the company consists of a fixed and a variable part;

(d) the company's shareholders can only transfer shares to third parties that are specifically nominated in the charter or that belong to a specific category of potential transferees that is defined in the charter; and

71

(e) each share carries the right to one vote, unless the charter otherwise provides, on issues of corporate governance that must be submitted to the company's shareholders.

In addition, the co-operative company with unlimited liability has a number of unique additional features worth noting:

(1) No notarial deed is required to establish it (although there must be a written document).

(2) Since its shareholders are jointly and severally liable for its debts, the rules relating to the protection of the capital which are mainly applicable to limited liability companies do not apply. Thus, there is no minimum requirement for the invariable part of such a company's capital, its shares need not be fully paid up, it does not need to complete a financial plan and there is no founding shareholders' liability for failure to provide sufficient capital, and there are no limitations on its distribution of profits.

(3) The company's managers must deposit a list of all shareholders with the Trade Registry every six months.

(4) The company's annual accounts do not need to be audited or published.

B.1.5.3 *Limited liability companies*

B.1.5.3.1 Co-operative company with limited liability (Cooperative Vennootschap met Beperkte Aansprakelijkheid/Société Coopérative à Responsabilité Limitée, abbreviated "C.V.B.A."/"S.C.R.L.") The co-operative company with limited liability must be formed by at least three members or shareholders who invest capital that is partly fixed and partly variable. The liability of these members or shareholders for the debts of the company is limited to their investments. As noted, this type of company has a number of features in common with the co-operative company with unlimited liability. It also has the following specific features:

(a) The company can only be established by a notarial deed which must specifically indicate the fixed portion of its share capital.

(b) The fixed part of the capital must be at least 750,000 Bfr (250,000 Bfr if the company is established with a social motive) of which at least 250,000 Bfr (100,000 Bfr if the company is established with a social motive) must be paid in at the time of its incorporation.

(c) Each share that represents contributions of cash or in kind must be paid up to at least one-quarter of its par value.

(d) Contributions in kind are only valid if their value can be objectively assessed in accordance with economic criteria.

(e) The amount of the required fixed part of the capital must be justified in a financial plan and must be paid into a special bank account.

(f) All signatories of the articles of incorporation who effectively make an investment are subject to founding shareholders' liability; and

(g) The annual accounts of the company must be audited by a statutory auditor (Bedrijfsrevisor/Réviseur d'entreprise) and published.

B.1.5.3.2 Economic interest grouping (Economisch Samenwerkingsverband/ Groupement d'Intérêt Économique, abbreviated "EIG"/"GIE") European Council Regulation (EEC) No. 2137/85 of July 25, 1985 on the European Economic Interest Grouping ("EEIG") ([1985] O.J. L199/1) was implemented into Belgian law by the Law of July 12, 1989. The EEIG, which applies to multinational business groups is not further discussed for the purposes of this chapter. However, we note that the Belgian equivalent, the so-called Economic Interest Grouping ("EIG") which was introduced into Belgian law by the Law of July 17, 1989, is governed by approximately the same rule as the EEIG, except that there is no multinational requirement. All members of the EIG may have the Belgian nationality.

The EIG is a grouping set up by contract, for a definite or indefinite period between two or more parties (natural persons or legal entities). The aim of the EIG may be to promote the economic activities of its members or improve or increase the profits generated by their activities. The activities of the grouping itself must be related, at least in an ancillary manner, to the activities of its members.

The EIG is often used as a vehicle for co-operation on a diverse range of subjects, including advertising, research and development, joint purchasing of materials, and lobbying.

A contract establishing an EIG can require that members make contributions in cash or in kind or to contribute their labour. For each contribution in kind, a statutory auditor must evaluate the contribution and draw up a valuation report. The contract itself must be registered with the Registry for Economic Interest Groupings (Register van de economisch samenwerkingsverbanden/Registre des groupements d'intérêt économique) of the judicial district in which the official office of the EIG is situated.

An EIG must be managed by one or more natural persons. Such managers can be appointed in the contract establishing the EIG or by the EIG's members. The managers may, but need not, be members of the EIG. Only the manager or each of the managers when there are two or more, can represent the EIG in relations with third parties. The contract for the establishment of the EIG may provide that the EIG can only be validly contractually committed by two or more managers acting jointly.

The EIG may not have as its main purpose the making of profits for itself. However, it may seek profits in the course of its activities, which profits will be deemed to belong to the EIG's members and must be allocated to them in accordance with the contract establishing the EIG. These profits must then also be taxed at the level applicable to the EIG members that receive them.

B.1.5.3.3   Private limited liability company (Besloten Vennootschap met Beperkte Aansprakelijkheid/Société Privée à Responsabilité Limitée, abbreviated "B.V.B.A."/"S.P.R.L.")   The private limited liability company is in principle formed by at least two natural persons or legal entities whose liability is limited to the amount of their investments and whose rights can only be transferred under specific conditions. The company may either be given a specific name or may be named after one of its members.

The following conditions must be satisfied to incorporate a private limited liability company:

(a)   Its capital must be fully subscribed. No calls may be made on the capital market for this subscription.

(b)   The company must be incorporated with a minimum capital of 750,000 Bfr.

(c)   At least 250,000 Bfr of the capital must have been paid in as of the day of incorporation.

(d)   The capital must be divided into equal shares of at least 1,000 Bfr per share, all of which must be registered in a register held at the registered office in order to preserve the private character of the company. Only capital shares may be issued.

(e)   Each share representing a contribution in cash must be paid up to at least one-fifth of its par value.

(d)   The shares representing contributions in kind must be fully paid up.

(g)   Certain rules applicable to a public limited liability company also apply to a private limited liability company. These include reporting requirements for contributions in kind and the completion of a financial plan.

The private limited liability company can only be established by a notarial deed. Excerpts of the deed must be published in the annexes to the *Belgian Official Journal* and must be registered with the Trade Registry of the judicial district in which the registered office of the company is situated.

Each party that participates in the incorporation of a private limited liability company will be considered a founder and may therefore incur specific founding sharcholders' liability. Thus, it is not possible to participate merely as a subscriber in the incorporation of such a company's capital.

The most specific feature of a private limited liability company is the limited transferability of its shares. Transfers of shares in such a company must be approved at a special or general shareholders' meeting by at least one-half of the shareholders and at least three-quarters of total votes cast. The company's charter may provide for an even stricter share transfer system. For example, it can require unanimous shareholder approval for transfers of shares. Unless otherwise provided in the charter, these rules do not apply to transfers of shares between shareholders, between a shareholder and a spouse, or between a shareholder and an ascendant or descendant. Also, other share transfers to other categories of persons can be exempted in the charter from shareholder approval requirements. Because of the ability to control shareholder succession in the charter, this type of company is often used in Belgium for small family enterprises.

The management of the private limited liability company can be entrusted to one or more paid or unpaid persons, either for a limited or an unlimited duration. Managers can also be appointed in the charter, which procedure allows for the guaranteed continuity of management. Unless otherwise provided in the charter, such managers are deemed appointed for the duration of the existence of a company. They can only be dismissed by unanimous decision of the shareholders or for serious grounds. The powers of managers can be limited in the charter, but such limitations are not enforceable against third parties, even if they are published.

A specific feature of a private limited liability company is that it can also be incorporated by one person. This person must be a natural person for the limited liability rule to apply. In principle, the same rules apply as for a private limited liability company with more than one shareholder. Other rules applicable to a "one-person private limited liability company" (Eénpersoons-BVBA./SPRL à une personne, abbreviated "EBVBA"/"SPRLU") are set forth in the Law of July 14, 1987. This type of company is often established by practitioners of liberal professions who want to separate their professional from their private capital and who want to escape the progressivity of individual income taxes.

B.1.5.3.4 Public limited liability company (Naamloze Vennootschap/Société Anonyme, abbreviated "NV"/"SA") The public limited liability company is formed by at least two shareholders whose potential liability is normally limited to their individual investments. It is the corporate form most often used by foreign investors to operate in Belgium. The rules governing its incorporation and operation are set forth in section 2.

B.1.6 Restrictions on Foreign Companies and Persons

In principle, no special permits are required for foreign companies to establish themselves in Belgium. However, certain activities, such as banking, insurance or transport, are regulated by Belgian law and require prior regulatory authorisation. In addition, non-EEA nationals taking up employment with a Belgium based employer must obtain a work permit. Non-EEA nationals exercising a self-employed activity require a professional card. With their work permit or professional card, these non-EEA nationals can obtain a residence permit.

INCORPORATING A COMPANY IN BELGIUM—THE EXAMPLE OF THE PUBLIC LIMITED LIABILITY COMPANY

B.2.1   Introduction—Definition

The public limited liability company is the form of commercial company most widely used by foreign companies and investors to establish subsidiaries in Belgium. This form of company has the following characteristics: (i) it has an independent legal personality separate from its shareholders; (ii) its shareholders may be natural persons or legal entities, such as other public limited liability companies, and they may be residents or non-residents of Belgium; (iii) the potential liability of its shareholders is, in principle, limited to their specific individual investments; and (iv) its shareholders' investments may be in cash or in kind.

The main body of law governing public limited liability companies is the Royal Decree of November 30, 1935 co-ordinating the Laws on Commercial Companies (the "Law"), as amended. The most recent substantial amendments to the Law are contained in the Law of April 13, 1995.

The Law contains a number of specific rules and requirements applicable to public limited liability companies that are deemed to have made a public offer of securities, *i.e.* companies whose shares are quoted on a stock exchange market or whose shares are distributed among the public. A company's shares are deemed to have been distributed among the public if the company has offered its securities by (i) use of advertising materials, including but not limited to newspapers, advertisements, television or radio broadcasts and circular letters; (ii) contacting more than 50 persons, or (iii) use of specific intermediaries such as banks.

B.2.2   Requirements Prior to the Incorporation

The first step in incorporating a public limited liability company is the drafting of the company's charter. The charter sets forth the basic terms for the company's operation and governance. As such, it fulfils the same function as that fulfilled by the memorandum and articles of association under English corporate law.

The Law requires that the charter meet certain minimum information require-ments and that it also contain certain substantive provisions. The main provisions that are included in the charter of a public limited liability company are reviewed in sections B.2.4 through B.2.11 below. Although a company charter does not need to be drafted by a Belgian notary public, once drafted, it must be placed in the form of a deed (the deed of incorporation), with all requisite formalities, by such a notary public. Thus, the necessary information and, if not drafted by the notary public, the text of the charter are usually supplied to a notary public by a company's founding shareholders at least one week prior to the desired incorporation of the public limited liability company.

As part of the formalities related to putting the charter in the form of a deed, the notary public reads aloud, the founding shareholders execute, and the notary public applies necessary stamps to the charter. The public limited liability company is deemed incorporated from that moment, although the company only acquires legal personality at a later stage (see section B.2.3 below). The incorporation of the company before the notary public does not require the physical presence of the founding shareholders, provided that they are represented by proxyholders. Proxyholders must hold valid special proxies that specify the proxyholders' authority. When a founding shareholder's investment in the company includes the contribution of real estate, a proxy authorising such contribution by a proxyholder must be prepared by a notary public in the form of a deed.

Prior to a public limited liability company's incorporation, the founding shareholders must also submit the following documents to the notary public:

(1) A *financial plan* establishing that the company's share capital will be sufficient to enable the company to conduct normal business operations of a type described in the charter for at least the first two years after its incorporation. The content of the financial plan is not subject to any legal requirement, and the notary public will not examine its merits. He or she will merely keep it, in confidence, with the original of the charter. However if the company goes into bankruptcy within three years after its incorporation, a court may review the financial plan to determine whether the capital, along with other financial resources such as bank loans and credit arrangements with suppliers, was adequate to sustain the company's normal business operations for this initial two-year period. If the court determines that the capital was manifestly insufficient, it can hold the company's founding shareholders jointly and severally liable for all or part of the debts of the company. Thus, the financial plan should be prepared carefully, and it is advisable to seek the assistance of an accountant or a statutory auditor for its preparation.

(2) *Bank certificates* confirming that investments of cash have been deposited with a Belgian financial institution in a special blocked account in the name of the company to be incorporated. This account must be reserved solely for funds invested to incorporate the company. When it receives these funds, the bank will issue a certificate of receipt to the depositor. The notary public will not proceed with the company's incorporation unless all such certificates have been obtained. The funds will be released to the company by the financial

institution upon presentation of a certificate from the incorporating notary public that the company has been incorporated.

(3) *Two special reports* regarding the valuation and usefulness of investments in kind, if any. One report, which must be prepared by a statutory auditor appointed by the founding shareholders, must describe the assets and the valuation methods used to determine their value. The second report, which must be prepared by the founding shareholders, must set forth their estimates of the value of the invested assets and the reasons why such assets are "in the interest of" the company. Each report must be completed prior to a company's incorporation and will have to be deposited with the Companies' Registry with a copy of the company's deed of incorporation (*see* point B.2.3(1) below). The founding shareholders should show great care in determining the value of the assets concerned, since they will be jointly and severally liable for any damages that are a direct result of a manifest overvaluation of such assets. It should also be noted that investments in kind can only consist of assets that can be valued using economic criteria; an agreement to perform labour or provide services in the future would not be considered a valid investment in kind.

Pursuant to mandatory Belgian regulations on the use of languages, the charter as well as all other corporate documents that are legally required, must be drafted in French, Dutch or German, depending on the geographical area in which the company's principal place of business is located. If the company is established in Brussels, it has the option of drawing up all documents in either Dutch or French.

B.2.3 Post-incorporation Matters

A company's shareholders or management must comply with several additional legal formalities once the company has been incorporated. These formalities are set forth below:

(1) Within two weeks from the date of incorporation of a company, an excerpt of its deed of incorporation (also known as its charter) must be deposited with the Companies' Registry of the Commercial Court with jurisdiction over such company's registered office. This excerpt must include certain mandatory information about such company, including the names of its founding shareholders, its name, its corporate purpose, the address of its registered office and a statement of its capital. A company acquires legal personality from the moment that the excerpt of its deed of incorporation is filed.

(2) A company must then register with and obtain a registration number from the Trade Registry of the Commercial Court with jurisdiction over its registered office. This must be done before such company can start operating. Such registration number must be included on all documents of a company.

(3) The excerpt of a company's deed of incorporation must be published in the annexes to the *Belgian Official Journal*. Until its date of publication, the deed of incorporation may not be relied upon as against third parties, unless the company can prove that such third parties had prior knowledge thereof.

(4) A company that has as its principal purpose the provision of goods or services will be subject to VAT, and must obtain a VAT registration number before it begins operating. In fact, a company's VAT number must be included on all of its documents. To obtain a VAT registration, the managing director of the company must complete a form issued for this purpose by the VAT authorities (the so-called "Declaration of Initiation of Economic Activity").

(5) Under Belgian law, a company must establish a register of registered shares, which should be kept at the registered office of the company. It is also a standard practice to keep the minutes of a company's board of directors' meetings and general shareholders' meetings in corporate books at the company's registered office.

B.2.4 Corporate Purpose

The specific purpose for which the company is formed must be stated in the charter. As in England, it is standard practice in Belgium to describe the particular corporate purpose(s) of the company and to also include a more general provision covering ancillary objectives and enabling powers related to the company's operations. It should be noted that certain activities, such as banking, insurance or transport, are regulated by Belgian law and require prior regulatory authorisation.

B.2.5 Corporate Name

The name selected for the company must be indicated in the Charter. There are no particular restrictions on the choice of a company name, except that the name must differ from that of any other company. In addition, companies are not permitted to use words that might mislead consumers as to the nature or quality of the business.

If a company's name is identical or similar to another company name or to a trade mark owned by a third party, such third party may require the company to amend its name and may claim damages from the company, where there are grounds therefore. It is usual practice to perform a prior informal examination of existing company names and trade marks. There is, however, no formal repository of company names in the Belgian system.

B.2.6   Registered Office

The location of a company's registered office must be specified in its charter. The office specified should be the office that serves as the principal place of business for the company's management. In principle, a transfer of a registered office to another location requires a modification of the charter. This would, in turn, require the holding of a general meeting of shareholders before a notary public. To avoid this type of situation, the charter often grants to the board of directors the authority to transfer the company's registered office by a board resolution. Any such resolution must be published in the annexes to the *Belgian Official Journal*.

B.2.7   Share Capital and Shares

Shares in a public limited liability company may be in registered, bearer or dematerialised form. Shares in a dematerialised form are represented by an account inscription in the name of the shareholder with an authorised account holder. No specific par value is required for a company's shares. As long as a company's share capital has not been fully paid up, its shares must be in registered form.

B.2.7.1   *Minimum share capital*

Pursuant to the last substantial revision of the Law, the minimum stated capital for public limited liability companies was increased from 1,250,000 Bfr to 2,500,000 Bfr. The transitional provisions of the Law stipulate that, as of July 1, 1996, existing companies have a five-year period to comply with this minimum stated capital. Notwithstanding this long grace period, it is advisable for all companies that fall under the scope of this provision to increase their minimum stated capital when they next modify their charters. To induce compliance, the Law provides that directors will be jointly and severally liable for the amount by which a company's actual stated capital is less than the new minimum capital requirement at the expiration of the transition period. In addition, any interested party may also request the Commercial Court with jurisdiction over a non-complying company to dissolve such company.

B.2.7.2   *Amount to be paid up*

At the time of incorporation, the entire share capital must be subscribed. The subscribed share capital must be paid up to an amount of at least 2,500,000 Bfr, *i.e.* the minimum share capital. In addition, at least 25 per cent of each share must be paid up. Share capital corresponding fully or partially with an investment in kind must be paid up within five years of the date of incorporation.

B.2.7.3 Increase of share capital

Capital increases normally must be approved at a shareholder's meeting by a majority in capital of a company's shareholders present and the affirmative vote of not less than three-quarters of all votes cast. Once approved, an increase in share capital requires the modification of a company's charter. As with its original charter, such a modification must be placed into the form of a deed by a notary public.

Alternatively, the charter of a company may provide its board of directors with the authority to increase the company's capital up to a specified amount (the "authorised capital"). However, such a charter provision will only be valid for a specified period of time, which may not exceed five years. Any decision by the board of directors to exercise such authority must be enacted in the form of a deed drawn up by a notary public. A board of directors' right to increase a company's share capital without specific shareholder approval may be reauthorised by the company's shareholders after it lapses under certain conditions (special report, quorum and majority requirements, notarial deed).

A board of directors' right to increase share capital is limited in two additional respects. First, the Law prohibits the board from increasing share capital when such increase will be mainly in the form of contributions in kind by a single shareholder who holds at least 10 per cent of company shareholders' total voting rights. In addition, a Board may not increase a company's capital after the company has received notice of a public takeover bid for its shares.

With respect to companies that are deemed to have made a public offer of securities, the amount of a company's authorised capital may not exceed that of its share capital.

B.2.7.4 Transfer of shares

Unless otherwise provided for in the company's charter, registered, bearer and dematerialised shares can be freely transferred. Non-fully paid up shares as well as shares of a company in formation can also be transferred.

The transfer of shares can be restricted by any type of clause, even in agreements involving non-shareholders. In order to be valid, these clauses must be limited in time. In addition, they must be "in the interest of" the company, which concept will need to be clarified by the courts. With regard to approval and pre-emption clauses, however, the Law specifically provides that these clauses cannot restrict the transfer of shares for a period exceeding six months. An approval clause subjects any transfer of shares to the prior approval of the Board of Directors or of another decision-making body of the company. A pre-emption clause requires a shareholder wishing to sell his or her shares to offer these shares to the other shareholders of a company before selling them to a third party.

B.2.8 Shareholders

Incorporation of a public limited liability company requires a minimum of two shareholders. A shareholder may be a natural person or a legal entity. If after the incorporation the number of a company's shareholders drops below two for any period longer than 12 months, the remaining shareholder shall be jointly and severally liable, together with the company, for all commitments undertaken by the company while he/she was the only shareholder. A company is not allowed to directly or indirectly subscribe for its own shares.

B.2.8.1 *Purchase of own shares*

Whilst not permitted to subscribe for its own shares, a company may purchase its own shares following their initial issuance and subscription, provided that the following restrictive conditions are met:

(a) the nominal value, or, in the absence thereof, the net asset value of the acquired shares (including those previously acquired by the company or those acquired by a subsidiary) does not exceed 10 per cent of the company's stated capital;

(b) only company funds available for the payment of dividends are used to acquire its shares;

(c) only fully paid shares are acquired by the company;

(d) the company offers to purchase shares and executes such purchases so as to treat shareholders equally.

A company's purchase of its shares must normally be approved at a shareholders' meeting by shareholders holding at least three-quarters of the votes cast. The charter may empower the board of directors to purchase the company's shares, provided that such purchase is necessary to prevent the company from sustaining significant and imminent harm. Such an authorisation can only remain valid for a period of three years, but it may be renewed.

B.2.8.2 *Voting arrangements*

The exercise of shareholders' voting rights may be regulated by shareholders' agreements. The Law no longer specifies a maximum time-limit for such agreements.

Previously it required that shareholders' agreements governing the exercise of shareholders' voting rights not exceed five years' duration. However, to be valid, such agreements must still have a definite duration and must be deemed to be consistent with the interests of the company.

B.2.8.3 *Disputes between shareholders*

One or more shareholders of a company who jointly represent at least 30 per cent of the company's voting rights (or 20 per cent of the company's voting rights if the company has issued non-equity securities) or at least 30 per cent of the company's share capital can, provided they have valid reasons, request the commercial court with jurisdiction over the company to order another shareholder to transfer his or her shares to them. The counterpart of this compulsory sale procedure is that each shareholder can, provided he has valid reasons, request such commercial court to order that his shares be purchased by the shareholders to whom these reasons relate. Finally, any shareholder who owns or shareholders who jointly own shares representing 95 per cent of all shareholder voting rights has the possibility to compel the remaining minority shareholders to sell their shares, regardless of the existence of a conflict between shareholders.

B.2.9 Shareholders' Meetings

A company must convene an ordinary shareholders' meeting at least once each year for, *inter alia*, the following purposes:

(a) to approve the company's annual accounts and auditor's report;

(b) to approve the board of directors' annual report;

(c) to decide upon profit distribution;

(d) to fix the remuneration of the members of the board of directors and to evaluate each director's performance during the preceding year.

In addition, extra-ordinary shareholders' meetings can be called during the year as and when the interests of the company so require.

B.2.9.1 *Calling a shareholders' meeting*

An ordinary or extra-ordinary shareholders' meeting may be convened in any one of the following ways:

(a) by a company's board of directors;

(b)   by a company's statutory auditor;

(c)   by a company's shareholders representing at least one-fifth of the company's share capital.

B.2.9.2   *Notices*

A notice of a shareholders' meeting must state the location, time and agenda of the meeting and must be published (i) in the *Belgian Official Journal* eight days prior to the meeting and (ii) on two separate occasions, at least eight days apart and with the second publication being at least eight days prior to the meeting, in a national newspaper and a regional newspaper. If all of a company's shares are in registered form, notice may be given by registered mail only to all of its registered shareholders at least eight days prior to the meeting. Copies of a company's annual report of its board of directors, its annual accounts and its auditors' report must also be made available for inspection at the registered office of the company at least 15 days before an ordinary shareholders' meeting.

B.2.9.3   *Quorum and majority at shareholders' meetings*

In principle, no quorum requirement exists for the holding of a shareholders' meeting. Shareholders' decisions are normally taken by a simple majority of the votes cast at the meeting. However, special quorum and majority requirements are applicable to a number of specific matters, as set out in the table opposite. At a shareholders' meeting, a company's shareholders may only deliberate and validly resolve matters subject to special quorum and majority requirements provided that the following requirements are met:

(a)   such matters have been disclosed as part of the meeting's agenda in the notice of the meeting; and

(b)   shareholders holding shares representing at least half of the stated capital are present or represented at such a meeting. Where this second condition is not satisfied, a new shareholders' meeting must be convened, which may, in principle, validly vote on such matters without application of a quorum requirement.

B.2.10   Directors

A public limited liability company is managed by a board of directors which must, in principle, consist of at least three directors.

Where there are only two shareholders at the time of a company's incorporation,

	Quorum First Meeting (%)	Quorum Second Meeting (%)	Majority (%)
1. Modification of the "purpose clause" of the company's charter	50	None	80
2. A company's acquisition or pledge of its own shares	50	None	80
3. Ordinary amendments to the charter	50	None	75
4. Increase or decrease of a company's stated capital	50	None	75
5. Extension of the life of the company	50	None	75
6. Early dissolution or merger of the company	50	None	75
7. Issuance of shares below par value	50	None	75
8. Cancellation or limitation of preferential subscription rights	50	None	75
9. Early dissolution of the company when one-half to three-quarters of the company's capital has been lost	50	None	75
10. Early dissolution of the company when three-quarters or more of its capital has been lost	50	None	25

or where it is established at the time of a shareholders' meeting that the company has only two shareholders, the board of directors can be composed of only two directors. A third director must be appointed at the next shareholders' meeting at which the company has more than two shareholders.

Directors are, in principle, appointed by a company's shareholders at a shareholders' meeting. Directors do not need to meet any residence or nationality requirement, and a director may be a natural person or a legal entity. A director's term may not exceed six years, but it may be renewed unless otherwise provided in the charter. A director may be removed from the board at any time by a vote of the shareholders at a shareholders' meeting.

A notice must be published in the annexes to the *Belgian Official Journal* when a director is appointed or dismissed.

Unless otherwise provided in the charter, members of a company's board of directors may appoint a director to fill temporarily a vacancy on the board until the next shareholders' meeting. At such a meeting a new permanent director must be elected to fill such vacancy.

Usually, a company's board of directors elects a chairman and a vice-chairman from among its members. However, these positions confer no special powers to the directors holding them unless so specified in the charter.

B.2.10.1 *Duties and liabilities of directors*

A company's directors have both the power and responsibility to manage all of the company's affairs, except for those affairs entrusted by the Law to the shareholders' meeting. A company is generally bound by all acts of its directors and of persons to whom the board of directors entrusts the daily management of the company, even if these acts do not fall within the corporate purpose (*i.e.* acts which are *ultra vires*). The exception to this rule is when a company can prove that a third person was actually aware of the *ultra vires* character of an act or that, in view of the circumstances, he could reasonably not have been unaware of it (*i.e.* that the third party had a "constructive knowledge" of the same). The mere publication of a company's charter does not give rise to such constructive knowledge.

A company's directors are jointly and severally liable *vis-à-vis* the company and third parties for all damages that are the result of violations of their specific duties, as set forth in the company's charter or in the Law. A director will only be exempted from such liability for any breach in which he or she had no part provided no fault can be imputed to him or her and provided he or she denounced this infringement at the first shareholders' meeting after he or she became aware thereof.

A company's directors are also individually liable *vis-à-vis* their company (but not to third parties) for failure to carry out the duties entrusted to them and for any management errors, provided that these errors are "manifest" in nature when made. The Law also provides for the special liability of directors for failure to file a company's annual accounts. If a company's annual accounts are not presented at the company's shareholders' meeting within six months after the closing date of the preceding financial year, or if the annual accounts have not been filed with the National Bank of Belgium within one month following their approval at the shareholders' meeting, then third parties will be assumed to have been harmed by this failure. The company's directors will have the burden of proving that no such harm has occurred. The effect of this presumption of causality remains to be seen, since it would be sufficient to prove that any damage already existed before the formalities had to be satisfied.

B.2.10.2 *Day-to-day management*

The daily management of a company is usually entrusted to a member of the board who acts as the company's managing director or to an employee of the company who acts as the company's general manager. Appointments, including details of the powers conferred, and dismissals of managing directors and general managers must be published in the annexes to the *Belgian Official Journal*. Within the limits of day-to-day management, a company may be validly represented by the person to whom daily management power has been entrusted. His or her authority to deal with third parties in this role cannot be limited.

B.2.10.3 *Conflicts of interests*

A director who has a conflict of interest, *i.e.* a direct or indirect conflicting interest of an economic nature with a decision or action of the board of directors, must inform the board of this conflict before the board takes a decision on a matter where such a conflict arises. This information must be specifically disclosed in the minutes of the board's meeting together with (i) the nature of the decision or action in relation to which the conflict has occurred; (ii) the reasons for the board for taking the decision notwithstanding the conflict; and (iii) the economic consequences of this decision for the company. The statutory auditor of the company must be informed of the conflict as well.

For a company deemed to have made a public offer of securities, a director with such a conflict of interest may neither deliberate nor vote with the company's board in respect of the transaction which raises the conflict of interest. For a company not deemed to have made a public offer of securities, the Law does not prevent such a director from participating in the decision making process. Special rules apply for companies that are listed on a stock exchange.

Any transaction in which a company's director has a conflict of interest and the economic consequences of such a transaction must be described in the annual report of the company's board and of its statutory auditor to the shareholders' meeting.

If the information procedure is not followed and the company's board takes a decision that unjustifiably advantages a director with a direct or indirect conflicting interest of an economic nature, the directors shall be held personally and jointly liable for all damages suffered by the company or by third parties. The regulation of conflicts of interest and the above procedure does not apply to relationships between a parent company and a subsidiary in which it owns 95 per cent or more of the subsidiary's voting equity; nor does it apply to ordinary transactions that take place at arm's length.

B.2.11 Board of Directors' Meeting

The proceedings of a company's board of directors are governed by rules laid down in the company's charter. In the absence of such rules, they are governed by the Law. The charter usually provides that the board shall meet upon notice from and under the direction of its chairman, when the interest of the company so requires or when a fixed number of board members so demands. A board of directors normally only validly meets and votes if at least one-half of its members are present or represented. Unless otherwise provided for in the charter, all decisions of the board are taken by a majority vote of the members present or represented, and in case of the abstention of one or more of them, by a majority of the other board members. The charter of a company may provide that minutes of a board's meeting signed by all directors will be considered valid, even when the board has not met physically, in case of emergency justified by the interest of the company.

B.2.12   Duration

As a general rule, companies are established for an indefinite duration, unless the charter provides otherwise. If a company's founding shareholders decide to limit its duration to a certain period, such company will be wound up at the end of this period. However, a company's duration may be extended prior to its dissolution, provided that such an extension is approved at a shareholders' meeting at which holders of at least one-half of the company's voting equity are present or represented by three-quarters of all votes cast.

B.2.13   Audit

Each company that does not qualify as a small or medium-sized enterprise is subject to a periodic (usually annual) audit of its accounts by statutory auditors appointed by its ordinary shareholders' meeting. A small or medium-sized enterprise is a company that does not satisfy more than one of the following criteria:

—personnel: 50;

—turnover: 200,000,000 Bfr;

—balance sheet total: 100,000,000 Bfr;

However, a company will not be deemed a small or medium-sized enterprise if it has more than 100 employees.

A company must be considered on a consolidated basis for the application of these criteria where (i) it forms part of a group which is required to draw up and publish consolidated annual accounts; (ii) it is a holding company; or (iii) its securities are listed on a stock exchange.

Not later than one month before an ordinary shareholders' meeting, a company's statutory auditor must receive a copy of the company's annual report and the accounts to enable him to prepare his auditor's report for presentation to the shareholders. As noted above, the auditor's report must be available for inspection at the offices of the company at least 15 days prior to its shareholders' meeting.

Section 3

COSTS OF INCORPORATION

B.3.1   At present, incorporation costs for public or private limited liability companies consist of:

(i)   A 0.5 per cent registration tax on the amount of the share capital;

(ii)   The notary fees calculated as a percentage on the amount of share capital:

Range of share capital	Private limited liability companies (%)	Public limited liability companies (%)
1 −1,500,000	0.570	0.855
1,500,000–4,000,000	0.399	0.570
4,000,000–9,000,000	0.285	0.399
9,000,000–21,500,000	0.171	0.228
21,500,000–71,500,000	0.057	0.114
71,500,000–134,000,000	0.0228	0.0456
134,000,000–.	0.0114	0.0228

(iii)   Other expenses such as publication costs in the *Belgian Official Journal*, registration with the Trade Registry and other related costs (approximately 30,000 Bfr).

BULGARIA

CLASSIFICATION OF BUSINESS ORGANISATIONS IN BULGARIA: INTRODUCTION*

C.1.0 The purpose of this study is to present a brief overview of the different legal forms by which a company may be formed in Bulgaria. Upon repeal of the old commercial legislation (1951), the Commercial Law (CL) has ceased to exist as a branch of Bulgarian law. A recovery of the positions of CL as a basic branch in private law was made in 1991 by the adoption of the new Trade Act. The commercial legislation now in force in Bulgaria aims at regulating the legal relations established in trade; trade perceived as economic activity directed to the exchange of wealth in general. Business deals are a legal form of manifested trade activity. A trader is deemed to be any natural person or body corporate whose occupation it is to do business deals under Bulgarian law.

The three possible legal organisational forms for carrying on business activities are as follows:

—a sole trader

—commercial companies and associations thereof

—co-operatives

Business activities maybe carried on by civil companies (partnerships) although they do not perform the functions of a trader and have other functions as a rule, as well as by co-partnerships (a form of civil company). The last two forms of partnership have not been regulated by Bulgarian positive law but their existence is to be acknowledged on the strength of the principle of freedom of contracting.

C.1.1 The Sole Trader (ST)

C.1.1.1 *The sole trader (ST)*

A sole trader is that individual who is engaged and may carry on business activities. Any capable Bulgarian citizen or foreigner who is a local resident by statute may register as a sole trader. Persons declared insolvent or in insolvency proceedings

---

* *Boyan Stanoev, Bazliankov, Stanoev & Tashev (full particulars are listed in the Appendix).*

and persons convicted of bankruptcy are excluded from this category. All rights and obligations resulting from the business activities are united by the personality of the individual recognised as a trader. The principle is one person—one ST. As a ST the natural person is liable to the extent of his whole property. The trade name of ST must include his forename and surname/father's name and it is subject to transfer only together with his business. Any natural person may register as a ST when his occupation is to do business deals or the business set up by him requires conduct of affairs in commercial manner due to its objects and size.

SECTION 2

COMMERCIAL COMPANIES

C.2.1 Introduction

Commercial companies (CCs) are bodies corporate. They are associations of two or more persons for the object of commercial dealing by joint means. Under Bulgarian law CCs are *numerus clausus*. Formation of any other types of company not provided for by law is deemed illegal. Depending on the economic organisation of CCs two categories are differentiated:

(1) CCs of persons (including general partnership and limited partnership). Companies of persons are essentially characterised by the personality of the members. They are companies established *intuitu personae*. Each partner is liable to make personal efforts and perform labour which requires special mutual trust. The persons assume personal and unlimited liability and their interests are non-transferrable.

(2) Capital CCs (including limited liability companies, joint-stock companies and partnership companies limited by shares). The nature of activities of a capital commercial company requires concentration of large sums of money irrespective of the persons putting in the financial means. A major role in a capital commercial company is played by shares in the capital whereby the right to vote and to a part of the members' profits is formed proportionately. In contrast to companies of persons the capital shares of the members are transferable and if a member terminates his membership no dissolution is caused to the company. The risk to the company's business activities is limited to the amount of the members' contribution to the capital of the company.

C.2.2 Commercial Companies of Persons—General Partnership (GP)

A general partnership (GP) consists of two or more natural persons or bodies corporate, incorporated for the object of commercial dealing by occupation and under a common trade name where partners assume joint and unlimited liability.

C.2.2.1 *Formation*

A general partnership is deemed set up provided that a valid partnership deed has been drawn up and an entry in the Commercial Register at the place of residence of the partnership has been made. The minimum contractual contents must include the legally individualising characteristics of the partners and the partnership itself; it must define the type and amount of contributions made by each partner, as well as the rules for distribution of profit and loss. The management and representation of the partnership must be specified as well.

C.2.2.2 *Legal relations between the partners*

The partners enter into relations to one another which they are free to regulate by the partnership deed. Furthermore they enter into legal relations with the partnership itself. The contents of these legal relations is expressed in heterogeneous rights and obligation which in their aggregate characterise the legal status of the partners.

A basic right of each partner is the right to receive part of the profits. This right covers such part of the partnership's net profit as proportionate to the contribution of the relevant partner. Moreover the partner is entitled to two types of indemnity. In respect of such necessary expenses as he incurs in the conduct of the partnership's business and for such damage as he suffers in the same. These rights correlate with the basic property obligation of the partner, *i.e.* to make contributions in cash or in kind to the partnership. Unless otherwise provided for in the partnership deed each partner may manage the affairs of the partnership alone and at his own discretion and at all times exercise his right to veto thus opposing to certain actions of the remaining partners. Each partner has a supervisory power which provides opportunity for him to get personally informed on the affairs of the partnership, to inspect the partnership books and ask for an account on the part of the managers. With regard to this a ban on engaging in competitive activities is imposed on the partner. He may not participate in another company having the same or similar objects nor for his own account conclude such deals that are related to the objects of the partnership.

C.2.2.3 *Representation*

In principle each partner may alone represent the partnership. The partnership deed may provide for the following:

(a) power of representation is given to only some of the partners (one or several of them);

(b) collective representation is established (the affairs of the partnership are managed jointly by the persons authorised).

The presentation in a GP may be legal and contractual. The law gives priority to the contractual presentation. In case of such presentation the legal one is excluded. Legal representation covers all legal actions and in contrast to the contractual representation is not subject to restrictions and is valid throughout the partnership's duration.

C.2.2.4 *Liability of a GP*

The inherent characteristic of a GP is the personal joint and unlimited liability of the partners. For the debts incurred by the partnership the partners are liable to the extent of their private ownership. In this sense their liability is a subsidiary and a guarantee one. This liability is *ex tunc*, *i.e.* the incoming partner is also liable for the obligation of the partnership assumed prior to his admittance to the partnership.

C.2.2.5 *Dissolution of a GP*

Dissolution of a GP is caused automatically: by the termination of the agreed term (if any); by the insolvency of the partnership; by the death or insolvency of any partner (at the request of the syndic). Other hypotheses for dissolution include: by the consent of all partners or by advance notice by a partner. Dissolution is also possible by a court ruling in case of faulty conduct of a partner who fails to fulfil a contractual obligation or his conduct prejudices the interests of the partnership.

C.2.3 Commercial Companies of Persons—Limited Partnership (LP)

The limited partnership (LP) consists of two or more persons for the object of carrying on business under a common trade name whereby one or more partners assume unlimited liability and the liability of the rest of the partners is limited to their agreed contribution. Through its trade name the partnership is individualised in the turnover and therefore it must include the abbreviated appendage "LP" and the name of at least one of the partners of unlimited liability.

C.2.3.1 *Formation*

A LP is formed by a partnership deed and registered with the Commercial Register at its residence. The partnership deed must be in writing and signed by the partners as witnessed by a notary public. The contents of a partnership deed must meet a certain minimum of requirements which include: legally individualising characteristics of the partnership and of the partners; the type and the amount of contribution and the rules for distribution of profit and loss respectively, as well as the type of management and representation. Upon registration of the partnership with the Commercial Register the partnership deed and the specimen signatures of the general partners should be attached to the application for registration.

C.2.3.2 *Legal relations among partners*

The partners in a LP may be as follows:

(a) general partners—assuming personal unlimited and joint liability for the obligations of the partnership. Their legal status is the same as that of the partners in a GP;

(b) limited partners—assuming limited liability to the amount of their agreed contribution.

The differences in the legal nature of the two types of partners affect their rights and obligations. General partners have the right to a part of the profits, to indemnity and interest and to a liquidation quota. They have the right to manage and exercise control over the affairs of the partnership. In return for it they are bound to make a contribution and refrain from competitive activities.

The rights and obligations of the limited partners are affected by the special liability assumed by this category of partners. They are obliged to make the agreed contribution in return for which they are granted the right to a share in the profits and access to the partnership books and the annual financial statement.

C.2.3.3 *Representation*

A limited partnership is represented by the general partners. Each general partner may alone represent the partnership in so far as he is not explicitly excluded from the representation or the partners have not set up collective representation. Exclusion from, or restriction of, the representation is inadmissible provided that there is only one general partner in a LP. The power of representation of the general partners includes the commitment of all legal actions, both court and non-court. Where a limited partner concludes deals without a proxy he is liable personally unless the partnership ratifies the deal.

C.2.3.4   *Liability of a LP*

A limited partnership is liable for its obligations to the extent of the partnership's assets, which are distinguished from the property of its partners. In case of insufficient partnership's assets the execution is directed as a rule to the private ownership of the general partners. They are liable personally, unlimitedly, jointly and *ex tunc*. The liability of the limited partners is limited to the amount of the agreed contribution.

C.2.3.5   *Dissolution of a LP*

Dissolution of a LP is caused by rights, by the termination of the agreed term (if any) and by the insolvency of the partnership. Grounds for dissolution may also be the death or insolvency of a general partner.

C.2.4   Capital Commercial Companies—Limited Liability Company (LLC)

A limited liability company (LLC) is a body corporate which is liable on its own for the obligation of the company with all of its assets. A LLC may be formed by one or more persons who are liable up to the amount of their contribution to the capital. Association of new members is allowed subject to a unanimous resolution of the general meeting which characterises the LLC as a closed commercial company. As a type of commercial company LLC may be used in all businesses whereas the formation of LLC in insurance and banking businesses is expressly excluded. LLC is a convenient form for setting up a commercial company with mixed Bulgarian and foreign participation.

C.2.4.1   *Formation of a LLC*

Incorporators of a LLC may be any capable Bulgarian or foreign natural persons or bodies corporate. The law makes no provision for the maximum number of members. Written articles of association are signed and they must include the signatures of the incorporators without any reservations or remarks. The mandatory contents of the articles of association include: specification of the elements individualising the company and the members, the objects for which the company is established, the stock of capital and the interest of each member in the capital stock and the management and representation of the company. The company should be entered in the Commercial Register at the respective district court.

C.2.4.2 *Capital of a LLC*

The value of the capital amounts to the sum total of the contributions of all individual members. The Trade Act provides for a minimum authorised capital of a LLC to the amount of 50,000 lei; there is no fixed maximum amount of capital. When a LLC is incorporated the entire capital must be subscribed whereas at least 70 per cent thereof must be paid in prior to the entry in the Commercial Register.

C.2.4.3 *Equities and shareholders' equity*

The equity is the nominal sum which a member's contribution to the capital amounts to. It is due on incorporation of a LLC or on subsequent association of a member to a LLC.

Shareholder's equity is equivalent to membership perceived as an aggregate of rights and obligations of any member with regard to the LLC. In this respect shareholder's equity is inheritable and transferable.

C.2.4.4 *Management of a LLC*

The management of a LLC is deemed to be a law regulated activity with respect to the formation and expression of the company's will and arrangements for implementation thereof. Management is effected by decision making and engaging in actions for their implementation. An outward expression of such decision making and actions are the acts of the limited liability company. These are statements of definite persons designated as company bodies.

The mandatory and required bodies of each LLC are the general meeting and the manager.

C.2.4.5 *General meeting of members*

The general meeting (GM) of members is a supreme organ of the LLC. It elects the other company bodies which give an account of their activities before the GM. The GM has wide terms of reference with respect to issues related to the existence of the LLC, the contents of the company's articles of associations, the membership and the capital. The GM is called by the manager at least once annually to approve the annual report and balance sheet and to resolve on the distribution of profits and payment of amounts thus distributed. The GM is a discursive and decision-making body and to this effect extraordinary sessions of the general meeting may be held depending on company's needs. All members have the right to participate in the GM and take decisions which are binding both on them and all persons engaged in the LLC.

Resolutions of the GM may be adopted by participants or by proxies. The number of votes of any member is determined by his relative share in the company's capital. In principle, resolutions are adopted by the affirmative vote of more than half of the voting capital except as may be otherwise provided for in the articles of association.

C.2.4.6 *Manager of a LLC*

The manager is a mandatory and legally required body of the LLC. The manager is to be elected on signing the articles of association and takes up his duties immediately. The manager organises and directs the company activities in conformity with the law and the resolutions of the GM. He is an executive organ who runs and manages the company and is responsible for the regular keeping of company books. The company is represented by the manager who may authorise other persons to represent the LLC as well. The manager's functions are terminated on his death, resignation, dismissal, expiration of the agreed term or transformation and liquidation of the company. The manager is liable with his property for damages inflicted on the company and he is also under penalty for crimes committed against the company.

C.2.4.7 *Increase and decrease of capital*

Increase of capital is connected with amendment of the articles of association. Any increase is deemed effective when new contributions are made , and nominal when such increase is made at the expense of the company's own funds. An increase of the capital of a LLC may be caused in two ways:

(a)   by allocation of larger shares;

(b)   by association of new members who subscribe for new shares.

In case of decrease of capital there is a threshold of 50,000 lei which is the minimum capital stock required for the existence of a LLC. The resolution to reduce the capital should explicitly specify the reasons therefore. The reduction of capital may be caused by:

(a)   allocation of smaller shares;

(b)   by repayment of the relevant share to a retiring member;

(c)   by remission of the obligation to pay up the amounts outstanding in respect of shares.

C.2.4.8 *Dissolution of a LLC*

Dissolution of a LLC may be caused either with or without liquidation. In case of dissolution with liquidation the company remains in existence but its active business activities are terminated and the process of liquidation is initiated.

Liquidation procedures include: cashing the assets of the dissolved company, redeeming liabilities and forming liquidation quotas. When all liabilities have been settled and remaining assets distributed the body corporate is deleted.

In case of dissolving a LLC without liquidation there is legal succession, *i.e.* the activities together with the property pass over to other bodies corporate. These are the hypotheses of: merging, acquiring and dividing the LLC, as well as transforming the LLC into another type of company. A LLC may be dissolved by a resolution of the members, by the expiration of the agreed term as specified in the articles of association or by a decree of the District Court which the company has been registered with.

C.2.4.9 *Sole-proprietor limited liability company*

This form of organisation is a variety of LLC where the total stock of capital is paid in and owned by one person. The sole-proprietor limited liability company (SPLLC) is not identified with the capital owner.

The form of a SPLLC is appropriate for traders and natural persons, who may use this form to limit the property with which they are liable for their business activity. The SPLLC is also suitable for formation of daughter companies. This form may also be used by non-profit organisations for the purpose of setting apart the business activities carried on by such organisations.

C.2.5   Capital Commercial Companies—Joint Stock Company (JSC)

A joint stock company (JSC) is a convenient legal form for the accumulation of financial resources and organisation of large-scale business activities. As a type of commercial company a JSC possesses all features common to commercial companies. It is a body corporate that assumes liability up to the value of its property. Both natural persons and bodies corporate can be shareholders in it. They subscribe to shares against which they make contributions in cash and/or in kind in expectation of receiving dividends. Shareholders have the right to a liquidation quota. The most important peculiarity of JSC pertains to the method of dividing the capital—its capital is divided into parts called shares. The membership in a JSC becomes effective upon acquisition of shares and is valid as long as the member is in possession of shares. The liability of the shareholder is limited to the amount of the par value of shares held by him.

C.2.5.1 Incorporation of a JSC

Under Bulgarian law any natural person or body corporate, no matter whether a shareholder or not, may be an incorporator of a JSC. Incorporators are the persons who draw up, sign and announce a public offering for the raising of capital for the company. Incorporation of a JSC can be made with or without a public offering for subscription. The incorporation of a JSC with a public offering includes drawing up a public offering for the purpose of raising the capital for the company, holding a constituent meeting and registration of the JSC. In this case the constituent meeting is to pass a resolution on the incorporation of the JSC and adopt the articles of association.

Hypothetically, whenever the capital of JSC could be raised by persons ready to incorporate JSC, opening of a public offering for subscription is not required. In this case incorporation is made on the spot, *i.e.* the capital is raised at the very constituent meeting and any other resolutions required are taken thereat.

C.2.5.2 Articles of association of a JSC

With respect to its legal nature this is a contract between the incorporators. The articles of association include the organisational structure of a JSC, the amount of its capital, classes of shares, rights and obligations of shareholders, management and power of representation.

C.2.5.3 Capital of a JSC

This is a value which expresses the nominal cash sum of the contributions made by shareholders. The capital of a JSC is always denominated in Bulgarian lei. Whenever a company is formed by a public offering the minimum amount of capital is 5,000,000 lei, while when formation is without a public offering it is 1,000,000 lei. Provided that a JSC carries on banking or insurance activities the minimum amount of capital is specified by a special law. For a full licence, any joint-stock bank should have a minimum amount of 1,200,000,000 lei.

C.2.5.4 Shares

A share is a security which certifies that its holder owns interest in the capital equivalent to the nominal value of the share as printed thereon. Shares may be either registered or bearer. Registered shares are transferable by endorsement. The transfer is recorded in the shareholders register kept at the JCS. Bearer shares are anonymous and are owned by the respective bearer. This is a class of shares that are transferable simply by their handing over, and on the condition that their nominal or issuance value is paid up. Shares may also be ordinary and preference ones. Ordinary shares grant the right to one vote at the GM, to a dividend and a liquidation quota in proportion to the share's face value. Usually preference shares offer additional rights to shareholders, *e.g.* the right to more than one vote.

C.2.5.5 *Legal status of a shareholder*

The share materialises membership in a JSC and for that reason its holder becomes a member of a JSC on its acquisition, *i.e.* a shareholder. The only obligation of a shareholder is to make contributions against the shares subscribed by him. In return for this he is granted a number of property, non-property and management rights like a voting right at the GM, right to a dividend and a liquidation quota. A shareholder is free to substitute registered shares for bearer shares and vice versa. He has the right to a proportionate part of the new shares in case of an increase of the company capital. In principle membership rights and obligations of a shareholder are specified by law for all shareholders alike. The provisions are imperative and no deviations from them to the detriment of shareholder's rights are allowed.

C.2.5.6 *Management of a JSC*

There are two structural forms of management and each JSC is free to choose between them. A JSC may change the existing form and substitute it for the other one.

The general meeting is common to both forms. The difference lies in the number of standing executive bodies, their terms of reference and relationship. In case of one-tier system there is one managing body—the board of directors while in a two-tier system there are two bodies, the managing board and supervisory board.

C.2.5.7 *General meeting of a JSC*

The general meeting is the organ of a JSC where shareholders exercise their rights. This is a meeting called and constituted under the provisions of the law where shareholders with voting rights are legally enabled to participate and where there should be the quorum of the shareholders stipulated in the articles of association.

The terms of reference of the GM are specified first and foremost by law. They include issues relevant to the status of the JSC and to its organisational and legal position. Those are the questions concerning the articles of association, capital, transformation and dissolution of the company and issuance of debentures. The GM also resolve a number of matters of operative nature as placed within its terms of reference, *i.e.* election and recall of the members of the board of directors or the supervisory board, as the case may be, approval of the annual financial statement and appointment of a liquidator.

C.2.5.8 *Managing board*

This body consists of persons appointed by the supervisory board. Its membership may not exceed nine persons and its specific number is determined in the articles of association. The minimum number of members may be two. The members of the managing board may be either natural persons or bodies corporate if provided for in the articles of association. The managing board adopts its own rules of procedure which must be approved by the supervisory board.

C.2.5.9 *Supervisory board*

The member's of the supervisory board are elected and recalled by the GM. The number of its members may vary from three to seven. The supervisory board may have both management powers and representative and supervisory powers over the activities of the managing board.

C.2.5.10 *Board of directors*

This is a standing managing body in the one-tier management system. It consists of three to nine members elected and recalled by the general meeting. The board of directors may delegate the management of the company to one or several of its members—the so-called executive directors.

C.2.5.11 *Increase and decrease of capital of a JSC*

An increase of the capital of a JSC is made when the company funds are not sufficient for the business activities carried on by the company. This is a regular method for an increase of the financial means of the company by using its own sources. The capital may be increased as follows:

(a) by issuance of new shares;

(b) by appreciation of the nominal value of shares already issued;

(c) by partial capitalisation of profits;

(d) by conversion of debentures into shares.

The capital of a JSC may be reduced when its amount exceeds the needs of the JSC for financial resources or the company suffers losses. In the former case there is an effective capital reduction while in the latter, a nominal capital reduction. The methods of capital reduction are as follows:

(a) by depreciation of the nominal value of shares;

(b) by invalidation of shares.

C.2.5.12 *Debentures*

The debenture is a security issued by the JSC where, against a sum paid in, the JSC guarantees payment of the nominal value printed on the debenture and the respective interest within a fixed term. At the same time, the debenture holder is a creditor of the JSC for money receipts. Debenture holders are chirographic creditors. Upon liquidation of a JSC they take precedence over shareholders.

C.2.5.13 *Annual closing of accounts*

The annual closing of accounts finds expression in drawing up of the annual financial statement and its audit by certified public accountants. This audit shows whether the book entries are in conformity with the law. After the audit, the managing board or the board of directors as the case may be draws up a draft resolution on distribution of profits. In case of the two-tier system the supervisory board verifies the annual financial statement and the draft on distribution of profits.

The last stage of the annual closing of accounts is the approval of the annual financial statement and the draft on distribution of profits by the general meeting.

C.2.6 Capital Commercial Companies—Partnership Limited by Shares (PLS)

A partnership limited by shares (PLS) is a form of commercial company where elements of a limited partnership and a joint-stock company are combined. It belongs to the group of capital commercial companies (since the features of JSC are prevailing).

Partners in a PLS are of two types, general partners and limited partners. They may be both natural persons and bodies corporate. According to the stipulations of the Trade Act the limited partners must number at least three.

Only general partners can be incorporators of a PLS. They have the right to select the shareholders, draw up the articles of association and call the constituent meeting. A PLS must apply the one-tier management system. The board of directors comprises the general partners only. The liquidation quota of each partner, no matter whether general or limited, is proportionate to his contribution to the partnership.

C.2.7   Association of Commercial Companies

These are also called economic groups and are characterised by general management of the enterprises which preserve their juridical independence. Both commercial companies and sole traders may participate in such associations. The Bulgarian Trade Act has restricted itself to the regulation of only two types of associations—consortia and holding companies.

C.2.7.1   *Consortium*

This is a contractual association of traders for a definite object. The members of a consortium are associated for temporary conduct of a specific economic operation whereby sharing the risks and the profits respectively. Consortia find application in bank operations and especially in crediting major projects. Consortia may be incorporated in the form of civil or commercial company.

C.2.7.2   *Holding company*

A holding company is a capital commercial company established to participate in the capital or management of other commercial companies. The holding company has no specific organisational form of its own, it may be set up as a type of a capital commercial company. There are two types of holding companies pursuant to their objects, *i.e.* commercial and financial. Commercial holding companies carry on direct business activities and work for a profit. Financial holding companies restrict themselves to managing the companies they incorporate, collecting dividends from such companies and distributing the finances amongst the companies in question.

A holding company may be formed in two ways: first, a capital commercial company may set up its own subsidiary companies; or, secondly, the participants in two or more commercial companies may form a capital commercial company in which they contribute their interest in the capital of the subsidiary commercial companies. In return for this contribution they receive shares in the holding company.

SECTION 3

CO-OPERATIVES

C.3.1 Co-operatives

The co-operative society is a body corporate. The legal regulation of co-operatives is dealt with in a special law, the Co-operative Act of 1991. Under Bulgarian law a co-operative is a voluntary partnership of natural persons with variable capital and variable membership who carry on economic and other activities for securing their interests through mutual aid and co-operation. A co-operative may be formed by at least seven capable natural persons. They call a constituent meeting where the Byelaws are adopted and the co-operative bodies elected.

The co-operative society is characterised by variable capital and variable membership. This is an open-type society, open membership to anyone who accepts the byelaws.

The democratic management of the co-operative affairs is a specific feature of co-operative societies. Irrespective of the amount of his contributions each member has the right to one vote which he exercises in person.

Co-operatives are the only economic form which the state supports and fosters by tax, credit interest, customs and other economic privileges.

C.3.2 Inter Co-operative Enterprise

The inter co-operative enterprise is a body corporate. It is a society of co-operatives for carrying on business or other activities of common interest. This is a closed-type society. Free application for membership in this type of society is not allowed. Decision on formation of an inter co-operative enterprise is within the terms of reference of the general meetings of the member co-operatives.

CZECH REPUBLIC

INTRODUCTION*

D.1.0   The primary source of business company law in the Czech Republic is Act no. 513/1991 Coll., the Commercial Code, as amended.[1] The principal effect of the Commercial Code is described in Section 1 which states, amongst other things, that the Commercial Code regulates the position of entrepreneurs and certain legal entities.

Under the Commercial Code, general commercial partnerships, limited partnerships, limited liability companies, joint stock companies and co-operatives are all legal entities. A legal business entity does not come into existence until it has been registered in the Commercial Register and terminates upon its deletion from the Commercial Register. Individuals who have been authorised to carry on a particular trade in the Czech Republic as well as foreign persons intending to undertake business activities there must also be entered in the Commercial Register.

The Civil Code (Act no. 40/1964 Coll., as amended), which is a governing regulation in relation to the Commercial Code, constitutes another source of business company law. With regard to business relationships, a special amendment of the Commercial Code prevails over the Civil Code.

In addition to civil law regulations, other source of business company law, which are regulations of a public-law nature, are as follows:

—Act no. 63/1991 Coll., on the Protection of Economic Competition, as amended

—Act no. 185/1991 Coll., as amended by Act no. 320/1993 Coll., on Insurance Companies

—Act no. 328/1991 Coll., on Bankruptcy and Composition, as amended

—Act no. 455/1991 Coll., on Trades Licensing, as amended

—Act no. 563/1991 Coll., on Accounting, as amended

—Act no. 21/1991 Coll., on Banking, as amended

—Act no. 214/1992 Coll., on Stock Exchange

—Act no. 248/1992 Coll., on Investment Companies and Investment Funds, as amended

---

* *Petr Pešek, Kocián Šolc Balaštík (full particulars are listed in the Appendix).*
[1] By Act no. 264/1992 Coll., Act no. 591/1992 Coll., on Securities, Act no. 28/1993 Coll. and by Act no. 142/1996 Coll.

—Act no. 42/1994 Coll., on Supplementary Pension Insurance, and

—Act no. 591/1992 Coll., on Securities, as amended

—and other generally binding legal regulations.

D.1.1   Classification of Business Companies

A business company can be defined as a legal entity organised for the purposes of carrying out business activity. Although not expressly stated in the Commercial Code, business companies under Czech law, both in theory and practice, are classified as follows:

—personal business companies

—capital business companies

—co-operatives.

D.1.2   Personal Business Companies—General Information

Personal business companies are those firms in which the personal component prevails over the property capital component. In such a company the partner[2] plays a significant role, while his/her/its capital participation in the company is less significant. The basic features of a personal business company are as follows:

(1)   As a rule, neither the registered capital of the company[3] nor the partner's contribution to the company are obligatory and a personal business company may be organised without investment or registered capital. A partner's investment obligation may arise under a Memorandum of Association concluded by the partners for the purposes of the creation of a business company. Neither the investment details nor the registered capital amount are entered into the Commercial Register.

(2)   Partners are obliged to participate in the company's activity in person and are entitled to act on behalf of the company in all matters. Termination of a partner's participation in a company may result in termination of the company.

(3)   Liability of partners for the company's obligations is unlimited.

---

[2] A business company's partner is (i) a natural person, or (ii) a legal entity which either (a) provided capital contribution into a company (a capital company's partner), or (b) has personal abilities, knowledge or characteristics relevant to a company (a personal company's partner).

[3] A company's registered capital consists of the aggregate of partners' contributions into a company. It represents the internal registered capital and is the source of the company's financing.

(4) Personal business is managed and controlled by its partners. The formal structure of management is not required by law and, as a rule, is generally a matter for agreement between the parties.

(5) A partner's business interest in a company is, by its nature, untransferable. In the event of a partner's withdrawal from the company upon notice (provided that this notice does not result in termination of the company), that partner is entitled to the return of its investments (if any) in the form of settlement interest.

Under Czech law, a personal business company can be either:

—a general partnership, or

—a limited partnership in which one or more partners has limited liability but then remains at least one partner whose liability is unlimited.

D.1.3 Capital Business Companies—General Information

A typical feature of capital business companies is the dominant position of the property capitals aspect over the personal components or, in other words, in this case it is the partner's contribution to the registered capital of a business company which prevails over the personal component.

Characteristic features of capital business companies are as follows:

(1) Partners of a capital business company have a contribution obligation. This contribution and the registered capital of a company are mandatory. The minimum amount of registered capital of each individual type of capital business company is stipulated by law. The law also sets out the procedure for increasing or decreasing the registered capital. The amount of a partner's contribution usually influences the amount of that partner's interest in the company's profits.

(2) The establishment of the company and its legal organisation are subject to the creation of its minimum registered capital.

(3) Partners need not participate in the activity of the company in person; they are obliged to provide and pay up contributions.

(4) As regards individual types of capital business companies, the law provides for an internal structure of executive and supervisory bodies which are constituted upon resolution of the partners (at the general meeting, etc.).

(5) When resolving company matters, the importance of each partner's vote is usually determined by the amount of his/her/its capital contribution.

(6) A partner's ownership interest in a company is transferable. However, for the

113

term of duration of the company, partners can neither unilaterally withdraw from the company nor request a refund of their contributions.

(7) The liability of partners for the company's obligations is limited.

Under Czech law, a capital business company can be either:

—a limited liability company or

—a joint stock company.

SECTION 2

INDIVIDUAL TYPES OF PERSONAL BUSINESS COMPANIES

D.2.1 General Partnership

The Commercial Code defines a general partnership as a company in which at lest two entities (natural or legal) carry on business activity under a common business name and who bear joint and several liability for their obligations on their entire property. The following can be deemed basic features of a general partnership:

(1) A general partnership is a legal entity is comprised of at least two (natural or legal) entities.

(2) A general partnership cannot be organised for any purpose other than entrepreneurial purposes.

(3) The business name of a general partnership must include the designation "veřejná obchodní společnost" (this can be replaced by the abbreviation "veř.obch.spol." or "v.o.s").

(4) The partners bear joint and several unlimited liability for their partnership obligations throughout the term of the partnership. A partner who joins the partnership after its incorporation is liable even for those obligations which arose before he became a partner (subject to a right to compensation from the other partners) but he is not liable for those obligations which arise after he leaves the partnership.

(5) The property of the partnership includes the monetary and non-monetary

114

contributions of the partners. The amount of each individual partner's contribution is specified in partnership agreement.

The general principles which apply to the organisation of a business company also apply to the organisation of a general partnership.

D.2.1.1   *The partnership agreement*

A general commercial partnership is founded on the basis of a partnership agreement which governs the rights and obligations of the partners. Under this agreement, certain provisions of the Commercial Code may be amended to reflect agreement between the partners. Under its special provision relating to a general partnership, the Commercial Code stipulates necessary substantial prerequisites of the partnership agreement:

(a)   the business name and the registered office of the partnership;

(b)   details of the partners by stating a business name and the registered office in the case of a legal entity or the name and domicile in the case of a natural person;

(c)   participation in a general partnership may be excluded for some persons, due to (i) reasons of creditors protection (a natural person or a legal entity may be a partner with unlimited liability in one company only) or (ii) reasons in the public interest (*e.g.* limitation under relevant and binding legal regulations relating to the state administration employees, territorial self-government officers, judges, state counsels and professional soldiers);

(d)   the business objective of the company.

D.2.1.2   *Management and duties of partners*

Each of the partners is entitled to exercise commercial management of the general partnership within a framework of principles agreed on by the partners. Should the partners authorise one or more partners to exercise partial or full commercial management under the partnership agreement, the remaining partners will lose their entitlement to this extent. An authorised partner is obliged to abide by the partners' decision if approved by a majority vote. Unless otherwise stipulated by the partnership agreement, each partner is entitled to one vote. Also, again unless the partnership agreement stipulates otherwise, a partner's authorisation may be recalled if the other partners so agree. Should the authorised partner be in substantial breach of his/her/its duties, the authorisation may be cancelled upon the suggestion of any partner even in the event that such authorisation is irrevocable under the partnership agreement. For the purposes of a judgement and the decision as to whether or not a partner's breach of duties is considered to be substantial, the

115

Commercial Code refers to the provision defining a substantial breach of duties for the purposes of withdrawal from the agreement. This provision indicates that a breach of a partner's duty is substantial if that partner knew, or could have reasonably anticipated, having regard to the purposes of the partnership agreement, that the remaining partners would not be in agreement with the breaching partner's further performance of commercial management of the partnership in the event of such a breach of the agreement. The partner authorised to manage the partnership is obliged, upon request, to inform the other partners of any and all affairs of the company. Each partner may view any of the partnership documents.

D.2.1.3   *Prohibition on competition*

Prohibition on competition is dealt with under section 84 of the Commercial Code which sets out that a partner may not engage in business activity which is in the same field as the company's business objective, even if such activity benefits other persons. This provision can, however, be altered by the partnership agreement.

D.2.1.4   *Rights and obligations of partners*

Each partner has a basic right to receive a portion of profits. The manner of profit distribution depends on agreement between the partners and is stipulated in the partnership agreement. If the partnership agreement has not been amended to reflect any such agreement on the manner of profit distribution, the profits should be distributed among the partners in equal shares by force of law.

A partner's position in the partnership can be described as an interest in a business company. It ensues from the nature of a general partnership that all partners have an equal interest in the company and, as such, must also bear equally any losses. On the basis of the nature of a general partnership interest, the partners have no rights of disposal of their ownership interests but they may, however, leave the partnership provided the partnership agreement is amended accordingly. In the event that the partnership is wound up and liquidated, the partners are entitled to receive a proportionate part of any remaining assets.

D.2.1.5   *Bodies*

A general partnership does not give rise to the establishment of any special internal bodies (as, for example, in the case of a joint stock company when a supervisory board must be formed).

Each of the partners has the right to act as a statutory body on behalf of the company in its dealings with third persons. The partnership agreement usually amends this legal entitlement to authorise a certain partner or partners to act on behalf of the company in its dealings with third persons, in which case only the authorised partner or partners is a statutory body.

D.2.2 Limited Partnership

A limited partnership represents another type of personal business company under Czech law. It is noted for the following features:

(1) It is a legal entity representing the association of at least two natural persons or legal entities. At least one of these persons or entities must have a position similar in all respects to that of a partner in a general partnership, including unlimited liability (such a person is designated as a general partner). Other partners (designated as limited partners) participate in the company with their property contribution and bear limited liability up to the amount of their contribution.

(2) A limited partnership, as in the case of a general partnership, may be organised only for the purposes of carrying out business activity.

(3) The limited partnership's business name must include the designation "komanditní společnost" or the abbreviation thereof, "kom.spol," or "k.s.".

(4) As mentioned above, the liability of individual partners for the partnership's obligations is not equal. A general partner or partners bears unlimited liability for the partnership's obligations with his/her/its entire property and this liability is joint and several. On the other hand, the liability of a limited partner or partners is limited to a specific time as well as to a specific amount, the extent of their liability being an amount equal to the amount of the unpaid portion of their contribution as recorded in the Commercial Register.

D.2.2.1 *The partnership agreement*

The partnership agreement must include:

(a) the business name and the registered office of the partnership,

(b) a description of the partners—the name and domicile in the case of a natural person, the business name and the registered office in the case of a legal entity and the identity of those partners who are general partners and those who are limited partners.

(c) the business objective of the company,

(d) the amount of each limited partner's contribution which contribution can be monetary as well as non-monetary. The minimum amount which a partner must contribute is CZK 20,000 (as in the case of a limited liability company). The actual amount of the contribution may be increased by the partnership agreement.

D.2.2.2 *Management*

Only general partners are entitled to exercise commercial management of the company. Unless the partnership agreement states otherwise, other company matters are resolved by a majority vote of both the general partners and limited partners who each have one vote. Limited partners are entitled to view the accounting books and documents of the company and to receive a counterpart of the annual financial statement.

D.2.2.3 *Rights and obligations of partners*

Having regard to the above mentioned facts, it is clear that the rights and duties of a partner in a limited partnership depend on the status of partner in question, *i.e.* whether they are a general partner or a limited partner. The legal status of both types of partners is different as regards proprietary as well as non-proprietary rights and obligations. The legal status of the general partner shall be regulated by the relevant articles which are valid for the general partnership. Regarding the legal status of the limited partner, the articles of a limited liability company shall apply.

Both types of partners have a basic obligation pay up their contribution. This obligation is imposed on a general partner exclusively by the partnership agreement. The limited partner's obligation to pay up the contribution is a basic and legal obligation and cannot be excluded. The partnership agreement details the amount of the contribution and the date on which it becomes due. The limited partner may not withdraw from the partnership for the duration of this term. But he/she/it can transfer his/her/its partnership to another limited partner or to a third person. Such transfer, however, has to be approved by all partners unless the partnership agreement requires otherwise. However, upon termination of the partnership, the limited partner is entitled to settlement of property and, in the event of liquidation of the partnership, it is entitled to any remaining assets.

Profits are divided in half between the general partners and the limited partners. The general partners each receive an equal share of their half of the profits whereas the limited partners each receive, from their half, a share of the profits in an amount proportionate to the amount of their paid up contributions. These provisions may be amended by the partnership agreement.

D.2.2.4 *Prohibition on competition*

Prohibition on competition as regards limited partnerships applies to general partners only, and applies to the same extent as it does to general partnership partners. The provisions of section 99 of the Commercial Code amending the prohibition of competition in limited partnerships do not apply to limited partners unless the partnership agreement states otherwise.

D.2.2.5 *Statutory body*

Only general partners, being in the position of a statutory body, are entitled to act on behalf of the company. Unless the partnership agreement sets out otherwise, each general partner is entitled to act for the company independently. If a limited partner, without proper authorisation, acts on behalf of the company, he will be liable to third persons to the same extent as a general partner for any obligations arising out of the unauthorised act.

SECTION 3

INDIVIDUAL TYPES OF CAPITAL COMPANIES

D.3.1 Limited Liability Company

A limited liability company is a capital business company. Its basic characteristic features are as follows:

(1) Mandatory creation of a registered capital in a minimum amount of CZK 100,000 made up of the members' contributions. The minimum contribution of one partner permissible by law is CZK 20,000. Contributions by individual members need not be equal but must be divisible by one thousand. At lest 30 per cent of each monetary contribution must be paid up prior to incorporation (100 per cent in the case of a sole founder) and the total of the registered capital must amount to at least CZK 50,000. Non-monetary contributions are permissible provided that the value of such contributions are calculated by an expert(s) whose decision, along with the acceptance of the company, is

recorded in either the memorandum of association or in a written declaration of acceptance.

(2) A limited liability company can be formed by one or more entities (natural or legal) but the members must not exceed 50 in number.

(3) The company can be organised not only for the purposes of carrying on business activities but also for another activity (*i.e.* an administrative company).

(4) The company is liable for a breach of its obligations with its entire property.

(5) Under the law, a member bears liability for the company's obligations up to the amount of the unpaid portion of its contribution as recorded in the Commercial Register. If a member makes a payment on behalf of the company on the grounds of his liability, he will either receive credit equal to the amount of the payment as part of his contribution or he will be reimbursed with this amount by the company or its members by way of compensation.

(7) The business name of a company must include the designation "společnost s ručením omezeným" or the abbreviation "spol. s.r.o." or "s.r.o.".

D.3.1.1 *Memorandum of association/foundation deed*

The basic foundation document is a memorandum of association or a deed of foundation (the latter deed applies in the case of a company organised by a sole founder). The memorandum of association or the foundation deed must contain the following details:

(a) the business name and the registered office of the company;

(b) the identity of the members by stating the commercial name and registered office in the case of a legal entity and the full name and residential address in the case of a natural person;

(c) the business objective of the company;

(d) the amount of the registered capital and the amount of the contribution required from each individual member as well as the method and the time-limit for payment of the contribution;

(e) the names and addresses of the initial executives of the company and details of how they may act in the name of the company;

(f) the names and addresses of the members of the initial supervisory board (if any).

The memorandum of association may also stipulate that the company shall issue the statutes (articles of association) to regulate its internal organisation and to provide more detailed regulations relating to particular matters included in memorandum of association.

The consent of all members is required for any amendment of the memorandum of association, unless the law or the memorandum of association confers this competence on the general meeting.

D.3.1.2 *Rights and obligations of a member*

The rights and obligations of a member are expressed by reference to his/her/its ownership interest in a company. Unless the partnership agreement states otherwise, the size of the ownership interest is determined by the ratio of the amount of contribution made by a particular member to the amount of the registered capital of the company. The ownership interest is transferable (but may not be transferred to the company itself) and can pass to members' heirs and legal successors according to the conditions stipulated in the memorandum of association, statutes or the Commercial Code. Liability for the members' obligations passes to the transferee upon registration of the transfer in both the Commercial Register and the list of members. If the ownership interests are transferred to one single member, the member must either pay up the full monetary contributions within three months or transfer part of the ownership interest to another person. The law allows the ownership interest to be divided and to be held jointly and severally by more than one person. Any rights arising from such ownership interest must be exercised by a common representative of the owners. Each member must pay up his contribution within time-limits set out in the memorandum of association or the statutes but, in any event, within five years of incorporation.

Members may be required, on resolution of the company, to contribute a monetary amount in proportion to the size of their ownership interests of up to one half of the registered capital to create a fund for the purpose of compensating for losses suffered by the company.

D.3.1.3 *Reserve fund*

The company must also create a reserve fund from the net profits of the first year in which profits are made, the amount of which must be equal to at least five per cent of net profits but no greater than 5 per cent of the value of the registered capital. The fund should be annually replenished by an amount equal to at least five per cent of the net profits for each year until the fund reaches a level stipulated in the memorandum of articles or the statutes which level shall equal at least 10 per cent of the registered capital. The purpose of this reserve fund is to cover the company's losses or to take bridging measures to rectify an unfavorable financial situation in the company.

D.3.1.4 *Increase and reduction in registered capital*

Registered capital may be increased by new monetary contribution only after the hitherto approved monetary contributions have been duly paid. However, the registered capital may be increased by non-monetary contributions prior to payment in full of the hitherto approved monetary contributions. Undertaking to make new contribution may be assumed on a priority basis by the existing members of the company in portion to their ownership interest unless the memorandum of association provides otherwise. If the company members do not make use of their priority within time-limit stipulated in the memorandum of association/the statutes or in the Commercial Code, any other person may assume the commitment to make new contributions, provided that the general meeting approves. A decision to reduce the company's registered capital is made by the general meeting approves. A decision to reduce the company's registered capital is made by the general meeting. The amount of the registered capital of the company and amount of each member's contribution cannot be reduced below the amounts stipulated in section D.3.1(1) above.

D.3.1.5 *Bodies—general*

The affairs of a company are managed by the company's bodies which are:

—the general meeting (the highest body)

—one or more executives (the statutory body)

—the supervisory board (not obligatory)

D.3.1.6 *General meeting*

The general meeting, which must be convened at least once a year, comprises all members of the company. If a company has only one single member, a general meeting is not required. Its powers are broad and include, *inter alia*, decisions on amendments to the memorandum of association and the statutes, approval of company accounts matters, decisions on the increase or reduction of the registered capital, appointment of executives and members of the supervisory board, expulsion of members in certain circumstances and decisions on winding up of the company.

Each member has one vote for every CZK 1,000 of contributions (unless the memorandum of association or the statutes stipulate otherwise) and is entitled to vote at the general meeting either in person or through a proxy under a power of attorney provided such proxy is neither an Executive of the company nor a member of the supervisory board. The general meeting constitutes a quorum when members having at least one-half of all votes are present. In most cases, a simple majority vote of members present is sufficient to pass a resolution, unless the memorandum of association states otherwise. If a resolution is passed which is contradictory to the legal provisions, the memorandum of association or the statutes, any member has the right (which must be exercised within three months of the general meeting) to request the court to declare the resolution null and void. Any such decision by the court does not affect rights acquired in good faith by third parties.

D.3.1.7 *Executives/prohibition on competition*

The statutory body of a limited liability company is made up of one or more executives who are appointed by the general meeting, chosen from amongst the partners or other natural persons. The executives shall make arrangements to the proper keeping of prescribed records and accounting, maintain a list of members of company and inform the members about the affairs of the company. Unless the memorandum of association or the statutes state otherwise, each executive is entitled, under the Commercial Code, to act independently on behalf of the company. Executives' rights may be limited by the memorandum of associations, the statutes or by resolution of the general meeting to allow only some of the executives to conclude agreements up to a certain amount and, if the subject of the agreement exceeds this amount, to state that the agreement must be concluded by all executives jointly. This restriction is effective only when it relates to the internal relationship between the executive and the company and is ineffective against third parties. Any decisions on company management made by the executives require a majority vote.

The Commercial Code deals with prohibition on competition imposed on an executive of a company (see section D.5.1. hereto).

D.3.1.8 *Supervisory board*

A supervisory board is only established if required by the memorandum of association. It consists of at least three company members (who cannot also be executives) elected by the general meeting. Supervisory board members have the right to attend the general meeting or, if the executives fail to do so when required by law, to convene the general meeting themselves.

The functions of the supervisory board are:

(a) supervision of the executives' activities;

(b) inspection and verification of documents relating to the company (including commercial documents and accounts);

(c) review of the annual financial statement;

(d) submission of reports to the general meeting.

D.3.1.9 *Termination of membership*

A member of a company may not withdraw his participation in the company by his/her/its own decision. However he may apply to the court of termination if he/she/it cannot reasonably be expected to remain in the company any longer. The company may file a motion with the court asking it to order the expulsion of a company member who has seriously breached of his/her/its duties, despite the fact that he/she/it was requested to fulfil them and was in writing notified of possibility of expulsion. Participation of a member of a company may also be terminated by an agreement of all members in that company. In the event of such termination the member would be entitled to receive a settlement share from the company.

D.3.2   Joint Stock Company

A joint stock company is a capital business company, the registered capital of which is distributed into a certain number of securities called shares. These shares have a certain nominal value and the sum of the nominal values of the shares must always be equal to the registered capital of the company. Other characteristic features are as follows:

(1)   Obligatory creation of registered capital. The minimum amount of registered capital permissible under law is CZK 1 million. The law does not stipulate the minimum nor the maximum allowable amount of the nominal value of one share.

(2)   The company may be formed by one single person (who must be a legal entity) or two or more persons (natural or legal).

(3)   The principal document necessary to establish a joint stock company is a Founders Agreement (in the case of two or more founders) or a Founders Deed (in the case of one founder) to which must be attached draft company statutes. The foundation documents contain details on the company including its name, registered address, its business objective, the proposed amount of registered capital, number, type and nominal value of shares and, if there is to be a call for share subscription, the place, time and manner of such subscription. The practical significance of the foundation documents is restricted to the period up until the date of incorporation of the company after which date the company is governed by the rules set out in the company statutes.

(4)   A joint stock company may be organised for the purposes of carrying out business or other activities.

(5)   The company (not the individual shareholders) is liable for its obligations with its entire property.

(6)   The joint stock company's business name must always include a supplement designating the legal form of the company, either in full, *i.e.* "akciová společnost", or the abbreviation "akc. spol." or "a.s".

D.3.2.1   *Shares and incorporation*

Shares may be made out to name (a registered share) or to bearer and may be one of three types, *i.e.* ordinary, reference or employee shares. Shares may be issued either as certificated shares (shares in physical form) or as uncertificated shares (only book-entered shares). Registered shares are entered into a "list of shareholders" and bearer shares (in case of uncertified shares) into a register in conformity with a special law. Shares can also be issued as publicly tradeable or publicly non-tradeable shares. The rights and obligations of shareholders are based on the nature of the shares held. The shares are basically always transferable although their transferability may be limited by the company statutes. The shares may pass to a shareholders's estate under the laws of inheritance or may be jointly owned by several persons. Certain rights attached to shares, *e.g.* the right to receive a dividend, may be separately transferred.

Once all shares have been effectively subscribed and any share premium and at least 30 per cent of the nominal value of the shares have been paid, a constituent general meeting is held prior to incorporation of the company. Incorporation will take place upon entry of the company into the commercial register. This general meeting approves the company statutes, elects the company bodies and may also make a decision to increase the registered capital. The company statutes contain the information set out in the foundation document as well as other rules relating to the day-to-day running of the company including share details, the manner of paying up shares distribution of profits, etc.

D.3.2.2   *Rights and obligations of shareholders of a joint stock company*

A shareholder is entitled to a proportion of the company profits which the general meeting sets aside for distribution to shareholders (*i.e.* a dividend), taking into account the company's financial results. Unless the company statutes state otherwise, this proportion shall be determined by the ratio between the nominal value of the particular shareholder's share and the nominal value of all shareholders' shares.

Each shareholder is entitled to attend and vote at the general meeting, demand and receive explanations regarding matters relating to the company forming the subject of discussion at the general meeting and to make proposals and counter-proposals. The voting right is attached to a share.

D.3.2.3 *The statutes of joint stock company*

The company statutes of a joint stock company represent, besides the founders deed or founding agreement, one of the most important corporate documents. According to the Commercial Code the company statutes must contain:

(a) the commercial name and registered office of the company;

(b) the business objective of the company;

(c) the amount of the capital stock and the manner of paying up shares;

(d) the number and nominal value of shares, the form of shares, specification as to whether shares are registered in name or made out to bearer and the numbers of registered shares and bearer shares;

(e) the number of votes attached to one share and the manner of voting at the general meeting; and, if the company has issued shares in different nominal values, the number of votes pertaining to a share of a certain nominal value;

(f) the procedure for convening a general meeting, its powers and the rules governing its decision-making;

(g) the number of members of the board of directors, the supervisory board and other bodies, if established, as well as a definition of their powers and the rules governing their decision-making;

(h) the method of creating the reserve fund, the amount up to which it must be replenished and the procedure for its replenishment;

(i) the method to be used for distribution of profits and covering losses;

(j) the consequences of breaching the duty to pay up the subscribed shares on time;

(k) the method for increasing or reducing capital stock, particularly the possibility of reducing capital stock by withdrawing shares from circulation,

(l) the procedure for supplementing and amending the statutes;

(m) any other facts required by law.

D.3.2.4 *Bodies—general*

The bodies of a joint stock company are:

—the general meeting (not applicable in the case of a single founder)

—the board of directors

—the supervisory board (obligatory, unlike in the case of a limited liability company).

D.3.2.5 *General meeting*

The general meeting is held at least once a year within the time-limit stipulated in the statutes, but no later than eight months after the end of the last day of the accounting period (year). Shareholders may participate in the general meeting, which is convened by the board of directors, either in person or through a representative under a power of attorney. The company statutes usually set out the procedure to be adopted when inviting the shareholders to attend.

As in the case of a limited liability company, the powers of the general meeting are broad and include, *inter alia*, decisions on amendments to the company statutes, approval of an increase or decrease in the capital stock, appointment of the board of directors or supervisory board members, approval of financial statements, decisions on winding-up of the company and, (unless the articles of association state otherwise), decisions on the sale of the company. Minutes of the meeting must always be kept. In most cases, the general meeting may pass resolutions on a simple majority vote providing the meeting has a quorum, *i.e.* that shareholders whose shares have a total nominal value exceeding 30 per cent of the capital stock of the company are in attendance. However, certain decisions, such as an amendment to the company statutes, an increase or decrease of the capital stock and decisions on winding-up of the company, require a two-thirds' majority vote. For a resolution by the general meeting on the change of the type or form of shares, a change of rights related to a certain type of shares, restrictions on transferability of registered shares and on cancellation of the public tradeability of shares, the consent of at least three-quarters of attending shareholders holding such shares is required. Certain other resolutions, *e.g.* on the exclusion or restriction of pre-emptive rights to subscribe for new shares under the Commercial Code and to increase the registered capital by non-monetary contributions also require the consent of at least three-quarters of the votes of attending shareholders.

The right to vote may not be exercised if the shareholder is in default of payment on a partially paid-up share. Additionally the shareholder may not exercise his voting right on a general meeting resolution on the evaluation of his non-monetary contribution, on a general meeting resolution on whether to enter into an agreement with him or whether he is to be excused from discharging his duty and in other cases stipulated in Commercial Code.

D.3.2.6 *Board of directors/prohibition on competition*

The statutory body of a joint stock company is the board of directors whose members are elected either by the general meeting of the company or by the supervisory board and whose names are incorporated into the Commercial Register. It must have at least three members including a chairman.

Members of the board of directors are elected for a period which is set out in the company statutes which must not be longer than five years. The board of directors manages the activities of the company, ensures the proper keeping of

127

company accounts and, unless the company statutes stipulate otherwise, each member of the board of directors may act on behalf of the company in its dealings with third persons. In practice, powers granted to the board of directors are usually defined in the company statutes requiring that each legal act is carried out by at least two board members. The general meeting or supervisory board may, as in the case of a limited liability company, also restrict the right of the board of directors or its individual members to act on behalf of the company in its relations with third persons. This restriction, however, applies only to internal relations between members of the board of directors and the company and has no bearing on transactions concluded with bona fide third parties.

Board members must act with due diligence and respect the company's confidentiality and are jointly and severally liable for damage caused to the company following a breach of the law. However, if the damage occurred as a result of a decision made by the general meeting and, provided the damage caused did not result from an illegal act, members cannot be held liable if at least one member of the board made an objection to the decision at the general meeting and such objection was recorded in the minutes of the meeting.

Prohibition on competition for members of the board of directors is covered under the relevant provisions of the Commercial Code (see section D.5.1. hereto).

D.3.2.7 *Supervisory board*

The supervisory board consists of at least three members (natural persons), two-thirds of whom are elected by the general meeting and one-third by the employees of the company provided that there are more than 50 employees for whom such employment is their main job at the time of the election. A member cannot sit on the board for a period exceeding five years and must not be a member of the board of directors, a procurator of the company or a person designated in the Commercial Register as being entrusted to act in the name of the company. The supervisory board oversees the activities of the board of directors, reviews the annual financial statement, inspects documents and records relating to the company's activities and ensures that those activities are legal and are in accordance with the company statutes and the instructions of the general meeting.

The supervisory board has the power to convene a general meeting if it is in the interests of the company to do so. In the event that there is a difference of opinion between any member of the supervisory board who was elected from among employees and the other members then this fact must be reported to the general meeting.

In order for the supervisory board to pass a resolution, a majority vote is required. Minutes of the meeting must be kept.

D.3.2.8 *Increase or decrease of share capital stock*[4]

Any increase in the capital stock shall be decided upon by the general meeting. The capital stock may be increased by a subscription for new shares only if all previously subscribed shares have been paid for. This restriction does not apply if the capital stock is to be increased by a subscription for shares and their issue price is to be paid only by non-monetary contributions.

Each shareholder has a pre-emptive right to subscribe for a part of the company's new shares if these new shares are intended to increase the capital stock by way of also increasing the shareholder's portion of the existing capital stock and provided that such shares are to be subscribed by monetary contributions. Shareholders' pre-emptive rights may not be restricted or eliminated by the company statutes; a resolution of the general meeting to increase the capital stock may restrict or eliminate pre-emptive rights only if there is a serious reason to do so on the part of the company. If pre-emptive rights are to be restricted or eliminated, these changes must be applied in equal manner to the shares of all holders of the same class of shares.

After approving an annual or extraordinary financial statement and allotting the relevant amount to the reserve fund, the general meeting may decide to use all or part of the profits, or other company resources shown in the financial statement as being liabilities of the company, to increase the capital stock.

A decision to reduce the capital stock is made by the general meeting. The amount of the capital stock of the company cannot be reduced below the minimum amount stipulated in section D.3.2.(1) above.

D.3.2.9 *Reserve fund*

A company can create a reserve fund at a time, in an amount determined by the company statutes and the Commercial Code. The reserve fund is created from profits shown in the financial statement for the year in which it first makes a profit. The company must transfer at least 20 per cent of the profits to the fund but no more than 10 per cent of the value of the capital stock. The fund is replenished by an amount determined in the company statutes (but not by an amount less than five per cent of the profits), until the level of the amount of reserve fund as stipulated in the company statutes is reached (such amount being equal to 20 per cent of the capital stock). The reserve fund, created in this way, may be used by the company only to settle its losses. Unless the statutes or Commercial Code provide otherwise, it is the board of directors which makes decisions on how the reserve fund is spent.

---

[4] The provisions of the Commercial Code which deal with an increase or decrease of share capital stock are complex and extensive. For the purposes of this book we have provided only general information on the subject.

SECTION 4

CO-OPERATIVES

D.4.0 A co-operative is a legal entity associating an unlimited number of persons founded either for the purpose of undertaking business activity or to satisfy the economic, social or other needs of its members. The following can be deemed basic features of a co-operative:

(1) A co-operative must have at least five members unless two or more members are legal entities.

(2) A co-operative is liable for a breach of its obligations with its entire property.

(3) The business name of a co-operative must include the designation "družstvo".

(4) Members are not individually liable for the obligations of the co-operative unless stipulated in the statues of the co-operative.

(5) The registered capital (known as the recorded basic capital) of a co-operative must amount to at least CZK 50,000 and consists of the total sum of membership contributions which the members have undertaken to pay. Membership is conditional upon payment of or part payment of a basic membership contribution determined by the company statutes.

(6) The co-operative must create an indivisible fund (which may not be distributed among members during the existence of the co-operative) in an amount of no less than 10 per cent of the recorded basic registered capital with this amount eventually increasing to one-half of the recorded basic registered capital achieved by adding a portion of the co-operative's profits each year.

(7) Unless the company statutes state otherwise, a member may transfer his/her/its membership rights and obligations on approval from the management board (this approval not being required in the case of a housing co-operative).

D.4.1 Foundation of the Co-operative

A constituent general meeting comprising those persons who have made application to join the co-operative is required for the founding of a co-operative. This constituent general meeting passes resolutions on a simple majority vote to determine the amount of the recorded basic capital, approve the statutes of the co-operative and to elect a managing board and an auditing commission. However, the co-operative will still not legally come into being until such time as it has been registered in the Commercial Register for which it is a condition precedent that at least one-half of the proposed basic capital has been paid.

The statutes of the co-operative must detail, amongst other things, the business name and registered office address of the co-operative, scope of business activity, rights and obligations of the co-operative and its members, amount of basic membership contribution, details of the co-operative's bodies, distribution of profit arrangements, particulars of the indivisible fund and may also stipulate that membership of the co-operative is conditional upon employment by the co-operative.

D.4.2   Termination of Membership

Membership expires on the death of an individual (although an heir to a members' rights and obligations is entitled to apply for membership in the co-operative), by written agreement, expulsion or if the co-operative ceases to exist due to its deletion from the Commercial Register. A member is entitled to receive a settlement share upon expiry of the membership.

D.4.3   Bodies—General

The bodies of a co-operative are:

—the members' meeting (*i.e.* the general meeting)

—the managing board (the statutory body)

—the auditing commission

—other bodies established under the statutes of the co-operative.

D.4.4   Members' Meeting

The members' meeting must be convened at least once a year and its powers include decisions on amendments to the statutes of the co-operative, election of members of the managing board and the auditing commission, approval of the annual financial statement, decisions on the distribution and use of profits, decisions on an increase or decrease in the recorded basic capital and decisions on a merger or winding-up of the co-operative. If the size of the co-operative is such that it is not practical for all members to be present at the meeting, an assembly of delegates may replace the members' meeting. Each member usually has one vote and

131

resolutions are made following a majority vote of members present (provided more than half of the co-operative's members are in attendance at the meeting). Minutes of the members' meeting must be kept.

D.4.5   Managing Board

The managing board manages the activities of the co-operative and implements decisions of the members' meeting. It is accountable to the members' meeting. Unless the statutes of the co-operative provide otherwise, the managing board elects a chairman and/or vice-chairman from among its members who not only chairs the board but, if the statutes so provide, will organise and manage the co-operative's daily activities.

D.4.6   Auditing Commission

The auditing commission audits the activities of the co-operative, comments on the annual financial report and deals with members' complaints. It is accountable to the members' meeting, meets at least once every three months and must have a minimum of three members. It has the authority to demand from the managing board any information relating to the management of the co-operative and receives reports from the managing board concerning all matters which may seriously affect the management of the co-operative.

D.4.7   Other Bodies

If a co-operative has less than 50 members, the statutes of the co-operative may stipulate that the powers of the managing board and the auditing commission may be exercised by the members' meeting. The chairman of such a co-operative would become the statutory body. However, if the members consist of solely legal entities, the method of decision-making and the statutory body are determined by the statutes of the co-operative.

SECTION 5

JOINT PROVISIONS ON BUSINESS COMPANIES

D.5.1   Prohibition on Competition

Persons may be identified in individual legal regulations or in the memorandum of association or the statutes of a business company as being prohibited from performing certain acts which represent unfair competition in relation to the business company and its business activities. These provisions on prohibition exist to deal with cases in which persons could use or abuse their knowledge, experience and information obtained from the company, for their own benefit or for the benefit of other persons, and who, by performing such acts, could impair the company in some way.

The extent of the legal provisions on prohibition on competition are valid only for the group of persons to which they apply and are amended to relate to each form of business company individually.

The general legal provisions relating to business companies provide for the company's rights arising from a breach of this prohibition on competition. The company is entitled to require that the person breaching the prohibition either give up the benefit of the business transaction which resulted from the breach of the prohibition, or transfer its rights thereto to the company. These rights must be enforced against the relevant sub-supplier within three months of the date on which the company learned about the breach of the prohibition but, in any event, within one year from the origin of rights relating to the breach of the prohibition of competition.

Prohibition on competition in a limited liability company relates to both the executives of the company and to the members of the supervisory board. The law stipulates that executives and members of the supervisory board may not:

(a)   conclude, in their own name and on their own account, commercial transactions which are connected with the business activity of the company;

(b)   act as broker for other parties in business transactions of the company;

(c)   be involved as a partner with unlimited liability in another business entity;

(d)   act as a statutory body or be a member of the statutory or other body of another legal entity whose business objective is similar to that of the

133

company, unless the company in whose name the executive acts has an ownership interest in such other legal entity.

The memorandum of association or the statutes may only extend, and cannot limit, the scope of the prohibition on competition of the executives or the members of the supervisory board. The prohibition on competition may also be extended to the company's members.

Prohibition on competition in the case of a joint stock company is based on principles similar to those concerning a limited liability company. The first three prohibitions listed above as valid for a limited liability company also apply to a joint stock company. The fourth prohibition states that neither a member of the board of directors nor a member of the supervisory board may act as a statutory body or be a member of the statutory or other body of another legal entity whose business objective is similar to that of the company, unless the company is a controlling person of the legal entity.[5]

The Commercial Code also sets out provisions on prohibition on competition as regards a cooperative prohibiting members of the managing board and the auditing commission from simultaneously being engaged in outside business activity or from being a member of a statutory body or supervisory body of another legal entity which has a business objective similar to that of the co-operative. However, the scope of this prohibition may be amended by the statutes of the co-operative.

---

[5] A controlling person is defined in the Commercial Code. It relates to the existence of a group of several legal entities, being either joint stock companies or limited liability companies, which are in association or mutual proprietary connection and the majority of the shares or the decisive ownership interest of one of these companies are included in the property of one of the other companies. Basically, a controlling person is a legal entity which is entitled to exercise a majority vote in another company due to the fact that it has a sufficient interest or sufficient shares in that business company to allow it a majority vote, or due to the fact that it acquired such a position by means of an agreement with another legal entity, regardless of the validity or invalidity of such an agreement.

A share in voting rights is further increased by the voting rights:

(a) attached to other persons' interests in the controlled persons or attached to shares in the controlled person held by other persons provided such other persons are controlled directly or indirectly by the controlling person.

(b) which are exercised by other persons in their own name but on behalf of the controlling person.

A share in voting rights is reduced by the voting rights attached to interests in a controlled person or attached to shares in such a controlled person, if;

(a) the controlling person exercises them on behalf of a person who is not a person which it directly or indirectly controls, or if it exercises them on behalf of a person controlling this person,

(b) the interest or shares are transferred to a controlling person in the form of a security or on the basis of a securities loan and the controlling person is obliged to abide by received instructions when exercising voting rights,

(c) the controlling person is a securities dealer owning shares of the controlled person simply for the purpose of their sale and does not exercise the voting rights attached to the shares.

The controlled person is a legal entity, *i.e.* it is a partner of an association or a proprietary connected group and the majority of its shares or decisive ownership interest are included in the property of another entity. Accordingly, the controlled person is a company in which the controlling person owns a majority interest in voting rights due to the fact that it has an interest in a company or shares of a company to which a majority of voting rights is attached.

D.5.2   Commercial Register

As mentioned above, all business companies have to be registered in the Commercial Register. The Commercial Register is a public list in which entries are made of legally required data pertaining to business persons and, where applicable, also data pertaining to other persons in accordance with a special law.

The facts entered in the Commercial Register take effect in relation to any party, as of the day, as of the date on which the entry is made. A person to whom an entry in the Commercial Register relates cannot raise an objection to a third party who has acted in reliance of the entry in the Commercial Register that the entry is incorrect. The Commercial Register is kept by a court which is designated to do so by a special law.

The Commercial Register is accessible to everyone and persons may look at any Commercial Register and make copies of its entries and extracts. On request, the registration court will make an official copy of an entry or of a document which is kept in the registry of documents, provide an extract or confirm a particular entry or, alternatively, confirm that a particular entry is not made in the Commercial Register.

The Commercial Register includes a registry of documents which contains the following:

(a)   the memorandum of association (or partnership agreement, founder's deed or founding agreement), the notarial record of any resolution of the constituent general meeting of a joint stock company or of the constituent members' meeting of a particular co-operative, the founders' decision substituting a resolution of the constituent general meeting of a joint stock company, statutes of a joint stock company or a limited liability company, statutes of a co-operative (if, according to the relevant memorandum of association or founding agreement, statutes are to be issued and documents recording subsequent amendments; in the case of such subsequent amendments, the wording of the founding document must be kept in the registry in its entirety;

(b)   decisions on the election or appointment, or on the removal from office or other termination of office, of persons (natural) forming or being the statutory body or being a member of a legal entity's body authorised to represent such entity before a court;

(c)   financial statements and auditor's reports in the event that the law requires verification of such statements by an auditor;

(d)   decisions on the winding-up of a legal entity;

(e)   proposals for a merger, consolidation, division or transformation accompanied by reports and expert opinions;

(f)   expert opinions on the valuation of a non-monetary investment contribution made on the foundation of a limited liability company or joint stock company or on an increase in its registered capital;

(g) judicial decisions issued under the Bankruptcy and Composition Act provided such decisions apply to persons entered in the Commercial Register.

D.5.2.1 *Data registered in the Commercial Register*

1. The following data shall be entered in the Commercial Register:

   (a) the commercial name; in the case of legal entities, their registered office, and in the case of natural persons (individuals), their residence and place of business, if the latter differs from the former;

   (b) the identification number of the business;

   (c) the business objective of the company;

   (d) the legal form of the legal entity;

   (e) the name and residential address of individuals forming the statutory body or being its members and details of the manner in which such individuals will act in the name of the legal entity;

   (f) the designation, location and object of business activity of a branch of an enterprise or of another organisational component of the enterprise, the name of its manager and his/her residential address;

   (g) the name and residential address of the procurator;

   (h) any other facts required by law.

2. The following additional data shall also be entered into the Commercial Register:

   (a) in the case of a general commercial partnership (*i.e.* an unlimited partnership), the names and addresses of the partners and the business name or designation and registered office of a legal entity if such legal entity is a partner in the general commercial partnership;

   (b) in the case of a limited partnership the names and residential addresses of the individuals who are partners, as well as the business name or designation and registered office of a legal entity if such legal entity is a partner in the limited partnership, the identity of general partners and limited partners, the amount of each limited partner's investment contribution and the extent to which it has been paid up;

   (c) in the case of a limited liability company, the names and addresses of the individuals who are members of the company as well as the business name or designation and registered office of any legal entity which is a member of the limited liability company, the amount of the registered capital, the individual amount of each member's investment contribution, and the extent to which each member's contribution has been paid up, as well as the names and residential addresses of the members of the supervisory board, if established;

(d) in the case of a joint stock company, the amount of its registered capital (capital stock) and the extent to which it has been paid up, the number, class and type of shares and their nominal value, any restrictions applying to transferability of shares and the name and residential address of each member of the supervisory board; should the joint stock company have a single shareholder, such shareholder's commercial name or designation and registered office or full name[6] and residential address must also be recorded;

(e) in the case of a co-operative, the amount of its registered capital and the amount of the basic membership contributions.

In the case of foreign persons, the entry in the Commercial Register shall include the data listed in subsection (1)(a), (c) and (d) above, the location of the branch or other organisational component owned by the foreign person in the Czech Republic, and the name and residential address (or if appropriate, the temporary place of stay) of its manager.

The following events shall also be recorded in the Commercial Register where appropriate; commencement of liquidation proceedings together with the name and address of the liquidator(s), adjudication of a bankruptcy order together with the name and address of the bankruptcy trustee, rejection of a bankruptcy petition due to a lack of assets, commencement of composition proceedings, and the legal grounds on which a business person was deleted from the Commercial Register.

Any amendment or extinguishment of facts entered in the Commercial Register must be recorded without undue delay.

D.5.2.2 *Application for an entry to be made in the Commercial Register*

An application for an entry to be made in the Commercial Register is to be filed either by the person whom the entry concerns, by persons who have been authorised in writing to do so by that person or by persons authorised to do so pursuant to the law. An application for an entry to be made in the Commercial Register must be accompanied by documents verifying the facts which are to be registered.

The signatures of persons applying for an entry in the Commercial Register and those contained in a power of attorney, must be officially authenticated.

---

[6] This is inconsistent with the provisions on joint stock companies.

D.5.3   Founding a Company

A company is founded on the basis of a memorandum of association founding agreement or partnership agreement) which must be signed by each founder, unless the provisions of the Commercial Code stipulate otherwise. The authenticity of founders' signatures must be officially certified. The founder may also authorise another person to sign the memorandum of association[7] on his/her/its behalf. A power of attorney accompanied by the officially authenticated signature of the founder, must accompany the memorandum of association partnership agreement, founding agreement).

In those cases where the Commercial Code permits the founding of a company by a single person, the memorandum of association is replaced by a founders deed in the form of a notarial record[8], unless the law provides otherwise. The founders deed must include the same essential data as the memorandum of association.

D.5.4   Incorporation of a Company

A company is incorporated (*i.e.* officially comes into being) on the day on which it is entered in the Commercial Register. An application for entry in the Commercial Register must be submitted within 90 days of the company's founding or within 90 days of the date on which a trade or similar business authorisation was delivered.

Unless it is explicitly stated that a company is founded for a specific period of time, it is assumed that the company has been founded for an indefinite period.

Unless the special law stipulates otherwise, an applicant for registration in the Commercial Register is required to prove, on the day the entry is to be made, that he/she/it has an effective trade licence or other authorisation required under the Trades Licensing Act (or by other acts), to engage in the activity which is to be entered in the Commercial Register as being the object of his/her/its business activity.

D.5.5   Winding-up and Dissolution of a Company

A company is dissolved on the day it is deleted from the Commercial Register.

The dissolution of a company is preceded by its winding-up, either with or

---

[7] The Czech name "Společenská smlouva" is translated into English as memorandum of association, while in the United States the relevant term is articles of incorporation; in the case of partnerships, the term partnership agreement is used, whereas "zakladatelská smlouva" in respect of joint stock companies is translated as founding agreement. References to a memorandum of association in this Chapter are also to be understood as referring to a founding agreement and a partnership agreement.

[8] A notarial record, in Czech notářský zápis, is also translated as a notarial protocol.

without liquidation; the latter applies if the company's business assets are transferred to its legal successor. Liquidation is not required if a bankruptcy petition is rejected because of a lack of assets or if there are no assets remaining following bankruptcy proceedings.

A company shall be wound up:

(a) on expiration of the period of time for which it was founded;

(b) on attainment of the purpose for which it was founded;

(c) on a date specified in a resolution of the participants or by an appropriate company body, as being the date on which the company will be wound up; otherwise, on the date when such a resolution was adopted;

(d) on the date stated in a judicial decision as being the day of the company's winding-up; otherwise, on the date when such judicial decision comes into legal effect;

(e) by a resolution of the company's participants or the competent company body, on the merger, consolidation or division of the company or by its transformation into another type of business company or a co-operative; or

(f) (i) on cancellation of a bankruptcy order following fulfilment of the distribution schedule or where the bankrupt's assets are insufficient to cover the costs of bankruptcy proceedings or
(ii) on rejection of a bankruptcy petition due to a lack of assets.

On the basis of an application by a state authority or by a person who has been able to prove a legal interest in the matter, the court may rule on the winding-up of a company and its liquidation in the following instances;

(a) if a general meeting has not been held for two years or if an appointment to a company body has not taken place for two years (and at the same time the term of office of a company body expired more than two years previously) or if the company has not been engaged in any activity for more than two years;

(b) if the company is no longer authorised to undertake business activity;

(c) if the legal prerequisites for incorporation of the company no longer apply or if the company's merger or consolidation is in violation of the law;

(d) if the company is in breach of its duty to create a reserve fund;

(e) if the company's business is not being conducted by authorised persons;

(f) if the company has failed to fulfil its duty as prescribed by the Ministry for Economic Competition in accordance to Act no. 63/1991 Coll., on the Protection of Economic Competition (also known as the Antitrust Act).

Prior to reaching a decision on the winding-up of a company, the court may set a time-limit during which the company may eliminate the grounds for which the winding-up of the company was proposed.

D.5.6   Winding-up a Company without Liquidation

In the case of voluntary winding-up of a company, if the company simultaneously decides to transform into another type of company or into a co-operative or that it will merge or consolidate with another company or that it shall be divided up, this shall not affect any restrictions stipulated by special laws.

In the event of a company's transformation, the hitherto existing company shall be wound up without liquidation provided that, on the day an application is filed for deletion of the existing company, all prerequisites for incorporation of the successor company or co-operative are met. The wound-up company's business assets pass to its successor company or co-operative.

In the event of consolidation, the business assets of the wound-up companies again pass to the successor company; in the case of a merger, the business assets of the wound-up company pass to the company with which the wound-up company is merged.

In the case of division of a wound-up company the business assets pass to the newly established successor companies of the divided company. Each new company, formed in this way, is liable for obligations assigned to them from the wound-up company up to the amount of the net business assets received from the wound-up company.

D.5.7   Transformation, Merger, Consolidation and Division

Only companies having an identical legal form may be merged or consolidated. Companies established on division of a wound-up company must have the same legal form as the wound-up company.

Merger, consolidation, division or transformation of a company must be decided upon by the company's general meeting or, should there be no general meeting, by all the members.

A project plan concerning a merger, consolidation, division or transformation must be prepared by the statutory bodies of the participating companies before a decision can be made.

SECTION 6

COSTS OF INCORPORATION

D.6.1 The amount of fees currently payable to the Commercial Registry for registration of a business company is governed by the provisions of Act No. 549/1991 Coll., as amended, which sets out that the registration fee payable shall be an amount equal to 0.5 per cent of the registered capital of the company. However, there is a minimum fee payable of CZK 3,000 and a maximum fee payable of CZK 20,000. It should also be noted that signatures on all documents which are included in the application for registration must be notarised, the cost of which is CZK 30 per signature.

Following registration, a fee of CZK 500 is charged for each individual application to amend or supplement the company's entry into the Commercial Register except that this does not apply in the case of an application to record a change in the registered capital in which case the fee is an amount equal to 0.5 per cent of the new recorded registered capital. The registration fee payable for an application to cancel the company's entry in the Commercial Register is CZK 1,000.[9]

[9] Fees correspond with those in 1997.

DENMARK

DENMARK

CLASSIFICATION OF BUSINESS ORGANISATIONS: INTRODUCTION*

E.1.1   Introduction

The business organisations most commonly used in Denmark are:

—stock corporations;

—private limited companies;

—partnerships;

—sole proprietorships.

Furthermore, business organisations like limited partnerships, partnership companies, co-operative societies, and corporate funds are used in Denmark, but not so commonly as the above mentioned organisations.

Foreign enterprises generally prefer to do business in the form of a limited liability company, and only a few operate through a local branch or a partnership.

Danish company law provides for two forms of limited liability companies. One form is the Aktieselskab, in short A/S (hereinafter called "stock corporation"), and the other the Anpartsselskab, in short ApS (hereinafter called "private limited company"), a form of limited company corresponding to the English private limited company, to the German GmbH, and to the French SARL.

All stock corporations, private limited companies, and branch offices of foreign corporations are to be registered with the Danish Commerce and Companies Agency and the registrations are published in the *Danish Official Gazette*.

The law concerning limited liability companies is set out in Section 2. In the remainder of this section, an introduction is given concerning other entities.

---

* *Henrik Petyz, Kromann & Münter (full particulars are listed in the Appendix).*

E.1.2   Sole Proprietorship (Enkeltmandsfirma)

The sole proprietorship is owned by private individuals. There is no distinction between the business capital and the private capital of the sole proprietor.

E.1.3   Partnerships (Interessentskaber)

There is no general legislation in Denmark governing partnerships apart from the Act on Commercial Undertakings (Act No. 123/1994) which sets out certain common rules above names and representation. The rules on partnerships are normally contained in rather detailed partnership agreements. Partnerships are subject to the rule that general partners are jointly and severally liable for the obligations of the partnership, and that income tax is imposed on the general or limited partners as individuals and not on the partnership as such, the exemption being the Amba. The distinguishing characteristics of the various forms of partnerships are as follows:

E.1.3.1   *Partnership (Interessentskab: I/S)*

The lack of legislation makes it possible to arrange the partnership and to give it a structure in accordance with the individual aims that the partners seek to achieve. Often partnerships are established with a structure corresponding to that of stock corporations or private limited companies. The partners may be individual persons and/or companies. The foundation of the partnership takes place on the signing of the partnership agreement or by agreement between the parties. In general the partnership agreement provides that each partner has power to carry on the day-to-day business whereas extraordinary arrangements require the unanimous consent of the partners. The parts of the partnership are not transferable without the consent of the other partners. If the partnership agreement does not provide otherwise, each partner can terminate the partnership on giving reasonable notice (*e.g.* three to six months). Annual accounts of the above partnership are not open for public inspection.

E.1.3.2   *Limited partnership (Kommanditselskab: K/S)*

A limited partnership must consist of one or more general partners and one or more limited partners. Any of the general or limited partners may be natural or legal persons. The firm name must indicate that the firm is a limited partnership by the initials K/S. The names of the partners need not appear in the firm name. As for organisation, limited partnerships follow the guidelines of partner-ships.

E.1.3.3 *Partnership company (Kommanditaktieselskab)*

A partnership company is a business enterprise in which a stock corporation is a limited partner for the whole of its capital or in which the limited partners have contributed a fixed sum which is divided into shares. In general, a partnership company is subject to the same regulations as a stock corporation, and the annual accounts are open for public inspection.

E.1.4 Association with Limited Liability (Andelsselskab med begrænset ansvar: Amba)

This type of enterprise is found more frequently in Scandinavia than elsewhere. The profit of this type of firm is normally distributed on the basis of the capital invested or on the turnover or volume of each member's transactions.

This entity is subject to the provisions in the Act on Commercial Undertakings concerning, *inter alia*, name, registration, competence, publication and annual accounts. It differs from the partnership in that the liability of the members is limited and further it is subject to taxation as an entity.

A person's name may not be used in the firm name, and the initials "Amba" must be used to indicate that it is an association with limited liability.

This form of entity is normally used by co-operative societies who wish to limit their members' liability and other entities with at least two limited partners. Normally the organisation in an association with limited liability is established in the same manner as for limited liability companies, *i.e.* with a general meeting, a board of directors and a management. Associations with limited liability must be registered with the Commerce and Companies Agency. The annual accounts are open for public inspection.

E.1.5 Branch Office (Filial)

E.1.5.1 *Introduction*

If a foreign company does not want to establish a subsidiary company in Denmark either as an A/S or as an ApS, it is possible to carry on business activities in Denmark through a registered branch office. For foreign stock corporations, private limited companies, partnership companies and similar entities, it is a condition that the foreign company is lawfully existing in its home country and that the establishment in Denmark of the branch office is allowed by international agreements or by the Danish Ministry of Industry. Companies with a registered office within one of the other E.U./EEA Member States are free to establish a branch in Denmark without a permission from the Danish Ministry of Industry. The Danish Companies Act, the Private Companies Act and the Commercial Undertakings Act govern the branch office.

Sections E.1.5.2–E.1.5.4 set out the regulation in the two acts which apply to branches of foreign stock corporations, private limited companies, partnership companies and similar entities. For other foreign limited companies other rules apply under the Commercial Undertakings Act.

E.1.5.2 *Formation procedure*

The application for registration with the Commerce and Companies Agency must be signed by the branch manager and accompanied by:

(a) official evidence that the company abroad is lawfully existing in its home country;

(b) a copy of the memorandum of association and the articles of association of the company;

(c) a power of attorney from the company to the branch manager, and

(d) proof that the branch manager fulfils the requirements described below.

The name of the branch office must show its nationality and its status as a foreign limited liability company. The branch office cannot initiate its activities in Denmark until it has applied for registration with the Commerce and Companies Agency. If registration is denied, the branch office must discontinue its activities. Danish company law does not require any minimum capital as the company operating through the branch is liable for the debts of the branch.

E.1.5.3 *Organisation and management*

The branch must be managed by one or more branch managers who can sign for the branch and grant powers of attorney. Branch managers must be of age and enjoying personal rights and domiciled in Denmark or in another country within the European Union/EEA. The branch manager is personally liable for the fulfilment by the branch office of a number of public obligations such as the payment of taxes withheld and filing tax returns, VAT reports, etc.

E.1.5.4 *Dissolution*

The branch office shall be struck off the Commerce and Companies Agency in the following circumstances:

(a) if the company files a notice to the effect that it wants the branch to be struck off the Agency;

(b) at the request of a creditor who provides documentation to the effect that it has not been possible for him out of the company's funds in Denmark to obtain settlement in full of his claim arising out of the company's operations in Denmark;

(c) if there is no branch manager, and this defect is not remedied within a period specified by the Commerce and Companies Agency;

(d) if the branch manager has not submitted annual accounts of the parent company and group accounts, if any, in accordance with the Company Accounts Act, and the defect has not been remedied within a period specified by the Commerce and Companies Agency.

SECTION 2

LIMITED LIABILITY COMPANIES

E.2.1 Introduction

The Danish Companies Act No. 370 of June 13, 1973, as amended (most recently by Act No. 545 of June 20, 1996), governs the stock corporations. The act conforms to present E.U. rules governing stock corporations.

The Private Companies Act No. 545 of June 20, 1996 governs the private limited companies.

E.2.2 Stock Corporation (Aktieselskab: A/S)

The stock corporation is a legal entity different from the holder or holders of the shares. The responsibility of the shareholders is limited to the capital contribution.

The stock corporations can under certain conditions be listed on the Stock Exchange.

The supreme authority of a stock corporation is with the shareholders acting in general meeting. Next, stock corporations shall have a two-tier management system which includes a supervisory board of directors and a management organ.

E.2.3   Private Limited Company (Anpartsselskab: ApS)

A private limited company is in many respects similar to a stock corporation but is normally a rather small company. In view of the far reaching regulations contemplated by the European Union in respect of company legislation the Danish government thought it advisable to enable small companies and companies with a small number of members to choose a less complex structure than that of stock corporations.

The Private Companies Act provides greater freedom to the shareholders as to how to organise the company.

The supreme authority of a private limited Company is with the shareholders, but the use of general meetings is not mandatory. A one-tier or two-tier management system can be used and a private limited company may therefore have either a board of directors or a general management organ or both.

The liability of the members of a private limited company is the same as for stock corporations, *i.e.* liability is limited to the capital contribution.

E.2.4   Incorporation

E.2.4.1   *Articles of association/formation procedure*

A stock corporation or a private limited company is formed by promoters acting in accordance with the procedures of the Companies Act and the Private Companies Act respectively.

The promoters of a stock corporation must draw up and sign a memorandum of association which must contain:

(a)   draft articles of association;

(b)   the names, occupations and addresses of the promoters;

(c)   the price of issue of the shares,

(d)   the periods fixed for subscription and payment for the shares;

(e)   the period within which the statutory meeting is to be held and in which manner and at which notice the calling of the meeting is to take place; and

(f) whether the company is to pay the costs of the formation, and in the affirmative, the estimated amount of the costs of the company.

The articles of association must be drawn up in conformity with the memorandum of association and contain as a minimum the provisions required by the Companies Act, *i.e.*:

(a) the name of the company and any secondary names;

(b) the municipality in Denmark in which the registered office of the company is to be situated;

(c) the objects of the company;

(d) the amount of share capital, the denomination of the shares (the nominal value), and the shareholders' voting rights;

(e) the number or the minimum number and maximum number of the members of the board of directors, and any deputy directors, and the term of office of the directors;

(f) the number or the minimum number and maximum number of auditors and the term of office of the auditors;

(g) notice calling general meetings;

(h) the business to be transacted at ordinary general meetings;

(i) the period comprised by the financial year of the company;

(j) whether the shares are to be issued to a registered holder, or may be issued to bearer; and

(k) whether the shares of the company shall be non-negotiable instruments.

Furthermore, the articles of association may contain provisions as to:

(a) an obligation on shareholders to have their shares redeemed in full or in part by the company or others;

(b) restrictions on the negotiability of the shares;

(c) special rights attached to certain shares;

(d) restrictions on the power to bind the company; and

(e) a management of more than three members.

At least one promoter must be resident of Denmark or national of another E.U./EEA country. Exemption from this rule, however may be granted by the Ministry of Industry. Legal persons such as stock corporations and partnerships having their registered office in Denmark are considered Danish residents irrespective of the nationality of the owners. The promoters need not subscribe any shares and all shareholders may be non-residents.

A decision on the stock corporation's formation must be taken at the first general meeting (the constituting meeting of shareholders) at which meeting the election of a board of directors and of one or more auditors also takes place.

The board of directors must apply for registration of the stock corporation with the Danish Commerce and Companies Agency not later than six months after the date of the signing of the memorandum of association. The company cannot be registered unless the subscribed capital, including a possible premium has been paid up.

Private limited companies are formed substantially in the same manner as stock corporations. However, no constituting meeting of shareholders is required, and the full share capital must be subscribed by the promoters. Application for registration shall take place not later than eight weeks after the date of signing of the memorandum of association.

E.2.4.2   *Registered office*

The municipality in Denmark in which the registered office of the company is to be situated must be specified in the articles of association. The registered office must be located in Denmark. If the company moves to another municipality the articles of association have to be amended.

E.2.4.3   *Company name*

The name selected for the stock corporation/private limited company must be included in the articles of association. The names shall be clearly distinguishable from the names of other companies. Unless a company is entitled thereto its name shall not include any family name, name characteristic of any real property, trademark, distinctive business name or the like, or anything which might be mistaken therefore.

The Commerce and Companies Agency checks on incorporation whether or not a proposed name would conflict with the above regulation. The name may not be misleading and must have a certain degree of distinctiveness. Stock corporations and private limited companies shall be liable to use and shall have the exclusive right of using the word "aktieselskab" respectively "anpartsselskab" or any abbreviation thereof, including, but not limited to, "A/S" and "ApS" respectively.

E.2.4.4   *Duration*

Both company laws allow the stock corporation/private limited company to be established for an unlimited period and this is the normal situation. The articles of association of a stock corporation or private limited company can determine otherwise, but this is in practice rarely seen.

E.2.5   Shares

The whole share capital of a stock corporation may be owned by one shareholder. Shares may be in either bearer or registered form (both transferable).

In principle, all shares have equal rights unless otherwise stated in the articles of association. All shares must have voting rights, but the articles of association may stipulate that certain shares have another voting power, which however, may not constitute more than 10 times the voting power of any other share of the same denomination.

Shares are not required to have a minimum face value, and different classes of shares may have different face values. The company may issue share certificates. If one shareholder demands it, or if the shares are negotiable or bearer shares, share certificates must be issued for all shares, unless the shares are issued through the Danish Securities Centre ("Værdipapircentralen", also known as the VP Centre). A share certificate can comprise any number of shares.

Shares quoted on the Stock Exchange shall be issued through Værdipapircentralen, with the effect that no physical shares are actually issued. Instead, the stock of shares will be registered electronically by way of EDP.

Members of private limited companies receive no share certificates for their capital contribution. A confirmation of the registration of the owner of the shares may, however, be issued. Such documents are not negotiable. In no event would a private limited company qualify for listing at the Stock Exchange.

A stock corporation is allowed, according to certain procedures, to take contracting loans against the issue of debentures and any other instruments of debt entitling the lender to convert his claim into shares in the company sometime in the future.

E.2.5.1   *Share capital*

Shares subscribed at the formation of the company shall be fully paid up prior to registration in cash or in kind (non-capital contribution). The share capital of a stock corporation or a private limited company must not be less than 500,000 Dkr or 125,000 Dkr respectively. Shares may be issued at a premium but not at a discount.

E.2.5.2   *Transfer of shares*

In principle all shares are freely transferable unless otherwise stated in the articles of association. However, only the transferability of the shares registered in the name of the holder may be restricted.

Where the articles of association in a stock corporation provide that the shareholders or any other persons shall in case of transfer of shares have a pre-emption right, the articles of association shall specify rules to the effect in particular with respect to the period within which to exercise such pre-emption rights.

Where the articles of association contain provisions concerning content to a transfer of shares a decision shall be made as soon as possible after receipt of a request for such consent. The party requesting the consent shall be notified of the decision without delay. If no notice has been given within eight weeks of submission of the request consent is deemed to have been given.

In connection with the transfer of shares in a stock corporation issued to registered holders, the name of the new shareholder shall be registered in the register of shareholders provided the new shareholder makes a request to that effect and proves his title. Under Danish law no contract is needed in connection with the transfer of shares in a stock corporation or in a private limited company but a change of ownership of shares in a private limited company must be notified to the company within four weeks. For transfer of shares in a stock corporation a share transfer duty of 0.5 per cent of the consideration for the shares has to be paid to the Danish tax authorities unless the transfer of shares takes place between two non-residents or from a non-resident to a resident. The transfer duty does not apply in connection with the transfer of shares in a private limited company.

E.2.5.3 *Increase/decrease of capital*

An increase or decrease of the share capital requires an amendment of the articles of association. An increase of the share capital by subscription for new shares or by transfer of the reserves of the company to share capital may, in a stock corporation, only be made subject to the approval of the shareholders at a general meeting. However, the general meeting may, via articles of the articles of association, authorise the board of the directors to increase the share capital by subscription of new shares. Such authorisation may be given for one or several periods of up to five years at a time.

The shareholders shall have a right to proportional subscription of the new shares in the case of any increase of share capital. However, the general meeting may, with the majority of votes required for an alteration of the articles of association, decide to depart from this rule.

A resolution for reducing share capital shall be passed by the general meeting (or by the shareholders in a private limited company) and the amount of the reduction may only be used in the following ways:

(a)   to cover losses:

(b)   to pay the shareholders;

(c)   to be allocated to a special fund to be used only according to the decision of the company in general meeting.

If the reduction is to be applied wholly or partly for the purposes mentioned under

(b) or (c) above, then unless the share capital is at the same time increased by means of a subscription of corresponding size, the company's creditors shall be requested by a notice in the *Danish Official Gazette* to notify their claims to the company within a period of at least three months.

E.2.5.4 *Form of subscription*

Subscription of share capital can take place in cash or in kind. Subscription in the form of contracts of employment or services are prohibited. Subscription in kind must be accompanied by a valuation report prepared by one or more impartial expert valuers. In practice the expert valuers will often be the accountant of the company.

The report shall contain:

(a) a description of its contribution or acquisition;

(b) information about the method of valuation used;

(c) a statement of the consideration fixed for the acquisition; and

(d) a declaration to the effect that the value fixed corresponds at least to the consideration agreed upon, *i.e.* the nominal value of the shares to be issued with the addition of any premium.

Provided the company takes over a going concern in connection with the capital increase the valuation report shall also contain a preliminary statement of account for the company provided with an unqualified auditors' certificate.

A company is not permitted to subscribe for its own shares, or shares in its parent company.

E.2.5.5 *Purchase of own shares*

Whilst a private limited company is not permitted to purchase its own shares, a stock corporation may acquire its own shares provided that:

(a) the nominal value of the company and its subsidiary companies' aggregate holding of shares in the company does not exceed or as a consequence of the acquisition will not exceed 10 per cent of the share capital;

(b) the board of directors have been authorised by the company in general meeting to acquire the shares;

(c) the share capital less the company's own shares shall not be less than 500,000 Dkr after the acquisition; and

(d) the acquisition shall only include fully paid up shares.

E.2.5.6 *Register of shares*

The board of directors shall keep a register for all the shares of a company (Register of Shareholders). The shares shall be entered in numerical order and in the case of shares issued to registered holders, the names of the shareholders shall be entered as well. For companies which have not issued share certificates or have issued shares through Værdipapircentralen the register shall include the name and address of all the shareholders as well as their amount of shares. Unless otherwise decided in the articles of association, the register of shareholders is not open for public inspection except in private limited companies with a share capital of 500,000 Dkr or more.

E.2.6 Company Bodies

E.2.6.1 *Board of directors (Bestyrelse)*

E.2.6.1.1 Appointment/dismissal of directors The board of directors of a stock corporation shall consist of at least three members. Only individuals may be elected. The board of directors shall normally be elected by the general meeting except for the employees' representatives who are elected directly by the employees (see below).

For a private limited company it is optional to have a board of directors unless the company shall have employee representation.

The election of directors shall be registered with the Commerce and Companies Agency and at least half the number of directors must be domiciled in Denmark. Danish citizenship is not required. The requirement of domicile does not apply to E.U./EEA citizens. Exemptions may be granted by the Ministry of Industry.

Normally a director is elected for a period of one year at a time, and he can be re-elected.

A member of the board of directors may retire from the board at any time. Furthermore, a member of the board of directors may be removed at any time by the body that elected or nominated such member.

E.2.6.1.1.1 Employees' representation The Companies Act and the Private Companies Act contain special provisions relating to the right of employees to be represented on the board. If a company during the immediately preceding three years has on average employed at least 35 employees, the employees are entitled to elect half of the number of the directors elected by the shareholders and at least two. If a company holds the voting majority in one or more companies, it is regarded as parent company under the Companies Act/Private Companies Act, and the employees in the subsidiary and the parent company are entitled to elect half of the members of the board of directors in the parent company and at least three, provided the group of companies during the immediately preceding three years have employed an average of not less than 35 employees.

Whenever calculating the half number of directors it has to be rounded up. The employees elect their directors for four years running, irrespective of the election period of the directors elected by the shareholders. The directors elected by the employees have equal rights and responsibilities as the directors elected by the shareholders. This also applies to the remuneration of directors, conflict of interest, disclosure, liability, etc.

E.2.6.1.2 Duties/powers of the board of directors The duties of the board of directors are to supervise the activities of the company, and the board of directors shall arrange for the proper and warrantable organisation of the activities of the company. The board of directors of a stock corporation shall assess whether the capital resources of the company, at any time, are adequate compared to the operations, and the board of directors shall, also in private limited companies, ensure that the control of the keeping of the books of accounts and the administration of property are carried out in a satisfactory way considering the position of the company.

The individual members of the board of directors in a stock corporation shall, when taking up their posts as members of the board of directors, inform the board of directors of their holdings of shares in the company and in stock corporations and private limited companies within the same group, and they shall later give notice of their acquisition and sale of such shares. Such notice shall be recorded in a special register.

Directors in a stock corporation shall not embark upon or participate in any speculative transactions relating to shares in the company or in stock corporations or private limited companies within the same group. Furthermore, under Danish law listed securities may not be brought or sold by anyone who has inside information about the corporate affairs of the issuer before it is announced to the public, if the nature of such information is likely to influence the price of the shares.

Under the rules of the Companies Act and the Private Companies Act loans and guarantees from the company to a shareholder, to the members of the board of directors, and to the managers or persons close to them are illegal.

No member of the board of directors of a stock corporation may vote on any matter relating to contracts between the company and himself or to lawsuits against himself. Power to bind the company is vested in each member of the board of directors and each manager. The articles of association may provide that joint signature by one or more members of the board of directors or the management is required.

E.2.6.1.3 Board meetings According to the Companies Act, the board of directors shall elect its own chairman. A manager shall not be elected chairman. The chairman shall arrange for the board of directors to hold meetings whenever this is necessary and shall ensure that all directors are being convened. A director or a manager may at any time request that a meeting of directors be convened. The board of directors shall, by rules of procedure, lay down further provisions as to the duties and powers of directors. The rules of procedure must, in publicly listed companies and in state-owned stock corporations include detailed minimum obligations in accordance with the Companies Act. Proceedings at meetings of directors shall be recorded in a minute book to be signed by all directors attending the meeting. A director or a manager who does not agree to a resolution passed by the board of directors shall be entitled to have his opinion entered in the minute book.

The board of directors shall be deemed to form a quorum provided more than half of all the directors are attending the meeting unless the articles of association provided for a higher number. The business transacted by the board of directors shall, provided the articles of association do not prescribe a special majority of votes, be decided by a simple majority of votes. The articles of association may provide that in the case of parity of votes the chairman shall be given a casting vote.

E.2.6.1.4   Legal liabilities of directors   Directors who have, in the performance of their duties, deliberately or negligently caused loss or harm to the company shall be liable to pay compensation for such loss or harm. The same shall apply where such loss or harm has been sustained by shareholders, creditors of the company or third parties by violation of the Companies Act, the Private Companies Act or the articles of association of the company. Compensation may be reduced where such reduction is deemed reasonable considering the seriousness of the offence, the extent of the loss or harm caused and other relevant circumstances. Where several of the directors are liable to pay compensation at the same time they shall be jointly and severally liable for the compensation.

The board of directors in a stock corporation must see to it that a general meeting is convened not later than six months after the company has lost half of its share capital. At the general meeting the board of directors shall give an account of the financial situation of the company and submit proposals for appropriate actions and if necessary, submit a proposal for dissolution of the company.

In private limited companies the supreme management organ (the board of directors or the management, as the case may be) shall inform the shareholders, at the latest six months after the company has lost 40 per cent of its share capital, about the financial situation of the company and propose either a decision leading to full coverage of the share capital, however at least 125,000 Dkr, or the dissolution of the company. The Commerce and Companies Agency may cause the company to be dissolved if the company does not resolve to rectify the subscribed capital of the company within a period fixed by the Agency.

The members of the board of directors are personally responsible for loss a third party might suffer due to the above rules not being observed.

E.2.6.1.5   The general manager   The board of directors of a stock corporation must appoint one or several managers to be responsible for the day-to-day business of the company. It means that the managers shall supervise the daily conduct of the company in accordance with the policy determined by the board of directors. Only individuals may be appointed.

A private limited company is not obliged to but may have one or several general managers. If the private limited company has no board of directors its duties under the law shall be assumed by the management.

The appointment of managers shall be registered with the Commerce and Companies Agency. A registered manager must be domiciled in Denmark or be an E.U./EEA citizen. However, exemptions may under certain conditions be granted by the Ministry of Industry.

A manager in a stock corporation shall not participate in the transaction of business or matters in respect of contracts between the company and himself or in respect of legal actions against the manager or in respect of contracts between the company and any third party or in respect of legal actions against any third party, if there is a material conflict of interest between the manager and the company.

Neither the general manager nor any of the directors in a stock corporation shall act in such a way that certain shareholders or others, may clearly obtain an undue advantage at the expense of other shareholders or the company. Nor shall any such person carry out resolutions passed by the company in general meeting or by other company bodies if such resolutions might be void as contrary to the Companies Act or to the articles of association of the company.

The post of general manager is not protected by the Danish Employers and Salaried Employees Act or Holidays with Pay Act. Accordingly, a general manager needs a contract in which the provisions, *e.g.* in relation to remuneration, holiday, pension, illness and termination are stipulated. The termination period for a general manager is normally longer than the termination period for an employee laid down in the Employees Act. Often the termination period runs for six to twelve months for a general manager.

E.2.6.2 *Committee of shareholders*

The articles of association of a stock corporation may provide that besides a board of directors there shall be a committee of shareholders.

The committee of shareholders shall consist of not less than five members. The articles of association may provide another mode of appointment for one or more members, but the majority of members of the committee of shareholders shall be elected by the company in general meeting. Managers and directors shall not be members of the committee of shareholders. The articles of association shall contain specified provisions for the composition of the committee of shareholders and the term of office of the members. As controlling authority the committee of shareholders shall supervise the board of directors and the management's administration of the company's affairs.

The articles of association may provide that the board of directors shall in so far as possible inform the committee of shareholders in advance of certain specified arrangements which do not fall within the scope of the day-to-day management.

Furthermore, the articles of association may provide that the committee of share-holders shall elect directors and fix their remuneration. Further powers shall not be conferred on the committee of shareholders.

A committee of shareholders may not be able to amend a decision made by the board of directors or the management.

It is not mandatory to have a committee of shareholders and it is rather seldom that a committee of shareholders is elected in Danish companies. The Private Companies Act does not contain any rules about a committee of shareholders.

E.2.6.3 The (Annual) General Meeting

E.2.6.3.1 General provisions The right of the shareholders to pass resolutions with respect to the company shall, in a stock corporation, be exercised at a general meeting. Any shareholder shall be entitled to attend a general meeting and to speak there. At least one shareholders' meeting must be held annually.

In a private limited company the use of general meetings is optional (cf. E.2.6.4 below). Normally the board of directors or, in a private limited company without a board of directors, the management convenes a general meeting. If a stock corporation has no board of directors or if the board of directors fails to convene a general meeting which shall be held in pursuance of the Companies Act, the articles of association of the company, or a resolution passed by a general meeting, the meeting shall (at the request of a director, a member of the committee of shareholders, a manager, the auditor or a shareholder) be convened by the Commerce and Companies Agency.

In a stock corporation, at least one shareholders' meeting must be held for the purpose of approving the annual accounts. In addition shareholder's meetings can be convened during the year as and when required for special business.

E.2.6.3.2 The convening of the (annual) general meeting An annual general meeting shall be held each year not later than five months after the end of the financial year. An extraordinary general meeting shall be convened if the board of directors, the auditor, or the committee of shareholders request it. An extraordinary general meeting shall also be convened within two weeks of the written request of shareholders holding one-tenth of the share capital or any smaller fraction thereof as might be provided by the articles of association for the purpose of transacting specified business to be stated in the request.

The board of directors shall cause a general meeting to be held not later than six months of the company having lost half of its share capital. At this general meeting the board of directors shall give an account of the financial position of the company and, if necessary, propose such measures as should be taken including the dissolution of the company. If the general meeting is not convened the members of the board may be held personally responsible for any loss which a third party may suffer.

E.2.6.3.3 Notices for the (annual) general meeting General meetings in a stock corporation shall be convened not earlier than four weeks and, unless the articles of association provide a longer period, not later than eight days prior to a general meeting. General meetings shall be convened in accordance with the provisions laid down in the articles of association. Notice in writing convening a meeting shall, however, be sent to all shareholders registered in the register of shareholders who have requested such notice. Where the shares of the company may be issued to the bearer, the notice convening a general meeting shall be made public, normally by publishing in a national newspaper.

The notice calling a general meeting shall specify the nature of the business to be transacted. If a motion for alteration of the articles of association is to be dealt with, the essence of such a motion shall be stated in the notice. The agenda and proposed resolutions in detail and, in the case of the annual general meeting, the annual accounts, shall be open for inspection by the shareholders at the office of the company not later than eight days prior to the general meeting, and shall be sent to registered shareholders upon their request.

E.2.6.3.4 Place of the (annual) general meeting The location for the general meeting shall be at the registered office of the company, or, elsewhere, if specified in the articles of association of the company. If the Danish company is a subsidiary of a foreign company it is normally stated in the articles of association that general meetings may take place at the registered office of the parent company abroad.

E.2.6.3.5 Duties/powers of the (annual) general meeting Pursuant to the Companies Act the general meeting has the supreme authority in all matters relating to the company. However, the normal supervision of the affairs of the company is taken care of by the board of directors and the management.

At the annual general meeting the annual accounts duly endorsed by an auditor and accompanied by the annual report, shall be presented. At the annual general meeting decisions are made on approval of the accounts, allocation of net earnings or deficit according to the adopted accounts and on other matters which according to the articles of association have been vested in the general meeting, *i.e.* election of directors and auditors and alteration of the articles of association.

At the general meeting, unless otherwise provided by the Companies Act or by the articles of association of the company all resolutions shall be passed by a simple majority. However, any resolution for alteration of the articles of association shall be valid only if carried by not less than two-thirds of the votes cast and, in stock corporations, also by members representing two-thirds of the share capital attending the general meeting and carrying voting rights.

The resolutions shall in all other cases comply with any other provisions which might be laid down in the articles of association and with certain provisions of the Companies Act according to which some resolutions are only valid if adopted by all the shareholders of the company and other resolutions only valid if adopted by members having a right to vote and representing at the general meeting more than three-quarters of the share capital. As a main rule the company in general meeting

161

shall not pass any resolution whereby certain shareholders or other persons may clearly obtain in unfair advantage at the expense of other shareholders or the company.

E.2.6.3.6 Voting rights and restrictions In a stock corporation each share must carry at least one vote. The articles of association may provide that the voting value carried by certain shares be increased provided always that no share shall carry more than 10 times the voting value carried by any other share of the same denomination.

The articles of association may provide that a shareholder who has acquired shares by transfer shall not exercise any voting rights attached to such shares at the general meeting of shareholders convened, unless the shares have been entered in the register of shareholders or he has given notice of and proved his acquisition. However, the shares acquired shall be considered represented at the general meeting of shareholders even though the voting rights cannot be exercised prior to the holding of the general meeting of shareholders or he has given notice of and proved his acquisition.

The shareholder can exercise his voting rights through a proxy. Shareholders agreements stating how to exercise voting rights are recognised as binding between the parties. No voting right shall be exercised on the basis of a company's own shares or a subsidiary company's shares in the parent company. No shareholder shall, in person, by proxy, or in his capacity as proxy for others vote at a general meeting concerning any legal action against himself or his own liability towards the company or concerning legal action against others or the liability of others if he has any material interests therein which may be contrary to the company's interest.

E.2.6.4 *Shareholder resolutions in private limited companies*

In a private limited company the use of general meetings is partly optional as the shareholders acting unanimously can agree to take the necessary decisions using other procedures which can be set out in the articles of association.

To the extent general meetings are used, they benefit from the simpler rules in the Private Companies Act as compared to the rules for stock corporation described above. Unless an alternative procedure is used (*cf.* above) the annual general meeting shall be held not later than five months after the end of the financial year. The decisions to be taken by the company in the annual general meeting are the same as for stock corporations (*cf.* E.2.6.3.5 above). An extraordinary general meeting shall be held when requested by the supreme management organ (board of directors or management as the case may be), the auditor, or a shareholder.

General meetings are convened by the supreme management organ setting the agenda, not later than eight days prior to the meeting, unless a shorter period is sufficient according to the articles of association.

Decisions in general meetings are taken by simple majority, unless otherwise decided in the articles of association or the Private Companies Act. Alterations of the articles of association require that two-thirds of the votes cast are in favour. Certain far-reaching decisions, such as a decision increasing shareholder obligations, require the consent of all shareholders.

It is possible to have shares without voting rights, or to have shares with different voting value. Contrary to stock corporations, no special limitations exist in this respect.

No decisions may be taken whereby certain shareholders or others clearly may obtain an unfair advantage at the expense of other shareholders or the company.

E.2.7   Audit/Accounts

E.2.7.1   *Appointment and dismissal of auditors*

Stock corporations and private limited companies must each year file a balance sheet and income statement pursuant to Danish Company Accounts Act (Order No. 574 of June 24, 1994 as last amended by Act No. 526 of June 17, 1996). The act conforms with the present E.C. regulations.

The annual accounts have to be audited by one or more auditors appointed by the general meeting of the company. However, in stock corporations listed on the Stock Exchange two auditors shall be appointed. Auditors shall be appointed for a certain term of years or for an indefinite period. At least one of the auditors shall be a state authorised or registered public accountant (in companies listed on a stock exchange at least one state authorised auditor shall be used). The articles of association may confer upon public authorities or others a right to appoint one or more additional auditors.

The duties of the auditor shall come to an end at the termination of the ordinary general meeting held after the final financial year of his term of office; or if the auditor has been appointed for an indefinite period, when another auditor has been appointed in his place. However, an auditor may at any time resign his duties or be removed by the person or body who appointed him.

E.2.7.2   *Duties and powers of auditors*

The auditor shall audit the annual accounts in accordance with generally accepted auditing principles including a critical examination of the accounting records and general state of affairs of the company. Further, the auditor shall ensure that the board of directors fulfil its obligations according to law to adopt rules of procedure, introduce and maintain the necessary books and records, and properly produce and sign the auditor's records as set out below.

The auditor shall further meet such requirements concerning the audit as might be made by the company in general meeting and so far as such requirements are not contrary to the Danish Company Accounts Act, to the articles of association of the company, or to generally accepted auditing principles.

The board of directors and the management shall give the auditor the information which is important for the assessment of the company, or in parent companies, of the group. Further, the auditor shall have right of access to examine such records as he deems necessary, and shall ensure that he obtains the information and the assistance he requires for the performance of his duties. When the audit has been completed the auditor shall certify the accounts confirming that he has audited the annual accounts. Furthermore, the auditor's certificate shall include a statement as to whether the annual accounts have been prepared in compliance with the provisions of the law and the articles of association, concerning the submission of accounts.

The auditor shall make a note in the auditor's certificate and provide any supplementary information necessary if the annual accounts or the annual report do not contain information about the company's assets and liabilities, financial position and profit or loss or any other information which shall be given or if the annual report conflicts with the annual accounts. If, in the opinion of the auditor, the annual accounts should not be adopted, he shall make a note to that effect in the auditor's certificate.

For the use of the board of directors, the auditor shall keep auditor's records in which he shall note work performed and any weaknesses and inefficiencies in the book-keeping and accounting system of the company which he may have discovered. The records shall be produced at all meetings of the board of directors and each entry shall be signed by all the directors.

Auditors who have, in the performance of their duties, deliberately or negligently caused loss or harm to the company shall be liable to pay compensation for such loss or harm. The same shall apply where any loss or harm has been sustained by shareholders, creditors of the company, or third parties by violation of the law or the articles of association of the company. Accordingly an auditor can be held liable for errors, omissions and false information in the annual accounts.

E.2.7.3   *Confidentiality of auditors*

If in the course of the audit the auditor has disclosed matters which may involve liability for the directors or managers, or if the auditor of a parent company lacks necessary information about the affairs of a subsidiary, such matters shall be stated in the auditor's certificate. In his certificate the auditor may, furthermore, include any such information as, in his opinion, it would be right to bring to the knowledge of the members of the company. The auditor and his staff shall not be entitled to disclose any information about the affairs of the company to individual shareholders or any unauthorised persons. An auditor who resigns his duty shall be obliged to inform the auditor replacing him about the reason for his resignation.

SECTION 3

COSTS OF INCORPORATION

E.3.1   The major expenses incurred in forming a stock corporation/private limited company consist of:

(a)   registration fee to be paid to the Commerce and Companies Agency; the fee is presently 3,000 Dkr for stock corporations and 2,300 Dkr for private limited companies;

(b)   by non-capital contributions of real property stamp duty (0.6 to 1.2 per cent) has to be paid of the value of the real property invested;

(c)   legal fees involved with setting up of a company depend on the time spent.

The major expenses incurred in forming a branch office consist of:

(a)   registration fee amounting to at present 1,700 Dkr has to be paid to the Commerce and Companies Agency;

(b)   the legal fees depend on the time spent.

ESTONIA

Section 1

INTRODUCTION*

F.1.1 The Estonian Commercial Code was adopted by the Estonian Parliament on February 15, 1995 and came into force on September 1, 1995. The law was substantially amended on May 28, 1996. Respective German and Swiss codes, as well as the E.U. Company Law Directives, have had a great influence on the drafting of the Estonian Commercial Code.

The Commercial Code provides for five types of business organisations: partnership, limited partnership, limited liability company, stock corporation and commune for profit. The latter is very rarely used and is mainly in specific fields of economic activity (*e.g.* agriculture) and hence will not be dealt with below. The Code also contains special provisions for the sole trader.

In addition, a foreign company may establish a branch in Estonia in order permanently to offer goods or services in the name of a foreign company. The branch is not a legal entity, and therefore such foreign company shall be liable for the obligations arising from the activities of the branch. A foreign company must appoint the director(s) to manage the day-to-day business of the branch. The branch is more like a representative office of a foreign company that is planning to enter the Estonian market, and wants to make some preliminary investigations here.

Besides the specific provisions about each business organisation, the Estonian Commercial Code contains general provisions, provisions about the Commercial Register, mergers and division of companies.

In the general provisions, the Code provides for, among other issues, the successor liability and corporate groups. Because of limited practice it is not possible to give clear interpretation for these provisions. The term "corporate group" is defined in the general provisions, but is not used in any regulatory provisions.

---

* *Risto Vahimets, Advokaadibüroo Tark & Co. (full particulars are listed in the Appendix).*

SECTION 2

SOLE TRADER, PARTNERSHIP AND LIMITED PARTNERSHIP

F.2.1 A sole trader is a legal term for an individual who trades in his own name. The sole trader is liable for all his debts and all his assets. Generally the sole trader has to register himself in the Commercial Register only if he has registered himself as a VAT obligee in the Tax Department. VAT obligees are persons whose turnover exceeds 250,000 Estonian crowns (about U.S. $19,200) per year.

A partnership is a business organisation, where two or more partners act under a common commercial name. A partnership is formed on the basis of a partnership agreement. Partners are liable for the debts of the partnership with all their assets. It is forbidden for the Republic of Estonia and its municipalities to be partners in a partnership. All individuals and legal entities however, can be partners in a partnership. A partner needs the consent of other partners in order to participate in other partnerships, to be a full partner in limited partnerships or to be a sole trader. Partners are entitled to distribution of profits and are obliged to pay the debts of the partnership pro rata to their initial capital contributions.

A limited partnership is otherwise similar to partnership, except there are two types of partners. There has to be at least one full partner and one limited partner. The full partner is liable for the debts of the partnership with all his assets. The limited partner is liable for the debts of the partnership to the extent of his capital contribution. It is significant that the limited partnership may not issue a security for the share of a limited partner. A limited partner can act as the manager of the partnership only if this is provided for in the partnership agreement. A limited partner has equal voting rights with the full partner at the general meetings of the partnership.

The two most popular forms of business organisations in Estonia are a stock corporation and a limited liability company. General and limited partnerships involve unlimited liability, and are used only in extraordinary circumstances.

SECTION 3

LIMITED LIABILITY COMPANY

F.3.1 Shares

A limited liability company is an enterprise whose share capital has been divided into shares with the nominal value of 100 Estonian crowns (about U.S. $10) or its full multiple. Each shareholder may have only one share. When a shareholder acquires an additional share, the nominal value of the initial share increases respectively. No security may be issued for a share.

A share can be freely transferred to another shareholder. In case a shareholder wants to transfer a share to a third person, other shareholders may, within one month, exercise their pre-emption right. The articles of association may stipulate a different order of transfer of shares than mentioned above (*e.g.* omitting the pre-emption right, etc.).

The number of votes provided by a share is proportional to the nominal value of the share.

F.3.2 Share Capital

Until September 1, 1999 the amount of minimum share capital must be at least 10,000 Estonian crowns (about U.S. $830). After September 1, 1999 the amount of required minimum share capital shall be 40,000 Estonian crowns (about U.S. $3,330).

Both monetary and non-monetary contributions can be made into the share capital. A non-monetary contribution must be something that can be assessed in money or a property right that can be claimed. The assessment of the value of a non-monetary contribution has to be confirmed by an auditor if the value of the non-monetary contribution exceeds 40,000 Estonian crowns, or if non-monetary contributions form more than half of the total share capital.

The issue price of a share has to correspond to *de minimis* the nominal value of the share.

F.3.3   Management

The administrative bodies of a limited liability company are the meeting of shareholders, the board of directors and, on certain conditions, the council.

F.3.3.1   *Meeting of shareholders*

The meeting of shareholders is authorised to pass resolutions if at least half of the votes determined by the shares are represented at the meeting. It is also allowed to pass resolutions without convening a meeting. Conditions for passing resolutions are the same as for a stock corporation. A resolution of the general meeting will be adopted when at least half of the votes represented at the general meeting are in favour of the proposal. A two-thirds majority of votes is required in resolving amendments to the articles of association, to increase or reduce the share capital and to terminate the activity of the limited liability company. Articles of association may stipulate a higher quorum requirement, and requirements for a higher majority of votes for passing the resolutions.

F.3.3.2   *Council*

A limited liability company may have a council. The council is obligatory only if the share capital is over 400,000 Estonian crowns and the board of directors consists of less than three members. The council of a limited liability company is subject to the same legal requirements as the council of a stock corporation. The council plans the activity of the limited liability company, organises its administration and supervises the activity of the board. The council is authorised to decide important issues concerning the economic activity of the limited liability company. The articles of association may further specify these issues.

The council must have at least three members. A member of the council cannot be a member of the management board nor a procurator. Members of the council are elected and dismissed by the meeting of the shareholders. There is no requirement as to the residence of the members of the council. A member of the council is prohibited from competing with the company, obligated to keep business secrets and is liable for damages incurred to the company or its creditors, due to wilful infringement of the law and the articles of association or due to neglecting his duties.

F.3.3.3 *Board of directors*

The board of directors of a limited liability company is, in general, subject to the same legal requirements as the board of a stock corporation. The board of directors is an administrative body of a limited liability company that represents and administers the day-to-day economic activities of the company. If there is a council in the limited liability company, then the board has to follow the stipulations of the council and transactions that exceed the limits of day-to-day economic activities may be made by the board of directors only if approved by the council.

There must be a minimum of one person on the board of directors. A member of the board cannot be a member of the council. At least half of the members of the board of directors must be residents of Estonia. Members of the board are elected and dismissed by the council. If a limited liability company has no council, the board is elected by the meeting of shareholders. Each member of the board has the right to represent the limited liability company individually, unless otherwise provided by the articles of association.

A member of the board of directors is prohibited from competing with the company, obligated to keep business secrets and is liable for damages incurred to the limited liability company or its creditors, due to infringement of the law or the articles of association or due to neglecting his duties.

F.3.3.4 *Auditor*

A limited liability company must have an auditor, if its share capital exceeds 400,000 Estonian crowns.

SECTION 4

STOCK CORPORATION

F.4.1 Shares

The stock corporation is an enterprise the share capital of which has been divided into shares with the nominal value of 10 Estonian crowns (less than U.S. $1) or its full multiple. A stock corporation can issue both registered shares and bearer shares. Bearer shares are freely transferable, in case of transfer of registered nominal shares,

173

the articles of association of a company may provide for a two-month pre-emption right of other shareholders.

Each share, except a preference share, gives the right to vote. Shares with equal nominal value give an equal number of votes, shares with different nominal value give the number of votes that correspond to the difference in nominal value. It is possible to issue non-voting preference shares that carry the priority in receipt of dividends and distribution of assets that have remained after the liquidation of a stock corporation. The sum of nominal values of preference shares cannot exceed the amount equalling one third of the share capital.

F.4.2   Share Capital

Until September 1, 1999 the amount of minimum share capital must be at least 100,000 Estonian crowns (about U.S. $8,300). After September 1, 1999 the amount of minimum share capital shall be 400,000 Estonian crowns.

Both monetary and non-monetary contributions can be made into the share capital. A non-monetary contribution must be something that can be assessed in money or a property right that can be claimed. The assessment of the value of a non-monetary contribution has to be confirmed by an auditor. The issue price of a share has to correspond to *de minimis* the nominal value of the share.

F.4.3   Management

The management of a joint stock company has three levels: the general meeting of shareholders, the supervisory board (council), and the management board.

F.4.3.1   *Meeting of shareholders*

The general meeting is authorised to pass resolutions if at least half of the votes determined by the shares are represented at the meeting. A resolution of the general meeting will be adopted when at least half of the votes represented at the general meeting are in favour of the proposal. A two thirds majority of votes is required in resolving amendments to the articles of association, to increase or reduce the share capital and to terminate the activity of the stock corporation. Articles of association may stipulate a higher quorum requirement, and requirements for a higher majority of votes for passing the resolutions.

F.4.3.2   Council

The council plans the activity of the stock corporation, organises its administration and supervises the activity of the board. The council is authorised to decide important issues of the economic activity of the stock corporation. The articles of association may further specify these issues.

The council must have at least three members. A member of the council cannot be a member of the management board nor a procurator. Members of the council are elected and dismissed by the general meeting, unless otherwise specified in the articles of association. There is no requirement as to the residence of the members of the council. A member of the council is prohibited from competing with the company, obligated to keep business secrets and liable for damages incurred to the company or its creditors, due to wilful infringement of the law and the articles of association or due to neglecting his duties.

F.4.3.3   Board of directors

The board of directors is an administrative body of a stock corporation that represents and administers the day-to-day economic activities of the company. In its activity, the board has to follow the stipulations of the council and transactions that exceed the limits of day-to-day economic activities may be made by the board of directors only if approved by the council.

There must be a minimum of one member on the board of directors. A member of the board cannot be a member of the council. At least half of the members of the board of directors must be residents of Estonia. Members of the board are elected and dismissed by the council. Each member of the board has the right to represent the stock corporation individually, unless otherwise provided by the articles of association.

A member of the board is prohibited from competing with the company, obligated to keep business secrets and is liable for damages incurred to the stock corporation or its creditors due to infringement of the law or the articles of association or due to neglecting his duties.

F.4.3.4   Auditor

A joint stock company must have an auditor(s) who is (are) elected by the general meeting that also determines the number of auditors.

SECTION 5

PROCEDURE AND COSTS OF INCORPORATION

F.5.1 The proceedings, timetable, and costs of establishing a company in Estonia depend on what type of business is to be established. There are several pieces of information that a client has to provide to his attorney during the course of completing paper work, for example names and addresses of the shareholders, members of the council and the board, etc. The communication between the attorney and the client has to be co-operative during the entire course of the establishment of a company.

One of the crucial matters is the drafting of the articles of association, because the provisions of that document must exactly reflect the interests of the client in order to avoid potential problems in the future. The paper work can take more than two weeks. Practice has shown that communication with foreign clients can take more time than with local clients. Once the documents are drafted, certain documents (the application for registration as well as the specimens of the signatures of the members of the board of directors) must be duly signed and notarised. It has to be pointed out that if some of the persons who must sign these documents that need notarisation, cannot be present here in Estonia, their signatures must be duly notarised by a foreign notary. Foreign notarisation is not valid in Estonia without following a legalisation procedure in the Embassy of Estonia in that foreign country or in the Estonian Foreign Ministry (which in turn needs the legalisation by the Foreign Ministry or Ministry of Justice of the country where the notary public is situated). This procedure involves some additional time and costs.

It is also worth mentioning that if a company plans some activities for which a licence is needed, the licence should be obtained before submitting the registration application for registration to the Commercial Register. That procedure can also take additional time. There are several fields of business which require licences from different government agencies, the respective list includes for example construction, medical services, telecommunications, etc.

When all documents are ready, signed and notarised, they will be submitted to the Commercial Register which has to make a decision about the application within 15 business days after the submission of the document. (The re-registration of companies can take two months.) In practice, the 15 business days term is sometimes not followed by the Commercial Register.

In conclusion, it is difficult to predict the exact timetable for the process of establishing a company, it differs from case to case. Quality should have a priority over speed.

The costs of establishing a company include, besides out-of-pocket costs, stamp duty that is accounted as follows:

(a) for the registration of a stock corporation—0.2 per cent of its share capital, but not less than 1,000 Estonian crowns and not more than 40,000 Estonian crowns;

(b) for the registration of a limited liability company—0.2 per cent of its share capital, but not less than 700 Estonian crowns and not more than 20,000 Estonian crowns.

(c) for the registration of a sole trader, partnership, limited partnership or a branch of a foreign company—700 Estonian crowns.

The fee for the establishment of a company by the Law office Tark & Co. is currently 20,000 Estonian crowns (1 DEM = 8 EEK) and more depending on the complexity of the matter. More complex are the foundations of companies which have to apply for licences, register trade marks, etc.

FINLAND

CLASSIFICATION OF BUSINESS ORGANISATIONS: INTRODUCTION*

G.1.0 Business can be carried on in Finland either by a private entrepreneur or in the form of a company formed by one or more persons or organisations. The most common forms of business organisations are the following:

—general partnership (Avoin yhtiö)

—limited partnership (Kommandiittiyhtiö)

—co-operative (Osuuskunta)

—limited company (Osakeyhtiö)

—branch (Sivuliike)

—European Economic Investment Grouping (EEIG)

Trade is divided by law into free and regulated forms of trade. Permission is not normally required to carry on a free trade. Foreigners not domiciled within the European Economic Area (EEA), however, always need a permit to carry on trade in Finland.

Before a business is started a trade notice must be filed with the Trade Register, maintained by the National Board of Patents and Registration.

G.1.1 Private Entrepreneur

There is no special legislation regarding private entrepreneurs. According to the Accountancy Act of 1973, every person carrying on a trade or business has to keep accounts of that activity. The business of a private entrepreneur with all its assets and liabilities can only be separated from his other assets and liabilities in the records. Hence his private assets may be used to pay debts incurred in connection with his business and vice versa.

The trade name of a private entrepreneur may not contain the name of any other

* *Magnus Pousette, Hannes Snellmann, Asianajotomisto (full particulars are listed in the Appendix).*

181

person except the proprietor. Otherwise the general rules of the Trade Name Act of 1979 are applied.

G.1.2 Co-operatives

A co-operative is the most important form of trade society. Under the Co-operative Act (1954/247), a co-operative society is a society whose number of members and amount of capital are not determined in advance and whose purpose is to carry on business operations in order to support the finances or trade of its members by having the members use the services of the society.

The members of a co-operative society are not personally liable for the debts of a co-operative; the byelaws may, however, stipulate a so-called additional fee for members. If so, the members are up to the amount of that additional fee, liable for the debts of the co-operative in liquidation or bankruptcy. This liability is secondary to the liability of co-operative itself.

A co-operative is formed by a written agreement containing its byelaws. A co-operative must be entered in the Trade Register and the entry constitutes the co-operative as a legal entity.

G.1.3 Branch

According to Finnish law a branch (of a foreign company) is not considered to be an independent legal subject, *i.e.* the branch is not entitled to acquire rights and obligations in its own name. The business of the branch is conducted by a local manager who shall be explicitly authorised to represent the (foreign) company in Finnish courts in all matters related to the business in Finland. Furthermore, the branch shall have one or several persons authorised to sign for the branch/company in Finland separately or together. Essential is, however, that the person acting on behalf of the foreign company has, and exercises an authority to conclude contracts in the name of the enterprise. If his activities are limited to purchasing and sales promotion this, according to double taxation conventions, generally does not constitute a branch.

The branch and the persons entitled to sign for the company shall be reported to the Trade Register.

G.1.4   European Economic Interest Grouping (EEIG)

The Act on European Economic Interest Grouping (EEIG) (229/1994) enforces the E.C. regulations on EEIG (2137/85). The formation of an EEIG shall be notified to the Trade Register.

SECTION 2

PARTNERSHIPS

G.2.1   General Partnership

General partnerships are governed by the General and Limited Partnership Act of 1988. A general partnership has to have the minimum of two partners, either natural or legal persons, who carry on trade together on the basis of a partnership agreement and who are personally liable for the obligations of the partnership.

The entry of a general partnership in the Trade Register has no constitutive effect, as it exists from the moment the agreement is made. The trade name of a general partnership must contain the words "avoin yhtiö" (or in Swedish "öppet bolag"), which denote a general partnership, and the trade name may not contain the name of any person who is not a partner.

The partners may basically arrange their mutual relations as they see fit. They may for instance agree that certain managerial acts, such as conveyance of real property, requires the consent of all of them. Such agreements concerning the management of the partnership are, however, binding only between the partners. They cannot be invoked against third persons who are unaware of them. Unless otherwise agreed, all partners have an equal share in the management of the partnership and each of them also has the authority to act alone in partnership matters. Each partner is legally authorised to represent the partnership in dealings with third persons. The limits of this authorisation are set by the purpose and field of trade of the partnership, and the partners cannot effectively restrict this authorisation by mutual agreements.

Partners may without restriction agree on partnership matters as, *e.g.* their investments in the partnership and the sharing of the profit and loss. The partners are liable for the obligations of the partnership with all their assets. This responsibility is joint and primary. A partner that withdraws from the partnership is still liable for its obligations and may even become liable for debts incurred after his resignation. Not until his resignation has been entered in the Trade Register and duly published can he rely on the partnership not incurring debts for which he may be held liable.

Partnership assets may not be resorted to in order to satisfy creditors of a partner. A share in partnership as such is distrainable. It following a distraint a buyer enters the partnership the other partners are entitled to redeem the share sold. If a partner goes bankrupt, the official receiver takes over his role in the management of the partnership. The grounds for dissolution of the partnership may be included in the partnership agreement. If the partnership agreement is entered for an indefinite time, a partner may cancel it at any time by giving notice. The period of notice is six months. Under the law a partner is entitled to demand dissolution of the partnership in the following cases:

(a) when a partner has cancelled the partnership agreement and the period of notice has ended, or when the agreement contains a fixed partnership period;

(b) when a partner is declared bankrupt or his share is distrained;

(c) upon death of a partner; and

(d) if it is impossible to continue the partnership due to changed circumstances.

G.2.2   Limited Partnership

A limited partnership is basically ruled by the same laws and provisions as a general partnership. The main difference between a general partnership and a limited partnership is that a limited partnership has two kinds of partners: general partners with unlimited liability and those with limited liability. The position of the general partners is roughly the same as that of partners in a general partnership. The limited partners take part in the limited partnerships only by financing its activity and their liability for any obligations is limited to the amount of their investment.

Like a general partnership, a limited partnership is created at the time the agreement is made. Entry in the Trade Register thus has a declaratory effect only. The trade name of a limited partnership must contain a term indicating its nature (in Finnish "Kommandiittiyhtiö" and in Swedish "Kommanditbolag") or an acknowledged abbreviation thereof (e.g. Ky or Kb) and it may not contain the name of any other person but a general partner.

The general partners decide on partnership matters, manage the partnership and represent it. The limited partners have no managerial power. Liquidation is carried out by the general partners. When the debts have been paid, the limited partners receive their shares, i.e. what they have invested. Any remainder is divided among the general partners unless the partnership agreement stipulates otherwise.

SECTION 3

LIMITED COMPANY

G.3.1   Introduction

The limited company is the most advanced form of business organisation and the most significant trade in Finland is carried on by limited companies. In a limited company the shareholders have no personal liability for the obligations of the company.

The Finnish Companies Act (78/734) has been amended (Act 175/97) to comply with E.C. directives and regulations aimed at harmonising company laws within the European Union. The amendments become effective on September 1, 1997.

The major amendments include the introduction of the following:

—The division into public limited companies and private limited companies. Only the shares of a public limited company may be traded on the Helsinki Stock Exchange.

—Capital requirements for public limited companies are set at 500,000 Mk and for private limited companies at 50,000 Mk; both replacing the prior minimum requirement of 15,000 Mk. The new capital requirement applies to companies founded under the amended law and also to companies founded prior to the amendment, granting a transitional period of seven years for meeting the new requirements.

—The group definition is extended to comprise all legal entities, except for foundations or subsidiaries where the parent company holds the controlling power.

—Enlarged majority voting requirements are needed for a number of situations.

—New means of hybrid equity financing: preferred shares with restricted voting rights and with certain preferential rights to profits; capital loans, where the interest may only be paid out of the accumulated profit and loss account as stated in the Annual Report of the previous year's accounting period; and furthermore, options without—as is currently the case—any attachment to a loan.

—The possibility for a limited company to acquire its own shares in certain circumstances.

—Changes in the rules concerning mergers and divisions in order to comply with the requirements set forth in the Merger Directive.

G.3.2 Incorporation

G.3.2.1 *General*

A limited company may be founded by one or more natural or legal persons. The founder is responsible for the practical work involved in the establishment. The founder may subscribe shares in the company, but he need not do so. At least half of the founders have to be domiciled within the EEA. The founder has to draw up a memorandum of association, to be signed by him, as well as to hold a constituent meeting of shareholders. The memorandum of association must include a proposal for the articles of association.

G.3.2.2 *Articles of association (Yhtiöjärjestys)*

The articles of association must always include:

(a) The name of the company containing a word showing a reference to its limited liability status in Finnish or Swedish (or a generally known abbreviation thereof), *i.e.* in Finnish "osakeyhtiö" (Oy) or "julkinen osakeyhtiö" (Oyj) as concerns the new public limited company; in Swedish "aktiebolag" (Ab) and "publikt aktiebolag" (Abp). The name may also contain another symbol indicating the type of company, such as Ltd or AG, for example "Oy XXXX Ltd". A limited company may use a subsidiary company name for a certain part of its business activities;

(b) The Finnish municipality which is the company domicile.

(c) The purpose of the company. The purpose refers to the field in which the company intends to operate.

(d) The share capital or the minimum and maximum share capital. The articles of association can either state a fixed amount of share capital or a minimum and maximum amount, in which case the minimum share capital must be at least one-quarter of the maximum share capital. Normally a minimum and maximum share capital are stated in the articles of association, in which case the share capital of the company may, after the registration of the company, be decreased or increased within those limits without amending the articles of association.

(e) The par value of the shares which must be equal for all shares.

(f) The number, or minimum and maximum number, of the members of the board of directors, any deputy members, and of the auditors as well as their terms of office.

(g) The manner in which a general meeting of the shareholders is to be convened.

(h) The matters to be handled at the general meeting of the shareholders; and

(i) The fiscal period of the company.

In addition to the above mandatory information, the articles of association may contain other provisions as well. These include stipulations whose effect is based on the articles of association (*e.g.* redemption clauses and provisions for a supervisory board), stipulations differing from non-mandatory provisions of the law and other stipulations. The articles of association may furthermore, for instance, include provisions dividing the shares into different categories with different voting rights or different rights to profits.

G.3.2.3 *Subscription to the stock of shares*

In practice, the whole stock of shares in a company is subscribed to in connection with the signing of the memorandum of association. When the company is being established, the subscription price is usually their par value.

G.3.2.4 *The constituent meeting of the shareholders*

The constituent meeting of the shareholders is normally held on the same date as the memorandum of association is signed. The meeting decides on the establishment of the company and elects the members of the board of directors and the auditors.

G.3.2.5 *Registration notice*

Within six months after the signing of the memorandum of association notice is to be given of the formation of the limited company for entry in the Trade Register. Where no notice is given within the above period, the formation is abandoned. A condition for registration is that at least half of the share capital has been paid up. The share capital must be fully paid up within a year after registration of the company. The notice is made by two copies of a form, on which the information to be entered in the Trade Register is given. However, the amended Act includes a stipulation according to which the total share capital shall be paid prior to the registration.

A limited company is created through entry in the Trade Register. The registration incorporates the company as a legal entity. After registration, the company may acquire rights and undertake obligations. As proof of the registration, the National

Board of Patents and Registration will send the company an extract from the Trade Register and a certified copy of its articles of association. In addition to the information entered in the Trade Register, the extract contains the date of registration and the registration number of the company.

G.3.3 Shares and Share Capital

G.3.3.1 Shares (Osake)

Basically, all shares of a limited company have equal rights in the company. The articles of association may, however, provide that the company shall have different categories of shares or that such shares may be issued. In the event of such a provision the differences between the categories of shares, the number of shares within each category and shareholders' entitlement to new shares when the share capital is increased, shall be stated. The differences between share categories may concern the right to part of the profit, the right to a share at dissolution, or voting rights. No share can, however, have a voting power exceeding 20 times the voting power of any other share. The proposed preferred shares however, do not normally carry any voting rights, and shall thus not be included in the aforesaid ratio.

In the company, the shares are entered in a share register, kept by the board of directors. A person acquiring shares in the corporation is not entitled to exercise a shareholder's rights until he has been entered in the share register or he has communicated his acquisition to the corporation together with an account thereof. This is not, however, the case with regard to financial rights. In order to realise his right to dividend, a shareholder need not have himself entered in the share register.

It is not mandatory to issue share certificates representing the shares. A list of shares and shareholders must, however, at all times be kept by the company, and be open to public inspection. A shareholder has the right to require the company to issue share certificates. Share certificates may not be issued in bearer form. The Companies Act provides that the company may elect to enter its shares in a dematerialised book-entry system where share certificates are replaced by book-entries on a shareholder book-entry account kept with authorised registers. Publicly quoted companies are obliged to enter their shares in the book-entry system.

G.3.3.2 Share capital (Osakepääoma)

As stated above the minimum share capital was until September 1, 1997, 15,000 Mk but is pursuant to the amendment 50,000 Mk for limited companies and 500,000 Mk for public limited companies. The share capital may be increased any time after the registration of the company. If the articles of association contain provisions on a minimum and maximum amount of share capital, a general meeting of the shareholders may increase it within these limits by simple majority, but if the increase exceeds the maximum share capital or if the articles of association provide for a fixed amount of share capital only, the raising of the share capital requires an amendment of the articles of association, which in turn requires a qualified majority.

The increase may be realised either in the form of a new issue or a bonus issue. A new issue resembles the subscription of shares upon the incorporation. The shareholders have the right to subscribe the new shares in proportion to their present holdings in the company. The shareholders' meeting may, however, decide to remove or alter that right. A qualified majority is required for that decision. In the case of a new issue, the subscribers invest new capital in the company, whereas a bonus issue is only a transfer of funds of the balance sheet: the share capital may for instance be increased by decreasing the reserve fund. The Companies Act contains provisions for convertible promissory notes and option loans and under the amendments options (without loans), capital loans and preference shares.

In the event that the board of directors finds that the company's stockholders' equity is less than one third of the share capital, the board shall convene a general stockholders' meeting as soon as possible to discuss liquidation of the company. The company is required to enter liquidation unless, at the latest during the next fiscal period, the annual general meeting dealing with the final accounts, adopts a balance sheet audited by the auditors and indicating that the stockholders' equity is at least one half of the share capital.

These provisions on mandatory liquidation have been tightened by the amendments to the Companies Act. The above mentioned threshold of one third is increased to one half of the share capital. The liability of the board would also be stricter as the new provisions require the board continuously to monitor the capital status. Furthermore, the duration of the liquidation procedure is proposed to be shortened. The liquidation must be initiated within 12 months after the first shareholders' meeting, should the capital requirement of one half of the share capital not be met within this period.

G.3.4 Management of a Limited Company

G.3.4.1 *General remarks*

The mandatory company bodies are a general meeting of the shareholders, a board of directors and auditors. Companies with a share capital of 500,000 Mk or more, must have a managing director. A supervisory board cannot be set in a company with a share capital of less than 500,000 Mk according to the amendment.

G.3.4.2 *General meeting (Yhtiökokous)*

At the general meeting the shareholders exercise their decision-making power. Each shareholder usually has as many votes as he has shares. The articles of association may, however, provide for a different number of votes per shareholder. Nevertheless, each shareholder must have at least one vote save for the proposed preference shares. With a few exceptions, the resolutions are carried by a simple majority.

General meetings are either ordinary or extraordinary. An ordinary general meeting must be held within six months after the end of the fiscal period. At the meeting, the annual report and the audit report are presented and a resolution is passed *e.g.* on the adoption of the income statement and the balance sheet, on the measures necessitated by the profit or loss shown on the balance sheet adopted, as well as on the discharge from liability of the members of the board of directors and the supervisory board and of the managing director. The ordinary general meeting elects the board of directors and the auditors.

An extraordinary general meeting is held when the board of directors or the supervisory board consider it necessary. It must likewise be held in case an auditor or shareholders with a minimum of 10 per cent of the shares so demand.

G.3.4.3 *Supervisory board (Hallintoneuvosto)*

If a company has a supervisory board, it must have at least five members. Its main function is to supervise the activities of the board of directors and the managing director. This supervision is mainly retrospective. The managing director or a member of the board of directors cannot be a member of the supervisory board.

G.3.4.4 *Board of directors (Hallitus)*

The board of directors has to have at least one ordinary and one deputy member. It must always have a deputy member if the number of the ordinary members is only one or two. If the share capital or maximum share capital is at least 500,000 Mk, the board of directors has to have at least three ordinary members.

It is the duty of the board to manage the company and to arrange the proper running of its operations. It must keep the share register, convene the general meetings, make sure that the supervision of the book-keeping and financial management of the company has been properly organised, etc.

At least half of the ordinary and deputy members of the board of directors must be domiciled within the EEA, unless the Ministry of Trade and Industry grants an exemption from this requirement.

G.3.4.5 *Managing director (Toimitusjohtaja)*

A limited company may have a managing director, who is appointed by the board of directors. The managing director is in charge of the current affairs of the company in accordance with instructions issued by the board of directors. The managing director may also be a member of the board of directors. A company whose share capital or maximum share capital is at least 500,000 Mk, must always have a managing director.

The managing director of a limited company has to be domiciled within the EEA unless the Ministry of Trade and Industry grants an exemption from this requirement.

G.3.4.6 *Representation*

Under the law, the board of directors of a limited company has the right to sign the company name. Usually, however, a provision on the right to sign the company name is included in the articles of association.

G.3.4.7 *Legal liability of the board of directors and the managing director*

Should the members of the board of directors or the managing director in their work, either wilfully or through negligence, cause damage to the company, they are liable to compensate such damage. If damage has been caused to a shareholder or a third person they are liable only if the damage was caused by breaching the Companies Act or the articles of association. The same rules apply to the liability of the auditors to the extent they have caused damage. In addition to this there are some special rules on tax liability.

G.3.5 Auditors

A company must have one or more auditors, elected by the general meeting. An auditor need not be a natural person; it may also be an auditing company authorised by the central, or local, Chamber of Commerce. According to the new provisions at least one of the auditors shall be authorised by the central Chamber of Commerce where the limited company is public.

The auditor must have such knowledge of, and skill in, business accounting and financial matters as is necessary for the job in view of the nature and scope of the corporate operations. In addition, special stipulations exist as to larger companies.

It is the duty of the auditors to inspect the management and the books of the company. The result of the inspection must be included in the annual report and a separate audit report must be issued. These form the basis on which the general meeting will have to consider whether the board of directors and the managing director can be discharged from liability.

G.3.6 Duration

A limited company is dissolved through liquidation, merger or bankruptcy.

FRANCE

CLASSIFICATION OF BUSINESS ORGANISATIONS: INTRODUCTION*

H.1.0 French law makes a series of distinctions which need to be borne in mind when considering the types of economic activity, business operation and legal and corporate structures involved. The main distinctions are:

—between traders (commerçants) and non-traders;

—between companies and other structures;

—between companies of persons and capital companies.

These distinctions result from the differences between commercial and civil companies generally, and the principles governing the most frequently used type of business vehicle, the capital company.

H.1.1 Traders and Non-traders/Commercial and Civil Companies

Not all business activities are classified as commercial under French law. The classification of a legal person or business activity as "commercial" has important consequences concerning the legal rules, procedures and courts applicable. Briefly, most businesses involving manufacture, purchase and resale of goods, provision of services of financing or leasing operations are deemed commercial. A number of activities are, however, not considered commercial, including "liberal" professions involving purely "intellectual" services such as architects, accountants and lawyers.

The business that is deemed commercial will also have what is known as a "fonds de commerce" or the elements of a commercial business, which is a separate legally defined asset which can itself be sold. The "fonds de commerce" will include notably intangible assets such as the trade name or other industrial property, commercial lease, custom and certain tangible movable assets such as equipment, furniture, etc.

Consideration therefore needs to be given as to whether a given economic activity

---

* *Thierry Jacomet and Hicham Naciri, Gide Loyrette Nouel (full particulars are listed in the Appendix).*

is legally classified as commercial and it is also important to note that French law deems certain types of company to be Commercial rather than Civil.

Civil companies are regulated by the Civil Code and may be formed for the following types of activity which are traditionally considered as inherently civil rather than commercial: farming (unless transformation of purchased foodstuffs becomes the dominant activity), extraction of minerals (transformation again remaining the minority activity); intellectual activities such as novel writing, artists, creative photographers, isolated sale of patents and trade marks by their inventors; screenwriting (but not film production); and purely intellectual research activities; so-called "liberal" professions such as doctors, lawyers, architects, accountants, dentists, as long as the dominant activity remains "intellectual" but now with some exceptions; purchase of land for development and letting of buildings; artisanal activities and certain co-operatives and mutualist organisations.

The civil company must be registered at the local Companies Registry and will have a separate legal personality from its members who will be individually liable for the debts of the company in proportion to their shareholding.

The rules governing civil companies tend to be generally more flexible than for commercial companies but certain types of civil activity such as lawyers and land development companies are specially regulated.

In the rest of this study we shall be concerned with commercial rather than civil companies. For example, the Société en Nom Collectif (SNC), Société Anonyme and SARL companies are deemed commercial companies.

H.1.2   Other Structures

A distinction is made between companies and other structures. For example, associations are created by two or more persons for the purpose of carrying on non-profit-making activities.

The economic interest grouping (Groupement d'Intérêt Economique) should be an extension or prolongation of the activities of the members and is not intended to make profits.

H.1.2.1 *Special forms of company*

A further distinction is made between general companies and certain types of companies active in particular areas of the economy.

Special forms of company are required, for example, for most financial and lending activities, insurance, real estate, agriculture and liberal professions. These are not discussed in further detail in this study.

H.1.3   Companies of Persons

Companies of persons are characterised by the essentially personal nature and identity of the members, and include notably the société en nom collectif and the société en commandite simple (see below).

The société à responsabilité limitée (see below) is an example of a commercial company involving the characteristics of both a company of persons and a capital company, to the extent of being able to have a tax position similar to that of a capital company.

H.1.3.1   *Société en Nom Collectif: SNC*

The SNC is a registered commercial company with a separate legal identity and of which the members, of whom there must be at least two, are deemed traders, who are each fully liable for the debts of the company. Share transfers are in principle subject to unanimous consent of the members.

The company is run by a legal manager (gérant), and the accounts must be audited annually by an independent statutory auditor (Commissaire aux Comptes) only if some limits are exceeded in a financial year (see H.2.1.7). In view of the unlimited liability, as well as restrictions and tax costs on transfer of shares (currently 4.8 per cent registration tax), this type of company is most commonly found in groups of companies in order to enable consolidation of results for tax purposes.

H.1.3.2   *Société en Commandite (limited partnership company)*

This is a form of company where there are members with unlimited liability (commandités) and members with limited liability as long as they do not become involved in day-to-day management (commanditaires). The commandités are the managers of the company. There must be at least two members and there is no minimum capital. This type of company is not frequently used, although a more complex version with issued shares, and treated as a capital company, is now used as an anti-takeover device (société en commandite par action).

H.1.3.3   *Société en participation; Société de fait*

Finally, it is worth very briefly mentioning the société en participation and société de fait which are companies that are not registered, and have no legal personality; where two or more persons bring together capital, goods or services, with a view to carrying on a common activity; and sharing profits, costs-savings and losses.

The société en participation is intentionally created by the partners, whereas the société de fait arises by operation of law. In the société en participation the partners will be responsible for debts in the same proportion as their shares in the capital; where, as is usually the case, the existence of the company relationship is not revealed to third parties, it is only the manager or partner dealing with third parties who will be fully liable for all debts to third parties. However, where the existence of the company is revealed with the authority of the partners, then each partner is jointly liable for the debts of the company. In the société de fait the partners will each be fully liable for the debts of the company. These types of company will be treated as commercial or civil depending on their objects.

SECTION 2

FORMS OF CAPITAL COMPANY

H.2.0 The capital company is not based essentially on the identity of the persons who are members, but rather on the common contribution of capital for the purposes of the company's objects with a view to profit-making. The société anonyme company dealt with below is the main example.

H.2.1 Société à Responsabilité Limitée: SARL

H.2.1.1 *Introduction*

H.2.1.1.1 Company legislation applicable The law of July 24, 1966 on commercial companies, and particularly Articles L34 to L69, L423 to L431 and Articles 20 to 53 of the Decree of 1967.

H.2.1.1.2 Definitions The SARL is a private limited liability company, with a maximum initial duration of 99 years, created by one or several members who are responsible for the company's losses up to the limit of their contribution to the capital of the company which has to be fully paid upon incorporation (Article 34 of the law of July 24, 1966).

Shares in the capital are not represented by issued shares and transfers are restricted. Shares in the capital cannot be offered to the public.

H.2.1.1.3 Commercial nature of the company The SARL limited liability company is always considered as a commercial company, whatever its object.

H.2.1.1.4 Activities not permitted Insurance business by capitalisation and by savings may not be carried on by a SARL.

H.2.1.1.5 Number of members Except for special cases and particularly the EURL mentioned below, the SARL limited liability company must have at least two founding members, but cannot have more than 50 members.

H.2.1.1.6 Company capital The minimum capital for a SARL limited liability company is 50,000 French francs and has to be fully paid on the day of incorporation. This amount is relatively low compared to the 250,000 FF minimum share capital necessary for a Société Anonyme limited company.

H.2.1.1.7 Taxation Taxation of SARL private liability companies is the same as for limited companies with shares (SA) except for the special case mentioned below. Cash contributions are subject to a registration fee of 500 FF.

Contributions in kind are in principle subject to a registration fee of 500 FF but can be up to 11.4 per cent when applying to real property rights, clientele, etc.

The income of the private limited company is subject to corporation tax (41.66 per cent both on retained earnings and on distributed income in 1997 and 1998 and 36.66 per cent for companies: (i) whose turnover (VAT excluded) does not exceed 50 million FF; (ii) which are not head of a tax integrated group; and (iii) which are held at least 75 per cent by individuals or a company held itself at 75 per cent by individuals), unless ordinary personal income taxation in the hands of the members has been chosen.

H.2.1.1.8 Particular types of SARL Since 1985 it has been possible to create a SARL with only one shareholder. Such a company is known as a EURL (Entreprise Unipersonnelle à Responsabilité Limitée). By this method an individual trader may limit his or her liability to the business capital contributed to the company.

H.2.1.2 *Incorporation and articles of association (Status)*

Written articles of association are required which must include provisions dealing with the: objects; legal form; duration of the company; name; registered office; amount of capital; details of contributions in kind; the extent of the interests of each member in the capital of the company; and date of contribution and details of the deposit of the capital at the bank; appointment of the legal manager and relevant powers and limitations thereon; provisions for transfers of interests in the capital of the company; general meetings; financial year; distribution of profits; and winding up. The articles must be signed by all shareholders or their authorised representatives.

After filing of the articles at the local tax office where the registered office is situated, the following steps have to be taken:

(a) notice of proposed incorporation published in a local paper;

(b) filing of personal details of the legal manager at the local Commercial and Companies Registry;

(c) filing of articles of incorporation at the Commercial and Companies Registry;

(d) publication of a notice of incorporation in an official Legal Journal.

The capital paid in cannot be withdrawn from the bank account before registration has been effected and a certificate of incorporation (K Bis) issued by the Commercial and Companies Registry, *i.e.* usually about a month from signing the articles of association; although this can sometimes be achieved more quickly.

H.2.1.3 *Members and shares in capital (Parts Sociales)*

The situation of the members in a SARL limited liability company is defined by the following rules;

(1) the members themselves are not deemed to be traders by reason of their membership of the company;

(2) their financial liabilities are, in principle, limited to the amount of their contribution to capital. In practice, if the capital of the company is insufficient for bank loans, the legal manager or shareholders may be called on to give personal guarantees. If any member acts as a *de facto* manager, he will be liable for any act of negligence committed in such management.

(3) their rights in the company result from the ownership of their share in the capital mentioned in the articles of association. Voting rights cannot be restricted or diluted;

(4) transfer of shares can be submitted to more or less strict control. There must always be a restriction on transfers to third parties. Transfer between members is in principle unrestricted but is usually limited by the articles. Likewise it is possible to control transfer of shares *inter vivos* or to legal successors in case of death;

(5) shares can be charged but the other members must usually be consulted.

Shares are transferred by written or notarised transfer agreement which must be registered at the local tax office.

Registration tax is at present 4.8 per cent of the purchase price indicated in the transfer agreement.

These limitations on the right to transfer shares which are among the particular characteristics of the SARL limited liability company, when compared with the

Société Anonyme, are generally viewed as advantageous when strict control of share ownership is desired.

On the other hand, if a transfer of shares does become necessary, the tax cost following registration of the transfer deed with the tax authorities is considered to be a drawback.

The members may resolve that the company acquire shares in capital from a member willing to sell, by way of a reduction in capital, the price of which has to be determined by an independent expert. There are substantial fiscal consequences which need to be considered where this is envisaged.

There is no share register as such, the company being formally notified of any proposed transfer or charge of shares.

H.2.1.4 *Company's management organs*

The SARL private limited liability company is represented by one or several legal managers (gérants), who can be a member, but must be a physical person. The gérant's powers are determined for internal purposes in the articles of association. The gérant is appointed by and can be freely dismissed by the members in general meeting. If the person is a member owning a majority of the capital, then the minority can apply to the court for dismissal.

The day-to-day management and administration are carried out directly by the legal manager who has full power to bind the company. Any limitations on the legal manager's powers in the articles do not affect third parties.

The gérant may delegate certain of his or her functions but not the whole of the gérant's functions.

The gérant is personally liable under civil law to the company and third parties for breaches of the law or of the Articles of Association, as well as for acts of negligence in the management of the company.

The gérant must present to the general meeting each year (or more frequently if provided in the articles) a report on the company's activities and management as well as an inventory and accounts for the company for the preceding financial year.

If the gérant is a minority shareholder, he or she will be considered as a salaried employee for income tax and social security purposes. If however, the gérant is a majority shareholder, he or she is treated as a self-employed trader. Social security protection is in that case less favourable than for employees, but on the other hand contributions are lower.

H.2.1.4.1 Supervisory board It is possible for the members of a SARL to agree on the appointment of a supervisory board to keep the legal manager's actions under review. However, this is an unusual, cumbersome arrangement, that can be achieved more easily by providing for more frequent shareholders' meetings.

H.2.1.5 *Meetings of shareholders*

H.2.1.5.1 General meetings There must be one ordinary general meeting within six months of the end of each financial year to approve the annual accounts by a simple majority of shares or if not at a second meeting by a majority of members present and voting.

Any member or members holding a quarter of the shares and representing at least one-quarter in number of the members, or holding at least one-half of the shares in capital, may call a meeting at any time.

Notice of meetings is given by registered letter with the agenda for the meeting, by the gérant, or in the case of his failure, by a person appointed by the court. The meetings may be held wherever is decided by the members and this is usually provided in the articles.

Ordinary general meetings can in general deal with any question not involving an alteration of the memorandum and articles, which must therefore be passed by an extraordinary general meeting with a 75 per cent majority. The legal manager may be dismissed by a simple majority.

The members may also decide to transform the company into a société anonyme by simple majority if the net assets exceed 5 million FF and in particular if the members have approved the first two years' accounts.

However, the unanimous decision of members is required for the transformation of the company into a SNC or limited partnership (société en commandite). Where the members' liabilities are to be increased in the case of increase in capital, share transfers or charging of shares, then there must be a decision by a majority of the members holding at least three-quarters of the capital.

H.2.1.5.2 Extraordinary general meetings Extraordinary general meetings must be held:

(a) to modify the articles which must be voted by members holding at least three-quarters of the capital;

(b) to increase capital or approve new members;

(c) to transform the company into a société anonyme.

For transfers of shares to third parties, a three-quarter majority of shares and members is required.

H.2.1.6 *Employee delegates and works council (Délégués de personnel et comité d'entreprise)*

French law provides for three types of representation of employees, applicable to all business enterprises with a certain minimum number of employees. This is dealt with fully in the section on the société anonyme (below).

H.2.1.7   *Audit/accounts (Commissaire aux comptes)*

Audited financial statements approved by a statutory auditor have to be published by the SARL only if two of the following three limits are exceeded in a financial year:

(a)   total assets: 10 million FF;

(b)   sales turnover ex. VAT: 20 million FF;

(c)   average number of employees: 50.

In addition, any member holding at least one-tenth of the capital of the company may apply to the President of the Commercial Court for the appoint of a statutory auditor.

In most cases, the auditors are appointed for a minimum period of six years by members holding three-quarters or more of the capital.

The auditors have a duty to independently audit the books of accounts and must be given notice of shareholders' meetings and have a right to attend. They must have access to the books and legal manager's report. The statutory auditor has a professional duty of confidentiality.

H.2.2   Société Anonyme

H.2.2.1   *Introduction*

H.2.2.1.1   Legal sources   The law of July 24, 1966, on commercial companies.

H.2.2.1.2   Definitions   The société anonyme is defined as the company of which the capital is divided into shares and created by the shareholders who are liable for losses within the limit of their obligation to contribute to the share capital (Article 73 of the law of July 24, 1966). The maximum initial duration of the company is 99 years.

It may, subject to certain conditions, issue shares to the public.

H.2.2.1.3   Commercial nature of the company   The société anonyme will always be deemed to have a commercial activity whatever its object.

H.2.2.1.4   Activities reserved to société anonyme companies   Certain activities must be carried out only by a company using the form of a société anonyme, for example companies involved in investment in stocks and shares and certain types of real estate investment projects.

H.2.2.1.5 Statutory auditors A société anonyme must appoint a statutory auditor (commissaire aux comptes) together with a deputy statutory auditor.

H.2.2.1.6 Taxation The société anonyme is subject to corporation tax (see H.2.1.1.7, above) for both retained earnings and distributed earnings.

H.2.2.2 *Incorporation formalities*

The company is formed by the signature of the written memorandum and articles of association by the shareholders and which must contain a certain number of obligatory matters similar to those found in the SARL except that in particular there will need to be a provision for the board of directors (see below) and in some cases the supervisory board.

The procedure for incorporation of the société anonyme, not selling shares to the public, includes the following steps:

(a) drafting of the memorandum and articles;

(b) payment of the share capital either in cash or in kind which in the latter case is subject to a special procedure;

(c) deposit of the share capital with the list of subscribers at the bank;

(d) issue of a certificate of deposit of the capital by the bank;

(e) signature of the memorandum and articles of association;

(f) appointment of the members of the board at a first board meeting;

(g) publication of notice of the creation of the company in an official journal;

(h) issue of the certificate of incorporation by the Companies Registry;

(i) transfer of the funds representing the share capital paid up in cash to the new company's commercial account.

H.2.2.3 *Shareholders and shares*

H.2.2.3.1 Number of shareholders A société anonyme may only be incorporated if it has at least seven shareholders and there is no maximum number of shareholders.

H.2.2.3.2 Share capital The minimum share capital is 250,000 FF for companies which do not sell shares to the public (the minimum capital for a company selling shares to the public is 1,500,000 FF; and such companies are subject to precise and rigorous rules which are not dealt with here).

As regards the ordinary SA, the share capital need only be paid up as to one-quarter of the total amount with the balance being paid up within the first five years.

H.2.2.3.3 Shareholders' status The position of shareholders in the société anonyme can be summarised as follows:

(a) The shareholders are not deemed to be commercial traders by virtue of their position as shareholder.

(b) Their liability is limited to the amount of their obligation to pay up the shares issued to each of them; but it should be recalled that in practice, banks or other creditors may require personal guarantees if the assets of the SA are not sufficient to support the credit needed.

(c) The law gives shareholders of the société anonyme a relatively broad right to be kept informed of the company's activities; and in particular:

   (i) Rights to be kept informed on a permanent basis:
A shareholder may require communication notably of the accounts, board and statutory auditors' reports, board's and shareholders' resolutions and the list of board directors and certain of the higher remunerations paid, minutes and attendance registers of shareholders' meetings, and for companies with more than 300 employees, a report on the employment position. In each case, the information will cover the last three financial years.

   (ii) Rights to receive information prior to shareholders' meetings:
This will include the right to have a copy of the agenda, draft resolutions, details of the company's financial position and business activity, and a résumé of the company's results over the last five years.
More detailed information should be available prior to the annual general meeting; and shareholders also have a right to inspect a wide range of documents and registers at the registered office prior to meetings, including a list of shareholders and directors.

(d) The shareholder's rights in relation to the capital of the company flows from the ownership of shares, of which the transfer to third parties may be subject to approval of the board or the general meeting of shareholders. In general, it is usually the board which approves share transfers.

H.2.2.3.4 Share transfers Transfers are subject to the simple formality of signature of a form of share transfer by the transferor. The share transfer form does not refer to the transfer price. No registration tax is payable provided that the transfer is not the subject of a deed. In the event that the transfer is effected by the deed, the registration tax is 1 per cent of the transfer price as of 1997, subject to an upper limit of registration tax payable of 20,000 FF per transfer.

The simplicity and absence of cost in relation to the transfer of shares is a fundamental characteristic of the société anonyme.

H.2.2.3.5 Purchase of company's own shares A SA may not, as a matter of legal principle, purchase its own shares directly or indirectly.

There are some limited exceptions allowed by law which are:

(a) reduction in capital with cancellation of the shares not arising from losses of the company;

(b) for the purpose of attributing shares to employees;

(c) for the purpose of regularising the share price where the company is quoted on the stock exchange in certain situations and subject to certain conditions, notably the approval of an ordinary general meeting.

H.2.2.4 *Company's management organs*

The day-to-day management of a société anonyme may be organised in two different ways: either with a board of directors or with a supervisory board and board of directors. There are also, or course, shareholders' meetings, both general and extraordinary.

H.2.2.4.1 The société anonyme with a board of directors In this case, the company is managed by a board of directors of at least three and not more than 24 members (since 1994) chosen from amongst the shareholders. The board appoints a president (Président Directeur Général) who must be a physical person, and who is responsible for the management of the company; and there may also be one or more general directors (Directeurs Généraux) who will also be physical persons. Board decisions are usually taken by simple majority.

While a board director is prohibited from becoming an employee of the company, an employee can become a board director, to the extent that: (i) its employment contract is anterior to his office as board director; (ii) the employment contract corresponds to an effective employment; and (iii) the number of board directors employed by the company does not exceed one-third of the board directors.

Normally, the day-to-day management of the société anonyme is undertaken by the Président Directeur Général assisted by a general director if required, reporting to the board.

Board directors will be liable under civil law in respect of any breach of the law governing sociétés anonymes and for any violation of the memorandum and articles, as well as for any act contrary to the interests of the company and in particular negligence in the conduct of the company's affairs, misuse of company funds, lack of proper surveillance of the employees and the Président Directeur Général. The liability will extend to third parties suffering loss as a result of negligent management, and in particular liability may arise to creditors for trading while insolvent.

Shareholders may bring an individual or collective action. In the latter case, they must represent at least 5 per cent of the share capital (a degressive percentage is applied to companies with a share capital of more than 5 million FF). The advantage of the collective action is the sharing of legal and court costs.

There is a wide range of criminal offences related to the non-compliance with regulations concerning the incorporation and operation of the SA which go beyond the scope of the present study.

H.2.2.4.2 The société anonyme with a board of directors and a supervisory board (SA à Directoire et Conseil de Surveillance) This type of société anonyme, which is inspired by the system widely used in Germany, offers the possibility of having a management system which is made up as follows:

(1) a board of directors (known as the Directoire) made up of physical persons who may or may not be shareholders and who are responsible for the day-to-day management of the company in the widest sense;

(2) a supervisory board made up of physical or corporate persons, who must be shareholders and whose main role is to appoint the members of the board and to internally supervise the management. From a practical point of view, it is appropriate to note that this system is relatively cumbersome in practice and is usually only used where the particular characteristics of the shareholders and the company's activity require it.

The members of the Directoire are appointed by the supervisory board. The Directoire may not have more than five directors and if the capital is less than 1 million FF, the Directoire may only consist of one director who is known as the Directeur Général unique.

A member of the Directoire may have a contract of employment and an employee may be appointed as a member of the Directoire without restriction. The members of the Directoire have the same liabilities as members of the board of directors of an ordinary SA.

The supervisory board is made up of at least three members with a maximum of 24, chosen from amongst the shareholders of the company. The members of the supervisory board may not have contracts of employment with the company. The supervisory board exercises permanent internal supervision of the management carried on by the Directoire. The supervisory board should not become involved in day-to-day management of dealings with third parties, otherwise the members of the supervisory board may themselves become liable as members of the Directoire. On the other hand, the failure of the members of the Conseil de Surveillance to exercise the necessary supervision and control of the Directoire may result in personal liability. In summary, the supervisory board should receive quarterly reports from the Directoire on the business and financial position of the company, and they may look at the company's books at any time. In addition, the supervisory board must be consulted for its approval before any guarantees are given by the company or sale of real property or securities. The memorandum and articles may extend the scope of approvals to be given by the supervisory board.

H.2.2.4.3 Meetings of shareholders The ordinary general meeting, of which the decisions are by ordinary majority, will appoint and replace members of the boards, and, where appropriate, the supervisory board. The general meeting appoints the statutory auditors and approves the annual accounts, and will determine the distribution of dividends. The general meeting must also approve certain regulated agreements, *e.g.* with directors, payment of dividends by issue of shares, and purchase of the company's own shares.

The extraordinary general meeting which takes decisions by a two thirds majority will take, in particular, all decisions concerning changes in the memorandum and articles of association.

The detailed rules on meetings differ depending on whether the company has issued shares to the public or not. We will only deal with companies that do not issue shares to the public.

Meetings of shareholders are usually convened by the board or Directoire as appropriate. They may also be convened by the supervisory board or the statutory auditors at any time and by the majority of votes or capital in the case of a takeover bid or transfer of a controlling block of shares.

In addition, any person who can demonstrate having an interest and the existence of urgency, *including a creditor of the company*, or, any person or persons holding at least a tenth of the capital, who do not need to justify urgency, may request the court to appoint a representative to call a general meeting.

Notices are usually to be given by registered letter with return receipt and by the insertion of a notice in a local newspaper authorised to publish such notices, at least two weeks prior to the meeting. Meetings must be held at the registered office or within the same administrative district (département) unless the articles provide otherwise. All shareholders have the right to attend or to be represented at meetings. Shareholders also have the right to vote by correspondence.

The quorum required is as follows:

(a) Ordinary meetings:

   (i) on first date convened for the meeting: one-quarter of voting shares;

   (ii) on second date convened for the meeting if no quorum attained at the first meeting: no quorum is required.

(b) Extraordinary meetings:

   (i) on first meeting convened: half of the voting shares;

   (ii) on second meeting in the absence of a quorum at first meeting: one-quarter of the voting shares.

In principle, no shareholder can be deprived of the right to vote; nor can attendance or freedom of voting be restricted.

However, there are certain exceptions, for example shares with preferential dividend rights, and cases where voting rights may not be exercised, such as where the shareholder has a personal interest in the outcome of the vote.

Certain shares may be given double voting rights; and where there are different categories of shares in a company, special meetings may need to be called to deal with questions affecting their rights.

H.2.2.5   *Employee delegates and works council (Délégués du personnel et comité d'entreprise)*

French law provides for three types of representation of employees applicable to all business enterprises with a certain minimum number of employees.

H.2.2.5.1 Personnel delegates (Délégués du personnel) Any business establishment with 11 or more employees must organise elections of personnel delegates who may present individual or collective claims relating to salaries, working conditions and social protection, and compliance with relevant regulations, particularly health and safety.

H.2.2.5.2 Works committee (Comité d'entreprise)   This is required for any business establishment with at least 50 employees.

The committee is presided over by the employer with elected representatives of the employees, and with trade unions having a consultative role. The works committee has to be informed of most aspects of the company's organisation and activities. The committee must be consulted on matters affecting employment (including dismissals) in the company, and changes in the company's legal structure or in the business activities.

H.2.2.5.3 Union representatives The trade unions may appoint union representatives in establishments with at least 50 employees to represent union members and interests.

H.2.2.6   *Audit/accounts (Commissaire aux Comptes)*

Every société anonyme is obliged to appoint a statutory auditor and assistant statutory auditor who is a member of the regulated profession of accountants and specifically authorised to be appointed as Commissaire aux comptes, of which a list is held by each Court of Appeal.

Companies with subsidiaries or participations with consolidated assets must have two statutory auditors. See also the comments relating to the SARL, above.

H.2.3   Société par Actions Simplifiée: SAS

This new simplified type of company has been created by a law dated January 3, 1994.

The main advantage of this SAS is its flexibility as to the organisation of the management powers and the operation of its management bodies according to the wishes of the shareholders. Besides these aspects, it works like a SA:

H.2.3.1 *Shareholders*

The SAS requires at least two shareholders, which must be legal entities, the capital of which must amount at least to the countervalue in foreign currency of 1,500,000 FF and be fully paid up.

H.2.3.2 *Share capital*

The minimum share capital requirement for the SAS is 250,000 FF. It must be fully paid up at the time of incorporation.

H.2.3.3 *Management*

The various voting majorities required may be set out freely in the articles of incorporation.

The SAS is represented by a president (in French, Président) who may be a legal entity. But the articles of incorporation may freely organise the management of the company around him.

With regard to share, it is noticeable that lock up clauses may be integrated into the articles of incorporation for maximum periods of 10 years.

This type of company may in some cases be well adapted for joint-ventures.

Furthermore, this corporate form may be adopted for the purpose of simplification of subsidiaries management as to constitution's general meeting's requirements.

Section 3

COSTS OF INCORPORATION

H.3.1 It should first be noted that there is no widespread trade in "off-the-shelf" companies in France and most companies are created on a "made to measure" basis.

Apart from the minimum share capital, the costs shown in the table opposite should be taken into account.

	SARL	SA	SAS
Name search:	500 FF approx.	500 FF approx.	500 FF approx.
Official notices:	1,500 to 2,000 FF	1,500 to 2,000 FF approx.	1,500 to 2,000 FF approx.
Registration duty (shares paid up in cash):	500 FF	500 FF	500 FF
Filing at Companies Registry:	1,500 to 2,000 FF	1,500 to 2,000 FF	1,500 to 2,000 FF
Legal costs:	variable (but approx. 10,000 FF on average in the Paris area	variable (but approx. 20,000 FF on average in the Paris area)	variable (but approx. between 20,000 FF and 50,000 FF)

GERMANY

GERMANY

CLASSIFICATION OF BUSINESS ORGANISATIONS: INTRODUCTION*

I.1.0   Three principal categories of business are recognised:

—sole proprietorship;

—commercial (general or limited) partnership;

—legal entities (company with limited liability; stock corporation company).

In addition to the above main forms, German law provides for civil partnerships which are in particular used for small enterprises, holding activities, joint ventures and the management of real estate. Of course, German law also knows the concept of sub-participations and silent partnerships (typical and non-typical, depending on their structure). Since the last-mentioned organisations are of minor importance, they will not be reviewed here.

I.1.1   Sole Proprietorship

A natural person doing business (*i.e.* not rendering professional services such as lawyers, auditors, physicians) himself is considered a merchant if, in principle, his business activities are of such size that a business organisation is necessary.

The sole proprietor, as owner, takes all the profits and losses and personally bears all risks. There is no distinction between his private and business capital so that both, private and business creditors, may take recourse to his entire assets. As a merchant he is subject to the provisions of the German Commercial Code (Handelsgesetzbuch: HGB). He has therefore to apply for registration in the commercial register, where his business as merchant is registered under his trade name (Firma). He is obliged to keep books and draw up a balance sheet once a year. As a merchant a sole proprietor is less protected than a private individual, *i.e.* consumer orientated laws, etc., do not apply to his benefit.

---

* *Dr Jürgen J. Seiger and Dr Ludwig Leyendecker, Deringer Tessin Herrmann & Sedemund (full particulars are listed in the Appendix).*

I.1.1.1 *Branch*

A sole proprietor or a (domestic or foreign) company may set up a branch. A branch is not a legal entity, but rather a registered place of business. It does not have legal representatives of its own or own assets. It has, however, to be registered with the commercial register. In addition, a branch is subject to the same law as its owner.

I.1.2 Partnerships

The commercial partnerships (general and limited partnership) are governed by the Commercial Code and, secondarily, the Civil Code. Civil partnerships are merely subject to the Civil Code. There is no legal limitation to the number of partners in a civil or commercial partnership. Neither partnership requires a deed or a written partnership agreement. Hence, a notarisation or the obtaining of a licence are not necessary. Whereas partnership agreements as such do not have to be filed with the commercial register, commercial partnerships have to register their trade name, domicile, name and status (general or limited) of their partners and, in case of a limited partnership, the amount of the liable contributions of the limited partners. Although the applications to the commercial register do not require notarial form, the signatures of the partners have to be certified by a notary.

I.1.2.1 *General partnership (Offene Handelsgesellschaft: OHG)*

An OHG consists of two or more persons, which may be legal entities, jointly establishing and running a business. It has no legal personality of its own, but it may sue or be sued in its own name. It may acquire rights including the title to real property and incur liabilities. But, despite its own assets, its partners are personally, jointly and severally liable for all debts incurred by the partnership. Registration (*cf.* above) is mandatory for reasons of publicity, but not necessary in a sense that the OHG's legal existence depends on it.

The structure of an OHG is subject to rather few mandatory legal provisions. In principle, each partner is entitled and obliged to represent and manage the OHG. The partnership agreement may amend this principle. Unless the partnership agreement provides differently, any issue being of basic interest for an OHG must be decided upon unanimously by the partners' meeting.

A statutory or minimum capital is not required. The partners are free to choose the amounts they are willing to invest. Usually, it is contractually stipulated that each partner has a fixed capital account in the amount of his contribution, which determines the ratio in which he participates in profits and losses, and a running account, where all contributions, profits, losses, withdrawals, etc., are recorded.

I.1.2.2 Limited partnership (Kommanditgesellschaft: KG)

The KG differs from an OHG in so far that it has one or more partners not being personally liable for the partnership's liabilities (limited partners: Kommanditisten). There must, however, be at least one general partner (Komplementär) being responsible for the management and representation of the KG. Whereas his liability is unlimited, the limited partners are liable for the partnership's liabilities only up to the amount of capital they are obliged to invest according to the provisions of the partnership agreement (liable contribution). There is no further liability once a limited partner has paid in this amount; his liability revives, however, when and in so far as the contribution is refunded to him. The partners are free to determine the amount of capital to be put up by the limited partners; there is no legal minimum. The name of the limited partners and the amount of their liability must be registered in the commercial register. This is fairly important since, before registration, the liability of a limited partner is unlimited. The limited partners have equal voting rights in the partners' meetings but do not participate in the partnership's management. The partnership agreement may, however, provide otherwise with respect to both. The limited partner's rights in the partners' meetings may be reduced, alternatively a limited partner may be appointed managing partner, without affecting the limitation of his liability.

I.1.2.3 The "GmbH & Co. KG"

The most common form of business organisation is the GmbH & Co. KG, *i.e.* a limited partnership, whose general partner is a company with limited liability. It combines the benefits of a partnership (great flexibility of structure, tax treatment as partner, somewhat restricted publicity) with those of a company with limited liability (*i.e.* liability limited to the assets of the limited company; as general partner, there would otherwise be unlimited liability). A GmbH & Co. KG is established by founding two companies. First, a GmbH (Gesellschaft mit beschränkter Haftung) is incorporated whereupon the newly established GmbH enters into a limited partnership agreement with the limited partner(s), which in practice are most often identical with the GmbH's shareholders. In recent years, there have been some decisions allowing the establishment of limited partnerships in which the general partner is a company incorporated under foreign law. Thus, for instance, a "Ltd (British Law) & Co. KG" has been held admissible. For the time being, however, it is not certain to what extent German courts are willing to acknowledge all kinds of foreign companies to act as general partner of a German limited partnership. Legally, a GmbH & Co. KG is treated, in principle, as a limited partnership. However, certain rules on the protection of the share capital of a GmbH also apply to a GmbH & Co. KG.

217

I.1.2.4   *The civil partnership (Gesellschaft bürgerlichen Rechtes: GbR)*

A civil partnership comes into existence *ipso jure*, if two or more persons associate for the purpose of operating an enterprise. A GbR does not have a corporate organisation, legal capacity or a trade name. Typically, a GbR enters into legal relations with special assets serving the GbR's purpose. The GbR's assets are jointly owned by its partners. The contributions may be made in cash, in kind, with claims or intangible assets as well as services. Although the individual partner has his private assets, he is both jointly and severally liable without limit for all debts of the GbR. Such personal liability may, however, be excluded by agreement with the GbR's creditors so that only the partnership assets are subject to liability. In principle, the partners are jointly responsible for the management and, since the power of representation depends on the authority to manage, there is joint power of representation. Due to the permissive character of these provisions, it has to be noted that for practical purposes the partnership agreement usually provides differently.

SECTION 2

THE STOCK CORPORATION (AKTIENGESELLSCHAFT: AG)

I.2.1   Introduction

The law concerning Aktiengesellschaften (AG) is embodied in the Stock Corporation Act (Aktiengesetz: AktG) of 1965, as amended. Other laws of particular impact are the Co-determination Act of 1976, the Shop Constitution Act of 1952, both determining the representation of employees on the AG's supervisory board, and the Commercial Code (Handelsgesetzbuch: HGB) containing general provisions applicable to all fully qualified merchants such as an AG, as well as general accounting and disclosure requirements.

An AG is characterised by its own legal personality, the limited liability of its shareholders, a fixed share capital, incorporated organisation (three tier system: general shareholders meeting; managing board; and supervisory board with manda-tory representation of employees) and anonymous membership. Shareholders can

218

be private individuals as well as corporate bodies, both domestic and foreign. All shares may be held by one shareholder.

The form of an AG is the suitable legal form for large enterprises being able to turn to the public capital market. It offers to the investor relative protection by far reaching mandatory disclosure requirements, special protective provisions and its largely obligatory law thus preserving the (minority) shareholders' right, to a great extent.

I.2.2 Incorporation

In principle, it is not necessary to obtain a licence in order to set up an AG (exceptions are the forming of banks, insurance and investment companies). The forming of an AG involves three steps:

(1) The articles of association ("articles") and the minutes of the formation have to be set up in full notarial form (powers of attorney have to be certified by a notary public). The formation instrument includes the articles and must specify:

(a) the founders;

(b) the par value, the issue price and, if any different classes of shares, those to which each incorporator subscribes; and

(c) the amount of the capital paid in.

(2) Thereafter, the incorporators must subscribe in notarial form to all the shares (the future AG may not subscribe for its own shares), whereby a sort of pre-company without legal personality is established, *i.e.* is not yet an AG. With respect to the shares, at least one-quarter of the nominal value and, if any, the entire premium must be paid in. Any contributions in kind must be fully rendered prior to application for registration. Special mandatory precautionary measures require:

(a) the rendering of a written formation report by the incorporators;

(b) the examination of the formation process by the first managing board and first supervisory board;

(c) the making of a respective examination report; and

(d) under special circumstances (*e.g.* if incorporators are to be members of the supervisory/management board, the making of contributions in kind, etc.) a separate examination report by a court appointed auditor.

(3) Finally, upon application to the commercial register (administered by the local district court) and approval of the formation process by the court, the company

219

is entered into the commercial register, whereby it acquires its legal existence as an AG.

Registration in the commercial register along with details of the newly established AG are published in the official *Federal Gazette* (*Bundesanzeiger*) and the newspapers designated in the articles. All information filed with the commercial register is available for inspection by the public.

I.2.2.1   *Articles of association (Satzung)*

The minimum contents are name, domicile and purpose of the AG, amount of share capital, par value of each share, number of shares of each par value, eventual classes of shares, issue of bearer or registered shares, number of members of the managing board and form of publications. Besides, the articles may contain provisions regarding the managing board, the supervisory board, general shareholders' meeting, annual financial reports and allocation of profits. The extent to which the articles may deviate from the principles contained in the AktG is rather limited, in particular the allocation of responsibility among the AG's three bodies may not be changed.

I.2.2.2   *Domicile (Sitz)*

The domicile must be located in Germany and have an actual relationship to the business of the AG. It is sufficient that a business establishment of the AG or the location of the management is situated or the administration is carried out at the domicile. The legal domicile determines which commercial register is responsible for the AG's registration and other filing and registration matters.

I.2.2.3   *Company name (Firma)*

The name selected has to include the full words "Aktiengesellschaft". The name itself is normally derived from the purpose of the enterprise, although an additional adaption of a personal name is permissible. Coined expressions are acceptable only if they conform with a known trademark or if they have acquired a secondary meaning. Of course the name has to be sufficiently different from all firms registered at the same place or community and may not contain deceptive elements.

I.2.2.4   *Duration*

German law allows the AG to be established for a limited period of time. Such limitation to be made by means of its articles is, however, a rare exception.

I.2.3   Shares (Aktien)

An AG may issue different classes of shares, *i.e.* common and preference shares (Vorzugsaktien), the latter representing special rights with respect to dividends, liquidation proceeds and voting rights. Whereas preferred shares may be issued without voting rights provided they have preferential rights to dividends, preferential voting rights or multiple voting rights are in principle not admissible. Issue of shares and "interim certificates" (documents that may be issued as a preliminary substitute for the final share certificates) are not permissible prior to registration of the AG. All classes of shares must have a certain par value to be 5 DM or a multiple of this amount, *e.g.* the issue of proportional/fractional shares is not possible. An AG may issue convertible bonds (Wandelschuldverschreibungen) and option warrants.

I.2.3.1   *Share capital (Grundkapital)*

The share capital must be stipulated in the articles and be denominated in Deutsche Marks. It had to amount to at least 100,000 DM. Prior to application for registration all shares must be subscribed to and at least 25 per cent of the nominal amount of the cash contributions, any premium of an over pa-par issue and all contributions in kind must have been made. Shares issued before paying in the full par-value must be registered shares.

The articles may authorise the board of management to increase the share capital up to a certain nominal amount (authorised capital) by issuing new shares against contributions during a period not exceeding five years. The nominal amount of the authorised capital may, however, not exceed one-half of the share capital existing at the date of the respective authorisation. There are strict rules on the preservation of the share capital including the prohibition to return paid contributions and, in principle, to acquire own shares, the rule that only retained earnings may be distributed, strict provisions on valuation and the requirement to form statutory reserves.

I.2.3.2   *Transfer of shares*

Bearer shares are transferred by agreement and delivery of the share certificate. Registered shares and interim certificates are legal instruments to order, whose transfer is effectuated by agreement and delivery with an endorsement of the certificates. Registered shares have to be registered in the share register book of the AG. The transfer of registered shares is contingent upon the consent of the AG which is granted by the managing board. The articles may, however, stipulate that such consent may only be granted if the supervisory board and/or the shareholders pass a consenting resolution.

I.2.3.3 *Increase/decrease of capital*

A capital increase to be specified in the articles and thus requiring an alteration of the statutes may be funded either by new funds, *i.e.* contributions by (new) shareholders, or from the AG's own funds, *i.e.* the conversion of capital reserves or revenue reserves into share capital (for authorised capital, *cf.* I.2.3.1). All existing shareholders have a pre-emptive right on the issue of new shares, which can be excluded only:

(a) by an express resolution passed with a majority of at least 75 per cent of the share capital represented; and

(b) if the exclusion is a suitable and necessary means for realising the goal of the capital increase; and

(c) the benefits for the AG resulting therefrom objectively outweigh the proportional loss of the excluded shareholders. A conditional increase is only permissible for certain objects.

Other means of increasing the financial means of the company are the issue of:

(a) bonds;

(b) convertible bonds granting the creditor a right of conversion or subscription to shares under certain conditions;

(c) income bonds granting the holder/creditor a right to interest and repayment of the capital in linkage with the shareholder's share in the profit; and

(d) usufructary (participation) rights. Existing shareholders have a right of pre-emption.

Three forms of a capital reduction are available:

(1) An ordinary capital reduction may provide for a reduction of the nominal amount or for a consolidation of shares in order to distribute the released assets to the shareholders or to form a reserve as well as to numerically reduce the share capital in order to eliminate a deficit balance.

(2) A simplified capital reduction procedure is available to offset declines in the value of assets, to cover other losses or to transfer amounts to the capital reserve.

(3) A redemption of shares is only permissible, if the shares to be redeemed have been acquired by the AG, or, if compulsory, if the redemption was provided for in the articles before the shareholders concerned acquired or subscribed to the shares The AktG provides for strict protection of creditors.

I.2.3.4 *Form of subscription*

Subscription of shares to an AG can take place in cash or in kind. Contributions in the form of contracts of employment or services are not possible. Additional precautionary matters apply to contributions in kind, in particular the need for an audit and a certificate of evaluation to be prepared by a public accountant. It is not possible to issue shares under-par. If issued over-par, which is permissible, the resulting premium is to be allocated to the capital reserves.

I.2.3.5 *Purchase of own shares*

An AG is not permitted to subscribe for its own shares. The purchase of own shares is permissible only if:

(a) it is necessary to protect the AG from severe damage;

(b) the shares are to be offered to the employees of the AG;

(c) if the acquisition is made to indemnify shareholders in connection with a contract of domination or an integration by majority resolution;

(d) if the nominal amount or a higher amount for the issue has been fully paid on the shares and the acquisition is free or the AG executes a purchase order therewith;

(e) by means of legal succession; or

(f) on the basis of a resolution of the shareholders' meeting concerning the redemption of shares.

In cases (a) to (c) the number of shares to be acquired is limited to 10 per cent of the share capital.

I.2.3.6 *Register of shares*

Registered shares are registered in the share register book setting out the holder's name, residence and occupation, which is in principle not open to the public. It may be inspected only by shareholders (both of bearer or registered shares) and those persons who have a legal interest in inspection (§ 810 German Civil Code). *Vis-à-vis* the company only those who are registered are considered to be a stockholder In the case of bearer shares possession is sufficient proof of ownership.

I.2.4   Company's Bodies

The mandatory three-tier system separates the managing board being alone competent for the management and representation, the supervisory board competent for the supervision and controlling of the management and the shareholders' meeting, which is, in principle, excluded from the management of the AG and decides only on items assigned to it by the AktG or the articles.

I.2.4.1   *Managing board (Vorstand)*

I.2.4.1.1   Appointment/dismissal of managing directors   The managing board consisting of one or more persons (and a labour relations director with equal status if the AG employs more than 2,000 employees) is appointed by the supervisory board, *i.e.* it is not possible for the shareholders' meeting to appoint or revoke the appointment of members of the managing board. Only a natural person may be appointed. There are no residential or nationality requirements for the managing directors. The maximum term of office is five years, although an appointment is renewable. A removal from office may only be made by the supervisory board and only for good cause (gross violation of duties, incapability of proper management, non-arbitrary withdrawal of confidence by the shareholders' meeting). Both appointment and removal must be registered in the commercial register.

I.2.4.1.2   Duties/powers of the managing board   The main responsibilities for the management of the AG include all measures for realising the AG's purpose in the broadest sense. The managing board further represents the AG in and out of court. If the managing board consists of several members, all of them are, in principle, only jointly responsible for the management and representation. Unless sole power of representation is granted, an AG is typically represented by two members jointly or by one member together with a Prokurist. Whereas its power of representation is unlimited and not capable of limitation, the managing board is bound by internal rules with respect to its power of management. The articles or the supervisory board may order that certain transactions require the consent of the supervisory board. If such consent is not given, the shareholders' meeting has to decide thereon if requested by the managing board. German law does not know the "*ultra vires* doctrine" so that an AG is bound by all actions even if the managing board exceeds the internal rules or the objects of the AG. The only exception applies if the third party was acting in "bad faith", *i.e.* he or she knew that the managing board was exceeding its internal power of management and was acting deliberately against the interests of the AG.

I.2.4.1.3   Rules of procedure; board meetings   The specific allocation of rights and duties among the board members and the procedures to be observed are typically set out in internal rules of procedure (Geschäftsordnung), determined by the managing board itself unless the articles provide that only the supervisory board may determine such rules, or the supervisory board does so. Resolutions of the managing board are taken unanimously unless the rules of procedure provide otherwise. In the case of a tie, the vote of one member (typically the chairman) may be the casting vote. It is not permissible that one or more board members may take decisions against the majority of the other members in the case of differences of opinion. The rules of procedure may also determine the number of board meetings, the quorum and all related procedural questions.

I.2.4.1.4 Legal liability of managing directors The managing directors have to apply a standard of care exercised by a "diligent and prudent manager" and are subject to a far reaching prohibition to compete. They are jointly and separately liable if they violate their duties. The strictness of liability is enhanced by a reversal of the burden of proof. The liability cannot be abrogated in advance nor may the AG, in principle, waive or settle a respective claim for damages. If a member grossly violates his duty of care, creditors who cannot obtain satisfaction from the AG are entitled to sue the managing directors. Finally, the AktG contains several provisions which, if violated by the managing board, result in their liability. The violation of certain statutory duties is a criminal offence.

I.2.4.2 *Supervisory board (Aufsichtsrat)*

I.2.4.2.1 Appointment, dismissal and composition The supervisory board is composed of representatives of the shareholders and employees, both having the same rights and duties. For companies which employ more than 2,000 employees the supervisory board is to be composed of equal parts of representatives of shareholders and employees. For companies with a lesser amount of employees, only one-third of the members are employees' representatives.

The supervisory board consists of at least three members up to 21 depending on the share capital. If the company is subject to full (equal number of representatives of shareholders and employees) co-determination the number is 12 to 20. Only natural persons may be elected with no restrictions on nationality or profession, unless the articles set personal requirements to be met by representatives of the shareholders. The accumulation of supervisory board posts is limited to 10 and interlocking boards are prohibited.

The shareholders' representatives are elected by the shareholders' meeting for a maximum of four years (re-election is possible) unless the articles contain a right to delegate members to certain shareholders (limited to one-third of all members). The employees' representatives are in principle, directly elected by the employees. Members of the supervisory board may be removed before the expiration of their term of office by a respective shareholders' resolution with a majority of 75 per cent of the votes cast. In the case of representatives of the employees an approving resolution by a three-quarters' majority of all employees entitled to vote is necessary.

The members of the supervisory board are not registered in the commercial register but their appointment, dismissal or resignation are published in the company's journals.

I.2.4.2.2   Duties/powers of supervisory board   The main duties are the supervision of the management by the managing board, and the appointment and removal of the managing board (for good cause only). The managing board is required to disclose all relevant information and to report regularly, at lest once per calendar quarter, to the supervisory board, each member of which has extensive information rights. For certain kinds of transactions the supervisory board must grant its consent if so required by law, the articles or the supervisory board itself. An allocation of the management duties to the supervisory board is not possible. The power of representation is limited to the representation of the AG *vis-à-vis* the managing board.

I.2.4.2.3   Rules of procedure; board meetings   The internal organisation is determined by the AktG, where applicable the Co-determination Act, the articles and, in addition, by rules of procedure as determined by the supervisory board itself. Decisions are taken by special resolutions to be passed, in principle, by a simple majority. In companies with full co-determination the chairman has a casting vote in certain cases. Quarterly board meetings are the rule but, if not, board meetings have to take place at least once per calender half year. Meetings may be called by each member or the managing board.

I.2.4.2.4   Legal liability of the supervisory board   The liability of the members of the supervisory board follows the same pattern as those of the managing board. Members of the supervisory board are, however, not subject to a prohibition against competition.

I.2.4.3   *The (annual) shareholders' meeting (Hauptversammlung)*

I.2.4.3.1   General provisions   The AktG does not differentiate between an annual and an extraordinary shareholders' meeting but at least one meeting must be held annually to decide on the appropriation of retained earnings, the appointment of the annual auditor and the release from responsibility of the managing and supervisory board.

I.2.4.3.2   The convening of a shareholders' meeting   The shareholders' meeting is called by the managing board if required under the AktG, the articles or for the benefit of the AG. The supervisory board is also entitled and obliged to call a shareholders' meeting if necessary in the interest of the AG. Shareholders representing at least 5 per cent of the share capital may request the calling of a shareholders' meeting. If such a request is not honoured, the minority shareholders may be authorised to convene the general meeting by a respective court order.

I.2.4.3.3 Notices for the shareholders' meeting The notice period for calling a shareholders' meeting is at least one month. The notice must be published in a prescribed form along with an announcement of the agenda, which has to contain the proposals of the administration on each item on which the shareholders' meeting should decide. Shareholders representing at least 5 per cent of the share capital are entitled to have further items put on the agenda. No decision may be taken on items not properly published.

I.2.4.3.4 Place of the shareholders' meeting Unless the articles provide differently, the location will be at the domicile of the AG. However, the place of the meeting must, in principle, be located in Germany.

I.2.4.3.5 Duties/powers of the shareholders' meeting The shareholders' meeting has no comprehensive competence but is restricted to the duties assigned to it by the AktG or the articles. Besides the items of the annual meeting (*cf.* I.2.4.3.1), the shareholders' meeting decides exclusively on all questions related to the legal and economic organisation of the AG, in particular on amendments to the articles or in the capital base, so-called enterprise agreements (*e.g.* contracts on domination; profit and loss pooling agreements), integration, merger and transformation, transfer of all assets as well as the dissolution and liquidation of the AG. On questions of management the shareholders' meeting may only decide at the request of the managing board and in cases of extreme importance ("Holzmüller" case).

All resolutions of the shareholders must be recorded in notarial form and, in principle, are passed by a simple majority of the votes cast. For certain resolutions of special significance (*e.g.* amendment to the articles) a qualified capital majority of at least three-quarters of the capital stock represented is also necessary. If several classes of shares have been issued, often special resolutions of the disadvantaged shareholders are required.

I.2.4.3.6 Voting rights and restrictions In principle, each issued share grants a voting right in accordance with the par-value of the share. If a preference dividend which is a prerequisite for the issue of non-voting preference shares is not fully paid in a year and if the arrears are not paid up in the next year together with the full benefit of that year, then the preference shareholders have a voting right until the arrears have been paid up. Multiple voting rights are in principle impermissible. It is, however, possible to provide for a maximum number of votes to be exercised by a shareholder regardless of his actual shareholding or otherwise limit voting rights by graduation as long as such limitations do not aim at individual shareholders (*e.g.* foreign shareholders) only. The voting rights for own shares held by the AG or a controlled enterprise are fully suspended.

A voting right might be exercised by a holder of a written proxy. In most cases the articles make the exercise of the right to vote conditional upon the shareholder depositing his shares by a certain date prior to the meeting. All shareholders present are listed in a roster of participants available for inspection prior to the vote. In principle, contracts of shareholders stating how to exercise their voting rights (pooling agreement) are valid.

Each shareholder, including those holding non-voting preference shares, is entitled to participate in the meeting and has a right to information concerning the AG to the extent necessary for an appropriate evaluation of the items on the agenda. Resolutions may be contested in court, but there are special provisions on the right to rescind, the time limits to be observed and a possible ratification of resolutions.

I.2.4.4 *Works council (Betriebsrat)*

A works council may be established in every enterprise with more than five employees. The works council is to be informed and consulted and partly has a certain right of co-determination on various internal matters affecting the employees. There is, however, no co-determination regarding the management of the company. The employees' rights are exercised through their representation on the supervisory board.

I.2.5   Accounting and Auditing

After the implementation of the E.C. Accounting Directives, the German regulations concerning accounting, auditing and publications are basically the same as in the other E.C. countries.

I.2.5.1 *Appointment and dismissal of auditors*

Each AG which is not considered to be a small company must be examined by a qualified auditor annually elected by the general meeting. If not appointed by the end of the financial year, a court will appoint an auditor. A small company is defined as not exceeding at least two of the following criteria:

(a) 3.9 million DM balance sheet total after deducting a deficit disclosed on the assets side;

(b) 8 million DM sales;

(c) annual average of 50 employees.

I.2.5.2 *Duties and powers of auditors*

The auditor must report in writing on the results of his examination and, in the absence of objections, the examination must be confirmed by a respective statement to the effect that the accounting records and the financial statements comply with the legal regulations. Unless left to the determination by the shareholders' meeting, the annual financial statements are determined by being approved by the managing board and the supervisory board. In principle, the financial statements together with the auditor's certificate have to be filed with the commercial register where they are open for public inspection. In addition, details of which commercial register the documents have been filed have to be published in the *Federal Gazette*. The extent of the disclosure requirements varies according to the size of the AG. The auditors are obliged to perform a conscientious and independent audit and to maintain confidentiality. In case of a violation of such duties the auditor is liable to pay damages.

I.2.6 Partnership Limited by Shares (Kommanditgesellschaft auf Aktien)

The AktG provides for another legal form, namely the Kommanditgesellschaft auf Aktien which is a hybrid form of a limited partnership and an AG.

I.2.7 Costs of Incorporating an Aktiengesellschaft

The major expenses incurred in forming an AG consists of:

(a) The public notary's fees include drawing up and executing the articles. The fee is subject to the size of the capital up to a maximum of 10 million DM. The fee will vary between 520 DM (capital of 100,000 DM) and 30,000 DM (capital of 10 million DM). For the notarisation of the appointment of the first supervisory board and the auditor a further fee is payable (160 DM: capital of 100,000 DM; 1,566 DM: capital of 10 million DM). Notarial fees have also to be paid for the notarisation of the application to the commercial register (130 DM: capital of 100,000 DM; 805 DM; capital of 10 million DM).

(b) There are no charges payable to the Chamber of Commerce.

(c) Upon entry of the AG into the commercial register, court fees are payable (260 DM: capital of 100,000 DM; 15,000 DM: capital of 10 million DM).

(d) The above-mentioned fees are minimum charges. Additional fees will be charged when problems result in more correspondence, translations or discussions and further consultation of the public notary or other professional advisors.

THE LIMITED LIABILITY COMPANY (GESELLSCHAFT MIT BESCHRÄNKTER HAFTUNG: GmbH)

I.3.1 Introduction

The limited liability company is one of the success stories in German business legislation. The newly created legal form, particularly designed to serve small and medium-sized enterprises or large enterprises with only a few shareholders, has won general acceptance within the business community. By the end of 1989, the number of GmbHs had risen to almost 400,000 with an aggregate share capital of approximately 180 billion DM. The vast majority of all German subsidiaries of foreign corporations are GmbHs. The GmbH, more generally speaking, is also the adequate legal form for all enterprises which secure their financing from other sources than the public capital market.

The GmbH is a legal entity (§ 13 sect. 1 GmbH-Act) which offers a wide range of flexibility in its structure. After a reform of the GmbH-Act in 1980 (and in line with applicable E.C. directives), it may now be formed from the outset as a one-person company with limited liability. The major advantage of the GmbH compared to the various existing forms of partnerships is the limited personal liability of its shareholders. Generally speaking, the shareholders are not liable to the company's creditors for the company's debts so that the entrepreneurial risk can effectively be limited to the minimum capital stock of 50,000 DM. Compared to the AG, the GmbH offers more flexibility, simplified internal decision-making and, in principle, lower transaction costs. It affords the shareholder(s) better control of the company than they would have in case of an AG. The transfer of GmbH participations ("Geschäftsanteile", hereafter simply referred to as "shares") and the access to the capital market, on the other hand, are more difficult to accomplish than in case of an AG.

I.3.2 Formation of the Company

In comparison to the AG, the GmbH is procedurally less complicated to form. Three subsequent stages characterise the formation process:

(a) the execution of the articles of association;

(b) the subscription to the original capital contributions; and

(c) the registration in the commercial register of the court district where the company has chosen its domicile. The latter must be within German national territory and is usually the place of its corporate office or principal place of business activity.

I.3.2.1 *Articles of association*

In order to assure a proper formation, § 3 of the GmbH-Act demands certain minimum contents of the articles of association. They include the purpose of the business, the name of the company, its domicile, both the amount of the share capital and of the individual contributions. If appropriate, the articles should identify the duration of the company's existence.

I.3.2.1.1 Company name Some attention has to be paid to the selection of the company's name. In order to facilitate identification of the company in business, its name must either be derived from the company's purpose, or contain the name(s) of (one or several) shareholder(s) together with an indication of a corporate relationship. Also a combination of both ways to name the company is possible. The use of foreign language elements, trademarks or proper names is permitted, subject to applicable legislation.

In order to avoid confusion with existing companies, the selection of the name requires the approval of the local Chamber of Commerce at the company's domicile. This requirement and the commercial register's monitoring of the name selection often create problems to which non-German shareholders are not used.

I.3.2.1.2 Share capital subscription and payment The shareholders have to sub-scribe to the entire original capital before registration. An application for entry of the company into the commercial register can only be made, if at least one-quarter of each original capital contribution has been paid in and the total amount of the paid-in contributions equals 25,000 DM. For the formation of a one-shareholder company, the GmbH-Act additionally requires a security for the remaining contribution(s).

I.3.2.2 *Formation procedure*

The articles of association must be signed by all shareholders and recorded by a notary. In addition, the shareholders' signatures must be authenticated by a notary. The notarial form may also be satisfied by a German consular officer acting outside of German territory.

I.3.2.2.1 Appointment of managing directors Unless an appointment is already made in the articles, the managing directors have to be appointed before an application for registration can be filed. Each managing director has to give a sample signature in front of a notary or consular officer, who will also inform the director about the statutory obligations imposed on him in the new office. The managing directors may then apply for registration of the GmbH, once they have ensured payment of the minimum capital contributions (*cf.* I.3.2.1.2).

I.3.2.2.2 The application The application has to contain information on the formation of the GmbH in compliance with the provisions of the GmbH-Act. It has to be accompanied by all documents necessary to enable the local court to control the proper formation. In particular, the articles, proof of the appointment of the managing directors and a list of all shareholders with their respective capital subscriptions have to be attached.

I.3.2.3 *Registration, costs and time-frame*

The local court of registration is obliged to examine all formal requirements for a GmbH-formation. With the registration, the GmbH comes into existence as a legal entity. The following publication of the registration is merely for declaratory purposes. From the moment of registration, the concept of limited liability of the GmbH is applicable and the shareholders' unlimited liability during the period of formation (*cf.* I.3.6) ceases.

The costs of registration include the notary's fees and the court fees for registration and publication. The fees vary depending on the stated capital of the company. For a GmbH with the (minimum) stated capital of 50,000 DM, the total fees would generally amount to approximately 3,000 DM. For companies with an elevated share capital, the fees may increase to, for instance, around DM 50,000 for a company with a share capital of 10 million DM. The legal fees of the lawyers involved will obviously depend on whether standard language can be used or whether any specific issues require in-depth consideration and drafting.

The process of formation, from the signing of the articles up to the registration in the commercial register, usually takes between four and six weeks.

I.3.3 Shares, Shareholders and Contributions

I.3.3.1 *Share Capital*

The basic function of the share capital is to ensure a minimum satisfaction of creditors' claims and to enable an evaluation of the company's standing. The minimum amount of share capital required is 50,000 DM. The minimum participation of each shareholder is fixed at 500 DM, but any amount may be agreed upon as long as it is a multiple of 100 DM. The general rule of contributions to the GmbH is a share capital contribution in an amount of money, expressed in DM. Such a cash contribution may validly be made by crediting the company's bank account in Germany. The shareholders may not be released from their obligations to make the contributions. Equally, a set-off against the obligation to contribute is not possible.

I.3.3.2 Contributions in kind

As an exception to the rule of capital contributions in money, the GmbH-Act allows contributions in kind. This possibility has led to a variety of problems concerning the process of formation and shareholder liability. In order to constitute a valuable contribution in kind, transferable assets of whatever nature have to be definitely and fully placed to the free disposal of the managing directors prior to the registration. Furthermore, they have to be evaluated within the articles of association. In addition, it is necessary to prepare a formal report on the formation and consideration of contributions in kind which must set forth the essential circumstances from which the evaluation of these contributions results, a requirement which often leads to practical difficulties and inevitably to a substantial extension of the time period for the establishment of a GmbH. The local court of registration has to review the value stated in the articles and may reject an application for registration, if the value does not reach the stated amount of the share capital contribution(s).

I.3.3.3 Transfer of shares

The transfer of shares is subject to certain formalities. Both the agreement to transfer and the effective transfer require the notarial form. The lack of proper form of an agreement to undertake a transfer is remedied by a transfer agreement respecting the required notarial form. This requirement of notarial form applies as well to agreements containing options to sell or to purchase, pre-emptive rights or pre-contracts. It is even considered necessary for mere sale offers and respective acceptances. In principle, any transfer of GmbH shares must be notarised by a German notary. Under German regulations, the fees of the notary depend on the (actual, not stated) value of the shares. These fees may be astronomical if interests in important companies are transferred. This is the reason why a significant practice has developed of having such transfers, particularly in the context of mergers and acquisitions, notarised by a non-German (notably Swiss or Dutch) notary. German courts have accepted this practice on a case-by-case basis. As their decisions continue to be challenged by lower courts and some commentators, it is essential to fully comply with the requirements established for a non-German notarisation (as otherwise the transaction may be held void by a German court or fiscal authority).

The articles of association can (and often do) require additional formalities or impose restrictions on the possibility of transfer. Such restrictions may require the prior consent of the company to any kind of transfer or impose a particular qualification upon the transfer. The transfer of shares may be subordinated to the approval of the company. In this case, the articles have to state which organ of the company is competent to pronounce such an approval.

Upon the transfer, the company has to be supplied with a copy of the transfer document. This notification may be performed by either party or by their representatives. Since the transfer of shares is not publicly registered, it is advisable to demand, prior to the conclusion of a transfer agreement, the presentation of an uninterrupted sequence of transfer documents in notarial form. This is the only way to ascertain that the transferor is in fact owner of the share.

I.3.3.4 *Acquisition of own shares*

If not otherwise stated in the articles, the company itself may acquire shares. A GmbH may only acquire own shares on which the share capital contributions have been fully paid in so far as the acquisition can be paid out of assets existing in excess of the amount of the share capital. Apart from this requirement, there is no limitation on the amount of own shares to be acquired by a GmbH.

I.3.3.5 *Shareholder rights and obligations*

I.3.3.5.1 Shareholder rights The shareholders' rights to be involved in the administration of the company essentially consist of the right to vote, the right to participate in shareholder meetings and the right to receive information on the activities of the company. Each of these rights may be defined in more detail in the company's articles. The right to vote can even be excluded by the issuance of non-voting shares. The voting right is generally exercised according to the amount of capital share contributions and may be cast by proxy. A shareholder has no right to vote if the passing of a resolution creates a particularly important conflict of interest, such as for a legal transaction between the company and himself. The individual shareholder is generally free in the way in which he exercises his voting right, but may not acquire advantages or abuse his majority position to the detriment of the company.

Share ownership also carries the right to receive a part of the profits according to the proportion of shares. § 29 GmbH-Act states that this right may be modified or excluded by the articles or a resolution voted by the shareholders. The individual shareholder only has a right to receive payment, however, once a determination on the distribution of the annual profits has been made.

I.3.3.5.2   Shareholder obligations   The principal obligation imposed on the share-holders is to fulfil the subscribed original capital contribution. In order to ensure this obligation, the GmbH-Act imposes a particular liability upon the shareholders. Defaulting shareholders must pay overdue interest. Furthermore, the articles may impose all kinds of duties upon the shareholders such as collaboration, availability as a consultant, service as a managing director and refraining from competition (the latter obligation may also exist as a statutory obligation without a specific provision in the articles).

I.3.3.6   Repayments

The GmbH-Act establishes the principle of preservation of the share capital. As far as the assets of the company are required for maintaining the share capital, the company is prevented from effecting payments to its shareholders, unless a full consideration for such payment is rendered to the company. The prohibition enters into force, if the net worth of the GmbH no longer equals the amount of the stated capital.

I.3.3.6.1   Refund of prohibited payments   If payments have been effected to a shareholder in violation of the prohibition to repay the share capital of the company, the recipient is obliged to refund what he has received. If he acted in good faith, the refund may only be claimed to the extent necessary for the satisfaction of the company's creditors. If a refund cannot be obtained from the recipient, the remaining shareholders are liable as far as is necessary to pay the company's creditors. Their liability depends on the proportion of their subscribed share capital contributions.

I.3.3.6.2   "Capital replacing loans"   Once the shareholders have made their con-tributions they are no longer obliged to provide additional funds. If a shareholder nevertheless provides the company with extra funds by means of loans, his right to receive repayment is not a mere shareholder right, but a third-party right equivalent to the rights of other creditors. The legal position of the respective shareholder, therefore, would be considerably stronger than in case of a supplementary con-tribution. In order to avoid abuse of this possibility, the GmbH-Act restricts the repayment of loans considered as "capital-replacing", if the company if in financial difficulties.

The definition of capital-replacing loans is quite broad. A loan is considered to have such an effect, if it is "made by a shareholder at a time when shareholders acting as orderly merchants would instead have provided capital to the company". The GmbH-Act even takes a further step and declares the limitation on repayments applicable for other legal transactions of a shareholder or a third party "which are the commercial equivalent of the granting of a loan". A legal transaction or a loan is of "capital-replacing" nature, if the company would not have been able to obtain the same conditions on the market from a third party.

Capital-replacing loans may not be reclaimed in case of bankruptcy or composition proceedings. If the company has repaid during the last year preceding bankruptcy proceedings a loan guaranteed or otherwise secured by a shareholder, this shareholder is obliged to refund the amount repaid by the company to the extent that a third party cannot be compensated from the bankruptcy proceeds. If the repayment has reduced the share capital, the shareholder has to pay back the amount necessary to restore the share capital.

I.3.3.6.3 "Hidden contributions in kind" If contributions in kind are to be made, the articles must clearly specify their nature and state the amount of the share capital contributions which they are intended to cover (see I.3.3.2). If the articles provide for a cash contribution and the company subsequently purchases assets from a shareholder which would qualify for a contribution in kind, such purchase may be considered as a repayment of the share capital contribution and might give rise to a liability up to the amount of the repaid share capital contribution. This doctrine which prohibits hidden contributions in kind intends to protect the strict rules on the raising of a GmbH's stated capital. It is of critical importance particularly in the context of leveraged buy-outs. The essential tests which the German courts apply to determine whether a transaction qualifies as a hidden contribution in kind is whether there is a correlation in time and substance between the fulfilment of the share capital contribution and the purchase of assets from a shareholder.

I.3.4 Corporate Structure

The structure of the GmbH is characterised by two main organs: the managing director(s) and the shareholder(s). The articles of association may additionally provide for a supervisory board. For companies with more than 500 employees, a supervisory board is mandatory.

I.3.4.1 *The managing director(s) (Geschäftsführer)*

The main task of the managing directors is to ensure management and representation of the company. If several managing directors are appointed, they may only jointly represent and act for the company. This legal principle can be altered by the articles. Individual representation of managing directors or joint representation of two managing directors or of one together with a holder of the power of Prokura (Prokurist) are all very common. The managing directors themselves have to follow instructions given by the shareholders and have to observe all limitations imposed upon them by the articles. Such limitations of the authority of the managing directors, however, remain without legal effect towards third persons. Additionally, the company is liable towards third persons for the acts of the managing directors.

I.3.4.1.1 Liability Managing directors who violate their obligations are jointly and severally liable to the company for the resulting damage. The standard of diligence is the one of an orderly businessman. A particularly important example of liability to the company concerns any payments effected after an insolvency or over-indebtedness of the company.

I.3.4.1.2 Appointment and dismissal Managing directors can either be appointed in the articles or by a resolution of the shareholders. The right of appointment may be transferred to another organ, such as the supervisory board. If a GmbH has a mandatory supervisory board, the competence to appoint the managing directors is with such a board. In general, the duration of the appointment of the managing directors is not limited in time. Dismissal of managing directors is permitted at any time notwithstanding claims resulting from employment contracts.

I.3.4.1.3 Qualification In general, there is no particular qualification required for appointment as a managing director. Every natural person capable of contracting may serve, unless he or she has been convicted because of certain offences. Nationality, domicile or permissions from public authorities do not constitute obstacles to the appointment as managing directors, but the articles of association may establish additional requirements for an appointment.

I.3.4.2 *Shareholder meetings (Gesellschafterversammlungen)*

Although control and management rights belong to the individual shareholder, their exercise in general is collective. With regard to all matters of the company, the shareholders constitute the ultimate authority of the GmbH. Shareholder resolutions are normally passed by simple majority votes, but different majorities may be stipulated in the articles.

The general procedure is to take resolutions in meetings. This is only mandatory for resolutions carrying amendments to the articles (such amendments have to be notarised). For all other kinds of resolutions no meeting is required, if all shareholders either consent in writing to a proposed resolution or agree to cast the votes in writing. Additional facilitations can be stated by the articles, *e.g.* the exchange of telefax messages as long as individual shareholders do not object.

A shareholder meeting has to be called by the managing directors or the supervisory board if it appears to be necessary in the interest of the company. The place of meeting, if not established by the articles, is determined at the reasonable discretion of the authority competent to call the meeting. It can take place on or out of German territory.

Notice of the meeting is to be sent by registered letter at least one week in advance. With the convocation, the purpose of the meeting shall be announced. If a procedural defect occurs, valid resolutions may nevertheless be passed, if all shareholders are present in the meeting.

I.3.4.3   *Supervision of the management*

GmbHs need not have a supervisory board. Frequently, shareholders nevertheless opt for the establishment of such a board in order to facilitate corporate governance and management control. Such a "voluntary" supervisory board may, but need not, be governed by the rules on supervisory boards of share corporations (see above I.2.4.2). The shareholders have a large amount of discretion to determine the rules on the structure, competence, and decision-making of such board. If the board is not structured along the lines of an AG's supervisory board, it is often called an "advisory board" (Beirat).

I.3.4.3.1   **Mandatory supervisory board**   The establishment of a supervisory board is mandatory in the following circumstances:

(a)   GmbHs with more than 500 employees are obliged to establish a supervisory board composed of one-third of employee representatives (§§ 76, 77 Shop Constitution Act).

(b)   For even larger GmbHs with more than 2,000 employees, the Co-determination Act of 1976 requires an equal number of representatives from the shareholders and from the employees (the details are the same as for the supervisory board of share corporations of that size, see I.2.4.1.1 above).

I.3.4.3.2   **Accounting and auditing**   The statutory rules on the accounting and auditing of a GmbH are basically the same ones as for an AG. If the GmbH does not have a supervisory board, the annual financial statements have to be approved by the shareholders. If there is a supervisory board, the managing directors have to submit to the board the annual financial statement together with a business report. The supervisory board is then entitled to review the results and to report these in writing to the shareholders. The final adoption of the results is generally made by the shareholders.

I.3.5   Amendment of the Articles of Association

Since the articles govern both the organisational structure and business activities of the company, an amendment is perceived as a major change. It is therefore subject to particular procedural requirements.

I.3.5.1   *Resolution, application, registration*

To effect an amendment, a shareholder resolution has to be voted by a majority of three-quarters. In this respect, the articles may establish further requirements, but no facilitations so that the articles may not allow an amendment to be passed by smaller majorities than three-quarters. Amendments concerning basic principles, such as the equal treatment or the ranting of preferential rights need the consent of all shareholders. Furthermore, the amending resolution must be recorded in notarial form, registered by the local court and published.

I.3.5.2   *Increase and decrease of capital*

Increases and decreases of capital are, generally speaking, the most important amendments to be made to the articles. In case of an increase of capital, the minimum amount required by law has to be paid prior to registration. The provisions to assure a proper formation of the GmbH apply accordingly. The procedure to realise a reduction in capital is even more demanding. It has to be published three times together with the request to the creditors to report to the company. Additionally, a registration of the resolution to decrease the capital can only come into effect after a waiting period of one year.

As this procedure of capital reduction proved to be too complicated in many cases of recapitalisation, the GmbH-Act now offers, similar to the Stock Corporation Act (AktG), the possibility of a simplified procedure. Oppressing the rules concerning the protection of creditors, this simplified procedure applies if the reduction is supposed to offset declines in the value of assets or to cover other losses.

I.3.6   Cases of Unlimited Shareholder Liability

Despite the fact that limited liability constitutes the principal characteristic of a GmbH, an unlimited liability of the shareholders is possible under certain circumstances.

I.3.6.1   *Pre-registration liability*

As described above (*cf.* I.3.2.3), the GmbH comes into legal existence with registration. Even before this formal act, a company exists from the moment of adoption of the articles. This pre-incorporation company is liable to third parties with the company assets.

A quite different and far-reaching liability is on the managing directors during the process of formation. In this period, the managing directors are personally, jointly and severally liable to any third party. This liability is *not* limited to the amount of capital share contributions, and therefore constitutes a rather serious form of liability. Before the company' registration, it can only be excluded by explicit agreement with the third party concerned.

I.3.6.2   *Liability for pre-registration losses*

After registration, the shareholders remain liable for so-called pre-registration losses. If the net assets of the GmbH in the moment of registration do not equal the subscribed share capital contributions, the shareholders are liable for the difference in the amount of the underfunding.

I.3.6.3   *Piercing the corporate veil*

In a number of cases, the German courts have developed the circumstances in which a shareholder may not rely on a GmbH's limited liability. The most important ones of these are thin capitalisation and the mixing-up between the company's and the shareholders' assets. If a GmbH is a member of a group of companies (Konzern), the parent company may be liable for the subsidiary's obligations, if it exercises corporate governance on a permanent basis. The details of these liabilities are fairly complex and depend very much on the particular circumstances of a case.

I.3.7   Dissolution and Liquidation

Dissolution generally is caused by expiration of the company's determined duration, by a resolution of the shareholders voted with a three-quarters' majority, by judgment or following bankruptcy proceedings. Upon dissolution, liquidation takes place unless bankruptcy proceedings have been initiated. The liquidation is, in principle, executed by the managing directors; the applicable procedure is described in detail in the GmbH-Act.

SECTION 4

TRANSFORMATION

I.4.1   German law now offers the possibility to transform commercial partnerships, companies and other legal entities. The new Transformation Act (Umwandlungsgesetz) provides for four forms of transformation: merger and splitting off of companies, transfer of all assets and change of legal structure. The detailed provisions of the Transformation Act are supplemented by the Transformation Tax Act (Umwandlungssteuergesetz)), which makes it possible to transform a company without triggering capital gain taxes in most of the cases.

240

GREECE

SECTION 1

CLASSIFICATION OF BUSINESS ORGANISATIONS: INTRODUCTION*

J.1.0 The following categories are the main business organisations recognised and regulated by Greek law:

—individual enterprise (Atomiki Epihirisi).

—partnerships:

(a) partnership of unlimited liability (Omorrithmos Eteria: OE).

(b) partnership of limited liability (Eterorrithmos Eteria: EE).

—limited liability companies:

(a) limited liability company (Eteria Periorismenis Efthinis: EPE).

(b) public limited company (Anonimos Eteria: AE).

In this section a short reference will be made to two other forms of business operations, namely, branch offices, and Law 89/67 offices of foreign enterprises.

In addition to the above, there exist some other forms of business organisations regulated usually by specific legislation such as co-operative societies, football public limited companies, banking institutions, insurance companies, stock-broking companies, civil law partnerships, joint ventures, shipping companies, etc., which are beyond the scope of this work.

J.1.1 Individual Enterprise (Atomiki Epihirisi)

This is an enterprise run by a single person. It is the simplest form of business organisation and there are no specific laws and regulations to deal with it. Anyone who is able to transact validly under civil law is entitled to engage himself as an individual in business activity.

The individual is the only one to decide on all business affairs throughout the life of the enterprise. He earns the profits and suffers the losses of his business activity. There is no minimum capital requirement and he may invest in his business

* Costas Vainanidis, Vainanidis, Schina & Economou (full particulars are listed in the Appendix).

243

without any formality at any time and to such amount as he thinks proper. The property of the enterprise is not distinguished from the personal property of the entrepreneur. In other words, whatever belongs to the enterprise belongs at the same time to the individual himself and whatever belongs to the individual is subject to claims by the business or private creditors of the individual in question.

Of course, once the entrepreneur starts his business activities he must notify this fact to the competent tax authorities and register himself and any employees he may have with the appropriate insurance fund.

J.1.2 Branch Offices or Agencies of Foreign Enterprises

Foreign limited liability companies or public liability companies may establish branches or agencies in Greece. In order to effect this a license of establishment is required.

If the foreign company is a limited liability company, in order to obtain such a license, it must produce evidence that:

(a) it is lawfully established in the foreign country where it has its place of establishment;

(b) it has appointed a local representative and process agent, by power of attorney executed by the foreign competent organ of the company before a consular authority or legalised by the same;

(c) a Greek company may establish a branch in the foreign country where the foreign company has its place of establishment (reciprocity).

The license is issued following a decision of the competent prefect. Such decision is registered with the relevant registry kept with the court of first instance of the district of the place of establishment of the branch or agency in question.

Foreign public limited companies, apart from the appointment by power of attorney of a local representative and process agent, have to make known to the authorities the year of incorporation and have to submit to the competent prefecture a list of the names of the company's representatives at its place of establishment. Any subsequent change to such elements should be notified to the prefecture. Moreover, public limited companies operating a branch or agency in Greece must, within three months of the annual general assembly's meeting, submit to the Ministry a copy of its balance sheet together with a report referring to the activities of the Greek branch or agency during the last fiscal year.

Branches and agencies have no legal personality and they may not sue or be sued as such.

J.1.3 Law 89/67 on Offices of Foreign Enterprises

Foreign commercial and industrial companies and foreign individual entrepreneurs of any type and kind, lawfully operating in their home-country and dealing exclusively with commercial operations whose object is outside Greece, may establish an office in Greece under the provisions of Law 89/67 as amended. The permit of establishment is granted by the Ministry of National Economy.

Offices operating under the status of Law 89/67 enjoy certain benefits, for example, they are exempted from Greek taxes, they may keep their books in a foreign language, they may import free from custom duties and other charges all necessary office equipment, vehicles, household equipment and private cars of its foreign employees, who are also entitled to obtain work permits regardless of their nationality etc.

In return, all expenses for the operation of Law 89/67 offices must be met by imported foreign currency converted to Greek drachmas. At present, the yearly minimum requirement of imported foreign currency is U.S. $50,000. Moreover, a bank guarantee of U.S. $50,000 must be deposited with the competent Ministry. The guarantee is forfeited in favour of the state in case of breach of the relevant legislation by the personnel of the Law 89/67 office.

SECTION 2

PARTNERSHIPS

J.2.1 General

Commercial partnerships, in general, are regulated by the Commercial Code and subsidiarily by the Civil Code. Such partnerships are mainly used by small-sized businesses. Two or more partners, either individuals or legal entities, may establish by private instrument a partnership in order to carry out joint commercial transactions. On the basis of tax considerations, partnerships are appropriate in particular when anticipated profits are not very high, when the registered capital is small and when the partners wish to keep the establishment and running costs low. Partnerships have a fixed capital which is recorded in the articles of incorporation, but there is no minimum capital requirement.

Running costs may be kept low because the keeping of partnership books does not require sophisticated accounting techniques: a book to record purchases or gross income and expenses is sufficient. Moreover, partnership articles of association are executed by the parties concerned in private without using the services of a notary public and without the need to publish notices in the *Government Gazette* or in any other newspaper. No shares are issued. The administration of the firm (unless stated to the contrary in the articles of incorporation) is entrusted to all the partners acting collectively. Nevertheless, normally one or more administrators, partners or third parties, are appointed as administrators by common agreement.

Decisions on all company affairs are normally taken unanimously, unless the articles of incorporation provide otherwise. The private agreement of the parties concerned incorporating the articles of association is merely submitted to the competent tax authority and it is then registered at the companies registry kept with the court of first instance of the district where the partnership has its registered office. The partners are obliged to register themselves and the employees of the partnership to the appropriate insurance fund. Partnerships possess legal personality therefore they have the ability to sue and to be sued in their own name.

There exist two main types of partnerships depending on whether all or some of the partners have unlimited personal liability for the debts of the partnership.

J.2.2   Partnership of Unlimited Liability (Omorrithmos Eteria: OE)

The characteristic feature of a partnership of unlimited liability (known as OE), is the unlimited, joint and several liability of each individual partner for all the debts and liabilities of the partnership. As a result, the personal property of each partner is subject to claims by creditors of the partnership for the whole amount due by the partnership to third parties. Court judgments issued against the partnership are executed against the individual partners without the need to prove that the assets of the partnership are not sufficient to satisfy such claims. Where a partner has satisfied a creditor of the company from personal funds, he is entitled to claim from the other partners and/or from the partnership the amount paid to the creditors. Any partner who resigns from the company is liable for debts and liabilities of the partnership to third parties having arisen up to the day of his resignation.

J.2.3   Partnership of Limited Liability (Eterorrithmos Eteria: EE)

The general features referring to commercial partnerships as outlined above are equally applicable to partnerships of limited liability.

The characteristic feature of a partnership of limited liability (known as EE) is that at least one of its partners (unlimited partner) has unlimited liability for all the debts and liabilities of the partnership, whereas the liability of the remaining partners (limited partners) is restricted to their capital contributions only. It should be noted that once the name of a limited partner is included in the company name or he is involved in the management of the partnership his liability becomes unlimited.

SECTION 3

LIMITED LIABILITY COMPANIES

J.3.1 General

One could argue that the title "limited liability companies" is misleading. In reality, the companies themselves are fully liable for debts to their creditors. It is the partners or shareholders of such companies who have limited liability in the sense that they merely take the risk of losing the capital contributed to such companies whereas they are not liable to company creditors through their personal assets.

Two more types of limited liability companies will be examined here, namely;

(a) the eteria periorismenis efthinis (EPE) which is a company introduced to fill the gap between public limited companies (Anonimos Eteria: AE) and partnerships, and

(b) the anonimos eteria, which is a public company similar to the british public limited company or the french société anonyme.

J.3.2 Limited Liability Company (Eteria Periorismenis Efthinis: EPE)

J.3.2.1 Introduction

The eteria periorismenis efthinis (EPE) is a company combining features of a partnership and of a public limited company. One or more persons, irrespective of nationality, may establish a limited liability company. This type of company has its own legal personality and it is fully and solely responsible through its property for its corporate obligations. The liability of its partners is limited to the amount contributed by them to the corporate capital of the company. Limited liability companies are regulated by Law 3190/1955 "on limited liability companies", as amended.

The main advantages of this type of company, which is normally chosen by small and medium-sized businesses, are as follows:

(a) the liability of the partners is limited to their capital contributions: as a result the personal assets of the partners are not subject to claims by company creditors;

(b) the minimum capital requirement for the formation of a limited liability company is low (3,000,000 dr) compared to the capital of a public limited company (10,000,000 dr);

(c) it is more flexible, in the sense that the formalities for running such a company are less complicated than in case of public liability companies;

(d) the partners play a vital role in the operation and decision making process of the company.

J.3.2.2   Articles of association

The articles of association are executed by the partners of the company, or by their proxies before a notary public. The notarial deed which incorporates the agreement of the partners must contain the following:

(a) the name, profession, residence and nationality of the partners;

(b) the name of the company;

(c) the place of establishment and the objects of the company;

(d) the designation of the company as a "limited liability company";

(e) the capital of the company, the share of participation and the multiple company parts, if any, of each partner, and certificate by the partners confirming that the capital of the company has been paid in;

(f) the contributions in kind, their valuation and the name of the contributor;

(g) the duration of the company.

Within one month from the execution of the notarial deed, a certified copy of the same must be registered with the secretary of the court of first instance in the place of establishment of the company concerned. An entry of a summary of the articles of incorporation is also published in the *Government Gazette*.

J.3.2.3   Duration

It is a fixed period of time.

J.3.2.4   Capital requirement-share capital-company parts

There is a minimum capital requirement of 3,000,000 dr which must be fully paid up at the time that the notarial deed is signed. At least 1,500,000 dr must be paid in cash. Contributions in kind are valued by an Experts' Committee provided by Art. 9 of codified Law 2190/1920. An EPE is not allowed to issue shares. The capital is divided into "company parts" the nominal value of which cannot be less than 10,000 dr each or a multiple thereof. Each partner has one "share of participation" but he may have one or more "company parts".

J.3.2.5   Transfer of company parts

Unless the articles of incorporation provide otherwise, company parts are freely transferable. Quite often, the articles of incorporation provide that the existing holders of company parts have pre-emption rights over company parts offered for sale in priority to third parties. Transfer takes place always by notarial deed. The company may not acquire its own company parts.

J.3.2.6   Administration-management

The partners' general meeting is the executive organ of the company which decides on all company affairs. It meets at least once a year. Unless the law provides otherwise, decisions at the general meeting are taken on the basis of a dual majority, namely a majority of more than one half of the partners representing a majority of more than one half of all company parts. The partners' general meeting alone, is competent to decide on:

(a) amendments of the articles of incorporation:

(b) appointment or dismissal of administrators and their discharge from any responsibility;

(c) approval of the balance sheet and the distribution of profits;

(d) bringing an action against the organs of the company or the partners as individuals to enforce claims of the company against them for damages;

(e) the extension of the duration of the company and on the appointment and removal of administrators.

A qualified majority, namely at least three-quarters of the total number of partners representing at least three-quarters of the total capital of the company is required for any of the following decisions:

(a) amendment of the articles of incorporation;

(b) additional contributions by the partners to cover company losses provided the articles of incorporation provide for additional contributions;

(c) increase or decrease of the share capital;

(d) mergers of limited liability companies either by absorption or by formation of a new limited liability company;

(e) premature dissolution of the company.

Finally, the following decisions may only be taken on a unanimous vote of the General Meeting:

(a) change of nationality of the company;

(b) increase of the duties and obligations of the partners or decrease of the rights attributed to them by the articles of incorporation.

Unless the articles of incorporation provide otherwise, the administration of the affairs and the representation of the company is entrusted to all the partners acting collectively. In practice, EPEs are managed by one or more administrators appointed for a fixed or an indefinite period of time either through the articles of incorporation or on appointment by the general meeting of the partners. If numbering more than one, such administrators act collectively and they bind the company with their signature in all respects, unless otherwise provided as above. They may be or may not be partners. Administrators who are partners appointed by the articles of incorporation for a definite period of time may only be dismissed upon serious reasons by a court decision following a resolution of the partner's general meeting to that end. The articles of incorporation may provide for a supervisory board, but in practice, very few companies do so.

J.3.2.7   Single member limited liability company

In 1993 Presidential Decree 279/93 harmonised the relevant legislation with the twelfth E.C. Company Law Directive on "single member limited liability company" and introduced the above type of company in the Greek legal order.

Each natural or legal person is allowed to participate only in one single member limited liability company. Moreover, it is prohibited to a single member limited liability company to have as a sole partner another single member limited liability company. The words single member limited liability company should be included in the name of the company.

The sole partner of a single member limited liability company exercises all the powers entrusted by law to the partners' general meeting of a limited liability company having two or more partners. However, the resolutions of the sole partner of a single member limited liability company should be executed in writing in the presence of a notary public.

J.3.2.8   Dissolution

Unless the articles of incorporation provide otherwise, the bankruptcy or the death of one or more partners does not result in the dissolution of the company. The company will be dissolved.

(a)   whenever the law or the articles of incorporation so provide;

(b)   by resolution of the partners' general meeting;

(c)   in case of serious grounds, by court decision following an application to the court by partners who own at least 10 per cent of the company capital;

(d)   in case of bankruptcy.

3.3   Public Limited Company (Anonimos Eteria: AE)

J.3.3.1   Introduction

Public limited companies are regulated by codified Law 2190/1920 on sociétés anonymes as amended. This type of company suits industrial and commercial companies of some substance. It is formed by notarial deed by at least two natural or legal persons. It has legal personality and it is solely and fully responsible through its own assets for its corporate obligations. The company capital is divided into shares. Shareholders are not liable to third parties for debts or obligations of the company. They only take the risk of losing the share capital invested.

J.3.3.2   Incorporation

The articles of incorporation of an AE are always executed before a notary public by two or more natural or legal persons (or their proxies), of any nationality. A certified copy of the articles of incorporation is then submitted for consideration and eventual approval to the competent department of the prefecture where the registered office of the company is to be established. The approval is granted by decisions of the prefect confirming that the articles of incorporation comply with the provisions of codified Law 2190/90 as amended. The establishment of the company is concluded by registration of the company in the relevant book of Public Limited Companies kept with the prefecture. A summary of the articles of incorporation and the approving decision is published in the *Government Gazette*. The records of the prefecture are open to inspection by the public.

J.3.3.2.1 Articles of association The articles of association must contain provisions concerning:

(a) the name and the objects of the company;

(b) the place of establishment of the company;

(c) the duration of the company;

(d) the amount of the share capital and the method of its payment;

(e) the type, number, nominal value and issue of the shares;

(f) the number of shares of each category, if there exist more than one category;

(g) the manner of conversion of registered shares into bearer shares and vice versa;

(h) the convening, composition, operation and the powers of the board of directors;

(i) the convening, composition, operation and the powers of the general meeting of the shareholders (hereinafter called the general assembly);

(j) the auditors;

(k) the rights of the shareholders;

(l) the balance sheet and the distribution of profits;

(m) the dissolution of the company and the liquidation of its assets;

(n) the particulars of the founders;

(o) the approximate cost for the establishment of the company.

J.3.3.2.2 Registered office The place of establishment of the AE must be recorded in the statutes. It is sufficient to refer to the district where the company will have its registered office without it being necessary to specify the actual address (street and number) where the AE will have its registered office.

J.3.3.2.3 Company name The name of the AE must be designated in the company statutes. It must reflect the main activity of the company (commercial, industrial, tourist, etc.) but the name(s) of any of the founders of or any third party may also be included. The company name must always include the words "anonimos eteria" (AE)

J.3.3.2.4 Duration It is accepted that AE companies are established for a fixed period of time. In practice their duration is normally fixed from 30 to 50 years, the duration of the company can be further extended by decision of the general assembly.

J.3.3.3 *Shares*

The capital is divided into shares. There can be bearer shares or registered shares. Their nominal value cannot be less than 100 dr or more than 30,000 dr each. The issue of preferential shares (with or without voting rights) and of founders' shares is also possible. Banking, insurance, railroad, and aviation public limited companies, companies producing gas, generating and distributing electricity, those operating city water and drainage, those engaged in telecommunications activities, those operating radio and television stations, stock-broking companies, publishing companies of newspapers and periodicals, football teams, and companies producing war material are obliged to have registered shares only.

J.3.3.3.1 Share capital There is a minimum share capital requirement of 10 million dr. Higher thresholds are applicable for companies having their shares listed in the Stock Exchange, banking institutions, insurance companies, and companies whose share capital or a debenture loan are offered to public subscription. The minimum capital of 10 million dr must be fully paid up either in money or in kind by at least two founders. Contributions in kind are valued by an Experts' Committee set up with the Ministry of Commerce. Where the share capital exceeds 10 million dr the excess may be paid in instalments within a maximum period of ten years. In that case the paid up part of each share may never be less than one quarter of its nominal value. The amount of the share capital must appear on the letter-head and any other printed material of the company.

J.3.3.3.2 Transfer of shares Shares to the bearer are transferred by agreement and delivery from the seller to the buyer. Registered shares, if not listed on the Stock Exchange, are transferred by recording the transfer in a special registry of the AE whereas, if listed, they are transferred by endorsement before a stockbroker or by notarial deed.

J.3.3.3.3 Increase/decrease of capital The increase of the company capital takes place by decision of the general assembly and it requires an amendment of the company statutes. If the statutes of the company so provide, the board of directors may also decide an increase of the company capital without an amendment of the statutes being necessary. The general assembly is solely competent to decide the decrease of the company capital which always entails an amendment of the statutes.

J.3.3.3.4 Forms of subscription Subscription may take place in cash or in kind but not in the form of rendering services or expecting any works.

J.3.3.3.5 Purchase of own shares It is prohibited for an AE company to acquire directly or indirectly its own shares. There exist some exceptions to the rule, the most notable one being an acquisition made with the intention of decreasing the share capital following a decision of the general assembly. In that case the shares must be cancelled immediately.

J.3.3.3.6 Register of shares There is a special book (register) kept by the AE company for the registration of transactions related to registered shares.

J.3.3.4 Board of directors

J.3.3.4.1 Appointment/dismissal of directors The first directors are appointed in the statutes and they are subsequently elected or dismissed by the general assembly. The board consists of at least three directors. No maximum number is fixed. The term of their office may not exceed six years, but they can be re-elected. The directors can be of any nationality, living in Greece or abroad.

J.3.3.4.2 Duties/powers of the board of directors AE companies are managed and are normally represented in court and/or extra judicially by the board of directors. Nevertheless, the articles of incorporation may provide that one or more members of the board may also represent the company either in general or for certain acts only. Representation of the board of directors cannot be entrusted to persons who are not members of the board. The board of directors has the power to decide on all matters related to the management of the company, the administration of its property and the attainment of the objectives of the company. Acts of the board of directors, even if outside the objects of the company, are binding upon the company, unless it is proved that the third party acted in bad faith.

Restrictions of the powers of the board based either on the statutes or on resolutions of the general assembly cannot be invoked to the detriment of third parties who acted in good faith, even if the relevant publicity formalities have been followed. The members of the board are obliged to keep strict confidentiality on all matters of the company made known to them during their term.

J.3.3.4.3 Board meetings The board meets at least once every calendar month at the district where the company has its registered office or exceptionally, if the statutes so provide, elsewhere in Greece, or even outside Greece by special permission of the Minister of Commerce. Such a permission is not required, when all the members of the board of directors are present or represented and no one objects to the meeting of the board of directors and to the taking of decisions on the items to be discussed. The board of directors is quorate if half of the directors plus one are present or represented (by proxy given to a fellow director) at the meeting. It should be noted that at every meeting each director may represent only one director by proxy. Moreover, in order that the board meeting is valid, the number of the directors actually present cannot be less than three. Unless otherwise provided by the articles of incorporation decisions of the board are taken by an absolute majority of the directors present and represented at the meeting.

J.3.3.4.4 Legal liability of directors Each member of the board of directors is liable to the company for any fault committed by him during the management of the company's affairs. Each one of the directors, with the exception of the managing director, may escape liability if he proves that he has exercised the care of a prudent "pater familias". The managing director is obliged to carry out his duties with more care than the other members of the board.

J.3.3.5 *The general meeting of shareholders (general assembly)*

The general assembly decides on all corporate matters. It holds annually an ordinary meeting for the approval of the financial statements and the directors' report. Extraordinary meetings are also convened when it is deemed necessary for the benefit of the company in general.

J.3.3.5.1 Convening of the GA The general assembly is always convened by the board of directors. In case the board of directors refuses or fails to call a general assembly, it can be forced to do so by judgment of the competent court following a petition by shareholders representing at least 5 per cent of the share capital.

J.3.3.5.2 Notices for the GA The notice of convocation of the general assembly, specifying at least the building, the day and hour of the meeting and the items of the agenda must be posted at a prominent place in the company offices. The notice must also be published in the *Government Gazette*, in one political daily newspaper, and in one daily financial newspaper. A copy of the items of the agenda with an explanatory statement of such items must be submitted to the local prefecture at least 20 days before the meeting of the general assembly. Such a notice of convocation is not required in case all shareholders are present or represented at the general assembly and no one objects to the convocation of the general assembly and to the taking of decisions on the items to be discussed.

J.3.3.5.3 Place of the GA The general assembly always convenes at the head office of the AE. Exceptionally the general assembly may also convene at another place in Greece other than the head office of the company, following a special permission of the Minister of Commerce. Such a permission is not required, when all shareholders are present or represented at the general assembly and no one objects to the convocation of the general assembly and to the taking of decisions on the items to be discussed.

J.3.3.5.4 Duties/powers of the GA The general assembly is the supreme organ of the company and it is exclusively competent to decide upon:

(a) amendments of the company statutes, including increases and decreases of the share capital;

(b) election of directors and of the auditors;

(c) the approval of the balance sheet;

(d) the appropriation of the annual profits;

(e) the issue of debenture loans;

(f) the merger, division, conversion, revival, extension of the duration or dissolution of the company;

(g) the appointment of liquidators.

The usual quorum for the general assembly is one-fifth of the paid up capital; if no such quorum is present, the general assembly shall be reconvened with a quorum formed no matter how many shares are present. In these cases the general assembly decides by an absolute majority (50 per cent plus one share) of the votes present at the meeting.

Exceptionally, a quorum of two-thirds of the paid up capital is necessary when resolutions are to be taken relating to:

(a) the change of the company's nationality;

(b) the change of its object;

(c) the increase of the shareholders' obligations;

(d) the increase or decrease of the share capital;

(e) the issue of a debenture loan;

(f) the amendment in the way of distribution of profits;

(g) the merger, division, conversion, revival, the extension of the duration or the premature dissolution of the company.

(h) the assignment or renewal of an authorisation to the board of directors for the increase of the share capital or for the issue of a debenture loan.

If no such quorum is present, the general assembly shall meet again and this time a quorum of one-half is needed; if, once again, no such quorum is present, in order to form a quorum at least one-third of the paid up capital should be present. In these cases the resolutions can be adopted by a two-thirds majority of the votes represented at the general assembly.

The articles of incorporation may provide that for a quorum or for certain resolutions higher percentages are required.

J.3.3.5.5 Voting rights Each voting share gives the right to one vote at the general assembly. The rights of each shareholder deriving from his shares are in proportion to the share capital represented by his shares.

J.3.3.6 *Audit/accounts*

The annual financial statements of the AE company must be audited at least by two auditors.

J.3.3.6.1 Appointment and dismissal of auditors The two auditors with an equal number of substitutes are appointed by the preceding general assembly sitting in ordinary session with the exception of the auditors appointed by the articles of incorporation for the first financial year. The general assembly of large companies (those meeting at least two out of three criteria referring to the value of their assets, their turnover and the number of their employees) is obliged to appoint certified auditors, who are members of the Official Body of Certified Auditors.

J.3.3.6.2 Duties and powers of auditors The duties and the powers of the auditors are specified in the law. In particular, the auditors are obliged during the financial year to check the accounting and administrative situation of the company. They have full access to the company books and accounts. At the end of the financial year they have to check the balance sheet and the profit and loss account and to prepare and submit to the ordinary general assembly a report on the results of their audit. The auditors are liable to the company for any fault committed by them during the exercise of their duties.

J.3.3.6.3 Confidentiality of auditors The auditors have the duty of confidentiality of what they observed in the operation of the company. Criminal sanctions are provided for failure to observe absolute secrecy.

J.3.3.7 *Dissolution*

The company is resolved when one of the following events occurs:

(a) the duration of the company provided by the articles of association expires;

(b) the general assembly decides to dissolve the company;

(c) the company is declared bankrupt.

257

SECTION 4

COSTS OF INCORPORATION

J.4.0 The fees mentioned below are minimum obligatory charges. Additional fees are charged from professional advisers (lawyers, accountants, economic consultants etc.)

J.4.1 Individual Enterprise

Stamp duty: not less than 2,000 dr and not more than 20,000 dr, depending on the district and town where the business activity will be carried out.

J.4.2 Partnership (OE and EE)

Capital Issue Tax: 1 per cent of the capital.
Stamp Duty: 10,000 dr for the company (OE or EE), not less than 2,000 dr and not more than 20,000 dr as above for each partner with unlimited liability, not less than 3,000 dr and not more than 30,000 dr as above for each partner with limited liability.
Lawyers' Pension Fund: 1.8 per cent of the capital.
Lawyer's Health Fund: 1 per cent of the capital.

J.4.3 Limited Liability Companies (EPE)

Capital Issue Tax: 1 per cent of the capital.
Stamp Duty: 50,000 dr for the company, not less than 3,000 dr and not more than 30,000 dr as above for each of the partners.
Lawyers' Pension Fund: 1.8 per cent of the capital.
Lawyer's Health Fund: 1 per cent of the capital.
Public Notary's fee and copies of the statutes of incorporation about 100,000 dr.
Registration with the court of first instance: about 1,000 dr.
Publication in the *Government Gazette* and related duties: 80,000 dr.
It is estimated that the incorporation expenses for an EPE company with two

partners and the minimum possible capital (3 million dr), to be established in a big town are 400,000 dr.

J.4.4   Public Limited Companies (AE)

Capital Issue Tax: 1 per cent of the capital.
Stamp Duty: Drs 150,000.
Lawyers' minimum obligatory fee: If the corporate capital exceeds 5 million dr (*i.e.* from 5,000,001 dr onwards) a minimum obligatory fee is paid in advance at the Lawyers' Pension Fund amounting to 1 per cent of the capital up to 5 million dr and 0.5 per cent to the excess.
Public Notary's fees and copies of the statutes of incorporation: about 300,000 dr.
Publication in the *Government Gazette* and related duties 140,000 dr.
It is estimated that the incorporation expenses for an AE company having the minimum possible capital (10 million dr) are approximately 800,000 dr.

HUNGARY

SECTION 1

CLASSIFICATION OF BUSINESS ORGANISATIONS*

K.1.1   General Introduction

With respect to the huge political changes in Hungary, the economy has also changed. The first step to establishing the new market economy in Hungary was the Act on Economic Association, enacted by the Parliament in 1988 (Law No. VI of 1988.)

This law gave a complete framework for the establishment and operation of companies. Previously this was contained partly in a law decree of the Ministry of Finance and partly within several areas of the old Corporate Law Act dating from the last century.

According to the new law, economic associations may acquire rights and undertake obligations under their own firm names. The law basically established two types of organisations, the "unincorporated" and the "incorporated economic associations". Unincorporated economic associations are:

—unlimited partnerships
—limited partnerships.

Incorporated economic associations are:

—unions
—joint enterprises
—limited liability companies
—companies limited by shares.

The Act does not deal with the co-operatives, specialised groups, water-management societies, incorporated work teams, societies and other unifications of natural persons serving purposes not requiring economic activities.

Such economic associations can be established by the state, by legal entities, by companies having no legal entity and by natural persons. The law states that such economic associations may carry out any activities, but they have to take into consideration the special requirements of the different law acts.

Like this, those activities, which fall under the regulations of the Act on

* Dr László Kárpárti Jr, S.B.G. & K. Patent and Law Office (full particulars are listed in the Appendix).

Concessions (XVI of 1991), may be carried out exclusively in accordance with the above-mentioned regulations.

Banks and the so-called financial institutions also have special regulations.

Where an Act requires a permit from the authorities to carry out a special activity, the company may start and continue such activity only in the possession of such permission.

Unless the law provides otherwise, at least two founding members are required to establish an economic association.

The law establishes further requirements concerning the founding members. According to these regulations, a person who—by law—bears unlimited liability in an economic association, may not be a founding member with similar liability in another company; furthermore, only legal entities may be members of a union or a joint enterprise.

K.1.2 Protection of Foreigners

Here attention should be called to the fact that both this Act and Act XXIV of 1988 on the Protection of Foreign Investments in Hungary offer special protection to foreigners.

In this respect I would mention the following basic regulations:

(1) An international treaty may determine conditions which deviate from the Act for the participation of foreigners.

(2) The interests of foreigners in economic associations shall enjoy full protection and security.

(3) A foreigner's share of the profit of the economic association, the amount due to him at the termination of the economic association, or the partial or complete sale of a foreigner's interest, and the share due to a foreigner through the reduction of the stock capital (registered capital), may, based on the foreigner's instruction, be freely transferred in the currency in which the foreigner made his investment, provided the economic association has the necessary financial background.

When the foreigner has performed his contribution to the assets exclusively in kind, or has reinvested his dividend in Hungary, the official currency of the foreigner's country shall be regarded as the currency of the investment.

K.1.3   Legal Supervision

It is the Registration Court which carries out legal supervision of companies. The court will examine whether the statutes and other documents of the organisation and operation of the economic association are in accordance with the legal rules, and, whether the resolutions of the bodies of the given company are in accordance with the legal rules.

It is prohibited, with the exception of a company limited by shares, to issue shares representing membership rights. Any such shares shall be null and void, and the issuers thereof shall be jointly and severally liable for damages incurred as a result of issuance.

SECTION 2

COMMON RULES FOR ECONOMIC ASSOCIATIONS

K.2.1   Foundation of Economic Associations

An economic association may be founded by articles of association. The documents shall be incorporated into a notarial document or a document countersigned by an attorney-at-law. Each member has to sign the articles of association, personally or through a duly empowered representative.

The members of the company may freely determine the contents of the articles of association with respect to their relationship to one another, and may depart from the provisions of this Act provided the law does not prohibit such departure. [1]

The articles of association shall determine at least the following issues:

(a)   name and seat of the company;

(b)   members, indicating their names and addresses;

[1] Please take into consideration that the above is a *summary* of the basic rules of the Corporate Law Act *for your information only*. Concerning the detailed regulations you should contact a legal advisor, as the strict regulations of the Act on Economical Associations in many cases do not allow any alterations on one hand and on the other hand in establishing any type of corporations the regulations of several other laws have to be taken into consideration.

(c) the sphere of activity of the company (which has to be determined by the official statistical numbers);

(d) the amount of the stock capital and the manner and time by which it is to be made available;

(e) all that the Act stipulates as mandatory for the individual forms of the given company form.

The articles of association that do not contain these items shall be null and void.

The assets of a company may be contributed in cash or in the form of contribution in kind. A contribution in kind may be any kind of marketable thing of pecuniary value, intellectual property or rights of pecuniary value. A member providing a contribution in kind shall be liable to the economic association for five years from the date of the provision of the contribution to ensure that the value of his contribution is really as much, as it was specified in the document.

The foundation, and any changes thereof, of an economic association shall be reported to the Registration Court for entry and publication.

The company shall come into existence upon being entered in the Companies Register. It has retroactive effect to the date of the conclusion of the articles of association, or to the date of the adoption of the statutes in the case of a company limited by shares. Registration shall only be refused in the case of an infringement of the legal rules.

Those members who, prior to the registration of the company, have acted on behalf of the economic association, shall be jointly and severally liable for obligations undertaken under the common name.

Where an economic association commences activity prior to registration, it may not assert lack of company registration against third parties.

K.2.2 Managing Clerks, Supervisory Board, Auditors

Managing clerks are the director in the case of a "union" or a joint enterprise, the managing directors in the case of a limited liability company, and members of the board of directors in the case of a company limited by shares. Where an unlimited partnership, or a limited partnership has authorised one or several of its members to represent the company these provisions shall apply to them.

The duties of a managing clerk may also be performed by a legal entity member of the company. In this case, the rules relating to the managing clerks shall apply to the representative of the legal entity. The law describes the reasons of excluding somebody from accepting such a position. These provisions shall apply to supervisory board members and auditors, too.

Managing clerks, members of the supervisory board and auditors shall be elected for a definite period of time, being no more than five years. They may be re-elected, or removed at any time. Managing clerks and their close relatives, as described in the Civil Code, shall not be elected as supervisory board members.

Managing clerks, supervisory board members and auditors shall act with the care generally expected of persons in such offices. If they breach their duties, they shall be, in accordance with the general provisions of civil law, liable for any damage caused to the economic association, even if they have a contract of employment with the economic association.

It is mandatory to establish a supervisory board

(a) for a company limited by shares;

(b) for a limited liability company, where the stock capital of the company exceeds 20 million florin, or the number of members exceeds 25, and

(c) for any economic association, where the number of full-time employees with the economic association exceeds an annual average of 200.

In the case of a one-man limited liability company, the establishment of a supervisory board shall be mandatory only in case of (c) above.

The supervisory board shall control the management of the company. It shall examine all major reports submitted to the supreme body of the economic association, and furthermore, it shall examine the balance sheet and the assets statement. In the absence thereof, no valid resolution may be adopted concerning the balance sheet and the apportionment of profits.

An appointment as a senior officer or supervisory board member shall cease:

(a) upon expiry of the period of appointment;

(b) upon removal

(c) upon registration;

(d) upon death;

(e) upon disqualification as regulated by law.

These provisions shall apply to the auditor too.

It is obligatory to elect an auditor for

(a) a company limited by shares,

(b) one-man company and

(c) limited liability company with stock capital exceeding 50 million HUF.

Founders, members, shareholders, managing clerks, supervisory board members and their close relatives as well as the employees of the company may not act as auditors within three years of the termination of this office, mandate of theirs.

The auditor may examine the books of the company, request information from the managers and the employees and may inspect the pay office, stock of securities and merchandise, contracts and bank accounts. The auditor shall be permitted to attend meetings of the supreme body of the company, and of the supervisory board. Furthermore, the auditor shall examine all reports submitted to the supreme body, in particular, the balance sheet and the assets statement to assess the accuracy of the information and compliance with the legal rules, in order to prepare his report. In the absence of such a report, no valid resolution may be adopted on the report.

K.2.3 Procuration of Economic Association

Procuration shall be carried out in such a way, that the authorised representatives of the company shall join their signatures to the firm name of the company. If the Act or the articles of association do not provide otherwise, managing clerks have the right of sole signature. In case of other representatives the joint signatures of two persons having power of representation shall be required. This same requirement shall also apply to disposition over the bank account.

K.2.4 Judicial Review of Resolutions of Economic Associations

Any member may request the court to review a resolution adopted by the company of its bodies that violates the provisions of this Act, other legal rules or the articles of association.

The member shall not be entitled to this right, if, with the exception of the cases listed under Section 210 of the Civil Code, he has contributed by his vote to the adoption of the resolution.

Action aimed at review of the unlawful resolution shall, under forfeiture of right, be brought against the economic association within 30 days of the resolution having been adopted. The court shall make void any unlawful resolution.

K.2.5 The Termination of an Economic Association

A company shall cease to exist when:

(a) the period of time stipulated in the articles of association has expired, or another condition for termination has realised;

(b) the company decides its termination, without a legal successor;

(c) the company merges into another company, de-merges or is transformed into another form of economic association;

(d) the number of the members of the company—with the exception of a limited liability company and a company limited by shares—is reduced to one, and a new member is not registered with the Registration Court within six months;

(e) the Registration Court declares the economic association terminated;

(f) the court dissolves the economic association in the course of liquidation proceedings;

(g) provisions of the Act relating to the various forms of economic association so stipulate.

The economic association shall cease to exist upon being removed from the Companies Register. The removal shall be published by the Court of Registration in its *Official Gazette*.

SECTION 3

CORPORATIONS

K.3.1 Unlimited Partnership

In an unlimited partnership (in Hungarian: KKT) the partners undertake the obligation to continue joint business activity with unlimited, joint and several liability and to make the assets so required available to the partnership.

K.3.1.1 *Foundation of a partnership*

The articles of association has to list (besides the general conditions, mentioned above) the contributions of the parties and the manner of their personal participation. Unless the articles of association provide otherwise, the contribution in cash has to be made available to the partnership upon the foundation of the partnership.

A partner of a partnership may not, with the exception of a company limited by shares, be a member of another economic association which pursues an activity similar to the activities of the partnership, unless approved by the other partners.

K.3.1.2 *Internal legal relations of a partnership*

The contribution in cash and in other usable or substitutable items shall become the property of the partnership, while other cash contributions shall, according to the provisions of the articles of association, be transferred into the property or use of the partnership. In case of doubt the contribution in cash shall be considered as the property of the company.

During the existence of the partnership, a partner may not withdraw assets from the partnership, and shall not alienate or encumber the contribution in cash he made, without the approval of all the partners.

Withdrawal of the contribution in cash may only be claimed upon the termination of the partnership, or the partner relationship.

Each partner shall be entitled to manage the business of the partnership, except for the partner sentenced validly to enforceable imprisonment for a criminal offence, until he should have a clean criminal record (*i.e.* completes his sentence).

If the partners appoint one or more partners to manage the business in the articles of association, the other partners shall not be entitled to manage the business.

If, according to the articles of association, all or several partners are entitled to manage the business, they will act jointly and shall bring their decisions by a majority vote. Emergency measures may be brought independently by any one of them, provided that this partner protects the partnership from damages. He shall inform the other partners entitled to manage the business of the partnership about emergency measure implemented, without delay.

A unanimous resolution shall be required:

(a) for the modification of the articles of association;

(b) for matters that do not belong to the usual business activities of the partnership; and

(c) in other cases stipulated in the articles of association.

A "qualified majority" resolution passed by at least a two-thirds majority of votes shall be required:

(a) to withdraw the appointment for the management, and to appoint another partner to business management;

(b) to withdraw the right of representation and to appoint a new representative;

(c) to exclude a partner;

(d) in other cases stipulated in the articles of association.

During the normal business activity of the company, profits or losses shall be divided among partners in proportion to their pecuniary contributions.

Obligations of the partnership shall be satisfied first from the partnership assets. If such assets do not cover claims against the partnership, the partners shall personally be jointly and severally liable with their own property. Exclusion or limitation of liability with respect to third party claims shall be void.

K.3.1.3   *Termination*

Partner relations shall terminate:

(a)   upon a joint agreement of the partners;

(b)   upon the exclusion of a partner;

(c)   upon termination by notice with immediate effect;

(d)   upon termination by ordinary notice;

(e)   upon the death of a partner, or upon its termination without a legal successor;

(f)   where its subsistence violates a legal rule.

The Act prescribes detailed regulations for the final account with the partners in case of termination.

K.3.2   Limited Partnership

In this type of partnership (known in Hungary as Bt), the partners undertake the obligation to conduct joint economic activity, in such a way that at least one (full) partner shall bear unlimited liability, borne jointly and severally with the other full partners for the partnership obligations, while at least one other (silent or limited) partner shall bear liability limited to his contribution to the capital.

The regulations governing unlimited partnerships shall apply to a limited partnership, unless otherwise stipulated by the Act.

K.3.2.1   *Foundation of the partnership*

The publication of the partnership by the Registration Court includes only the number of silent partners and the amount of their deposits; without the permission of the silent partner, the register may not contain the name of the silent partner.

K.3.2.2   *Internal legal relations of the partnership*

The silent partner shall not be entitled to the management of the partnership. The active and silent partners of a partnership shall adopt joint resolutions regarding any objection to a measure to be taken by a partner entitled to manage the business of the partnership and regarding matters that do not belong to the ordinary business activity of the partnership. A silent partner shall bear the same liability as an active partner if his name appears in the firm name of the partnership.

If, on the basis of an agreement with the other partners of the partnership, the silent partner reduces his deposit, until the new amount of deposit is registered in the company register, the liability of the silent partner against third parties shall be to the extent of the original amount.

K.3.2.3   *Termination of the partnership*

The partnership shall cease to exist if all active partners leave the partnership. If only the active partners remain, the partnership shall cease to exist, unless the partners decide in writing to continue the partnership as an unlimited partnership. This amendment of the articles of association shall be submitted to the Registration Court within 30 days of the leaving of the last silent partner.

K.3.3   Union

A union is an economic association established by legal entities to co-ordinate their business activities, and to represent their joint trade interests. The union shall not be entitled to make an own profit, except of services and business activities and its members shall bear unlimited and joint and several liability for its debts exceeding its assets.

K.3.3.1   *Formation of a union*

The articles of association have to state the tasks aimed, the distribution of costs of operation among the members, the rules for refunding assets due to a departing member and the order of distribution of the assets remaining following the termination of the union.

The operational costs of the union shall be borne by the members, who shall also provide the assets required for the servicing and business activity.

Members of the association may undertake an obligation to provide additional services. The member shall be entitled to additional remuneration in respect of the additional services.

The services provided by the union shall be available for the members free of charge, the members also shall receive a share of the profits from the servicing and business activity performed for others.

The distribution of profits made in the course of servicing and business activity shall be calculated in proportion to the pecuniary contribution of each member; otherwise the profit shall be divided among the members in equal proportions.

K.3.3.2 *Organisation of the union*

K.3.3.3 *Board of directors*

Every member shall delegate one representative to the board of directors. The tasks of the board include the following:

(a) establishing the internal organisation of the union,

(b) determining the strategy for the activity of co-ordination and representation of trade interests, and the servicing and business activity;

(c) establishing the balance sheet of the association;

(d) distributing the profits generated by servicing and business activity;

(e) defining the duties of each member;

(f) approving contracts concluded on behalf of the union prior to registration at the Registration Court;

(g) decisions to terminate, transform, consolidate with another economic association, merge or demerge the union;

(h) admitting new members;

(i) electing and removing the director, and exercising employer's rights in respect of the director;

(j) electing the supervisory board if it exists, removing its members, and fixing their remuneration;

(k) appointing the auditor where the parties decided to have one, withdrawing his appointment and defining his remuneration;

(l) modification of the articles of association;

(m) excluding members;

(n) decision on all issues referred by the articles of association to the competence of the board.

The board of directors shall be convened as it is necessary, but at least once each year. It shall be convened by the director, but members representing at least one-tenth of the votes may, at any time, request a meeting of the board of directors. If the director fails to do so within thirty days, the members themselves may convene the meeting of the board of directors. The meeting has a quorum if members representing at least three-quarters of the votes attend the meeting.

Each member has one vote in relation to co-ordinating activities and representation of interests. In relation to servicing and business activity, and, in certain cases listed by law, voting rights shall be defined in proportion to the contribution of each member or, in the absence thereof, in equal proportions.

The member with whom a contract is to be concluded, or against whom an action is to be brought according to the resolution to be adopted, may not vote on that resolution.

The board shall bring its decisions by a simple majority vote of the members present. At least a three-quarter majority of votes shall be required for a resolution to terminate, transform, consolidate with another economic association, merge or de-merge the union, to incorporate a new member, to exclude a member, as well as to modify the articles of association.

The board of directors may adopt a resolution without convening a meeting. In that case the draft of the decision shall be delivered in writing to the members, who shall cast their votes in writing. The members shall be informed of the outcome of the vote by the director within eight days of the receipt of the last vote.

K.3.3.4 The director

The union shall be managed by an elected director with personal liability, and he shall represent the union against third parties, in court and at other authorities. The director shall exercise the union's employer's rights.

K.3.3.4.1 Leaving the union A member may leave the union at the end of the year. A member shall notify the board of directors of the intention to depart at least six months in advance.

The member who leaves a union shall be liable for five years from the date of departure, for the debts of the union incurred prior to departure. In case of such leave, the board of directors shall determine, within the framework of the articles of association, when and in what instalments the union shall refund the contribution of the leaving member, and the share due to him of the assets acquired up to the date of the leave.

K.3.3.5 Termination of the union

In the event of a union being terminated without a legal successor, the provisions pertaining to final accounting shall apply, together with the additional provisions under the law. Following the satisfaction of all debts, the remaining assets shall be distributed among the members in equal proportions or in proportion to their contributions.

K.3.4   Joint Enterprise

A joint enterprise (in Hungarian: KV) is established by legal entities which are liable for obligations to the extent of the registered capital supplied by its members and its other assets. If the assets of the enterprise do not cover its liabilities, the members shall be jointly liable, as guarantors for the liabilities of the enterprise in proportion to their contributions. The articles of association may not determine more favourable conditions than these.

K.3.4.1   *Foundation of an enterprise*

The articles of association have to dispose of the following issues:

(a)   the organs of the enterprise;

(b)   the rules of voting;

(c)   the rules for the distribution of the profits and for bearing losses;

(d)   in the case of a departing member, the conditions for the refund of assets due to him;

(e)   order of the distribution of the assets remaining after the termination of the enterprise;

(f)   the contribution in kind of each member;

(g)   other services (ancillary) services;

(h)   establishing a limit in respect of contracts, above which the approval of such contracts will belong to the board of directors.

Profits and losses shall be distributed among members in proportion to their pecuniary contributions.

K.3.4.2   *Board of directors*

Each member shall delegate one representative to the board of directors.
The following shall fall within the competence of the board of directors:

(a)   establishing of the organisation of the enterprise;

(b)   approving of plans and business strategy for the enterprise;

(c)   determining the balance sheet of the enterprise, and the distribution of profit;

(d) decision to terminate, transform, consolidate with other economic associations, merge or de-merge the enterprise;

(e) admission of new members;

(f) the election and removal of a director, and the exercise of employer's rights in respect of the director;

(g) where the enterprise has a directorate, election of the directorate, removal of its members, and the approval of its rules of procedure;

(h) where the enterprise has a supervisory board, election and removal of the supervisory board, and the determination of remuneration for its members;

(i) if the company has an auditor, his appointment, withdrawal, and determination of remuneration;

(j) deciding on contracts, where the contractual value is over the limit as set by the articles of association, and concluding contracts the enterprise enters into with its own members;

(k) approval of contracts concluded on behalf of the enterprise prior to registration at the Registration Court;

(l) modification of the articles of association;

(m) exclusion of a member;

(n) decisions on every issue referred by the articles of association to the competence of the board of directors.

The board of directors shall hold a meeting as required, but at least once a year. The meetings shall be convened by the director, but members representing at least one-tenth of the votes may at any time request the convening of a meeting. If the director fails to do so within thirty days, the members themselves may convene the meeting.

The meeting of the board of directors has a quorum if the meeting is attended by members representing at least three-quarters of the votes. Members shall be entitled to vote in proportion to their contributions.

The meeting shall bring its decisions with a simple majority. At least a three-quarters majority of votes shall be required for a decision to terminate, transform, consolidate with another economic association, merge or de-merge the enterprise, to permit a new member to join, to exclude a member and to modify the articles of association.

The board of directors may adopt a resolution without holding a meeting, in this case the draft shall be sent to the members in writing and the members shall cast their votes in writing. The director shall inform members of the outcome of the vote within eight days of the receipt of the last vote.

K.3.4.3   *The directorate*

Where the number of members in the enterprise make it necessary, the articles of association may provide for the establishment of a directorate. Members of the directorate shall be elected by the board of directors from among their members. The tasks and competence of the directorate shall be defined in the articles of association. The directorate shall report to the board of directors.

K.3.4.4   *Director*

The enterprise shall be managed and represented by an elected director, with personal liability. The director shall exercise the employer's rights of the enterprise.

K.3.4.5   *Supervisory board*

The members of the supervisory board shall be elected by the board of directors; it may not elect employees of the enterprise to the board.

K.3.4.5.1   Joining the enterprise   If new legal entities wish to join the enterprise, the board of directors (directorate) shall decide whether to admit a new member.

A joining member shall be liable for debts the enterprise has incurred prior to his joining. This liability of the joining member may be limited upon joining in a statement addressed to the board. In this case, the joining member shall be liable for debts incurred prior to joining only to the extent of his contribution. This limitation of the liability shall be entered in the companies register, in this case such limitation shall be effective towards third parties as from registration.

K.3.4.6   *Leaving the enterprise*

A member may leave the enterprise at the end of the year. This intention shall be announced to the board at least six months in advance. The leaving member shall be liable for five years thereafter for debts incurred by the enterprise prior to departure. The board of directors shall determine, when and in what instalments the enterprise shall refund the contribution of the leaving member and the share of the assets acquired until the date of the leave.

Leaving the enterprise is also possible by transferring the "member's right" to another member. In this case the departing member shall not be liable for the debts incurred by the enterprise prior to departure.

K.3.4.7 *Exclusion*

The board may exclude any member that does not fulfil the obligations as determined under the law or in the articles of association, or if the further participation of the member in the joint enterprise would seriously endanger the interests of the enterprise. An excluded member shall be liable for five years from the date of exclusion for debts incurred by the enterprise prior to exclusion.

K.3.4.8 *Termination of the enterprise*

If the enterprise is terminated without a legal successor, the provisions of a final accounting shall apply. The assets remaining after the settlement of all debts shall be distributed among the members in proportion to their contributions.

K.3.5 Limited Liability Company

A limited liability company (in Hungarian: Kft) is established with a stock capital, in which the liability of members towards the company is limited to provide the contribution to the stock capital, but the members shall not be liable for the obligations of the company.

K.3.5.1 *Foundation of a company*

The company can also be established by one member only. Although, it is forbidden to publicly recruit members.

The articles of association shall dispose of the following issues:

(a) the amount of the stock capital and the business parts of each member;

(b) the manner and date of payment of cash contributions that have not been paid up in full;

(c) the rules of voting and the procedure to be followed in the case of deadlock;

(d) the first managing director or, in the case of several managing directors, the procedure for management, representation and signing on behalf of the company;

(e) where the establishment of a supervisory board is mandatory, members of the first supervisory board;

(f) where the election of an auditor is mandatory, the first auditor.

If necessary, the articles of association shall dispose of the following too:

(a) contributions in kind and the value thereof;

(b) subsidiary services, the conditions thereof;

(c) regulations of additional payments;

(d) in the case of legal succession, the exclusion of the transfer of the business parts, and of the division of the business parts;

(e) approving the withdrawal of business parts;

(f) empowering every member to manage the business and to represent the company;

(g) limiting the right of the managing directors to represent the company;

(h) establishing a supervisory board, where not mandatory;

(i) electing an auditor, where not mandatory.

In case of a one-man company the articles of association, will be replaced by a deed of foundation. In such cases the rights of the meeting of the member will be replaced by the decisions of the founder.

The amount of the stock capital may not be less than 1 million florin. (This will probably change in the near future). The business parts of the members may be different, however they cannot be less than 100,000 florin. The business parts must be expressed in florins and be divisible by 10,000. Each member shall have one business part, one business part may, however, have several owners.

When the company is established, the total amount of cash contributions may not be less than 30 per cent of the stock capital and 500,000 florin.

The foundation of the company shall be notified to the court of registration for registration and publication. In the case of a one-man company, the fact that the company has only one founder shall also be reported.

Registration shall be executed when the company proves that one-half of each cash contribution, a total of at least 500,000 florin, or in the case of one-man companies, the total amount had been fully paid up by the time the application for registration was submitted, and all contributions in kind had been put at the disposal of the company. Following the submission of the application for registration, the company may freely dispose of any part of the stock capital put at its disposal.

A contribution in kind is accepted if it is an enforceable object or is intellectual property or a right which the company may subsequently transfer, without the approval or agreement of any third party.

If the contributions are not paid up in full at the foundation, the rules of further payment have to be established, and all cash contributions shall be paid up within one year from the registration of the company. It is forbidden to set the value of the contribution in kind higher than it was determined by the auditor.

Members of a company may undertake to provide other subsidiary services. The articles of association shall contain provision for the remuneration thereof.

The articles of association may authorise the meeting of the members to prescribe a supplementary payment for the members to cover losses. It shall determine the maximum amount a member may be obliged to pay. The supplementary payment shall not increase the stock stake of the member. Supplementary payments shall be defined and performed in proportion to the participation in the stock capital.

The rights of members and the portion of the company assets due to them shall be expressed by the business parts. Each member may only have one business part. If a member acquires additional business parts, his business part shall increase.

One business part may have several owners. In relation to the company, such owners shall be considered as one member; such owners shall exercise their rights through a common representative, and shall be jointly and severally liable for the obligations of the member. The business parts can be freely transferable to the members of the company. The approval of the company is required if the articles of association deems it so.

A business part may only be transferred to an outsider if the member has paid up his contribution to the stock capital in full, and with the condition that the other members, the company, or the person appointed by the meeting of the members shall have, in that order, a pre-emptive right, within 15 days. The company may purchase the business part for itself from the assets exceeding its stock capital.

Division of the business part may only be permitted in the event of transfer, legal succession where a member has ceased to exist, and in the event of inheritance. The division of a business part requires the approval of the company.

During the existence of the company, members may not reclaim their contributions from the company.

Distribution of the profits shall be executed among the members in proportion to their participation in the stock capital.

The company may purchase not more than one-third of the business parts, from its assets exceeding its stock capital. These business parts shall not provide voting rights; the profit due to such a business part shall be distributed among the members.

The withdrawal of a business part may take place where a member is excluded, where the company acquires the business part, or where the articles of association so permit. A one-man company may not acquire or withdraw business part for itself.

The meeting of the members may, with at least a three-quarters majority of votes, exclude a member who does not perform his duties as defined by the Act and in the articles of association, despite having been given written notice thereto, or whose continued membership in the company would seriously endanger the objectives of the company. The notice of the exclusion shall indicate the reason thereof. The member may appeal against such exclusion within 30 days of the notice of the resolution to the court.

K.3.5.2 *Company organisation*

K.3.5.3 *The meeting of the members*

The meeting of the members is the highest decision making body of the company. The following items are within the exclusive competence of the meeting:

(a) approval of the balance sheet and distributing profits;

(b) ordering supplementary payments and their repayment, and the increase and reduction of stock capital;

(c) dividing and withdrawing business parts;

(d) excluding a member;

(e) electing, removing and fixing the remuneration of managing directors, and exercising employer's rights in respect of managing directors;

(f) electing, removing and fixing the remuneration of supervisory board members;

(g) stock capital, and approving contracts which are to be concluded with the members of the company, the managing director or the close relatives thereof (paragraph (b), section 685 of the Civil Code), except if the latter contracts are part of the normal business activity of the company;

(h) approving contracts concluded on behalf of the company prior to registration of the company with the Registration Court;

(i) claims for damages against members responsible for the foundation, managing directors and supervisory board members, and providing for representation of the company in legal actions brought against the managing directors;

(j) resolving the termination, transformation, consolidation merger and demerger of the company, and the foundation of another company or the joining as a member of an existing company;

(k) modification of the articles of association;

(l) any matters referred by the Act or the articles of association to the exclusive competence of the meeting of the members.

The meeting of the members, unless the Act or the articles of association otherwise stipulate, shall adopt its resolutions by the simple majority of votes of the members present.

The meeting has a quorum if at least half the stock capital is presented at the meeting. If the meeting does not have a quorum, the following meeting shall have a quorum in respect of matters listed on the original agenda, regardless of the proportion of the stock capital represented.

The procedure to be followed in the event of a deadlock shall be regulated by the articles of association.

A member may not vote on any resolution which exempts him from duty or liability, or which grants the above member some other advantage at the expense of the company, and may not vote if the resolution stipulates that a contract is to be concluded with that member, or that an action shall be brought against that member, or where that member is otherwise interested.

The meeting of the members shall be convened by the managers but members representing at least one-tenth of the stock capital may request at any time, indicating the reasons and the purpose thereof, the convening of the meeting. If the managing director fails to do so, within eight days of the request, or where there is no one to whom this request can be addressed, the members may themselves convene the members meeting.

If the meeting is not convened in accordance with the rules, it may only adopt resolutions if every member is present and they do not object to the members meeting being held.

Any member shall be entitled to request discussion of an item of agenda proposed by him. The member shall make known the proposal to the members at least three days prior to the meeting. Issues not included in the invitation, or issues not made known subsequently to members, may only be discussed at the meeting if every member is present and they do not object thereto.

The members may bring decisions without even holding a meeting in a way, that the draft resolution shall be delivered to all members in writing and the members shall cast their votes in writing. If any member so requests, a meeting of the members shall be convened for the discussion of the draft resolution.

The managing directors shall keep a continuous record of the decisions of the meeting of the members ("book of decisions"). The resolution shall become effective only when it is registered in the book of decisions, thereafter, with the authentication of one member having participated in its adoption.

If the meeting of the members rejects a proposal that an expert inspect the balance sheet of the previous year or any event of the previous two years related to management, or if the meeting fails to bring a resolution on this proposal, the Registration Court may order this upon the application of members representing at least one-tenth of the stock capital.

In the frame of the protection of minority rights, should the majority shareholders refuse to file a claim against the founding members for damages, the minority shareholders (representing at least 10 per cent of the stock capital) may file such claim themselves, even though the shareholders' meeting refused such decision or did not bring decision on this subject.

K.3.5.4 *Managing directors*

The members elect one or more managers for the management and representation of the company. The first managing directors shall be appointed in the articles of association. In the case of a one-man company, if the founder is a natural person, the deed of foundation may stipulate that the founder shall be entitled to manage and to represent the company. The employer's rights shall be exercised by the managing director, or where there are several managing directors, by the managing director appointed thereto.

Without the approval of the meeting of the members, the managing director:

(a) may not, on his own behalf, continue any business activity falling within the scope of activity of the company;

(b) may not bear unlimited liability in another company which is pursuing activities similar to those of his own company;

(c) may not be a managing clerk in another company which carries out similar activities to those of his own company.

If the managing director violates any of these prohibitions,

(a) the company may claim compensation for damages,

(b) the company may claim that, instead of compensation, the managing director shall assign to the company any profit arising from any agreement concluded on behalf of another party, or shall assign his claim thereto to the company.

The managing directors shall keep records of the company members ("list of members"). Such list shall indicate:

(a) the names of the members, their place of residence (registered office), and participation in stock capital;

(b) the provisions in the articles of association relating to any supplementary payments and subsidiary services;

(c) the provisions relating to the pre-emptive rights;

(d) any changes concerning the above.

Any person may inspect the register of members upon proving a relevant interest.

K.3.5.5 *Supervisory board*

Members of the supervisory board shall be elected by the meeting of the members. Employees of the company may not be elected, except those who, in accordance with the regulations, are elected by the employees themselves. The removal of a member of a supervisory board elected by the meeting shall require at least a three-quarter majority of votes.

The amendment of the articles of association shall require a resolution adopted by the members meeting with at least a three-quarter majority of votes. An unanimous resolution of the meeting of the members shall be required to increase the obligations of members as prescribed in the articles of association, to determine new obligations and to limit the individual rights of certain members.

K.3.5.6   Increasing the stock capital

Where the meeting of the members decides to increase the stock capital, the increase has to be executed by the payment of new stock contributions. The stock capital may only be increased if all previous contributions to the stock capital have been paid up in full.

The members of the company registered prior to the increase in the stock capital shall have, within 30 days, a pre-emptive right in respect of the new stock, and they may exercise such right in proportion to their participation to the stock capital. In the absence thereof, any person may acquire the new stock.

The meeting of the members may resolve to increase the stock capital from the company assets which exceed the stock capital of the company. The increase of the stock capital shall be reported to the Court of Registration for registration and publication. Registration may only be effected if at least half of each cash contribution has been paid up, and if the contributions in kind have been fully put at the disposal of the company.

K.3.5.7   Reduction of the stock capital

The stock capital may not be reduced to an amount less than 1 million florin. If the reduction is effected through repayment of a portion of the contributions to the stock capital, the minimum amount of the remaining business parts may not be less than 100,000 florin.

The managing directors shall publish twice, at an interval of 30 days, a notice in the official gazette of the resolution announcing the reduction of the stock capital following the same having been reported to the Court of Registration. The resolution regarding the reduction of the stock capital shall be made known in the notice and at the same time, company creditors shall be invited to state their claims within three months of the last notice being published. Known creditors shall be invited separately to state their claims.

The claims of those creditors who have notified the company within the above time limit and who did not approve the reduction of the stock capital, shall be settled or security shall be provided for them.

On the basis of the reduction of the stock capital, repayments to members may only be effected after the reduction of capital has been recorded in the companies register.

K.3.5.8 Termination of a company

The termination of the company shall require a resolution, passed with at least a three-quarters majority of votes, by the meeting of the members. In the event of a company being terminated without a legal successor, the provisions pertaining to the final accounting shall apply.

From any assets remaining subsequent to the settlement of the claims of creditors, the supplementary payments made by members shall be repaid first, after which the amount remaining shall be distributed among the company members in proportion to their participation in the stock capital, but this is not permitted for six months following the third publication in the official gazette.

If the number of company members has decreased to one and no new member has been reported to the Court of Registration within six months, the company shall not cease to exist, but shall continue to operate as a one-man company.

K.3.6   Company Limited by Shares

K.3.6.1   General rules

A company limited by shares (in Hungarian: Rt) is a company established with a registered capital consisting of shares of a predetermined amount and nominal value, in which the liability of the shareholders is limited to the delivery of the nominal value of the share or the value of issue of the share. Otherwise, the shareholder has no liability for the obligations of the company.

It is an important regulation of the Law Act that alteration from the provisions of the Law relating to the company limited by shares shall only be possible where the Law so permits.

K.3.6.2   The shares

A share is a security embodying membership rights which shall provide identical membership rights. In accordance with the law, the statutes may provide for the issue of shares providing different membership rights.

Shares providing identical rights constitute one class of shares. The rights attached to the class of shares, and the number and nominal value of the shares that are to be issued within a certain class of shares shall be stated in the statutes. The issue of shares below nominal value shall be void. The following information must be indicated on the share:

(a)   name and seat of the company;

(b)   serial number, nominal value and type of the share, if it is registered the name of the holder;

(c)   the class of share and rights attached thereto as stated in the statutes;

(d)   date of issue, amount of registered capital and number of shares upon issue;

(e)   signature of the board of directors.

Prior to the registration, a share voucher may be drawn up in respect of the part of the registered capital already paid up, which cannot be transferred to any other person.

Subsequent to the registration of the company limited by shares in the Companies Register, an interim share may be drawn up in respect of the part of the registered capital already paid up, provided that the subscriber of the share has met the payment obligations. Both the share voucher and the interim share are registered documents which certify the sum of money paid up by the shareholder until the issue.

Following the registration and full payment of the registered capital, the shareholder may request delivery of the shares due to him.

The type of the shares may be bearer shares or registered shares. Bearer shares, without any indication as to its holder, shall be freely transferable. The transfer of a registered share or, of an interim share shall be effective with the company if the name of the new holder has been registered in the share register. Foreigners may hold only registered shares. If a foreigner acquires a bearer share through estate, that bearer share shall be converted into a registered share within one year of the delivery of the inheritance or, in all other cases, within three months of the acquisition of the share. A foreigner holding a bearer share may not exercise the shareholders rights.

The board of directors of the company limited by shares shall keep a share register of the registered shares, which shall contain a record of the names (firms) and addresses (registered offices) of the shareholders.

The law recognises so-called preference shares too, which entitle the holder to dividends from profits that may be distributed among shareholders in preference to other classes of share. Voting rights attached to preference shares may be restricted or precluded by the statutes. The rules governing dividend preference shall be established by the statutes. Such shares may be issued up to 50 per cent of the registered capital of the company.

In accordance with the provisions of the statutes, employee shares may also be issued free of charge or at a special discount price. These shares arise from assets exceeding the registered capital, through a simultaneous increase of the registered capital. Such shares may be transferred between existing and retired company employees only, i.e. are not to be transferred on the market.

Interest bearing shares entitling holders to a fixed interest rate may be issued not in excess of 10 per cent of the registered capital. The holder of such share shall be entitled to interest calculated on the basis of the interest rate specified in the share, even if the company limited by shares does not make a profit in the given year. In addition the shareholder shall also be entitled to other share-related rights, including the right to receive dividends.

A company may issue convertible bonds up to the value of one-half of its registered capital, which may be converted into shares upon the request of a bond holder.

A company limited by shares may acquire its own fully paid-up shares from the assets which exceed its registered capital, but not more than one-third of the registered capital. The company may withdraw the shares it owns, but it shall not reduce the amount of the registered capital.

A share may be owned by more than one person but they shall be considered as one shareholder. They will exercise their rights only through a joint representative, and shall bear joint and several liability for the obligations borne by shareholders.

K.3.6.3 Foundation of the company limited by shares

The founder of the company issues the draft of foundation. The company limited by shares may have only one founder.

The registered capital of the company limited by shares may not be less than 10 million florin (this will probably change in the near future) of which the cash part cannot be less than 30 per cent and 5 million florin.

K.3.6.4 Subscription of shares

The draft of foundation shall serve as the basis for the subscription of shares, which shall contain the following:

(a) name and seat of the company, scope of activity and period of duration;

(b) amount of planned registered capital;

(c) number, nominal value and price of shares, their classes, and rights attached thereto;

(d) place, and opening and closing dates for share subscription;

(e) benefits due to the founders, specially the right that they appoint the members of the board of directors for the first three years;

(f) nature and value of contributions in kind, number of shares to be provided in exchange, name and seat of the person, who contributes in kind;

(g) name and seat of the auditor, who evaluated the in kind contribution;

(h) procedure to be followed in the event of oversubscription;

(i) manner of convening the founding general meeting;

(j) other information prescribed in law.

In the draft of foundation, the value of the contributions in kind may only be considered at the value predetermined by the auditor. The subscriber of the share shall pay up not less than 10 per cent of the amount subscribed.

In case of oversubscription the founders may reject it. Where this has not been done, the first general meeting shall decide whether to accept or reject the oversubscribed shares, and such an amount shall be repaid to the subscribers within 15 days of rejection.

K.3.6.5 *Founding general meeting*

A founding general meeting has to be convened within 60 days of the closing date of a successful share subscription. If the founders fail to convene the founding general meeting, share subscribers shall become exempt from their obligations, and may demand the refund of the amount paid. The stock capital paid up has to be completed up to 30 per cent prior to the general meeting. The tasks of the general meeting will be as follows:

(a) establish that the registered capital has been subscribed and at least 30 per cent has been paid up;

(b) accept or reject any oversubscription;

(c) decide on the foundation of the company limited by shares;

(d) establish the statutes;

(e) decide on the privileges due to the founders;

(f) approval of contracts concluded prior to the meeting;

(g) approval of the value and date of the provision of contributions in kind;

(h) elect the members of the board of directors and the supervisory board, and elect the auditor.

The founding general meeting shall bring decisions by a simple majority of votes, but:

(a) may modify the draft of foundation only by a unanimous decision;

(b) may not determine the contributions in kind in a higher value;

(c) may not change the privileges due to the founders.

K.3.6.6 *Exclusive foundation (in camera)*

If the founders agree to buy all the shares, it is not necessary to issue a draft of foundation, share subscription or a founding general meeting, and they will prepare a deed of foundation instead of statutes.

The statutes shall dispose the following:

(a) name and seat of the company;

(b) term of the company;

(c) scope of activity;

(d) amount of registered capital;

(e) conditions for payment of shares;

(f) number, nominal value and type of shares;

(g) way of the procuration;

(h) rules of convening and operating the general meeting, including voting rights, etc.;

(i) numbers of members of the board of directors, supervisory board and number of auditors, their election and withdrawal;

(j) distribution of profit;

(k) publication of official announcements;

(l) consequences for failing to pay up for the shares.

And if necessary:

(m) agreements concerning the contributions in kind;

(n) number and rights attached to different classes of shares;

(o) rules of eventual pre-emption;

(p) rules of withdrawing shares;

(q) rules of an increase of the registered capital.

K.3.6.7 *Rights and duties of shareholders*

The full value of the shares shall be paid up within one year of the registration of the company. The shareholders shall pay when the board of directors call them to do so in accordance with the statutes.

The shareholders are entitled to a dividend defined by the general meeting for distribution in proportion to their shares.

The shareholder may not request repayment of any paid-up contribution either during the existence of the company limited by shares, or upon the termination thereof. Every shareholder shall be entitled to attend and vote on the general meetings, to request information and to make comments. The directorate shall publish, at least 30 days prior to the general meeting the details of the balance sheet, the proposal for the distribution of profits and the reports of the board of directors and the supervisory board. The manner in which voting rights are exercised shall be prescribed by the statutes. A shareholder shall not exercise his voting rights prior to providing the pecuniary contribution he owes.

If the company fails to pay or to pay in full the fixed dividend on preference shares, and does not cover the shortfall in the following year together with the dividend due in that year, preference shareholders shall be granted voting rights, and may exercise these rights until they receive all their dividends.

The general meeting shall also be convened if shareholders representing at least one-tenth of the registered capital request this in writing. If the board of directors fails to do so, the Registration Court shall convene a general meeting. Shareholders representing at least one-tenth of the registered capital and provided with voting rights may request within eight days from the publication of the coming general meeting, that the board of directors include a particular issue on the agenda of the general meeting. If the board of directors fails to meet its obligation, this shall be ordered by the Registration Court.

Shareholders representing at least one-tenth of the registered capital may request in writing the review of the management of the company by the supervisory board. If the supervisory board does not fulfil the request within 30 days, the shareholders may file a complaint to the general meeting.

K.3.6.8 *Organisation of the company*

K.3.6.9 *General meeting*

The general meeting consists of all the shareholders. The following items shall be within the exclusive competence of the general meeting:

(a) establishment and modification of the statutes;

(b) increase and reduction of the registered capital;

(c) change in the rights attached to the various classes of shares;

(d) the decision to merge into another company, to de-merge or terminate the company, or to transform the company into another corporate form;

(e) the election and removal of the supervisory board members, members of the board of directors and the auditor, and fixing their remuneration;

(f) approval of the balance sheet and distribution of the profit;

(g) transformation and overprinting of shares;

(h) decisions on the issue of convertible bonds or pre-emptive bonds;

(i) decisions on all issues referred to the exclusive competence of the general meeting.

The general meeting shall be convened by the board of directors in accordance with the statutes, but it must be held at least once each year. Notice shall be published at least 30 days prior to the general meeting.

The general meeting shall have a quorum where the attending shareholders represent more than 50 per cent of the voting shares. If the general meeting does not have quorum, the second general meeting convened within 15 days shall have a quorum with respect to the original agenda regardless of the number of persons attending.

The general meeting shall adopt resolutions by at least a three-quarters majority of votes regarding the matter listed by law, while on other matters, unless the statutes prescribe a qualified majority, it shall adopt resolutions by simple majority of votes.

K.3.6.10 *Board of directors*

The board of directors, which consist of not less than three and not more than eleven members, shall represent the company, establish and supervise the organisation of the company and shall exercise employers rights.

Each director shall be authorised to sign on behalf of the company. The statutes may prescribe joint procuration. The statutes or a general meeting decision or of the supervisory board may restrict the right of the board of directors to represent the company; the restriction shall be void in relation to third persons.

The board of directors will prepare the balance sheet, the statement on assets, the proposal for the distribution of profits and the annual report for the general meeting. It will convene a general meeting and notify the supervisory board if the company lost one-third of its registered capital, or the company stopped payments, and its assets do not cover its liabilities.

As far as non-competition is concerned, a member of the board of directors:

(a) may not conclude, on his own behalf, deals that fall within the scope of activity of the company;

(b) may not be a member of unlimited liability of another company which carries out activities similar to those of company;

(c) may not be a managing clerk of another company which carries out activities similar to those of the company.

If the director violates these prohibitions the company may claim compensation for damages and the company may claim, that he transfers the profit arising from such agreement, or shall assign his claim thereto to the company.

K.3.6.11 *Supervisory board*

The supervisory board shall exercise its rights as one body or through its members. The supervisory board may divide control among its members on a permanent basis. This shall not affect the liability of the supervisory board members.

K.3.6.12 *One-man company*

A company limited by shares may also be founded in such a way that the founder is the only shareholder, or when one shareholder acquires ownership of all shares. In such a company the shareholder shall bear liability for the company obligations to the extent of his shares.

If this fact is not reported to the Registration Court in due time, the shareholder shall bear unlimited liability for company obligations from the date when all of the shares were acquired by that party.

The same regulations of a company limited by shares shall apply to a one-man company, with the condition, that the rights of the general meeting shall be exercised by the founder/the shareholder.

K.3.6.13 *Increasing the registered capital*

The company may increase its capital if the nominal value of all the previously issued shares has been fully paid up. If the portion of the registered capital representing the increase is to be covered entirely by contributions in kind, the company may increase the registered capital even if the counter-value of all the shares has not yet been put at the disposal of the company.

The increase shall be effected through the issue of new shares or by converting the assets exceeding the registered capital into registered capital or by converting convertible bonds into shares. The increase can be executed through the subscription of new shares only in the case where the issuer (or its legal predecessor) has been in operation for at least one calendar year.

It is the general meeting who shall decide upon the increase of the registered capital, its method, time-schedule, the classes of shares and all other issues prescribed by law. The rules of the Act governing foundation shall accordingly apply to the increase.

The statutes may authorise the board of directors, specifying the conditions thereto, to increase the registered capital through a new share issue, or by converting the company assets exceeding the registered capital into registered capital.

The general meeting may decide upon a conditional increase of the registered capital, its method, time-schedule, the classes of shares and all other issues prescribed by law. The rules of the Act governing foundation shall accordingly apply to the increase.

The statutes may authorise the board of directors, specifying the conditions thereto, to increase the registered capital through a new share issue, or by converting the company assets exceeding the registered capital into registered capital.

The general meeting may decide upon a conditional increase of the registered capital if the purpose of the increase is to issue convertible bonds. Bond holders may apply for shares to the debit of the conditionally increased registered capital. Shareholder rights shall commence upon the issue of the new shares.

K.3.6.14 Reduction of the registered capital

The resolution of the general meeting which decides upon the reduction of the registered capital shall indicate the reason for and the manner in which the registered capital is to be reduced, the amount by which the registered is to be reduced and the time limit within which the shares shall be returned to the company. It must start with the redemption of the shares held by the company itself. The rules governing the nominal value of shares and the minimum amount of registered capital shall be taken into consideration in the case of a capital reduction, and the reduction may not influence the rights of the owners of convertible bonds. The board of directors shall report such decision to the court, and following the report, it shall publish twice the resolution in the *Official Gazette*.

Those creditors who have valid claims against the company may demand collateral from the company within 90 days of the last announcement. Missing such a deadline shall result in forfeiture of right. The company has to provide the appropriate collateral for the creditors who contact the company.

The reduction of the registered capital can be executed through:

(a) replacement or an overprinting of shares;

(b) reducing the number of shares;

(c) withdrawing shares.

K.3.6.15 Termination of the company

In the situation where the company is being terminated without a legal successor, the provisions of a final accounting shall apply.

Following the settlement of all debts, the remaining assets shall be divided among the shareholders in proportion to their shares. The distribution of assets is prohibited prior to six months having elapsed following the publication of the third notice to creditors in the *Official Gazette*.

K.3.6.16 Interests in other companies

The possibilities of having interest in another company are as follows:

K.3.6.16.1 Substantial interest acquisition of more than one-quarter of the registered capital of another company limited by shares, or similar votes. The company shall immediately notify the other company thereof, and such interest shall be published in the *Official Gazette*, indicating the acquired share and voting ratios.

K.3.6.16.2   A majority interest   acquisition of shares representing more than one-half of the registered capital, or similar votes. Prior to the acquisition of a majority interest, the other company shall be notified of such an intent and a bid shall be made to the shareholders of the controlled company to purchase the shares planned for the purpose of the acquisition of the majority interest. The notice and the bid shall be published in the *Official Gazette*. The shares may be purchased exclusively after the expiration of 30 days from the date of the publication.

If a company failed to meet its above-mentioned obligations, it may exercise its shareholder rights in relation to the controlled company only in accordance with the rules providing for the acquisition of a substantial interest.

In case of a majority interest the controlled company may not acquire additional shares in the company holding the majority interest, and may not exercise its voting rights arising from its existing shares and the same person may not be simultaneously a member of the board of directors or supervisory board of the company holding majority interest and the controlled company.

Within ninety days of the acquisition of the majority interest, the company holding a majority interest shall according to the choice of any of the shareholders of the controlled company, purchase shares from the share holder at least at the price identical to its own offer or pay a pre-determined dividend to the shareholders.

An important rule of the Act is that if the controlling company continues a business practice detrimental to the long-term interests of the controlled company the court may, upon a request from creditors representing no less than 20 per cent of the liabilities of the controlled company limited by shares, impose unlimited liability upon the company holding the majority interest in respect of the liabilities of the controlled company.

K.3.6.16.3   Direct control   If the company holding a majority interest has acquired shares representing more than three-quarters of the registered capital. The board of directors of the controlling company may issue instructions regarding the management of the controlled company. The controlling company limited by shares shall bear unlimited liability for the liabilities of the company under its direct control.

Shareholders of the controlled company may, at any time, require the controlling company to pay a pre-determined dividend, to purchase their shares at the value prevailing at the date the resolution was passed or to exchange their shares for the shares of the controlling company.

Creditors whose claims have arisen prior to the publication of obtaining control, may request collateral from the controlling company to the extent of their claims.

K.3.6.16.4   Mutual interest   where both companies limited by shares have acquired shares representing more than one-quarter of the registered capital of the other, or similar votes. In the event of a mutual interest the company which first delivers the notice to the other company may retain its acquired portion of the registered capital of the other company, while the other company shall reduce its portion to one-quarter of the registered capital, and the company may exercise its voting rights in the other company to a maximum of one-quarter of the votes that may be cast at the general meeting.

If the mutual interest is asserted through a majority interest, the rules governing majority interests shall apply to their relationship. With respect to these regulations one also has to take into consideration the provisions of the Act on the Prohibition of Unfair Market Practices.

SECTION 4

TRANSFORMATION

K.4.1   The last large chapter of the Act establishes the transformation of economic associations into other types of economic associations. These provisions will not apply to economic associations that are undergoing either liquidation or final accounting. Transformation has to be carried in accordance with these regulations, otherwise the Registration Court will not register the transformed company.

SECTION 5

CONSOLIDATION

K.5.1   According to the Law Act the following may consolidate with each other:

(a)   economic associations operating in the same form;

(b)   unlimited partnerships with limited partnerships;

(c)   limited liability companies with companies limited by shares.

A consolidation may be either merger or amalgamation.

In the case of merger: with the termination of one of the companies, its assets

295

as a whole shall be transferred to the ownership of the other company as the general legal successor.

In the case of amalgamation; the amalgamating companies cease to exist and their assets as a whole shall be transferred to the ownership of the new company as the general legal successor.

In the course of the consolidation, the provisions of the Act on the Prohibition of Unfair Market Practices relating to the control of organisational consolidations should also be taken into consideration. Merger and consolidation have to be executed in accordance with the detailed rules of the Law Act.

SECTION 6

DE-MERGER

K.6.1 The company may decide on a de-merger of the company into two or more economic associations. The de-merger requires the holding of two meetings of the members.

At the first meeting the members declare whether they agree with the intention of the de-merger, and in case there is an agreement, which legal successor economic association they wish to be the members of. Following this, the managing clerks shall prepare the de-merger agreement, which shall contain the draft property balance sheet concerning the assets of the company, the proposal on the division of assets and of the rights and obligations which all has to be reviewed by an auditor.

The second meeting shall decide on the de-merger and the division of assets and rights and obligations on the basis of the property balance sheet and the proposal on the division of assets.

The de-merging company ceases to exist while its rights and obligations shall devolve upon the new companies as legal successors. The legal successors shall be liable for the liabilities (debts) incurred prior to the de-merger in proportion to the division between themselves. If a liability arises only after the de-merger, the liability of the legal successor economic associations shall be joint and several.

Concerning the de-merger, the detailed rules of the Act have to be applied.

SECTION 7

COSTS OF INCORPORATION

K.7.1 With respect to incorporation, the following costs appear:

(1) State-stamp duty of the Registration Court:

   (a) in case of an incorporated legal entity, 2 per cent of the stock (registered) capital, but a minimum of 10,000 florin and a maximum of 300,000 florin;

   (b) in case of unincorporated entities 2 per cent, but a minimum of 5000 florin and a maximum of 150,000 florin.

(2) Publication fee—to be paid through bank transfer:

   (a) registration of an incorporated legal entity: 20,000 florin;

   (b) registration of an unincorporated entity: 10,000 florin;

   (c) modification of data: 10,000 florin and 5,000 florin.

(3) Notary public costs (certifying the specimen signatures) 1,400 florin/pieces

(4) Translation costs (originals of the trade registers of the founders have to be translated officially by the National Office of Translation):

   (a) 700–4900 florin/page, depending on the language and the deadline

   (b) stamp duty: 100 florin/page

   (c) authentic: 500 florin/page.

IRELAND

Section 1

CLASSIFICATION OF BUSINESS ORGANISATIONS: INTRODUCTION*

L.1.0   The main forms through which business may be conducted in Ireland are as follows:

—a sole trader;
—a foreign company having a place of business in Ireland (*i.e.* a branch);
—a partnership;
—a co-operative society;
—a building society;
—a European economic interest group;
—a private limited company;
—a public limited company; and
—an unlimited company.

L.1.1   Sole Trader

The sole trader constitutes the simplest form of business entity. A sole trader describes an individual who operates on his own rather than as a body corporate and typically all the property, profits, losses and risks of the enterprise vest in the sole trader. There is no distinction between the capital used in the business and the personal funds of the individual in determining the liabilities of the sole trader. As a result, the sole trader has unlimited liability for the obligations of his enterprise. A sole trader will be taxed on the profits of the business at personal income tax rates.

The sole trader is exempt from the rules and restrictions governing companies and, in particular, the restrictions on the distribution of assets of the business, the obligation to maintain capital which applies in the case of limited companies and the requirement which applies in the case of all companies to have their accounts independently audited.

No formal registration requirements must be observed for the establishment of the business of a sole trader other than those applicable to businesses generally,

* *Henry Ong and Stephen Hegarty, Arthur Cox (full particulars are listed in the Appendix).*

such as registration for VAT, if applicable. However, if a sole trader carries on business under a name other than his own then he must file details of that name (which may not include the word "limited") and his own name. This is to enable the public to establish the identity of the person with whom they are dealing.

L.1.2 Branch

A company incorporated outside Ireland may establish a branch in Ireland. The Irish branch of a company incorporated outside Ireland may in fact constitute its principal place of business.

The eleventh E.C. Directive on Company Law (concerning disclosure requirements of branches) has been implemented in Ireland. The documents and particulars which need to be filed by a branch with the Registrar of Companies include the following:—

(a) details of the company such as its legal form, place of registration and details of the branch itself;

(b) details of the activities of the branch;

(c) particulars of the person(s) resident in Ireland responsible for ensuring compliance of the directors and secretary of the company, and of the person(s) resident in Ireland who is/are authorised to accept service of process;

(d) a certified copy of the company's constitution;

(e) a copy of the most recent accounts of the company.

If any alteration is subsequently made to the documents or particulars registered, the company must file a return with the Registrar of Companies containing particulars of such alteration.

The business carried on in Ireland by a branch is regulated by the laws applicable to commercial entities generally.

L.1.3 Partnership

A group of individuals may carry on business in the form of a partnership. The principal rules governing partnerships and limited partnerships are set out in the Partnership Act 1890 and the Limited Partnership Act 1907, respectively. There is also a form of partnership which can be established under the Investment Limited Partnership Act 1994, but this is of limited application.

L.1.3.1 *General partnership*

A partnership is defined by the Partnership Act 1890 as the relationship subsisting between persons carrying on business together with a view to profit. The existence of a general partnership is a question both of law and of fact and no formalities need to be observed, nor is any registration required for the formation of a general partnership. Thus a partnership may be formed by way of an express or an implied contract.

Although partnerships are more commonly formed between individuals, they may exist between companies or between companies and individuals. A partnership consisting of more than 10 persons may not be formed for the purpose of carrying on the business of banking unless it is registered as a company. Except in the case of certain professions, a partnership consisting of more than 20 persons may not carry on business unless it is registered as a company (see L.1.3.3 below).

The partners constituting a partnership are referred to collectively as a firm. If the partnership's business is carried on under a name other than the surname of each of the partners then the partners must register details of the firm's name and their individual names in the Register of Business Names and this information must be shown on the firm's letterhead.

Although a firm is not a legal entity separate from its members, proceedings may be brought by and against the firm in its name. Each partner in a firm is liable jointly for all the debts and obligations of the firm incurred while he is a partner. In the absence of any agreement to the contrary, all the partners of a firm are entitled to equal shares of the profits and capital of the business. It is usual to provide that all property and capital contributed by the partners must be held and applied exclusively for the purposes of the partnership and in accordance with the partnership agreement. However, provided that the firm is solvent, the partners may agree to the withdrawal of assets from the partnership.

A partner is an agent of the firm for the purposes of the business of the firm. Accordingly, the firm is bound by the acts of each partner unless the partner did not have the authority to act and the third party with whom he was dealing was aware of that fact.

The partnership agreement may be entered for the joint lives of the partners or for any shorter period. If no term is fixed for the duration of the partnership, any partner may terminate the partnership upon giving notice to all of the other partners.

Where a partnership is composed of persons which are limited liability companies, there is a requirement that the accounts of the partnership be audited by independent auditors and filed with the Registrar of Companies.

L.1.3.2 *Limited partnership*

Except for certain rules and modifications set out in the Limited Partnership Act 1907, the laws applicable to partnerships generally apply also to limited partnerships.

A limited partnership must consist of at least one general partner, who has unlimited liability for all debts and obligations of the firm, and one or more limited partners, whose liability for the firm's debts and obligations is limited to the amount of any capital or property contributed by them. In addition, the limited partners may not participate in the management of the firm's business.

Unlike a general partnership, a limited partnership must be registered with the Registrar of Companies and the following disclosures made:

(a) the name of the business;

(b) the nature of business carried on;

(c) the place of business; and

(d) the names of each of the partners.

The registration details must also state that the partnership is limited and must disclose the names of the limited partners and the amount contributed by each limited partner. Any subsequent change in the constitution of the partnership must also be registered.

L.1.3.3 *Professional partnership*

Members of the same profession often operate in the form of a partnership. Indeed, the rules of certain professions preclude their members from operating in the form of a company.

The legislation and laws governing partnerships generally apply equally to professional partnerships. However, the rule that a partnership may not consist of more than 20 members does not apply to solicitors' or accountants' partnerships.

L.1.3.4 *General provisions*

The legislation governing partnerships is in many ways merely declaratory of the rules of the common law and equity as applied to partnerships. Accordingly, the rules of common law and equity apply to partnerships in so far as they are not inconsistent with the legislation.

L.1.4 Co-operative Society

Co-operative societies in Ireland have their origin in the middle of the last century. Given the agricultural basis for much of Ireland's industry, co-operative societies continue to play an important role in Ireland. Originally, co-operative societies were created by an agreement amongst several persons for a particular purpose. As such, co-operative societies are similar to partnerships but are distinguishable by the following four main principles which were usually incorporated in the agreement creating the society:

(a) democratic control;

(b) open membership;

(c) fixed or limited return on capital subscribed; and

(d) dividend on purchases.

Co-operative societies were first given statutory recognition in Ireland by the Industrial and Provident Society Act 1893. The 1893 Act, subject to various minor amendments, has continued to be the primary source of legislation governing the creation of co-operative societies in Ireland. The 1893 Act does not define what is a co-operative society. Instead, the 1893 Act provides that a society "for carrying on any industries, businesses or trades specified in or authorised by its rules, whether wholesale or retail, and including dealings of any description with land" may be registered under the Act. Registration of a society is made with the Registrar of Friendly Societies as provided for in the 1893 Act.

Registration under the 1893 Act renders the society a body corporate, with the power to sue and be sued, with perpetual succession, a common seal and with limited liability.

The 1893 Act provides that the society must register its rules in accordance with the Act, and requires that the rules incorporate various provisions but, in general, the Act remains silent on many points. These rules will govern such things as membership, transfer or termination of membership, meetings, capital of the society, management of the society and resolution of disputes. The 1893 Act also provides for the termination of a society, the transfer of its assets and the conversion of a society into a company. Given the absence of legislation in this area, co-operative societies are not subject to rules similar to those rules which have been introduced in many common law jurisdictions during this century for the purpose of protecting the rights of shareholders in companies. Such protection may only be obtained by ensuring the rules of the society are appropriately drafted. However, this protection can be circumvented as the rules may subsequently be amended.

In the case of agricultural and fisheries societies, there are some further legislative provisions governing their creation.

L.1.5   Building Society

Building societies in Ireland were originally another form of co-operative society and were traditionally constituted by an agreement amongst several persons for the purpose of raising funds (by the subscription of the members, and the acceptance of deposits and loans) for making loans to members. Building societies were first given statutory recognition by the Building Society Benefit Act 1836. Since then there have been several further pieces of legislation, culminating in the Building Societies Act 1989. All building societies are bodies corporate with perpetual succession.

A building society must have a memorandum stating its objects and powers and this must include the object of providing mortgage funds for housing. The building society must also have rules for the regulation of its business.

The range of services which may be provided by a building society include auctioneering, conveyancing and financial services relating to land. These services may only be exercised after being adopted by the society by means of a special resolution and with the approval of the Central Bank. Building societies are regulated by the Central Bank of Ireland. Subject to the satisfaction of a number of conditions, a building society may convert from mutual to public limited company status.

L.1.6 European Economic Interest Grouping

The European Economic Interest Grouping (EEIG) has its origin in Council Regulation 2137/85 of July 25, 1985 which has been implemented in Ireland. The EEIG Regulation is intended to simplify and harmonise the legal environment for co-operation between enterprises or individuals from different Member States in activities of common economic interest. By the creation of an EEIG such persons may come together in a joint venture which is not of itself profit-making and which is ancillary to the business activities of the constituent parties.

In implementing the EEIG Regulation, Ireland exercised the option in Article 1(3) to confer legal personality on EEIGs registered in Ireland. Registration is effected by the delivery of the contract for the formation of the EEIG to the Companies Registration Office which is the designated registry for the purposes of Articles 6, 7, 10 and 39 of the EEIG Regulation. Only an EEIG whose official address is located in Ireland may be so registered.

SECTION 2

LIMITED LIABILITY COMPANY

L.2.1 Introduction

The primary Irish legislation concerning companies is contained in the Companies Act 1963 followed by amending Acts in 1977, 1982, 1983, 1985, 1986 and 1990

(Companies (Amendment) Act 1990 and Companies Act 1990 (hereafter, the "1990 Act")). The first, second, third, fourth, sixth, seventh, eighth, eleventh and twelfth E.C. Directives on Company Law have been implemented in Ireland, together with the E.C. Stock Exchange Directives of 1979, 1980 (as amended) and 1982, the UCIT Directive, the EEIG Regulation, the Mutual Recognition Directive, the Disclosure of Major Shareholdings Directive, the Insider Dealing Directive and the Prospectus Directive.

The fundamental principles of Irish company law were derived from English company law. However, the differences between Irish and English company law are significant, particularly in the areas of insolvency, the Irish equivalent of company administration and securities regulations.

The liability of a member of a company for the debts of that company may either be limited or unlimited. Limited liability status may be achieved by providing in the memorandum of association that the members' liability is limited to either the amount remaining unpaid to the company on the shares held by them in the company, in which case the company will be known as a company limited by shares, or to the amount specified in the memorandum up to which the members agreed to contribute in the event of the company being wound up, in which case the company will be known as a company limited by guarantee. In the case of companies limited by shares, the Companies Acts further provide that they may be either public or private companies.

L.2.2 Public Company

A public company must be limited by shares and is registrable as a public limited company ("plc") under the provisions of the Companies (Amendment) Act 1983 if certain conditions have been complied with. Such conditions relate mainly to minimum capital requirements and capital maintenance. A plc must, in addition, have a minimum of seven shareholders and an allotted share capital of a specified minimum (currently IR £30,000). A plc is subject to more detailed disclosure requirements than those applicable to a private limited company. The 1983 Act implements the second E.C. Companies Directive and contains some similarities to corresponding legislation in the United Kingdom.

There is no requirement that the shares in a plc be traded on a stock exchange. If, however, its shares are listed on the Official List of the Irish Stock Exchange, the plc must comply with the requirements of the European Communities (Stock Exchange) Regulations 1984 which implement the E.C. Stock Exchange Directives. Compliance with the Irish Stock Exchange's Listing Rules will normally ensure compliance with these regulations. More flexible rules exist with respect to shares dealt in on the Developing Companies Market and the Exploration Market of the Irish Stock Exchange.

The Irish Stock Exchange and the London Stock Exchange were, in 1973, merged to form the International Stock Exchange of the United Kingdom and the Republic of Ireland Limited. Following the enactment of the Stock Exchange Act 1995, however, the two exchanges de-merged and the Irish exchange is now called The Irish Stock Exchange Limited.

The Irish Stock Exchange Limited, which is regulated by the Central Bank of Ireland, has three markets; the Official List, the Developing Companies Market and the Exploration Market.

Both natural persons and corporations may be shareholders in private limited companies and plcs. Similarly, persons not resident in Ireland may own shares in Irish companies.

L.2.3   Private Company

A private company may have between one and fifty shareholders. A private company is also subject to the following restrictions:

(a)   the right to transfer shares is restricted; and

(b)   any invitation to the public to subscribe for shares and debentures is prohibited.

L.2.4   Incorporation

To incorporate a company, the following must be delivered to the Registrar of Companies:

(a)   the memorandum and articles of association of the company;

(b)   details of the first directors and secretary of the company and the address of the company's registered office;

(c)   a capital duty statement for shares allotted;

(d)   a statutory declaration from the solicitor acting in the incorporation or a director or the secretary of the company certifying compliance with all requirements necessary for registration; and

(e)   a bank draft for the appropriate registration fee.

To register a plc, an additional statutory declaration made by a director or the secretary of the company must be delivered to the Registrar of Companies. The declaration must confirm:

(1)   that the nominal value of the company's allotted share capital is not less than the authorised minimum (currently IR £30,000);

(2)   the amount paid up on the allotted share capital of the company amounts to at least one-quarter of the nominal value of the allotted shares plus all of any premium paid;

(3)   details of preliminary expenses of the company; and

(4)   details of any payment made to a promoter of the company.

L.2.4.1   *Constitutional documents*

The constitutional documents of a company are its memorandum and articles of association. These documents, which must be registered with the Registrar of Companies, constitute a contract between the company and its members.

The memorandum contains the conditions upon which the company is incorporated and the 1963 Act stipulates that it must include certain clauses which set out, *inter alia*, the company's objects and authorised share capital.

The articles of association set out the regulations governing the internal management of the company's affairs. In particular, the articles regulate the conduct of board meetings, general meetings, the transfer and transmission of shares, and set out the rights and obligations of directors and shareholders and their respective powers and authorities.

A company's memorandum or articles of association may be altered by special resolution.

The 1963 Act sets out in Table A of the First Schedule a set of model form articles of association. If a company limited by shares does not register its articles, the provisions of Table A will apply automatically. If its articles are registered, the provisions of Table A will apply only in so far as they are not modified or excluded by the company's articles.

L.2.4.2   *Registered office*

The address of the registered office of a company must be given when applying for incorporation. A company must at all times have a registered office in the State, which need not necessarily be the company's place of business. The main purpose of this requirement is to enable the service of documents on the company, such as the process of a court. The Registrar of Companies must be notified of any change in the address of a company's registered office.

L.2.4.3   *Company name*

A company's memorandum must state the name of the company. If a company is limited by shares or by guarantee, the name must end with the word "Limited" or "Teoranta" (the Irish equivalent), or these may be abbreviated to "Ltd" or "Teo", respectively. If a company is a public limited company, its name must end with the words "public limited company" or "cuideachta phoibli theoranta" (the Irish equivalent) or these may be abbreviated to "plc" or "c.p.t.", respectively.

The consent of the Minister for Enterprise, Trade and Employment must be obtained for the use of a particular name, which consent may be refused if the name, in the opinion of the Minister, is undesirable. A right of appeal to the courts lies in respect of any such refusal. A company may change its name by special resolution, subject to the approval of the Minister for Enterprise, Trade and Employment.

The name of the company must be affixed outside every place of business of the company, engraved on the company's seal and printed on all business letters and other notices of the company.

L.2.4.4 *Duration*

Unlike unincorporated businesses, a company's existence is not dependent on the survival of its members. However, its members may fix the duration of the existence of the company by providing in its articles that the company's existence will terminate after the expiration of a specified period of time, or the occurrence of a specified event, and the passage of an ordinary resolution that the company be wound up voluntarily.

L.2.5   Shares

Section 25 of the 1963 Act states:

> "The memorandum and articles shall, when registered, bind the company and the members thereof to the same extent as if they respectively had been signed and sealed by each member, and contained covenants by each member to observe all the provisions of the memorandum and of the articles."

A share in a company is effectively a contract between the company and the shareholder, the terms of which are derived from the memorandum and articles of association and company law.

Companies are generally free to create and provide in their articles for different types and classes of shares with varying rights and obligations attached.

The most common types of shares are:

(1)   *Ordinary shares* It is usual for shares carrying voting rights to be called "ordinary" shares although the term "ordinary" is more appropriately used to distinguish such shares from other classes which carry preferential, dividend and/or other rights. Voting rights may take many different forms. For example,

310

it is common for the articles of companies formed for the purpose of a joint venture to provide for various classes of ordinary shares, each class carrying the right to appoint a specified number of directors and other rights.

(2) *Preference shares* Preference shares are so called because they carry the right to receive, in preference to all other classes of share capital, a dividend, which may be fixed and/or cumulative. Such shares usually confer on the holding priority in the return of capital in a winding-up.

(3) *Redeemable shares* If authorised by its articles, a company may issue redeemable shares provided that at least one-tenth in nominal value of the total issued share capital is not redeemable and the terms of redemption provide for repayment on redemption.

The redemption of shares is subject to several other restrictions set out in the 1990 Act. Redeemable shares may only be redeemed if they are fully paid up. Generally, the shares may be redeemed only out of profits available for distribution or, if it is proposed that the shares be cancelled, the proceeds of a fresh issue made for the purposes of the redemption. Likewise, any premium which is paid on redemption must be met out of such profits. The premium (if any) payable on redemption may be paid out of the proceeds of such issue only if such shares had been issued at a premium and only to the extent specified in the 1990 Act. The 1990 Act sets out detailed provisions in respect of shares cancelled on redemption.

A company may, instead of cancelling shares on redemption, retain them as treasury shares. The nominal value of treasury shares so retained may not exceed 10 per cent of the nominal value of the company's issued share capital.

Voting and dividend entitlements attached to such shares may not be exercised for as long as the shares are held by the company as treasury shares. Treasury shares may be reissued at any time by the company. A company whose shares are not listed or dealt in on a recognised stock exchange may reissue treasury shares only within the price range determined by special resolution of the company.

L.2.5.1 *Share capital*

The words "share capital" have a variety of meanings depending on the context in which they are used. For instance:

(a) the authorised share capital is the aggregate amount of share capital (divided into shares each of a fixed amount) which the company is authorised by its memorandum to issue or with which the company proposes to be registered;

(b) the issued share capital is the amount of authorised share capital which has been subscribed for and allotted. A plc must presently have a minimum issued share capital of IR £30,000;

(c) the paid-up share capital is that amount paid up by shareholders on the issued share capital;

(d) the reserve share capital is any portion of the issued share capital which has not already been called up and which the company has resolved by special resolution shall not be capable of being called up except in the event and for the purposes of the company being wound up; and

(e) the unissued share capital is that part of the authorised share capital which has not been issued and so equals the difference between the authorised share capital and the issued share capital at any given time.

The fundamental principle of capital maintenance is reflected in section 72(1) of the 1963 Act which states:

"Except insofar as this Act expressly permits, it shall not be lawful for a company limited by shares ... to reduce its share capital in any way."

The rationale for the rules governing the maintenance of capital is to prevent companies from making payments which would erode its capital and to secure the obligations on the part of its members to contribute to the assets of the company. This principle is subject to many exceptions, such as the reduction of capital with the sanction of the court (discussed in L.2.5.3 below), the purchase of own shares (discussed in L.2.5.5 below) and the redemption of redeemable shares (discussed above).

L.2.5.2   *Transfer of shares*

The 1963 Act requires a transfer of shares to be effected by "a proper instrument of transfer". In the case of a transfer of shares in a company limited by shares, the Stock Transfer Act 1963 provides that this may be effected by means of an instrument under hand in the form set out in the schedule to this Act and need only to be signed by the transferor. In the case of an unlimited company or a company limited by guarantee, the instrument of transfer will only be effective when executed by both parties.

Under regulations introduced in 1996, it is also possible for the shares in a company to be transferred in uncertificated form where this had been provided for either in the articles of association of the company or pursuant to a resolution passed in accordance with the regulations. These regulations are designed to operate in respect of large public companies whose shares are traded on a stock exchange. For uncertificated share transfers to take place, the company must have made arrangements with a "relevant operator" as defined in the regulations. Currently the only relevant operator is CRESTco Limited.

As will be discussed below, membership rights in respect of shares transferred will generally be vested in the transferee only when he is registered as the holder of the shares.

The articles of a private limited company must contain a provision restricting the right to transfer shares. This statutory requirement will be satisfied by a regulation which controls in some way the disposition of shares. For this reason articles of a private limited company normally provide that the directors may in their absolute discretion and without giving any reason, decline to register a transfer of shares.

The rules of the Irish Stock Exchange generally prohibit any restrictions on the transfer of fully paid shares in a plc whose shares are listed or dealt in on the Irish Stock Exchange.

L.2.5.3   *Increase and decrease of capital*

If so authorised by its articles, a company in general meeting may alter its memorandum and increase its authorised share capital or cancel shares which have not been taken or agreed to be taken by any person.

Directors may not exercise the power to allot shares or rights or options in shares (other than subscriber shares or shares allotted under an employee share scheme) unless they are so authorised by the company in general meeting or the articles of association. Such authority may be general and not limited to a particular allotment and may be unconditional or subject to conditions. The authorisation must comply with the requirements set out in section 20 of the 1983 Act and, in particular, the authority must state the maximum amount of shares which may be allotted and specify the date on which the authority will expire, which may not exceed five years. Section 20 also sets out the period of validity of the authority, the procedure to be observed and conditions relating to its variation, revocation and renewal.

Section 23 of the 1983 Act confers on shareholders (other than holders of shares which only carry rights to dividend and capital up to a specified amount generally) the right of pre-emption over a proposed allotment of "equity securities" in the company. "Equity securities" essentially means any shares other than shares which only carry rights to dividend and capital up to a specified amount and shares acquired or to be allotted in pursuance of an employees' share scheme. A private company may through its memorandum or articles of association exclude the right of pre-emption conferred by section 23.

This statutory right of pre-emption does not apply to an allotment if the shares are, or are to be, wholly or partly paid up otherwise than in cash.

If the directors are generally authorised to allot shares for the purposes of section 20 of the 1983 Act, they may also be empowered by special resolution of the company or by its articles of association to allot shares pursuant to such authority as if the statutory right of pre-emption did not apply to the allotment. Provided the directors so recommend, the company may by special resolution resolve that the right of pre-emption does not apply to a specified allotment or that such right applies only in a modified manner.

Section 72(2) of the 1963 Act provides an exception to the principle of capital maintenance. A company may, if so authorised by its articles and the passing of a special resolution, reduce its share capital.

The reduction of capital by whatever means is only effective when confirmation of the court has been obtained. The purpose of this requirement is for the protection of creditors of the company. Creditors have the right to object to the reduction and the court must be satisfied that they have either consented to it or that provision has been made in respect of the company's debts. A reduction of share capital may be challenged by minority shareholders or holders of different classes of shares if different treatment is given to holders of different classes of shares. Some protection is given to them under the 1983 Act which provides that any alteration of class rights connected with the reduction of share capital requires the separate consent (by special resolution or three-quarters consenting in writing) of the class of shareholders concerned.

L.2.5.4 *Form of subscription*

Although there is no requirement for an application for shares to be evidenced in writing, this is normally the case. Until such time as the applicant has been notified of the allotment in response to his application, it is generally open to him to revoke such application.

In the case of a private company, shares may be allotted for non-cash consideration but the contract constituting the title of the allottee to the allotment must be registered with the Registrar of Companies within one month of the allotment. It is not open to the court to question the adequacy of the consideration unless the transaction was fraudulent or the consideration was clearly inadequate.

The 1983 Act prohibits a plc from accepting, as payment for an allotment of its shares or any premium on them, an undertaking to do work or perform services for the company or any other person. A plc may not allot shares as fully or partly paid up otherwise than in cash if the consideration consists of or includes an undertaking which is to be or may be performed more than five years after the date of the allotment. Shares may not be allotted as fully or partly paid up otherwise than in cash unless the consideration has been valued in accordance with the provisions of section 30 of the same Act and a report obtained from the valuer and a copy thereof sent to the proposed allottee. The company must deliver a copy of the report to the Registrar of Companies at the same time the return of the allotments is filed.

L.2.5.5 *Purchase of own shares*

A company may purchase its own shares if:

(a) the shares to be purchased are fully paid up;

(b) the shares are purchased out of profits available for distribution or the proceeds of a fresh issue of shares;

(c) subject to one exception, any premium payable is paid out of such profits;

(d) a minimum of 10 per cent of the nominal value of the issued share capital is made up of non-redeemable shares (*i.e.* a company may purchase its own shares to the extent that this minimum level is maintained); and

(e) the company is so authorised by its articles of association.

Shares purchased on a recognised stock exchange, constitutes a "market purchase" and an ordinary resolution of the company is required. The resolution must specify certain matters set out in the 1990 Act which effectively restrict the number of shares that may be acquired, the price to be paid and the period in which such acquisition should be made.

The purchase by a company of its own shares other than on a recognised stock exchange constitutes "an off-market purchase". A company may not make an off-market purchase of its own shares unless the agreement to make such purchase has been authorised by a special resolution of the company and the agreement has been available for inspection by members of the company for a specified period.

L.2.5.6 *Financial assistance for purchase of own shares*

Section 60(1) of the 1963 Act provides that it is unlawful for a company "to give, whether directly or indirectly ... any financial assistance for the purpose of or in connection with a purchase or subscription ... of or for any shares in the company, or ... in its holding company". A breach of section 60 renders the transaction concerned voidable at the instance of the company and will constitute an offence on the part of all officers of the company involved.

A private company may provide financial assistance for the purchase of its own shares if it has been authorised by a special resolution passed within the preceding 12 months and if certain other conditions are fulfilled.

The prohibition in section 60(1) does not extend to a payment of a dividend properly declared by a company or the discharge of a liability lawfully incurred by it.

Section 60(13) provides that the following transactions are exempted from the prohibition in section 60(1):

(a) the lending of money by the company in the ordinary course of its business or where the lending of money is part of its ordinary course of business;

(b) the provision by the company of money in accordance with an employee share scheme as stated in the subsection; and

(c) the making of loans to persons other than directors bona fide in the employment of the company with a view to enabling them to acquire shares in the company.

A plc may give financial assistance under section 60(13) only if certain other conditions are met. These require that the net assets of the company are not reduced or that the financial assistance is only provided out of profits available for dividend.

A company may, however, acquire and hold shares in its holding company under certain conditions. The prohibition in section 60(1) of the 1963 Act does not apply to companies which are investment companies within the meaning of Part XIII of the 1990 Act.

L.2.5.7 Register of shares

Under Irish law, a company is not required to maintain a register of shares. Rather, it must keep a register of its members which may be inspected by anyone, regardless of whether or not he is a member of the company. The register of members must contain, inter alia, particulars of the members with a statement of the shares held by each member.

Membership rights will not normally arise until the holder of shares in the company has been registered as a member. If a company refuses to register a transfer of shares, notice of such refusal must be given to the transferee within a specified period. If the name of a person has been omitted from the register of members, that person may apply to the court for an order that the register be rectified by the inclusion of his name.

If the holder of shares is an existing member of the company and has taken a transfer of further shares in the company, he may seek relief under section 205 of the 1963 Act if his application to be registered has been refused. The court will grant relief under section 205 if it can be shown that the directors had exercised their powers in an oppressive manner or in disregard of the applicant's interests as a member.

The general rule is that no notice of any trusts, express, implied or constructive, will be entered in the register of members or be receivable by the company. The model form of articles in Table A provides that the company will not be bound to recognise any equitable interests in any share. However, the articles may reserve the right on the part of the company to require a member to reveal the beneficial ownership of any share.

The 1990 Act also imposes various requirements for the disclosure of interests in the shares of a company.

L.2.6 Corporate Management

Although the shareholders control the company, the management of the company's business will normally be vested by the articles of association in the board of directors who may delegate their powers and duties to the extent permitted by the articles of association.

L.2.6.1 *Board of directors*

The board of directors may be composed of executive directors and non-executive directors. Executive directors are also employees of the company. Executive directors will usually be responsible for the day-to-day management of the business of the company whereas non-executive directors will not usually be so involved but are usually appointed primarily for particular skills or expertise which they may possess.

L.2.6.1.1 Appointment and dismissal of directors The first directors of a newly incorporated company are determined by the subscribers to the memorandum but thereafter it is usual for the articles to empower both shareholders and directors to appoint new or additional directors on to the board of directors. The articles usually specify the maximum number of directors that may be appointed on to the board but the shareholders may vary this number by special resolution.

Subject to certain prohibitions imposed by the Companies Acts, any person may be appointed director and, unless the articles specify otherwise, a person need not possess any particular qualification to be eligible. The persons prohibited from acting as a director are as follows:

(a) a company;

(b) the auditors of the company;

(c) any person who has not obtained the appropriate share qualification in accordance with the company's articles (if required) within a period of two months after his appointment;

(d) an undischarged bankrupt; and

(e) a person disqualified by the court pursuant to section 160 of the 1990 Act.

A person subject to a restriction order imposed by the court under section 150 of the 1990 Act may be appointed a director of a company only if the company appointing him has complied with certain conditions. A person who is the subject of a disqualification order under section 160 of the 1990 Act is also prevented from acting as auditor, receiver, liquidator, examiner or other officer of a company for such period as the court sees fit.

The articles may also specify other situations when an individual is disqualified from acting as a director of the company or, if already a director, automatically ceases to be a director.

A director may be removed from office by the passing of a resolution at a general meeting of which 28 days' notice has been given of the intention to propose such a resolution. The articles may also empower the directors to remove any one or more of the directors from the board and appoint one or more in his or their place.

The articles may also provide for the retirement of directors by rotation. The articles may specify that a proportion of the directors retire at each annual general meeting and that the directors so retiring are eligible for re-election.

L.2.6.1.2 Duties and powers of directors The articles of association usually provide that the business of the company is the responsibility of the directors who may exercise all powers of the company as are not required by the Companies Acts and the articles to be exercisable only by the company in general meeting. Accordingly, the powers of the directors are subject to the articles, the Companies Acts and to such directions as may be given by the shareholders in general meeting. The powers of the directors may also be restricted by any shareholders' agreement entered into and by their service contracts. The directors must exercise their powers in good faith and for proper purposes.

The duties of the directors emanate from the articles, the Companies Acts, the common law and the rules of equity. In addition, environmental and consumer information legislation impose further duties on the directors, breach of which may result in severe penalties.

It is well established that a director is under a duty to act with skill and care in the performance of his functions. However, this is a subjective test and will vary depending on the qualifications and abilities of each director.

Directors' duties are usually owed to, and are enforceable by, the company only. However, the Irish courts have now accepted that directors may in certain circumstances owe fiduciary duties to creditors and to members of the company.

A director may be held personally liable for the debts of the company where he is held to have "traded recklessly". Two examples of conduct which will constitute trading in a reckless manner are given in the 1990 Act. These are:

(1) where, having regard to the general knowledge, skill and experience that may reasonably be expected of a person in the director's position, he ought to have known that his actions or those of the company would have caused loss to the creditors of the company; or

(2) where the company incurred a debt and a director did not honestly believe on reasonable grounds that the company would be able to pay the debt when it fell due, as well as all its other debts.

It should be noted that the two examples given above are not exhaustive.

Directors are also under a duty not to allow their own interests to conflict with their duties as directors. The 1990 Act sets out prohibitions and restrictions on a

318

wide range of transactions which essentially seek to prevent directors from abusing their positions for personal gain.

(1) A company is, as a general rule, prohibited from entering into the following transactions with a director:

    (a) the making of loans and quasi-loans as defined in the Act;

    (b) credit transactions, such as hire-purchase agreements and leasing arrangements; and

    (c) the provision of guarantees or other security for the benefit of a director.

    Such prohibitions are subject to certain exemptions, such as the *de minimis* rule which exempts transactions below a specified value. A director who enters into a prohibited transaction may be liable to account to the company for any gain made and he may also be liable for some or all of the company's debts in a winding-up. In addition, criminal penalties may be imposed. The transaction is also voidable at the instance of the company.

(2) It is an offence for a director of a company to buy an option to buy or sell certain shares or debentures of the company or its subsidiary or the company's holding company or its subsidiary. Generally, these are shares or debentures for which dealing facilities are provided on a stock exchange.

(3) Certain substantial (currently, IR £50,000 or 10 per cent of the company's assets) property transactions between the company and its directors (whether on an arm's length basis or otherwise) require the approval by a resolution of the company in general meeting. A breach of this restriction will entail similar sanctions to those in (1) above, except that a contravention of the relevant provisions is not a criminal offence.

(4) Directors are required to notify the company in writing of their interests in the company's shares and of any dealings by them in respect of such shares. "Interest" is very widely defined to include, *inter alia*, interests held in trust, option arrangements and other contractual interests. Companies must maintain a register of directors' shareholdings and all notifications made by them. If a director fails to notify the company within a specified time, his rights and interests in relation to the relevant shares may become unenforceable by him.

If a director enters into a contract with the company, or has a personal interest in a contract with the company or has entered into a transaction described in (3) above, he is required to disclose such interest to the directors at a board meeting. Such declarations of interest must be entered into a book kept for that purpose, which may be inspected by any officer or member of the company at its registered office and at every annual general meeting. In addition, particulars of such contracts and transactions are required to be included in the annual accounts of the company.

A director is also under a duty to ensure that the company keeps proper books of account.

The articles normally allow directors to delegate their powers to the managing director or managing directors and to committees formed for particular purposes.

L.2.6.1.3 Board meetings The proceedings of directors are regulated by the articles of association. The directors' functions are carried out through resolutions of the board of directors. The articles may fix the quorum required and the proportion of votes in favour necessary for the passing of a valid board resolution. The model form of articles in Table A fixes the quorum at two, provides that a resolution must be passed by a majority and that the chairman of the board has a casting vote.

The 1963 Act requires all board and committee meetings to be minuted. The articles normally provide that a resolution in writing signed by all directors for the time being is an effective resolution as if it had been passed at a meeting duly convened and held.

2.6.1.4 Liabilities of directors If a director has acted in breach of his duties an action may be brought against him by the company or, if applicable, by the company's liquidator. In certain circumstances, it is also possible for individual shareholders to bring a derivative, or even a direct, action against him. If a director exceeds his authority, he may be liable to the company in damages for any loss suffered. If in the process of the winding-up of a company, a director is found to have knowingly been a party to the carrying-on of any of the business of the company in a fraudulent or reckless manner, he may be held liable for some or all of the debts of the company.

If a company is unable to pay its debts and is in liquidation or receivership, the court will make a declaration prohibiting each director of that company from acting as a director of any other company unless certain requirements relating principally to the capitalisation of that other company are met. Such a restriction order will not be imposed if the court is satisfied that the director has acted honestly and responsibly.

The Act also gives the court wide powers in making a disqualification order against a director, thus preventing him from acting as an auditor, director or other officer, receiver, liquidator or examiner of any company for such period as the court sees fit. A person may be made the subject of a disqualification order if, *inter alia*, he has been found guilty of fraud, dishonesty or breach of duty.

Under the common law, certain wrongs of directors may be ratified by shareholders of the company, thereby absolving such directors of liability to the company. For example, a director will not be accountable for personal profits made out of his office if full disclosure of his interest in the relevant transaction is made to the company in general meeting. It is also possible for the company to refuse to bring proceedings against directors for any breach of their duty to exercise skill and care. However, fraud committed by the directors in connection with company property cannot be ratified by the members, nor can the company ratify any acts entered into by the directors in the absence of good faith. This situation is to be distinguished from an act entered into in good faith but for an improper purpose. The latter may be ratified by the company (see L.2.6.3.5 below).

The 1990 Act exposes directors to liability and, in some instances, criminal liability for certain transactions entered into for his own gain and to the detriment of the company and its creditors. This was discussed above (at L.2.6.1.2).

In addition, directors may incur criminal penalties for breach of certain legislation concerning anti-competitive practices, air and water pollution and dangerous substances. The Local Government (Water Pollution) Act 1990 also enables aggrieved third parties to claim against directors for certain losses suffered.

L.2.6.2 Supervisory board

Irish law does not provide for a supervisory board or any other body to supervise or advise the board of directors.

L.2.6.3 The general meeting

The functions and decisions of members of a company are carried out through the holding of a general meeting. Decisions are expressed by means of resolutions, which may be ordinary resolutions or special resolutions depending on the subject voted on.

L.2.6.3.1 General provisions

To validly constitute a general meeting, a chairman must be appointed in accordance with the articles and a valid quorum (which may be fixed by the articles) must exist.

An ordinary resolution is not defined in the Companies Act but is understood to mean a resolution which requires a simple majority. The passing of an ordinary resolution is sufficient for the ordinary business of the company. A special resolution is defined in the 1963 Act as a resolution passed by not less than 75 per cent of the members of the company present at the meeting and entitled to vote. The Companies Acts require the passing of special resolutions for certain special businesses of the company.

For example, special resolutions are required for:

(a) the alteration of the company's object clause;

(b) the alteration of the company's articles of association;

(c) the changing of the company's name;

(d) the reduction of share capital;

(e) the voluntary winding-up of the company (except where the duration of the company is specified in the articles, in which case an ordinary resolution will do); and

(f) the variation of class rights.

A company is required to maintain minutes of proceedings of all general meetings held. The minute book must be open to the inspection of any member of the company without charge. The minutes must be signed by the chairman of the company at the end of the meeting or by the chairman of the next succeeding meeting.

Provided that the articles so permit, the procedures and formalities required by the Companies Acts need not be observed if a resolution in writing is signed by all members for the time being entitled to attend and vote at general meeting. Such a resolution is valid and effective as if the resolution had been passed at a general meeting duly convened and held.

L.2.6.3.2 Convening a general meeting A company must hold an annual general meeting not more than 15 months after the previous meeting. Exception is made in the case of a newly incorporated company, when an annual meeting may be held at any time within an 18-month period after its incorporation. It is the duty of the directors and secretary of the company to convene the meeting and if they fail to do so after the period expires, the Minister for Enterprise, Trade and Employment may, on the application of any member of the company, convene the meeting.

An extraordinary general meeting may be convened by the directors of the company if so authorised by the articles, and by the court in certain circumstances. The 1963 Act provides that the holders of not less than one-tenth of the paid-up capital carrying voting rights at a general meeting may requisition the directors to convene an extraordinary general meeting.

L.2.6.3.3 Notices The articles must provide for:

(a) a minimum of 21 days' notice in writing for the calling of an annual general meeting;

(b) in relation to the calling of an extraordinary general meeting, a minimum notice period of 7 days in writing, in the case of a private limited company, and 14 days' notice in writing in the case of a plc.

However, shorter notice may be given if it is so agreed by the company's auditors and by all members entitled to attend and vote at the meeting. Notice of every general meeting must be served on every member so entitled under the articles.

A minimum of 21 days' notice must be given of the intention to propose a special resolution at a general meeting. However, shorter notice may be given if it is so agreed by a majority of shareholders representing at least 90 per cent nominal value of voting shares. Extended notice of 28 days is required in relation to certain resolutions such as a proposed resolution to remove a director.

The directors are under a duty to exercise good faith in serving notice to the members and the information disclosed in the notice must be true and accurate. The notice must also state that the members are entitled to appoint a proxy to attend the general meeting on their behalf, and that such person need not be a member of the company.

If any of the rules governing the giving of notice are breached, it is open to any shareholder to apply to the court for an order invalidating the meeting and the resolution passed thereunder.

L.2.6.3.4 Location   The annual general meeting of a company may be held outside Ireland if:

(a) either all the members entitled to attend and vote at such meeting consent in writing to it being held elsewhere or a resolution was passed at a preceding general meeting that it be held elsewhere, and

(b) the articles do not state that the annual general meeting must be held in Ireland.

Some companies conduct their board meetings and general meetings outside Ireland because this is one of several determining factors of the residency of a company under Irish revenue law.

L.2.6.3.5 Duties and powers of the general meeting   The annual general meeting deals with the ordinary business of the company such as:

(a) the declaration of a final dividend (if any);

(b) the consideration of the company's accounts, balance sheet and reports;

(c) the election of directors; and

(d) the appointment of the company's auditors.

The special business dealt with at an extraordinary general meeting may consist of such matters as the amendment of the company's articles of association, alteration of share capital, the conferring of authority on the directors to allot shares and the winding-up of the company.

As discussed above (at L.2.6.1.2), articles of association normally provide that the directors of the company are responsible for the conduct of the company's business. Essentially, the company in general meeting may interfere with the powers of the directors only to the extent to which the articles define the functions and duties between the board of directors and general meeting. In practice, however, the functions of the board of directors may be interfered with because the power to amend the company's constitutional documents is vested in the general meeting, as is the power to control the composition of the board of directors. This is particularly the case if a shareholder or a group of shareholders voting together have sufficient voting strength to pass a special resolution or ordinary resolution as the motion requires.

Certain functions and powers of the company are by law reserved to the company in general meeting. These functions have been examined above (at L.2.6.3.1).

Members of a company may ratify acts of directors which were done outside the powers delegated to them provided that such acts are within the powers of the company. It is also possible for the company to ratify a director's breach of fiduciary and other duties by deciding that the company will not seek damages for the loss suffered. However, if the directors fail to exercise their duties in good faith, such wrong is not ratifiable and an individual member may bring a derivative action against those directors.

Ratification by the company may not be a complete exoneration because in certain circumstances an action may lie under section 205 of the 1963 Act. This provision entitles a shareholder to apply to the court for relief when the affairs of the company are being conducted, or the powers of the directors are being exercised, in a manner oppressive to him or any of the members, or in disregard of his or their interests as members. If the company's affairs are being conducted in such a manner, the court may make any order it deems fit, including an order winding up the company.

L.2.6.3.6 Voting rights and restrictions

The articles may provide for different types and classes of shares with different voting rights attached. This has been discussed in L.2.5 above.

The model form of articles in Table A in the 1963 Act provides that every member entitled to vote at an annual general meeting is to have one vote and that every motion be initially decided by a show of hands. However, if a poll is validly demanded, each member has one vote for each voting share held by him. The 1963 Act prohibits a company's articles from excluding the right to demand a poll on any question other than the election of the chairman of the meeting or the adjournment of the meeting. The Act also renders void any provision in the articles which has the effect of restricting the right to demand a poll in certain specified ways.

A person entitled to more than one vote need not use all his votes or cast all the votes used in the same way.

A body corporate may by resolution of its directors authorise a person to act as its representative at any general meeting or class meeting of the company.

Any member of a company is entitled to appoint another person as his proxy to attend and vote in his stead. A proxy so appointed has the same rights as that member to speak and vote at the meeting. A proxy may be either a general proxy (*i.e.* a proxy authorised to represent the member at more than one general meeting) or a special proxy (*i.e.* a proxy authorised to represent the member for one general meeting only). It is open to a member of the company to avail of the two-way proxy system which would entitle the proxy to vote on any particular motion in accordance with the member's wishes.

The model form of articles in Table A provides for certain situations when the voting rights attached to shares are to be restricted or suspended.

L.2.6.4 *Works council*

The E.C. Works Council Directive has been implemented into Irish law. A company or group of companies with 1,000 or more employees in the European Union and at least 150 employees in each of at least two Member States is required to establish a works council. In addition, under the Worker Participation (State Enterprises) Acts 1977 and 1988, employees of specified corporations which are mostly State and semi-State bodies, are entitled to nominate specified numbers of directors to the board of the employer organisation.

L.2.7   Audits and Accounts

A company is required to prepare "proper books of account". "Proper books of account" will be deemed to be kept if the company's books comply with section 202 of the 1990 Act and give a true and fair view of the company's affairs and explain its transactions. The auditors of the company are required to prepare a report on the accounts, balance sheet, profit and loss account and group accounts of the company.

Officers and former officers who deliberately or negligently fail to ensure that proper books of accounts are kept will be guilty of an offence and, in certain circumstances, they may be made personally liable without any limitation of liability for all or some of the debts and other liabilities of the company. It is an offence for an officer of a company to give any information to the auditors that is materially misleading, false or deceptive. Any failure on the part of an officer to provide information to the auditors within two days of such request being made is also an offence.

The 1986 Act was enacted to implement the fourth E.C. Directive on Company Law. The Act requires companies to file with the Registrar of Companies financial statements in a certain format together with its annual return. The detail required in such financial statements varies according to which category the company falls into. All private limited companies which are categorised as "large companies" and all plcs are subjected to more detailed filing requirements than companies which fall into other categories. A company classified as a large company must file a profit and loss account and balance sheet in the prescribed form together with the appropriate notes, directors' report and auditors' report.

The seventh E.C. Directive on Company Law has also been implemented in Ireland. Under the relevant regulations, Irish limited companies which have subsidiary undertakings are required to draw up group accounts comprising a consolidated balance sheet, a consolidated profit and loss account and notes to the accounts. The regulations define when an undertaking is to be regarded as a subsidiary of another for the purposes of the preparation of group accounts in specified circumstances. The regulations also contain provisions governing the preparation of group accounts, the contents of those accounts, their format and the valuation of items to be included therein. They also specify information to be included in the notes to the group accounts.

E.C. Directive 90/605 has also been implemented into Irish law. This Directive extends the scope of the fourth and seventh Directives to partnerships, limited partnerships and unlimited companies, where all the members of such entities are themselves limited companies.

Finally, the eleventh E.C. Directive on Company Law has also been implemented into Irish law. This makes provision for various disclosure requirements in respect of foreign limited liability companies which establish a branch in Ireland.

L.2.7.1 Appointment and dismissal of auditors

Part X of the 1990 Act implements Council Directive 84/253 of April 10, 1984 on the approval of persons responsible for carrying out the statutory audits of accounting documents.

The Minister for Enterprise, Trade and Employment is empowered to grant recognition to accounting bodies, whether foreign or Irish, for the purposes of eligibility for appointment as auditors of a company. Certain persons may not act as auditors of a company. In particular, these include officers and employees of the company, the immediate relatives of officers and employees of the company, and bodies corporate.

The shareholders in general meeting appoint the company's auditors, who will generally hold office until, and be automatically reappointed at, the next annual general meeting of the company.

The 1990 Act extended the power of the company to remove the company's auditors and to replace them with other persons nominated for the office. Directors of a company, or the company in general meeting, may fill any casual vacancy in the office of auditor which may arise.

Auditors of a company may resign from office at any time. The auditors must state in their notice of resignation any circumstances relating to their resignation which ought to be notified to the members or creditors of the company, and if there are none, to make a negative statement to that effect. Such notice must be served by the auditors on the Registrar of Companies and the company may be required to send a copy of this notice to every shareholder so entitled. The auditors may also requisition the convening by the directors of an extraordinary general meeting to consider such circumstances connected with their resignation.

L.2.7.2 Duties and powers of auditors

The auditors must prepare a report on the accounts examined by them and the balance sheet, profit and loss account and group accounts to be laid before the general meeting. The auditors must state in their report such opinions which they may have on the matters set out in section 193(4) of the 1990 Act. This includes a statement of whether, in their opinion, proper books of account have been kept by the company. If the auditors are of the opinion that proper books of account have not been kept, they are under a duty to notify the Registrar of Companies and the company of this fact.

The auditors of a company have a right of access to the books, accounts and vouchers of the company and may request from the officers and employees such information and explanation they deem necessary.

The auditors of a company are entitled to receive notice of, and to attend, the general meetings of the company. They are also entitled to be heard on any part of the business of the general meeting which concerns them as auditors. The auditors of a subsidiary company are required to give to the auditors of its holding company such information and explanations reasonably required by the latter. If the subsidiary is not a company incorporated in Ireland, it is the duty of the auditors of the holding company to endeavour to obtain from the subsidiary such information as may be required.

L.2.7.3 *Confidentiality of auditors*

Section 193(6) of the 1990 Act states as follows:

> "A person who is appointed as auditor of a company or as a public auditor shall be under a general duty to carry out such audit with professional integrity".

Subject to the exceptions set out below, the auditors are under a duty to the company not to disclose confidential information and to take reasonable care in relation to documents entrusted to them. However, the extent of this duty is subject to the following exceptions:

(a) if the auditors of a company know that a company or its officers have committed a felony, they are under a duty to report this to the police;

(b) as auditors and accountants do not possess legal professional privilege, the court may make an order of discovery against them and order them to give evidence in court. Auditors and accountants are, for the same reasons, compellable witnesses in civil and criminal proceedings;

(c) if the auditors are a party to legal proceedings in which the company to which they are appointed auditors is not a party, they may disclose information relating to that company in so far as is necessary for the protection of their interest; and

(d) certain persons may be authorised by legislation to request the auditors of a company to disclose information or produce documents concerning the company's affairs.

327

SECTION 3

COSTS OF INCORPORATION

L.3.1 The Companies Registration Office presently charges a registration fee of IR £50 whether it is a private limited company or a plc. Capital duty of 1 per cent is charged on subscribed capital of the company with a minimum charge of IR £1.

Any subsequent changes to the memorandum and/or articles of association, any further allotment of shares and resolutions of general meetings must be filed with the Companies Registration Office. A filing fee of IR £5 is charged on each document, prescribed form or resolution filed. Other documents may be required to be filed or registered from time to time, such as the annual return, notice of increase in nominal capital, charges, etc. Such post-incorporation documents carry varying registration fees which range from IR £5 to IR £25. The Companies Registration Office charges a fee of IR £50 for a change of name.

Where articles in a form previously approved by the Companies Registration Office are adopted, a company can be incorporated within two weeks. Alternatively, where non-standard articles are adopted the process will take between three to four months. A change of name normally takes approximately three to four weeks.

ITALY

ITALY

SECTION 1

CLASSIFICATION OF BUSINESS ORGANISATIONS*

M.1.0 There are (apart from special forms of co-operative companies and governmental agencies) five categories of business organisations in Italy. They are mainly governed by the Civil Code and can be listed as follows:

—entrepreneur (imprenditore)
—joint venture (associazione in partecipazione)
—partnership (società di persone)

    (a)   general partnership (società in nome collettivo or Snc)

    (b)   limited partnership (società in accomandita semplice or Sas)

    (c)   civil partnership (società semplice)

—companies with limited liability (società di capitale)

    (a)   share company (società per azioni or SpA)

    (b)   limited liability company (società a responsabilitá limitata or Srl)

    (c)   limited partnership by shares (società in accomandita per azioni or Sapa)

—branch of foreign company (sede secondaria)

M.1.1 The Entrepreneur (Imprenditore)

An entrepreneur is a person who engages professionally in an economic (business) activity for the purpose of production or exchange of goods or services.

    The entrepreneur is not necessarily the owner of the assets of the enterprise (he can borrow or hire the means he needs) but he must be filed in a special register ("Register of Enterprises") with the Chamber of Commerce. As a consequence of the implementation of a new legislation the "Register of Economic Activities" was

---

* *Roberto Cociancich, Piergrossi Villa Manca Graziadei Studio Legale (full particulars are listed in the Appendix).*

also introduced in 1996. Both the above-mentioned registers are important sources of information on the life of the enterprises.

The company's code entered in such registers must be indicated in any correspondence and in the main documents of the company together with indication of its registered office, equity capital, fiscal code or VAT number.

Being an entrepreneur is the prerequisite for the applicability of several provisions of law concerning labour, trade marks, trade names, competition as well as fiscal and administrative rules, and, in particular, it entails the possibility of being declared in bankrupt.

The entrepreneur must keep, with diligence, a journal and an inventory book as well as all the other accounting and fiscal records as are required for an enterprise, including—for a period of 10 years—copies of correspondence and of invoices issues. In practice, the provisions laid out for the entrepreneur generally apply to all other forms of business.

In the case of a sole entrepreneur (imprenditore individuale), since there is no distinction between business capital and private capital, the sole entrepreneur is personally liable for all the obligations undertaken during his economic activity.

The Civil Code contains special provisions for the small entrepreneur and for the agricultural entrepreneur.

The intellectual activities (such as those of lawyers, architects, accountants, etc.) are regulated by specific provisions of law.

M.1.2 Joint Venture (Associazione in Partecipazione)

Although the expression "joint venture" is nowadays being used in many meanings, it is being used here in the very specific meaning described hereunder.

This is a form of business which does not imply any permanent establishment nor any administrative formalities in Italy. It is a contract under which an associating party grants an associate a share in the profits of a specific venture or transaction as consideration for an agreed contribution. Losses are usually shared on the same basis as profits but the losses to which the associated party is subject may not exceed the value of its contribution.

A variation to the standard set-up described above can be a contract without any sharing in losses or a contract whereby one contracting party grants to another a participation in the profits and the losses without a specific contribution.

Unless otherwise agreed, the associating party cannot grant participations in the same venture to other persons without the previous consent of the party or parties already associated.

The associated party may remain undisclosed to third parties who consequently acquire rights and assume obligations only toward the associating party. Indeed, the associating party is the only one who may act on behalf of the joint venture.

In all cases the associated party has the right to receive an accounting of the results of the venture or an annual account of operations of these last for more than one year. No public disclosure of such information nor audit of the joint venture is required by law.

M.1.3 Partnerships (Società di Persone)

Under Italian law the most relevant difference between companies with limited liability and partnerships is that the former, generally speaking, ensure limited liability and emphasise the paid-up capital of the company (as the limit of liability), whereas in the latter there is always at least one party with unlimited personal liability.

Partnerships are not legal entities and consequently the partners, or at least some partners (according to the form of the partnership and their position therein), are liable for the obligations of the partnership.

Moreover, under the prevailing interpretation of Italian courts, companies cannot become partners in a partnership.

M.1.3.1 *General partnership (Società in nome collettivo or Snc)*

In this form of partnership all partners are jointly and severally liable for an unlimited amount for the partnership's obligations. Any stipulation to the contrary has no effect with regard to third persons. However, the creditors of a partnership cannot demand payment from individual partners until after having exhausted remedies against the assets of the partnership.

On the other hand, the personal creditors of a partner cannot demand (as long as the partnership is in existence) the liquidation of the share (quota) of the partner who is their debtor.

To establish a general partnership there is no need for a public deed, but the services of a public notary are required in order to authenticate the signatures of partners and to file them together with the articles of association in the Register of Enterprises.

A partner may not exercise an activity in competition with that of the partnership for his own account or for the account of others without the consent of the other partners.

Any amendments to the articles of association must be notified to the Register of Enterprises within 30 days from the resolution of the partners.

Except in the case of final liquidation, there is no need to file the annual balance sheet, nor any financial statement, except with the annual tax return.

It is forbidden to distribute sums to the partners unless such sums represent profits actually earned. In case of losses, no distribution of money can take place until the capital is restored. No audit of accounts is required but each partner has the right to examine the documents concerning the operation of the business.

Partnerships can be dissolved in the following cases:

(a) by expiration of the period fixed for its duration;

(b) when its object has been fulfilled or fulfilment has become impossible;

(c) when all partners so desire;

(d) when there is only one member left;

(e) for any other reason set out in the articles of association.

M.1.3.2 Limited partnership (Società in accomandita semplice or Sas)

The main feature of this form of business organisation consists in a distinction between two categories of partners: general partners (soci accomandatari) who are jointly and severally liable for the obligations of the partnerships and to whom the management of the partnership is entrusted, and limited partners (soci accomandanti) who are liable only to the extent of their contribution.

The business name of the limited partnership must include the name of at least one general partner as well as the indication Sas.

Limited partners may not act on behalf of the company except by virtue of a special power of attorney for very specific transactions. A limited partner who breaches such prohibition meets two kinds of penalties: (a) he can be removed from the partnership (by the other partners) and (b) he becomes jointly and severally liable without limitation for the obligations of the partnership towards third parties, i.e. he forfeits the benefit of limited liability. He is subject to the latter penalty also if he consents that his name be included in the business name. In this way the law aims to protect third parties who can rely on the actual full liability of those partners whose name is part of the business name of the partnership.

The greater liability of the general partner or partners is justified by their weight in the management of the partnership. As a consequence of such principle, in order to appoint directors and to revoke them, the law requires the consent of all the general partners and of as many limited partners as represent the majority of the capital subscribed by limited partners. In any case limited partners are entitled to receive the balance sheet and the profit and loss account and to verify their accuracy by consulting the books and other documents of the partnership. They are not bound to return profits collected in good faith in accordance with a regularly approved balance sheet. The capital cannot be represented by shares.

Whereas the equity participation of a general partner cannot be transferred without the consent of all the other partners, the equity participation of a limited partner can be assigned subject to the consent of the partners representing the majority of the capital.

Except for the rules specifically applying to a limited partnership, the rules and principles relating to a general partnership govern.

M.1.3.3   *Civil partnership (Società semplice)*

Except for few agricultural activities this kind of partnership has a very residual importance since it cannot be used to carry on commercial or industrial operations.

All the partners participate directly in the management and represent the partnership. They are all jointly and severally liable for the obligations of the enterprise. Creditors of the partnership can enforce their rights against the assets of an individual partner, but the latter can demand the prior execution of the assets of the partnership by indicating the assets on which the creditors can satisfy themselves.

SECTION 2

COMPANIES WITH LIMITED LIABILITY

M.2.1   Differences between Società per Azioni and Società a Responsabilità Limitata

As explained below, there are basically two forms of company with limited liability, *i.e.* share company, Società per Azioni (SpA) and limited liability company, Società a responsabilita limitata (Srl).

The major differences between a SpA and an Srl can be summed up as follows:

(a)   minimum equity capital (for an SpA 200 million lire, for an Srl 20 million lire);

(b)   no share certificates are issued for an Srl;

(c)   an Srl may not issue debentures;

(d)   simplified procedure to call general meetings for an Srl; in fact, the publication of the notice of a shareholders' meeting in respect of an SpA has to be requested one month in advance (in order to meet the 15-day deadline under M.2.7.2.3 (b) below) and involves a cost of some 500,000 lire, as against mailing registered letters eight days in advance in respect of an Srl;

(e)   the term of office for directors may not exceed three years in an SpA.

The appointment of a committee of statutory auditors is not compulsory for an Srl unless its equity capital exceeds 200 million lire, or alternatively two of the following situations are satisfied: (1) the aggregate turnover exceeds 9,500 million lire; (2) the total assets exceed 4,700 million lire; (3) the number of employees is higher than 50.

Apart from these there are no differences as to accounting rules, tax returns and filing requirements. Therefore administrative costs are identical and taxation is the same.

There is however one indirect difference of a tax nature, namely that a withholding tax applies for a non-resident vendor, on the sale of an "equity share" of an Srl and does not apply on the sale of shares of an SpA.

Until quite recently, forming an SpA was found preferable for reasons of prestige, in as much as an Srl was considered either a family affair or a second-class entity. Since the late eighties, however, there is a new trend in favour of forming an Srl as a fully respectable alternative.

M.2.2 Share Company (Società per Azioni: SpA)

In a share company the company is only answerable with its assets for the obligations of the company.

The liability of the shareholders in a share company is limited to the amount of the participation subscribed by each of them. The share participation of the shareholders is represented by shares, and the minimum share capital is 200 million lire.

M.2.3 Limited Liability Company (Società a Responsabilità Limitata: Srl)

In a Srl (as for an SpA) the liability of participants is limited to their respective holding and the obligations of the company are guaranteed only by its assets.

The main difference is that the participations are not represented by shares but by portions (quote) which cannot be incorporated in certificates.

Since 1993 it is possible to form an Srl with a sole partner but in this case the name and the personal details of the latter must be filed with the Register of Enterprises. Mention of such "sole partnership" must be indicated in any correspondence and in any other documents of the company.

"Quote" (plural of quota) grant the same rights pro-rata to their par value. Any transfer of such equity portions ("quote") must be entered in the register of partners of the company and, as a consequence of a recent legislation, such entry must be authenticated by a Public Notary and filed with the Register of Enterprises within 30 days from the date of the transfer. The minimum equity capital is 20 million lire and the portion of a partner cannot be less than one thousand lire.

An SpA may be partner of an Srl (whereas this is not allowed for other forms of partnerships) together with other partners or even a "sole partner" but, in this case, it is fully liable with its entire share capital for the liabilities of the Srl. In the latter case an SpA cannot take advantage of the limitation to liabilities generally recognised to individuals who are (sole) partners of an Srl.

Except for the aforesaid difference and those listed under M.2.1 above, the functioning of the Srl is almost identical to that of an SpA.

M.2.4 Limited Partnership by Shares (Società in Accomandita per Azioni: Sapa)

This type of company, which has not met with much success in business practice, can be described as a middle way between a limited partnership and a share company.

Actually it borrows from the former, the difference between jointly and severally liable partners (accomandatari) and limited partners (accomandanti) who are liable within the limits of the portion of equity respectively subscribed. Except the differences connected with such distinction, the functioning is similar to that of the SpA.

M.2.5 Incorporation

M.2.5.1 *Instrument of incorporation or articles of association (Atto Costitutivo) Byelaws (Statuto)*

A company must be constituted by a public instrument attested by a Notary Public in either of the two following forms:

(1) *Private subscription (Costituzione simultanea)* All the participants (individuals or legal entities) meet before a Public Notary to draw up the instrument of incorporation (articles of association) consisting of two parts. The first one (atto costitutivo) records the will to incorporate a company and some essential information in respect thereof; the second part is the byelaws (Statuto) and indicates the rules concerning the operation, the organisation and the winding up of the company.

Individuals may participate directly or by proxy; legal entities through their legal representatives. Proxies are required to be in the form of a public instrument. The (Italian) fiscal code number of each shareholder must be indicated.

(2) *Public subscription (Pubblica sottoscrizione)* This kind of incorporation is far less frequent and consists of two stages:

337

(a) *Preparatory.* The promoters prepare a prospectus to be filed with a Public Notary setting forth the objects of the company, equity capital, major provisions of the instrument of incorporation, the share on profits, if any, which promoters intend to reserve to themselves and the time-limit within which the instrument of incorporation is to be executed.

Thereafter subscriptions are collected and subscribers are requested to pay, within one month, three-tenths of their subscription.

(b) *Constituent.* The subscribers (at least 50 per cent of them) meet together and after having ascertained the fulfilment of the conditions required for the formation of the company and having adopted a final version of the instrument of incorporation appoint the directors and the members of the committee of statutory auditors (collegio sindacale).

The promoters are jointly and severally liable for all the obligations assumed during the preparatory stage and in the event that the company is not established they bear all costs incurred. On the other hand, if the company is eventually formed, they are entitled to be reimbursed of all reasonable expenses incurred.

In both forms (1 and 2) above, the validity of the incorporation is conditional upon the following requirements:

(a) the equity capital must be fully subscribed;

(b) at least three-tenths of the equity subscribed must be deposited with a bank (this deposit is returned when the company has been duly filed in the Register of Enterprises).

An authorisation is required from the Treasury if the equity of the company exceeds 10,000 million lire;

(c) in particular fields of activity which are considered of national interest (*e.g.* banking, insurance, shipping, air transport) all required government authorisations must have been obtained.

Moreover the instrument of incorporation must indicate:

(a) the name of the company, the address of its registered office and of the branch offices, if any;

(b) the objects of the company;

(c) the amount of capital subscribed and paid up;;

(d) the par value and the number of shares;

(e) the name, date and place of birth, domicile and citizenship of each shareholder and the number of shares subscribed by each of them;

(f) the value of the contributions in kind, if any;

(g) the rules for distribution of profits;

(h) the participation, if any, in the profits granted to founding members or promoters;

(i) the number of directors and their powers and an indication as to which of them has or have authority to act in the company's name;

(j) the number and the names of members of the committee of statutory auditors (collegio sindacale);

(k) the duration of the company;

(l) the total amount of the expenses foreseen for the incorporation of the company which shall be borne by the company itself.

Within 30 days from the execution of the instrument of incorporation the Notary must apply for its filing at the Register of Enterprises with the clerk's office at the local Chamber of Commerce.

A magistrate, specifically appointed to supervise the Register of Enterprises, after having ascertained compliance with the conditions required by law for the incorporation and having heard the favourable opinion of the Public Prosecutor, will order the registration of the company in the Register of Enterprises (omologazione). As a result of such formalities the company becomes a "legal entity".

M.2.5.2 Registered office

The instrument of incorporation must indicate the complete address of the company (not only the town) as well as the address of branches, if any.

M.2.5.3 Company name

The name may be freely composed by names, initials and references to the object of the company, but must include the initials of the specific type of company (respectively SpA, or Srl, or Sapa).

Moreover, the name has to be selected in compliance with the general provisions of law prohibiting the use of a name identical or similar to those already used by other enterprises, or existing trademarks, tradenames, etc.

M.2.5.4 Duration

Companies may not be established for an unlimited period of time.

M.2.5.5 *Contribution*

Unless otherwise provided in the instrument of incorporation, contributions must be made in cash. Those who grant a contribution in kind must submit a sworn report of an expert appointed by the president of the local court (tribunale) containing a description of the assets contributed, the value given to them and the method of evaluation applied.

Within six months the directors and the statutory auditors must check such evaluation and, if well founded reasons exist, must revise the appraisal. If the revised value falls short by more than one-fifth of the value for which the contribution was made, the company must reduce its equity capital proportionally.

Until the valuations have been verified, the shares corresponding to any contribution in kind must remain deposited with the company and are not transferable.

M.2.6   Shares (Azioni)

The shareholders' participations are represented by shares. They are indivisible, of equal value and cannot be issued for an amount lower than their par value. A company may not make loans against its own shares nor accept its own shares as guarantee. The shares can be of different types:

(1) *Ordinary shares (Azioni ordinarie)* each share grants to the owner the right to one vote and to a pro-rata portion in the distribution of profits and of assets in case of liquidation, as well as the right to subscribe new shares in case of any capital increase. Shares carrying multiple voting rights are not allowed.

(2) *Preferred shares (Azioni privilegiate)* which grant some privileges in the distribution of profits and in the reimbursement at the moment of winding up of the company. The byelaws may limit their voting rights to matters requiring a resolution of a shareholders' extraordinary meeting (see below under M.2.7.2.1); shares with limited voting rights may not exceed 50 per cent of the equity capital.

(3) *Savings shares (Azioni di risparmio)* which have no voting rights but the following privileges:

   (a) upon distribution of profits a minimum annual dividend of no less than 5 per cent of their par value must be distributed to them and the residual profits must be distributed so that the savings shares be given an aggregate dividend exceeding the one given to ordinary shares by at least 2 per cent;

   (b) upon the winding up of the company they have priority in reimbursement (of their par value);

(c)   in case of reduction of the equity capital for losses their par value may be reduced only after the reduction of the par value of other shares.

Savings shares may be issued only by companies listed on the Stock Exchange.

(4) *Shares in favour of employees (Azioni a favore dei prestatori di lavoro)* special shares may be issued, with or without voting rights, in favour of employees for the purpose of distributing profits to the employees of the company.

(5) *"Enjoyment" shares (Azioni di godimento)* these shares, though seldom used, may be allotted in lieu of shares cancelled and do not give any voting rights. They entitle their holders to share in the annual profits after ordinary shares have received a dividend equal to "legal interest" (which is now determined each year by the Government) and to participate in the distribution of assets remaining on liquidation, after the other shares have been reimbursed at par value.

M.2.6.1   *Transfer of shares*

Except savings shares which may be issued also to the bearer (al portatore) all shares must be registered (nominative) and must be represented by certificates bearing the indication of their par value, the name of the company, the registered office, duration and share capital of the company as well as the signature of a director, and obviously the name and address of the shareholder.

Shares are transferred by an endorsement authenticated by a notary or bank. Moreover, any transfer of shares must be entered in the Register of Shareholders (Libro Soci).

Whether or not shares are freely transferable depends on the byelaws. Some byelaws require either that the transfer be approved by the board of directors or that shares be first offered to the other shareholders (first refusal).

In case the subscribed equity is not paid up in full the shares in respect thereof can be transferred by the shareholders. The latter remains liable, jointly with the buyer, for an amount equal to the payments still due for a period of three years subsequent to the transfer date.

A company listed on the Stock Exchange may not have any restriction as to the transferability of its shares. Furthermore, any liens or pledge on the shares must be noted on the share certificates and in the register of shareholders.

The limited liability companies (Srl) have no shares. Equity participations (quote) are represented only by the relevant entry in the register of equity holders and are transferred by a transfer note signed by the vendor and the buyer which has to be entered in the register of equity holders within 30 days from the date of the contract. Such signatures must be authenticated by a Public Notary and a note has to be filed with the Register of Enterprises.

M.2.6.2 Purchase of own shares (treasury shares)

A company may not purchase its own shares unless such purchase is authorised by a shareholders' meeting which determines terms and conditions of the purchase. The purchase is anyway subject to the following additional requisites:

(a) shares must be fully paid with distributable profits or available reserves on the basis of the last approved balance sheet;

(b) the aggregate par value of treasury shares may not exceed one-tenth of the share capital, taking into account, to such purpose, also the shares owned by controlled companies, if any.

Voting and dividend rights of treasury shares are suspended and proportionally assigned to the other shares until they remain in the ownership of the company. A special fund in respect thereof must be entered into the balance sheet.

Controlled companies may purchase shares of their holding company within the limit of their distributable profits and available reserves provided that the shares are fully paid up. However, they cannot exercise the voting rights at shareholders' meetings. The resolution to purchase such share must be approved by the shareholders.

Specific legislation was implemented in 1994 in order to forbid cross participation between controlling and controlled companies. Infringements by directors or statutory auditors of the new provisions of the law are now subject to the criminal law.

M.2.6.3 Increase/decrease of capital

For the benefit of third parties (particularly creditors) the Civil Code provides that all records and correspondence of the company must indicate the actual amount of the equity capital (as resulting from the instrument of incorporation and from the last approved balance sheet). Increases or decreases of such amount require amendment of the byelaws. Furthermore, increases of capital can be made free or against cash.

In no cases can a company (nor its controlled companies) subscribe to its own shares.

A free increase of capital can be the result of allocating to capital available reserves or special funds recorded in the balance sheet, or alternatively of a revaluation of assets. The increase takes place either by issuing new shares with the same characteristics of those outstanding and to be distributed proportionally to the shareholders, or by increasing the par value of existing shares. Increase against cash is obviously a way to finance the company through contribution of fresh money.

Upon an increase of capital the company will issue new shares (or convertible debentures) which must be offered proportionally to the existing shareholders (who have a pre-emption right in respect thereof).

If the increase of capital takes place by means of contributions in kind the rules concerning their evaluation for the case of incorporation apply (see above under M.2.5.5).

In case of losses exceeding one-third of the equity capital the board of directors must promptly call a shareholders' meeting and submit a report on the financial situation of the company. The shareholders may either cover the losses or reduce the capital or carry forward the losses.

If the loss is not reduced to less than one-third within the current fiscal period the shareholders must reduce the capital in proportion to the losses that have been ascertained.

If by reason of a loss exceeding one-third of the capital the latter falls below the legal minimum (200 million lire for an SpA and Sapa and 20 million lire for an Srl) the directors must call without delay a shareholders' meeting in order to resolve a reduction of the capital and a concurrent increase thereof to an amount not lower than the said minimum or alternatively the reorganisation of the company into a simpler form.

The Civil Code contains moreover, two instances of decrease of capital: in case of reimbursement of shares to a withdrawing shareholder and in case the capital is held to be excessive for the attainment of the company's objects. All changes in the capital structure are subject to court approval, as are any amendment of the byelaws.

M.2.6.4 *Sole shareholder*

Even if it is not allowed to form an SpA by a sole shareholder it is possible (and permitted by the law) that, as a consequence of subsequent transfer of shares, a person (either an individual or a company) become the only proprietor of the entire equity capital. In this case he (or it) is personally and fully liable (jointly with company) for any liability of the company incurred in the period he (or it) is sole shareholder.

M.2.7 Corporate Bodies

Italian law regards a company to comprise of three "corporate bodies": board of directors (or sole director), shareholders' meeting, committee of statutory auditors.

M.2.7.1 *Board of directors (Consiglio di Amministrazione)*

The directors are the management body of the company and have consequently the power to determine and implement the policies for the achievement of the objects

343

of the company. The management of the company may be entrusted to a sole director or a board of directors.

Unless otherwise provided for by the byelaws a board meeting is validly constituted only when the majority of its members is physically in attendance (not by proxy). Some courts are now allowing, however, the holding of board meetings by way of video conference or teleconference, provided that this is previously admitted by specific provision of the byelaws. No particular formalities are requested by the law for the calling of board meetings (specific notes may be indicated in the byelaws). Resolutions are validly passed by either a favourable vote of the majority of the members in office or of the members in attendance, depending on the byelaws. The minutes in respect thereof must be signed by the chairman and by the secretary of the meeting.

M.2.7.1.1 Appointment/dismissal of directors The directors are first appointed in the instrument of incorporation and subsequently by a shareholders' resolution.

Any person of age can be appointed as a director unless disqualified or disabled by court order, bankrupt or sentenced to a penalty entailing disqualification even temporary from public office or incapacity to exercise managerial functions. Should any of these facts occur during the term of office, the director would lapse from office by force of law. Directors need not be shareholders. Directors may be removed at any time by shareholders' resolution, subject to damages if the removal is without cause. In an SpA the appointment of directors cannot be for a period in excess of three years. They may, however, be reappointed. In an Srl directors may be appointed without limit as to term of office.

The appointment of directors, *i.e.* their acceptance and signatures, must be filed with the Register of Enterprises.

If during the course of a fiscal period a vacancy of one or more directors occurs the others—provided that the majority of the board is still in existence—may fill the vacancy by a board resolution which needs specific approval by the Committee of Statutory Auditors. Directors thus appointed remain in office until the next shareholders' meeting.

If, however, vacancies are in respect of the majority of directors, the remaining directors (or the committee of statutory auditors if necessary) must call a shareholders' meeting for the purpose of filling the vacancies.

Directors may resign at any time, the resignation being effective immediately if the majority of the board members remain in office. Otherwise the resignation becomes effective only when such majority has been re-established by new appointments.

Board members may be Italian or foreigners; the latter need not be residents, but they have to apply for a fiscal code number in Italy.

M.2.7.1.2 Chairman The board must appoint a chairman among its members (unless he has been appointed by the shareholders). The chairman is the legal representative and has the power to sign on behalf of the company. This does not mean that by force of law he has executive powers for the management of the company, but rather that he has power to represent the company in carrying out the resolutions of the board, calling board and shareholders' meetings when required by the law or the byelaws and in general to perform the duties expressly established by the law and the byelaws, sign reports, statements, etc. (so-called "active" representation) and receive notices addressed to the company ("passive" representation).

M.2.7.1.3 Managing director and executive committee The board of directors may delegate some of its powers to one or more of its members, in which case the company has one or more managing directors, or to an executive committee composed of some of its members.

M.2.7.1.4 Directors' fees The remuneration and the profit sharing, if any, payable to directors are established by the instrument of incorporation or by a shareholders' resolution. The fees of directors who are vested with specific offices (Chairman, Deputy Chairman, Managing Director) may be established by the board of directors after having heard the opinion of the committee of statutory auditors.

M.2.7.1.5 Duties/powers of the board of directors Delegation of powers by the board cannot be total and in any case the delegation does not exclude the powers of the board itself. Certain powers such as the drafting of the annual balance sheet must remain the duty of the board, that is ultimately liable for establishing the company policies and supervise the operation. In case of a sole director, the duties and responsibilities of the board will concentrate in one person.

The board has the specific power to call shareholders' meetings and to determine their agenda, to submit the balance sheet and the report thereon to the shareholders for approval and to carry out shareholders' resolutions.

The directors must fulfil their duties with the diligence to be expected from a person to whom the management of the property of third parties has been entrusted. They are jointly liable for damages arising to the company if they have failed to exercise a proper supervision over the company's operation or if they did not prevent (insofar as it was in their power) the consequences of any action prejudicial to the company.

A very broad listing of the duty of directors specifically mentioned in the Civil Code would include compliance with:

(a) the rules provided for the preservation of the equity and assets of the company and indirectly the rights of creditors, such as prohibition to issue shares at a price lower than par value or before the proper formation of the company, the duty of controlling any contribution in kind to the equity of the company, prohibition to distribute fictitious dividends or dividends not resulting from a duly approved annual balance sheet (interim dividends), prohibition of giving advances or loans from company funds to acquire shares of the company, prohibition of making transactions on shares of the company or controlling or associated companies, prohibition of making loans and giving guarantees in favour of the directors (and accepting such loans and guarantees), prompt action whenever the equity capital is reduced below certain levels because of losses; prompt application to the Tribunal for an insolvency procedure in case the company becomes insolvent. Violation of many of these prescriptions involves a penal liability;

(b)   the requirement that the company maintains true and complete accounting book and records, complies with the payment of taxes, social security contributions, tax withholdings from employees' salaries, etc. Violation of these prescriptions also involves a penal liability;

(c)   general duty of abstaining from any action that may damage the company, such as disclosure of false or confidential information, fraudulent acts affecting the securities of the company, etc.

Compliance by the directors with their duties is a matter of public interest and violation cannot be excluded by express or implied authorisation from the other directors or the shareholders, nor by the approval of the balance sheet of the year in which the violation took place.

A director who, in a given business transaction, has an interest which is in conflict with that of the company, either on his own account or for the account of third parties, must notify the other directors and the statutory auditors and abstain from voting on the resolutions in respect of said transaction. Directors may not carry on business activities which compete with that of the company without the consent of the shareholders.

M.2.7.1.6   Liabilities of the directors   Shareholders may sue the directors in case of damages suffered by the company as a consequence of lack of diligence in the performance of their duties. In particular, any violation (including omission) of a duty results in the joint and several liability of directors. In any case directors are jointly and severally liable if they have not carefully watched the operation of the company or, in case they were aware of any negative facts, have not acted to prevent them or to reduce the resulting negative consequences. Formal violation or omission of a duty must obviously result from clear evidence but once the facts have been ascertained there are usually no serious problems of interpretation. On the other hand, business decisions that eventually resulted in serious damage to the company (and indirectly to its creditors) must be judged with reference to the general duty of the directors to preserve the equity and the assets of the company in the interest of the shareholders and creditors in general. The principle is that business decisions, unless absolutely unreasonable or made under a conflict of interest or involving fraud, should not be subject to criticism and the eventual result should not be charged as a liability to the directors. Directors cannot be held liable for bad luck or error made in good faith. Also the company's creditors may act against directors for non-fulfilment of their duty to preserve the company's assets.

Directors are also liable to individual shareholders if the latter gives evidence that they have suffered prejudice in their rights connected with their relations with the company, as a consequence of guilt or negligence of the directors.

A specific liability of directors is the unlimited joint and several liability of directors for the debts of the company if the company continues to operate when losses have reduced the share capital below the statutory minimum (see M.2.6.3). The liability is joint and several when the violation or negligence must be attributed to directors collectively. A director is exempt from liability if he was not a party to the violation or negligence and provided that his dissent from the action of the other directors was promptly recorded in the minutes of a Board meeting and that notice was immediately given to the chairman of the committee of statutory auditors.

In criminal matters, however, it is obviously not sufficient for a director to record his dissent in the books of the company, especially if it is eventually proved that he was responsible for the criminal action. Tax liability is becoming a topical subject due to relatively new legislation which is trying to fight tax avoidance. Very briefly, directors incur liability of a penal nature mainly in the following cases:

—omission by the company of filing any required tax report
—omission of invoicing or registering sales or services in the accounting books
—incomplete declaration of income
—omission of paying to the Treasury the amount of tax withholdings
—fiscal fraud in general.

The penal nature of the fine resulting from the omission is usually connected with a violation in excess of 50 million lire. Arrest becomes compulsory when the violation is in excess of 100 or 150 million lire, depending on the various cases mentioned above. There is no allowance in the case of fiscal fraud.

The liability of directors for violation of their duties, negligence or fraud can be claimed by the company only. Individual shareholders as well as third parties have a claim only for damages caused directly to them and not for damages incurred by the company.

The legal action against the directors must be authorised by a shareholders' resolution. The latter may cause the revocation of the directors against whom the action was taken.

The action by the creditors of the company is based on the claim that the directors did not observe the duty of preserving the equity and assets of the company. The action is only admitted if the assets of the company are insufficient to satisfy the creditors' claims. Any third party, including shareholders, may act against the directors if they claim they were directly damaged by the negligent or fraudulent action of the directors. Limitation of actions is five years.

M.2.7.1.5   General managers (Direttori generali)   General managers are employees of the company and they are not necessarily members of the board. Nevertheless, if they are appointed by the shareholders, they share the same responsibilities as directors in respect of the duties entrusted to them.

347

M.2.7.2 *Shareholders' meeting (Assemblea degli azionisti)*

M.2.7.2.1 General provisions Shareholders' meetings may be ordinary or extra-ordinary according to the matters on the agenda.

An ordinary meeting (the one referred to in English as the AGM) must be held at least once a year within four months from the end of the financial period (the byelaws may provide for an extension of the term to six months when required by special circumstances) in order to approve the balance sheet.

The other matters which require a resolution of a shareholders' ordinary meeting are:

(a) appointment of directors and statutory auditors;

(b) determining the fees of directors and of statutory auditors (the latter must be determined by reference to the official tariff of the Certified Public Accountants);

(c) operational decisions reserved to a shareholders' resolution by the byelaws or submitted to its consideration by the board of directors, as well as resolutions on the liability of directors and statutory auditors.

Extraordinary meetings are those which deal with amendments to the byelaws and issuance of debentures, as well as with the appointment and powers of the liquidator (in case of voluntary liquidation).

The minutes of extraordinary meetings must be drafted and signed by a Public Notary.

(Note: in Italy a Public Notary has the same law degree as a solicitor; his commission is for life.)

M.2.7.2.2 The convening of a shareholders' meeting Shareholders' meetings are usually convened at the registered office of the company; alternatively elsewhere in Italy or in other specified countries abroad according to the byelaws. Shareholders' meetings are usually called by the directors. In some special cases a shareholders' meeting may be called by other persons, namely:

(a) by the committee of statutory auditors either when the directors fail to call a meeting when necessary or when all directors have ceased from office or when the statutory auditors receive from as many shareholders as represent at least one-twentieth of the equity capital, complaint of facts they deem objectionable;

(b) by the local court (tribunale) if so requested by shareholders representing at least one-fifth of the equity capital, when the same shareholders have already requested in vain that the directors and statutory auditors have a meeting convened.

(c) by the local court (tribunale) in case of serious irregularities pointed out by one-tenth of the shareholders.

(d) by the liquidator(s) in case of voluntary winding up of the company.

M.2.7.2.3 Notice of call for a shareholders' meeting Shareholders' meetings are called as follows:

(a) Srl: by notice of call sent by registered mail to all the shareholders (as well as to all directors and statutory auditors if any), at least eight days before the meeting, specifying date, hour, place and the agenda of the meeting;

(b) Spa (or Sapa): by notice published in the *Official Gazette of the Republic of Italy (Gazzetta Ufficiale)* at least 15 days before the date set for the meeting including the same information mentioned under (a).

   A "second call" meeting may be provided in the notice of call in case the attendance falls short of the prescribed quorum (see under M.2.7.2.4). Otherwise a second meeting must be called within 30 days by a second notice to be published as above at least eight days in advance.

In the absence of these formalities a meeting is nevertheless deemed duly constituted when the entire capital, all the directors and the statutory auditors are in attendance (the so-called "plenary" meeting—assemblea totalitaria). In this case, however, each of those present may refuse to discuss matters on which he does not feel sufficiently informed.

In order to be entitled to attend a shareholders' meeting, a shareholder must be registered in the shareholders' register at least five days before the date of the meeting and in the case of an SpA shares must be deposited at the company or at the bank within the same term. Shareholders may attend personally or by proxy.

M.2.7.2.4 Due constitution of a shareholders' meeting and validity of resolutions There are slight differences between an SpA and an Srl:

(1) SpA: Shareholders "ordinary" meetings are duly constituted with the attendance, personally or by proxy, of as many shareholders as represent at least 50 per cent of the share capital.

   Unless the byelaws require a higher majority, resolutions are passed if approved by the majority of voting shareholders.

   Resolutions of shareholders extraordinary meetings require the favourable vote of more than 50 per cent of the share capital, unless a higher majority is required in byelaws. On second (adjourned) call, resolutions of shareholders' ordinary meetings are approved whatever portion of the share capital is present or represented and resolutions of shareholders' extraordinary meetings require the favourable vote of more than one-third of the share capital (50 per cent is however required for changing the objects of the company, reorganisation, voluntary liquidation, etc.).

   A third meeting, requiring the attendance of only 20 per cent of the share capital is provided for companies listed on the Stock Exchange.

(2) Srl: Unless different provisions are set in the byelaws, resolutions of share-holders' ordinary meetings, whether held on first or on second call, are approved with the favourable vote of as many shareholders as represent a majority of the equity capital.

Resolutions of shareholders extraordinary meetings require the favourable vote of at least two thirds of the equity capital.

According to the byelaws, the shareholders appoint the chairman of the meeting who is assisted by a secretary and both are required to draft and sign the minutes of the meeting. The assistance of a secretary is not required for the minutes of an extraordinary meeting which are drawn up by a Public Notary.

The chairman is responsible for verifying that the meeting is regularly constituted.

M.2.7.2.5 Voting rights and restrictions Voting rights may be exercised also by proxy, unless otherwise provided in the byelaws, which may also establish that the proxies may be issued only to another shareholder.

The same person cannot represent more than ten shareholders or, in case of companies listed on the Stock Exchange, a number of shareholders which increases progressively according to the share capital of the company.

Proxies must be issued in writing and may not be granted to directors, statutory auditors or employees of the company or of owned companies, nor to credit institutions, banks or auditing firms.

Directors, if shareholders, have voting rights which however may nor be exercised in connection with the resolutions concerning their responsibilities. Shareholders may not exercise their voting rights on matters in which they have, on their own account or on behalf of third parties, an interest which conflicts with the interest of the Company.

M.2.7.3 *The committee of statutory auditors (Collegio Sindacale)*

M.2.7.3.1 General provisions All the companies with a capital exceeding 200 million lire (and thus all SpA) must have a so-called "committee of statutory auditors" that is responsible for supervising the company's accounts and ensuring that the company is operating in compliance with the law and the byelaws.

The committee of statutory auditors must not be confused with external auditors (see under 2.8).

M.2.7.3.2 Appointment of statutory auditors The committee of statutory auditors (called also "the auditors") is appointed by the shareholders for a period of three years and cannot be dismissed, except for cause and with the approval of the local court (Tribunale).

The committee is composed of three or five active members (persons, not entities) who may or may not be shareholders. Two supplementary auditors must also be appointed (for immediate filling of any vacancy).

All the auditors must be chosen among those enrolled in the Special Roll of Certified Public Accountants (Ruolo dei Revisori Contabili). They cannot be employees of the company nor members of the family of any director. The chairman of the committee must be selected by the shareholders. The appointment of the committee of statutory auditors must be filed with the Register of Enterprises within 15 days from the date of the shareholders' resolution in respect thereof.

The remuneration of the auditors is established by the same shareholders' resolution in conformity with a fee schedule laid out by a specific Law Decree.

2.7.3.3 Duties and powers of statutory auditors
The statutory auditors are responsible for supervising the accounts of the company and compliance with the law and the byelaws.

They must verify the regular keeping of the company's accounts, the consistency of the balance sheet and the loss and profit account with the company's books and its accounting records in general, as well as compliance with the provisions of law for the evaluation of the company's assets.

The committee of statutory auditors must also verify at least once every three months the amount of cash on hand and the existence of securities of all kind owned or received by the company in pledge or guarantee.

The auditors may at any time request directors to give information on the operation of the company or on particular transactions and may proceed, even individually, with acts of inspection and supervision.

The auditors must be notified of, and attend, all shareholders' and board meetings, without any voting rights. Their active intervention is however required in respect of certain specific issues, such as confirming that the previous capital is fully paid in case of any increase of capital and approving the remuneration of directors when voted by the board.

The auditors must perform their duties with diligence and may be held responsible for the truth of their statements. They are obviously held to business secrecy.

On the basis of the draft annual balance sheet approved by the board of directors and of the latter's annual report, the auditors must submit a report on the annual balance sheet to the AGM.

The auditors are jointly liable with the directors for damages arising from acts or omissions of the latter, when such damages would not have occurred if they had exercised proper vigilance.

Action for liability against the auditors may be brought by shareholders or by creditors in accordance with the same provisions applicable to directors (see under M.2.7.1.6).

Any shareholder may complain to the committee of the statutory auditors about facts he deems objectionable and the committee must take the complaint into account in its report to the annual general meeting.

If the complaint is made by as many shareholders as represent one-twentieth of the capital the auditors must investigate without delay and report their conclusions and suggestions to a shareholders' meeting.

M.2.8   External controls

M.2.8.1   *Auditing firms*

Law Decree 136 of March 31, 1975 introduced in Italy the concept of independent auditing as understood in Anglo-Saxon countries. The law laid out that all companies listed on the Stock Exchange must appoint independent auditors from those accounting firms which are approved by and registered with CONSOB (Commissione Nazionale per le Società e la Borsa), a Government agency with functions similar to the American SEC.

The appointment (resolved by the shareholders) is normally for three years and may be renewed. After nine years they cannot be reappointed until a further five-year period has elapsed.

Even though such an appointment is mandatory only for listed companies, in practice many companies (especially if part of multi-national groups) submit their balance sheets and accounts to external auditing.

M.2.8.2   *CONSOB*

CONSOB (Commissione Nazionale per le Società e la Borsa) which, as already mentioned above, is the Italian equivalent of the American SEC, has been granted some specific powers in order to ensure larger information to the market about the activities of listed companies.

In particular CONSOB may order companies to draw up consolidated balance sheets or require further information besides that given in the balance sheet and the reports. CONSOB may also proceed with inspections in order to check the exactness and the accuracy of the accounts. Moreover, CONSOB may contest the resolution of the shareholders' meeting which approves the balance sheet.

M.2.8.3   *Local court (Tribunale)*

Under the Civil Code if there is a basis to suspect that serious irregularities have been committed by directors and/or the statutory auditors a complaint may be filed with the local court (tribunale) by as many shareholders as represent one-tenth of the equity capital.

The court, having heard the directors and statutory auditors, may order an investigation. If it is found that abuses have been committed, the court may take the appropriate precautionary measures (*e.g.* sequestration) and call a shareholders' meeting or in the more serious cases the court may remove directors and auditors and appoint a trustee (amministratore giudiziario).

M.2.8.4 Branch of foreign company ("Sede secondaria")

According to the law of May 31, 1995, No. 218 (which modified the entire Italian system of international private law) a (foreign) company is disciplined by the law of the country where it was formed. Nevertheless, the Italian law applies when the administrative office of such company or its main activity are situated or performed in Italy. In this case the entire life of the company (and in particular the procedure of its constitution, the representative powers and the liabilities of its bodies) are fully regulated by Italian law.

On the other hand, foreign companies may also establish one or more branch offices with permanent representation within the territory of the Italian Republic. In this case they are subject, for each of such branch offices only, to the provisions of Italian law concerning the filing and registration of the instrument of incorporation and of the annual balance sheet of the parent company in the Register of Enterprises of the place where the branch is established.

Branches must also publish in the said Register, the full name of the persons who permanently represent the company in Italy and deposit their respective signatures. Normally one of them is described as being the responsible manager (Institore).

Until the prescribed formalities have been fulfilled the persons acting on behalf of the foreign company are personally liable without restrictions (jointly with the parent company) for the obligations of the company.

Since the branch is not a separate legal entity, when the formalities have been completed the parent company remains fully liable for all debts and obligations of the branch. This explains why, for the knowledge of third parties, the balance sheet together with the profit and loss account of the parent company must be filed with the Register of Enterprises.

On the other hand, as a taxable entity, the branch must keep separate accounting records and close its financial year with a balance sheet and profit and loss account, which must be filed annually with the Revenue Office together with the annual tax return. The branch is subject to all the formalities already mentioned in respect of the entrepreneur, as well as those of a limited company in respect of tax obligations.

From a tax point of view, a branch is a permanent establishment and therefore can be assumed to exist *de facto* in some cases where a foreign entity does business in Italy.

The branch does not have a board of directors, nor a committee of statutory auditors (see M.2.7.3 above) nor any shareholders' meeting, nor any capital subject to the provisions mentioned under point M.2.6.3 above.

SECTION 3

COSTS OF INCORPORATION

M.3.1 Apart from the cost connected with legal assistance and obviously the minimum capital to be paid, the expenses incurred in forming an SpA or an Srl basically consist of:

(a) Capital issue tax. This tax is charged at 1 per cent on the amount of paid in capital. If the capital is contributed in kind, the tax is payable on the value of the contribution.

(b) Notary's fees and costs. The Notary's fees include the drawing up and execution of the instrument of incorporation as well as the filing formalities. The fees are practically dependent on the amount of the authorised capital.

By way of example, for an Srl with a share capital of 50 million lire, overall fees and costs can be estimated to be approximately 9 million lire; for an Spa with a share capital of 500 million lire, fees and costs can be estimated to be approximately 20 million lire.

The foregoing figures include substantial filing dues payable to the Register of Enterprises and the Chamber of Commerce. Additional fees will obviously be charged when problems result in additional correspondence, consultations and translations.

LUXEMBOURG

CORPORATE OPTIONS*

N.1.1   Branch

A foreign company intending to establish a branch in Luxembourg must register the branch with the company register (registre de commerce et des sociétés). The mere registration of the branch at the company register does not require prior government authorisation.

A government permit is required (in the case of a branch and a subsidiary) in order to start any business activities (see N.2.12, below). No work and residence permits are required for E.U. nationals to settle in Luxembourg in order to be employed by the Luxembourg operation. A work and a residence permit are required for non-E.U. nationals.

The following documents must be submitted to the company register in the case of a non-E.U. company:

(a)   a copy of the updated articles of association of the foreign company;

(b)   a translation, in the French or German language, of the articles of association;

(c)   a certified copy of a resolution by the competent corporate body of the foreign company deciding for the establishment of a branch office in Luxembourg. The resolution should indicate the name and powers of the legal representative of the branch and the address of the branch office.

The Luxembourg branch or establishment must comply with certain publication rules. The articles of association filed with the company register must be published in the Luxembourg *Official Gazette* (*Memorial*). The particulars filed and published, together with the details of the powers of the persons entrusted with the management of the Luxembourg operation, must be kept up to date, in particular any change as to the identity or delegation of the local manager must be updated.

In the case of an E.U. company, the following information must be filed with the company register and published in the *Official Gazette*:

(a)   address of the branch;

(b)   indication of the activities of the branch;

---

* *Tom Loesch, Loesch & Wolter, Avocats (full particulars are listed in the Appendix).*

(c) company register where the company's file is kept and registration number of the company;

(d) name and form of the branch.

At the time of registration, the branch will be attributed a Register of Commerce number which must be printed on all documents used by the local operation, such as invoices, letters, order confirmations, etc.

The registration costs presently amount to 4,800 Lfr. For a branch of a non-E.U. incorporated company in addition a 1 per cent capital contribution tax assessed on the means (cash or equipment) made available to the branch is payable. The branch is required to keep separate books in accordance with standards of Luxembourg accounting law and file an annual tax return.

Every year, the foreign parent company must file with the company register its "annual accounts" (*i.e.* balance sheet, profit and loss statement and explanatory notes), together with a list of the directors and the name of the auditor(s) of the foreign company. These accounts need not follow the legal form imposed upon Luxembourg companies.

As a matter of principle, any company which has as its purpose the supply of goods or services must register with the government VAT authorities. VAT registration is free of charge.

The decision of the competent corporate body of the foreign company to close the branch must be filed with the register of commerce and an announcement must be published in the *Official Gazette*.

N.1.2 Partnerships

N.1.2.1 *General partnerships (Société en Nom Collectif)*

The "société en nom collectif" is a general partnership formed between two or more persons (the partners) who may or may not be corporate entitles. The partnership has legal personality; it can sue and be sued in court under its own name. All partners are jointly and severally liable for the debts of the partnership and each of the partners will be assumed to have authority to act on behalf of the partnership.

The duration of the partnership is, in principle, to be determined in the partnership agreement by the partners. The partnership agreement must be filed with the company register and published in the *Official Gazette*. The Civil Code and company law provide for a number of basic terms which must be included in the partnership agreement.

N.1.2.2   *Limited partnership (Société en Commandite Simple)*

The "société en commandite simple" is a limited partnership in which the structure is essentially the same as that of the general partnership (see N.1.2.1 above) provided that two or more partners (individual persons or corporate entities) act as the general partner and one or more partners (individual persons or corporate entities) act as the limited partner.

General partners are jointly and severally liable in respect of all debts of the partnership and they are solely entitled to act in the name of the partnership. Limited partners are merely liable for the debts of the partnership up to the amount contributed by them to the partnership.

The shares of the limited partnership are transferable to third parties if the terms of the partnership agreement so allow or all the partners specifically so agree.

N.1.3   Co-operative Company (Société Coopérative: SC)

The "société coopérative" is a co-operative association which may be formed by private deed to be made public (by way of filing with the company register and publication in the *Official Gazette*). The SC must at all times have at least seven shareholders. The SC has the form of a limited liability company without being subject to most of the mandatory rules applicable to public and private limited companies (see below).

The articles of association of the SC may provide that the shareholders/members are liable only up to the amount of their contribution. If no such provision is provided, the shareholders are jointly and severally liable for all the debts of the SC. The SC is not subject to any minimum capital requirement rules.

The SC is subject to certain mandatory rules imposed by law: the shares of the SC must be in registered form (in practice in the form of a "membership register") and may not be transferred to third parties because of their strictly personal character. The law imposes rather stringent rules with respect to the withdrawal, admission and exclusion of shareholders in an SC.

N.1.4   Limited Liability Company

N.1.4.1   *Private limited company (Société à responsibilité limitée: Sàrl)*

The Sàrl may be compared to the private limited company under English law. The Sàrl may be incorporated by and may have one or more (up to a maximum of 40) shareholders who may be individual persons or corporate entities and may be established for a limited or unlimited duration. The minimum corporate capital of the shareholder is 500,000 Lfr (or the equivalent thereof in anorther currency) which must be fully paid up at the time of incorporation. The articles of association must be recorded in a notarial deed which has to be published *in extenso* in the *Official Gazette*.

The Sàrl is primarily a "closed" corporation in that its shares, which must be in a registered form, cannot be transferred to non-shareholders without the consent of the other shareholders (affirmative vote of three-quarters of the other shareholders required). The articles of association may only deviate from these rules by imposing even stricter rules for any share transfer.

The Sàrl is prohibited by law to directly or indirectly publicly offer its shares for subscription or sale or to issue bonds (the creation of bonds or similar debt instruments on a purely private basis is permissible).

Each share must have a nominal value of at least 1,000 Lfr (or the equivalent thereof in another currency). All shares must carry equal voting rights and there is a prohibition on the creation of non-voting or multiple voting shares.

N.1.4.2 Public limited company (Société Anonyme: SA)

The SA may be compared to the English public limited company. As in the case of the Sàrl, individual persons and corporate entities may become shareholders of an SA. The minimum share capital is 1,250,000 Lfr (or the equivalent thereof in another currency) of which one-quarter must be paid up at the time of incorporation. The articles of association must be recorded in a notarial deed which has to be published *in extenso* in the *Official Gazette*.

Shares may be issued in either registered or bearer form, provided the articles of association do not contain limitations in this respect. For a transfer of registered shares to take place it is necessary that the transfer be recorded in the company's share register. Where bearer shares are issued, the transfer is effected by transfer of the share certificate itself. The transfer of shares is in principle free save where the articles of association contain restrictive provisions in that respect, provided, however, that an effective total prohibition on any share transfer is not valid.

All shares of the SA must have the same value (minimum par value: 50 Lfr (or the equivalent thereof in another currency), and in principle one vote. The law allows the creation of non-voting shares (for a maximum of 50 per cent of the total amount of the capital) which must carry the right to a preferred dividend and liquidation proceeds. The issue of multiple voting shares is prohibited.

SECTION 2

INCORPORATING A COMPANY IN LUXEMBOURG

N.2.1 The Articles of Association

The rules governing the conduct of the business of a public and private company are laid down in the company's articles of association. The founding shareholders must submit to the Notary Public drawing up the deed of incorporation of the company, a bank certificate with respect to the contributions in cash (see N.2.6.4) or an asset valuation report in the case of contributions in kind (see N.2.6.4).

The incorporation may be carried out by way of proxies signed under private deed by the founding shareholders. It is important to note that there are no nationality or residence requirements in relation to the founding shareholders (or their proxyholders) for the incorporation of the company.

Subsequent to incorporation, the articles of association must be filed with the register of commerce and published *in extenso* in the *Official Gazette*.

N.2.2 Objects Clause

The purpose for which the company is being formed must be described in the articles of association although it is possible to use a general wording to describe the purpose(s) and objective(s) for which the company is incorporated.

Certain activities are regulated by law (banking, insurance, professionals of the financial sector). A special government authorisation is required before the incorporation of a company carrying out such types of activity can take place.

N.2.3 Corporate Name

The name selected for the company must be indicated in the articles of association. There are no particular restrictions on the choice of company names although companies are not permitted to use a name which might be misleading or create confusion with an already existing company name.

There is no possibility to make a name reservation under Luxembourg law. Only a protection under the trade mark/service mark legislation could achieve a similar result.

N.2.4 Registered Office

The registered office of the company must be indicated in the articles of association. It is sufficient in this respect to indicate the name of the municipality. The office can only be changed by resolution of a shareholders' meeting. A change of the registered office must be published in the *Official Gazette*. In addition, the detailed address (a change of which may take place in principle by way of board resolution if the registered office is still within the same municipality) must be notified to the register of commerce at the time the entry is made at the register.

N.2.5 Duration

As a general rule, companies may be established for an indefinite duration unless the articles of association provide otherwise. If the founding shareholders decide to limit the duration of the company to a certain period, the company will be wound up automatically at the end of this period, unless its duration is being extended prior to this date by a shareholders' decision.

N.2.6 Share Capital and Shares

All shares in a private limited company must be in registered form and have a nominal value of at least 1,000 Lfr (or the equivalent thereof in another currency). For shares in a public limited company, the minimum nominal value is 50 Lfr. Shares in a public limited company may be in registered form or bearer form and may be with or without nominal value.

N.2.6.1 *Minimum subscribed share capital*

(a) Public limited company (SA) 1,250,000 Lfr;

(b) Private limited company (Sàrl) 500,000 Lfr

or their countervalue in any other currency.

N.2.6.2   Amount to be paid in

The entire subscribed share capital of an Sàrl must be paid in at incorporation. At least one-quarter of each share in an SA must be paid in at incorporation.

N.2.6.3   Increase of share capital

An increase of the company's capital normally requires a special resolution of the general shareholders' meeting in the form of a decision carried by a majority of two-thirds of the votes cast (resolution to be adopted in the presence of a Notary Public).

The board of directors of the SA may be given the power, pursuant to a specific delegation of power in the articles of association, to increase the company's capital up to a level specified in the articles of association (the "authorised share capital"). The board of directors may only make use of the right to increase the capital up to the limit of the authorised share capital within a period of five years after publication of the articles of association or the date of the notarial deed amending the articles of association. The five years' permission may be renewed.

N.2.6.4   Form of subscription

(a) Subscription may be either in cash or kind.

(b) Contributions in cash must take place in the form of money transfer equal to the sum to be paid in (see N.2.6.2 above) to a special blocked account opened with a bank in Luxembourg in the name of the company. Upon receipt of this sum, the bank will issue a certificate. The Notary Public will not proceed with the incorporation/capital increase if the registered certificate has not been made available to him. The sums will be released by the bank upon confirmation by the Notary Public that the company has been incorporated and/or the capital has been increased by shareholders' resolution.

(c) Contributions in kind (*i.e.* assets other than cash which may be valued on the basis of economic criteria) must be accompanied by a valuation report prepared by an independent auditor (réviseur d'entreprises). The report must be available prior to the incorporation of the company/capital increase and specific reference thereto must be made in the notarial deed.

N.2.7 Shareholders

In public companies, a minimum of two shareholders, individuals or corporate entities, is required at all times. A company is not allowed to directly or indirectly subscribe for its own shares.

N.2.7.1 *Repurchase of own shares*

Whilst not permitted to subscribe for its own shares, a company may acquire its own shares provided the following restrictive conditions are met:

(a) the holding of shares may not exceed 10 per cent of the total capital;

(b) the shares must be fully paid in;

(c) the repurchase must be effected out of the net assets;

(d) the repurchased shares must be set against a special reserve in the balance sheet;

(e) the shares cannot be held for a period exceeding two years.

The company may also, under certain conditions imposed by the law, issue repurchasable shares.

N.2.8 Directors

Directors are appointed by the shareholders' meeting and must be at least three in number (public company). Private companies are normally managed by a manager (gérant) designated in the articles of association or elected by the shareholders. Private companies may also be managed by a board of directors.

The appointment must be for a term not exceeding six years. At the expiration of this term, the directors are eligible for re-election. They may be dismissed by the shareholders at any time with or without cause (in the case of public companies). A note concerning the appointment and the dismissal of directors must be published in the *Official Gazette*. There are no restrictions or requirements as to residence or nationality for the directors who may be corporate entities as well as individuals (a residence requirement may be imposed by specific legislation in certain cases).

N.2.8.1 *Duties and liabilities of directors*

The directors have the power and the responsibility to manage all the company's affairs, except such matters which are by law or by the articles of association specifically entrusted to the general meeting of shareholders. The company is bound by all acts of its directors and of the persons to whom the daily management of the company is entrusted even (in principle) if these acts exceed the corporate purpose (*i.e.* acts which are *ultra vires*), unless the company can prove that the third person has been aware of the *ultra vires*.

The directors are jointly and severally liable to the company and third parties for any damages which are the result of a violation of specific duties imposed by the company's articles of association or by company law. A director will only be exempted from such liability if he has not himself committed any fault and if he is protesting against any infringement of company law at the general meeting of shareholders.

N.2.8.2 *Day-to-day management*

The directors normally appoint one or more managing directors or general managers to carry out the day-to-day management. The appointment together with any details of the powers so conferred must be published in the *Official Gazette*. The delegation of the daily management to a director (*i.e.* to the managing director) is subject to prior authorisation by the general meeting of shareholders.

N.2.9 Board Meetings

The proceedings of board meetings are organised by the articles of association. Failing any rules in the articles of association they are governed by company law. The articles of association may provide that any director may be represented by proxy by another director at any board meeting.

The directors are appointed by the general meeting of shareholders which determines their number. In case of vacancy the remaining directors may appoint a new director until the next coming general meeting of shareholders which must ratify the new appointment.

N.2.10 Shareholders' Meetings

At least one general meeting of shareholders must be held annually at the date mentioned in the articles of association for the purpose, *inter alia*, of:

(a) approving the annual accounts and the statutory auditor's report;

(b) approving the directors' annual report;

(c) deciding upon the appropriation of profit (if any);

(d) fixing the directors' remuneration and conferring discharge to the directors and the statutory auditor.

In addition, an extraordinary general meeting of shareholders may be called by the board of directors as and when required for special business.

N.2.10.1 *Calling a shareholders' meeting*

General meetings of shareholders are convened by the board of directors or the statutory auditor. The board of directors has the duty to call for a general meeting if so requested by shareholders representing at least one-fifth of the share capital.

N.2.10.2 *Notices*

Notices of annual general meetings of shareholders setting out the agenda must be published twice in the *Official Gazette* eight days prior to the meeting with an interval between the two publications of at least eight days if bearer shares have been issued. If the shares are in registered form only, convening notices may be sent by registered letter to all shareholders at least eight days prior to the meeting. Copies of the annual report of the directors, the annual accounts and the auditor's report must be available to the shareholders at the registered office of the company at least 15 days before the date of the general meeting.

N.2.10.3 *Voting rights and restrictions*

The voting rights and restrictions are set out in the articles of association of the company.

N.2.10.4 *Quorum and majority at shareholders' meetings*

In principle, no quorum is imposed for general meetings of shareholders. Shareholders' decisions are normally taken by a simple majority of the votes cast at the meeting. Special quorum and majority requirements are imposed in specific cases.

	Quorum First Meeting (%)	Quorum Second Meeting (%)	Majority (%)
1 Change of nationality	100	100	100
2 Ordinary amendments to the articles of association	50	None	66.6
3 Increase or reduction of capital	50	None	66.6
4 Extension of the life of the company	50	None	66.6
5 Early dissolution or merger of the company	50	None	66.6
6 Cancellation or limitation of the preferred subscription right	50	None	66.6
7 Early dissolution of the company when one half of the capital has been lost	50	None	66.6

N.2.11   Audit

Public limited companies and private limited companies (having a number of associates exceeding 25) must submit their accounts to a periodic (normally annual) audit of the statutory auditor appointed by the general meeting of shareholders.

No later than one month before the annual general meeting, the auditor must receive copies of the board's annual report and the accounts to enable him to prepare his audit report for submission to the shareholders. The audit report must be available for inspection at the offices of the company at least 15 days prior to the meeting.

N.2.12   Licence to do Business

A company engaging in any kind of business activity is required to obtain a licence from the government. The licence is delivered upon representation of a file comprising the following documents:

(a)   a copy of the articles of association;

(b)   a copy of the decision appointing the person responsible for the day-to-day management of the company;

(c) the CV and school/university diploma of the person responsible for the day-to-day management of the company (professional qualification will be examined on the basis of these documents);

(d) an affidavit or excerpt of the criminal register stating that the person responsible for the day-to-day management has not been declared bankrupt;

(e) a duly completed application form (duty of 1,000 Lfr payable upon collection of the application form).

The engaging in a business activity prior to the date of delivery of the licence is a criminal offence.

SECTION 3

COSTS OF INCORPORATION

N.3.1 The incorporation costs for public or private limited liability companies may be summarised as follows:

(a) 1 per cent capital duty tax assessed on the amount of the corporate capital (and any subsequent capital increase);

(b) 50,000 Lfr (for a company with the minimum required share capital), for Notary Public fees, publication costs of the notarial deed in the *Official Gazette* and entry in the company register.

NETHERLANDS

CLASSIFICATION OF BUSINESS ORGANISATIONS: INTRODUCTION*

O.1.0 Dutch law recognises four principal categories of business organisations:

—the sole proprietorship (with the branch of a foreign enterprise as a subdivision);
—the (limited) partnership;
—the limited liability company;
—the co-operative society.

O.1.1 Sole Proprietorship

The sole proprietorship can be considered the most basic and simplest form of business enterprise. On the whole, this form of business organisation is owned by private individuals. The individual, as owner, takes all the profits and the risks. The sole proprietor is manager, employer, owner of the assets and stock and everything else in the enterprise.

This form of business organisation is not regulated by any special rules of law. Nevertheless, the rules and provisions of law which apply to business enterprises in general will also affect the sole proprietor. The main feature of this form is, of course, that there is no distinction between the business capital and the private capital of the sole proprietor. The capital is considered to form one unit, especially for the private and business creditors.

O.1.1.2   *The branch*

A branch in the Netherlands is not recognised as a separate legal entity but as part of, and identified with the foreign company. The registration of a branch is, however, almost equivalent to that of an NV/BV (naamloze vennootschap/de besloten vennootschap met beperkte aansprakelijkheid). The information which must be published in the Trade Register of the place where the branch is established must include:

---

* *Gerard Carrière, Nauta Dutilh (full particulars are listed in the Appendix).*

(a)   name and address of the foreign enterprise setting up the branch;

(b)   the constitution documents of the foreign company (in the Dutch language);

(c)   the amount of capital of the foreign company;

(d)   names and addresses of directors of the foreign company as well as the date of their appointment as such;

(e)   any information that the foreign company requires for registration in the Trade Register of its own country;

(f)   the legal domicile in the Netherlands;

(g)   the name of the branch;

(h)   the names and addresses of branch manager(s) empowered to conclude contracts on behalf of the branch;

(i)   all subsequent changes to the above.

Since a branch is not a separate legal entity, the foreign enterprise (company) is fully responsible for its debts, obligations and liabilities.

O.1.2   Partnerships

Dutch law recognises the general partnership (vennootschap onder firma), and the so-called limited partnership (commanditaire vennootschap). These forms of business organisations are covered by the Dutch Commercial and Civil Code.

Next to the above mentioned forms, Dutch law also recognises the civil partnership governed by civil law (de maatschap). The latter organisation, governed by the Civil Code, is often used as a tool for co-operation between members of independent professions, such as dentists, lawyers or auditors. All partnerships have a contractual basis.

O.1.2.1   *The general partnership (vennootschap onder firma: VOF)*

This partnership is established as a result of a contract between two or more individuals. Corporate bodies may also establish a VOF. The purpose of establishing a VOF is to operate a business (rather than a profession) under a common name and to share profits derived from the partnership ventures. At the beginning of the partnership, each partner undertakes to bring an agreed contribution to the partnership. The VOF is not a separate legal entity. Nevertheless, it is able to sue and to be sued in its own name. Furthermore, the VOF has its own capital separate from the capital owned by the individual partners engaged in the VOF; the civil partnerships (see below) lack such a distinction.

All partners (vennoten) will be subject to joint and several liability and each of the partners will be assumed to have authority to act on behalf of the partnership as a whole. Liabilities of the VOF must first be satisfied from the capital owned by the partnership itself. If, however, the capital of the partnership is insufficient to satisfy all liabilities of the partnership, the creditors can turn to each individual partner for the satisfaction of the whole amount.

The contractual basis of the partnership means that the remaining terms of the partnership have to be embodied in the contract. The Commercial and Civil Code are far from exhaustive in determining the provisions which will apply to the partnership and, therefore, leave it, except for some basic terms, up to the contract between the partners.

O.1.2.2   The limited partnership (commanditaire vennootschap: CV)

This partnership differs from the general partnership, the VOF. The main objective is to enable the participation in the CV of a limited (or silent) partner whose liability will be restricted to the amount of his (initial) contribution and who will not be engaged in the (day-to-day) management. The main difference between the two partnerships, the VOF and the CV is the different classes of partners. Unlike the VOF, the limited partnership has two classes of partners: the general partner, also called the managing partner (de beherende vennoot), and the limited partner (de stille vennoot). The liability of the general partner in the limited partnership is similar to that of the partners in the general partnership, *i.e.* unlimited. Limited partners are liable to the extent of their capital contributions. The limited liability will only remain in place subject to the condition that the limited partner does not engage in one way or another with the (external) management of the limited partnership. If the limited partner does get involved with the management of the partnership his liability will convert from limited into unlimited. The management task is solely reserved for the managing partner. Consequently, each limited partnership must have at least one partner who is fully liable for all debts of the partnership.

O.1.2.3   The civil partnership (maatschap)

The civil partnership also differs from the general partnership, the VOF. The general partnership is governed by the Commercial and Civil Code while the civil partnership is governed by the Civil Code only.

Contrary to the general partnership, the partners of the civil partnership are not authorised to act individually on behalf of the partnership. Only the partners jointly are entitled to act on behalf of the civil partnership. The second main difference between the civil partnership and the VOF is that in the former the partners cannot be held jointly liable. The partners of a civil partnership can be held liable for the debts of the civil partnership in equal parts only. The statutes can determine

373

otherwise, such as, liability in proportion to the contributions. Nevertheless, this is all on the presumption that the partners acted jointly; if not, the general rule will apply that one partner cannot bind the others without their consent. The third major distinction, already mentioned, is the lack of separate capital.

O.1.2.4 *General provisions*

There are no formal requirements laid down in the Commercial or Civil Code concerning the establishment of the partnerships. The main feature of formation is the contract between the two or more parties involved.

A deed is not required. There is no legal maximum to the number of partners, and partnerships can sometimes be quite large organisations. The general and civil partnerships allow the contribution to be in cash, kind, labour or goodwill. The limited partnership only allows the contribution to be in cash, as it concerns the limited partner.

O.1.3 Co-operative Societies (Coöperaties)

This form of business enterprise takes the form of an association (vereniging) which is recognised in Dutch law as a separate legal entity. The members of the association remain, under certain circumstances, liable along with the association for the latter's liabilities. This form of business enterprise has often been used for insurance businesses, residential building societies and industrial business in the agrarian sector.

SECTION 2

LIMITED LIABILITY COMPANIES

O.2.1 Introduction: Sources of Law

The principal source of Dutch corporate law is Book 2 of the Dutch Civil Code. In addition, the Ministry of Justice has issued guidelines as to the procedures to be observed in establishing companies and as to the contents of the deed of incorporation, also to reflect the initial articles of association of the company concerned. In addition, the E.C. Directives are an important source of information. Apart from

374

the statutory and non-statutory instruments, case law, especially the judgments of the Supreme Court (De Hoge Raad) are also important sources of Dutch company law. The above mentioned list of sources of law does not purport to be exhaustive.

O.2.2 The Public Company (De Naamloze Vennootschap: NV)

Since 1971 Dutch company law recognises two types of limited liability companies; the NV (naamloze vennootschap/public limited liability company) and the BV (besloten vennootschap met beperkte aansprakelijkheid/private limited liability company). The main existing differences relate to:

(a) the type of shares and the restrictions on the transfer of shares (an NV may have bearer shares a BV can only have registered shares);

(b) the acquisition by the company of its own shares;

(c) the prohibition against giving financial assistance with respect to the acquisition of shares;

(d) the issuance of shares;

(e) the pre-emptive rights of shareholders; and

(f) the minimum capital.

O.2.3 The Private Company (De Besloten Vennootschap met Beperkte Aansprakelijkheid: BV)

The BV is similar to the private limited company under English law. Public funding and the issuing of bearer shares are not allowed. There is no required minimum of shareholders for the BV. Shareholders can be private individuals as well as corporate bodies.

O.2.4 Incorporation

O.2.4.1 Articles of association/the statutes (De Statuten)

In order to establish a NV or a BV the following procedure should be observed. A deed of incorporation (Akte van oprichting) should be prepared reflecting also the initial articles of association (Statuten: Statutes) of the company to be incorporated.

The statutes should, *inter alia*, reflect the corporate seat (statutaire zetel), the

375

objects and the capital structure as well as the manner in which the company is represented *vis-à-vis* third parties.

The deed of incorporation should also reflect who subscribes to the capital to be issued at incorporation, and how this capital has to be paid up (cash or kind) as well as the name(s) of the initial member(s) of the board of managing directors. The draft deed of incorporation is subsequently submitted to the Ministry of Justice (together with financial and other information on the proposed shareholders and initial directors) in order to obtain the so-called "declaration of no-objection" (verklaring van geen bezwaar). Once the said declaration has been obtained and the initial share capital has been duly paid-up, the company may be established by passing (executing) the deed of incorporation before a civil law notary. The time necessary to complete the above process may vary between one and two months. In exceptional circumstances the process may be accelerated. The company should (prior to or immediately after its incorporation) be recorded with the Trade Register of the Chamber of Commerce of the district in which it has its corporate seat and registered office, *inter alia* by filing a copy of the deed of incorporation as well as the names of the members of the board of directors and the sole shareholder (the latter *only* if the company concerned has one shareholder).

The Trade Registers are organised as departments of the local Chambers of Commerce. All information filed with the Trade Register is available for inspection by the public. Registration in the Trade Register is automatically reported in the Dutch *Official Gazette (De Nederlandse Staatscourant)*.

O.2.4.2   *Registered office (de zetel)*

The registered office (or corporate seat) of the NV/BV (de zetel) must be specified in the statutes. The registered office must be located in the Netherlands. Nevertheless, the location of the registered office can be changed by amending the statutes. However, it may only move within the Netherlands. The NV/BV needs to be registered in the local Trade Register of the district where it has its registered office. Nevertheless, the NV/BV can have its principal place of business elsewhere in which case it must also be registered with the Trade Register of this other district.

O.2.4.3   *Company name*

The name selected for the NV/BV must be included in the statutes. The public notary will on incorporation check whether or not a proposed name would conflict with the name of an enterprise already recorded with any of the Trade Registers in the Netherlands. The said check does not fully protect the company against a claim of a third party pursuant to the Trade Name Act (Handelsnaamwet). The said act prohibits the use of a name which resembles too closely the name of an existing business or other company engaged in similar activities. The name may not be misleading and must have a certain degree of distinctiveness. In practice, the public notary will seek unofficial approval of the Trade Register before incorporation. A business name, if different from the company name, needs also to be filed in the time-limit.

The company name must include the full words "de naamloze vennootschap" or "de besloten vennootschap met beperkte aansprakelijkheid" or the abbreviations NV or BV at the beginning or the end of the proposed company name.

O.2.4.4 *Duration*

The Dutch Civil Code Book 2 allows the NV/BV to be established for an unlimited period. However, the NV/BV by means of its statutes can determine otherwise.

O.2.5 Shares (Aandelen)

The Dutch Civil Code allows the company to issue different shares. The NV/BV can determine to issue:

(a) ordinary shares;

(b) priority shares (prioriteitsaandelen);

(c) preferential shares (preferente aandelen) with cumulative rights or not;

(d) founders' shares (oprichtersaandelen);

(e) bonus shares (bonus aandelen).

The nominal value of the (different classes of) shares will be specified in the statutes. The nominal value must be expressed in the Dutch currency. In addition, the NV/BV are allowed to issue debentures (obligatielening), convertible debentures and depositary receipts. For the BV, however, there is a stricter regime. Convertible debentures can be exchanged against shares sometime in the future. The depositary receipts can be issued as convertible, partly convertible or non-convertible against shares. The idea behind the depositary receipts is that an office independent from the company holds (all) shares and receipts for them. The receipt holder has therefore only the economic property; in other words he may claim dividends. The legal property is with the independent office. Inevitably, the right to vote rests in the hands of the independent office. The main reason for the company to use depositary receipts is the centralise the voting power, preserve some independence and be protected against possible hostile takeover bids.

O.2.5.1 *Share capital*

The authorised capital, specified in the statutes, is the maximum capital which the NV/BV can issue. For the NV/BV the issued capital must be at least one-fifth of the authorised capital. Of the issued capital at least 25 per cent must be paid up in cash or in kind. The minimum issued and paid-up capital for the BV is fl 40,000 and for the NV fl 100,000. The BV is not permitted to issue share certificates in respect of its shares. Non-conclusive evidence as to ownership may be obtained by way of an excerpt from the shareholders' register.

O.2.5.2 *Transfer of shares*

The transfer of registered shares, for the NV/BV is effected by way of a notarial deed of transfer to be served on the company by a Dutch bailiff or acknowledged by the company in writing. Where bearer shares are issued, the transfer is effected by the handing over of the share certificate itself. In contrast to the BV (see below) the NV may restrict the transfer of shares. An absolute prohibition on transfer will be forbidden. For the BV, other rules are applicable. The Dutch Civil Code prescribes that the share transfer for the BV must be restricted in one way or another. The transfer of shares can be unrestricted if the shares are transferred to a spouse or other shareholders. The statutes are free to determine in what way they restrict the scope of the transferability. For any transfer other than just mentioned above, the Civil Code prescribes that the transfer will be restricted along the lines of the "consent system" or the "offer system". The first one requires the shareholder to obtain the consent of the relevant body of the company before he may transfer his shares to a third party. Refusal by the relevant body to approve the requested transfer without offering an alternative transferee within three months is deemed to be an approval of the transfer. The second system requires the shareholder to offer his shares first to the remaining shareholders of the company. If the remaining shareholders refuse to purchase, the statutes can prescribe reversion to the consent system or disposal without restriction within three months following refusal. The BV must include one of the above-mentioned systems in its statutes. Again, an absolute prohibition on the transfer is forbidden.

O.2.5.3 *Increase or decrease of capital*

The increase or decrease of the authorised capital specified in the statutes requires an alteration of the statutes. The increase of the issued capital up to the level of the authorised capital permitted by the statutes can be authorised by a decision of an (A)GM or by the decision of the board of directors which has been given the power by the (A)GM or the statutes to increase the issued capital. However, this power may only last for five years. In addition, the authorisation must contain the exact amount of shares which may be issued.

The existing shareholders do not have a pre-emption right on the issue of new shares *per se*. In most cases, however, the statutes provide for pre-emption rights.

O.2.5.4   *Form of subscription*

Subscription of the NV/BV can take place in cash or in kind. Subscription in the form of contracts of employment or services is prohibited. Subscription in kind must be accompanied by a description of the relevant assets as well as by a certificate of valuation prepared by a chartered accountant (registeraccountant).

O.2.5.5.   *Purchase of own shares*

Whilst not permitted to subscribe for its own shares, the NV/BV may acquire its own shares provided they are fully paid up and:

(a)   the acquisition is for free; or

(b)   the company's equity, less the acquisition price, is not less than the sum of the paid up and called up part of its issued share capital and the reserves which it must maintain according to statutory provisions and its statutes. Moreover, the nominal value of the own shares acquired by the NV/BV or its subsidiaries will not amount to more than 50 per cent of the issued capital of the BV and not more than 10 per cent of the issued capital of the NV, the statutes do allow the acquisition and an authorisation for the acquiring of the own shares is given by the (A)GM or other body authorised by an (A)GM or the statutes.

O.2.5.6   *Register of shareholders*

The board of directors is obliged to keep a register of shareholders in which the shares of the company are registered (to the extent the company is an NV only if it has issued registered shares). The register should among other things list the names and addresses of the shareholders. The register is in principle not open to the public. Only the register of partly paid shares of the NV/BV can be inspected by the public. Furthermore, the NV/BV has the duty to file the information concerning the partly paid shares with the Trade Register.

O.2.6   Company's Bodies

O.2.6.1   *Board of directors (Directie/Raad van Bestuur)*

O.2.6.1.1   Appointment/dismissal of directors   In the case of the NV/BV the first directors are appointed in the deed of incorporation. Subsequent directors are appointed and dismissed by the (A)GM. Unless, it concerns a "large NV/BV" (see below). In the case of a "large NV/BV" the supervisory board appoints and dismisses the subsequent directors. There is no required minimum or maximum for the number of directors. The appointment of directors has no time limit and can be reselected or discussed as the shareholders may, from time to time decide. A note of both appointment and dismissal of directors must be registered in the Trade Register of the local Chamber of Commerce. There are no residential or nationality requirements for the directors. Directors may be individuals as well as corporate bodies.

O.2.6.1.2   Duties/powers of the board of directors   Directors have both the power and responsibility to manage the company's affairs. The directors have a contractual liability to perform their duties properly. Internally management tasks may be divided among the directors. Externally the board of directors will, save for a few exceptions, be collectively responsible and liable for the management as conducted. The board of directors may delegate part of its tasks to other employees to assist the board in its managing task. The company is represented by each of its managing directors acting alone unless their authority is restricted in its statutes. Any such restriction can—if it has to have external effect—only be in the sense that the company is to be represented by two or more managing directors acting jointly. Once a director or directors (individually or jointly) are authorised to represent the NV/BV, it is not possible to restrict the power itself. Any such restrictions (except those prescribed by law) imposed will only have internal effect and will not affect third parties. In addition, the board of directors may grant an employee of the NV/BV the power to represent the NV/BV. Contrary to the representation by the directors, the power of the employee can be restricted. In cases where a director/directors act *ultra vires* to the objects of the NV/BV laid down in the statutes, there is no binding effect upon the company if the company can prove that the third party knew that this act was *ultra vires* the objects or could not have been ignorant of this fact. In other words the third party must have acted in "bad faith". To prove "bad faith" of the third party it is not sufficient to state that the third party could have inspected the statutes of the company in the Trade Register. The third party may not rely on this doctrine as a means of avoiding his obligations. Consequently, if the director is authorised the company cannot deny the binding effect of any lawful act by the authorised director (except for those limited cases described above) on behalf of the company. If the director is not authorised, the company can. This underlines the necessity to know which directors are authorised to represent the NV/BV and which are not. Therefore it is of the utmost importance that the appointment of the directors, together with the details of whether or not they are entitled to represent the NV/BV, are verified by the third parties in the Trade Register. Nevertheless, if the NV/BV acts in a way that the third party is made to believe that a director is authorised to represent the NV/BV, the company is bound by the acts of the director irrespective of the fact whether he is authorised or not.

O.2.6.1.3 Board meetings The Civil Code is silent in respect of rules governing the task of the board of directors. The only provision that the Civil Code contains is that the board of directors must "manage" the NV/BV. Because the Civil Code contains no specified rules, the statutes are free to determine the procedure. Normally, the statutes will not reflect extensive rules as to the operations of the board of directors. The statutes are also at liberty to determine the number of board meetings as well as the number of directors which must be physically present to hold a meeting. If, according to the statutes, at least two or more directors need to be present, the statutes can provide for representation in the board meetings by proxy. This proxy, however, may only be given to a fellow director. Normally, board resolutions are passed by a simple majority of those voting: again the statutes can determine otherwise. A casting vote of the chairman of the board of directors is one of the possibilities.

O.2.6.1.4 Legal liability of directors The law contains several provisions on the basis of which a managing director or supervisory director (see below) of an NV/BV can be held personally liable. The different legal sources of liability can be divided into several categories: internal liability, external liability, liability for special debts, liability in the event of bankruptcy and criminal liability. Hereinafter, only the main provisions relating to the civil liability will be addressed.

With respect to the liability towards the company (internal liability) the most important provision is that each managing director is responsible for the proper performance of the duties assigned to him.

The general liability towards third parties is that a person who commits an unlawful act towards another which can be imputed to him must repair the damage which the other person suffers as a consequence thereof. A separate provision deals with the furnishing of so-called misleading information. A person who publishes or allows to be published a statement concerning goods or services offered in the course of business (by himself or his principal) commits a tort if it is misleading in one or more aspects. If, however, the annual accounts, the annual report, or interim figures published by a BV or an NV misrepresent the condition of the company, the directors are jointly and severally liable towards third parties for any loss sustained by them as a result thereof. A director is, however, not liable if he proves that he was not to blame.

The liability for special debts rests in principle upon each (former) managing director and each person with respect to whom it may reasonably be believed that he (co-)determined the management of the BV or NV as if he were a managing director. The BV or NV is under the obligation to give immediate (within 14 days) notice to the relevant authorities as soon as it has become clear that the company will not be able to pay any (tax or social security) debt. If the company has duly complied with this obligation, a director is only liable for the debts if it is plausible that he was to blame for the non-payment as a result of his clearly improper management during a period of three years prior to the time the relevant authorities were notified of the inability to pay. If no immediate and proper notice has been given, a director is (unless he proves the contrary) presumed to be to blame for the non-payment as a result of his clearly improper management.

Liability (to the estate for the deficit) exists when a company is declared bankrupt if the management has clearly performed its duties improperly and if it is plausible that this is to any significant extent a cause of the involuntary liquidation of the company. The failure of the management to comply with its obligations with respect to bookkeeping and filing of the annual accounts constitutes such improper performance and it is presumed that such improper performance constitutes an important cause of the involuntary liquidation. No liability exists if a director proves that he was not to blame for the improper performance and that he was not negligent and did not fail in his duty to prevent the consequences thereof.

O.2.6.2 *Supervisory board (Raad van Commissarissen)*

O.2.6.2.1 Small and large NV/BV Apart from the distinction NV/BV, there is a second distinction, namely between that of the normal (or small) and the large NV/BV. The large NV/BV is called "structuurvennootschap". A special regime is called "structuurregime". To fall within this regime, the NV/BV should comply with the following requirements:

(a) The issued capital and the free reserves must be at least fl 25 million.

(b) The NV/BV or one of its subsidiaries has a works council (employers are obliged to form a works council if they employ more than 34 people).

(c) The NV/BV and the subsidiaries together have at least 100 employees employed in the Netherlands.

If a NV/BV does comply with the above-mentioned requirements, it is obliged to register this in the Trade Register. Three years after registration as a large NV/BV the company will fall within, and has to comply with the aforementioned special regime applicable to a large NV/BV. In addition, a further distinction must be made between different classes of the large NV/BV. The large NV/BV seek classification as an exempted, mitigated or structured NV/BV. This latter distinction concerns solely the degree of applicability of the special regime.

O.2.6.2.2 Appointment and dismissal of supervisors Only the large NV/BV are required to have a supervisory board. The small or normal NV/BV can adopt a supervisory board voluntarily. In the case of a voluntary supervisory board, the first supervisors are appointed by the deed of incorporation. Further appointments will be made by the (A)GM. In the case of the compulsory supervisory board, the first supervisors are also appointed by the deed of incorporation. Further appointments, however, are made by the supervisory board itself. Nevertheless, the (A)GM, the works council and the board of directors can make recommendations. The ultimate decision, however, remains with the supervisory board. The minimum required number of supervisors for the compulsory supervisory board is three. The voluntary supervisory board does not have a prescribed minimum. The compulsory and voluntary supervisory boards must consist of individuals only. The appointment of supervisors in the case of the compulsory supervisory board can only be done up to a maximum period of four years. For both the large and the regular NV/BV there is a maximum age for the supervisor of 72 years.

In the case of a small NV/BV, the supervisors are dismissed by the (A)GM. In the case of a compulsory supervisory board, only the Enterprise Chamber (de ondernemingskamer) of the Court of Appeal in Amsterdam can dismiss the supervisors. The compulsory supervisor must resign at the latest, four years after his appointment. During this time, only the Enterprise Chamber of the Court of Appeal in Amsterdam can dismiss the supervisor on application of the NV/BV represented by the supervisory board, or a representative of the (A)GM or the works council.

Both the appointment and dismissal of the supervisors of normal and large NV/BVs must be registered in the Trade Register.

O.2.6.2.3 Duties and powers of the supervisory board The supervisory board means basically that instead of a one-tier there is a two-tier management system. This, however, does not mean that both the board of directors and the supervisory board are engaged in daily management. Although certain decision require the prior approval of the supervisory board (having no external effect), the daily management is reserved solely for the board of directors. The primary task of the supervisory board is to supervise and to advise the board of directors.

The board of directors has the duty to disclose all relevant information to the supervisory board in order to enable the supervisory board to exercise sufficient supervision over the management of the NV/BV. In addition, the supervisory board can exercise some powers of the board of directors in case the latter is not willing or capable to fulfil its task properly. The compulsory supervisory board has more extensive powers than the voluntary one, such as the appointment and dismissal of directors. In the case of a voluntary supervisory board the appointment and dismissal of directors remains with the (A)GM.

O.2.6.2.4 Legal liability of supervisors See under O.2.6.1.4 above.

O.2.6.3   *The (annual) general meeting (De algemene vergadering van aandeelhouders)*

O.2.6.3.1   General provisions   There is no difference between an annual general meeting and an extraordinary general meeting. At least one shareholders' meeting must be held annually. The Civil Code states that the board of directors and the supervisory board are entitled to call a general meeting. However, the statutes can determine otherwise. At least one shareholders' meeting must be held for the purpose of approving the annual accounts. In addition shareholders' meetings can be called during the year as and when required for special business.

O.2.6.3.2   The convening of an (annual) general meeting of a NV/BV   The shareholders' meeting may be convened in any of the following ways:

(a)   by the board of directors;

(b)   by the supervisory board;

(c)   by the person or persons authorised by the statutes;

(d)   by shareholders representing at least one-tenth of the company's issued capital authorised by the President of the District Court in the district of the NV/BV (President van de Rechtbank);

(e)   by any shareholder on the authorisation of the President of the District Court if it turns out that the relevant bodies are not capable or are not willing to convene an (A)GM.

O.2.6.3.3   Notices for the (A)GM of the NV/BV   *The NV:* Notices of shareholders' meetings must be published in a national newspaper where bearer shares are issued. If all the shares are registered, the statutes can determine how to convene an (A)GM. The notice does not need to include the agenda of the general meeting. However, the agenda must be present at the registered office before the (A)GM for inspection by the shareholders.

The BV: Notices of shareholders' meeting setting out the agenda must be sent to all registered shareholders. Unlike the requirements for the NV, the BV notice must contain the agenda.

The call for the (A)GM of the NV/BV must be made at least 15 days before the meeting is held. If the NV/BV does not comply with the aforementioned period or the call for the meeting did not take place at all, no valid decisions can be taken during the meeting unless with unanimity of the whole issued capital present.

O.2.6.3.4   Place of the (A)GM   The location for the (A)GM is specified in the statutes or will be the registered office of the NV/BV. In addition, the place of the meeting must, in principle, be located somewhere in the Netherlands; with the approval of all shareholders this can be changed.

O.2.6.3.5 Duties and powers of the (A)GM Generally speaking, the (A)GM is the body which has the exclusive power to decide on matters relating to the "internal structure" of the company, whereas the board of directors has the exclusive power to "manage" the company. The general provisions regarding the powers of the (A)GM are residual in nature, stating that the "powers not conferred upon the board of directors or other persons are—within the limits set by the law and the statutes—vested in the (A)GM". However, a number of specific provisions allocate certain decisions exclusively to the (A)GM. These decisions relate to the structure/organisaton of and the internal relations within the company and comprise, *inter alia*, the

(a) issuance of shares (delegation of this power is possible);

(b) reduction of the issued capital;

(c) adoption of the annual accounts;

(d) amendment of the articles of association;

(e) appointment, dismissal and suspension of members of the board of directors (except in case of large companies; see above);

(f) liquidation of the company.

Some of these powers may be limited or restricted (but not excluded) by the statutes. Furthermore, with respect to certain other decisions, mandatory legal provisions require that the prior approval or authorisation of the shareholders' meeting be obtained.

The Civil Code prescribes that decisions taken by the (A)GM do not require anything more than a simple majority. Save for a few exceptions the statutes can determine the qualified majority voting in general and also specify qualified majority voting requirements for different classes of shares. Furthermore, the statutes can state that a certain decision requires a minimum amount of votes. The latter provision also implies the quorum.

Although the statutes are free to determine the quorum, in respect of certain decisions such as the appointment and dismissal of directors and supervisors the Civil Code prescribes an upper limit. Nevertheless, if the quorum is not satisfied at the (A)GM, the Civil Code allows the statutes to determine that no quorum at all will apply to those decisions which are referred to the following (A)GM. The fact that the quorum is not satisfied means that the particular decision for which the quorum is prescribed cannot be taken.

O.2.6.3.6 Voting rights and restrictions The voting rights of the shareholders can be restricted. There is, however, an absolute prohibition on non-voting shares. Every shareholder must have at least one vote. However, the NV/BV itself may not exercise the voting rights of its own shares. The shareholder can exercise his voting rights through a proxy. Contracts of shareholders stating how to exercise their voting rights can be valid. However, the shareholders will always remain authorised to exercise his voting right despite the proxy or the contract. The voting rights and restrictions to the extent permitted, can be set out in the statutes of the NV/BV.

O.2.6.4 *Works council (de ondernemingsraad)*

Every enterprise having more than 34 employees must establish a works council. The works council advises on various matters such as labour, safety, relocation and reorganisation. In addition the works council has the right to advise on proposed appointments of managing directors and make recommendations for vacancies on the supervisory board of the large NV/BV.

O.2.7 Audit/Accounts

O.2.7.1 *Appointment and dismissal of auditors (accountant)*

Each year, within five months after the end of the financial year (book year), the board of directors must prepare the annual accounts. The annual accounts consist of the balance sheet and the profit and loss account with explanatory notes thereon. In special circumstances the (A)GM may extend the period of five months by a maximum of six months. The annual accounts must be signed by the directors and, if a supervisory board exists, by the supervisory directors. If one or more of their signatures is missing this must be stated in the annual acounts together with the reasons why. Both the annual accounts and the annual report have to be deposited for inspection by the shareholders. The adoption of the annual accounts takes place by the (A)GM.

The law provides detailed rules with respect to the contents of the annual accounts and the annual report. Based on the size of the company some exemptions from these detailed rules (and the rules with respect to the publication of the annual accounts) apply.

The annual accounts must be published within eight days after adoption by depositing a copy at the office of the Trade Register. If the annual accounts have not been adopted in conformity with the above-mentioned legal provisions within two months from the end of the period set out for their preparation, the board of directors must (without delay) publish the annual accounts as prepared, together with a statement in the annual accounts to the effect that they have not yet been adopted. Publication must, in any event, take place within 13 months from the end of the financial year. Non-publication is an economic offence and may result in personal liability of the directors in the event of bankruptcy (see above).

O.2.7.2 *Duties and powers of auditors*

The auditor has no special rights. The duty of the auditor comprises the issue of an auditor's report to the board of directors and the supervisory board and the issue of an auditor's statement to the (A)GM. The auditor's report is solely addressed to the board of directors and the supervisory board, and plays no major role in the life of a NV/BV. The auditor's statement, however, is far more important. The auditor's statement must state whether or not the annual accounts of the NV/BV are made in compliance with the requirements set out in the Civil Code. Subsequently, the auditor's statement (de accountantsverklaring) must be reported with the annual accounts and the annual report to the shareholders.

O.2.7.3 *Confidentiality of an auditor*

The Civil Code is silent on the confidentiality of the auditor. However, the organisation of Dutch accountants, the Royal NIVRA, has adopted a code of conduct for auditors comprising a duty of confidentiality for the individual auditor. The auditor must keep confidential all information which will be revealed to him in the exercise of his profession. This is in stark contrast with what is applicable, for example, in French law. In France the auditor (Verifacateur de Comptes) is obliged to disclose all facts which involve or relate to criminal offences to the public prosecutor. Non-disclosure of those facts by the Fraud auditor will amount to a criminal offence committed by the auditor himself.

O.2.7.4 *Single-member companies*

The Act implementing the twelfth E.C. Council Directive on Company Law contains, *inter alia*, provisions obliging both NV and BV to register in the Trade Register the fact that all its shares are held by a single natural or legal person as well as the identity of the single shareholder. Only the holders of bearer shares are under the obligation to notify the company as soon as they become the sole shareholder.

SECTION 3

COSTS OF INCORPORATION

O.3.1   The major expenses incurred in forming a NV/BV consist of:

(a)   *Capital Issue Tax*. This tax is charged at 1 per cent on the amount of paid-up capital. If the capital is furnished other than in cash, the tax is payable on the value of the consideration.

(b)   *The Public Notary's Fee*. The Public Notary's fee includes drawing up and executing the deed of incorporation.

(c)   *The Chamber of Commerce fee*, charged for filing the company's documents in the Trade Register. This fee is based on the share capital, the long-term loans (more than one year) and the reserves. For the NV/BV, this fee will amount to fl 195 in the case of share/loan/reserve capital of fl 40,000, fl 830 in the case of a "total" capital of fl 500,000 and a fee of fl 1,256 in the case of a "total" capital of fl 1,000,000.

(d)   *The Ministry of Justice fee*, charged for the issue of the No Objection Statement, amounts to fl 175.

The above-mentioned fees are the minimum charges. Any additional fees will be charged when problems result in more correspondence, translation or discussions and further consultation of the public notary or other professional advisers.

Finally, one should bear in mind that the minimal paid-up capital for the NV is fl 100,000 and for the BV fl 40,000.

NORWAY

SECTION 1

CLASSIFICATION OF BUSINESS ORGANISATIONS IN NORWAY: INTRODUCTION*

P.1.0   A variety of organisational forms are available to the business man who is about to establish himself in Norway. However, the organisational forms fall into three main groups:

—sole proprietorship (including the "branch office")
—partnerships (with limited, unlimited or mixed liability)
—other forms (trusts, co-operatives, etc.).

In practice, one will often meet a variety of terms that describe business enterprises, such as "consortiums", "pool-agreements", "joint ventures", etc.

These terms have no precise legal definition, and in content may cover various contract agreements ranging from very loose co-operation agreements, to companies with unlimited liability.

P.1.1   Sole Proprietorship

Sole proprietorship (Enmannsforetak) exists where a person is engaged in a business activity, alone, or with employees.

No regulations apply to the formation of a sole proprietorship. The decisive factors in the establishment of the business is the decision to do so, and the subsequent enactment of this decision.

P.1.2   Formation and Formal Requirements

Although there are generally no formal requirements to the establishment of a sole proprietorship, certain business activities might need an official permit. There are, in addition, a host of detailed requirements that apply to specific areas of business.

* *Bjorn Blix, Bull & Co. (full particulars are listed in the Appendix).*

The sole proprietor of a business will be obliged to keep accounts, and to draw up a balance sheet once a year. Also, certain activities (for instance "the trading of goods acquired for this purpose") lead to a requirement for registration of the business in the Register of Business Enterprises (Foretaksregisteret).

P.1.3   The Branch Office

A branch office is defined as a "permanent place of business", and the exact interpretation of this term is not clear. Whether or not a foreign enterprise does have a permanent place of business within this country depends on the extent of the activity. One criterion will be whether or not the activity is under "separate leadership" from the enterprise itself. Foreign enterprises with a branch office in Norway are required to register with the Register of Business Enterprises.

P.1.4   Restrictions for Foreigners

There are no general restrictions that apply to foreigners wishing to establish a business in Norway. However, there are quite a few regulations that will apply to, and to some extent restrict the actions of foreigners. For some activities a foreign person or enterprise will need a special permit, and there are general requirements for work and residence permits for foreign nationals. Other regulations stipulate requirements for Norwegian domicile of a certain length of time, and foreign nationals or enterprises are restricted in the ability to purchase or acquire long term leases to real estate.

SECTION 2

LIMITED PARTNERSHIPS: THE LIMITED LIABILITY COMPANY (AKSJESELSKAP: AS/ASA)

P.2.0   Partnerships comprise all organisational forms where the company is structured to accommodate more than one participant. Accordingly, the limited liability company, or the "stock corporation" (Aksjeselskap; hereinafter called "AS" or "ASA", see below P.2.2 and P.2.3) in which the partners' liability is restricted to the payment of the share capital, is technically a partnership, although all shares may be owned by a single person or entity.

This is clearly the most important company form in Norway, comprising all the major industrial and financial enterprises, and in actual numbers is second only to sole proprietorships. For this reason the AS will be discussed separately in this section, while the other partnership forms are described in sections 3 and 4.

P.2.1 Introduction and Definition

In practice, the only permissible form of business partnership that allows a limited liability for all participants, is the limited liability company. The legal regime for the formation and operation of the AS is described in the Limited Company Act (Aksjeloven) of June 4, 1976 (No. 59), as amended. This act will apply to all partnerships where none of the participants have full liability for the commitments of the company. There are, however, other laws and acts that apply to specific types of limited companies, such as banks, insurance companies and financing companies. The AS is also subject to regulations covering topics from mandatory registration to taxation.

The primary objectives of the Limited Company Act are to protect the share capital for the benefit of the company's contracting partners, to protect the shareholders through requirements for publicity, to protect minority shareholders, and, finally, to protect the employees of the company by giving them a certain influence in the management of the company.

P.2.1.1 *The public limited company (Allment Aksjeselskap, ASA) and the Private Limited company*

To obtain a wider public participation from others than the founders of the company, the company must be a public limited company, hereinafter called "ASA". For the private limited company, called "AS", public funding is not allowed.

The division between the ASA and AS is a result of the implementation of the E.C. Directives through the EEA Agreement.

The most important differences between the ASA and the AS lie in the requirements on public funding and minimum share capital.

P.2.2   Incorporation

No permit or licence is required to set up an AS/ASA except for certain types of companies, such as banks, insurance companies or financing companies. An AS/ASA can be established by one or more persons or legal entities ("the founders"). At least half of the founders must have Norwegian domicile, and must have had domicile in Norway or one of the other Nordic countries for the last two years.

The incorporation of an AS/ASA involves four steps:

(a) the drawing up and signature by the founders of a dated memorandum of association, which shall include the proposed articles of association, as well as other information relevant to the subscription of shares;

(b) the subscription of shares;

(c) the holding of a constituting general assembly of shareholders;

(d) the filing for registration with the Register of Business Enterprises.

The memorandum of association must include the proposed articles of association, and must also specify:

(a) the issue price for each share;

(b) the time for share subscription and payment of share capital;

(c) the time for the holding of the constituting general assembly;

(d) all relevant information pertaining to intended contribution in kind;

(e) whether the costs of incorporation are to be borne by the company;

(f) if the company is an ASA; the name and personal number/company registration number of the company's founders.

The memorandum of association may designate a minimum share capital which must be subscribed for the founding of the company, and a higher amount which may be subscribed. The subscription of shares shall be made on the memorandum of association itself, or on a document which records the memorandum of association. If shares are to be subscribed by persons or entities other than the founders or persons or entities represented by the founders, there are special provisions dealing with the timing of the subscriptions, the publishing of the memorandum of association, etc.

Provided that all shares are intended to be subscribed by the founders or by persons or entities represented by the founders, and provided that the founders and shareholders are all duly represented, the subscription of shares can be done immediately following the signature of the memorandum of association. Provided that all shares have been subscribed to in accordance with the memorandum of association and that the memorandum specifies this timing, the constituting general meeting of shareholders can be held immediately. The decision to constitute the company is made by the general meeting, which then shall elect the members of the board and appoint an auditor.

Within six months of the signing of the memorandum of association, the company must file for registration with the Register of Business Enterprises. On approval of the formation process, the company is entered into the Register, and only then does it achieve full status as a legal entity. In the interim period, from the decision by the general meeting to constitute the company to the entry into the Register, the company has a limited legal personality; it is not allowed to acquire any rights or obligations towards third parties that are not explicitly mentioned in the memorandum of association. An extract of the registration is then published.

P.2.2.1   *Articles of association (Vedtekter)*

The minimum contents are:

(a)   the company name (Firma);

(b)   the county in which the company shall have its registered office;

(c)   the object of the company's activities;

(d)   the amount of share capital;

(e)   the par value of the shares;

(f)   the number of board members;

(g)   which matters are to be decided by the annual general meeting of shareholders;

(h)   if the company is an ASA, the articles of association must specify the company as "allment aksjeselskap", and state whether the company shall have more than one managing director or if the number of managing directors can be decided by the board of directors, by the corporate assembly or by the representative assembly.

If the company should not have as its object the generation of profit for the participants, the articles must contain provisions for the distribution of profits and of the assets in case of liquidation.

If the shares are to be registered in the Verdipapirsentralen, this must be provided for in the articles. The articles may contain other regulations, such as restrictions on the transfer of shares, regulation of voting rights, etc.

P.2.2.2   Registered office

The registered office must be located within Norway. The county in which the registered office is located must be included in the articles.

P.2.2.3   Company name (Firma)

The company name will be the official designation of the legal entity, and accordingly must be recognisable as separate from other entities. The name of the private limited company must include the word "aksjeselskap" or the abbreviation "AS". The name of the public limited company must include the words "allment aksjeselskap" or the abbreviation "ASA". The company name must not be misleading. There are certain other restrictions in the choice of a name, particularly to the protection of the established rights of third parties.

P.2.2.4   Duration

An AS/ASA will exist as a legal entity until it is dissolved according to the procedures for liquidation, following a proper decision by the general meeting or a court order. The articles may contain provisions for the dissolution of the company following a period of time or the occurrence of a given event. The dissolution of the company will still have to be decided by the general meeting, or by the courts.

P.2.3   Shares (Aksjer)

Normally, all shares shall have equal rights. However, the articles may establish different classes of shares. The articles must then contain a description of the differences between the classes of shares, as well as the total par value of the shares within each class.

Share certificates shall be issued for all shares, unless the shares are to be registered in "Verdipapirsentralen" (VPS). This is an official register of securities (stocks and bonds), and registration is mandatory for all Norwegian companies whose shares are quoted in a Norwegian stock exchange. Other shares may be registered in VPS, if the company so desires. The registration in VPS will replace the share certificates, and make these redundant.

Share certificates shall be dated and signed by the board, or a minimum of two board members. They shall contain the name of the shareholder and the company, the par value of the share and the number of shares that the certificate is valid for. If there are different classes of shares, the certificate shall state the specific regulations pertaining to the shares, and if there are any other special regulations connected with the shares (such as limited transfer rights, etc.), these shall be specified in the certificate.

"Interim certificates" may be issued, and shall contain the same basic information as the final share certificates. No share certificate may be issued before the company is registered, or before the shares in question have been paid in full.

P.2.3.1 *Share capital (Aksjekapital)*

The share capital must be stipulated in the articles. For private limited companies the share capital must amount to at least 50,000 Nkr, for public limited companies at least 1 million Nkr. Apart from these, there are no directives as to the size of the share capital, but there is a general assumption that a company must not be under-capitalised in relation to the company's activities, and that such under-capitalisation might ultimately lead to liability for the persons responsible.

There are no specific requirements as to the par value of each share or the number of shares to be issued, so the company may be founded with as little as one share, or as many as one might wish. All shares must, however, be of the same par value. If the total subscription of shares does not amount to the share capital stipulated in the articles (or to the minimum amount stipulated in the memorandum of association), the company cannot be founded.

Prior to application for registration, all shares must be subscribed to, and at least half of the share capital as well as half of any over-par premium must be paid by the shareholders. All contributions in kind must have been made. Increases or decreases of the capital must be done according to the regulations in chapters 4 and 6 of the Limited Company Act (see P.2.3.3 below).

Should the company's year-end balance sheet show that two-thirds of the share capital has been lost, the board of directors must address this in the annual report, with suggestions for what might have to be done to ensure the future operations of the company, or whether the company should be dissolved.

If the company is an ASA and the shareholders' equity is less than half of the share capital, the board of directors must ensure there is held a general meeting of shareholders. Then, the board must account for the company's financial position and how to balance the shareholders' equity and share capital. The board of directors are obligated to propose a liquidation of the company if balancing the equity/share capital is futile.

P.2.3.2 *Transfer of shares*

Under the Act on Acquisition of Business Enterprises 1994, any acquisition of one-third, one-half or two-thirds of the shares in a Norwegian enterprise with more than 50 employees, must be reported to the Ministry of Trade and Industry. Such a duty to report an acquisition, also exists if the yearly sales of the enterprise is more than 50 million Nkr, or if the enterprise has received governmental funding for R&D of more than 5 million Nkr to one project during the last eight years. To protect public interest, the Government may prohibit the acquisition. Approval from the Government is also necessary to acquire one-third, one-half or two-thirds of the shares in a limited company that owns real estate.

There are also restrictions on ownership of certain companies, such as banks and financing companies, whereby no person or entity may own more than ten per cent of such companies. There are modifications in these restrictions, relating to subsidiaries.

Apart from the restrictions above, the general rule is that shares are freely negotiable, unless the articles contain restrictions. The articles may reserve current shareholders or other designated persons or entities the right to purchase shares that have been or are about to be transferred. The articles may also state that the transfer of shares must be approved by the company, and that the purchaser shall have certain qualities. Other restrictions on the transfer of shares may not be incorporated in the articles.

Share certificates are legal instruments to order, whose transfer is effected by delivery with an endorsement of the certificate. Shares that are registered in VPS are transferred by the filing of the appropriate record of transfer. For the purchaser to be able to exercise the rights of a shareholder, the transfer must also be registered in the company's register of shares.

If a transfer of shares results in the purchaser becoming owner of more than ten per cent of the shares in a company which is quoted on the stock exchange, the transfer must be "flagged" immediately, by sending a report of the transfer to the company and to the stock exchange.

P.2.3.3 *Increase/decrease of capital*

An increase in the share capital can be based on either a subscription of new shares, whereby the company received added funds or contributions, or by the issue of shares through the conversion of the company's reserves to share capital. In private companies, AS, the increase of capital can only be based on subscription of new shares by the existing shareholders or specified persons.

Both transactions normally a decision by the general meeting of shareholders. However, on certain terms, the general meeting may give the board of directors the authority to increase the share capital by the issue of new shares against contributions. This authority can not be conferred upon the board until the company has been registered in the Register of Business Enterprises. The authority is limited to a period of five years, and may not exceed half the registered share capital at the date of the authorisation.

Existing shareholders have a pre-emptive right to the new shares in the same ratio as their existing shares in the company. This pre-emptive right can be excluded only by a decision of the general meeting, with a majority of two-thirds of the votes as well as of the share capital represented in the meeting.

If the company has more than one class of shares, the articles can restrict the pre-emptive rights to the class of shares in which a shareholder already has shares. The employees of the company shall have the right to subscribe to shares that have not been subscribed to by the shareholders according to their pre-emptive rights.

When the share capital is to be increased, the shareholders may demand a certificate for each of their shares, stating their pre-emptive rights, and how many certificates are required for the subscription of one new share or the receipt of one share of converted new share capital. If the shares are registered in VPS, this register will establish a separate list of the pre-emptive rights.

A decrease of capital must be based on a decision of the general meeting, with the same qualified majority vote that is required for amendments of the articles (two-thirds of the votes and of the represented share capital).

The decision must record the amount with which the capital is to be decreased, as well as whether the decrease is to be used to:

(a)   eliminate a deficit that cannot be eliminated any other way;

(b)   distribute the released assets to the shareholders;

(c)   reduce the shareholders obligations of payment;

(d)   form a reserve.

A capital decrease is permissible only if the decrease is to be employed in one of the four ways above, or a combination of them.

Decisions as mentioned in (ii), (iii) and (iv) above can only be made with the explicit consent of the board of directors, and may be only so large as to leave assets that fully cover the remaining share capital as well as any other restricted funds. The decision to decrease the capital must be registered with the Register of Business Enterprises within four months, or the decrease cannot be implemented.

P.2.3.4   *Form of subscription*

Subscription of shares can take place in cash or in kind. The memorandum of association must contain all relevant information concerning contributions in kind, such as a description of the factors relevant to the evaluation of the assets in question.

Contributions in kind cannot be made with assets that are incapable of being legally entered into the company's balance sheet, and the value of the shares subscribed with the contribution must not exceed the value the assets assumedly would have in the balance sheet. Shares cannot be issued under par.

P.2.3.5   *Purchase of own shares*

An AS is not permitted to subscribe to its own shares, nor to purchase such shares, or to accept them as security. Any agreement containing such subscription, purchase or pledge will be invalid.

Own shares may, however, be legally acquired by an AS/ASA through donation, through the merger with another AS/ASA through a court ordered restitution of a shareholder according to regulations in the Limited Company Act (Aksjeloven), or through the pursuance of the company's claims.

Own shares legally acquired as above, must either be eliminated through a decrease of share capital, or they must be sold as soon as possible, and not later than two years after they were acquired.

P.2.3.6   *Register of shares*

Upon incorporation, the board of every AS/ASA must establish a Register of Shares, containing the name and address of all shareholders, along with the number of shares held by each shareholder. If the shares are to be registered in VPS, a register of shares is to be established as a file with VPS. The Register of Shares is a public register, and the public shall have unrestricted access.

P.2.4   Corporate Structure

Every AS/ASA must have a minimum organisational structure, comprising a general meeting of shareholders, a board of directors and an auditor. If the company has a share capital of more than 1 million Nkr, the company must also have a managing director. This is also possible, but not mandatory for companies with lesser share capital. In addition, should the company over the last three years have had an average of at least 200 employees, the company shall also have a corporate assembly (Bedriftsforsamling), unless the company in question has agreed differently with its employees. Companies without a corporate assembly may have a representative assembly (Representantskap).

Other than the above, no other company bodies with executive powers may be established. There are, however, no restrictions on the creation of advisory bodies, intended for the preparation of matters for the executive bodies.

P.2.4.1   *General meeting of shareholders (Generalforsamling)*

P.2.4.1.1   General provisions   The annual (ordinary) shareholders' meeting shall decide on the annual financial report, including the company's balance sheet and

400

the handling of profits or losses. The notice of the shareholders' meeting forms the basis for which decisions the meeting may make in whatever topic is at hand.

P.2.4.1.2 The convening of the shareholders' meeting The annual shareholders' meeting shall be held within six months of the expiry of the fiscal year. An extraordinary shareholders' meeting may be held whenever deemed necessary by the board of directors, the corporate assembly, the representative assembly or the chairman of either of the two latter bodies. An extraordinary shareholders' meeting shall also be called when this is requested in writing by the auditor, or by shareholders representing at least one-tenth of the share capital.

The shareholders' meetings are called by the board of directors. If a shareholders' meeting has not been called when it should, it may be called by court order at the request of a member of one of the company's bodies, the managing director, the auditor, or a shareholder.

P.2.4.1.3 Notices for the shareholders' meeting The shareholders' meeting shall be called with a notice of at least one week, unless the articles of association specify a longer period. The summons shall be in writing, and shall be sent directly to every shareholder, unless the articles specify that a shareholders' meeting may be called by publishing the summons in at least two specifically identified newspapers.

The summons must provide the agenda, or give sufficient information on which matters are to be dealt with during the meeting. If the meeting is to decide proposed amendments of the articles, the summons must contain the main contents of the proposals. On items not properly publicised in the summons, the shareholders' meeting can make no decision without the consent of all shareholders.

P.2.4.1.4 Place of the shareholders' meeting The shareholders' meeting shall be held within the county of the company's registered office, unless the articles provide differently, or extraordinary circumstances necessitate a different location.

P.2.4.1.5 Duties/powers of the shareholders' meeting The general meeting of shareholders holds the supreme authority within the AS. This is the forum for the exercise of the rights of the shareholders, and the meeting holds the power to perform any act or make any decision that is not specifically vested in one of the other company bodies. This implies that as a general rule, the meeting may give instructions to the board on any matter, may overrule decisions made by the board, and may discuss and decide on any matter; subject, of course, to the matter being properly announced in the summons.

An important deviation from this general rule applies to companies that have a corporate assembly (or should have had a corporate assembly, if the company did not have a contrary agreement with the employees). In these companies, the corporate assembly (or the board of directors) is the supreme authority in certain important matters. The general meeting of shareholders elects the members of the board of directors, unless one of the special election procedures applies.

If the company has a corporate assembly, the general meeting of shareholders shall elect two-thirds of the members of the corporate assembly. If the company has a representative assembly, the general meeting shall elect all members of this assembly.

The general rule is that decisions of the shareholders' meeting require a simple majority of the votes cast. In the case of elections or appointments, the person that receives the most votes is elected, regardless of whether he or she has received fifty per cent of the votes cast.

Amendments to the articles of association normally require at least two-thirds of the votes cast as well as of the share capital represented in the meeting.

In certain instances the Limited Company Act draws up even stricter voting regulations for the protection of minority shareholders. The following decisions can only be made unanimously, or with the full consent of all those who are affected by the decision:

(a) the limiting of shareholders' right to receive dividends by amendment of the articles of association;

(b) the extension of the shareholders' obligations towards the company;

(c) restrictions on the transfer of shares;

(d) the establishment of inequality between groups of shares that have previously had equal rights.

The shareholders' meeting cannot legally make a decision that will grant an unreasonable benefit in favour of certain shareholders or others, to the detriment of other shareholders or the company.

Minutes of the shareholders' meeting shall be kept, recording all decisions made in the meeting.

P.2.4.1.6 Voting rights and restrictions

All shareholders have the right to participate in the shareholders' meeting. The articles may restrict the participation to shareholders who have confirmed their participation to the company within a given time limit. All shareholders have the right to be assisted in the meeting by an adviser, or to be represented by proxy, which must be granted in writing.

Through the presentation of the matters that are to be decided by the shareholders' meeting, the shareholders will receive substantial information about the company. In addition, the shareholders' meeting may decide by majority vote that information is to be submitted. If requested by a shareholder, the managing director or any member of one of the company's bodies is obliged to give certain information to the shareholders' meeting, provided that the submitting of the information will not damage the company.

Only shareholders have the right to vote in the meeting, and generally each share has one vote. Shares owned by the company itself or by a subsidiary have no votes, and are not computed in deciding questions of majority. A shareholder's voting rights are restricted in certain matters involving conflicts of interest.

The articles may stipulate that certain shares shall be without voting rights, or shall have restricted voting rights. Such restrictions can only be implemented if the number of shareholders within the relevant class of shares is lower than 20. The articles may also restrict the voting rights of any shareholder to a maximum number of votes or percentage of the share capital, regardless of the number of shares owned. In addition, voting rights may be suspended for shares that have been transferred, for a period of up to four weeks after the company has been notified of the transfer.

P.2.4.2 Corporate assembly (Bedriftsforsamling)

P.2.4.2.1 General provisions As a general rule, a corporate assembly must be established in any company that has had an average of 200 employees over the last three fiscal years. However, the company may enter into an agreement with its employees whereby the corporate assembly is waived, and the employees instead receive a more substantial representation on the board of directors, which assumes certain functions of the corporate assembly.

P.2.4.2.2 Appointment/dismissal of members The corporate assembly shall have a minimum of 12 members. Two-thirds of the members and their substitutes are elected by the shareholders' meeting. One-third are elected by and amongst the employees. The employees also have the right to demand that they in addition to the members shall elect half again as many observers.

The normal term of office is two years. A member may, however, be dismissed at any time by the company body that elected him or her. This does not apply to members elected by and amongst the employees.

Neither the managing director not a member of the board of directors may be elected to the corporate assembly. As a general rule, at least half the members of the corporate assembly must have Norwegian domicile, and have lived in Norway or one of the other Nordic countries for the last two years.

P.2.4.2.3 Meetings of the corporate assembly The chairman shall summon the corporate assembly as often as necessary, and whenever one-sixth of the members request a meeting. The members of the board of directors as well as the managing director are entitled to be present and to speak. Normally the chairman of the board and the managing director will be obliged to be present.

P.2.4.2.4 Duties/powers of the corporate assembly The corporate assembly appoints the members of the board of directors, including the chairman of the board. One-third of the members of the corporate assembly may demand a re-election of the members of the board, and that the election shall be by apportionment. A consequence of this is that the employee-elected members of the corporate assembly can ensure that up to one-third of the members of the board are candidates of the employees. The power to demand a re-election of the board does, of course, mean that the corporate assembly may dismiss the board at any time.

The corporate assembly shall, following a proposal from the board of directors, make the final decision in matters concerning:

(a) investments that are considerable in relation to the resources of the company;

(b) rationalisation or restructuring of the activities of the company, which will result in a substantial change in or reallocation of the company's workforce.

The corporate assembly also has certain supervisory functions. The members may demand the information they deem necessary from the company. The assembly may initiate investigations. It shall give its opinion to the general meeting of shareholders on the board of directors' proposals for year-end accounts and balance sheets, as well as on proposals for the handling of profits or losses. The corporate assembly may decide on recommendations to the board of directors on any subject.

P.2.4.3 *Representative assembly*

P.2.4.3.1 General provisions For companies that do not have a corporate assembly, the articles of association can stipulate that the company shall have a representative assembly.

P.2.4.3.2 Appointment/dismissal of members The representative assembly shall have a minimum of three members. All members are appointed by the general meeting of shareholders. The employees are not entitled to representation in the representative assembly. The normal term of office is two years. A member may, however, be dismissed at any time by the company body that appointed him or her.

Neither the managing director nor a member of the board of directors may be elected to the corporate assembly. As a general rule, at least half the members of the corporate assembly must have Norwegian domicile, and have lived in Norway or one of the other Nordic countries for the lat two years.

P.2.4.3.3 Meetings of the representative assembly The chairman shall summon the representative assembly as often as necessary, and whenever one-sixth of the members request a meeting. The members of the board of directors as well as the managing director are entitled to be present and to speak. Normally the chairman of the board and the managing director will be obliged to be present.

P.2.4.3.4 Duties/powers of the representative assembly Unless the articles of association provide for a different procedure, the representative assembly appoints all members of the board of directors, including the chairman of the board. When the representative assembly has the power of appointment of board members, the assembly may also dismiss the board at any time.

The representative assembly has certain supervisory functions. The members may demand the information they require from the company. The assembly may initiate investigations, and shall give its opinion to the general meeting of shareholders on the board of directors' proposals for year-end accounts and balance sheets, as well as on proposals for the handling of profits and losses. The representative assembly may also decide on recommendations to the board of directors on any subject.

P.2.4.4   Board of directors

P.2.4.4.1   General provisions   The board of directors of an ASA/AS must normally have at least three members. If, however, the company is an AS and the share capital is less than 1 million Nkr, one member of the board will suffice. If, on the other hand, the AS has a corporate assembly, the board must have at least five members. At least half of the members of the board of directors must have Norwegian domicile, and have lived in Norway or in one of the other Nordic countries for the last two years.

P.2.4.4.2   Appointment/dismissal of directors   The general rule is that the directors are appointed by election in the general meeting of shareholders. There are, however, important modifications to this rule, to ensure employee representation in the company's bodies.

The election of directors takes place by majority vote, which means that shareholders representing a majority of the votes in the general meeting of shareholders may elect all the directors. There are no regulations to ensure minority shareholders any representation on the board of directors. However, the articles may provide for an election by others (such as a certain class of shares, a single shareholder or company creditors) of up to half of the directors.

In companies that for the last three fiscal years have had an average of more than three employees, two-thirds of the employees may demand that one director and one observer be appointed by and amongst the employees of the company. If the company for the last three fiscal years has had an average of more than 50 employees, a majority of the employees may demand that up to one-third of the directors (and never less than two) are appointed by and amongst the employees.

In companies that have a corporate assembly, the entire board of directors is appointed by the corporate assembly. If the corporate assembly has been waived through agreement with the employees, the latter then have the right to appoint up to one-third of the directors plus one, or up to one-third of the directors plus two observers. If the company has a representative assembly, the directors are appointed by this assembly, unless the articles decide differently. This does, however, not infringe on the rights of the employees to appoint directors as stated above.

The normal term of office for a director is two years. The term may be shortened or lengthened as decided in the articles of association, but it must not exceed four years. The term of office for directors appointed by the employees will always be two years. A director may at any time be dismissed by the company body that appointed him or her. This does not apply to directors appointed by the employees.

405

P.2.4.4.3 Duties/powers of directors In general, the board of directors is the supreme management body of the company, which represents the company in and out of court, signs on behalf of the company, and is authorised to enter into any agreement in the name of the company. This general power of decision and representation is a joint power and responsibility, resting with the board of directors as a forum. Sole powers of representation may, however, be granted by board decision.

The board of directors is responsible for the management of the company in the broadest sense, and must ensure a satisfactory organisation of the activities of the company. The board is superior to the managing director, who must adhere to instructions from the board. On the other hand, the board must adhere to lawful instructions from the general meeting of shareholders, the corporate assembly or the representative assembly.

If the corporate assembly has been waived by agreement with the employees, the board shall make the final decision on matters relating to:

(a) investments that are considerable in relation to the resources of the company;

(b) rationalisation or restructuring of the activities of the company, which will result in a substantial change in or reallocation of the company's workforce.

According to regulations in the Limited Company Act (Aksjeloven), there are several specific tasks that should be performed by the board, such as the approval of share transfers (as applicable), the presentation of proposals to the corporate assembly, the compilation of proposals to the corporate assembly, the compilation of the end of year report, the proposals for the payment of dividends, etc.

The board also decides whether signatory rights shall be delegated to directors singly or jointly, to the managing director or to other specifically designated employees. All such delegations of representative powers must be registered with the Register of Business Enterprises.

The board of directors shall appoint the managing director, and may, in principle, dismiss him or her at will. This function of the board may be delegated to one of the other company bodies.

The board may not make any decision which will lead to an unequitable benefit to certain shareholders or others to the detriment of the company or other shareholders. Nor must the board abide by resolutions by the general meeting of shareholders or any other company body, if this decision would be illegal, or contrary to the articles of association.

P.2.4.4.4 Rules of procedure: board meetings The board shall have a chairman, who is to be elected by the board members, unless the articles of association assign this function to another company body. The chairman is responsible for calling board meetings whenever necessary. Board members and the managing director may demand that a board meeting be called. The managing director has the right to be present and to address the board.

The board of directors forms a quorum when more than half of the members are present unless the articles have stricter regulations. As a general rule, all decisions are made by majority vote amongst the members that are present in the meeting. However, the majority must never be less than one-third of the total number of directors. If the votes are tied, the vote of the chairman will be decisive. The articles may set up stricter voting regulations, such as requiring a two-thirds majority for a binding decision to be made.

Observers to the board, elected by the employees as described above, have the same right to be present, to speak and put forth proposals in board meetings as the members themselves. Observers do not, however, have the right to vote, and they will normally not be responsible for the decisions of the board.

Minutes are to be kept of every board meeting, and these are to be signed by all members who are present. A member or managing director who disagrees in a board decision, may demand that his or her opinion be recorded in the minutes. A board member may not participate in decisions relating to matters in which he or she directly or indirectly has a marked personal or financial interest.

P.2.4.5 *Managing director*

P.2.4.5.1 General provisions Any ASA/AS must normally have a managing director. Though, in a private limited company (AS) with a share capital less than 1 million Nkr, the board of directors can decide that the company shall be without a managing director.

P.2.4.5.2 Appointment/dismissal of the managing director The board of directors shall appoint the managing director. This function may be delegated to the corporate assembly or, if the company does not have a corporate assembly, in the representative assembly or the general meeting of shareholders, by regulations in the articles of association.

The managing director may have Norwegian domicile, and must have lived in Norway or one of the other Nordic countries for the last two years.

The managing director may, in principle, be dismissed at any time by the company body that installed him or her in office. However, as the managing director will be an employee of the company, he or she is protected by the regulations of the Employee Protection Act (Arbeidsmiljøloven) which, among other things, means that he or she cannot be fired without justification.

P.2.4.5.3 Duties/powers of the managing director The managing director shall undertake the day-to-day administration of the company. Normally, he or she is not empowered to make decisions that are of an unusual nature or of great importance to the company. However, the board may grant to the managing director the power to make such a decision in a specific instance. He or she will also be empowered to make such a decision if there is no time to get a decision by the board.

The managing director has powers of representation in matters concerning the daily operations of the company. Whether or not a specific matter falls within this definition will have to be decided on a case-by-case basis, taking into account the size and nature of the operations of the company.

P.2.5 Accounting and Auditing

P.2.5.1 *General provisions*

The Limited Company Act (Aksjeloven) contains strict requirements as to the accounts of an AS/ASA which in conjunction with regulations in the general Accounting Act (Regnskapsloven) are broadly in line with internationally approved accounting principles.

P.2.5.2 *Appointment and dismissal of auditors*

Every AS/ASA must have at least one qualified and officially approved auditor, who is to be appointed by the general meeting of shareholders. In certain instances, minority shareholders may demand the appointment of an additional auditor.

The term of office lasts until a new auditor is appointed by the general meeting of shareholders. The meeting may only appoint a new auditor after proper announcement of the intention to do so in the summons to the meeting. Under certain extraordinary circumstances, the auditor shall have the right to withdraw before his term of office is completed, subject to reasonable notice being given.

P.2.5.3 *Duties and powers of auditors*

The auditor shall examine the company's accounts, year-end reports and other relevant material to the extent required by accepted auditing principles. All officers of the company are required to assist the auditor in acquiring the necessary information.

The audit is to be performed in a conscientious manner, and the auditor is to maintain an independent status. Any time that has attracted comments from the auditor shall be entered into auditing minutes, which are to be kept by the board of directors.

At the end of every fiscal year, the auditor shall submit a written report of specified content. The report shall be addressed to the general meeting of shareholders, but must be submitted to the board of directors no later than two weeks before the meeting. The auditor is to maintain confidentiality.

The auditor has the right and the obligation to be present at the general meeting of shareholders. When requested by the meeting or by a shareholder or an officer of the company, the auditor is obliged to submit any information he has acquired in the course of his duties. A certain number of shareholders may request an extraordinary examination of the company, including but not limited to the accounts.

P.2.6 Legal Liability of Officers

All officers of an AS/ASA, including board members, members of the corporate of representative assembly, managing director and auditors, may be held liable for damages to the company, a shareholder or others, arising from wilful or negligent acts or omissions in the release of their duties. This will also apply to a shareholder who wilfully or negligently contributes to such damage. The violation of statutory regulations may also be a criminal offence.

P.2.7 Dissolution and Liquidation

The Limited Companies Act (Aksjeloven) has a separate chapter on dissolution and liquidation, which gives detailed procedures for this process. Generally, the decision to dissolve the company must be made by the general meeting of shareholders, by the same majority vote as is required to amend the articles of association. The decision to dissolve the company shall be registered in the Register of Business Enterprises, and the Register will take steps to publicise the decision.

During the liquidation process, the organisational structure of the company remains more or less intact. However, the board of directors must resign, to be replaced by a liquidation board. The company may continue its business to the extent that this is desirable. If the company maintains contact with third parties, it must add to its name on letterheads, etc., the words "under liquidation".

The liquidation board must register all the company's assets, and draw up a special "liquidation balance sheet", which must be held available to all shareholders. All assets must be sold to the extent necessary to pay the company's creditors and shareholders.

SECTION 3

UNLIMITED PARTNERSHIPS (ANSVARLIGE SELSKAPER: ANS)

P.3.1 Introduction and Definition

These partnerships are governed by the Companies Act of 1985 (Selskapsloven) which is applicable to any business activity with two or more participants where at least one of the partners has an unlimited, personal liability for the total commitments of the partnership.

The unlimited partnership (Ansvarlig selskap: ANS) is defined in the Companies Act as a partnership where the partners each have an unlimited, personal liability for the total commitments of the partnership (or for a part of the total commitments, as long as the sums of the parts they are liable for add up to the total commitments of the partnership), and where the partnership acts as an unlimited partnership towards third parties.

An unlimited partnership will have legal personality, and will generally be subject to similar accounting and auditing requirements as limited partnerships. The partners may be persons or companies, as long as they do have legal personality. There are no specific requirements of Norwegian citizenship or domicile, apart from such regulations that might apply to the intended activities of the partnership.

The Companies Act presumes that unless otherwise explicitly provided for in the partnership agreement, the partners will have joint and several, unlimited, personal liability for the partnership commitments. This liability does not, however, emerge until the creditor has sought payment from the partnership itself. Even if the partners do have a joint and several, unlimited and personal liability towards the partnership's creditors, they may agree on a different division of liabilities amongst themselves.

P.3.2 Incorporation

An unlimited partnership is normally formed by agreement between the partners. The Companies Act stipulates that the partnership agreement must be in writing, and must be signed and dated by all partners. Also, the following five items must be included in the agreement:

(a) the company name (Firma), which must include the words "ansvarlig

410

selskap" ("unlimited company"), or the abbreviation "ANS";

(b) the name and address of all partners;

(c) the objectives of the partnership;

(d) the county in which the partnership shall locate its registered office;

(e) whether or not the partners are to contribute in cash or in kind to the partnership, and the value of such contributions.

Every unlimited partnership must be registered in the Register of Business Enterprises, and such registration must take place before the commencement of business activities.

P.3.3   Shares (Andeler)

A partner's share in an unlimited partnership is not transferable without the consent of all other partners. The reason for this can partly be found in the personal nature of the participation, and partly in the fact that partners have joint and several liability. This general rule may, however, be waived in the partnership agreement, in whole (allowing absolute freedom of transfer), or part (allowing transfer to designated recipients such as family, or upon specific conditions).

A legal transfer of a share will mean that the recipient will assume the transferer's rights and obligations towards the other partners. Towards third parties, however, the transferer will remain responsible jointly and severally with the recipient for all obligations that rested upon him at the time of the transfer. The death of a partner does not lead to a transfer of his share to his successors, unless this is explicitly agreed among the partners. Instead, within six months, the remaining partners must pay to the successors an amount corresponding to the value of the share.

Under the Act on Acquisition of Business Enterprises 1994 any acquisition of one-third, one-half or two-thirds of the shares in a Norwegian enterprise with more than 50 employees, must be reported to the Ministry of Trade and Industry. Such duty to report an acquisition, also exists if the yearly sales of the enterprise is more than 50 million Nkr, or if the enterprise has received governmental funding for R& D of more than 5 million Nkr to one project during the last eight years. To protect public interest, the Government may prohibit the acquisition. Approval from the Government is also necessary to acquire one-third, one-half or two-thirds shares in a limited company that owns real estate.

P.3.4 Organisation (Partnership Structure)

Each partner has the right to act on behalf of the partnership to a certain extent, and apart from this, the Companies Act has certain requirements to the organisation of an ANS. These requirements are based on the organisational requirements for limited companies, but are simplified due to the unlimited liability of the partners. The unlimited partnership must have a partnership meeting, and may have a board of directors and a managing director, but these are not mandatory. However, these three are the only permissible company bodies with the right to make decisions on behalf of the partnership. Other fora or bodies may be established, but only with consultative functions.

P.3.4.1 *The partners' right of representation*

If the partnership does not have a board of directors or a managing director, each partner has the right to perform such acts as are natural and necessary for the administration of the partnership, as long as these acts have not been met with opposition from other partners. Each partner will always retain the right to perform such acts as might be necessary to prevent loss or damage, also after the appointment of a board/managing director.

As long as a partnership does not have a board of directors, each partner has the power of representation on behalf of the partnership. This power may be restricted by agreement. Such restrictions may be registered in the Register of Business Enterprises.

P.3.4.2 *Partnership meeting*

All unlimited partnerships must have partnership meetings, as this is the forum of the partners, and the highest authority of the partnership. In many ways the partnership meeting resembles the general meeting of shareholders in a limited company. The following decisions must, if applicable, be made in a partnership meeting:

(a) the appointment/dismissal of board members (note that in certain instances the employees are entitled to elect members of the board, and such members may not be dismissed by the partners);

(b) the appointment/dismissal of the managing director;

(c) the imposition of restrictions in the right to sign for or otherwise represent the partnership;

(d) approval of the partnership's year-end accounts and balance sheet;

(e) the exclusion of a partner;

(f) the dissolution of the partnership;

(g) whether to undertake the dissolution of the partnership, or to elect a dissolution board.

All partners have the right and the obligation to participate in partnership meetings, unless otherwise decided in the partnership agreement. If the partnership has a board of directors and/or a managing director, these are obliged to be present. Decisions in the partnership meeting must be unanimous, unless the partners have agreed differently. Only partners have voting rights in the partnership meeting.

The employees of the partnership have the right to be represented in the partnership meeting if the partnership during the last three accounting years has had an average of at least 30 employees.

P.3.4.3 *Board of directors*

A board of directors is not required in an unlimited partnership, but the partnership may choose to appoint a board, by stipulation in the partnership agreement. If there is to be a board, the appointment and dismissal of directors shall rest with the partnership meeting.

If the partnership has had an average of more than 30 employees over the last three accounting years, the employees may demand that one director as well as one observer be appointed by and amongst the employees. If the average number of employees exceeds 50, they may demand the appointment of two or one-third of the directors.

A board of directors will be responsible for the general management of the partnership, and will be superior to a managing director. The board will at all times, however, be subject to the instructions of the partnership meeting, which may dictate the actions of the board, and also overrule any decisions made by the board.

The board shall have a chairman, to be appointed by and amongst the directors, unless the partnership agreement or the partnership meeting should decide otherwise. More than half of the members of the board must be present to form a quorum.

Decisions are made by majority vote, unless the partnership agreement stipulates a different voting requirement. No decision is valid unless it receives more than one-third of the total votes of the board. The board of directors holds the power of representation for the partnership. The partnership meeting may grant the powers of representation to one director or a limited number of directors.

P.3.4.4   *The managing director*

An unlimited partnership may have a managing director, if the partners so decide. The appointment and dismissal of the managing director rests with the partnership meeting. The managing director shall be responsible for the day-to-day management of the partnership, but must comply with all instructions given by the board of directors and the partnership meeting.

The managing director has the power to represent the partnership in matters that fall within his responsibilities. The managing director's responsibilities do not include matters that may be termed unusual in nature or of great importance to the partnership. The managing director may only decide on such matters if the partnership meeting or board of directors in the specific instance has empowered him to do so, or if there is no time to seek the decision of the board or the partnership meeting, and a delay will damage the interests of the partnership.

P.3.5   Accounting and Auditing

An unlimited partnership will normally be subject to general regulations on accounting and auditing, although there are certain exceptions to this rule. When accounting and auditing requirements apply, the general provisions in the Accounting Act and the Auditing Act will apply. The Companies Act does not have any auditing provisions, as opposed to the Limited Companies Act.

P.3.6   Unilateral Withdrawal/Exclusion

Generally, a partner has the right to withdraw from further participation in the partnership by giving six months' notice of his intention to do so. No specific reason for the withdrawal is needed. Also, if there are special reasons for the partner's desire to withdraw, such as a violation of his rights by a breach of the partnership agreement, or a vote against him in the partnership meeting in a matter that is very important to him, the partner may demand to be released immediately.

Upon withdrawal, the withdrawing partner shall be reimbursed for the net capital value of his share in the partnership. The Companies Act contains regulations on how the share value is to be calculated, and these regulations will apply also in case of the death of a partner. The withdrawing partner will not automatically be free of his obligations towards the creditors of the partnership. He may request in writing that the creditors release him from these obligations, which leads to the creditors having to respond to his request within three months if they wish to prevent his release.

A partner may be excluded from the partnership by a decision of the partnership meeting following the request by another partner. A partner may be excluded:

(a) if he is declared bankrupt or is unable to meet his financial obligations;

(b) if he has abused the partnership by defaulting; or

(c) if there are other important grounds for exclusion.

If a partner holds the opinion that he has been unreasonably excluded, he may bring the matter before the courts. This course of action is also available to the partner who has demanded the exclusion of another, but not succeeded in getting the necessary decision from the partnership meeting.

A partner who is excluded shall be reimbursed for the net capital value of his share. The calculation is done in the same way as if he had withdrawn unilaterally. The excluded partner will not automatically be freed of his obligations towards the creditors.

P.3.7 Dissolution and Liquidation

The Companies Act contains regulations for the dissolution and liquidation of an unlimited partnership. The regulations are not very far removed from the corresponding regulations in the Limited Companies Act.

The partnership must be dissolved following a unanimous decision in a partnership meeting. A partner may also demand the immediate dissolution of the partnership if his rights as a partner have been abused by default and exclusion of the culprit(s) would not seem reasonable under the circumstances, or there are other important grounds for dissolution.

If the partnership meeting refuses to grant the dissolution of the partnership, the partner who raised the demand may bring the matter before the courts.

After a decision has been made to dissolve the partnership, the regulations on liquidation in the Companies Act will apply. Unless the partners have agreed differently, all assets shall be converted to cash and be distributed amongst the partners. Any partner may demand, however, that sufficient assets are put aside for the satisfaction of the creditors, before any distribution to the partners.

SECTION 4

MIXED PARTNERSHIPS

P.4.1   Introduction and Definition

Mixed partnerships exist where one or more of the partners are liable with their total assets for all the commitments of the partnership as in an unlimited partnership (ANS), while other partners are liable only with their share of the partnership capital as in a limited partnership (AS). The Companies Act recognises two forms of mixed partnerships: the "Kommandittselskap", and the silent partnership (Stille selskap).

P.4.2   Kommandittselskap: KS

This partnership has one or more partners with unlimited liability (Komplementar), while the other partners are only liable with their share of the partnership capital (Kommandittist). In practice, the partner with the unlimited liability will be a limited company, formed for the explicit purpose of being the unlimited partner of the KS. Thus, the unlimited liability of the Komplementar becomes rather fictitious, and the economic reality is very close to the limited company (AS). This partnership used to be very popular, due to beneficial tax effects for the participants. New tax regulations have, however, reduced the number of KS.

P.4.3   Silent Partnership (Stille Selskap)

This partnership form is primarily an agreement between the partners, as the very definition of the silent partner is that the partners have agreed not to disclose his participation to the outside world. The Companies Act grants the silent partner certain rights, such as the right to a share of any partnership profits. He also has a limited liability for the partnership losses.

SECTION 5

OTHER ORGANISATIONAL FORMS

P.5.1   Joint Ownership (Sameie)

If two or more persons hold joint ownership to an asset, the situation will be governed by the Joint Ownership Act, and any agreements between the parties. As soon as the owners start an enterprise that involves the asset, the question arises whether a partnership has in effect been established.

P.5.2   Co-operatives (Samvirkelag)

These are special joint efforts with limited liability for the participants, and might be termed "clubs with an economic objective". Often, however, these co-operatives have objectives relating to the customer or professional interests of their members, and they will fall outside the normal scope of company law.

P.5.3   Foundations (Stiftelser)

A foundation can be defined as "capital designated for a specific purpose or objective, with an autonomous leadership and its own administration". Most foundations are governed by the Foundations Act (Stiftelsesloven). A foundation is formed by a donation, a testament or another legal act whereby assets are designated to the purpose of fulfilling a specific objective of an ideal, humanitarian, social, educational, economic or other nature. All foundations must have a board of directors, which will be responsible for the satisfactory administration of anything connected with the foundation or its assets. The board will be responsible for accounting and the appointment of an auditor.

417

POLAND

INTRODUCTION*

Q.1.1 The political events of 1989 were followed by significant economic upheaval. The introduction of market rules into the Polish economy led to many changes in Polish law.

Privatisation of state enterprises has begun. State enterprises are transformed into companies whose shares are wholly owned by the State Treasury and shares in these companies may be sold to third parties. Alternatively, privatisation of state enterprises can be effected by the sale of the enterprise itself.

The basic regulations concerning the formation and operation of partnerships and companies are comprised in the following legislation:

(a) those provisions still in force, and the amended provisions of the Polish Commercial Code;

(b) the Polish Civil Code;

(c) the Act on Economic Activity 1988;

(d) the Act on Companies with Foreign Shareholdings 1991.

A subject carrying on economic activity may be:

(a) a natural person;

(b) a legal entity;

(c) an organisational unit having no legal personality, formed in compliance with the provisions of law, if its objects include carrying on economic activity.

Economic activity may be undertaken in the following forms:

(1) a natural person acting as an economic subject;

(2) partnerships:

(a) partnership,

(b) registered partnership,

(c) limited partnership;

* *Dr Tomasz Wardyński, Wardyński, Wierciński, Śledziński, Szesepińksi, Szaj & Lachert (full particulars are listed in the Appendix).*

(3) companies:

(a) limited liability company,

(b) joint stock company.

Foreign subjects may only establish businesses having their seats in Poland, in the form of limited liability or joint stock companies. They may acquire shares in companies.

The acquisition of shares by a foreign entity (natural or legal) in a commercial company with its seat within the territory of Poland, being the owner or perpetual usufructuary (użytkownik wieczysty) of certain types of real estate, requires a permit from the Minister of Internal Affairs and Administration. This rule applies only if the company is a controlled company and the shares are acquired by a foreign entity, or the company becomes a controlled company as a result of the acquisition. A controlled company is a company in which a foreign entity directly or indirectly owns at least 50 per cent of the initial share capital. The acquisition of certain types of real estate by a foreign entry also requires a permit of competent Ministers.

A foreign person is allowed to transfer abroad the benefits (dywidenda) from the companies in which he is a shareholder. However, the transfer of sums acquired by the sale of shares in companies is allowed only after an audit of the companies.

SECTION 2

PARTNERSHIPS (SPÓŁKI OSOBOWE)

Q.2.1 Partnership (Spółka Cywilna)

This form of activity is governed by the provisions of the Polish Civil Code. A partnership is an agreement between two or more individuals or incorporated bodies which comes into existence without any formalities. The Code stipulates that the partnership agreement should be made in writing, although this requirement is only for evidential purposes. The partners should undertake to promote the attainment of a common economic objective, in particular by making contributions to the partnership (i.e. property, rights, services).

A partnership is not a legal entity under Polish law. The partners are jointly and severally liable for the partnership's obligations to the extent of the value of all their assets (present and future).

During the partnership's existence none of the partners can make any disposition of their shares in the partners' common property.

Unless the provisions of the agreement state otherwise, each partner is entitled and bound to manage the partnership's affairs and to represent the partnership (*e.g.* by undertaking obligations and making contracts on behalf of the partnership). Any provisions of the agreement regulating representation are not binding on third parties and do not affect their rights as against the partnership.

A partner's share in profits and losses can be regulated by the provisions of the agreement and certain partners can be excluded from their share in losses. However, no partner can be deprived of his share in profits. In the absence of such provisions shares, both in profits and losses, are equal as amongst the partners.

The partnership can be dissolved in case of:

(a) lapse of time (if the partnership was created for a specified period of time);

(b) the mutual consent of all partners;

(c) the death of one of the partners (when there are only two partners);

(d) a court judgment.

Q.2.2 Registered Partnership (Spółka Jawna)

This form of activity is governed by those provisions of the Commercial Code 1934 still in force.

A registered partnership is a partnership which runs a profit-making "enterprise of a larger size" in the partners' joint names. At present the definition of an "enterprise of a larger size" does not exist and therefore, the main difference between a partnership and a registered partnership is unclear. Compared with the provisions governing simple partnerships, those concerning registered partnerships are far more detailed.

The agreement of the partnership should be in writing and the registered partnership should be registered in the Commercial Register. If the agreement is not registered in the Commercial Register it is considered to be an ordinary partnership. The initial entry of the registered partnership in the Commercial Register should include:

(a) the business name, seat, address and objects of the enterprise;

(b) the full names of each of the partners, as well as all the information relating to a partner's legal capacity;

(c) the full names of persons entitled to represent the partnership and the manner of such representation;

423

(d) any alteration of the above particulars.

A registered partnership may acquire rights and undertake obligations and may sue and be sued, although this does not mean that it is a legal entity. Partners are jointly and severally liable to creditors for a partnership's obligations, without limitation, to the value of all their assets (present and future). This also applies in the event of the bankruptcy of the partnership. Any person who joins an existing partnership is also liable for the obligations of the partnership undertaken before he joined. Provisions of the partnership agreement which are not in accordance with the above-mentioned rules, as stipulated by the law, have no legal effect upon third parties.

Contributions of the partners can be regulated by the provisions of the agreement. However, in case of doubt all partner's contributions are considered equal. A partner's contribution may consist of ownership or other rights, permission to use "things" or rights, or the performance of work.

Each partner is entitled to an equal share in both profits and losses, irrespective of the type and value of his contribution. However, the agreement may provide otherwise.

A partner has the right and duty to manage the partnership's affairs. The agreement or a later resolution may entrust the management of the partnership to one or several partners, however, the partnership agreement cannot entrust the management of the partnership's affairs to a third party to the exclusion of the partners.

In matters exceeding the scope of the ordinary activities of the partnership the consent of all the partners is required (even those excluded from management).

A partner should refrain from any activity contrary to the partnership's business. In particular he cannot be involved in any competitive business, nor become a partner or a member of the governing bodies of a competing partnership.

The registered partnership can be dissolved on the grounds of:

(a) reasons specified in the partnership agreement;

(b) the mutual consent of all the partners;

(c) a declaration of the partnership's bankruptcy;

(d) the death of a partner or declaration of his bankruptcy;

(e) a notice of termination;

(f) a court judgment.

If the partnership was created for an unspecified period of time a partner can give notice of termination prior to the end of the financial year.

In order to dissolve the partnership, liquidation should take place unless the partners agree to terminate the partnership's activities on a different basis.

All the partners are liquidators. However, by common consent they can appoint certain partners or third parties as liquidators. The court of registration may, in specific circumstances, also appoint certain partners or third persons to be liquidators.

Commencement of the liquidation must be registered in the commercial register.

If the partnership's assets are insufficient for the payment of the debts and shares, the deficit is divided amongst the partners in accordance with the partnership agreement, or in the absence of such provisions, in proportion to their share in the losses.

Termination of liquidation must be registered in the commercial register.

Q.2.3   Limited Partnership (Spółka Komandytowa)

This form of activity is governed by the provisions of the Commercial Code 1934 (reinstated in 1991), concerning limited partnerships and certain provisions relating to registered partnerships.

A limited partnership is a partnership whose purpose is to run a profit-making "enterprise of a larger size" under a joint business name, where at least one of the partners has unlimited liability and at least one has limited liability (limited partner—komandytariusz) to creditors for the obligations of the partnership.

The limited partnership agreement must be made in the form of a notarial deed. A limited partnership comes into existence at the moment of registration. Failure to register means that the partnership will be considered a simple partnership and each partner will be liable without limitation to the extent of all his assets.

The entry of the limited partnership should include:

(a)   the business name, seat, address and the objects of the enterprise;

(b)   the full names of each of the partners, as well as all information relating to a partner's legal capacity;

(c)   the full names of persons entitled to represent the partnership and the manner of such representation;

(d)   the form of the contribution of each limited partner;

(e)   information concerning the return of all, or a part of, the partners' contributions;

(f)   the financial limit of each limited partner's liability to the partnership's creditors (the commandite sum—suma komandytowa);

(g)   any alteration of the above particulars.

A limited partner is liable for partnership obligations only to the extent of the commandite sum. If any part of his contribution is returned he becomes liable to the partnership's creditors to the value of the amount returned. A partner who joins an existing limited partnership is liable for partnership obligations existing at

425

the moment of registration thereof in the Commercial Register, as a limited partner.

A limited partner has no right to represent a limited partnership unless he has a power of attorney. If he concludes a transaction on behalf of the limited partnership, without disclosing his power of attorney, he bears unlimited liability to third parties for this act.

Contractual provisions inconsistent with the above have no legal effect upon third parties.

Affairs exceeding the scope of ordinary acts of a partnership require the consent of the limited partner.

The limited partnership agreement should specify the form of distribution of profits and losses. In case of any doubt a limited partner participates in losses only to the amount of the agreed contribution.

Death of a limited partner does not constitute a valid reason for dissolution of the partnership.

SECTION 3

COMPANIES (SPÓŁKI KAPITALOWE)

Q.3.1 Limited Liability Company (Spółka z Ograniczona Odpowiedzialnościa: sp.z o.o.)

This form of activity is governed by those provisions of the Commercial Code 1934 still in force.

A limited liability company is a legal entity, which may be formed for economic purposes by one or more persons, unless statutory law provides otherwise. Shareholders do not bear any personal liability for a company's obligations. A sole shareholder of a limited liability company cannot be another limited liability company itself consisting of only one shareholder.

The following are required to form a limited liability company:

(a) the execution of the deed of company formation (the deed of company incorporation—umowa spółki z o.o.);

(b) the contribution of the entire initial share capital;

(c) the appointment of the company bodies;

(d) the registration in the commercial register.

Whenever the law refers to the "deed of company formation" it also means the founding act drawn up by a sole shareholder.

The deed of company formation must be executed in the form of a notarial deed, otherwise it is null and void. It shall specify:

(a) the business name and seat;

(b) the objects of the enterprise;

(c) the lifetime of the company, if limited;

(d) the value of the initial share capital;

(e) whether a shareholder may hold one or more shares;

(f) the number and value of shares held by individual shareholders.

The initial share capital is divided into shares having equal or unequal values. If a shareholder can hold more than one share all the shares in the initial capital must be equal and indivisible. The initial capital must amount to not less than 4,000 zloti and a share cannot amount to less than 50 zloti.

The subject of contribution can be either a cash or a non-cash asset. Non-cash assets include ownership and other rights.

The company bodies consist of:

(a) the board of directors;

(b) the supervisory board;

(c) the board of auditors;

(d) the general meeting of shareholders.

A member of the board of directors cannot be involved in competitive business, or participate in a competitive partnership or company as a registered partner, or as a member of their governing body unless he has been granted permission by the company. These rules also apply to joint stock companies and to the members of supervisory boards.

The board of directors represents the company and manages its affairs. There should be at least one director. Members of the board of directors are appointed by a resolution of the shareholders, unless the deed of company formation provides otherwise.

The deed of company formation may establish the supervisory board, the board of auditors or both. The supervisory board exercises permanent supervision over the activities of the company. The deed of company formation may extend the powers of the supervisory board (*e.g.* it may provide that the board of directors is obliged to obtain the consent of the supervisory board before performing certain activities).

The general meeting of shareholders should be convened by the board of directors. Certain matters specified in the deed of company formation, as well as in the Commercial Code, require the resolution of the shareholders (*e.g.* the transfer and lease of an enterprise). Unless the deed of company formation provides otherwise each 10 zloti value of shares carries with it the right to one vote. Each shareholder should have at least one vote.

Q.3.1.1 *Registration in the commercial register*

The board of directors is obliged to give notice of the formation of the company to be registered in the commercial register.

The company's initial entry in the commercial register should contain:

(a) the business name, seat, address and the objects of the enterprise;

(b) the value of the initial share capital;

(c) provisions stating whether a shareholder is allowed to have one or more shares;

(d) the full names of members of the board of directors entitled to represent the company and the manner of such representation;

(e) non-cash contributions, if any, made upon the formation of the company;

(f) the lifetime of the company, if limited.

The following must be enclosed in the application for registration by the board of directors:

(a) the deed of company formation;

(b) a declaration of the board of directors stating that cash contributions have been made and that the transfer of non-cash contributions to the company, upon its registration, have been secured.

Each amendment to the deed of company formation requires a resolution of the shareholders and must be recorded by a notary, otherwise it is null and void. Each amendment (*e.g.* resolutions increasing or reducing the initial share capital) should be reported in the commercial register.

Q.3.1.2 *Dissolution and liquidation of a company*

A company may be dissolved on the grounds of:

(a) reasons provided for by the deed of company formation;

(b) a resolution of shareholders on dissolution;

(c) a declaration of the company's bankruptcy;

(d) a court judgment.

Members of the board of directors become liquidators unless the deed of company formation, or a resolution of shareholders, provides otherwise.

Commencement of the liquidation should be registered in the commercial register and announced in *Monitor Sadowy i Gospodarczy*, an official publication intended for company announcements.

After satisfying or securing the assets necessary to meet the demands of a company's creditors, the remaining assets are distributed amongst shareholders in proportion to their shares, unless the deed of company formation provides otherwise. In case a company becomes bankrupt, the company cannot be dissolved until bankruptcy proceedings have been terminated.

Q.3.1.3 *Merger of companies*

A merger of companies may be effected by:

(a) transfer of all the assets of the company ("transferring company") to another ("acquiring company") in exchange for shares granted by the acquiring company to the shareholders of the transferring company;

(b) formation of a new limited liability company, to which the assets of all the merging companies are transferred in exchange for the shares in the new company.

The merger must be registered in the commercial register.

It should be noted that, in some cases, members of the board of directors and liquidators bear joint and several civil liability with the company. In certain situations (*e.g.* failure to declare bankruptcy of the company in spite of circumstances justifying such), they also bear criminal liability (and may be subject to imprisonment, a fine or both). They are also personally liable for the tax obligations of the company if it fails to fulfil them.

Q.3.2 Joint Stock Company (Spółka Akcyjna: SA)

This form of activity is governed by those provisions of the Commercial Code 1934 still in force.

A joint stock company acquires legal personality upon registration. It can be formed for any lawful purpose. Generally, there is no need for formal consent to run a business in this form, although there are certain situations in which it is required; for example, to create a bank in the form of a joint stock company, provisions of the Banking Law Act require the consent of the President of the National Bank of Poland and the competent Minister. Also, an insurance activity (both in the form of joint stock company and mutual insurance company) shall be carried on exclusively upon a permit granted by the competent Minister.

Q.3.2.1 *Formation of a company*

There should be at least three founders of the company (założyciełe). The articles of the joint stock company should be executed in the form of a notarial deed, otherwise they are null and void.

The articles of the joint stock company should contain, in addition to those requirements for a limited liability company:

(a) information as to whether the shares are registered shares or shares payable to bearer;

(b) the number of shares of each respective kind and the rights attached to them;

(c) the full names (business names) and addresses (seats) of the founders;

(d) the structure of managing and supervisory bodies.

The initial share capital is divided into shares of equal nominal value. Shareholders are not personally liable for obligations of the company. The minimum share capital of the company should be not less than 100,000 zloti. The share capital may be contributed in either a cash or non-cash form.

In case of non-cash contributions the founders are obliged to draw up a written report on the value and nature of non-cash assets and the amount and classes of shares issued in return. The founders' report should be examined by expert auditors.

The initial capital can be raised in two ways:

(a) by purchase of all the shares by the founders themselves, or in conjunction with other persons;

(b) public subscription.

The board of directors should apply for registration of the company in the commercial register.

There are many different kinds of shares including: ordinary shares, preference shares, registered and bearer shares and utility shares.

A shareholder is obliged to pay the amount due for shares in full. The time-frame for paying and the amount to be paid for shares is determined by the articles of the company or by a general meeting. If the shareholder fails to pay he may be deprived of his rights by cancellation of the shares. Bearer shares may not be issued before they have been fully paid for.

Generally shares are transferrable. Registered shares are transferred either by a written declaration made on a share certificate, or on a separate document and by the delivery of the share. Bearer shares are transferred by delivery. Agreements which restrict the transferability of shares for specified periods of time are valid. Shares (and other securities) may be the subject of public trading at stock exchange. However, it only refers to joint stock companies that have fulfilled specific requirements given by the Public Trading in Securities and Trust Funds Act 1991.

The company's governing bodies are:

(a) the board of directors;

(b) the supervisory board;

(c) the board of auditors;

(d) the general meeting.

The scope of activity of a joint stock company's governing bodies is similar to that of limited liability companies.

Q.3.2.2   Amendments of the articles of the company

The company may increase its share capital by issuing new shares. New shares may only be issued after the existing share capital has been fully paid for. This rule does not apply to insurance companies or mergers of companies.

The share capital may also be reduced by decreasing the nominal value of shares, or by redemption of a number of shares. Both increases in, and the reduction of share capital should be registered in the commercial register.

Dissolution of the company is effected upon the termination of liquidation and is caused by:

(a) the reasons provided for under the articles of the company;

(b) a resolution of the general meeting on dissolution of the company, or on the transfer abroad of the seat or principal establishment of the company;

(c) a declaration of company bankruptcy.

The regulations concerning the merger of joint-stock companies are similar to those for limited liability companies.

Likewise, the regulations concerning the civil and criminal liability of individual members of company bodies are similar for both joint stock and limited liability companies.

Q.3.2.3   Change in the status of a joint stock and limited liability company

Conversion of a joint stock company into a limited liability company does not cause any changes in its relations with third parties. It requires a resolution on conversion stating the value of shares and a draft deed of formation of the limited liability company. The resolution comes into force upon registration. These rules also apply to the conversion of a limited liability company into a joint stock company.

Section 4

THE COMMERCIAL REGISTER

Q.4.1 The Commercial Register is maintained for the registration of entries as stipulated by law. The register and all documents submitted for registration are open to inspection by the public. The Commercial Register is administered by the Court of Registration. All entries are announced in *Monitor Sadowy i Gospodarczy*, an official publication intended for company announcements.

PORTUGAL

CLASSIFICATION OF BUSINESS ORGANISATIONS: INTRODUCTION*

R.1.0   The purpose of this study is to present a brief overview of the different legal forms by which a company may be formed in Portugal. In addition to the different trading companies defined in the Companies Act (Código das Sociedades Comerciais), we describe the sole entrepreneur because of the important role he plays in the Portuguese economy, the various forms of setting up partnerships, co-operation between companies, branches, and finally, the cost of establishing a company.[1]

R.1.1   The Sole Entrepreneur

R.1.1.1   *The sole entrepreneur (empresário em nome individual)*

A sole entrepreneur is that individual who is engaged in a stable commercial activity. The word "commercial", commonly used in Portuguese law, also covers other forms of economic activities, namely industrial.

The assets which he uses for his commercial activity are not held to be separate from the remainder, as his total assets will be used for setting his commercial debts.

The sole entrepreneur's activities must be minimally organised, namely in that he must keep proper accounts and the compulsory records. His company shall be known by the entrepreneur's name, whether it be his full name, an abbreviated form of the same, or by a nickname by which he is known, to which he may add an expression which refers to the activities of his company.

According to available official data, there are more than 600,000 sole entrepreneurs in Portugal, by far the most numerous forms of commercial companies.

---

* *Dr Rui Peixoto Duarte, Rui Peixoto Duarte & Associados (full particulars are listed in the Appendix).*
[1] At the time of going to press there had been some changes in Portuguese company law, and reference should be made to a local lawyer before relying on the text of this Chapter.

R.1.1.2 *The sole entrepreneur with limited liability (estabelecimento individual de responsabilidade limitada)*

The legal entity of "sole entrepreneur of limited liability" was instituted in Portuguese law in 1986 and corresponds to a desire to limit the liability of the sole entrepreneur as regards any debts incurred by his company.

This new entity enables the sole entrepreneur, without setting up a company, in other words, without entering into a partnership with others, to set aside part of his personal assets for his business, thereby creating autonomous assets.

Any individual, thereby excluding companies, who is already engaged in or intends to become engaged in a form of commercial activity, may incorporate himself as a limited liability company for this purpose. An individual may only own one such company. The setting up of this form of company is done by means of a public deed.

The name of the company consists of the legal name of the owner, to which he may or may not add a reference to the object of his business, and shall mandatorily include the designation "Estabelecimento individual de responsabilidade limitada", or simply "EIRL".

The minimum capital required is of 400,000 escudos of which at least two-thirds must be realised in cash. The remainder may be pledged in goods or equipment.

The owner is responsible for managing his company. Only those assets attributed to the company are held as a guarantee for any debts incurred by the commercial activity in question. Should the entrepreneur, while he is engaged in this activity, not respect the principle of a separation of assets and thus cause the bankruptcy of his establishment, his total personal assets shall be applied to the settlement of his commercial debts.

The owner of an EIRL shall present accounts which must be filed with the Commercial Registry Office, accompanied by a mandatory report by a statutory auditor. In practice, few sole entrepreneurs have incorporated themselves in this manner.

R.1.2 Informal Partnerships (Sociedades Civis)

In informal partnerships (sociedades civis) two or more persons contributing with goods or services, jointly enter into a profit-making economic activity, though this may not be either commercial or industrial in nature. An example of this are partnerships of liberal professions such as those involving attorneys, statutory auditors (for which there are specific regulations), engineers, artists, etc. Informal partnerships may or may not constitute a legal entity.

The partnership agreement is not subject to any special formula other than that which is required by the nature of the goods which the partners bring into the partnership. Although these are not commercial partnerships, it is accepted that informal partnerships may wish to incorporate themselves in one of the manners foreseen by the Companies Acts (Código das Sociedades Comerciais), in which case they shall have to proceed in the legally prescribed manner.

The individual contribution of each partner is presumed to be of an equal value as those of the other partners, unless otherwise established in the partnership agreement. All the partners are responsible for managing the partnership and decisions are taken by majority vote, unless otherwise stipulated in the agreement or required by certain types of acts. The partnership is represented by its directors.

The partnership, and the partners altogether, are responsible for any debts incurred. The partner who is being sued for his debts may insist on the previous exclusion of the partnership's assets. There are few informal partnerships in Portugal.

R.1.3 Co-operation Between Companies

R.1.3.1 *Complementary grouping of companies (Agrupamento complementar de empresas)*

Introduced into Portuguese law in 1973, the complementary grouping of companies (Agrupamento Complementar de Empresas), or ACE, enables individuals or companies to group together in order to improve their trading conditions or the results of their activity. The principle object of an ACE may not be the obtaining of profits, although this may be an subsidiary objective.

The establishment of an ACE is by public deed. From the moment of the mandatory registration of the ACE, it becomes a legally constituted entity. This grouping is formed with or without share capital. The participation of its members may not be represented by negotiable securities.

The name of the ACE may consist of the names of the individuals or the companies involved, or it may be given a name of its own. The names of the individuals or the companies involved, or of at least of five of these when the total number of members is greater than this amount, must always be specified in all acts and contracts in which the ACE is involved. All companies thereby grouped are subsidiarily and jointly responsible for any debts incurred by the grouping.

An ACE is prohibited from the following:

(a) acquiring rights of ownership other than that of the building in which it is located;

(b) acquire holdings in companies; and

(c) hold positions in companies.

This grouping is managed by one or more persons who are appointed and exonerated by a general assembly of its members. The signature of any one director obligates the ACE when dealing with third parties. Deliberations of the members shall be approved by majority vote.

437

R.1.3.2 *Consortiums*

A consortium is an association between two or more persons, whether individuals or companies engaged in an economic activity, so that together they may perform material or legal acts in preparation for a set activity, implement a given undertaking, supply goods produced by their members to third parties, research or exploit natural resources or share, among the members, the production of set goods, etc. A written agreement is compulsory.

There may be two forms of consortiums: an internal consortium, when, as regards the activities in question, the identity of an individual or company as a member of the consortium is not made public; and an external consortium, when the identity of an individual or company as a member of a consortium is expressly made public. In the latter case, the consortium may adopt a name consisting of the names of the member individuals or companies.

In the case of an external consortium, one of the members shall be appointed as head of the consortium. Internally, he is responsible for organising the co-operation between members with a view to attaining the object of this association. Outwardly, he is given certain powers of representation, such as the power to negotiate contracts, receive monies due to the members by third parties, ship goods and merchandise, contract consultants. However, a special mandate is required for him to sign, amend, or rescind contracts.

As regards relations with third parties, it is presumed that there is no active nor passive solidarity between the members of the external consortium. Liability is limited to that member of the external consortium who is held liable according to the law. No consortium may constitute common funds.

R.1.3.3 *Reciprocal interest contracts*

The agreement by which an individual (the associatee) associates himself with an economic activity in which another (the associator) is engaged in is known as a Reciprocal Interest Contract.

The rights of the associatee shall be defined in a contract which is not subject to any particular formula, other than that which is required by the nature of the goods contributed by the associatee. His contribution shall, however, be attributed a monetary value.

The duties of the associator, in addition to any other which may be expressly defined in the contract, are to administer the contract with the due care of a discerning manager, to give information, to render accounts, etc.

Unless otherwise stipulated, the share in the profits and losses of the activity of the associator shall be proportional to the value of the associatee's contribution, and in the case of a loss, to the limit of the value of the latter's contribution.

R.1.4 Branches of Foreign Companies

Foreign companies may establish branch offices in Portugal. These branch offices are not considered to be a separate legal entity; they are considered dependent on the foreign company which established them, thereby only representing this company in Portugal.

Their constitution must comply with formalities similar to those required for the incorporation of companies, namely, they must register with the Register of Companies and with the National Registry of Collective Bodies (Registo Nacional de Pessoas Colectivas). The only difference is that they are not required to execute a instrument of incorporation at a Notary Public's.

Branch offices must have a representative and are subject to the same financial and accounting obligations as companies.

SECTION 2

COMPANIES (SOCIEDADES COMERCIAIS)

R.2.1 Introduction

Portuguese law on companies with substantially updated in 1986, the year which coincided with Portugal's accession to the European Economic Community. In effect, the 1986 Companies Act revoked several laws, including the 1888 Commercial Code (Código Comercial). These amendments were the result, not only of the need to adjust the legislation to the changes in the national economy, but also to incorporate the various community Directives on Company Law.

Four types of companies are described in the Companies Act:

—partnerships;

—private companies;

—joint stock companies;

—limited partnerships (simple or by shares).

Private companies and joint stock companies are the most common in Portugal. Plain and limited partnerships are infrequently used.

We shall first describe those aspects which are common to the different types of companies and then discuss each type individually, naturally highlighting private companies and joint stock companies as they are of greater practical interest.

The following must always be included in the deed of incorporation which itself must be signed in the presence of a Notary Public:

(a) the complete names and trade names of all the founding members, together with details of all documents so identifying them;

(b) the type of company formed;

(c) the name of the new company;

(d) the object of the company;

(e) the location of the head office;

(f) the share capital, except in the case of partnerships where the partners contribute only with their work;

(g) the distribution of the share capital and the amount held by each partner;

(h) in the case of a non-monetary contribution to the capital, a description of each item and its equivalent monetary value.

Schematically, the proceedings for the establishment of a company in Portugal are the following ones:

(1) Propose to the National Company Register three names, by order of preference, for the company and ask for the issue of a provisional company registration card.

(2) Lawyers prepare the proposed memorandum and articles of association of the company and submit it to a notary for his comments.

(3) Deposit the amount of the paid-up capital into a bank account in the name of the company.

(4) Sign the company constitution deed before a notary.

(5) Publish the memorandum and the articles of association in the *Official Gazette* and in a newspaper published where the company has its registered office.

(6) File a declaration of "start-up of activities" with the local tax authorities.

(7) Request the registration of the company's formation and of the issue of the definitive "company registration card" and register with the Commercial Registry.

(8) If the company will be an industrial one, it will be necessary to obtain an industrial licence from the regional office of the Ministry of Industry.

(9) Register the company with the regional social security office closest to the company's registered office.

440

(10) Obtain authorisation of working hours from the Ministry of Employment and Social Security.

(11) Register the official books with the tax authorities.

(12) Other formalities: obligatory insurance, registration of employees with the social security office, registration of foreign employees and employment contracts with the Ministry of Employment and Social Security.

R.2.2 Incorporation

R.2.2.1 *The company*

The name/trade name is, in companies, the manner by which they are identified and this is subject to certain general rules which are common to all types of companies, and to certain specific rules according to each type. The name is formed by the names of all or some of the shareholders/founding members. The trade name is formed by a word which alludes to the activity of the company. One can also join a name and a trade name and create a mixed denomination for the company.

As regards the general rules for the name, trade name, denomination or denominations used, these must be correctly spelt in the Portuguese language. Foreign words or parts of foreign words may be used when:

(a) they are part of names or denominations which have already been registered;

(b) they correspond to common terms or words which have no appropriate translation into Portuguese or which are in general use;

(c) they correspond, totally or partially, to the trade names or denominations of associates;

(d) they represent a legal commercial or industrial brand;

(e) they are the result of a merger of Portuguese or acceptable foreign words or parts of words which are directly related to the specific object of the company or part of the remaining parts of the trade names or names of associates;

(f) they are directed at making it easier for the activities of the company to penetrate foreign markets;

(g) they result from the correct use of classical Latin or Greek.

The trade name or denomination must be distinct and not liable to be confused with or mistaken for other registered names or denominations. No words or elements which suggest an activity different from that engaged in by the company

441

may be used. The exclusive right to a trade name or denomination is only granted after the company has been duly registered.

R.2.2.2 *Object*

The deed of incorporation must indicate, in exact and precise terms, which activities the shareholders/members wish the company to engage in. Unspecific expressions such as "and other activities" are expressly prohibited.

R.2.2.3 *Head office*

The location of the head office which represents the company's official domicile, must be given as a specific address.

R.2.2.4 *Duration*

It is not compulsory to mention the duration of the agreement, since companies, unless otherwise specified in the deed of incorporation, may exist for an unspecific period of time.

R.2.2.5 *Capital*

The corporate capital consists of the sum of the amounts contributed by the shareholders/partners, and is subject to general rules which are common to all types of companies and to specific rules according to the particular form of company concerned.

General rules require that the deed of incorporation must indicate the nature of each shareholder's/partner's contribution. This may be of two types: in cash or in kind (except for partnerships which accept a contribution in the form of a partner's expertise or labour).

Contributions in kind are subject to a prior appraisal, by a statutory auditor, of the value of the goods in question. The contributions may be made at the time of the setting of the date for the signing of the deed of incorporation. Private companies and joint stock companies may, under certain conditions, defer part of the contributions. Contributions in kind may not be deferred. The total amount of cash contributions must be deposited, prior to the signing of the deed of incorporation, with a financial institution, in an account in the name of the company wherever possible, or as soon as a date has been set for the signing of the deed. These monies may be withdrawn by the management following the signing whenever authorised by the shareholders/partners.

R.2.2.6   *Registration*

The company must be registered at the official registry within 90 days following the date the deed of incorporation is signed. It is only after registration that the company becomes a legal entity.

R.2.3   General Partnerships (Sociedades em Nome Colectivo)

Under Portuguese law, a general partnership, in an association of individuals, as opposed to an association of capital as is the case of the joint stock company. This personal element is clearly present in the various provisions which regulate this type of company, namely:

(a)   the name of the company must include the name of at least one of the partners, to which the word "Companhia" is added;

(b)   the manner of deliberation which, unless otherwise stipulated, grants one vote to each partner;

(c)   the prohibition that any of the partners engage in an activity which would compete with the company, or of being limited liability partners in another company;

(d)   the acceptance of a contribution to the corporate capital in the form of a contribution in industry;

(e)   the principle that the management of the company is in the hands of all the partners who have equal and independent powers to direct and represent the company, and that decisions are taking by majority vote;

(f)   the transfer of the respective shareholdings without the express consent of the other partners.

Liability of a partner in a general partnership is unlimited, subsidiary in relation to the company, and joint with that of the other partners. A partner is not liable for any debts incurred by the company after his withdrawal from the partnership, although he is liable for any incurred before.

R.2.4   Partnership Association (Sociedades em Comandita)

There are two types of partners/shareholders in a partnership association (sociedades em comandita): those whose responsibility is limited to the value of their shareholding (comanditários), and those who are subsequently and jointly liable, without limits for any debts incurred by the partnership (comanditados).

443

Partnership associations may also be general partnerships in which the capital is not represented by shares (sociedades em comandita simples), or a partnership association in which the shareholdings of the partners are represented by shares (sociedades em comandita por acções).

The trade name of a partnership association consists of the name or denomination of at least one partner to which the expression "em comandita" or "& comandita", "em comandita por acções" or "& comandita por acções" must be added.

The management of a partnership association must be exercised exclusively by the comanditados, unless otherwise authorised in the statutes. As regards resolutions, the ensemble of the comanditados must be ensured voting rights equal to at least one-half of the voting rights of those pertaining to the ensemble of comanditários.

R.2.5 Limited Liability Companies (Sociedades por Quotas)

This is the most frequent type of company in Portugal. According to official data, there are approximately 135,000 such companies. This is the preferred model for small and medium-sized companies given their great flexibility. In addition to the compulsory forms defined by law, it is left to the founding members to select from the various regulations available.

Two is the minimum number of shareholders for a limited liability company and a married couple may, jointly, set up a limited liability company. The company is only answerable with its assets for any debts it may incur. The company statues must specify the sum value of each shareholding and indicate the name of the holder.

The minimum capital required is 400,000 Esc which must be totally realised at the time of the execution of the instrument of incorporation. The monies comprising the initial capital must be deposited with a financial institution before the date for the execution of the said instrument is set, in an account in the name of the future company, and proof of which must be presented to the Notary Public. It is usual, at the time of the execution of the instrument at the Notary Public's, that the directors be granted permission to withdraw the monies deposited.

R.2.5.1 *The company*

The trade name of a limited liability company consists of the name or trade name of all or of one shareholder, to which a logo may or not be added, or by a particular denomination, or by a combination of these, to which the word "Limitada", or simply "Lda", must be added.

R.2.5.2 *Shares*

The corporate capital is divided into shareholdings and these are not represented by share certificates. The nominal value of each shareholding may not be less than 20,000 Esc and the value of each must be multiple of 250 Esc.

The transfer of a shareholding is done by public instrument except when this is the result of a judiciary procedure. Unless otherwise stipulated in the company statutes and other than the transfer of shares between spouses, ascendents, descendents, or other shareholders, the surrender of a shareholding must be approved by the company. The company must be informed or acknowledge, in writing, the intention of a surrender of shares, in which case the name of the person surrendering and the conditions of the surrender must be given. The company must deliberate as to whether it shall approve or refuse the said surrender and so inform the person surrendering within 60 days of his application. Should it fail to do so within this period, no further approval is required.

Should the company refuse the application for surrender, it must, in its notification to the surrendering shareholder, present a proposal for the redemption or acquisition of the shares in question, guaranteeing to pay an equivalent sum as that indicated in the application.

R.2.5.3 *Shareholder's meetings (Assembleia Geral)*

All those acts which require the shareholders' approval are described in detail in the law, yet the company statutes may indicate others. Resolutions of the shareholders are taken by a written ballot, unless otherwise prohibited in the statutes, or during the course of a shareholder's meeting or general assembly.

There is a set procedure both for written ballots and for voting in a general assembly.

A written ballot is only permissible when all shareholders agree that resolutions are to be taken in this manner. In order to obtain the consent of all shareholders, the directors shall consult each by registered letter indicating the object of the deliberation and informing the addressee that unless he replies within 15 days he shall be deemed to approve this form of ballot. Once all the shareholders have given their approval, in accordance with this procedure, the directors shall inform each shareholders of the resolutions to be approved together with all relevant information and, a set of deadline of not less than 10 days for the return of their vote.

The returned ballot must indicate which resolution is approved and indicate whether the voter is in favour or against the resolution which he may not amend in any manner whatsoever upon pain of this being considered a rejection of the proposed resolution.

General assemblies are convened by the directors of a company, on their initiative or as requested, in writing, by any one of the shareholders. Those shareholders who request that the directors convene such a meeting must, in their application, indicate exactly which issues are to be included in the agenda.

Meetings must be convened by a registered letter sent to each shareholder no less than 15 days prior to the date of the meeting, together with a copy of the respective agenda. This formality may be dispensed with as long as all the shareholders are present and all express their desire for such a meeting to be held to discuss a given issue. The law does not foresee any quorum for general assemblies. The company statutes may however stipulate otherwise and require a quorum for all resolutions to be considered valid.

Each shareholder is entitled to one vote for each 250 Esc he holds. Generally speaking, resolutions are considered to have been passed when approved by majority vote. Exceptions to this rule are those resolutions whereby the company statues, or the law, stipulate a number of votes equal to a given amount of the capital for the approval of a resolution. This is known as a "qualified majority". An example of such a requirement is an amendment to the company statutes for which the minimum number of votes required must correspond to three-quarters of the capital.

R.2.5.4   Management

The company is managed and represented by one or more directors who must be individual persons and may also be appointed from persons not pertaining to the company. Directors are responsible for all those acts required for attaining the object of the company. Directors obligate the company in dealings with third parties. Unless otherwise specifically stipulated in the company statutes, a director, or directors, may be dismissed if the company so decides. A director who is dismissed without just cause may seek damages.

R.2.5.5   Auditing of the company

A committee of auditors or a statutory auditor is only compulsory for companies of a certain size. Limited liability companies who during two consecutive years go beyond the following limits are required to deposit a management report and a balance of accounts with the Commercial Registry Office:

(a)   total balance of 180 million Esc;

(b)   total net sales and other income of 370 million Esc;

(c)   more than 50 employees.

2.5.6   Right to information

Shareholders of limited liability companies have the right to information. The management is required to supply any shareholder who so requests it, true and full information regarding the management of the company. Should he wish to consult the books and records of the company, the shareholder may be accompanied by an expert. Consultation or examination of the books and records may only be refused when it is feared that the said shareholder may use this information for purposes which are incompatible with and damaging to the interests of the company. Any shareholder who has been refused the information he requested or who has been given false or incomplete information may request that the courts order an audit of the company.

R.2.5.7 *Right to profits*

Unless otherwise stipulated in the company statutes or following a deliberation taken by a majority of three-quarters of the votes corresponding to the total capital during the course of an extraordinary general assembly expressly convened for this purpose, the shareholders are entitled to receive one-half of the available profits of a given financial year.

R.2.6   Joint Stock Companies (Sociedades Anónimas)

As capital is the determining element in joint stock companies (sociedades anónimas), this is the type of company which is most often used by corporations of which, according to official data, there are more than 3,000 in Portugal. In the joint stock company the capital is divided into shares and the liability of each shareholder is limited to the value of his shareholding. Five is the minimum number of shareholders for the incorporation of a joint stock company.

R.2.6.1   *The company*

The trade name of the joint stock company consists of the name or trade name of one or more of the shareholders with or without a logo, or a particular denomination, or a combination of these; the words "Sociedade Anónima" or, more usually, SA, must be added.

The joint stock company is the type required for engaging in certain activities which, in addition to the regulations of the Company's Act regarding joint stock companies, are subject to specific regulations, as are merchant and investment banks, venture capital companies, credit and loan companies, property management and investment companies, factoring companies, regional development companies, etc.

R.2.6.2 *Capital*

The capital is divided into shares, all of which have the same nominal value which may never be less than 1,000 Esc. 5 million Esc is the minimum capital necessary for a S.A. The realisation, in cash, of up to 70 per cent of the nominal value of the shares may be deferred for up to five years.

The monies realised must be deposited with a financial institution prior to the setting of the date for the execution of the instrument of incorporation, in an account in the name of the future company, and a document proving such a deposit must be presented to the Notary Public. At the time of the execution of the instrument of incorporation at the Notary Public's, the directors or managers are usually authorised to withdraw the amount deposited.

A joint stock company may also be incorporated by a public subscription promoted by one or more persons who assume responsibility required by law. The promoters shall always be required to subscribe to and realise the minimum capital of 5 million Esc and these shares shall be held unalienable for two years.

R.2.6.3 *Shares*

Unless otherwise stipulated by law or by the company statutes, named or bearer shares may be issued, and these are represented by share certificates.

Given the nature of the joint stock companies in which the relevant element is the capital and less the people, shares in S.A.s may usually be freely transferred. The company statutes may however, determine certain restrictions to the free transfer of shares, requiring that these be subject to the consent of the company, giving preference, in the alienation, to other shareholders, or subjecting the transfer to certain conditions. The company statutes cannot prohibit the transfer of shares.

Should the company statutes determine certain limitations to the alienation of shares, these must be named shares. The share certificates must clearly transcribe the limiting clauses otherwise ownership will transfer to anyone who acquires them in good faith.

R.2.6.4 *Bonds*

A joint stock company may, under certain conditions, issue bonds and this issue must be approved by the shareholders, unless the company statutes enable the directors to so decide. S.A.s may not, unless otherwise authorised by the Minister of Justice and Finance, issue bonds whose value exceeds the amount of realised and existing capital.

R.2.6.5   *Shareholders' meetings (Assembleia Geral)*

As in the case of limited liability companies, joint stock companies are also permitted to have unanimous decisions, written ballots, and general assembly resolutions. Given that in the S.A. the capital is usually distributed among a wide number of shareholders, resolutions by general assembly are naturally the most usual means of decision-making.

The general assembly has at least a chairman and a secretary who together make up what in Portugal is called the "mesa da Assembleia Geral". General assemblies are convened by the chairman of the general assembly at those times required by law, when deemed necessary by one of the corporate bodies, or when requested by one or more shareholders representing at least five per cent of the capital. In the last case, the request must be made in a letter addressed to the chairman of the general assembly, giving precise details of the issues which are to be included in the agenda and justifying the need for the extraordinary meeting.

The chairman of the general assembly usually convenes the meetings except in those cases where there are doubts as to his royalties, in which case the meeting is convened by the court; or when the chairman does not convene a meeting as requested by a corporate body, in which case the meeting is convened by the board of directors of the committee of auditors. Notices convening meetings of the general assembly must be published at least one month prior to the date of each meeting.

An ordinary meeting of the general assembly must be held during the first quarter of each year to:

(a)   consider the management report and the balance of accounts;

(b)   consider the proposed application of the profits;

(c)   make a general appraisal of the management and auditing of the company and, if necessary (although these matters may not be on the agenda), dismiss, where allowable, or express a vote of no confidence regarding the management or the directors;

(d)   elect individuals within the framework of its duties.

All shareholders with a right to vote are entitled to be present at meetings of the general assembly and to discuss and vote on issues. The company statutes may stipulate the holding of a minimum number of shares in order to vote. In this case, those shareholders not owning the said minimum number of shares may combine their holdings in order to fulfill the requirement and then be represented by one of the group.

Generally speaking, the assembly may give consideration to items on the agenda regardless of the number of shareholders present or represented by proxy. The law, however, does stipulate that a minimum quorum of shareholders must be present for the discussion of certain issues, namely amendments to the company statutes.

Resolutions are usually approved by majority vote whereby one share corresponds to one vote, unless otherwise stipulated in the company statutes. There are cases, such as amendments to the company statutes, in which a special majority is required. Minutes must be written and signed by the chairman and secretary of the general assembly for each meeting which is held.

R.2.6.6   *The management of the joint stock company*

The Companies Act allows for two forms for the management of a joint stock company: a board of directors (conselho de administração) or a board of general directors (direcção).

The board of directors is comprised of an odd number of members, as stipulated in the company statutes. Should the capital not exceed 20 million Esc, the company statutes may allow for the company to have a board of directors with a single director, or administrador.

Members of the board (administradores) need not be shareholders. Members of the board are either elected by the general assembly or designated in the company statutes which also stipulates their term office. The latter may not exceed a period of four years, and members of the board are eligible for re-election. Members of the board may be dismissed by decision of the general assembly.

The board of directors is responsible for managing the activities of the company. Its members represent the company and engage the company in all their actions.

The board of general directors is comprised of an odd number of directors, up to a maximum number of five. Should the capital not exceed 20 million Esc, the company may have a single director.

Directors are usually designated in the company statutes or appointed by the board of shareholders (conselho geral). Their mandate may not exceed four financial years.

The board of shareholders may dismiss a director for a just cause. Should the dismissal not be founded on a just cause, the director is entitled to an indemnisation for damages he may have suffered.

The board of general directors is responsible for representing and managing the activities of the company, yet the practice of certain actions may be subject to approval of the board of shareholders who must be kept informed of its activities by means of quarterly reports on the company's business, in addition to the annual reports required by law.

R.2.6.7   *Auditing of the company*

As with the management of the company, there are also two distinct forms for the auditing of the company: joint stock companies with a board of directors have a committee of auditors, and joint stock companies with a board of general directors have a board of shareholders (conselho geral) and a statutory auditor.

The auditing of a company with a board of directors is in the hands of a committee of auditors consisting of three full members. This number may be increased to five if so stipulated in the company statutes. One of the full members must be a statutory auditor. In those companies where the capital does not exceed 20 million Esc, the committee of auditors may be reduced to one full member who must be a statutory auditor. The law defines a series of incompatibilities regarding the position of member of the committee of auditors of a joint stock company. Members of the committee of auditors are elected by the general assembly for a maximum term of four years and are eligible for re-election.

The committee of auditors is responsible namely for auditing the management of the company, seeing that the law and the terms of the company statutes are being complied with, regularly examining the accounts and all supporting documents, preparing an annual report on their activities, reporting on the accounts and the proposals submitted by the management.

During the course of their activities, the members of the committee of auditors may obtain information from the management regarding the activities of the company, examine the books and other company documents, and attend meetings of the board of directors whenever they deem it necessary. Members of the committee of auditors must ensure the confidentiality of all facts and information they may acquire during the course of their activities.

In the case of a joint stock company with a board of general directors, the auditing is performed by the board of shareholders and the statutory auditor.

The board of shareholders is comprised of an odd number of members which is stipulated in the company statutes and must always be greater than the number of directors, but never more than 15. Members of the general board must be shareholders and hold sufficient shares to entitle them to vote at the general assembly.

Members of the board of shareholders are either designated in the company statutes or elected by the general assembly for a maximum term of four years and are eligible for re-election. Directors may not be members of the board of shareholders.

The board of shareholders is responsible namely for appointing and dismissing directors, supervising the activities of the board of general directors, regularly examining the accounts and supporting documents, approving the management report and the balance of accounts prepared by the board, convening the general assembly whenever deemed necessary, and preparing a report on the activities of the company for the general assembly.

The statutory auditor has the same powers and duties attributed to the committee of auditors and is responsible for auditing the company accounts.

R.2.6.8   *Right to information*

All shareholders of a joint stock company are granted the right to information. This consists of the right to examine the various documents pertaining to the company, to request written information from the board of directors or the Direcção, and the mandatory giving of information by the appropriate corporate bodies during meetings of the general assembly. Each request for information cannot be refused without due cause. In certain situations, the law stipulates a minimum shareholding for the shareholder to exercise his right to information.

R.2.6.9 *Right to profits*

Unless otherwise stipulated in the company statutes or resolved by a majority of three-quarters of the total votes representing the entire share capital, at an extraordinary meeting of the general assembly expressly convened for this purpose, half of the profits of the financial year in question must be distributed among the shareholders.

SECTION 3

COST OF INCORPORATION

R.3.1 A Notary Public is required for the execution of the instrument of incorporation. Additionally, all companies are required to register with the respective Registry Office and apply for an identification number with the National Registry of Collective Bodies (Registo Nacional de Pessoas Colectivas).

The Notary's fees and the cost of the various registries are calculated on the basis of a set table. As an example, we quote those incurred by companies with a share capital of between 400,000 and 5,000,000 Esc, the minimum acceptable amount for limited liability and joint stock companies respectively, and also for companies with a capital of 30 million Esc.

Hence, according to the Table of Notary's Fees, the execution of the instrument of incorporation for a joint stock or a limited liability company would cost 9,400, 35,000, or 139,000 Esc, according to whether the capital is 400,000, 5,000,000, or 30,000,000 Esc.

The cost of registration with the Commercial Registry Office, according to its Table of Charges is, for companies with the above capital, 7,500, 8,500, or 106,500 Esc, respectively.

The same companies shall have to pay the following fees when registering with the National Registry of Collective Bodies: 5,000, 25,000, or 150,000,000 Esc, respectively.

452

ROMANIA

CLASSIFICATION OF BUSINESS ORGANISATIONS*

S.1.1   Introduction

Romanian law establishes the judicial status of business organisations within several general laws: the Romanian Commercial Code, Company Law No. 31/1990 as amended by Government Ordinance No. 32/1997, Government Ordinance No. 31/1997 regarding Foreign Investment in Romania, and the Commercial Register Law No. 31/1997. There are also certain specific laws, for the business organisations operating in the banking field, in the insurance field and for state-owned companies, etc.

The Company Law establishes five main types of companies:

—partnership (societate in nume colectiv)

—limited partnership (societate in comandita simpla)

—limited liability company (societate cu raspundere limitata)

—joint stock company (societate pe actiuni)

—limited partnership by shares (societate in comandita pe actiuni).

In addition to the above-mentioned entities, commercial practice also acknowledges the existence of sole traders, representative offices of foreign companies, and "autonomous regie" (regii autonome). These are established by Governmental Decisions in order to run public utilities.

Physical persons and business entities (sole traders or companies) may associate and create an association in participation (asociatie in participatie) which is a type of association established under the rules settled by the Romanian Commercial Code, by the parties to perform certain commercial activities, but having no legal personality distinct from that of its members.

---

* *Ion I. Nestor; Nestor Nestor Kingston Petersen SA (full particulars are listed in the Appendix).*

S.1.2 Sole Traders

The Romanian Commercial Code sets the rules under which a physical person may acquire the status of a sole trader. A sole trader is an individual who performs—with professional title and on his/her own behalf—certain objective commercial activities, as established by Article 3 of the Romanian Commercial Code. Sole traders may perform their activities only after acquiring an administrative authorisation, as required by Decree-Law No. 54/1990.

In accordance with Commercial Register Law No. 26/1990, sole traders have to be registered with the Commercial Register, the application for registration containing:

(a) personal data of the sole trader: name and surname, domicile, date and place of birth, civil status;

(b) data regarding the commercial name and the headquarters, as well as the administrative authorisation;

(c) data regarding the object of the trade.

S.1.3 Representative Offices of Foreign Companies

The juridical status of representative offices of foreign companies in Romania is established by the Decree-law No. 122/1990 regarding the authorisation and functioning of representative offices of foreign companies and foreign economic organisation, and by Government Decision No. 1222/1990.

Representative offices are not distinct legal persons, they are considered to be "extensions" of the legal personality of the parent company. While representative offices cannot perform commercial activities of their own, they are entitled to perform some activities on behalf of their parent companies.

Representative offices have to be authorised, upon the request of the parent company submitted to the Ministry of Commerce, with full details of the following:

(a) the object of activity;

(b) the headquarters;

(c) the duration for which the representative office is established;

(d) the number and the positions of the persons to be employed.

The application for authorisation must be submitted with the foreign company's statutes or equivalent, and its most recent accounts.

Within 15 days from the grant of authorisation, the representative office must be registered with the Romanian Chamber of Commerce and Industry and with the Financial Administration.

A yearly fee of U.S. $1,200 is levied for the grant of a licence, with an additional 10 per cent for each other company represented by the representative office.

S.1.4   Foreign Investment Facilities

Foreign investors, irrespective of their nationality or citizenship, may benefit from the legal regime established for the whole duration of the investment made in Romania.

Foreign investments, irrespective of their form, are granted national treatment, in accordance with current Romanian legislation and with international agreements to which Romania is party.

The Government Ordinance No. 31/1997 regarding Foreign Investment in Romania establishes the conditions under which fiscal incentives may be granted for foreign investments. In this respect, fiscal facilities are granted to Romanian legal persons with foreign equity, effectively paid in cash, representing at least 20 per cent of the share capital but no less than U.S. $350,000 or the equivalent in any other freely convertible currency or, to the extent permitted by law, in lei.

The tax on profits payable by companies meeting the above mentioned conditions shall be 15 per cent for the first two years of activity, starting from the date the project is put into commission or, as the case may be, from the effective date of starting activity, but no more than four years from the date the foreign investment is registered with the Trade Registry.[1]

Under certain circumstances, for Romanian legal persons with foriegn equity, effectively paid in cash, representing at least U.S. $5 million or the equivalent in any other freely convertible currency or, to the extent permitted by law, in lei, additional facilities may be granted, such as 15 per cent tax on profits applied to the profits obtained from the activity carried on for the next five years following the above-mentioned two-year period.

The extent to which the provisions of the previous paragraph may apply to Romanian insurance companies with foreign participation is not entirely clear. This issue and others relating to this new legislation is to be the subject of classification in an Emergency Ordinance due to be issued in the near future.

---

[1] The current profits tax rate is 38 per cent.

457

SECTION 2

MAIN FEATURES OF COMPANIES

S.2.1   Introduction

Companies set up in Romania are legal entities, subject to the Romanian legislation in force.

The five types of companies recognised by Romanian Company Law, No. 31/1990, are legal persons operating in their own right, their assets being distinct from those of the natural or legal persons that have created them.

S.2.2   Incorporation of Companies

S.2.2.1   *Incorporation documents*

These have to be drafted in accordance with the legal requirements for each type of company. The incorporation documents have to be authenticated.

S.2.2.2   *The registration of the company*

Company law requires that all companies must have authorisation before they may trade. Such authorisation is granted by the Commercial Register through a judge appointed annually by the President of the court.

Established in accordance with Law No. 26/1990, the Commercial Register is a public institution, located close to the Romanian Chamber of Commerce and Industry, with offices in Bucharest and every provincial/regional capital.

The registration with the Commercial Register is performed on the basis of an application submitted to the Office of the Commercial Register within 15 days from the authentication of the incorporation documents, together with certain documents:

(a)   the incorporation documents, *e.g.* statutes;

(b)   proof of subscription for shares under the conditions provided in the incorporation documents;

(c)   evidence as to ownership and value of contributions in kind and, in case of real property, details of any charges or mortgages;

(d) a statement of the company's opening balance sheet approved by the directors;

(e) the other acts and proofs provided by law.

The main effect of the registration of the company is the acquisition of legal personality.

S.2.2.3 *Publishing in the official gazette*

When the registration is completed, the decision of the judge is confirmed by publication in the *Official Gazette*.

Upon the associates'/partners'/shareholders' request, the incorporation document may also be published, in whole or in part, in the *Official Gazette*.

S.2.2.4 *Registration with the fiscal authorities*

Registration is made by application, submitted with the certificate of incorporation of the company and with the incorporation documents.

S.2.3 Registered Capital: Dividends

Company law admits three types of contributions to the registered capital of a company: contribution in cash, contribution in kind and contribution in labour (this latter not being accepted in case of a joint stock company).

Company law states that dividends may be distributed to the associates/shareholders only if they are real (meaning that the company actually has a net profit). Dividends may not be distributed out of the registered capital.

If the capital decreases during the functioning of the company, it has to be completed or reduced prior to any profit allocation or distribution.

S.2.4 Amendment of the Incorporation Documents

For the amendment of the incorporation documents, company law requires compliance with the same requirements as for incorporations, *i.e.* the document modifying the incorporation documents has to be authenticated, registered with the Trade Registry and published in the *Official Gazette*.

The main reasons for amendment of the incorporation documents are considered to be the increase or the decrease of the registered capital, the extension of the duration of the company, the prior dissolution of the company and the merger of the company.

S.2.5 Administrators

The associates or shareholders appoint one or several administrators or directors ("administrator"), who may be physical or legal persons, whose function is to implement the decisions of the general meeting of associates and to ensure the functioning of the company.

Company law does not define the administrators, but Romanian law provides that the relationship between the company and its administrators is governed by the rules of mandate and that administrators are trustees of the company's assets and interests.

Company law states that in a joint stock company and in a limited partnership by shares the sole administrator or the president of the administration council and at least half of the number of the administrators should be Romanian citizens. This legal provision is not mandatory, the parties are able to decide otherwise in the incorporation documents.

S.2.6 Dissolution of a Company

Dissolution does not produce any effects on the juridical personality of the company, the company still exists, but only for the purpose of its liquidation.

The general cases of dissolution of a company under Romanian company law are:

(a) the expiration of the period set for the duration of the company;

(b) the impossibility to attain the business object of the company;

(c) the decision of the general meeting of associates;

(d) insolvency of the company.

Following the dissolution of the company, the company may not develop new commercial activities. The dissolution of the company grants the right of any associate to ask for its liquidation.

S.2.7   Liquidation of a Company

The activity performed by the company within the liquidation phase shall be subordinated to the needs of liquidation, being limited to the execution of the operations existing in the moment of dissolution of the company.

The company shall appoint liquidators to perform the activities required by the liquidation phase.

SECTION 3

PARTNERSHIP (SOCIETATE IN NUME COLECTIV) ·

S.3.1   Definition and Main Features of Partnerships

According to the Company Law, a partnership is a company whose obligations are guaranteed by its social patrimony and by the unlimited and joint liability of the partners.

In this respect, partnerships have a definite *intuitu personae* character.

The commercial name of the partnership must include the name of at least one of the partners, with the fully written mention "partnership" (societate in nume colectiv).

S.3.2   Incorporation Documents

The partnership is incorporated on the basis of a partnership contract. The contract should be concluded in authentic form and must include:

(a)   name and surname, place and date of birth, domicile and citizenship of the associates physical persons; name, headquarters and nationality of the associates legal persons;

(b)   the juridical form of the company ("partnership"), its name and head-quarters, and, as the case may be, the logo of the partnership;

461

(c)   the scope of the partnership and its main object of activity;

(d)   the capital subscribed and deposited by partners, each partner's contribution in cash or other assets, the value of the contribution and the method of valuation, and the due date for payment in full of the subscribed capital;

(e)   the partners in charge of the partnership's administration and representation, and the limits of their powers;

(f)   each partner's share of profits and losses;

(g)   secondary headquarters of the partnership;

(h)   duration of the partnership;

(i)   procedures for dissolution and liquidation of the partnership.

S.3.3   Registered Capital

The company law does not provide a minimum amount for the registered capital of a partnership.

The registered capital is divided in "parts of interest" (parti de interes), which, under specific conditions settled by the law in respect with the *intuitu personae* character of the partnership, may be subject to an assignment. The parts of interest cannot be represented by negotiable instruments.

S.3.4   General Meeting of Partners

The decisions of the partners are validly taken with the majority of votes for the following issues:

(a)   appointment of the administrators, establishing their powers, the duration of their appointment and their remuneration, unless otherwise provided for in the partnership contact;

(b)   revocation of the administrators or the limitation of their powers, except in case that the administrators were appointed by the partnership contract.

The decision or the amendment of the partnership contract is validly taken with the unanimous vote of the partners.

S.3.5 Liability for the Obligations of the Partnership

Being a distinct legal person, the partnership is liable with its own patrimony for its obligations.

Company law states that the partners have an unlimited joint and several liability for the obligations of the partnership, their liability arising only after the assets of the partnership are exhausted.

SECTION 4

LIMITED PARTNERSHIP (SOCIETATE IN COMANDITA SIMPLA)

S.4.1 Definition and Main Features of Limited Partnerships

According to company law, a limited partnership is a company whose obligations are guaranteed by its social patrimony and joint liability of the general partners; the limited partners are liable only up to the value of their interest.

One of the characteristics of the limited partnerships is the existence of two types of partners:

(a) general partners, unlimitedly and jointly liable for the obligations of the limited partnership;

(b) limited partners, liable for the obligations of the limited partnership only up to the value of their interest.

The commercial name of a limited partnership shall comprise the name of at least one of the general partners, with a fully written mention of "limited partnership" (societate in comandita simpla).

The general features of partnerships apply also for limited partnerships (*e.g.* the rules regarding the contact of association, the registered capital, the parts of interest and their assignment, taking decisions in the general meeting of associates).

463

S.4.2 Administration of the Limited Partnerships

According to company law, only general partners may be appointed administrators of a limited partnership.

SECTION 5

LIMITED LIABILITY COMPANY (SOCIETATE CU RASPUNDERE LIMITATA)

S.5.1 Definition and Main Features of the Company

According to company law, a limited liability company is the company whose obligations are guaranteed by its social patrimony; the associates are liable only for the payment of their contribution.

The establishment of a limited company is based on the mutual trust of the associates, the company having an *intuitu personae* character.

The commercial name of a limited liability company has to point to the object of activity of the company and the mention of "limited liability company" (societate cu raspundere limitata) or "SRL".

. A limited liability company may not have more than 50 associates. Furthermore under the care of the administrators, the limited liability company must keep a register of associates recording:

(a) the name and surname/the commercial name of each associate;

(b) the domicile/headquarters of each associate;

(c) each associate's share of the registered capital;

(d) any transfer of shares;

(e) any changes in the above-mentioned particulars.

S.5.2   Registered Capital

Company law provides a minimum limit for the registered capital of a limited liability company of 1 million lei. The registered capital shall be paid up before commencing the activity of the company.

Company law also provides that contributions in kind to the registered capital of a limited liability company may not exceed 60 per cent of the registered capital. The assets representing contribution in kind have to be transferred at the time of the company's establishment.

The registered capital of a limited liability company is divided into "social parts" or shares ("parti sociale"), of an equal nominal value that may not be lower than 100,000 lei. The social parts may not be represented as negotiable instruments. Each social part gives right to a vote.

S.5.3   Incorporation Documents

Company law provides that a limited liability company shall be incorporated on the basis of the contract of association and of the statutes, the latter detailing the provisions of the contract of association. The law also allows the conclusion of a single document named the "constitutive act" of the company.

The incorporation documents should contain provisions regarding:

(a)   name and surname, place and date of birth, domicile and citizenship of the associates physical persons; name, headquarters and the nationality of the associates legal persons;

(b)   the juridical form of the company (limited liability company), its name and headquarters;

(c)   the scope and the object of activity of the company;

(d)   the capital subscribed and paid by the associates, each associate's contribution and the method of valuation;

(e)   the physical/legal persons in charge with the company's administration and representation, and the limits of their powers;

(f)   each associate's share of profits and losses;

(g)   secondary headquarters of the company;

(h)   duration of the company;

(j)   procedures for dissolution and liquidation of the company.

S.5.4   General Meeting of Associates

According to company law, the general meeting decides by a vote representing the absolute majority of the associates and shareholders. If there are no contrary provisions in the statutes, the vote of all associates is required for the decisions of amending the incorporation documents.

If the legally convened general meeting cannot make a valid decision because of a lack of the required majority, the general meeting convened again may decide on the matters on the agenda, whatever the number of social parts and associates represented by the attending associates.

S.5.5   Internal Auditors (Cenzori)

According to company law, the statutes of a limited liability company may provide the appointment of one or several auditors by the general meeting of the associates. The appointment of auditors is mandatory if there are more than 15 associates.

Company law also provides that, if no auditors are appointed, each shareholder who is not an administrator of the company shall exercise the control of the company.

S.5.6   Transfer of Shares (Social Parts)

In respect of the *intuitu personae* character of the limited liability company, company law provides restrictive conditions regarding the transfer of social parts. The social parts may be transferred between the associates. The transfer to persons outside the company is allowed only if it was approved by associates representing at least three-quarters of the registered capital.

The transfer of social parts has to be registered with the Commercial Register and with the company's register of associates. The transfer is effective against third parties only as of the moment of its registration with the Commercial Register.

SECTION 6

JOINT STOCK COMPANY (SOCIETATE PE ACTIUNI)

S.6.1 Definition and Main Features of Joint Stock Companies

According to company law, a joint stock company is a company whose obligations are guaranteed by its social patrimony, the shareholders being liable only for the payment of their shares.

For the incorporation of a joint stock company the law requires a minimum of five shareholders.

A joint stock company must have its own name which differentiates it from other companies' commercial names. The name must be followed by the words "joint stock company" (societate pe actiuni) or "S.A.".

Company Law provides a minimum limit for the registered capital of a joint stock company of 25 million lei. Initially the fully paid capital cannot be lower than 30 per cent. The rest of the registered capital has to be paid within six months of the registration of the company.

S.6.2 Incorporation Documents

Company law provides that a joint stock company shall be incorporated on the basis of the contract of association and of the statutes, the latter detailing the provisions of the contract of association. The law also allows the conclusion of a single document named the "constitutive act" of the company.

The contract of association and the statutes of a joint stock company shall include:

(a) name and surname, place and date of birth, domicile and citizenship of the associates physical persons; name, headquarters and nationality of the associates legal persons;

(b) the commercial name and headquarters of the joint stock company, of its branches and subsidiaries;

(c) the legal form of doing business, the scope of the company and its main object of activity;

(d) the amount of subscribed and deposited capital;

(e) value of the assets brought in as contribution in kind (if case), methods of valuation and number of shares issued in consideration for the mentioned assets;

(f) number and nominal value of shares, the type of the shares;

(g) number, name, surname and citizenship of the administrators, the guarantee that they have to deposit, their powers and their special rights of administration and representation;

(h) conditions for validity of the general meeting proceedings and procedure for exercising voting rights;

(i) information regarding the auditors;

(j) duration of the company;

(k) method of distribution of profits;

(l) transactions undertaken by shareholders on behalf of the company to be organised, which shall be assumed by the new entity and the amounts which will have to be paid on the account of these transactions.

S.6.3 Forms of Incorporation of a Joint Stock Company

Company law provides two ways of incorporating a joint stock company: "simultaneous incorporation" and "incorporation by public subscription".

S.6.3.1 *Simultaneous incorporation*

Simultaneous incorporation of a joint stock company is the simple way of incorporating such company, by the depositing of 30 per cent of the registered capital by at least five shareholders, and by concluding the incorporation documents and fulfilling the formalities required by law. The joint stock company incorporated this way is a "closed company" (for further details, see S.6.10).

S.6.3.2 *Incorporation by public subscription*

Incorporation by public subscription of a joint stock company requires the issue of a prospectus, the subscription for shares, the approval of subscription and the approval of the incorporation documents by the subscribers.

The prospectus is prepared by the founders of the company and presented in an authenticated form. It contains certain information regarding the future company, as well as the date of ending the subscription, the advantages reserved to the funders, etc.

The prospectus must be registered with the Commercial Register. Company law provides that the authorisation to publish the prospectus is granted by the judge delegated by the Commercial Register.

The issue of shares has also to be approved by the National Securities Committee, the authorisation is granted on the basis of the prospectus having been prepared according to company law.

The shares subscription will be written on one or more copies of the prospectus marked by the judge. Prospectuses which do not fulfil all legal requirements are void.

The results of the public subscription shall be verified and approved by the inaugural meeting of subscribers.

The joint stock company incorporated this way is an "opened company" (for further details, see S.6.10).

S.6.4 Shares

The shares of a joint stock company are equal fractions of the registered capital, indivisible and negotiable.

Company law mentions two types of shares: bearer shares and registered shares. The type of the shares issued by the company and their nominal value shall be determined by the contract of association. The nominal value of a share cannot be lower than 1,000 lei.

The shares may be issued only after the registration of the company with the Commercial Register. The shares cannot be issued for a value lower than the nominal value. The capital cannot be increased and new shares cannot be issued until the shares of the previous issue are fully paid.

The company has to keep a shareholders register as well as a shares register that contains mention of the modifications ocurred in the property of the shares.

Under Romanian law, there are two classes of shares: *ordinary shares* and *preference shares with no voting right*.

Preference shares with no voting right have the same nominal value as the ordinary shares. They may not exceed 25 per cent of the registered capital. The preference shares grant to their holders the following rights: the right to a priority dividend drawn from the distributable profits resulting from the fiscal year, before any other drawing; the rights acknowledged to the holders of ordinary shares, except the right to participate and to vote, under these shares, in the general meetings of the shareholders.

The holders of each class of shares meet at special meetings, under the terms established by the statutes of the company.

469

S.6.5 General Meeting of Shareholders

According to the company law, a general meeting of shareholders (GMS) may be ordinary or extraordinary.

S.6.5.1 *Ordinary GMS*

The ordinary GMS convenes at least once a year, no later than three months after the end of the fiscal year.

Besides the discussion of other issues included on the agenda, the ordinary GMS has the following duties:

(a) to discuss, approve and modify (as appropriate) the annual report after its presentation by the administrators and the auditors;

(b) to appoint the administrators and auditors and to set their remuneration;

(c) to evaluate the performance of the administrators;

(d) to determine the budget of revenues and expenses and, accordingly, the plan of operations for the next fiscal period;

(e) to decide the pledge, lease or dissolution of one or several of the company's units.

The law requires the presence of the shareholders holding at least half of the registered capital for the meeting to be validly constituted. The decisions must be taken by shareholders holding the absolute majority of the registered capital represented at the meeting. If these conditions are not met, the majority (of the shareholders) of the meeting which shall convene following a second notice may decide on the issues included on the agenda of the first meeting, whatever the number of the attending shareholders.

S.6.5.2 *Extraordinary GMS*

The extraordinary GMS is convened whenever a decision is needed:

(a) to change the type of the company;

(b) to change the headquarters' address;

(c) to change the objects of the company;

(d) to extend the duration of the company;

(e) to increase or decrease the company capital;

(f)   to issue new shares, the capital of the company;

(g)   to merge the company with other companies;

(h)   to dissolve the company;

(i)   to issue bonds;

(j)   to make any amendment to the contract of association and the statutes.

The extraordinary GMS may delegate to the council of administration subject to the conditions provided by the contract of association and/or statutes, the exercise of the following powers: to change the headquarters' address; to change the object of the company; to increase the company capital; to   decrease or increase, by issuing new shares, the capital of the company; and to issue bonds.

In order to ensure the validity of the proceedings of the extraordinary gms, if the contract of association or the statutes of the company do not provide otherwise, the following conditions are required:

1.   Upon the first notice, the attendance of the shareholders holding three-quarters of the registered capital; the decision may be taken by vote of the shareholders holding at least half of the registered capital.

2.   If the above-mentioned conditions are not met, upon the following notices the attendance of the shareholders holding half of the registered capital is required; decisions may be taken by the vote of the shareholders holding at least one-third of the registered capital.

Joint stock companies are required to maintain a Register containing the minutes of the meetings and mentioning the fulfilment of the legal requirements regarding shareholder's meetings.

The decisions of the GMS shall be submitted, within 15 days, to the Commercial Register. The decisions shall be also published in the *Official Gazette*.

S.6.6   Administration of a Joint Stock Company

If more administrators are appointed, the company law provides that they shall form an administration council (consiliu de administratie), lead by a president, who is also the general director of the company.

The administration council convenes whenever is necessary, but at least once a month, at the company's headquarters.

If the contract of association or the statutes of the company do not provide otherwise, the personal attendance of at least half of the number of the administrators is required for the validity of the decisions of the administration council.

The administration council may delegate part of its powers to a managing committee (comitet de directie), lead also by the president of the administration council and formed only by administrators.

The board of directors convenes at least once a week, at the headquarters of the company.

The managing committee may take decisions based on the absolute majority of its members. The decisions of the managing committee may be annulled or suspended by the administration council, and, *a fortiori*, by the GMS.

The company law provides that the execution of the operations of a joint stock company may be entrusted to one or more executive directors, employees of the company. The executive directors cannot be members of the administration council of the company.

Joint stock companies are compelled to keep a register of the meetings and debates of the administration council, as well as a register of the meetings and debates of the managing committee.

S.6.7   Internal Auditors of Joint Stock Companies

If the incorporation documents do not provide otherwise, a joint stock company shall have three auditors and the same number of deputies. The number of auditors must be odd in all cases.

At least one of the auditors must be an accountant legally certified or an expert accountant. Except the accountant auditors, the auditors must be shareholders.

The auditors have the obligation to check the administration of the company. They shall issue a detailed report to the GMS regarding the matters set by the law. The GMS may not approve the annual balance sheet and the profit and loss account if these are not accompanied by the auditor's report.

S.6.8   Bonds

Article 118 of the company law entitles joint-stock companies to issue bearer or registered bonds, for an amount not exceeding three-quarters of the paid and existing capital, according to the last approved annual report.

The bonds of the same issue must be of equal value and grant the same rights to their owners.

The issue of bonds is decided by the extraordinary general meeting of shareholders. For the issuance of bonds the administrators of the company shall prepare a prospectus containing certain information regarding the company, the date at which the decision of the general meeting which approved the bonds issue was published, the total amount of the bonds to be issued, the method of reimbursement, the nominal value of bonds and their interest.

Under specific conditions set forth by the laws and regulations ruling the legal regime of securities, the issuance of bonds is subject to the control of the National Committee of Securities.

The company law provides that bondholders may convene a general meeting to deliberate upon their interests. The meeting shall be convened at the expense of the company which issued the bonds upon the request of a number of bondholders representing one-quarter of the issued and unpaid bonds or, once they were appointed, upon the request of the representatives of bondholders.

S.6.9   Dissolution of Joint Stock Companies

Besides the general cases of dissolution of companies (see S.2.6), company law provides two specific cases of dissolution for a joint stock company:

(1)   In case of loss of half of the registered capital. According to the law, upon finding out about the loss of half of the registered capital, the administrators are compelled to convene an extraordinary GMS to decide about the recovering of the capital or the reduction of the registered capital to the actual value or the dissolution of the company. The incorporation documents may provide that the meeting be convened even for a lower loss.

(2)   In case that the number of the shareholders is reduced below the limit set by the law (to less than five associates), if there are more than six months since that reduction and the number was not completed.

S.6.10   "Opened" and "Closed" Joint Stock Companies

In view of the recent Romanian regulations on securities and the securities market, which created a new environment in this field, since 1994 a distinction may be made between "opened" and "closed" joint stock companies.

S.6.10.1   *Opened companies*

Under the above-mentioned regulations, an opened company is a joint stock company established by public subscription or whose shares or other securities convertible in shares, have been subject to a public offer regularly promoted and successfully closed.

Joint stock companies that have performed a public offer subsequent to which the offered shares have been subscribed and paid by minimum 50 persons, become opened companies.

473

If a joint stock company has, at the end of a fiscal year, a registered capital higher than 1 billion lei and more than 500 shareholders (except the employees of the respective company) that company is considered an opened company.

In order to become an opened company by an initial public offer or public subscription, the joint stock company must have a registered capital of at least 100 million lei.

Opened companies are subject to regulation by the National Securities Commission, providing special rules for the summon of the General Meeting of Shareholders, transfer of shares, reporting requirements towards the National Securities Commission.

S.6.10.2 *Closed companies*

A closed company is a joint stock company whose incorporation documents provide restriction regarding the free transferability of its shares, forbid any issuance of securities to the public or does not comply with the conditions mentioned above (see S.6.10.1).

SECTION 7

LIMITED PARTNERSHIP BY SHARES (SOCIETATE IN COMANDITA PE ACTIUNI)

S.7.1 Definition and Main Features of the Company

According to company law, a limited partnership by shares is a company whose obligations are guaranteed by its social patrimony and by the unlimited and joint liability of the general partners; the limited partners are liable only for the payment of their contribution.

The rules regarding the joint stock companies apply also for the limited partnerships by shares, with the observance of the specific of this type of company.

One of the characteristics of the limited partnerships by shares is the existence of two types of partners:

(a) general partners, unlimitedly and jointly liable for the obligations of the limited partnership;

(b)   limited partners, liable for the obligations of the limited partnership only up to the value of their interest.

The commercial name of a limited partnership by shares consists of its own denomination able to differentiate it from other companies' commercial names, and shall be followed by the fully written mention of "limited partnership by shares" (societate in comandita pe actiuni).

The administration of a limited partnership by shares is entrusted to one or more general partners.

The legal regime of general and limited partners is ruled by the legal provisions set for partnerships.

SPAIN

CLASSIFICATION OF BUSINESS ORGANISATIONS: INTRODUCTION*

T.1.1 This account shall only refer to corporations according to Spanish legislation, that is to say, to those entrepreneurs who exercise their commercial activity through a separate entity; there are, of course, entrepreneurs who are physical persons, governed by the rules of the Commercial Code which apply to the exercise of their activity, but in no case can they be considered as a "company".

Any examination of Spanish company law must be first based upon the distinction between civil law corporations and commercial corporations. Although there is not a clear distinction between them, those companies which adopt any of the forms provided for in the Commercial Code and in the special laws for particular corporations are considered commercial corporations. Civil law corporations are those which are not incorporated for the purpose of developing or exploiting an enterprise, and therefore they do not adopt any of the forms provided for the commercial corporations. They are regulated by Articles 1665, *et seq.*, of the Civil Code. For the purposes of this account we shall only refer to commercial corporations.

Concerning commercial corporations, the Spanish legislation and legal practice distinguish the following corporate forms:

1. Companies with unlimited liability

    (a)   accounts in participation (cuentas en participación);

    (b)   general partnerships (sociedades colectivas);

    (c)   limited partnerships (sociedades comanditarias);

    (d)   branches (sucursales).

2. Companies with limited liability

    (a)   share companies (sociedad anónima or SA)

    (b)   limited liability companies (sociedad de responsabilidad limitada or SRL)

    (c)   limited partnership by shares (sociedad en comandita por acciones)

---

* *Almudena Arpón de Mendívil, Gomez, Acebo & Pombo, Abogados (full particulars are listed in the Appendix).*

3. Special types of companies

    (a) co-operative companies (sociedades cooperativas)

    (b) mutual insurance companies (mutualidades de seguros)

    (c) mutual guarantee companies (sociedades de garantía reciproca)

SECTION 2

COMPANIES WITH UNLIMITED LIABILITY

T.2.1   Accounts in Participation (Cuentas en Participación)

This is not really a corporation, but more like a contract. One or more parties make only capital contributions (the so-called "participants") while the other party carries out the commercial activity (the so-called "manager") in order to obtain the mutually agreed objective. Therefore, this is a mere participation in the economic results of a certain business with no personal collaboration in the business activities.

These forms of collaboration are governed by the provisions contained in articles 239 to 243 of the Commercial Code. Sometimes this vehicle is referred to as an "accidental corporation" because it has some of the aspects of a corporation but not others: the accounts in participation neither lead to the creation of common assets (because the capital contributions of the participants are part of the wealth of the owner of the business), nor do they have legal personality.

The contract of accounts in participation does not need to be in any specially prescribed form or adopt any particular formalities, although it should, for ease of evidence, be set out in a written public or private document. The parties are obliged to transfer to the manager the agreed upon capital. The manager is bound to perform his duties as a reasonable businessman; to render accounts of his management, and to prepare information on the business accounts and results. He is responsible to third parties for whatever acts he may have carried out in the course of his business.

It should be noted that this legal entity is seldom used, basically due to the problems arising from the transfer of money to the manager and the sole responsibility of the latter to third parties.

T.2.2   General Partnership (Sociedad Colectiva)

General partnerships are defined in the Commercial Code as companies in which all the partners agree to have a share of equal rights and obligations in the proportions which they establish, under a firm name. Unlimited liability for the company debts can be added to that concept. The partner's individual circumstances are, in itself, the reason for the members' consent to associate. This implies that partnership is not transferable without the authorisation of all the members.

Company management is a major concern entrusted to all the partners, except those who have previously resigned from that commitment. Those partners who express their opposition to a decision adopted by the majority will not be bound by it. However, some partners may be specially appointed to deal with management. In this case, the rest of the partners shall not interfere, and disagreement will lead to withdrawal/expulsion from the partnership.

Only those partners who are granted specific power may represent the firm and act on its account. Profits and losses will be distributed in proportion to the interest of each and every member in the company. The creditors of a partnership shall not collect debts from individual partners unless the assets of the partnership have been completely liquidated.

Partners may contribute just with their personal work in the firm, rather than with capital. In that case, they are not entitled to take part in the company management, and they receive a share in profits equal to that obtained by the minor capital partner. They do not participate in losses.

Partners may not carry out, for their own account or for the account of other parties, any activity in direct competition with the partnership, without the authorisation of the rest of the partners. This permission will not be denied unless it is proved that great damage may result form such competing activities.

In principle, general partnerships are recommended for businesses run by few partners, who are very confident of one another, and whose weight in the management is comparably equal; businesses which require relatively small amounts of capital, are quite certain to be profitable, so that the partner's personal property is not at risk.

Finally, Articles 125, *et seq.*, of the Commercial Code apply to this type of companies.

T.2.3   Limited Partnership (Sociedad Comanditaria)

There are two different categories of members in limited partnerships: general partners (who remain jointly and severally liable for the partnership debts, as in general partnerships), and limited partners whose liability is limited to the extent of their contributions. The management is entrusted to the former, although the latter have a right to be informed pursuant to the articles of partnership. These should, at least, provide that the balance sheet must be communicated to limited partners.

Only general partners may represent the partnership, or add their personal names to the firm name. Limited partners cannot act on behalf of the partnership, their liability being extended if they fail to comply with such prohibition. Categories of partnership are not transferable.

Profits shall be received by limited partners, proportionally to their contributions. General partners will be entitled to earnings in proportion to their interest in the partnership.

Limited partnerships permit greater capital accumulation than general partnerships, and avoid the disadvantages which result from the participation of outside capital holders in the firm management. Limited partnerships by shares may ensure more capital contributions, but the number of limited partners would increase, which could lead to important problems concerning decision-making. (A general limited partners' meeting would have to be created).

However the number of general partnerships in Spain has already exceeded that of limited partnerships, due to the fact that the former are mainly family run businesses, and in the event that capital accumulation is required, conversion into limited liability companies may be easier and more convenient.

Limited partnerships are regulated by Articles 145, *et seq.*, of the Commercial Code.

T.2.4 Branches (Sucursales)

First of all it should be noted that branches do not have legal personality as they only are all establishment created by a corporation for the development of its activities. The Mercantile Registry Regulation describes branches as secondary establishments through which the company's activities are carried out, with their own permanent representatives and a certain amount of management autonomy.

There are no legal criteria that provide a distinction between branches and principal offices; and between branches and plain commercial facilities. Nevertheless, they can be identified by certain features. For example, branches are always subject to a unified economic supervision from the company's principal office, especially when they are part of a commercial network. However, they independently undertake those operations which are considered part of the business purpose of the company, and were initially performed by a single principal establishment.

On the other hand, they do not develop merely as an auxiliary or executive activity; from an economic point of view branches could survive independently, even if the main office ceased operations.

Branches have their own legal existence. The Mercantile Registry Regulation states that the company and its branches must be registered separately, at the Mercantile Registries which correspond to their respective domiciles.

The branch must be set up by means of a Public Deed which specifies the branch domicile, business purpose, capital assigned, and other compulsory information. Presentation of documentation certifying that the parent company is incorporated and authorised according to the legislation of the country of origin is also required. This is also applicable to branches and secondary establishments owned by individual entrepreneurs and other Spanish registrable entities and by foreign entities with legal capacity and a profit-making object.

SECTION 3

COMPANIES WITH LIMITED LIABILITY

T.3.1 Share Company (Sociedad Anónima: SA)

The essential features of limited corporations have been established by the Share Companies Act (SC Act) of December 22, 1989, which compiles the rules governing these commercial corporations, as amended for the purpose of adaptation to E.C. Directives. These are analysed in Section 4, focusing on: incorporation, transfer of shares, rights and obligations of shareholders, management, financing, accounting principles, transformation and termination.

T.3.2 Limited Liability Company (Sociedad de Responsabilidad Limitada: SRL):

The legal regime applicable to limited liability companies has been recently amended by the new Law 2/1995, of March 23, 1995, which substitutes the former Law on Limited Liability Companies, of July 17, 1953.

Limited liability companies (LLCs) have been traditionally considered as the appropriate legal form of corporation for small companies, where there are restrictions on transfers of shares and the personal circumstances of the partners are relevant, acting in practice as closed companies.

One of the aims of the new law is to adapt the legal regime applicable to these companies to the current economic and social circumstances, providing them with the necessary flexibility to act as an attractive vehicle for certain investments and commercial operations. With this purpose, it has also taken the legislative opportunity to modify the legal regime of share companies (SCs), by implementing the E.U. Directives and contemplating the possibility of unipersonal corporations, both LLCs and SCs.

Within both companies, the shareholders/partners have limited liability. The main difference between the two is that SCs have their capital divided into shares, whilst LLCs have their capital divided into cumulative and indivisible participations, which cannot be incorporated to negotiable instruments nor be called "shares".

Aside from this principal difference, the regulatory regime for LLCs is quite similar to that established in SC Act for Share Companies, but there are certain differences that should be mentioned.

T.3.3 Differences Between Share Companies and Limited Liability Companies

The most significant features of the new Law in comparison with the statutory provisions governing SCs, under the SC Act, of December 22, 1989, are as follows:

(1) Minimum share capital required: SCs are supposed to have a capital of at least 10 million Ptas, while the Limited Liability Companies Act requires a minimum capital of 500,000 Ptas.

(2) Paid-up capital: At least 25 per cent of a SC's capital must be paid up on incorporation, while it must be fully paid up in LLCs.

(3) Valuation of contributions: The rules of SCs require professional experts to make a valuation of the non-cash contributions to the company through a specified procedure, whilst the rules on LLCs do not impose such a formal valuation procedure. This implies a significant simplification of the procedure; but the founders, the partners in cases of capital increases, the acquirers of a paid up participation in change of contributions in kind, or the administrators in the event of a capital increase with these contributions, must set their own valuations, and shall all respond before the company and the corporate creditors with respect to the existence and valuation of such contributions.

(4) Foundation: Neither SCs nor LLCs require a specific number of persons to found the corporation. On the other hand, the LLC Act does not provide for the alternative of successive foundation applied for in the SC Act.

(5) Funding: The funding of SCs can be done by means of capital issue, raising debt or the granting of loans by shareholders or third parties. LLCs, however, cannot issue debt.

(6) Interests: It should be noted that SCs cannot issue shares which guarantee

the payment of an interest. Notwithstanding this, the Law provides for the existence of non-voting shares that cannot represent more than the half of the disbursed share capital. Said non-voting shares do not confer voting rights, but ensure the payment of a preferential interest of five per cent, provided that there are dividends to be distributed. On the contrary, it can be understood that LLCs may issue participations which guarantee the payment of an interest, notwithstanding the granting or not of voting rights. LLCs do not contain any limitation on the above and, therefore, it is possible to have different participations which, having the same nominal value, may grant different economic and voting rights.

(7) Proportionality: Control over SCs and LLCs will be exercised by the shareholders in the former or partners in the latter who hold the majority voting rights, in the sense that their vote will decide issues at the shareholders or partners meeting. SCs must keep proportionality between the nominal value of the shares and the voting and economic rights grants to each owner, although there can be different classes of shares which grant different rights to their owners. On the contrary, LLCs do not contain any limitation on the above and, therefore, it is possible to have different participations which, having the same nominal value, may grant different economic and voting rights.

(8) Transfer of shares/participations: The general rule is that shares of SCs can be freely transferable whilst participations of LLCs cannot, since the rest of the partners have a pre-emption right. This rule can be modified in the byelaws of both sets of companies. In LLCs, non-onerous or free transfers are only valid when the acquirer is another partner, a partner's spouse, ascendant or descendant, or a company of the same group. The LLC Law also regulates some cases of compulsory transfers.

(9) Capital increases and decreases: Increases and reductions of capital are regulated in a more simplified manner than in the SC Act. The Act states the exclusive competence of the general meeting (without delegation) and requires the favourable vote of two-thirds of votes corresponding to all participations.

(10) General meeting: In SCs, a majority of valid votes of those attending the meeting is required in order to validly decide on an issue, whilst in LLCs, only one-third of the votes corresponding to all participations is necessary in order to adopt general decisions. However, in the LLC regime, there are some exceptions: capital increases and decreases and any other modifications of byelaws require qualified majorities such as the vote of more than a half of the total votes corresponding to all participations; transformation, merger or split up of the corporation, suppression of the pre-emption rights in capital increases, partners' exclusion and authorisation to the administrators in order to carry out an activity identical or similar to the corporate purpose of the company, will need the vote of two-thirds of the total votes corresponding to all participations. Similarly, the byelaws could require a higher percentage

(never unanimity) or the vote of a certain number of partners for specific issues.

(11)   Administrators: The administration of SCs can correspond to a sole administrator, to various administrators acting individually, to two joint administrators or to a board of directors composed of a minimum of three members, it being necessary that the byelaws establish which of the different systems of administration will be applicable. On the contrary, the byelaws of LLCs can contain alternative administration systems, it being possible for the general partners' meeting to decide at any moment which administration system will be applicable. It is not necessary to modify the byelaws in case of change of that system, provided that this is so ruled in the byelaws.

The LLC Act does not limit the number of administrators acting jointly; on the contrary, in the SC Act, if said number exceeds from two, the company's administration body will necessarily take the form of a board of directors. In LLCs, the board of directors must be composed of a minimum of three and a maximum of 12 members.

Administrators of SCs can be appointed for a maximum term of five years, although they can be re-elected, whilst administrators of LLCs can be appointed for an indefinite period of time.

LLCs may appoint substitute administrators, but this is something prohibited for SCs.

(12)   Unipersonal corporations: One of the changes introduced by the LLCs Act is the allowance of the existence of unipersonal corporations, either from the moment of incorporation or at a later stage by acquisition by a sole partner of 100 per cent of the stock capital. This can apply, not only for LLCs, but also for SCs, by modifying their own regulation (suppression of the need of three founders). These circumstances must be recorded in a public deed and registered at the Mercantile Registry.

The sole partner will exercise the general meeting functions, and his decision will be recorded in minutes.

The aim of this legal modification is to suppress a prohibition already breached in the ordinary practice, where individuals and/or entities who wanted to limit their liability used to incorporate corporations through cat's-paws.

T.3.4   Limited Partnership by Shares (Sociedad Comanditaria por Acciones)

It is equivalent to a limited partnership in which the limited partners' participants are represented by shares. The share capital should exceed 10 million Ptas; it must be totally subscribed and at least 25 per cent of it must be paid up on incorporation.

Shares are transferable with the same restrictions which apply to share companies. Company representation, decision making and partners' liability are similar to those in simple limited partnerships.

These corporations are ruled primarily by Articles 151 to 157 of the Commercial Code, and secondly by the Share Companies Act.

SECTION 4

SHARE COMPANIES

T.4.1 Incorporation

Share companies must be incorporated by means of a public deed granted before a Spanish Notary Public and thereafter registered at the Mercantile Registry of the appropriate Spanish province. Registration results in the corporation acquiring its legal personality.

The public deed must include the following:

(a) the names and personal data of the individuals or legal persons granting the public deed, as well as their nationality and domicile;

(b) their intent to grant a share company;

(c) the cash, goods or rights that each shareholder undertakes to contribute to the corporation and the number of shares attributed to such contribution;

(d) an estimate of the cost of incorporation;

(e) the byelaws which are to govern the corporation;

(f) the names and personal data of those initially in charge of the management of the corporation, and of the auditors.

Moreover, the public deed may include whatever agreements and conditions that the shareholders may consider appropriate, as long as they are not contrary to the Law or the essential principles applicable to SAs.

The Share Companies' Act establishes two procedures for the incorporation of a share company: the simultaneous incorporation which is currently used in Spain, and the successive incorporation. According to the former, the founder or founders grant the public deed and subscribe all the shares of the corporation.

487

T.4.2 Byelaws

The corporation will be subject to the rules contained in the byelaws, which should include the following:

(a) the name of the corporation;

(b) the corporate purpose describing the activities included within the same;

(c) the duration of the corporation;

(d) the date at which it shall start its operations;

(e) the social domicile;

(f) the stock capital expressing, if necessary, its non-paid-up value, and the maximum term and manner in which it shall be disbursed; the number of shares into which it is divided, its nominal value, classes, series, and their representation;

(g) the structure of the body in charge of the representation and management of the corporation, appointment of the administrators to whom the power of representation is granted, stating the number of the said administrators or at least the minimum and maximum number;

(h) the duration of their post and their disciplinary procedure if they are entitled to receive remuneration;

(i) the procedure for discussing and adopting decisions by the executive bodies of the corporation;

(j) the relevant date for end-of-year accounts and financial reports;

(k) the restrictions on the free transfer of shares, if appropriate;

(l) the procedure for ancillary contributions, if applicable and the special rights that the founders of the corporation may have reserved for themselves.

T.4.3 Registered Office

The company byelaws should express the domicile, and state which corporate body is entitled to decide the settlement, dismantlement and change of domicile of branches. Corporations are bound to have their domicile wherever their management and administration are performed, or where the principal office or establishment is located. If the registered office differs from the aforementioned, third parties may consider as domicile either the former or the latter.

T.4.4   Company Name

The corporation name must include the expression "Sociedad Anónima" (share company) or the abbreviation "SA". No company may adopt the name of another previously registered or a similar name.

Corporations may have an objective or subjective name. The former may refer to economic activities, but only to those which are part of the business purpose of the company. The latter is taken from the name of a person, who is usually a partner.

The company name will not include any expression which might lead to misunderstanding as to the identity of the entity or corporation or the nature of their activities.

T.4.5   Duration

The company byelaws must state the period of time during which the corporation will be carrying out its activities. The Mercantile Registry Regulation provides that if a certain period is fixed and no reference to the date of its commencement is made, it will start from the date of the incorporation deed. Alternatively, the company duration may be indefinite.

T.4.6   Contributions

Shareholders may make contributions either in cash or in kind, these bring goods or rights which may be subject to economic valuation. Personal work contributions are not allowed.

Contributions in cash will be nominated in pesetas, and must be attested by the Public Notary. Contributions in kind will require a report by one or several independent experts appointed by the Mercantile Registrar. The report should describe each and every contribution and express the criteria upon which their economic value has been settled. It should also state if the valuation corresponds to the number and total nominal value of the shares to be issued. The report will be attached to the deed of incorporation or to the deed of capital increase.

The subscribed capital should be fully paid up within a period which must be established in the byelaws, or decided by the directors of the company. This period shall not exceed five years in the case of contributions in kind. If shareholders fail to comply within that period, their voting rights will be suspended. In addition, they shall neither receive any share in the company earnings nor exercise their preferential right to subscribe to new shares or bonds.

T.4.7   Shares

T.4.7.1   *Transfer of shares*

An essential feature of share companies is that their capital is divided up into shares. In addition, these shares grant certain rights to their holders and are treated as negotiable instruments.

Shares may be represented by titles or by book entries. Those represented by titles may be registered (when the name of the holder appears in the title), or bearer shares. Shares represented by book entries are subject to the rules contained in the Spanish Securities Market Act. It should be noted that the SC Act requires that shares be represented by registered titles when they have not been fully paid up, when there are restrictions to their transfer, when they entail ancillary contributions, and whenever special rules require it.

In principle, shares are freely transferable as of the moment the corporation is registered at the Mercantile Registry. However, the byelaws may contain restrictions on the freedom of transfer of registered shares, so long as they do not make them non-transferable in fact. Private agreements limiting the transfer of shares shall not affect the corporation, which shall recognise the valid ownership of the share as that of the purchaser, although the private agreement shall be valid as between the contracting parties.

Concerning the methods of transferring, if the titles have not yet been printed and delivered to the shareholders they are governed by the rules concerning transfer of credits and other immaterial rights.

Once the titles are physically held by a shareholder, if they are bearer shares they may be transferred by the simple delivery of the title to the purchaser with the intervention of a Notary Public, a Securities Society or Securities Agency. If they are registered shares they may likewise be transferred by delivery of the title, and in addition the transfer must be recorded in the stub-book held by the Company. Shares represented by book entries are transferred through an accounting procedure in accordance with the rules of the Spanish Securities Market Act.

T.4.7.2   *Acquisition of own shares (treasury stock)*

A company must neither subscribe its own shares, nor the shares issued by its parent company, although purchases are permitted provided that certain requirements are fulfilled. First, the purchase must be authorised by the general shareholders' meeting, by means of an agreement which identifies the terms and conditions of the purchase, the procedure, and the period of validity of the authorisation, which will not exceed 18 months.

In addition, the face value of the shares acquired, together with that of the shares already owned by the company may not exceed 10 per cent of the share capital. The shares must be completely paid up, and the company must be provided with reserves for an amount equal to the value of the shares that have been purchased. That should neither imply a share capital decrease, nor affect the reserves already established.

The Share Companies Act imposes a number of sanctions on those companies which fail to comply with the legal requirements already mentioned, apart from the obligation to transfer the shares acquired. Nevertheless, there are four cases of acquisition exempted from the legal conditions. In these cases the shares must also be transferred, but the law permits that the transfer be made within a longer period of time.

The law also regulates for the company's own shares, once they have been purchased. It states that the voting and economic rights which are inherent to the shares are suspended.

A corporation may accept its own shares (or the shares of its parent company) as pledge, or any other form of guarantee, with the conditions and within the limits established for the purchase of such shares; consequently, suspension will also be applicable.

T.4.7.3 *Increase/decrease of capital*

Corporations may increase capital upon the issue of new shares as well as upon an increase in the face value of the already existing shares. Capital increase will be decided for the purpose of receiving new capital contributions from the shareholders, or in order to transform earnings or reserves into share capital. Capital increase decisions may also be adopted for the purpose of satisfying the company's debts (for instance, in the case of conversion of bonds into shares).

The increase must be decided in a general shareholders' meeting, and the procedure should follow the method for deciding a change in the company's byelaws. If new contributions in cash are proposed, at least 97 per cent of the share capital must be paid up. Once the capital has been increased, 25 per cent of the value of the new shares must be paid up.

The general shareholders' meeting may delegate to the directors the necessary authority to decide the execution of the increase up to the amount decided by the shareholders' meeting within a term of one year, or to decide themselves to increase the share capital up to a certain amount when they decide it convenient. In this latter case, the increases may not exceed half of the share capital and have to be executed upon contributions in cash over a period of five years from the date of the delegation.

If new shares are to be issued, shareholders and convertible bondholders are entitled to subscribe to a number of such shares in proportion to the nominal face value of their shares (in the case of convertible bondholders, in proportion to the value of the shares which they should receive if conversion took place at that moment). This right of preferential subscription must be exercised within the period established by the directors to that effect, which should exceed one month. This right is transferable, under the conditions which govern the transfer of shares. The

491

general shareholders' meeting may decide the suppression of this right in the interest of the company, provided that certain legal conditions are fulfilled.

Notice that it is possible to issue new shares with a premium (an amount over their nominal value) or as a preference share (which grants a privilege with respect to ordinary shares), or as a voteless share (which grants to the holder a special economic right in the receipt of a minimum yearly profit, while suppressing voting rights and thereby not allowing participation in the management of the corporation).

Capital increases may be carried out through a public offer for the subscription of the shares, and it is also possible to request the listing of the new shares on the Stock Exchange. In both cases it will be necessary to comply with the notice and disclosure requirements contained in the Spanish Securities Market Law.

Capital decrease may be decided for the purpose of refunding contributions to shareholders; creation or improvement of reserves; compensation of unpaid capital; and restoration of the balance between capital and assets, in case of company losses. This type of capital decrease is compulsory whenever losses exceed 33 per cent of the share capital over a period of two years. In this case, the operation must affect equally all the shares, in proportion to their nominal value.

Capital decrease must be decided by the general shareholders' meeting, according to the same conditions imposed on capital increase. In addition, the agreement shall express the amount, purpose, period and procedure for decreasing the share capital. Whenever the operation implies refunding contributions to shareholders, and it does not affect them equally, the decision should be approved by the majority of those shareholders who are affected.

The Share Companies Act grants certain company creditors a right to oppose the capital decrease until the company guarantees the payment of such debts which will be due and payable after the decision is adopted. This right is excluded when the purpose of the capital decrease is to balance capital and assets, or create reserves, or is made with profits, free reserves or redemption of shares freely acquired by the corporation.

Capital decreases to zero or below the legal minimum amount may only be decided when an increase beyond that minimum is simultaneously decided.

T.4.7.4 *Rights and obligations of shareholders*

The SC Act provides the following rights for shareholders:

(a) participation in the corporation's profits, *i.e.* a dividend;

(b) participation in the proceeds resulting from the winding up of the corporation;

(c) a preferential subscription right;

(d) voting rights at general shareholders' meetings and to challenge the corporate resolutions;

(e) information.

With regard to shareholder obligations, the main duty is to carry out the disbursement of a call on share capital regarding partly paid shares.

T.4.8 Corporate Bodies

The decision-making process in a limited corporation is entrusted to its shareholders. This is exercised through the general shareholders' meeting, and to some extent through the administrators appointed at the shareholders' meeting.

T.4.8.1 *The administrative body*

The corporation is managed and represented by administrators appointed by the general shareholders' meeting. It may decide to entrust these tasks either to a single administrator or to several administrators who can act individually or jointly, thereby forming a board of directors (if the number of directors exceeds two). If the management is entrusted to a single administrator, he will have the power to act on behalf of the company.

An administrator is not required to be a shareholder. The law states that those who are affected by certain circumstances (bankruptcy, minority, lack of legal capacity, conviction for serious infringement of law, legal disqualification for public charges, etc.) are not allowed to be administrators.

If several administrators are appointed to act individually on behalf of the Company, any provision in the byelaws or any decision adopted by the general shareholders' meeting concerning distribution of functions will be ineffective for third parties.

T.4.8.2 *The board of directors (Consejo de Administración)*

T.4.8.2.1 Appointment and dismissal of directors The appointment of directors, and how many (if the byelaws establish only the maximum and minimum number) is entrusted to the general shareholders' meeting. The board of directors must comprise of at least three directors.

The SC act establishes a system of proportional representation according to which any shareholder or group of shareholders owning shares representing an amount of capital equal to or higher than the result of dividing the capital stock by the number of board members, shall be entitled to appoint a proportional number of directors, not counting fractions.

If there are vacancies on the board, whilst the appointments are still valid, the board members may appoint as many shareholders as necessary to cover the vacancies until the general shareholders' meeting is convened. Dismissal of directors may be decided at any time by the general shareholders' meeting. The Law provides two special cases of dismissal, upon the request of any of the shareholders:

(a) those company administrators who act for competing corporations, or whose interests are opposed to those of the company, will be dismissed from the board by decision of the general shareholders' meeting;

(b) those administrators who are affected by any of the prohibitions established by law (*e.g.* bankrupts, convicted criminals, minors, incapables, etc., may not be appointed administrators), will be immediately dismissed.

The appointment of a director will be effective form the time of the nominee's acceptance. It will be presented for registration at the Mercantile Registry within the next 10 days. The name, age, condition, nationality, and domicile of the directors should be mentioned, stating if they should act jointly or may act individually on behalf of the company.

The duration of the appointments will be established by the byelaws, and will not exceed five years. Re-election is not restricted by law.

T.4.8.2.2 Attendance quorum and voting rights The SC Act establishes the general rules for board meetings which shall apply in all cases, unless otherwise provided for in the byelaws. These rules are as follows: the quorum is fixed at one-half plus one of its members present or duly represented and resolutions are adopted with the affirmative vote of the majority of the directors attending the meeting.

T.4.8.2.3 Managing director (Consejero delegado) and executive committee (Comisión Ejecutiva). According to the Share Companies Act, the board may approve rules concerning the performance of its duties, accept the resignation of its members; and appoint a president as well as an executive committee (or one or several managing directors), in addition to granting specific powers to any person when it is necessary (provided that the byelaws do not contain different regulations).

The board may delegate to the committee or to the managing directors many of its functions. The presentation of the company's balance sheets and accountancy to the general shareholders' meeting. The permanent delegation of powers to the committee or to the managing director, as well as their appointment must be approved by two-thirds of the directors and shall be ineffective unless they are registered.

T.4.8.2.4 Directors' fees The byelaws must specify the directors' remuneration. If it consists of a share in the company earnings, this shall be allocated from the net earnings, after the legal requirements concerning accounting reserves are fulfilled, and once the shareholders have been granted a dividend equal to 4 per cent (or higher if established in the byelaws).

494

In any case, the registration of the byelaw provisions concerning directors' fees is subject to the strict description and definition of the remuneration, be it a share in the earnings, or a fixed amount of money, or both.

T.4.8.2.5 Duties and powers of the board The administrators must perform their duties with the diligence of an orderly businessman and loyal representative; they are bound to secrecy on confidential information, even after the termination of their duties.

Directors are entitled to act on behalf of the company, within the scope of those activities which are connected with the company's business purpose as specified in the byelaws. Restrictions imposed on this power will be ineffective for contracting third parties, even though they have been registered. In addition, the company will be liable in damages to bona fide third parties for the directors' actions, even when the object mentioned in the byelaws clearly does not comprise those acts.

The power to represent the company is granted by the law to all the members of the board. However, the byelaws may entitle one or several specific members to represent the company, jointly or individually. In this case, and where an executive committee or managing director has been appointed by means of a delegation agreement, the actions of those who have power of representation must be strictly regulated.

T.4.8.3 *General shareholders' meeting (Junta de Accionistas): GSM*

T.4.8.3.1 General provisions A general shareholders' meeting may be ordinary or extraordinary. The first must be held periodically, at the time fixed in the byelaws. The SC Act establishes that an ordinary meeting must be held within the first six months of the financial year in order to examine the management of the corporation, approve the annual accounts and determine the profit distribution.

An extraordinary meeting is held for matters other than those of the ordinary meeting. The SC Act also provides, as a procedure for holding shareholders' meeting, the universal extraordinary meeting, at which shareholders attend representing all of the share capital, and who unanimously decide to hold the meeting.

T.4.8.3.2 The convening of a shareholders' meeting A meeting either ordinary or extraordinary, needs to be convened by the corporate administrators. Meeting will be convened whenever the administrators consider it convenient for the functioning of the corporation or when shareholders representing five per cent of the share capital request them to do so.

T.4.8.3.3 Notice of call for a shareholders' meeting General shareholders' meetings are called by means of a notice published in the *Official Gazette* of the Mercantile Registry and in one of the newspapers having a major circulation in the province, at least 15 days before the date set for the meeting. The notice will specify the agenda, date, hour and place for the meeting.

The notice may also include a second call for the meeting, in case the number of shareholders attending the meeting does not meet the prescribed quorum. Shareholders can meet again 24 hours after the first attempt.

If the notice does not contain a call for a second meeting, this must be called within 15 days by means of a second notice, to be published at least eight days in advance.

Nevertheless, as mentioned above, a meeting will be duly constituted whenever the entire capital is in attendance, and nobody present expresses opposition. This general shareholders' meeting is called a plenary or universal meeting (Junta Universal).

T.4.8.3.4 Due constitution and validity of resolutions On matters concerning the attendance and voting requirements of the general shareholders' meeting, the SC Act fixes general rules. Thus, the meeting is validly constituted when the shareholders attending represent 25 per cent of the paid-up stock capital at the first call. At the second call, the SC Act does not impose any quorums for attendance.

However, when the meeting has to decide on specific matters such as the issue of bonds, increase or reduction in share capital, transformation, merger, division or dissolution of the corporation, and generally, any amendment of the corporate byelaws, it must be attended, on first call, by shareholders who own at least 50 per cent of the paid-up stock capital. On the second call, the attendance of 25 per cent of such capital shall be sufficient. If shareholders representing less than 50 per cent of the paid-up voting stock are present then the above mentioned resolutions may only be validly adopted if two-thirds of the share capital present or represented at the meeting vote in favour thereof.

T.4.8.3.5 Voting rights and restrictions As regards the general rule on voting, the SC Act establishes that to obtain passage of an issue before the general shareholders' meeting approval must be given by a majority of those attending the meeting.

The SC Act states that the byelaws may require shareholders to possess a minimum number of shares in order to attend the meeting. Any shareholder having the right to attend the meeting may appoint another person, who need not be a shareholder, to represent him.

It should be pointed out that attendance and voting requirements may be altered in the byelaws, as long as they do not require that decisions should be adopted unanimously.

T.4.9 Accounting, Auditing and Financial Statements

The administrators of share companies must produce within three months following the end of the corporation's financial year, the annual accounts (consisting of the balance, profit and loss accounts, and the annual report), the management report and the proposal for the distribution of profits.

Share companies must prepare consolidated accounts when, as a partner of another corporation, the relationship towards the corporation falls within any of the following cases:

(a) when it has the majority voting right;

(b) when it has the power of appointing or removing the majority of the members of the management body;

(c) when it may exercise the majority of the voting rights by virtue of agreements concluded with other partners;

(d) when it has appointed, exclusively with its votes, the majority of members of the management body who are in office the moment in which the accounts should be prepared and for the two previous years, except if the corporation whose administrators had been appointed is related to another corporation as in the cases provided for in points (a) and (b) above.

The SC Act contains detailed rules on the structure of the balance, the profit and loss accounts, the valuation of the items appearing on said accounts and of the contents of the annual report.

The annual accounts and the management report must be audited by the auditors appointed by the general shareholders' meeting. They are to verify that the documents contain a honest description of the corporation's assets, financial situation, economic results, as well as the concurrence between the management report and the annual accounts. The auditors must submit the report to the ordinary meeting, which is held for the approval of the accounts. The annual accounts, the management report and the auditor's report have to be deposited for publication during the month following the ordinary meeting at the corresponding Commercial Registry.

It should be noted that "small" companies are exempted from the obligation of having their accounts audited and may prepare an abbreviated balance when they meet the conditions mentioned in the following point.

T.4.10   External Controls

T.4.10.1   *The auditors*

The annual accounts and the management report must be audited by the auditors appointed by the general shareholders' meeting for a period between three and nine years (re-election is possible, after three years from the termination of the previous period). Those companies which are entitled to present an abbreviated balance are exempted from this obligation.

Corporations will be excepted from the compulsory appointment of auditors, given that two of the following conditions are fulfilled within a period of two consecutive years:

(a) the assets side of the balance sheet amounts to less than 395 million Ptas;

(b) annual sales revenue does not exceed 690 million Ptas;

(c) the workforce comprises less than 50 workers.

Auditors are bound to present a report to the general shareholders' meeting, at least one month after the management report and annual accounts have been presented to them. They must supervise the company's accounts and verify that the company is operating in compliance with the law and the byelaws. They ensure the regular keeping of the company's accounts, and the fulfilment of the legal provisions for the evaluation of the company's assets.

The auditors must perform their duties with diligence being responsible for the truth of their statements. Actions against the auditors are governed by the same rules which apply to directors' liabilities.

Whenever the shareholders' meeting has not appointed the auditors, or those who were appointed do not accept their responsibilities, or cannot perform their duties, the corporate administrators, and the shareholders may request the Mercantile Registrar to appoint the person or persons who should carry out the audit.

The auditors' remuneration will be established before they start the performance of their duties, and it shall not be modified. Auditors cannot be removed, unless there are circumstances that justify it.

T.4.10.2 *The national stock exchange commission (Comisión Nacional del Mercado de Valores, CNMV)*

The Spanish Securities Market Act of 1988 describes the NSEC as an administrative entity, with its own legal personality and full public and private capacity to carry out its functions, the main being:

(a) to supervise and inspect the Securities Exchanges and the activities of its members;

(b) to act as an advisor for the Government and the Ministry of Economy and Finance, proposing the adoption of the necessary legal measures;

(c) to guarantee the openness of the Securities Exchanges and the protection of the investors, through the distribution of all kinds of information;

(d) to issue legal dispositions (Circulares) in order to enforce and develop the rules contained in the Royal Decrees enacted by the Government and the Ministry of Economy.

In particular, the Commission is responsible for verifying the fulfilment of the requirements established by law, prior to the acceptance of securities for trading. It also decides the suspension of delisting of securities for trading. It also decides the suspension or delisting of securities when certain conditions are not duly met, or when special circumstances occur that may disturb trading. The Commission also registers the information of different types provided by the issuers of listed securities, in compliance with the Securities Market Act dispositions, being entitled to ask for explanatory notes or additional information when necessary.

The CNMV also supervises and protects the interest of the investors when purchase and sale tender offers are intended. The Royal Decree No. 1197 of July 26, 1991 establishes its functions and faculties regarding such cases.

T.4.10.3   *The local courts*

The Share Companies Act provides for a judicial convening of the general shareholders' meeting, which is ordered by the first instance court (Juez de Primera Instancia) of the corporate domicile, whenever the meeting has not been duly convened by the administrators.

The Law also provides for judicial intervention in connection with the appointment of auditors. When justifying circumstances occur, the company administrators, and those who are entitled to ask the Mercantile Registrar for the appointment, may request the first instance court for the annulment of the appointment previously made by the meeting or by the Registrar, and for a new appointment.

Those general shareholders' meeting agreements which infringe the Law, breach the byelaws or damage the interest of the company, in favour of one or several shareholders or company creditors may be legally attacked by the shareholders, the administrators and third parties with lawful interest, before the first instance court of the social domicile.

Action for liability against the company administrators and auditors may be brought by the shareholders and the company creditors also before the local first instance court.

The local courts also intervene in many other moments of the existence of the company, such as for deciding its termination, if there was a bankruptcy, and in general wherever there is a need of protecting the rights of any interested party (shareholders and creditors basically).

T.4.11   Transformation of Share Companies

A share company may be transformed into a general partnership, a limited partnership or a private limited company. This transformation may be carried out at any moment during the corporation's life, whenever the general shareholders' meeting so decides. Those shareholders who voted against the transformation have the right to leave the corporation, receiving a reimbursement for their shares. Lastly, the transformation may also be effected into an Economic Interest Grouping.

T.4.12   Termination of Share Companies

Share companies may be terminated for any of the following reasons:

(a) by decision of the general shareholders' meeting;

(b) by fulfilling a term fixed in the byelaws;

(c) by the cessation of the business which constitutes the corporate object or the proven impossibility of carrying out the corporate purpose, or the blocking of the corporate bodies so that the running of the corporation becomes impossible;

(d) by the existence of losses that reduce the assets in more than one-half of the share capital, unless the latter was proportionally increased or decreased;

(e) by the decrease of the share capital below 10 million Ptas;

(f) by the merger or complete division of the corporation;

(g) by any other cause fixed in the byelaws;

(h) by the bankruptcy of the corporation, if the court decided such termination.

The decision to terminate the corporation may be made by the general shareholders' meeting, or by the court when so requested by the administrators or by any interest party. The decision has to be made public. Thereafter, the liquidation process commences. This involves the termination of the administrators' office and the appointment of the so-called "liquidators" appointed by the general shareholders' meeting who then represent the corporation during liquidation. Shareholders representing 5 per cent of the paid-up stock capital may request the court to appoint a controller for the supervision of the liquidation operations. The liquidators' function is to direct the distribution of the corporation's assets between shareholders after the corporation's creditors have been paid.

T.4.13   Financing Share Companies

Share companies may be financed either through the injection of funds by shareholders (that is, stockholders' equity) or by third parties (that is, debt funds).

Shareholder's equity is obtained by means of an increase of the share capital of the corporation (see increases/decreases of capital, T.4.6.3 above).

As regards debt, it may be created by issuing bonds. These may have a fixed or variable interest rate; they may be ordinary or come with special guarantees; they may be issued at a premium; they may be convertible into shares and they may be represented by registered or bearer titles or by book entries. The contents and formalities regarding security bond issues need to be communicated to the National Stock Exchange Commission.

It is also possible for a corporation to borrow funds from any third party in the form of loans. In the case of obtaining credit from financial institutions, the lender usually requires some form of guarantee for the payment of the interest rate and the return of the principal. The guarantees may be granted by the shareholders or by the corporation. In the first case, shareholders may act as bonders, pledging their shares or granting a mortgage on their assets. The corporation may likewise grant mortgages on its own assets and, if it has treasury stock, it may pledge its own shares.

SECTION 5

COSTS OF INCORPORATION

T.5.1 The costs of incorporation of commercial companies, (including corporate forms, such as accounts in participation), basically comprise:

(a) transfer tax levied on the issue of capital; this tax is charged at 1 per cent the total nominal value of the issue plus the premium, in the case of companies with limited liability: in any other case, the taxable base will consist in the real value of the partners' contributions;

(b) notary fees and costs; the former vary according to the amount of the capital issued: the latter comprise the drawing up and execution of the incorporation deed.

(c) registration costs; the cost of registrations of the corporation before the Mercantile Registry is approximately half of the notary fees.

SECTION 6

SPECIAL TYPES OF COMPANIES

T.6.1   Co-operative Company (Sociedad Cooperativa: SCoop)

These companies associate partners with common economic requirements and interests in terms of free incorporation and separation, and subject to a regime of variable capital and democratic structure and management.

The main feature of a co-operative company is its closed nature, based on the existence of some reciprocal services between the co-operative company and its own members, by the development of the commercial activity. Despite its unique nature, the Law contemplates different types of co-operative companies.

The incorporation of a SCoop, that may be made by successive or simultaneous foundation, must be recorded in public deed and registered at the special Registry existing in the Ministry of Employment.

There is no minimum capital required. Traditionally the law distinguishes between first-degree co-operatives, that will be comprised at least of five partners, and second-degree co-operatives, comprised at least of two partners, and created when, under the principle of co-operation between them, several co-operatives incorporate another one to achieve common interests. To acquire the status of a partner in a SCoop, it is necessary to comply with the requirements fixed in the byelaws and to make a compulsory contribution in cash, assets or rights, taking into account that a minimum of 25 per cent needs to be paid up. Associated members can only make capital contributions of less than 33 per cent of the whole sum.

Contributions are represented by registered bonds or registered notes of participation, and are only transferable to other partners.

The partners' liability is limited to their contributions, unless the byelaws state the opposite.

Benefits will be distributed in the following form: 30 per cent for the reserve fund and/or the instruction and promotion fund; and 70 per cent for the partners (proportionally to the services supplied), participation of workers, increasing the compulsory funds or creating a free reserve fund.

The adoption of resolutions is entrusted to the partners by means of a general meeting, and a regulatory board is responsible for management.

Co-operative companies are regulated by the Law of April 2, 1987. Currently, although this type of company is provided for in the Spanish Constitution and enjoys with it some tax benefits, it is not sufficiently used in Spain due to the competition with other corporate types within its same sector and the absence of an effective access to the market of capitals.

T.6.2 Mutual Guarantee Company (Sociedad de Garantia Reciproca: SGR)

These are financial entities with variable capital, whose partners are entrepreneurs. They are set up to guarantee the operations that the members may carry out in the exercise of their respective businesses. Similarly, they are an instrument of mercantile promotion, which allows assessing and promoting the investment made by small and medium-size enterprises.

The incorporation of a SGR requires authorisation from the Ministry of Economy and Finance. They are incorporated by means of a formal public deed, and must be registered at the Mercantile Registry and the special Registry of the Bank of Spain. At least 150 participants must participate in the act of incorporation.

There are two different types of members: "participants" and, if allowed in the byelaws, "protectors". The former are entitled to obtain guarantees for their operations; the latter just make contributions and receive dividends.

The capital of mutual guarantee companies should amount to at least 300 million Ptas and must be divided into participations, which are not easily transferable and can not be considered as shares. The capital should be totally subscribed and paid up on incorporation. Capital can be increased or decreased merely be decision of the board of directors, with certain limits.

The partners may not have a number of votes exceeding 5 per cent of the total, unless the byelaws establish a lower limit.

Mutual guarantee companies are governed by a general meeting and a board of directors, which follow the rules established by the SC Act. They are also subject to administrative control by the Ministry of Finance.

These corporations are designed to facilitate the financing of medium-and-small-size enterprises, by means of a technical provisions fund, which is part of the company assets.

Finally, they are ruled by Law 1/1994 of March 11, 1994, and have had an extensive development in Spain due to the guarantee provided by the Administration for their operations.

T.6.3 Mutual Insurance Company (Mutuas de Seguros)

The Private Insurance Regulation and Supervision Law of November 8, 1995, provides regulation for this type of company based upon the distinction between fixed premium and variable premium companies. The former are set up to cover those risks insured by means of a premium which is paid in advance by its members. These will not be responsible unless the byelaws establish such liability, in any case limited to an amount equal to the annual premium and may make capital contributions. Variable premium companies are based on the "mutual aid principle", and their purpose is the coverage of risks, by means of the distribution of damages after its occurrence among the members. These will be jointly liable, only for the amount of the insured capital.

Members should exceed 50 in number, and maintain a double liaison with the company: partnership, which entitles them to receive the interest accrued by their contributions to the capital and to the mutual funds, or a share in the earnings, if any; and insurance, which entitles them to receive compensation in case of damage. The Insurance Contract Law of 1980 applies to this relationship.

Variable premium companies are subject to a programme of their activities, which is approved by the Ministry of Economy and Finance, and may not carry out their operations within certain sectors. Directors will not receive remuneration and members must make initial contributions to a working fund.

SWEDEN

Section 1

TRADING COMPANIES*

U.1.1 Introduction

Two or more persons who have agreed to jointly carry on business in a company can do this in the form of a trading company. A trading company is regulated by the law (1980:1102) on trading companies and partnerships, and may acquire rights and assume obligations and also bring or defend actions in a court of law or before any other authority.

U.1.2 Registration

A trading company exists as soon as an agreement has been made between two or more parties jointly to carry on business in form of a company and the company has been registered in the Commercial Register. The documents shall be registered at the National Patent and Registration Office (Patent-och registreringsverket, "PRV"). From that date the company is an independent legal entity. Anyone has the right to ask PRV for a registration certificate regarding a certain trading company and from the registration certificate it is possible to see the names of the partners, their personal data, the name of the trading company and which types of business activity are conducted.

U.1.3 The Partners' Rights and Liabilities

Regarding the trading company the partners are jointly and severally liable for the company's obligations. Each partner represents the company, unless otherwise agreed or especially prescribed in law. A partner is obliged to be loyal to the other partners and an infringement of the loyalty clause may result in a cancellation of the agreement and the company is thereby dissolved.

* Mats Koffner, Advokatfirman Glimstedt (full particulars are listed in the Appendix).

507

A trading company can have a board handling the company's administration. The trading company is, however, usually managed by its partners without the constitution of a special board. A trading company entered in the commercial register can report to the register that a certain person is the procuration holder of the company. A procuration holder has the right to make agreements with binding effect for the trading company, but not agreements regarding business transactions as to real estate.

A creditor having claims against a trading company may direct his claim to the company or to one or more of the partners. It is not unusual that regarding disputes before a court of law the trading company as well as its partners are sued.

A partner who has left the company is liable for the obligations that the company has entered into before his departure. When a new partner joins the company he will also be liable for the obligations made before he joined the company.

U.1.4 Termination of Trading Companies

A trading company exists as long as the company agreement is valid. If the company agreement is to remain in force for an indefinite period, one of the partners may cancel the agreement at any time. The company shall then be entered into liquidation not later than six months after the cancellation, unless otherwise agreed. A trading company shall also be entered into liquidation if one of the partners dies or is declared bankrupt, unless otherwise agreed. At a liquidation the debts shall be paid, the assets disposed of and the surplus, if any, distributed among the partners.

U.1.5 Limited Partnership Company

A limited partnership company is under the same provisions as a trading company. The difference is that one or more of the partners are only liable for the debts of the limited partnership company to a certain extent, equivalent to a specially agreed investment. The investment is usually rather low, generally no more than 1,000 Skr. However, at least one partner must be fully liable for all of the obligations of the limited partnership company. The Swedish word for the partner who is fully liable for the company's obligations is "komplementär" (complementary partner). Those who have a limited liability equal to their investment are called "kommanditdelägare" (limited partner).

A limited partner may not represent the company. A legal act taken by a limited partner on behalf of the company shall, however, be binding on the company if the person (or company) against whom the transaction was taken could not have been aware of, or could not have been expected to be aware of, the fact that the person taking this action was a limited partner. Consequently, it is very important to get information about the contents of the Commercial Register. If a limited partner is entered as a limited partner in the Commercial Register third parties are deemed to have received notice of this fact.

U.1.6   Foundations

The Foundation Act (1994:1220) stipulates under what circumstances a foundation can be formed. A foundation is an independent legal entity and in general the rules for the board of directors, the auditors and book-keeping are the same as those which apply for normal trading companies. Not all foundations are obliged to be registered.

A foundation is normally characterised by the fact that a person has contributed money to a foundation and given the right of decision to another person or group of persons to administer the assets of the foundation. The income from the foundation's property shall go to someone whose purposes the foundation shall promote.

A foundation may carry on business activities, even if it usually has another function, as for instance to pay pensions to specially stated persons or to give contributions to scientific work or to persons in great need.

In order to form a foundation a memorandum of association is required wherein the purpose of the foundation shall be stated. A foundation formed in this way is an independent legal entity. A foundation carrying on business activities shall, however, in some cases be entered in the commercial register of the County Administration.

SECTION 2

CO-OPERATIVE AND UNINCORPORATED ASSOCIATIONS

U.2.1   Introduction

A distinction is made between co-operative and unincorporated associations. Associations with the purpose of promoting the economic interests of the members

509

through economic activities are called co-operative associations, while the other associations are called unincorporated associations.

The law (1987:667) regarding incorporated associations (Lag (1987:667) om ekonomiska föreningar) prescribes the provisions under which the economic activities of an incorporated association shall be carried on. These associations are usually buying associations.

U.2.2   Co-operative Associations

U.2.2.1   *Registration*

A co-operative association must have at least three members.

A co-operative association becomes a legal person when it is entered in the register of associations at PRV. Before the registration the association must have accepted certain rules and it must have appointed a board and auditors. The rules shall state, *inter alia*, the name of the association, the object of the association, the field of activities, the registered office of the board, the capital invested, the number of board members and auditors, the financial year, the date and calling of the association meeting and the rules regarding allocation of profit.

PRV studies, amongst other things, if the activities of the association really are such that it may be entered as an incorporated association. As soon as the association has been entered in the register it becomes a legal person and thereby an independent legal entity. The name of an incorporated association shall include the words "ekonomisk förening" (co-operative association) which also may be abbreviated to "ek för". A registration certificate can be ordered from PRV.

U.2.2.2   *Association meeting*

The highest decision-making body of an incorporated association is the association meeting. The right of decision is allocated in much the same way as in limited liability companies. Each member of the association normally has one vote at the association meeting, unless otherwise agreed.

U.2.2.3   *Appointment/dismissal of directors*

The board members of the co-operative association are appointed at the association meeting. The board shall consist of at least three members. The chairman is appointed by the board. At least one of the members of the board of directors shall be resident within the European Economic Area unless otherwise authorised in special circumstances by the Government or the public authority designated by the Government. The board decides who shall sign for the company.

U.2.2.4 *Duties/powers of directors*

The board is responsible for the organisation of the co-operative association and for the administration of its activities.

The majority principle is used for decisions within the board. A board member of a co-operative association has, on the whole, the same rights and liabilities as a board member in a limited liability company.

The board can appoint a managing director, which shall normally be done if the number of employees in the association exceeds 200. The managing director has in principle the same rights and liabilities as a managing director in a limited liability company.

For limited liability companies as well as for co-operative companies the rule is that the persons being entered in the register as board members and managing director have the right to sign for the company or the association in question.

U.2.2.5 *Audit/accounts*

The accounts shall be kept according to roughly the same rules as apply to limited liability companies. A co-operative association shall in its accounts divide its paid-up capital into restricted equity and non-restricted equity. Under the heading "restricted equity" the investments made by the members shall be stated. This investment can be compared with the share capital of a limited liability company. The association is free to state in its rules the size of the investment, which can be returned to a member who wishes to leave the association. Regarding the auditing of the accounts there must be at least one auditor. There are different requirements as to the auditor's qualifications, depending on the book value of the company.

U.2.2.6 *Exclusion of member*

The association meeting decides whether to exclude a member. The exclusion shall be made according to the rules of the association. A member who has been acting in an extremely disloyal way against a co-operative association can always be excluded from the association.

U.2.2.7 *Liquidation*

A co-operative association enters into liquidation according to the same rules as regards limited liability companies. The association is dissolved as soon as the liquidation procedure has been terminated. This rule also applies to bankruptcies.

U.2.3   Unincorporated Associations

Economic activities may be carried on in unincorporated associations. However, the unincorporated association is generally not working for profit, but its activities may have some economic elements. Trade unions, political parties, different sport associations, religious societies and professional organisations (for instance the Swedish Bar Association) are unincorporated associations. There is no legislation to regulate the activities of the unincorporated associations. The rules regarding limited liability companies and co-operative associations will therefore have to be complied with, where appropriate. The rules that the members have agreed upon are therefore an important instrument when analysing the activities of the association. These rules are usually accepted, unless they are contrary to other regulations.

SECTION 3

LIMITED LIABILITY COMPANIES

U.3.1   Introduction

The limited liability company is the most developed company form. The regulations regarding limited liability companies are subscribed in the Companies Act (1975:1385) (Aktiebolagslag (1975:1385)). There are two types of limited liability companies, public and private. A limited liability company becomes an independent legal entity as soon as it has been registered. Registration is made at PRV. Unless otherwise provided, the Company Act applies to all companies.

A private company shall possess a share capital of not less than 100,000 Skr and a public company shall possess a share capital of not less than 500,000 Skr. When the share capital is divided into several shares, all shares shall have the same value.

A private company, or a shareholder of such a company, may not attempt through advertising to distribute shares or debentures or warrants issued by the company. The restrictions set forth do not apply to offerings made to not more than ten purchases.

A number of laws are directly related to the activities of a limited liability company. Consequently, there is, *inter alia*, legislation concerning the right of the employees to be represented on the board of the limited liability company, special laws concerning the activities in bank companies, financial companies, stock market companies and a number of laws regulating the fiscal matters of a limited liability company.

U.3.2   Incorporation

U.3.2.1   *Articles of association (Bolagsordning)*

A limited company is formed by one or more founders. A founder should be residing in an E.C. country, be a Swedish legal person or be a legal person formed and having its activities within an E.C. country. Partnerships or corresponding legal entities, which are formed pursuant to the laws of a member state of the European Economic Area may, however, act as incorporators provided that each partner with unlimited liability is domiciled within the same area. The founders shall state the incorporation terms and they shall draw up and sign a dated memorandum of association, which amongst other things must include a proposal as to the articles of association. The articles of association must include the name of the company and where in Sweden the board of the company will have its registered office. Other important data that must be stated in the articles of association includes the object of the company's activities, the size of the share capital, the number of board members and which financial year shall be used. With regard to public companies, the names of which do not contain the word "public", the symbol (publ) shall be set forth in the articles of association following the company's name.

The incorporation documents including the articles of association and the minutes kept at the statutory meeting shall be sent to PRV to be registered. At the registration the limited company gets an organisation number of ten figures, always beginning with the figures 556. As soon as a limited company is registered it becomes an independent legal entity. PRV makes sure that the rules of the Companies Act have been complied with and that the chosen name does not infringe the right of another person to the name in question.

U.3.2.2   *Registered office (Säte)*

The registered office of the limited company must be stated in the articles of association. The registered office must be located in Sweden. A limited company may change its registered office by altering the articles of association and then register this anew.

U.3.2.3 *Company name (Firma)*

The company name must include the word "Aktiebolag", usually abbreviated "AB". PRV decides whether the chosen name may be registered. One hinderance may be that another company already had taken the name or that a well-known trade mark is included in the name but without permission. The name of a limited liability company must not be misleading to the public. Also note what is said above that public companies must include information hereabout in the name.

A limited liability company may register a so called subsidiary company for part of the company activities. The name of a subsidiary company must not include the word "aktiebolag" or the word "bolag" as the subsidiary company is not an independent legal entity.

U.3.2.4 *Duration*

A limited liability company exists until the day it has been dissolved by a liquidation procedure or declared bankrupt and the bankruptcy proceedings have been terminated without any surplus. If a bankruptcy has been terminated with some surplus a liquidation procedure shall be followed, after which the company is dissolved.

U.3.3 Shares (Aktier)

Normally, all shares have the same rights. The articles of association may decide that different kinds of shares shall be at hand or that such shares shall be possible to issue. In case of such a provision the articles shall state:

(a) the difference between the shares;

(b) the number of each kind of share;

(c) if the shares are not to have the same right to take part in the company's assets or profits, the shareholders' right of priority at an increase of the share capital.

The difference between the shares lies in the voting power, no share can have a voting power exceeding 10 times the voting power of another share.

A share certificate shall be issued to a particular person. It may be given to the shareholder only if his name has been entered in the share register and not until full payment has been made for share(s) stated in the share certificate. Share certificates shall be signed by the board or according to the board's power of attorney by a bank. Before a share certificate is issued the company may issue a warrant stating the right to one or more shares, "interimsbevis" (interim certificates).

The board of directors shall maintain a register (share register) of all of the company's shares and shareholders.

The articles of association may contain provisions to the effect that any person who, on a specified record date, is registered in the share register shall be deemed to be authorised to receive dividends and, where bonus issues are made, to receive new shares which vest in shareholders and to exercise shareholder's pre-emption rights to participate in share issues. Companies whose articles of association contain such provisions are referred to as VPC companies. For such VPC companies the Share Accounts Act (1989:827) stipulates that Värdepapperscentralen VPC AB (the Swedish Central Securities Depository) shall:

(a) maintain share registers;

(b) deal with matters regarding registration of shareholders in share registers;

(c) provide print-outs of share registers;

(d) distribute dividends and other questions in connection with registration.

U.3.3.1   *Share capital (Aktiekapital)*

The share capital of a private limited company shall be at least 100,000 Skr and for a public limited company at least 500,000 Skr. If the share capital is distributed on additional shares, these shares shall be of equal par value. At the incorporation of a limited liability company the whole share capital shall be paid up.

The minimum share capital shall be stated in the articles of association and it may be increased to a maximum amount equivalent to four times the minimum share capital, without having to alter the articles of association.

If the share capital of a company during its business activities, due to losses, is less than half of the registered minimum share capital the company shall be entered into liquidation, unless the annual general meeting within eight months has accepted a new balance sheet showing that the registered share capital has been restituted.

U.3.3.2   *Transfer of shares*

Shares in private limited liability companies may be connected with an obligation regarding offer of first refusal. The meaning of this is that if a person who is not already a shareholder in a certain private limited liability company acquires shares in this company, he shall report his acquisition to the company board, whereby the board, within a specified time-limit, shall offer these shares to the other shareholders. If this offer is not utilised the new owner shall be entered as shareholder in the share register.

Shares in public limited liability companies are normally traded on the Stock Exchange.

U.3.3.3 *Increase/decrease of capital*

The share capital must never be lower than 100,000 Skr for a private and 500,000 Skr for a public limited liability company. An increase of the share capital within the limit stated in the articles of association, equivalent to four times the specified lowest share capital, may be made without any alterations of the articles of association. Any other increase of the share capital requires an alteration of the articles of association, to be decided by the board and the meeting of the shareholders. The procedure is the same regarding decrease of the share capital.

At the issue of new shares a shareholder has a prior right to the new shares in proportion to the number of shares that he already holds, unless otherwise prescribed in the articles of association or decided in connection with the decision to issue. A share capital is not considered to be increased until the decided issue of new shares has been registered at PRV.

U.3.3.4 *Form of subscription*

The share capital should be paid either in cash or by other real kinds, "apportegendom". If the payment is made in cash, it shall be effected at the incorporation by deposition money on the company's bank account. The bank issues a bank certificate of the deposit.

If the payment is made in kind rather than cash, the memorandum of association shall state how the property has been valued and that the property is a benefit for the company. A certificate issued by a chartered accountant or an approved auditor shall be attached to the memorandum of association, stating that the property has been valued in a correct way and that it has been transferred to the company.

U.3.3.5 *Purchase of own shares*

The main rule is that a limited company must not acquire, or as a security receive, its own shares. A subsidiary must not either acquire, or as a security receive, shares in the parent company. Agreements contrary to this restriction are invalid. However, in connection with the taking over of a business or at a public auction a limited liability company is allowed to buy its own shares. Such shares shall be disposed of as soon as possible, at the latest three years after the date of acquisition.

U.3.3.6 *Register of shares*

All shares are entered in the share register where the name of the shareholder is also stated. As can be seen from the above the share register of some specific companies, mainly listed public limited companies, is kept by Värdepapperscentralen VPC AB.

U.3.4 Companies' Bodies

U.3.4.1 *General meeting (Bolagsstämma)*

The shareholder's right is exercised at a meeting of all the shareholders, the general meeting. The legislation makes no distinction between large and small companies as regards the general meeting, but in practice the differences are considerable.

In small private companies with one or a few shareholders the general meeting is often held in such way that minutes of the general meeting are written out and are thereafter signed by the keeper of the minutes, the chairman and the minutes-checker appointed at the meeting.

A shareholder shall be called to the general meeting as stated in the articles of association. The notice shall be sent four weeks before the general meeting at the earliest and usually no later than two weeks before the general meeting. The notice shall provide information about what issues will be dealt with at the meeting.

A general meeting shall be held at least once a year, not later than six months from the expiration of the company's financial year. At the ordinary general meeting the board and the auditors are appointed and the meeting shall decide how to handle the profits or the losses. At the ordinary general meeting the annual financial report including the calculation of results, the balance sheet, the audit report and the board's report concerning its administration of the company are presented.

An extraordinary general meeting shall be held whenever the board finds it necessary. The auditor of the company has also the right to demand that an extraordinary general meeting shall be held, as well as the owners of one-tenth of the shares in the company.

Only shareholders entered in the share register have the right to be present at the general meeting. With respect to VPC companies, the right to participate at shareholders' meetings vest in any person, who is registered as a shareholder in print-outs held by VPC at a certain day. Minutes shall be kept of the general meeting.

U.3.4.2 *Board of directors*

U.3.4.2.1 Appointment/dismissal of directors   A limited liability company shall have a board of at least three members. If the share capital does not exceed 1 million Skr the board may, however, consist of one or two members, if there is at least one deputy member. The board is appointed by the annual general meeting, unless it is prescribed in the articles of association that one or more members of the board shall be appointed in any other way.

The appointment of a board member is for the period as stated in the articles of association, usually one year, and for the period between the ordinary general meetings. A board member may be re-elected an unlimited number of times.

A board member can be dismissed from his post during his term of office by a decision at an extraordinary general meeting. A board member may also resign during his term of office. Any change in the board shall be registered at PRV.

The managing director and not less than one-half of the members of the board of directors shall be resident within the European Economic Area, unless otherwise authorised in special circumstances by the Government or the public authority designated by the Government. A board member must be at least 18 years of age and he must not be declared bankrupt.

U.3.4.2.2 Duties/powers of directors The board is responsible for the organ-isation of the company and for its administration. If a limited liability company has a managing director he shall handle the day-to-day administration according to the guidelines and the instructions stated by the board. The board and the managing director shall see to it that the activities of the company are carried on in accordance with law and that the book-keeping and the administration of the funds are being controlled in a satisfactory way.

The board decides who shall sign for the company. The board may authorise a director, the managing director or another person to represent the company and to sign the company name, unless otherwise prohibited by the articles of association. The right to sign for the company shall be reported to PRV for registration purposes.

A managing director is appointed by the company's board. He may always sign for the company in the day-to-day management. The board may at any time dismiss the managing director from his post. In a limited company carrying on rather extensive business activities it is not unusual that the managing director has a so called "parachute agreement", which entitles him to a salary during a certain period of time after the date of his dismissal.

The general rule is that the board members and the managing director are obliged to work for the interests of the company and to be loyal to the company. A board member or a managing director can be made responsible for failing to ensure, to a reasonable extent, that the company has paid its taxes and general fees and he is thereby becoming jointly liable for payment to the government of the unpaid amounts.

U.3.4.2.3 Board meetings One of the board members shall be appointed chairman of the board. The board forms a quorum when at least 50 per cent of the board members are present. Decisions of the board are subject to a majority vote. If not all the members of the board are present, at least one-third of the total number of board members must agree in order to pass a decision. Minutes shall be kept of the board meetings.

One important rule is that a board member or a managing director must not participate in decisions concerning any agreements between himself and the company or any agreements with a third party, in which he has a considerable interest, and which may be contrary to the interest of the company.

The chairman of the board shall ensure that board meetings are held whenever it is considered necessary. If a board member or a managing director demands that a board meeting shall be held, such a demand shall be complied with. A managing director, even if he is not a member of the board, has the right to be present and to speak at the board meetings, unless otherwise decided by the board.

U.3.4.2.4 Legal liabilities of directors Board members and managing directors are, as can be seen from the above, obliged to work for the interests of the company. If a board member or a managing director in his work is acting wilfully or with negligence, he can be made liable, and forced to pay for the damage which has arisen. If the Companies Act or other legislation is not followed the board members and the managing director may be convicted regarding this offence and punished by fines or imprisonment.

U.3.5 Audit/Accounts

U.3.5.1 *Appointment/dismissal of auditors*

All limited liability companies shall have at least one auditor. The auditor is appointed for the period of time stated in the articles of association. The auditor is usually appointed for the period between two ordinary general meetings. There are different requirements as to the auditor's qualifications, depending on the book value of the company.

An auditor may be dismissed during his term of office, but this does not prevent him from informing about the company's accounts and should he be dismissed he is obliged to inform about the facts that he has found at his auditing work during the part of the financial year that he has been working.

U.3.5.2 *Duties/powers of auditors*

The auditor shall present an annual audit report of the company's accounts. The audit report shall be presented at the ordinary general meeting. The auditor has the right to be present at the general meeting.

U.3.5.3 *Confidentiality of auditors*

An auditor is not allowed to give information to any unconcerned persons, regarding the company, which has come to his knowledge during the performance of his work, if this would be to the prejudice of the company.

519

SWITZERLAND

THE CORPORATION LIMITED BY SHARES*

V.1.1 Introduction

The corporation limited by shares (or simply referred to as the corporation) is by far the most widespread form of corporate organisation in Switzerland. Virtually all public companies are organised in the form of corporations. The appeal of the corporation to the business community may be explained by the fact that Swiss law preserves the parties' flexibility to adapt a corporation to their specific needs. The relevant section of the law governing the corporation is in Articles 620 to 763 of the Code of Obligations (CO). This section has recently been revised by the Swiss legislator and the amendments became effective as of July 1, 1992, with a transitory period expiring on June 30, 1997 (see in particular, V.1.3.1 below).

V.1.2 Incorporation

V.1.2.1 Articles of incorporation

A corporation limited by shares is formed by three or more natural persons or legal entities. Subsequent to its formation, the number of shareholders may fall to one (a so-called single member corporation). It is not required that the founders be Swiss citizens or companies registered in Switzerland. In the public deed of incorporation the founders declare to form a corporation, they determine the articles of incorporation and appoint the corporation's executive body (board of directors) and the auditors. Among other information, the articles or incorporation have to indicate:

(a) the name and the registered office of the corporation;

(b) the corporate purpose;

(c) the amount and composition of the share capital and the amount thereof which is paid in;

* *Jean-Paul Aeschimann and François Rayroux, Lenz & Staehelin (full particulars are listed in the Appendix).*

(d)   the number, nominal value and type of shares;

(e)   the convocation of the general shareholders' meeting;

(f)   the voting rights of the shareholders; and

(g)   the form of public announcements of the company.

Furthermore, a number of provisions are only binding on the shareholders and third parties if they are included in the articles of incorporation, such as:

(a)   provisions regarding the conversion of registered shares into bearer shares or vice versa;

(b)   the restriction of the transferability of registered shares;

(c)   the issuance of preferred shares and profit-sharing certificates; and

(d)   the restriction of voting rights.

Although not required by law, provisions on the distribution of dividends, the liquidation of the company and the business year are usually also part of the articles of incorporation.

The incorporation becomes effective with its registration in the Commercial Register. Before such registration, the founders form a simple partnership. The Commercial Registry then publishes the relevant information on the new corporation in short form in the Swiss *Official Gazette of Commerce*. It also examines summarily if the formation of the new corporation was done in compliance with the law.

V.1.2.2   *Registered office*

The registered office or statutory seat of the corporation must be stated in the articles of incorporation. The seat can be chosen freely within Switzerland and it is considered irrelevant if the registered office corresponds to the corporation's actual principal place of business. The corporation is free to move its registered office to a different place within Switzerland by simply modifying its articles of incorporation accordingly and by registering with the Commercial Register at its new seat.

V.1.2.3   *Company name*

The corporation may at will choose its name. The only restrictions imposed are that:

(a)   the name must not infringe the registered and protected name of another company; and

(b) if the name of a person is selected, an indication as to the legal form must be added (usually "AG" or "SA").

Furthermore, as a general principle, the name of the corporation must not be misleading to the public. As a practical matter, it is standard procedure to submit the proposed name to the Swiss Federal Commercial Register for approval.

A special consent of the Swiss Federal Commercial Registry is necessary if the name includes any national, territorial or regional designation, such as "Swiss Bank Corporation" or "Zurich Life". The authorisation is required not only with respect to references to Switzerland but also to foreign nations, regions and territories, including such terms as "international" or "overseas".

V.1.2.4 *Duration*

A corporation may be formed for a definite or an indefinite period of time. The majority of Swiss corporations are established for an indefinite period of time. If no term is fixed, it lies in the discretion of the shareholders to pass a resolution to dissolve the company, which will then have to be liquidated. It does not cease to exist as a legal entity, however, until it is deleted from the Commercial Register. The corporation may also be dissolved as a result of a bankruptcy proceeding, a court decree based on important reasons, or by way of merger. The dissolution by court order is an *ultima ratio* and may only be resorted to if there is a permanent deadlock situation in the corporation or if the majority shareholder is subject to systematic abuse by the majority shareholder.

V.1.3   Shares

V.1.3.1 *Share capital*

The minimum share capital of a company amounts to 100,000 Sfr. Corporations that were formed prior to January 1, 1985 are not required to adjust their capital to the new minimum standard. All other companies were given a transition period of five years which expired on June 30, 1997, to comply with the new minimum capital requirement. Pursuant to the new law, at least 50,000 Sfr have to be paid in as opposed to previously 20,000 Sfr. There is no maximum amount for a corporation's share capital. The revised law offers Swiss companies the possibility to provide for authorised as well as for contingent share capital (contingent share capital is created in connection with the issue of convertible debts or options, etc.).

The share capital represents the extent of the shareholders' liability for debts incurred by the corporation. As a protective measure the law prescribes that a general shareholders' meeting has to be called for if the annual balance sheet shows that half of the share capital is no longer covered by the company's assets.

525

Moreover, if the claims of the corporation's creditors are no longer covered by its assets, the management (and, as the case may be, the auditors) has to notify the judge who will then decide whether the company should be placed in bankruptcy.

V.1.3.2 *Increase and decrease of share capital*

Under the revised 1992 law, three types of share capital increases are provided for: the ordinary capital increase, the authorised capital increase and the contingent capital increase. Each of these types requires a change of the corporation's articles of incorporation, and is therefore subject to a shareholders' resolution. However, under the authorised capital increase, it is the board of directors which decides within two years of the vote of the relevant shareholders' resolution and within the limits set by such resolution, on the actual amount of the capital increase. As to the contingent capital increase, the new capital is created whenever conversion or option rights are exercised. New shares may be issued in the form of the existing shares or in any other form, depending on the shareholders' meeting. Unless waived for important reasons in the relevant shareholders' resolution, each shareholder is entitled to receive new shares in proportion to his existing shareholding. The capital increase will become effective at the time of its recording in the Commercial Register.

The decrease of a corporation's share capital requires a shareholders' resolution to that effect. Any such resolution is subject to a special audit report stating unequivocally that despite the decrease of the share capital all creditor claims will be fully covered. Under no circumstances may the share capital be decreased below 100,000 Sfr. After the general shareholders' meeting has resolved to decrease the share capital, the creditors are to be notified of such resolution by public announcement and are given the opportunity to ask for payment or security for their claims within a delay of two months. Upon the lapse of the two months' period, the corporation may proceed to reduce its share capital which will become effective with its entry in the Commercial Register.

V.1.3.3 *Forms of subscription*

The share capital may be paid in cash or by means of a contribution in kind or by way of set-off. If payment is made in cash, it needs to be deposited with a bank in an account in the name of the corporation. The bank will issue a certificate of deposit in escrow. If payment is made by means of a contribution in kind, the articles of incorporation must indicate the type of assets contributed, their evaluation, the person making the contribution and the number of shares given in consideration thereof. In addition, under the amended statute, a special audit report has to confirm the evaluation of the contribution in kind or the existence of the claim against which the set-off is applied, as the case may be.

V.1.3.4 *Purchase of own shares*

Traditionally, and except under very limited circumstances, a Swiss corporation was not allowed to purchase its own shares. Such circumstances included the implementation of a reduction of the share capital, the acquisition in settlement of claims of the corporation or as a result of an acquisition of an estate or a business. Shares acquired under such circumstances either had to be cancelled immediately or sold as soon as possible. Shares acquired by the corporation could not be voted and had to be recorded in the corporation's annual report. The revised law is more lenient with respect to the purchase of own shares. The company shall be permitted to repurchase up to 10 per cent of its own share capital, provided the purchase price is paid out of net profits, retained earnings or other free reserves. The purchase of shares of a corporation by its subsidiary is treated like a repurchase of the corporations's own shares. The revised law preserves the rule pursuant to which the corporation is not permitted to vote using its own shares.

V.1.3.5 *Share register*

All registered shares are entered in the company's share register where the names and address of each shareholder and each usufructary are listed. Each corporation with registered shares outstanding keeps its own share register, which is not available for public inspection. There is no register for bearer shares.

V.1.4 Corporate Structure

V.1.4.1 *General shareholders' meeting*

A Swiss corporation is required to hold annual shareholders' meetings, so-called "ordinary shareholders' meetings". They must be convened within six months following the close of the corporation's business year. The meeting is called by the board of directors which also selects the date and place thereof. Special shareholders' meetings, so-called "extraordinary shareholders' meetings", may be held at the request of:

(a) the board of directors;

(b) the auditors;

(c) the representatives of holders of bonds issued by the corporation, if any;

(d) the liquidators; and

(e) shareholders representing at least 10 per cent of the share capital.

527

If all shareholders are present or represented at the general shareholders' meeting (the so-called "universal meeting"), all notice requirements may be waived. This is particularly relevant for closely-held companies with one or only a few shareholders.

Shareholders are convened to the shareholders' meeting in the manner stated in the articles of incorporation. By law, registered shareholders must be given special notice, usually by way of registered mail, while holders of bearer shares must be given notice through a press announcement in the Swiss *Official Gazette of Commerce*. In the case of publicly-held corporations, they are usually also given notice in daily newspapers. Previously, the notice had to be given at least 10 days prior to the date of the meeting; under the revised law, this notice period is extended to 20 days. Together with the notice of such meeting, the shareholders have to be provided with the agenda stating all items that will be discussed at the meeting. Specific information that needs to be made available to the shareholders is the balance sheet and profit and loss statement, the auditors' report, the business report, the proposals concerning allocation of net profits and proposals to amend the articles of incorporation.

The revised law has abolished all existing statutory quorum requirements, but decisions that are subject to quorum requirements may be provided for under the articles of incorporation.

Unless provided otherwise in the articles of incorporation, all shareholders' resolutions are passed by simple majority of votes represented at the relevant shareholders' meeting. For a number of resolutions, however, a majority of two-thirds of the represented share capital is mandatory. Such resolutions include the capital increase against contribution in kind, the conveyance of preferential rights in connection with a capital increase, the change of the corporate purpose or the creation of voting rights.

Subject to the articles of incorporation, voting by proxy is permissible.

V.1.4.1.1 Shareholders' rights in general

V.1.4.1.1.1 Overview Swiss company law distinguishes between (i) shareholders' rights which are inalienable, *i.e.* of which the shareholders cannot be deprived ("vested rights"), and (ii) shareholders' rights which may be restricted or suppressed (as the case may be subject to additional requirements, such as voting quorums and/or the existence of qualified reasons).

Vested rights include, in particular, (i) the shareholders' rights of equal treatment, (ii) the right to exercise voting rights at shareholders' meetings, and (iii) the right to challenge a decision of the shareholders' general meeting in court.

Shareholders' rights which may only be restricted subject to qualified conditions include (i) the suppression of subscription rights (see V.1.4.1.5 below), (ii) the creation of an "authorised" or "conditional" capital (as defined in V.1.4.1.4 below), a capital increase out of equity or against contributions in kind as well as (iii) the dissolution of the company without liquidation (*i.e.* by way of merger).

For example: the merger of the company into a parent company would be subject to the approval of the general meeting of shareholders which must be passed by at least two-thirds of the votes represented and the absolute majority of the par value of shares represented at the meeting.

V.1.4.1.1.2 Right of equal treatment The minority shareholders may, in circumstances being equal, claim the right of equal treatment with the majority shareholder.

For example: the minority shareholders would be entitled to claim, in the context of the company's merger into a parent company controlled by the majority shareholder, to be treated equally with the majority shareholder. Further, in the event that the company resolves to buy back its own shares, the board of directors must treat all shareholders equally. Subject to the existence of qualified reasons, the board of directors may formulate different offers to different categories of shareholders. In this context, the term "category of shareholders" means different classes of shares as expressed in terms of voting rights or financial claims. Minority shareholders do not represent, as such, a different category of shareholders which would justify that they be subject to a different treatment as compared to the majority shareholder.

Further, the offer formulated by the company's board of directors must correspond to market prices, *i.e.* the determination of the offer price must correspond to the intrinsic value of the shares, or to their stock exchange price. Considerations paid to shareholders accepting to present their shares for repurchase by the company must be equal not only as regards their amount, but also in respect of the other terms and conditions of the purchase price payment (time-limit, formalities, etc.).

For the present, the question remains open whether, in the context of the acquisition of the company's shares by a third party (as opposed to a merger), the company's board of directors would, pursuant to the right to equal treatment, be obliged to arrange for the offer of that third party to be based on equal terms for *all* shareholders, *i.e.* to exclude the payment of a "control premium" to the majority shareholder and to deprive the minority shareholders of such premium. This question has never been tested in Swiss courts.

In our analysis, Swiss company law would not provide for a legal basis which would allow such a claim by a minority shareholder to be enforced. However, it is to be noted that under the new Swiss Stock Exchange Law ("SESTA"), the price offered in the context of a public takeover offer must be at least as high as the stock exchange price and may not be lower than 25 per cent of the highest price paid by the offeror for equity securities of the offeree company in the preceding 12 months (Art. 32, para. 4, SESTA).

V.1.4.1.1.3 No fiduciary duties of the majority shareholder towards the minority shareholders? Swiss company law and case law do not provide for a basis which would allow to derive a particular fiduciary duty of the majority shareholder towards the minority shareholders, as opposed to, for example, the United States. Certain textbook authors have, however, recently taken the position that such a fiduciary duty could be construed in special and exceptional cases.

V.1.4.1.2 Transparency of important shareholdings Pursuant to Art. 663c CO, companies whose shares are listed on a Swiss or foreign stock exchange are obliged to publish, in the attachment to their annual financial statements, a list reflecting the company's "important shareholders and their participations".

This disclosure obligation is imposed on the company, but not on the shareholders. The latter are obliged under Arts 20, *et seq.*, of SESTA, in the context of listed companies, to disclose important shareholdings in the event their participations fall below or exceed the threshold percentages of 5, 10, $33\frac{1}{3}$, 50 or $66\frac{2}{3}$ per cent of the voting rights.

V.1.4.1.3 Transparency of financial statements The 1992 Swiss Company Law provides through enhanced accounting rules for more information as compared to the previous regime, *inter alia*, for the benefit of minority shareholders. In this context, we note:

(a) minimum requirements as to the structure and content of the financial statements (Art. 662a CO, Art. 663 CO and Art. 663a CO);

(b) the obligation to contain the previous year's figures (Art. 662 para. 1 CO);

(c) the obligation to provide for an attachment to the balance sheet containing certain minimum information;

(d) the obligation to issue consolidated statements of accounts in the event the company is in control of a group of companies (Arts 663e CO).

Enhanced requirements as to the auditing of the financial statements further strengthen the information provided to minority shareholders (Arts 727, *et seq.*, CO).

However, Swiss accounting principles, as laid down in the CO, do not ensure a "true and fair view" of the company's financial position, as provided by international accounting standards (such as IAS or GAAP) as "hidden reserves" through (i) the undervaluation of assets, or (ii) the overvaluation of liabilities, are permitted to the extent justified with regard to the continuing prosperity of the company and taking into account the interests of the shareholders (Art. 669 CO).

In respect of listed companies, more stringent rules apply as the 1996 Listing Regulations require companies listed on the Swiss Stock Exchange to prepare their consolidated financial statements so as to provide for a "true and fair view" of their financial position, the results of operations and the cash flows of the group. See V.1.4.1.13 below.

V.1.4.1.4 Capital restructuring

V.1.4.1.4.1 Ordinary share capital, authorised share capital and conditional share capital As a reminder, we note that a share corporation organised under the laws of Switzerland must have a minimum capital of 100,000 Sfr, of which at least 50 per cent or 50,000 Sfr must be paid in cash or in kind. Shares are issued in registered or in bearer form.

An increase of the company's ordinary share capital requires a simple majority of the votes represented at the shareholders' meeting. That resolution must be made in the form of a notarised deed and contain certain minimum information.

In the event of the creation of an "authorised capital" or of a "conditional capital", a resolution of the general meeting of shareholders passed by at least two-thirds of the votes represented and the absolute majority of the par value of shares represented is required. The same quorum applies in the event of the increase of the Company's share capital out of equity, or against contributions in kind. In this context:

—"Authorised share capital" is defined as the power conferred by the shareholders to the company's board of directors to increase the share capital within a period of no more than two years; the authorised share capital may not exceed half of the outstanding ordinary share capital.

—The "conditional capital" allows the increase of the company's capital for the benefit of obligees of new bond issues, or similar debt instruments (options, etc.) of the company, or its group companies, as well as employees, whereby the company's share capital is increased each time such obligees or employees exercise their conversion or option rights to acquire shares in the company; the amount of the conditional capital may not exceed half of the amount of the company's share capital.

For an example, see V.1.4.1.1.1 hereof.

V.1.4.1.4.2 Shares with privileged voting rights   The articles of association may provide for shares with privileged voting rights, *i.e.* providing for voting rights based on the number of shares held by each shareholder irrespective of the par value (*e.g.* shares of a par value of 100 Sfr bearing the same voting rights as those with a par value of 1,000 Sfr).

In such a case, the shares with a smaller par value, *i.e.* those with privileged voting rights, must be issued as registered shares and be fully paid in. The par value of the remaining shares may not exceed 10 times the par value of the shares with privileged voting rights. It is to be noted that shares which, while providing for the same par value, confer different voting rights to one or more classes of shares, are not permitted under Swiss law.

The determination of the voting rights in accordance with the number of shares, *i.e.* the exercise of the "privilege", is inapplicable to:

(a) the election of auditors;

(b) the appointment of experts for the review of the management of the company;

(c) the resolution concerning special audit (see V.1.4.1.10.2 below);

(d) the decision of the initiation of an action for responsibility against directors, auditors, etc. (see V.1.4.1.11.4 below).

V.1.4.1.5 Pre-emptive rights In the event of the increase of the company's share capital, each shareholder is by law entitled to a portion of the newly issued shares corresponding to his prior participation. The same rule applies in the context of the issue of bonds, or of similar debt instruments, connected with conversion or option rights, or "bare" options, which confer the right to subscribe for shares as a result of the exercise of the "conditional capital" (see V.1.4.1.4 above). In this case, such debt instruments or options must be previously offered for subscription to all other shareholders in proportion of their participations.

These pre-emptive rights are, in particular, designed to protect the interests of the minority shareholder, *i.e.* to maintain their proportional shareholdering in the event shares or debt instruments with conversion rights are issued below their market value.

Pre-emptive rights may only be restricted:

(a) for "valid reasons" which are defined to encompass, in particular, the takeover of an enterprise, or part of an enterprise, or of participations as well as for the participation of employees, whereby no one shall be advantaged or disadvantaged by such withdrawal without proper reasons (Arts 652b and 643 CO); and

(b) by a resolution of the general meeting of shareholders passed by at least two-thirds of the votes represented and the absolute majority of the par value of shares represented (Art. 704, subpara. 1, cipher 6 CO).

V.1.4.1.6 Calling and agenda of a general meeting of shareholders Minority shareholders representing together at least 10 per cent of the share capital have the right to request the calling of the general meeting of shareholders. Further, shareholders representing shares of a par value of 1 million Sfr at least may request the inclusion of items on the agenda. The calling and the inclusion on the agenda is to be requested in writing and with details of the items and motions to be placed on the agenda. In the event the board of directors fails to comply with such request, the judge at the registered office of the company may be asked to order the calling of the meeting, as requested by the minority shareholders.

V.1.4.1.7 Transfer restrictions Under Swiss company law, the company's articles of association may provide for restrictions applicable to the transfer of registered shares (but not of bearer shares).

In the event of registered shares which are listed, the only restriction which may apply, if the company's articles of association so provide, is a percentage limit which, when exceeded, confers to the company the right to refuse the registration of the shareholder in respect of those shares which exceed that limit. As opposed to the old law, the company may not anymore refuse the registration of shareholders based on other reasons than the passing beyond the percentage limit. This enhances the liquidity of the shares and serves the interests of the minority shareholders.

It is to be noted that the relevant regime applicable to shares which are not listed on a stock exchange is different and that further restrictions may apply.

V.1.4.1.8 Special quorums for important resolutions The protection of minority shareholders is further achieved through the application of particular quorums in the event of important resolutions which, as already indicated, require the approval of at least two-thirds of the votes represented and the absolute majority of the par value of the shares represented at the shareholders' meeting. These voting quorums apply in the event of:

(a) the change of the company's object;

(b) the creation of shares with privileged voting rights (see V.1.4.1.4.2 hereof);

(c) the introduction of restrictions on the transfer of registered shares (see V.1.4.1.7 hereof);

(d) the creation of an authorised or conditional capital (see V.1.4.1.4.1 hereof);

(e) the increase of capital out of equity, against contribution in kind, or for the purpose of the acquisition of assets and the granting of special benefits;

(f) the limitation or withdrawal of pre-emptive rights (see V.1.4.1.5 hereof);

(g) the change of the company's domicile;

(h) the dissolution of the company without liquidation (see V.1.4.1.11.1 hereof).

The required approval of the absolute majority of the par value of the shares represented limits the voting power of the privileged shares (see V.1.4.1.4.2 hereof).

V.1.4.1.9 Board representation Pursuant to Art. 709 CO, the company's articles of association must ensure to the shareholders, in case there are several classes of shares as expressed in terms of voting rights or financial claims, the election of at least one representative for each class to the board of directors. Minority shareholders do not, as such, represent *per se* a class entitled to appoint a representative to the company's board of directors.

V.1.4.1.10 Right of information

V.1.4.1.10.1 Shareholders' meeting Pursuant to Art. 697 CO, shareholders may request at the general meeting of shareholders information from the board of directors concerning the affairs of the company as well as information from the auditors concerning the execution and the results of their examination.

That information must, however, only be given by the company to the extent necessary for the exercise of the shareholders' rights, and may be refused if business secrets or other interests of the company worth being protected are jeopardised.

The company's books and correspondence may only be inspected with the express authorisation of the general meeting of shareholders or by a resolution of the board of directors and subject to the safeguarding of business secrets. In the event information requests are unjustifiedly refused by the company, the shareholders may seize the judge at the company's domicile and request that the company be ordered to comply with their request.

V.1.4.1.10.2 Special audit   An important means in the hands of minority share-holders has been introduced in the 1992 revision of Swiss company law. This is the shareholders' right to request, at the general meeting of shareholders, that certain facts be subject to a special audit in accordance with Arts 697, *et seq.*, CO. The special audit may only be granted if it is necessary for the exercise of shareholders' rights and if the right of information or the right of inspection, described under V.1.4.10.1 hereof, has been previously exercised. In the event the general meeting of shareholders approves that motion, the company or any shareholder may, within 30 days, request the judge to appoint a special auditor.

In case of refusal of that motion by the general shareholders' meeting, shareholders representing together at least 10 per cent of the share capital, or representing shares with a par value of 2 million Sfr, may request the judge to appoint a special auditor. The applicants are entitled to the appointment of the special auditor if they credibly establish that founders, or corporate bodies, have violated the law or the articles of association and, thereby, damaged the company or the shareholders.

The special auditor, once appointed, shall within reasonable time issue a detailed report on the results of his special audit and submit that report to the judge who then must send the report to the company and decide, upon the latter's request, if parts of the report violate business secrets or interests of the company worth being protected and, therefore, may not be presented to the applicants. Both the company and the applicants must have an opportunity to take a position on the audit report and to ask supplementary questions.

The board of directors must submit the report and positions thereon to the next general meeting of shareholders. Any shareholder may, during one year after the general meeting of shareholders, request a copy of the report and of the positions.

The special report is an important means in the hands of minority shareholders for the filing of subsequent actions against members of the board of directors for damages caused to the company.

V.1.4.1.10.3 Right of information and inspection of board members   Members of the board of directors may, pursuant to Art. 715a CO, request information about all matters concerning the company. At meetings of the board of directors, all members are obliged to provide information requested. Outside such meetings, any member may request from the persons entrusted with the management information concerning the course of the business and, with the authorisation of the chairman, information concerning specific matters. Further, any member of the board of directors has the right, to the extent necessary for the performance of his duties, to apply to the chairman to be shown the books and the files of the company. If the chairman declines such a request for information, a hearing or an inspection, the board of directors shall decide.

V.1.4.1.11.1 Remedies

V.1.4.11.1.1 Challenging of resolutions of the general meeting of shareholders Any shareholder, including the minority shareholders, as well as the board of directors may take legal actions against the company to challenge resolutions of the general meeting of shareholders which violate the law or the articles of association. Decisions which are challengeable include those which:

(a) withdraw or limit shareholders' rights thereby violating the law or the articles of association;

(b) withdraw or limit shareholders' rights without proper reason;

(c) discriminate against or disadvantage shareholders in a manner not justified by the company's purpose;

(d) withdraw the profit orientation of the company without the consent of all shareholders.

For example, the resolution of the general shareholders' meeting to merge the company into the parent would be subject to challenge, *e.g.* in case the valuation methods used for the calculation of the exchange ratios of the shares were clearly unjustified, discriminating or false.

The right to challenge decisions of the general shareholders' meeting lapses if a suit is not filed within two months with the general shareholders' meeting.

V.1.4.1.11.2 Nullity of certain resolutions of the general shareholders' meeting Certain decisions of the general shareholders' meeting are deemed to be null and void in case of severe violations of the articles of association or Swiss company law, *i.e.* those resolutions which:

(a) withdraw or limit the shareholders' right to participate in the general shareholders' meeting, the minimum voting right, the right to sue as well as other rights granted by mandatory provisions of law; and

(b) limit the shareholders' voting right to control beyond the extent provided by law.

V.1.4.1.11.3 Opposition with the Register of Commerce Under Article 32 of the Federal Ordinance on the Register of Commerce, any opponent to the registration of a modification in the company's status with the Register of Commerce may file an opposition with the Head of the Register of Commerce, who is obliged to suspend such registration and to fix to the opponent a time limit for filing with the competent court at the company's seat for a temporary restraining order. In the event the court does not grant that temporary restraining order, the head of the

Register of Commerce must proceed with the registration of the proposed modification which, accordingly, becomes effective. In practice, the threat of such opposition with the Head of the Register of Commerce, which is not subject to any particular requirements as to form and content, is an important means in the hand of the minority shareholders to defend their rights against the majority shareholder.

V.1.4.1.11.4 Actions against board members, officers, auditors, etc. Members of the board of directors, as well as all persons who have participated in the management of the company, may become liable to the company, to the shareholders and the company's obligees for any damage caused as a result of an intentional or negligent violation of their duties.

Directors or officers delegating the fulfilment of duties to another corporate body remain liable for any damage caused by the latter unless they prove that they have applied the necessary care in selection, instruction and supervision required under the circumstances.

In addition to the company, each shareholder is entitled to file an action for damages caused to the company (*i.e.* "derivative suit"). The claim of the shareholders is for performance to the company.

In the case of bankruptcy of the company, the obligees of the company are also entitled to request that damages suffered by the company be compensated.

In the event that several persons are liable for damages caused to the company, any one of them is liable jointly and severally towards the others to the extent that the damage is attributable to such a person based on the latter's fault under circumstances. The plaintiff may sue several participants jointly for the total damage and request that the judge sets the liability for each individual defendant in the same proceeding.

Claims for compensation of damages against persons responsible for the management of the company are time barred after five years calculated from the day the plaintiff received knowledge of the damages and of the persons liable, but in any case after expiration of ten years, calculated from the day of the act causing the damage. Actions are to be filed at the place of the company's registered office.

For example, the company's board of directors, or the management, resolves to enter into an uneconomic transaction to the detriment of the company, but for the benefit of the majority shareholder in violation of its duties (*i.e.* an action which is in contradiction to their obligation not to enter into transactions which are unilaterally to the detriment of the company). In such an event, Swiss courts apply stringent standards for the appreciation of the liability of members of the board of directors and of the management.

1.4.1.12 Swiss stock exchange law The SESTA calls for mandatory takeover of Swiss listed companies when a shareholder (or a group of shareholders acting "in concert" or constituting an "organised group") exceeds the threshold of $33\frac{1}{3}$ per cent of the votes. Minority shareholders may, but are not obliged to present their shares in the context of public takeover offers within the meaning of Arts 22, *et seq.*, SESTA.

This being said, Article 33 of the SESTA provides for the possibility to cancel outstanding equity securities in the event that an offeror, following a public takeover offer, owns more than 98 per cent of the voting rights of the offeree company. In this case, the offeror may request through judicial proceedings that the outstanding equity securities be cancelled. To this effect, the offeror has to commence an action against the company. The remaining minority shareholders may participate in these proceedings.

In case of success of the offeror's request, the company must reissue equity securities and allot them to the offeror either against payment of the offer price, or the fulfilment of the exchange in favour of the holders of the equity securities which have been cancelled.

Offerors have the obligation, in the context of public takeover offers, to provide in the prospectus for true and complete information. The principle of equal treatment is implemented through an express provision stating that all holders of equity securities of the same class must be treated equally (Article 24 of the SESTA).

Minority shareholders are further protected by Article 27, paragraph 2 of the SESTA, which provides that, in the event the conditions of the offer are met, the offeror must extend the offer period for those holders of shares and other equity securities who have not yet accepted the offer.

The principle of equal treatment does however not apply without restrictions. Holders of control blocks may be offered a premium. However, the minimum price in the context of a mandatory public takeover is the stock exchange price, and the maximum price may not be higher than an amount exceeding 25 per cent of the highest price paid by the offeror for the relevant equity securities in the preceding 12 months.

V.1.4.1.13 Listing rules

V.1.4.1.13.1 Financial statements Financial statements of listed companies must be established in accordance with the (domestic) "FER/RPC" principles. These ensure a "true and fair" presentation of the company's assets and liabilities (as opposed to Swiss company law; see V.1.4.1.3 hereof).

V.1.4.1.13.2 "Ad hoc" publicity Any issuer is, under the new listing rules, obliged to inform the market forthwith of any price sensible facts which have arisen in its sphere of activity and are not public knowledge. The term "price sensible facts" means new facts which, because of their considerable effect on the issuer's assets and liabilities, or financial position, or on the general course of business, are likely to result in substantial movements in the price of the securities.

The issuer must provide such information without delay as soon as it has knowledge of the main points of the price sensible facts in question. A postponement of the disclosure of such material information is only admitted if the new facts are based on a plan or a decision of the issuer and if its dissemination is likely to prejudice the legitimate interests of the issuer. In such a case, the issuer must guarantee the complete confidentiality of such facts. Any disclosure must be carried out so as to ensure equal treatment of all market participants.

V.1.4.1.13.3 Delisting procedure The procedure in view of the delisting of a company's share would not be subject to particular requirements as to form and content. The company would be required to submit a request to the Admission Board of the Swiss Stock Exchange. With the Admission board's approval, the company would proceed with the publication of the information that it will proceed with the delisting of its shares. However, the Admission board would only issue such an approval if it is satisfied that the interests of the minority shareholders are sufficiently protected.

V.1.4.2 Board of directors

V.1.4.2.1 Appointment and dismissal of directors There is a single-tier board system in Switzerland where the board directly instructs and supervises the management. The board of directors consists of one or several directors who must be shareholders of the corporation. If the board is composed of more than one member, the majority must be Swiss citizens resident in Switzerland; in the case of a single member, he must be a Swiss citizen resident in Switzerland. If there is more than one class of shares outstanding, each class is entitled to appoint one representative to the board.

The directors are elected by the general shareholders' meeting. They may be appointed for a tenure of up to six years, the typical period being three years. There are no limitations as to their re-election. A director may be dismissed from office during his regular tenure by a decision of an extraordinary general shareholders' meeting. A board member may also resign during his term of office. Any such change needs to be recorded in the Commercial Register.

V.1.4.2.2 Duties and authority of directors Generally speaking, the board is responsible for the organisation, administration and operation of the company. For this purpose, the board may enact regulations and guidelines. More specifically, the board has to prepare the business of the general shareholders' meetings and execute their resolutions, supervise management, prepare an annual business report containing the annual financial statement, and notify the judge as soon as the claims of creditors are no longer covered by the corporation's assets.

The board is authorised to delegate certain of its powers to committees or individual directors, such as managing directors. Furthermore, it appoints the persons authorised to sign on behalf of the company.

As to the extent of authority, the board of directors may perform all legal acts on behalf and in the name of the corporation that are not excluded by the general corporate purpose as described in the articles of incorporation. Restrictions on these powers to act have no effect with regard to bona fide third parties unless such restrictions are entered in the Commercial Register and relate to the exclusive representation of the principal office or of a branch office or to the collective representation of the corporation.

The board is under an obligation to act exclusively in the best interest of the corporation, as distinct from the selfish interest of the shareholders. Each director is liable to the company and its shareholder for any breach of his fiduciary duties. In determining their responsibility, decisions made and actions taken by the directors are measured against a general standard applying to the duty of care under Swiss law. Among the directors there is joint and several liability with respect to damages caused by their negligence or wilful misconduct (see V.1.4.1.11.4).

V.1.4.2.3 Board meetings The chairman of the board usually calls board meetings, but any member of the board may request that a meeting be held. Unless stipulated otherwise in the articles of incorporation, there are no quorum requirements and resolutions are typically passed by a simple majority of member present at the meeting. By law, minutes are to be kept of all board meetings. Resolutions in writing, so-called "circular resolutions", are permissible, provided no director requests a meeting.

V.1.5 Auditors and Accounts

V.1.5.1 *Appointment and dismissal of auditors*

Each corporation must have one or more auditors who may not be directors or employees of the company. Auditing firms or companies are eligible. The general shareholders' meeting elects the auditors, initially for one year and, subsequently, for a maximum of three years. The outgoing auditors are immediately eligible for re-election. Under the new law, there are certain qualification standards required for auditors as well as independence from the board of directors and from any shareholder controlling the company.

An auditor may be removed from office by an extraordinary shareholders' meeting. No reasons have to be stated for such removal.

V.1.5.2 *Duties and authority of auditors*

The auditors are required to conduct an examination to determine whether the books of the company are kept properly, whether the statements of profit and loss and the balance sheet agree with the books and whether the business results and financial position, as represented in the financial statements, comply with the legal requirements as to valuation of assets and expenses as well as with any special provisions of the articles of incorporation. The board of directors must submit to the auditors, under court order if necessary, the corporate books and records and, if requested, furnish explanations concerning particular subjects. The auditors must submit to the general shareholders' meeting a written report on the balance sheet and statement of profit and loss furnished to them by the board of directors. The auditors must also render an opinion on the proposal of the board of directors concerning the distribution of profits. Swiss law requires that the auditors attend the general shareholders' meeting, although in practice this requirement is often waived.

Like members of the board of directors and managers, the auditors are responsible to the corporation as well as to individual shareholders for damage intentionally or negligently caused by a breach of their duties (see V.1.4.1.11.4).

V.1.5.3 *Confidentiality of auditors*

The auditors are not permitted to inform individual shareholders, or third parties, of information obtained in carrying out their duties.

V.1.5.4 *Accounts*

The new law raises the minimum standard with respect to accounting principles to be adopted by corporations, but still offers the option to adhere to a higher standard. The annual accounts consists of the profit and loss statement, the balance sheet and the annex. Under certain circumstances, *e.g.* if the corporation is publicly traded, has bond issues outstanding or is of a certain size in terms of its assets, turnover or employees, the corporation is required to prepare consolidated accounts. Under the new law, public corporations also have to disclose major shareholders in the annex to their balance sheets, *i.e.* persons holding more than 5 per cent of the voting rights.

SECTION 2

THE CORPORATION WITH GENERAL PARTNERS

V.2.1 The corporation with general partners is governed by Articles 764 to 771 CO. It is an extremely rare form of business organisation in Switzerland (nine such companies were registered in 1989). It combines elements of a corporation limited by shares and a general partnership as it is made up of two different groups of members: there are shareholders who hold the stock of the company and who are in a position largely equal to that of the shareholders of a corporation. In addition, there are one or more members of the company whose liability for the company's debts is unlimited, as in a general partnership. The members with unlimited liability by law constitute the company's board of directors and exercise all powers with respect to the management of the company's affairs. In all other respects, the corporation with general partners is subject to the same rules as the corporation limited by shares.

SECTION 3

THE LIMITED LIABILITY COMPANY

V.3.1 Introduction

The limited liability company is regulated in Articles 772 to 827 CO. It is formed by two or more natural persons or companies with a predetermined capital. The liability of the company is limited to the capital amount entered into with the Commercial Register. Compared to the corporation, the limited liability company is not a very common form of business organisation in Switzerland.

V.3.2 Incorporation

The limited liability company is formed by two or more natural persons or companies. The articles of incorporation must contain the name and registered office of the company, the corporate purpose, the amount of the company capital and the amount of the contribution of each of its members, as well as the form of notice given by the company. Upon its registration with the Commercial Register, the limited liability company acquires its status as a separate legal entity. The company in formation is treated as a simple partnership.

The limited liability company may choose its company name freely, but an indication as to its legal form must be added if its name is made up of a person's name rather than a fantasy name. The limited liability company is typically established for an indefinite period of time, but its duration may also be limited.

541

V.3.3   Company Capital

The capital of the limited liability company is divided into shares with a par value of at least 1,000 Sfr. The minimum capital is 20,000 Sfr and the maximum is 2 million Sfr. The share evidencing the equity participation is not freely transferable as any such transfer by law requires the consent of three-quarters of the members representing at least three-quarters of the company's capital.

The amount of the capital share of each member of the company is recorded in the Commercial Register. Such amount represents the extent to which each member is liable for debt incurred by the company. However, in the event that any of the members fail to pay in their full share, the other members are jointly and severally liable for the amount no so paid in. At the beginning of each year, the company has to furnish to the Commercial Register an updated list containing the names of all member, their respective capital shares and the amounts paid in on such shares. This list is publicly available. The members of the company are entitled to receive profits in proportion to their capital contributions. It is not permissible to pay interest on the capital shares.

V.3.4   General Meeting

A general meeting is convened annually within six months of the close of the business year. It may also be called by one or more members of the company who represent at least 10 per cent of the company capital. The powers of the general meeting include the amendment of the articles of incorporation, the appointment and removal of managers, the appointment of auditors, the approval of the profit and loss statement and the decision as to allocation of profits, exoneration of managers and splitting of company's shares.

Unless stated otherwise in the articles of incorporation, resolutions are passed by the absolute majority of votes represented at the general meeting. The voting rights is measured in relation to the amount of the capital contribution, 1,000 Sfr representing one vote. These provisions may be altered by the articles of incorporation.

V.3.5   Management

Subject to the articles of incorporation, all members of the company are entitled to collectively manage the limited liability company. In practice, the managing powers are often conferred upon one or more members of the company or upon managers who need not themselves be members of the company. In contrast to the corporation, it is sufficient if one manager is resident in Switzerland; Swiss citizenship is not necessary.

V.3.6 Auditors

Given that the members of the company are also its managers, a separate controlling body is not necessary. Auditors will usually be appointed, however, in the event that management is in the hands of persons who are not members of the company. The auditors have the same duties and powers as the auditors of a corporation.

SECTION 4

THE CO-OPERATIVE

V.4.1 Introduction

The co-operative is a form of business organisation designed to foster or secure certain economic interests of its members by self-help (under the principle of "mutuality"). The co-operative generally limits the liability of its members, but unlimited personal liability may be provided for. In Switzerland, although there are some very large businesses organised in the form of co-operatives (especially food retail distributors), the co-operative is a common form of business organisation mainly for smaller businesses in rural areas. It is governed by Articles 828 to 926 CO.

V.4.2 Incorporation

The co-operative is formed by at least seven natural persons or companies. The articles of incorporation have to state the name and registered office of the co-operative, the corporate purpose, obligations of the members against the company, if any, the management and auditors, as well as the form of notice given by the co-operative. The co-operative is incorporated by virtue of registration with the

Commercial Register at its principal place of business. Before such registration, the co-operative in formation constitutes a simple partnership.

V.4.3   Membership

The co-operative may elect to establish a company capital to which each member has to contribute. However, to predetermine the amount of the capital in the articles of incorporation is not permissible since membership must be available to interested new members at any time (no closed-end co-operatives).

Anyone may apply for membership in writing. Management, or the general meeting, decides on the acceptance of new members. Unless stated otherwise in the articles of incorporation, membership may be waived at any time. By resolution of the general meeting, a member may also be expelled from the co-operative for important reasons or for reasons stated in the articles of incorporation. Transfer of membership is subject to the approval of the co-operative's management or general meeting, as the case may be.

V.4.4   General Meeting

The general meeting is convened by the management, if necessary by the auditors, or by 10 per cent of the members of the co-operative. The general meeting has the power to amend the articles of incorporation, appoint the management and the auditors, approve the profit and loss statement and balance sheet and decide on the distribution of profits, the exoneration of the managers and generally take all decisions on matters reserved to the general meeting by the articles of incorporation or by law.

Irrespective of any capital contributions, each member of the co-operative has one vote. Unless provided otherwise in the articles or incorporation, resolutions are passed by a majority of the votes represented at the general meeting. Resolutions regarding the dissolution, merger or the amendment of the articles of incorporation require a majority of two-thirds of the votes cast at the general meeting.

V.4.5   Management

The management of the co-operative consists of at least three persons, the majority of whom have to be members of the company and have to be Swiss citizens resident in Switzerland. Members of management are elected for a maximum term of office of four years and are eligible for re-election. Management functions may be delegated to management committees. The powers and duties of management are similar to those described with respect to the corporation limited by shares. In particular, all restrictions on a manager's signing authority need to be entered in the Commercial Register to be effective against third parties. Managers may be removed from office by resolution of the general meeting at any time.

V.4.6   Auditors

The provisions governing the powers and duties of the auditors are by and large those applicable to the corporation limited by shares.

UNITED KINGDOM

CLASSIFICATION OF BUSINESS ORGANISATIONS*

W.1.1 Introduction

The United Kingdom comprises three distinct legal jurisdictions: England and Wales, Scotland and Northern Ireland. The principles of company law and much of the legislation is similar. This chapter will focus on the company laws of England and Wales but the reader should bear in mind that there may be slight differences in dealing with companies incorporated in other jurisdictions within the United Kingdom.[1]

There are five main types of business entity recognised under English law as a vehicle for engaging in a commercial trade or business:

—sole trader

—partnership

—incorporated company

—branch of foreign incorporated company

—European Economic Interest Grouping (EEIG).[2]

In addition to the above, there continue to be a number of old trading companies which were incorporated by Royal Charter and statutory companies established to run public utilities and governmental or quasi-governmental entities will have no corporate status at all but are essentially government agencies carrying out commercial activities, *e.g.* The Crow Estate.

Individuals or companies may also combine in consortia syndicates and joint ventures whether for particular projects or on a long term basis. Such arrangements will be regulated in accordance with the contractual terms agreed between the parties but would have no legal personality distinct from that of its members.

---

* *Julian Maitland-Walker, Maitland Walker Solicitors (full particulars are listed in the Appendix).*
[1] Note also that similar but different company laws exist for the Isle of Man and the Channel Islands which are also separate jurisdictions within the British Isles.
[2] See chapter on the European Community, X.4.1, below.

W.1.2   The Sole Trader

A sole trader is an individual carrying on a business, trade or profession on his own account.

There are no registration or other formalities required prior to commencement of business by a sole trader although there is an obligation to maintain proper accounts for taxation purposes and to maintain proper records where the business is registered for VAT purposes. The accounts of a sole trader do not need to be audited nor do they have to be publicly disclosed.

The business man or professional person engaged in business as a sole trader has no separate legal persona distinct from the business which he operates. Accordingly, the sole trader will own and be personally responsible for the assets and liabilities, profits and losses of the business which he may have entered into with third parties as to the ownership of assets, *e.g.* mortgages and charges, or in relation to liabilities, *e.g.* insurance.

W.1.3   Partnership

There are two types of partnerships under English law and both are governed principally by statute:

(a)   a general partnership in which two or more partners agree to join together to pursue a business jointly is governed by the Partnership Act 1890;

(b)   a limited partnership in which one or more of the partners enjoys limited liability is governed by the Limited Partnership Act 1907.

Generally, partnerships are limited to a maximum of 20 partners. Exceptionally, however, certain professions such as lawyers and accountants may have partnerships exceeding that number of partners. This is because, historically, such professions have not been permitted to operate through limited liability companies so as to ensure that the public may rely on the unlimited liability of individual partners. In recent years, however, the professional rules have been relaxed so as to enable professional partnerships to place certain of their activities in limited liability companies but the principle of unlimited professional liability remains intact.

W.1.3.1   *General partnership*

A partnership will come into existence without the need for any formalities, where two or more individuals or corporate bodies carry on business in common with a view to making a profit.

As stated above, the rights and duties of the partners are governed by the

Partnership Act 1890, which refers to a partnership as a "firm".

The key legal consequences of the formation of the partnership is that the partners are personally liable, both jointly with their partners and individually, for the liabilities of the firm as a whole. A partnership is not a legal entity, under English law, separate from the identity of each of its constituent partners, though in Scotland a firm is a legal person distinct from the partners. However, even a Scottish partner can be compelled to pay the firm's debts.

The liability of each partner is unlimited, each partner being the agent of the other partners with the authority to make contracts, undertake obligations and dispose of partnership property in the ordinary course of the business on behalf of the firm as a whole.

Partnerships are regulated by the Partnership Act 1890 in the absence of a contrary agreement between the partners. The provisions of the Partnership Act are somewhat limited and for that reason most partnerships are governed by a formal written partnership agreement. This agreement will govern the division of capital, property, profits, management and will also provide for the distribution of assets on a winding up. The existence of such an express agreement does not affect the rights of third parties in their dealings with the firm, but merely governs the relationship of the partners between themselves. There are also statutory provisions governing the use of firm names and publicity as to the names of individual partners both on the firm's stationery and at the firm's premises.

W.1.3.2 *Limited partnership*

A limited partnership may be formed under and must be registered under the Limited Partnership Act 1907.

The expression "limited partnership" is misleading, in that the liability of the firm to its creditors is unlimited, and it is simply the liability of some (but not all) of the partners which is limited. There must be at least one general partner who bears unlimited liability for the debts of the firm in the same way as any partner in an ordinary partnership. Many of the benefits of limited liability may be obtained by making the general partner a limited liability company, but even so limited partnerships are relatively rare in the United Kingdom.

In order to obtain limited liability for some of its members, the limited partnership must be registered at the Companies Registry. Such registered particulars must include:

(a) the name;

(b) the general nature of the business;

(c) the principal place of business;

(d) the full name of each partner;

(e) the term (if any) of the partnership;

(f) the date of its commencement;

(g) a statement that the partnership is limited; and

(h) a description of every limited partner as such.

They must also specify the sum contributed by each limited partner and state whether it is in cash or otherwise. Failure to register means that the partnership will be considered to be an ordinary general partnership and each limited partner will therefore be liable for all the debts and obligations of the firm.

A limited partner has no power to bind the firm and may not take part in the management of the business, on penalty of losing the benefits of limited liability. A limited partner may also be at risk if he directly or indirectly draws out or receives back any part of his contribution, in which case he becomes liable to third parties up to the amount so drawn out or received back. A limited partnership structure is normally selected for tax reasons.

SECTION 2

COMPANIES LIMITED BY SHARES

W.2.1 Introduction

Public and private companies limited by shares are regulated primarily by the Companies Act 1985 which consolidated the various Acts passed between 1948 and 1983.

The 1985 Act continues to be the primary Act governing company law although it has itself been amended principally by the Companies Act 1989.[3]

In addition, issues of solvency and liquidation of companies are regulated by the Insolvency Act 1986. Issues relating to the conduct of investment business are covered by the Financial Services Act 1986.

There are also numerous statutory instruments governing such areas as disclosures of interests in shares, the content of investment advertisements, the official listing of securities, merger pre-notification regulations, etc. While the law governing corporations is mainly statute-based, there is also a substantial body of case law in which the courts have interpreted and supplemented the relevant statutes.

---

[3] References herein to section numbers of the Act are references to the 1985 Act as amended unless otherwise stated.

A registered limited company may be a public company or a private company. A public limited company is not necessarily a publicly quoted company, as there are certain public companies whose shares are not listed on the London Stock Exchange. However, a company whose ordinary shares are quoted on the Stock Exchange will invariably be a public company.

W.2.2 Public Limited Company (plc)

In order to register a company as a public limited company three conditions must be satisfied:

(1) the fact that it is a public company must be stated specification in its memorandum of association[4] and in its name. The name of the company must end with the words, "public limited company" or "plc".

(2) the memorandum must be in the form specified in Table F of the Companies (Tables A to F) Regulations 1985.

(3) the company must have an authorised capital (*i.e.* the number of shares it may issue to the public) of not less than the authorised minimum which is currently £50,000.

Public companies are subject to stricter requirements than private companies on:

(a) payment and maintenance of capital—as stated above, a company must have an authorised capital of not less than £50,000. A public company cannot start business or exercise any borrowing powers unless it has actually allotted shares up to the authorised minimum and has received at least one-quarter of that amount from its shareholders;

(b) where shares are subscribed for in specie as opposed to cash, the asset funding the subscription must be valued in accordance with detailed valuation procedures laid down by the Act;

(c) distribution of dividends—all companies may only distribute accumulated realised profits by way of dividend so far as they are not already distributed or capitalised. However, public companies may only make a distribution if at the time of distribution the amount of net assets is not less than the aggregate called-up share capital and its undistributable reserves and the amount of the proposed distribution will not lower the amount of those assets to less than that aggregate;

(d) loans to directors and to persons connected with them—section 330 of the Act prohibits making loans to, or guarantees for directors. In addition,

---

[4] The memorandum and articles of association are the equivalent of a company's "statutes" in other jurisdictions.

public companies and companies within a group including a public company may not make loans, give guarantees or securities to persons connected with such directors;

(e)   content and publication of accounts;

(f)   purchase and redemption of their own shares;

(g)   disclosure of interests in shares;

(h)   the granting of financial assistance for the acquisition of their shares;

(i)   minimum shareholders—the minimum number of shareholders is two;

(j)   minimum directors—the minimum number of directors is two.

The memorandum of a public company must state that it is to be a public company. The name must also include the words "public limited company" or the abbreviation "plc".

W.2.3   Private Company Limited by Shares (Limited)

A private company is any company registered under the Act which is not a public company. The main difference is that it is an offence for a private company limited by shares to offer to the public (whether for cash or otherwise) any shares in or debentures of the company. There is no single definition in English law of what constitutes "the public", but there is some statutory guidance to the effect that an offer or invitation shall not be treated as made "to the public" if it is not likely to result, directly or indirectly, in the shares or debentures becoming available for subscription or purchase by persons other than those receiving the offer or invitation. Further, the existing shareholders and employees of a company, together with the family members of such shareholders and employees, or an existing lender to the company are not treated as constituting "the public".

A private company has a number of advantages over a public company including the following:

(a)   no authorised minimum share capital;

(b)   shares can be issued in exchange for assets without the need for the complex valuation procedures laid down by the Act for public companies;

(c)   directors of private companies are much less restricted in their financial dealings with the company;

(d)   small private companies are excused publication of some or all their accounts;

(e)   private companies may provide financial assistance to purchase their own shares;

(f) there is no obligation to disclose true ownership of private company however large the holding.

W.2.4 Incorporation

W.2.4.1 *The memorandum of association*

Every registered company must have a memorandum of association which is the registered company's charter.

The memorandum establishes the basis of a company's statute for the incorporation and continued operation of the company. The regulations governing the way in which the company's objects may be achieved, and the conduct of the internal management and affairs of the company, are set out in the articles of association which are the company's statutes. The memorandum prevails over the articles and may only be altered in limited circumstances.

The memorandum must state:

(a) the name of the company, which must end with the word limited (or the Welsh equivalent) or an abbreviation thereof in the case of a private company, and with the words public limited company (or the Welsh equivalent) or an abbreviation thereof in the case of a public company;

(c) the objects of the company (see W.2.4.2 below);

(d) that the liability of its shareholders is limited;

(e) in the case of a company having a share capital, the amount of the share capital with which the company proposes to be registered and the division of that share capital into shares of a fixed amount. No subscriber of the memorandum may take less than one share, and the number of shares taken must be shown opposite the name of each subscriber.

(f) the memorandum of a public company must also state that the company is to be a public company.

W.2.4.2 *The objects*

The single most important statutory particular required to be registered in the memorandum used to be the "objects clause", which defines the nature and extent of the business which the company may transact. A company may not do anything which is not expressly or impliedly authorised by the objects set out in the memorandum since such activity would be *"ultra vires"*. The result of this doctrine was that in addition to the "main object" of the company, it became customary to add some 20 or 30 specific objects subsidiary to the main object, such as the power to invest or lend, and to do anything else which may be conducive to the attainment of the main object.

The *ultra vires* doctrine caused considerable hardship for third parties who found themselves without a remedy against a company acting outside its powers. In addition, the first E.C. Directive required a change in the *ultra vires* law. Accordingly the Act now provides that if a company is described as a general commercial company it is deemed to be able to carry on any trade or business whatsoever and have the power to do anything which is conducive to the conduct of any trade or business by it.

In addition, there are powers to vary the objects of a company by special resolution at any time and for any reason.

There is now also statutory protection for third parties who deal with a company in good faith, though the directors may be liable for acts which are *ultra vires* of the powers containeddin the memorandum.

The memorandum must be delivered to the Registrar of Companies for England and Wales (if the memorandum states that the registered office is to be locate din England and Wales) or the Registrar of Companies for Scotland (if it states that the registered office is to be situated in Scotland). The memorandum so delivered must be subscribed by at least two persons (or only one in the case of a private company), who must each take at least one share. "Subscription" means the signing of the memorandum by each subscriber in the presence of at least one witness who must attest the signature. The memorandum may be subscribed by an individual or corporate body, and there is no prohibition on all or any of the subscribers being foreigners. There must also be delivered to the Registrar a statement of the identity of the first directors and secretary of the company.

W.2.4.3 *The articles of association*

A company's management and administrative structure are set out in the articles, which constitute a contract between each shareholder and the company. The articles must be printed, divided into consecutively numbered paragraphs and, in the case of articles registered on incorporation, must be signed by each subscriber. The formalities of subscribing the articles are substantially the same as those relating to the memorandum. Guidance on the content of the articles is provided in the form of model regulations for limited companies, both public and private, known as Table A. A company may adopt as its articles all or any of the regulations set out in Table A. However, it is common for a company to adopt Table with modifications and exclusions.

The extent to which a company disapplies or varies Table A will depend, subject to the greater statutory constraints imposed on public companies, on the circumstances and wishes of the shareholders. Public limited companies quoted on the London Stock Exchange tend to disapply the whole of Table A and adopt long-form articles, some provisions of which reproduce Table A and others are specially drafted. It is also common to adopt long-form articles where the company is a

United Kingdom subsidiary of a foreign corporation or a company with many non-resident shareholders, who find it more convenient to have the articles set out in a single document, rather than have to cross-refer to Table A. Subsidiaries of group companies will often have extended short-form articles enabling consistency of administration by the parent.

The Articles will regulate, *inter alia*, the following:

(a) share capital, and the rights and liabilities attaching to the shares;

(b) alteration of share capital, issue, transfer and transmission of shares;

(c) conduct of shareholders' meetings and exercise of voting rights;

(d) appointment and removal of directors;

(e) conduct of meetings of directors, exercise of their powers and their remuneration, expenses and other interests;

(f) general administrative and financial provisions for the keeping of minutes, notices, distribution of assets on winding up, declaration and payment of dividends, treatment of reserves and capitalisation of profits.

W.2.4.4 Registered office

The memorandum must state whether the registered office is to be situated in England and Wales or in Scotland, or only in Wales. If it is to be only in Wales, the company may take advantage of the Welsh language provisions of the Companies Act. The part of Great Britain stated in the memorandum to be the site of the registered office is important, as it dictates the place of jurisdiction. A company may not elect to move its registered office to another part of Great Britain, say from England and Wales to Scotland, as this would involve a change in the domicile of the company. However, it is possible for a company with its registered office in England and Wales to change its address to anywhere else within England and Wales.

Every company is required at all times to have a registered office to which all communications and notices may be addressed. It is a company's duty to keep at its registered office, or make available for public inspection there, any register, index or other document of the company. It is also its duty to mention the address of its registered office in any document, and to display legibly, on all business letters and order forms, the place of registration and the company number.

W.2.4.5 Company name

The name of a company, which must be stated in its memorandum, must end in the case of a private company, with the words "limited", or, in the case of a public company, the words "public limited company". If the registered office of the

557

company is to be in Wales, the Welsh equivalents may be used, "cyfyngedig" and "cwmni cyfyngedig cyhoeddus". The statutory suffixes may be abbreviated by using the abbreviations "Ltd" and "plc", or their Welsh equivalents "cyf" and "ccc".

There are a number of statutory restrictions on the use of certain words and expressions in business names generally without the consent of a named government department or professional body. Restricted names are generally those which my import a connection with the Crown, with a profession or with a particular trade or may otherwise be misleading, such as apothecary, assurance, chartered, English, European, international, royal or trust. Also, a name will not be accepted for registration if it is the same as one already appearing in the index kept by the Registrar of Companies. A company may also be required to change its name within 12 months of registration on the ground that its name is too similar to that of an existing company name. Nor will a name be accepted for registration if it is offensive or its use would constitute a criminal offence. There are further important restrictions on the use of either the company name or the business name or a company which has gone into insolvent liquidation.

The use of a name too similar to the name of a company already on the register may lead to claims in passing off.

W.2.4.6 *Duration*

Companies are normally set up for an unlimited period, although it is possible to provide in the articles that the duration of the company will be for a limited period or that the company is to be dissolved on the occurrence of a particular event.

W.2.5 Shares

W.2.5.1 *Introduction*

The rights which a shareholder enjoys under the memorandum and articles determine the precise nature of the share itself. Different classes of shares may have different rights as to dividends, participation in surplus assets and voting. Shares are required to have a nominal or par value. Except for public company shares, shares may remain nil paid, partly paid or fully paid. However, where the shares are not fully paid up there remains an underlying liability on the part of the shareholder to pay up the nominal amount in the event of a call or on a winding up. Multi-currency share capital is lawful. A company may also, if it has the authority to do so in its articles, issue a share warrant in respect of any fully paid shares.

It is almost impossible to classify every type of share in a company, but the most common classes of share, which are often used in combination, are:

(a)   ordinary shares;

(b)   preference shares;

(c)   non-voting shares;

(d)   redeemable shares;

(e)   convertible shares;

(f)   deferred shares.

It must be stated in the articles how the various classes rank for any distribution by way of dividend or otherwise, and there are statutory restrictions on the variation of class rights.

W.2.5.2   Share capital

The share capital of a company must be stated in the memorandum, but may be increased or reduced by following certain strict statutory procedures. As stated above, there is no minimum for the share capital of private companies but the current minimum capital for a public company is £50,000 (of which £12,500 must be fully paid up).

W.2.5.3   Transfer of shares

The transfer of the legal title to shares can only be affected by means of a proper instrument of transfer known as a stock transfer form. This requirement may not be waived by anything to the contrary in the articles, but does not apply to the transmission of shares on death or bankruptcy which occurs by operation of law.

The articles commonly provide that the directors may refuse to register the transfer of shares which are only partly paid or for other reasons, such as if the transfer form is not accompanied by the relevant share certificate or other evidence of title to the shares. A share certificate is *prima facie* evidence of title of a shareholder to his shares. Share warrants, however, are negotiable instruments transferable by delivery.

The articles of private companies often contain intricate pre-emption provisions designed to prevent control of the company passing out of the hands of a few founding or family shareholders, but public companies listed on the Stock Exchange are not permitted to impose restrictions on the transfer of their shares, as they would reduce marketability. If the articles set out any pre-emption provisions on transfer, such provisions must be substantially complied with before a sale of the shares can be made to an outsider. Pre-emption provisions commonly require share valuations to be carried out by the auditors of the company in circumstances where the price is not agreed.

W.2.5.4 *Increase of capital*

The power of a company to alter its share capital must first of all be contained in the articles. Provided a company has such a constitutional power, it then has a statutory power to increase its authorised share capital by such amount as it thinks fit. This statutory power must be exercised by the company in general meeting, and the articles may provide either for majority voting or for 75 per cent of votes in favour. A company may also consolidate and subdivide its share capital, convert shares into stock and cancel unissued shares.

The articles may grant the directors the power to issue the newly created or any unissued shares, but this power is restricted by statute: whether the authority is given by the articles or by a general meeting, it must state the maximum amount of shares which the directors may issue and the date when the authority will expire. The maximum period of the authority is generally five years, though this restriction can be waived for private companies.

There are also detailed legislative provisions restricting the issue of the new shares, so that a company may not issue the shares for cash without offering them first to its existing shareholders pro rata with their shareholdings. These statutory pre-emption rights may be excluded or varied by private companies. Any company whether public or private may also disapply the pre-emption rights provided that the directors have been given the requisite authority to issue shares and certain stringent conditions have been met.

W.2.5.5 *Reduction of capital*

Share capital may be lost if the business suffers losses, but share capital cannot generally be reduced unless this is permitted by the articles and a reduction is specifically sanctioned by the court.

A company may pass a special resolution to reduce share capital but the resolution will not take effect until it is first approved by the court.

Serious loss of capital—directors of a public company are obliged to call an extraordinary meeting of the company within 28 days from the earliest date on which any director knew that the company had suffered a serious loss of capital, *i.e.* where the net assets of the company are half or less of the amount of the company's called-up share capital.[5]

W.2.5.6 *Form of subscription*

The general rule is that shares may not be issued at a discount. The offering of shares at a discount is a criminal offence by the company and any officer in default.

---

[5] This provision was introduced in English law pursuant to Article 17, second E.C. Company Directive. (See chapter on the European Community, X.3.1.3, below.)

Note, however, that there is nothing to prevent debentures being issued at a discount and that the deduction of a commission by a person who agrees to subscribe or to procure subscriptions does not constitute sale at a discount.

Where a company issues shares at a premium, whether for cash or otherwise, a sum equal to the aggregate amount or value of the premium must be transferred to a share premium account, which must be maintained in the same way as capital. In the case of a public company, one quarter of the nominal value of the shares plus the whole of any premium must be paid up before the shares are allotted.

The shares of a private company may be paid up in money, or money's worth, including goodwill and know-how, but payment for public company shares otherwise than for cash must generally be supported by an expert's valuation report in accordance with statutory rules.

W.2.5.7 Purchase of own shares

Both public and private companies are generally able, subject to statutory procedural requirements, to purchase their own shares, including any redeemable shares. The conditions for such a purchase include:

(a) the purchase monies may only be found out of distributable profits or the proceeds of a fresh issue of shares (with a limited exception in favour of private companies);

(b) once purchased, the shares must be treated as cancelled and the issued share capital of the company reduced by their nominal amount;

(c) following the purchase, there must be at least one shareholder who holds non-redeemable shares.

W.2.5.8 Register of shareholders

The register of shareholders is considered to be of fundamental importance as giving publicity to the identity of the shareholders and the extent of their liability, though shareholders are often nominees. The following information must be entered on the register:

(a) the names and addresses of shareholder;

(b) a statement of the number and class of the shares held;

(c) the amount paid up on the shares;

(d) the date of entry on the register;

(e) the date of cessation of shareholding.

The register must be readily available and must be kept either at the company's registered office or at some other publicised place. It must also be available for inspection during business hours by any shareholder, free of charge, and by any other person for a nominal fee.

W.2.6   The Board of Directors

W.2.6.1   *Definition of a director*

There is no comprehensive statutory definition of the term "director", although statute provides that a director includes any person occupying the position of director, by whatever name called. A director is an officer of the company (but not necessarily an employee) and may be executive or non-executive, full or part-time.

A formal appointment to the board is not necessary for a person to become a "director", and there is an important concept in English law of a "shadow director", defined as "any person in accordance with whose directions or instructions, the directors of a company are accustomed to act". The existence of such a relationship is a question of fact rather than law. A person giving advice to the board in a professional capacity is not, however, regarded as a shadow director merely because that advice is acted on. A number of statutory provisions affecting directors also apply to shadow directors.

W.2.6.2   *Appointment/dismissal of directors*

Although there is no maximum number of directors, a public company must have at least two directors, and a private company may have a sole director only if such a sole director is not also the secretary of the company.

The first directors are appointed by the subscribers to the memorandum. The appointment of subsequent directors is primarily determined by the articles, which usually confer the power of appointment both on the directors and on the company in general meeting. Table A provides that a third of all the directors shall retire by rotation at successive AGMs, at which they are then eligible for reappointment by the shareholders. It is usually specified however that a managing director or other director holding executive office shall not be the subject to retirement by rotation.

Directors may resign from office at any time, and directors of public companies must retire at the age of 70 unless the continuance of their appointment is approved by a resolution in general meeting. It is also usual to provide in the articles that directors shall be required to vacate their office on the occurrence of certain events, such as becoming a mental patient or being absent without leave for more than a certain period of time, or if they have been disqualified under the Company Directors' Disqualification Act 1986.

Notwithstanding anything to the contrary in the articles or in a separate contract between the company and a director, the company may remove a director by ordinary resolution (requiring over 50 per cent of votes in favour) provided that special notice of 28 days has been given of such removal and certain other statutory procedures are followed. The board of directors also commonly has the power to remove one of their number from office, either by simple majority or by qualified majority set out in the articles.

W.2.6.3 *Duties/powers of the board of directors*

The management of a company is usually delegated to its directors by the articles, and the directors may exercise all the powers of the company through resolutions passed at duly convened board meetings. In practice, the day-to-day decision making is delegated to executive or managing directors or to committees of directors under empowering provisions in the articles.

Directors are agents of the company with a duty to act in its best interests. Accordingly, they have a fiduciary duty towards the company and are trustees of the company's assets.

When exercising his powers, a director must act not only in good faith and with honesty but also in the best interests of the company. He must not use company property or information gained in the course of his duties for his on personal gain. A director acting honestly and with reasonable care will usually be held to have performed his duty if he believed on reasonable grounds that the transaction he approved was for the benefit of the company. However, even this will not be sufficient if for example:

(a) the transaction is outside the scope of the company's objects or an abuse of the powers given to the directors;

(b) a personal profit was made by the director, even if the company also benefited; or

(c) the director did not declare his interest in the transaction.

The directors' duties are prescribed by both common law and statute. At common law, a director must exercise reasonable skill and care in carrying out his duties, must consider the position and interests of creditors if the company is insolvent, and must have regard to the interests of the company's employees in general as well as the interests of the company. Directors also owe a duty to the company's shareholders collectively rather than individually. Shareholders have important statutory rights to apply to the court on the ground that the company's affairs are being or have been conducted in a manner which is unfairly prejudicial to the interests of some or all of the shareholders.

In addition to these common law duties, the directors are responsible for the performance of the duties imposed by statute and non-compliance with any of these may give rise to a fine or to disqualification and even imprisonment if the default is serious or persistent. Their statutory duties are to maintain proper accounting and value added tax records, to ensure that the annual accounts are prepared in accordance with Companies Act requirements, and to maintain the various statutory books which must be kept at the company's registered office, *i.e.* the register of members, the register of directors and secretaries, the register of mortgages and charges, the register of debenture holders and the register of directors' interests, all of which must be open to public inspection.

The directors are also responsible for ensuring that the company complies with relevant legislation such as that relating to employees, health and safety at work and environmental protection.

W.2.6.4 *Board meetings*

Directors must ensure that the board meets sufficiently frequently to enable it to discharge its duties properly. Adequate notice should be given to allow the attendance of all directors and relevant papers should be circulate din advance. Minutes must be kept of all board meetings recording the names of the directors present, the decisions reached and the views expressed. The articles usually prescribe such mattes as period of notice, quorum, voting, chairman's casting vote, etc.

W.2.6.5 *Legal liability of directors*

The personal liabilities which can be imposed on directors for both civil and criminal offences are potentially very great and may arise in the following circumstances.

W.2.6.5.1 Abuse of powers Directors must not act outside the objects of the company as set out in its memorandum and must use the powers given to them only for their proper purpose, or else they may incur personal liability unless relieved by special resolution of the shareholders.

W.2.6.5.2 Breach of duties If a director is in breach of any of the duties imposed on him, he may be personally liable to pay to the company any profit he has made and/or reimburse the company for any loss suffered as a result of such breach. Relief is however available to any director who, although in breach of a non-statutory duty, has acted honestly and reasonably.

W.2.6.5.3 Liabilities to shareholders Directors may also be personally liable to the shareholders. Under criminal legislation, the directors are guilty as officers of the company of a criminal offence if they publish an account of the company's affairs with intent to deceive the shareholders or creditors and knowing that it is or may be false, misleading or deceptive. In addition, directors may be personally liable if a person suffers loss as a result of the directors knowingly permitting a contravention of any of the pre-emption rights on transfer of the existing shareholders.

W.2.6.5.4 Liabilities to investors Directors may incur liability for deceit or fraudulent misrepresentation, at common law in relation to dealings in the securities of a company, and under the Financial Services Act 1986 which requires prior authorisations to be obtained before any investment business (including offers and disposals of securities) may be lawfully conducted.

W.2.6.6 *Directors' transactions with the company*

In order to avoid any conflict of interest between the directors and the company, there is a wide range of statutory restrictions on directors, the principal ones being as follows:

W.2.6.6.1 Loans Subject to certain exceptions a company is prohibited from making loans to, or providing guarantees for a director or a director of its parent company, or from making quasi-loans or providing credit to such directors and to persons connected with them. A director receiving an unlawful loan is liable to account to the company for any gain made and to indemnify the company against any loss suffered as a result.

W.2.6.6.2 Contracts of service Broadly speaking, unless authorised by the shareholders in advance of general meetings, directors' contracts must not exceed five years and a register of contracts must be kept for inspection by the shareholders at any time.

W.2.6.6.3 Substantial property transactions Substantial property transactions by the company involving a director or connected person must be first approved by the company in general meeting. Substantial property transactions include those in which the director or connected person buys from or sells an asset to the company the value of which exceeds a set amount.

W.2.6.6.4 Interest in contracts A director must disclose to the board any interest he may have directly or indirectly, in a company contract. If the interest is material, it must also be disclosed in the accounts.

W.2.6.6.5 Insider dealing It is a criminal offence for a director of a listed company to deal in the securities of the company on the basis of unpublished price-sensitive information or to pass such information to a third party, if the director knows or has reason to believe that such third party may deal in the securities.

W.2.6.6.6 Interests in shares or debentures Directors have a duty to notify the company of any interests they and certain connected persons may have in its shares or debentures. Interests are defined as both beneficial and non-beneficial holdings and share options and similar rights.

W.2.6.7 *General meetings*

Meetings of shareholders fall into two categories: Annual General Meetings (AGMs) and Extraordinary General Meetings (EGMs). The rules governing the conduct of AGMs and EGMs are largely the same, though the length of the notice which must be given varies. All members may and attend and vote at general meetings, unless they only had shares of a particular class with not rights to attend. Meetings of debenture holders and creditors are often regulated in a similar way.

With some exceptions in favour of private companies, every company must hold an AGM in each calendar year and meetings must not be more than 15 months apart. The articles may provide what business must be conducted at an AGM, but it is usual for AGMs to conduct only "ordinary business", meaning the declaration of dividends, consideration of the accounts, the election of directors who are required to retire by rotation, and the appointment and remuneration of auditors. Private companies may elect to dispense with the holding of AGMs. Any meeting which is not an AGM is an EGM. EGMs are held as and when necessary.

W.2.6.7.1 The convening of meetings   If a company fails to hold an AGM when required, any shareholder may apply to the Department of Trade, which may then call an AGM and order that one person shall constitute a quorum for the meeting. Shareholders who are registered holders of not less than one-tenth of such of the paid up capital as carries the right of voting at general meetings may requisition the holding of an EGM. Following such notice, the directors must then call a meeting for a date not later than 28 days following the notice. There is also a separate power for two or more members holding not less than one-tenth of the issued share capital (*i.e.* not necessarily the paid up capital) to call a meeting themselves, subject to proper notice. Shareholders with 5 per cent or more of the voting rights may also insist that a particular resolution be included in the agenda of the next AGM, subject to notice.

The directors usually have the power under the articles to decide when to call the AGM and to call an EGM at any time and the vast majority of meetings will be called in this way.

W.2.6.7.2 Ordinary, special, extraordinary and elective resolutions   A company in general meeting may only transact business by passing the appropriate type of resolution. An ordinary resolution is one requiring a simple majority of votes in favour, in other words more votes in favour than against. An extraordinary resolution and a special resolution both require a three-quarters majority in favour of them to be passed.

The difference between an extraordinary resolution and a special resolution is that a special resolution requires 21 days' notice even if it is to be considered at an EGM, whereas an extraordinary resolution only requires the same length of notice as the meeting at which it is to be considered.

Statue generally requires a special resolution where minority shareholders might need protection, such as to alter the articles or objects, or to exclude pre-emption rights.

Private companies may dispense with the holding of AGMs and with the annual laying of accounts and reports by passing a resolution to that effect at a general meeting.

Private companies may also pass written resolutions to take certain decisions, which must be signed by all the shareholder, instead of having to hold formal meetings. Written resolutions may not be used to remove a director or an auditor from office.

W.2.6.7.3 Notice of meetings   Business at a meeting cannot be properly transacted unless proper notice has been given of the meeting to every member required to be given notice under the articles. This usually means all the members, although some articles provide that shareholders with no registered address in the United Kingdom are not entitled to notice.

For an AGM, 21 days' notice is required. For an EGM, 14 days' notice is required unless a special resolution or an elective resolution is to be proposed, in which case the period is 21 days. If all the shareholders agree to short notice, an AGM may be held without 21 days' notice. A majority in number owning at least 95 per cent (or not less than 90 per cent in the case of a private company which has so elected) of the voting shares may agree to shorter notice of an EGM.

Notices must specify the date, time and place of the meeting and describe the business to be considered in sufficient detail of shareholders to decide whether they wish to attend.

Certain resolutions, such as a shareholders' resolution to remove a director must be set out *verbatim* in the notice and require 28 days' notice, called "special notice".

Shareholders must also be informed in the notice of their right to appoint proxies.

W.2.6.7.4 Duties/powers of meetings   A meeting cannot validly consider the business in hand unless a quorum is present. Without a provision to the contrary in the articles, two members personally present would constitute a quorum. Amendments may be proposed but only within the scope of the notice, which means that no amendment of substance is permitted to special, elective or extraordinary resolutions, and amendments to ordinary resolutions are limited. Proxies may speak at meetings of a private company in the same way as shareholder themselves.

Voting on resolutions may be decided on a show of hands, where each member personally present has one vote (regardless of the number of shares held) and proxies are not entitled to vote unless empowered to do so by the articles. However, any five voting shareholders, or any shareholders with 10 per cent of the voting rights, or any shareholder with 10 per cent of the paid up voting capital, is entitled to demand a poll. Proxies have the same right to call for a poll as the shareholders whom they represent. On a poll, votes are counted according to the number of voting rights rather than the number of shareholders.

Minutes must be kept of all decisions taken at general meetings and remain available for inspection by shareholders at the registered office. Further, copies of certain resolutions must be sent to the Registrar of Companies within 15 days of being passed.

W.2.7 United Kingdom Branch of an Overseas Company

An overseas company is any company incorporated outside the United Kingdom which establishes a "place of business" in the United Kingdom. A place of business is one which has some degree of permanence and consists of office premises of the company, rather than merely the presence of agents or sales representatives.

Overseas companies must comply with certain provisions of company law within one month of establishment, which require them to deliver to the Registrar of Companies:

(a) a certified copy of their articles of association or byelaws duly certified as true copies by an official of the Government of the country where the company is incorporated, or by a notary public, or under oath by anyone empowered to administer oaths;

(b) a list of the directors and secretary, detailing their names, surnames, residential addresses, nationality, business occupation and directorship, together with the name of the secretary;

(c) the names and addresses of one or more United Kingdom residents authorised to accept, on behalf of the company, service of any notice to be served on the company;

(d) a formal notice of the balance sheet date;

(e) the date of establishment.

The Registrar of Companies must also receive notice within 21 days of any change in the registered particulars. An overseas company may be refused permission to use its corporate name for trading in the United Kingdom.

Overseas companies are required to submit to the Registrar of Companies copies of their annual accounts, including group accounts, within 13 months of the end of their accounting period. The accounts so submitted must generally comply with United Kingdom company law, with certain exceptions.

An overseas company must display its name, the name of the country in which it is incorporated, and a statement that its liability is limited, at every place of business in the United Kingdom and on all invoices and letterheads and all publications of the company. Certain charges over the United Kingdom assets of overseas companies need to be registered with the Registrar of Companies.

W.2.8   Accounts

With the exception of those private companies electing for special treatment as described below, the directors must lay before the company in general meeting in respect of each financial year copies of its accounts and the directors' and auditors' reports. Failure to do so within the statutory time periods renders the directors liable to fines.

The directors are also required to deliver copies of the accounts and the directors' and auditors' reports to the Registrar of Companies within the said statutory time periods.

The statutory time periods are normally 10 months after the reference period for a private company and seven months after the reference period for a public company.

Concessions are offered to small and medium sized companies or groups under which they may file abbreviated financial statements. Any private company whose annual turnover does not exceed £90,000 and whose balance sheet does not exceed £1.4 million is exempt from the statutory audit requirement.

W.2.9   The Audit

Subject to the concessionary exception for small companies referred to above, a company's accounts must be examined and reported on by an independent appropriately qualified person ("the auditor") who must indicate whether the accounts comply with the statutory requirements and give "a true and fair view" of the company's affairs and results.

In addition to their responsibility to report on the accounts, the auditors are required to make reports where, for example, a public company allots shares otherwise than for cash, or a private company redeems or purchases its shares out of capital.

Apart from the auditors' contractual duty of care to the company, he owes a duty of care to third parties with whom he is not in a contractual or fiduciary relationship if he is aware that reliance is being placed upon his actions and he does not make it clear that he accepts no responsibility for the information or advice which he gives.

A specific resolution appointing or reappointing the auditors must be passed at every AGM for all public companies and for many private companies. Such resolution must provide that an auditor's term of office runs from the conclusion of the general meeting at which the accounts are laid until the conclusion of the next. The first auditors may be appointed by the directors at any time before the first AGM. The directors may, or the company may in general meeting, fill any subsequent vacancy. Where a general meeting is called to fill a casual vacancy, or to reappoint an auditor, or to appoint someone other than a retiring auditor, special notice of 28 days is required to be given to the company.

Special notice must always be given for a resolution removing an auditor before the expiry of his term of office. An auditor can be removed by ordinary resolution of the company notwithstanding any agreement to the contrary between the auditor and the company.

The auditors are engaged by the shareholders and report to them. They are not empowered to disclose any information relating to the company's affairs without the company's permission, and their audit files are confidential. Audit files are however the property of the auditors and not of the company.

Auditors do not currently have a duty or the power to report to any third party on any aspect of a company's affairs without the authorisation of the company. There is not therefore any "public duty" to report irregularities to any legal, fiscal or other authority.

SECTION 3

COMPANIES LIMITED BY GUARANTEE AND UNLIMITED COMPANIES

W.3.1   Introduction

In addition to the registered company limited by shares a registered company may also be:

(a)   a company limited by guarantee in which case the liability of members to contribute to the company's assets is limited to the amount, if any, unpaid on his shares; or

(b)   an unlimited company, in which case the liability of a member is unlimited.

W.3.1.1   *Companies limited by guarantee*

A company limited by guarantee is subject to broadly the same requirements as that of a private company. The members are not required to contribute to the company on incorporation. The liability of members is limited to the amount they each undertake to contribute to the assets of the company in the event of it being wound up.

W.3.1.2 *Unlimited companies*

There is no limit on members' liability to contribute to the assets of the company and such companies are very rare. A limited private liability company can be re-registered as an unlimited company with the unanimous consent of its members although a public company cannot re-register without first converting to a private company.

SECTION 4

COSTS OF INCORPORATION

W.4.1 Introduction

The registration fee payable to Companies House on incorporation of a company is £50. In addition, there is additional fee for the swearing of a statutory declaration of compliance with incorporation requirements of £5. These costs are exclusive of the professional fees involved in the preparation of the memorandum and articles of association, the statement of first directors and secretaries, address of registered office, etc.

A company complete with standard memorandum and articles and the necessary minute books, share register, etc., can be purchased "off the shelf" for an all-in fee in the region of £250–500. A further fee would be payable in order to change the name of the company or alter the articles.

EUROPEAN COMMUNITY

SECTION 1

INTRODUCTION*

X.1.1 One of the primary objectives underlying the European Economic Community is the creation of a fully integrated European Single Market. The Treaty of Rome[1] sets out the means by which this Single Market is to be created through the elimination of internal frontiers and the abolition of restrictions both governmental and commercial inhibiting trade flows between Member States. These restrictions on trade are prohibited under the Treaty though provisions dealing with the free movement of goods, services and capital, free competition and the free movement of persons whether wage-earners or self-employed. National legislation which impedes these freedoms or discriminates on grounds of nationality is likely to be contrary to Community law and applying the doctrine of the supremacy of Community law, the National law may be found to be illegal as contravening the Community legislation.

The fundamental freedoms described above apply to legal as well as natural persons. Article 58 of the Treaty extends them to all companies formed in accordance with the law of a Member State and having their registered office, central administration or principal place of business within the Community. A company is defined as an undertaking constituted under civil or commercial law, including co-operative societies and other legal persons governed by public or private law, save for those which are non-profit making. National laws governing the establishment and operation of companies are all concerned with the protection of the interests of various categories of persons, *i.e.* shareholders, employees, creditors or third parties. The laws protecting these interests differ substantially from one Member State to another and this can give rise to obstacles to the development of an integrated single market. As the integrated European market develops, so cross border dealings between companies, their shareholders, creditors, etc., increase. The fact that such relationships are governed by different rules in different countries represents an obstacle to the growth of such integration.

The Treaty acknowledges this in Article 54(3) by conferring on the Council of Ministers and the European Commission the responsibility of:

---

* *Julian Maitland-Walker, Maitland Walker Solicitors (full particulars are listed in the Appendix).*
[1] The European Economic Community Treaty signed at Rome in 1957 between the original six Member States: the Federal Republic of Germany, France, Italy, Belgium, the Netherlands and Luxembourg, and subsequently through the various accession treaties by the United Kingdom, Denmark and Ireland with effect from January 1, 1973, Greece with effect from January 1, 1981, Spain and Portugal with effect from January 1, 1986 and Austria, Sweden and Finland with effect from January 1, 1995 (hereinafter referred to as "the Treaty").

"... coordinating to the necessary extent the safeguards which, for the protection of the interests of members and others, are required by Member States of companies or firms within the meaning of the second paragraph of Article 58 with a view to making such safeguards equivalent throughout the Community".

SECTION 2

THE DEVELOPMENT OF EUROPEAN COMPANY LAW

X.2.1 Harmonisation

Nine directives on company law have been adopted by the Council of Ministers while four other proposals are under consideration. These are as follows:

X.2.1.1 *Directives*

- The First Directive   On public disclosure
- The Second Directive   On the raising maintenance and alteration of capital of public limited companies (plcs)
- The Third Directive   On mergers of plcs
- The Fourth Directive   On company accounts
- The Sixth Directive   On the division or scission of plcs
- The Seventh Directive   On consolidated accounts
- The Eighth Directive   On statutory auditors
- The Eleventh Directive   On branch disclosure requirements
- The Twelfth Directive   On single-member private limited companies

X.2.1.2 *Proposals*

- The draft Fifth Directive   On the structure of plcs
- The draft Ninth Directive   On groups of companies
- The draft Tenth Directive   On cross border mergers
- The draft Thirteenth Directive   On cross border mergers

X.2.2 Community Regulation

In addition to the harmonisation directives referred to above by virtue of which Member States are required to bring national laws in line with the Community standard, the Community has also introduced the following regulations which have immediate effect throughout the Community as directly enforceable legislation.

X.2.2.1 *Regulations*

- The EEIG Regulation   A measure introducing the concept of a European Economic Interest Grouping
- The Merger Regulation   A measure imposing Community control of Community Dimension mergers

X.2.2.2 *Proposals*

- The draft European Company Statutes   A measure establishing rules for the creation of a European Company

SECTION 3

THE HARMONISATION DIRECTIVES

X.3.1 Measures Already Implemented

X3.1.2 *The first Directive (Directive 68/151)*[2]

This Directive was adopted in 1968 and applies to all types of companies both private and public. The Directive establishes a system of public disclosure. Member States are required to maintain an official public register of companies in addition to ensuring the publication of certain company information in an official gazette. The official register which must be accessible by the public is required to contain:

(a) the statutes/memorandum and articles of association of the company;

(b) particulars of those empowered to represent the company;

(c) procedures for winding up the company, etc.

Subsequent Directives have extended the application of this disclosure system to other categories of document or information.

Article 7 of the Directive establishes a uniform approach for the treatment of pre-incorporation contracts by providing that:

> "If, before a company being formed has acquired legal personality, action has been carried out in its name and the company does not assume the obligations arising from such action, the persons who acted shall without limit, be jointly and severally liable therefore, unless otherwise agreed."

The provision was enacted in English law under Section 36C of the Companies Act 1985 but has been given a narrow interpretation. In *Cotronic (UK) Ltd v. Dezonie* ((1991) B.C.C. 200) for example, the defendant had unknowingly made a contract on behalf of a company which had been struck off the register. A new company had been set up with the same name to carry on the business of the old one. Despite this the court held that the defendant was not personally liable on the basis that he had made the contract for the old company rather than the new one.

---

[2] O.J. Spec. Ed. Vol. 9, pp. 82–86.

X.3.1.3   The second Directive (Directive 77/91)[3]

This Directive was adopted in 1976 and covers the raising maintenance and alteration of the capital of plcs. Member States have been required to adopt a minimum subscribed capital of a plc at 25,000 ECUs[4] whether in the form of cash or in kind. In the latter case, the value of the subscription must be certified by an independent value. profits available for distribution are specifically defined so as to prevent the erosion of capital through distribution.

The Directive lays down certain rules requiring non-discrimination as between shareholders and also requires that any new issues of shares must first be offered to the existing shareholders.

The European Court of Justice has held that Articles 25 and 29 of the second Directive which relate to increases of capital had direct effect in the laws of the Member States and therefore a government was not permitted to direct an increase in share capital without the consent of existing shareholders: *Karella v. Minister for Industry and the Organisation for the Restructuring of Industry* (E.C.R. Joined Cases C-19 & 20/90, Judgment May 30, 1991) and *Syndesmos EEC, Vasco et al. v. Greece et al.* (E.C.R. Case 381/89, Judgment March 24, 1992). See also *Siemens AG v. Henry Nold* (E.C.R. Case C-42/95, Judgment November 19, 1996).

X.3.1.4   The third Directive (Directive 78/885)[5]

This Directive was adopted in 1978 and lays down common rules for company mergers taking place within a single Member State and involving the acquisition of one company by another. The directive lays down a procedure for valuation of the target company shares and the basis upon which such shares should be exchanged for shares in the acquiring company. The Directive also provides for creditor protection in the case of such mergers where the financial conditions of the participating enterprises require it.

3.1.5   The fourth Directive (Directive 78/660)[6]

This Directive was adopted in 1978 and provides for the introduction of a standard format for the balance sheet and profit and loss account and the minimum information to be published in the notes to a company's annual report.

The Directive requires that the balance sheet must give a true picture of the company's financial position adopting the general principles of consistency prudence and attribution to the financial year in question. Accounting standards are set for

---

[3] [1977] O.J. L26/1.
[4] 1 ECU (European Currency Unit)—approximately £0.70.
[5] [1978] O.J. L295/26.
[6] [1978] O.J. L222/11.

579

asset valuations requiring "current cost" valuation as the norm but with a right to allow "historical cost" valuation provided that:

(a) any additional value resulting is treated as a reserve rather than as profit; and

(b) the notes to the accounts incorporate a table showing the comparable figures adopting the two valuation approaches.

X.3.1.6 *The sixth Directive (Directive 82/891)*[7]

This Directive was adopted in 1982 and concerns the division or "scission" of a public limited company into several undertakings. Member States are not required to adopt legislation governing such restructuring arrangements but if they do so, the legislation must accord with the Directive. The Directive is particularly concerned to ensure that the rights of creditors of one undertaking are not prejudice by the transfer of assets into another corporate entity.

X.3.1.7 *The seventh Directive (Directive 83/349)*[8]

This Directive was adopted in 1983 and lays down the circumstances under which a group of companies may prepare consolidated accounts and the basis upon which such accounts are to be prepared. The directive also covers the rules for auditing such accounts and publication requirements.

X.3.1.8 *The eighth Directive (Directive 84/253)*[9]

This Directive, adopted in 1984 sets out common professional standards for statutory auditors to companies and requires a full audit to be carried out in respect of a company's accounts annually.

X.3.1.9 *The eleventh Directive (Directive 89/666)*[10]

This Directive was adopted on December 21, 1989 and is designed to harmonise the rules governing the establishment of a branch throughout the Community. The Commission has been concerned that different disclosure requirements from branches throughout the Community was an obstacle to establishment. Under the Directive, branches of companies established in other Member States will not have

[7] [1982] O.J. L378/47.
[8] [1983] O.J. L193/1.
[9] [1984] O.J. L126/30.
[10] [1989] O.J. L295/36.

to publish annual accounts of their own activities provided that they submit a consolidated and duly audited report for their parent company.

X.3.1.10   The twelfth Directive (Directive 89/667)[11]

This Directive was adopted on December 21, 1990 and requires Member States to permit the establishment of single-member private limited companies in order that individual business operations are able to take advantage of limited liability.

X.3.2   Proposals

X.3.2.1   The draft fifth Directive[12]

This Directive has attracted considerable controversy within the Community and most particularly within the United Kingdom because it seeks to regulate the structure of companies and in particular the question of supervision and worker participation. The latest draft proposal seeks a compromise between the conflicting views on worker participation by leaving Member States to choose from a variety of structures ranging from the two tier supervisory/management board system to the creation of a workers' representative council which is quite separate from the board.

The Directive requires that whichever structure is adopted, all worker representatives are elected by secret ballot of the work force. The Directive also lays down rules governing shareholders' general meetings. In particular, voting rights, proxy rights, etc.

X.3.2.2   The draft ninth Directive

In 1985, the Commission announced in response to a question in the European Parliament that it intended to issue a proposal for a ninth Company Law Directive which would deal with the transparency of relationships between enterprises. To date no such proposal has been published.

X.3.2.3   The draft tenth Directive[13]

The major differences in attitude within different Member States towards cross-border mergers has been the subject of much criticism. Some Member States have

---

[11] [1989] O.J. L395/40.
[12] [1983] O.J. C2402.
[13] COM (95) 655 final.

applied legislation which requires the unanimous approval of shareholders before a merger can proceed and such measures have severely inhibited the scale of co-operative alliances within the Community. The objective of the tenth Directive is to introduce a higher degree of "transparency" in relation to mergers and acquisitions throughout the Community.

As stated above, the merger provisions contained in the third Directive were limited to single state mergers. The tenth Directive extends the application of the third Directive to cross border mergers subject to some modifications.

X.3.2.4   *The draft thirteenth Directive*[14]

The original proposal was adopted by the Commission at the end of 1988 but replaced by a new draft in February 1996.

This proposal seeks to open up the market for cross frontier mergers and takeovers by making such transactions more transparent and ensuring that share-holders interests are protected in the context of such acquisition.

The draft Directive envisages that where a certain threshold of shareholding is achieved (currently one third of the shares) a formal announcement of the bid would have to be made requiring the acquirer to bid for all the remaining shares. The proposal also requires that the workforce are kept informed.

Section 4

EUROPEAN ECONOMIC INTEREST GROUPING (EEIG)

X.4.1   The EEIG is a form of Community-based partnership designed to facilitate co-operation between legal and natural persons established in more than one Member State. The rules governing the establishment and operation of the EEIG are laid down by E.C. Regulation 2137/85.[15] Basically, the EEIG is established by contract and is a business entity registrable within the Member States and with the Commission. All participating enterprises must be engaged in some form of

---

[14] [1989] O.J. C64/8; revised [1990] O.J. C240/7.
[15] [1985] O.J. L199/1.

economic activity and at least two members must come from different Member States.

An EEIG may not exercise a power of management over its members or another undertaking nor may it hold shares in a member or another company or participate in another EEIG. Furthermore, an EEIG may not employ more than 500 persons and is not permitted to invite investment by the public.

An EEIG is not a taxable entity distinct from its members. The profits made by an EEIG must be apportioned among the membership in accordance with the contract, and profits and losses from the EEIG are subject to tax only in the hands of its members.

An EEIG may not benefit from limited liability and all members of an EEIG will be jointly and severally liable in respect of debts or liabilities of an EEIG. For this reason and the tax transparency referred to above, EEIG's have tended to be used mainly in the services and consultancy sectors where joint investment costs are likely to be low so that the extent of the commitment of the parties is limited.

SECTION 5

THE MERGER REGULATION (REGULATION 4064/89)[16]

X.5.1 The Merger Regulation was adopted by the Council of Ministers on December 21, 1989 and came into force on September 21, 1990. The procedure in respect of merger pre-notification, time-limits and other administrative matters are dealt with by Commission Regulation 2367/90.[17]

The Merger Regulation requires that certain large scale mergers having "a Community Dimension" must be pre-notified to the Commission for appraisal. If the Commission finds that such merger "creates or strengthens a dominant position" as a result of which competition would be significantly impeded, it has the right to order that the merger does not proceed.

A Community Dimension Merger is defined as one where the combined worldwide turnover of all the parties involved exceeds 5 billion ECUs *and* the Community wide turnover of at least two of the parties is at least 250 million ECUs *unless* each of the undertakings concerned achieves more than two-thirds of its aggregate Community wide turnover in one Member State.

---

[16] [1989] O.J. L395/1 as amended [1990] O.J. L257/14.
[17] [1990] O.J. L219/5.

As currently drawn, the thresholds would cover only the very largest mergers; however, there is a proposal of the Commission that the thresholds be revised downwards currently being considered by the Council. Mergers below the threshold will continue to be regulated under the merger rules (if any) of the Member State but Community dimension mergers are, subject to certain special exemptions, the exclusive responsibility of the E.C. Commission.

SECTION 6

THE PROPOSED EUROPEAN COMPANY

X.6.1 The idea of a European company, Societas Europea (or SE) is by no means recent. The original proposal for a Regulation under Article 235 of the EEC Treaty dated from 1970 and was subsequently amended in 1975. Discussions ground to a halt on these proposals in 1982 in the Council because the Member States could not reach agreement either on the form or the coverage of the proposal.

The Commission's White Paper on the completion of the single market raised again the need for the SE and in July 1988, the Commission decided to relaunch the initiative. Following consultation with the member States, a revised proposal was prepared and published in August 1989. Unlike its predecessor, the revised proposal takes the form of a regulation under Article 100A of the Treaty, covering less contentious company law provisions, and a separate directive under Article 54 dealing with the more controversial proposals for worker participation which had created a major political obstacle to previous attempts to introduce the SE.

The SE seeks to give companies in different Member States a means of co-operation, integration and restructuring. Instead of having to choose between the corporate forms offered within the national jurisdictions forming the European Community, companies will have an option to use a single community structure. The proposal for a European Company Statute (*i.e.* combing the draft regulation and the draft directive) has the following key elements:

(1) The creation of a European Company will be *optional* for public limited companies of two different Member States that wish to merge or set up a holding company. The creation of a joint subsidiary is more open being possible for all companies and other legal entities coming from at least two different Member States.

(2) The text of the Regulation establishes the basic rules of European Company law incorporating common strands of legislation under national company laws

and those which have already been the subject of Commission harmonisation directives. Where other rules are required (*e.g.* on matters such as winding-up, insolvency, etc.), the national law of the Member State of the principle place of business for the SE will apply.

(3) Worker participation. A major obstacle to the SE regulation in the past was the attempt to adopt the "continental" approach towards worker participation which was strongly opposed particularly by the United Kingdom as alien to its corporate structures. As a result, the new Commission scheme seeks a compromise by offering a choice of three models of worker participation which may be adopted. In establishing National rules for the incorporation of an SE, a Member State may offer some or all of the available models within its territory.

The models are as follows:

Model 1 (German Style): Employee members on the company board (administrative board in the unitary system, supervisory board in the dualist system)

Model 2 (French Style): A separate body in the form of works council representing the employees alongside the board and informed and consulted before the implementation of major decisions

Model 3 (British Style): Collective bargaining giving the employees the same rights of information and consultation as in Models 1 and 2 above.

Progress towards adoption continues to be slow. In December 1995 the Commission issued a Communication on Worker Information & Consultation (COM (95) 547 final) which sets out a number of proposals to enable the adoption of the Regulation to proceed but a date for implementation has yet to be set.

APPENDIX

List of Contributors

Austria
Dr Franz Pegger
Greiter Pegger Kofler & Partner Rechtsanwalte
Maria-Theresien Strasse 24
A-6020 Innsbruck
Austria

Tel: + 43 512 57 18 11
Fax: + 43 512 58 49 25

Belgium
Steven De Schrijver and Markus Wellinger
Van Bael & Bellis, Avocats
Avenue Louise 165
B-1050 Brussels
Belgium

Tel: + 32 2 647 73 50
Fax: + 32 2 640 64 99

Bulgaria
Boyan Stanoev
Bazliankov, Stanoev & Tashev
5 Bogoridi Str
Plovdiv 4000
Bulgaria

Tel: + 359 32 266 620
Fax: + 359 32 266 620

Czech Republic
Petr Pešek
Kocián Šolc Balaštík
110 00 Praha 1
Jinkdřišská 24
Czech Republic

Tel: + 42 2 2410 3316
Fax: + 42 2 2410 3234

Denmark
Henrik Peytz
Kromann & Münter, Law Firm
14 Rådhuspladsen
DK-1550 Copenhagen V
Denmark

Tel: + 45 33 11 11 10
Fax: + 45 33 11 80 28

Estonia
Risto Vahimets
Advokaadibüroo Tark & Co.
Roosikrantsi 2
Tallinn EE000
Estonia

Tel: + 372 611 0900
Fax: + 372 611 0911
Email: tarkco@online.ee

Finland
Magnus Pousette
Hannes Snellmann, Asianajotoimisto
Eteläranta 8
00130 Helsinki
Finland

Tel: + 358 9 228 841
Fax: + 358 9 177 393

590

France
Thierry Jacomet and Hicham Naciri, Avocats à la Cour
Gide Loyrette Nouel
Association D'Avocats à la Cour de Paris
26, Cours Albert 1er
75008 Paris
France

Tel: + 33 1 40 75 60 00
Fax: + 33 1 43 59 37 79

Germany
Dr Jürgen J. Seiger and Dr Ludwig Leyendecker
Deringer Tessin Herrmann & Sedemund, Attorneys-at-law
Heumarkt 14
5000 Köln 1
Germany

Tel: + 49 221 20 50 70
Fax: + 49 221 20 50 7 90

Greece
Costas Vainanidis
Law Offices
Vainanidis, Schina & Economou
5 Akadimias Street
106 71 Athens
Greece

Tel: + 30 1 36 34 287
Fax: + 30 1 36 04 611

Hungary
Dr László Kárpárti Jr, Attorney-at-law
S.B.G. & K. Patent and Law Office
H-1062 Budapest
Andrassy ut 113
Hungary

Tel: + 36 1 342 4950
Fax: + 36 1 342 4323

Ireland
Henry Ong and Stephen Hegarty
Arthur Cox
41–45 St Stephen's Green
Dublin 2
Ireland

Tel: + 353 1 618 0000
Fax: + 353 1 618 0618

Italy
Roberto Cociancich
Piergrossi Villa Manca Graziadei Studio Legale
Via Festa del Perdono, 10
20122 Milano
Italy

Tel: + 39 2 58303657
Fax: + 39 2 58303818

Luxembourg
Tom Loesch
Loesch & Wolter, Avocats
11, rue Goethe
Boite postale 1107
L-1011 Luxembourg

Tel: + 352 48 11 481
Fax: + 353 49 49 44

Netherlands
Gerard Carrière
Nauta Dutilh
Advoaten Notarissen Belastingadviseurs
Postbus 1110
3000 BC Rotterdam
Weena 750
3014 DA Rotterdam
Netherlands

Tel: + 31 10 224 00 00
Fax: + 31 10 414 84 44

Norway
Bjorn Blix
Bull & Co.
PO Box 552 Sentrum
0105 Oslo
Norway

Tel: + 47 22 42 70 15
Fax: + 47 22 33 64 10

Poland
Dr Tomasz Wardyński
Wardyński, Wierciński, Śledziński, Szesepińksi, Szaj & Lachert
Aleje Ujazdowskie 12
00–478 Warsaw
Poland

Tel: + 48 22 622 04 00
Fax: + 48 22 628 90 40

Portugal
Dr Rui Peixoto Duarte
Rui Peixoto Duarte & Associados
Rua João Grave, 125–1/16
4150 Porto
Portugal

Tel: + 351 2 6067908
Fax: + 351 2 6001816
Email: ibereuro@mail.telepac.pt

Romania
Ion I. Nestor
Nestor Nestor Kingston Petersen SA
Strada Iuliu Teodori No. 1, Sector 5
Bucharest
Romania

Tel: + 401 312 51 96
Fax: + 401 311 06 46

Spain

Almudena Arpón de Mendívil
Gomez, Acebo & Pombo, Abogados
Castellana, 164
28046 Madrid
Spain

Tel: + 34 1 582 91 00
Fax: + 34 1 582 91 14

Sweden

Mats Koffner
Advokatfirman Glimstedt
Kungsgaten 42
Box 2259
S-403 14 Göteborg
Sweden

Tel: + 46 31 17 20 40
Fax: + 46 31 711 90 38

Switzerland

Jean-Paul Aeschimann and François Rayroux
Lenz & Staehelin, Avocats
25, Grand'Rue
CH-1211 Genève 11
Switzerland

Tel: + 41 22 319 06 19
Fax: + 41 22 319 06 00

United Kingdom

Julian Maitland-Walker
Maitland Walker Solicitors
Aldersmead
Alcombe Combe
Minehead
Somerset TA24 6EW

Tel: + 44 1643 707777
Fax: + 44 1643 705224

European Community
Julian Maitland-Walker
Maitland Walker Solicitors
Aldersmead
Alcombe Combe
Minehead
Somerset TA24 6EW

Tel: + 44 1643 707777
Fax: + 44 1643 705224

INDEX

United Kingdom—*cont.*
  companies limited by shares—*cont.*
    private companies, W.2.3
    public limited companies (plcs),
      W.2.2
    purchase of own shares, W.2.5.7
    registered office, W.2.4.4
    shareholders' register, W.2.5.8
    shares,
      generally, W.2.5.1
      purchase of own, W.2.5.7
      subscription, W.2.5.6
      transfer, W.2.5.3
  general partnerships, W.1.3.1

generally, W.1.1
limited partnerships, W.1.3.2
partnerships,
  general partnerships, W.1.3.1
  generally, W.1.3
  limited partnerships, W.1.3.2
private companies limited by shares.
  See companies limited by shares
  above.
public limited companies (plcs). *See*
  companies limited by shares
  above.
sole traders, W.1.2
unlimited companies, W.3.1, W.3.1.2